The Routledge Handbook of Disability Arts, Culture, and Media

Edited by Bree Hadley and Donna McDonald

LONDON AND NEW YORK

First published 2019
by Routledge
2 Park Square, Milton Park, Abingdon, Oxon OX14 4RN

and by Routledge
52 Vanderbilt Avenue, New York, NY 10017

First issued in paperback 2020

Routledge is an imprint of the Taylor & Francis Group, an informa business

© 2019 selection and editorial matter, Bree Hadley and Donna McDonald; individual chapters, the contributors

The right of Bree Hadley and Donna McDonald to be identified as the authors of the editorial material, and of the authors for their individual chapters, has been asserted in accordance with sections 77 and 78 of the Copyright, Designs and Patents Act 1988.

All rights reserved. No part of this book may be reprinted or reproduced or utilised in any form or by any electronic, mechanical, or other means, now known or hereafter invented, including photocopying and recording, or in any information storage or retrieval system, without permission in writing from the publishers.

Trademark notice: Product or corporate names may be trademarks or registered trademarks, and are used only for identification and explanation without intent to infringe.

British Library Cataloguing-in-Publication Data
A catalogue record for this book is available from the British Library

Library of Congress Cataloging-in-Publication Data
Names: Hadley, Bree, editor. | McDonald, Donna, 1955– editor. Title: The Routledge handbook of disability arts, culture, and media / edited by Bree Hadley and Donna McDonald.
Description: 1st Edition. | New York: Routledge, 2019. |
Series: Routledge international handbooks |
Includes bibliographical references and index.
Identifiers: LCCN 2018033986| ISBN 9780815368410 (hardback) | ISBN 9781351254687 (ebook)
Subjects: LCSH: People with disabilities—Handbooks, manuals, etc.
Classification: LCC HV1568 .R68 2019 | DDC 700/.4527—dc23
LC record available at https://lccn.loc.gov/2018033986

ISBN 13: 978-0-367-65966-0 (pbk)
ISBN 13: 978-0-8153-6841-0 (hbk)

Typeset in Bembo
by codeMantra

The Routledge Handbook of Disability Arts, Culture, and Media

In the last 30 years, a distinctive intersection between disability studies – including disability rights advocacy, disability rights activism, and disability law – and disability arts, culture, and media studies has developed. The two fields have worked in tandem to offer critique of representations of disability in dominant cultural systems, institutions, discourses, and architecture and to develop provocative new representations of what it means to be disabled.

Divided into five parts:

- Disability, identity, and representation
- Inclusion, well-being, and whole-of-life experience
- Access, artistry, and audiences
- Practices, politics, and the public sphere
- Activism, adaptation, and alternative futures

This handbook brings disability arts, disability culture, and disability media studies – traditionally treated separately in publications in the field to date – together for the first time.

It provides scholars, graduate students, upper-level undergraduate students, and others interested in the disability rights agenda with a broad-based, practical, and accessible introduction to key debates in the field of disability art, culture, and media studies. An internationally recognised selection of authors from around the world come together to articulate the theories, issues, interests, and practices that have come to define the field. Most critically, this book includes commentaries that forecast the pressing present and future concerns for the field as scholars, advocates, activists, and artists work to make a more inclusive society a reality.

Bree Hadley is Associate Professor in Drama at Queensland University of Technology. Her research on representations of disability in contemporary, pop cultural, and public space performance, and spectators' responses to these representations has appeared in *Theatre, Social Media and Meaning Making* (2017), *Disability, Public Space Performance and Spectatorship: Unconscious Performers* (2014), and numerous performance and media studies journals

Donna McDonald is an Adjunct Senior Research Fellow with Griffith University, an art therapist, and an artist. Her publications include two books, *Jack's Story* (1991) and *The Art of Being Deaf: A Memoir* (2014), and chapters in several books including *Complicated Grief* (2013), *Deaf Epistemologies* (2012), *Literature and Sensation* (2009), and *A Revealed Life: Australian Writers and Their Journeys in Memoir* (2007). McDonald regularly exhibits her paintings and mixed-media works in art shows.

Contents

List of figures	ix
List of contributors	xi
Acknowledgements	xvii

1 Introduction: disability arts, culture, and media studies – mapping a
maturing field   1
Bree Hadley and Donna McDonald

PART I
Disability, identity, and representation   **19**

2 Great reckonings in more accessible rooms: the provocative
reimaginings of disability theatre   21
Kirsty Johnston

3 Visual narratives: contemplating the storied images of disability and
disablement   36
Donna McDonald

4 Dis/ordered assemblages of disability in museums   48
Janice Rieger and Megan Strickfaden

5 The Down Syndrome novel: a microcosm for inclusion or parental
trauma narrative   62
Sarah Kanake

6 Paralympics, para-sport bodies, and legacies of media representation   74
Laura Misener, Kerri Bodin, and Nancy Quinn

Contents

PART II
Inclusion, well-being, and whole-of-life experience   **87**

7 *Beauty and the Beast*: providing access to the theatre for children
with autism   89
Andy Kempe

8 Moving beyond the art-as-service paradigm: the evolution of arts and
disability in Singapore   100
Justin Lee, Shawn Goh, Sarah Meisch Lionetto, Joanne Tay, and Alice Fox

9 Ten years of Touch Compass Dance Company's integrated education
programme under the spotlight: a reflective essay   114
Sue Cheesman

10 Inclusive capital, human value and cultural access: a case study of
disability access at Yosemite National Park   125
Simon Hayhoe

11 Gender representation, power, and identity in mental health
and art therapy   137
Susan Hogan

12 Demarcating dementia on the contemporary stage   148
Morgan Batch

PART III
Access, artistry, and audiences   **161**

13 Ways of watching: five aesthetics of learning disability theatre   163
Matthew Reason

14 History, performativity, and dialectics: critical spectatorship in
learning disabled performance   176
Dave Calvert

15 Institution, care, and emancipation in contemporary theatre
involving actors with intellectual disabilities   189
Tony McCaffrey

16 *Sweet Gongs Vibrating*: the politics of sensorial access   203
Amanda Cachia

Contents

17 Crip aesthetics in the work of Persimmon Blackbridge   218
    Ann Millett-Gallant

18 Exquisite model: Riva Lehrer, portraiture, and risk   227
    Ann M. Fox

PART IV
Practices, politics, and the public sphere   **241**

19 On the fringe of the Fringe: artmaking, access, rights,
    and community   243
    Brian Lobel and Jess Thom

20 The last avant garde?   251
    *Sarah Austin, Kath Duncan, Gerard Goggin, Lachlan MacDowall,
    Veronica Pardo, Eddie Paterson, and collaborators Jax Jacki Brown,
    Morwenna Collett, Fiona Cook, Bree Hadley, Kate Hood,
    Jess Kapuscinski-Evans, Donna McDonald, Julie McNamara,
    Gaelle Mellis, Eva Sifis, and Kate Sulan*

21 Seeing things differently: Danielle's place making   263
    Jori De Coster

22 ADAPT in space! Science fiction and disability: storying
    interdependence   276
    Petra Kuppers

23 Environments, ecologies, and climates of crises: engaging disability
    arts and cultures as creative wilderness   281
    Bronwyn Preece

PART V
Activism, adaptation, and alternative futures   **295**

24 Changing representations of disability in children's toys as
    popular culture   297
    Katie Ellis

25 Economies of scales (and chords): disability studies
    and adaptive music   310
    Alex Lubet

vii

Contents

26 Accidental leaders: inclusion, career pathways, and autonomy among
dancers with disabilities   323
Sarah Whatley

27 Performing disability: representation and power in 'Classical'
Indian dance   336
Akhila Vimal C.

28 Disability arts in an age of austerity   347
Bree Hadley

29 Conclusion: practicing interdependency, sharing vulnerability,
celebrating complexity – the future of disability arts, culture, and
media research   362
Bree Hadley, Donna McDonald, Sarah Austin, Kath Duncan, Gerard Goggin,
Lachlan MacDowall, Veronica Pardo, Eddie Paterson, with collaborators Dave
Calvert, Jori De Coster, Shawn Goh, Alice Fox, Ann M. Fox, Andy Kempe,
Petra Kuppers, Justin Lee, Alex Lubet, Sarah Meisch Lionetto,
Ann Millett-Gallant, Tony McCaffrey, Laura Misener, Bronwyn Preece,
Megan Strickfaden, Joanne Tay, Matthew Reason, Nancy Quinn,
and Sarah Whatley

30 Plain language summary   373
Bree Hadley and Donna McDonald

Index   *385*

Figures

8.1	Characterising the spectrum of arts	101
10.1	The development of inclusive capital and a *sense of inclusion*	129
13.1	Typology of five aesthetics of learning disability theatre	165
16.1	(a and b) Cooper Baker, *Giant Spectrum* (2016) in *Sweet Gongs Vibrating*, San Diego Art Institute, 2016, curated by Amanda Cachia	205
16.2	(a and b) Wendy Jacob, installation shots of visitors engaged with *Three threads an a thrum (for D.B.)*, (2016) at the opening reception of *Sweet Gongs Vibrating*, San Diego Art Institute, 2016, curated by Amanda Cachia	206
16.3	(a and b) Curator Amanda Cachia using the mallet to hit the gongs in Aaron McPeake's selection of gongs (2007–2010) in *Sweet Gongs Vibrating*, San Diego Art Institute, 2016, curated by Amanda Cachia	207
16.4	(a and b) Raphaëlle de Groot, installation shots of *Study 5, A New Place* (2015) in *Sweet Gongs Vibrating*, San Diego Art Institute, 2016, curated by Amanda Cachia	208
16.5	(a and b) Darrin Martin, installation shots of *Objects Unknown: Sounds Familiar* (2016) in *Sweet Gongs Vibrating*, San Diego Art Institute, 2016, curated by Amanda Cachia. Photos by Emily Corkery	209
16.6	Visitors engaging with Aaron McPeake's selection of gongs (2007–2010) at the opening reception of *Sweet Gongs Vibrating*, San Diego Art Institute, 26 March 2016, curated by Amanda Cachia	210
16.7	(a and b) Installation shots of the signage that accompanied Aaron McPeake's gong installation in *Sweet Gongs Vibrating*, San Diego Art Institute, 2016, curated by Amanda Cachia	212
16.8	(a and b) Installation shots of the "Please Do Not Touch" signage to accompany Anne Gibbs' work, *Crossing Boundaries* (2016), in *Sweet Gongs Vibrating*, San Diego Art Institute, 2016, curated by Amanda Cachia	213
16.9	Signage at the front entrance of the gallery warning visitors, "Please Handle All Objects Carefully" in *Sweet Gongs Vibrating*, San Diego Art Institute, 2016, curated by Amanda Cachia	214
18.1	Riva Lehrer, The Risk Pictures: Lennard Davis. Mixed media and collage on paper, 2016	231
18.2	Riva Lehrer, *Carrie Sandahl*, Acrylic on cradled wood panel, 2017	234
20.1	*Last Avant Garde* Inclusive Creative Workshop, Sydney, 4 May 2018. From left, foreground: lead facilitator Sarah-Vyne Vassallo, Mel Tyquin, Chris Bunton, James Penny, Holly Craig. Obscured on left: Riana Head-Toussaint. Image by Sue Wright	253

Figures

20.2 Images of Quippings production of *Risky Business*, Melba Spiegeltent, Melbourne, Australia, 1 December 2017. From left: Julie McNamara, Rachel High. Image by Angel Leggas, 3FatesMedia   256
23.1 Bronwyn Preece, site-specific improvisation, Huddersfield, United Kingdom, 12 May 2015. Image by Franc Chamberlain   283
24.1 © Rebecca Atkinson / #ToyLikeMe / Beth Moseley Photography   301

Contributors

Sarah Austin (Victorian College of the Arts, Australia). Sarah Austin is an award-winning theatre artist, working predominantly with children and young people, creating inclusive contemporary performance. She is a PhD candidate in Theatre at the Victorian College of the Arts, and a Research Associate at the University of Melbourne on *The Last Avant Garde* research project examining Disability Arts in Australia.

Morgan Batch (Queensland University of Technology, Australia). Morgan Batch is currently completing her PhD on representations of dementia in contemporary theatre at Queensland University of Technology, Australia.

Kerri Bodin (Western University, Canada). Kerri Bodin is a Master of Arts student in Sociocultural Studies of Kinesiology at Western University. Her research to date has involved media representation of athletes with a disability, integrated sport governance, and the Canadian sport system and sport events.

Amanda Cachia (Moreno Valley College, United States). Amanda Cachia is Assistant Professor in art history and Director of the Moreno College Art Gallery. She has curated over 40 exhibitions, many of which iterate disability politics in contemporary art. Her exhibition *Automatisme Ambulatoire: Hysteria, Imitation, Performance* opened at the Owens Art Gallery at Mount Allison University in New Brunswick in 2018.

Dave Calvert (University of Huddersfield, United Kingdom). Dave Calvert has written critical studies of various learning disabled performers and theatre companies, including Heavy Load, Mind the Gap, Susan Boyle, and Back to Back. These have appeared in various journals as well as the edited collections *Žižek and Performance* (2014) and *British Theatre Companies: 1995–2014* (2015). He is also the Chair of Dark Horse Theatre Company, UK.

Sue Cheesman (University of Waikato/Te Whare Wananga o Waikato, New Zealand). Sue Cheesman is Senior Lecturer in Dance Education at the University of Waikato, New Zealand. Her research interests include dance education in New Zealand and inclusive/integrated dance education, and she has been published in *Dance Research Aotearoa* and other journals.

Jori De Coster (University of Leuven, Belgium). Jori De Coster holds a Master of Literature and a Master of Social and Cultural Anthropology. She defended her doctoral thesis in Anthropology at the University of Leuven, Belgium. Her research interests are,

Contributors

among others, bodily difference, performance, and representation. She is co-organiser of a disABILITY film festival and co-author of a number of articles and book chapters.

Kath Duncan (University of Melbourne, Australia). Kath Duncan is NOT an academic's academic. She is an artist/producer with a background in electronic journalism with decent enough academic credentials. Kath co-founded *Quippings: Disability Unleashed*, Australia's first all-disabled, mostly queer cabaret spoken word troupe; Kath holds degrees from UTS, AFTRS, and SCU and is presently Research Associate/Chairperson with the groundbreaking ARC research project *Disability and the Performing Arts in Australia: Beyond the Social Model,* at the School of Culture and Communication, University of Melbourne, Australia.

Katie Ellis (Curtin University, Australia). Katie Ellis is an Associate Professor in the Internet Studies Department at Curtin University. She holds an Australian Research Council (ARC) Discovery Early Career Researcher Award studying disability and digital television. She has worked with people with disabilities in the community, government, and in academia. She has published 10 books on the topic and is series editor of Routledge Research in Disability and Media Studies.

Alice Fox (University of Brighton, United Kingdom). Alice Fox is acting Head of The School of Art, University of Brighton where she founded the pioneering MA Inclusive Arts Practice. Alice delivers Inclusive Arts performance and learning projects for Tate Exchange and The National Gallery. Alice won the Times Higher Education Award 2017 for Excellence and Innovation in the Arts.

Ann M. Fox (Davidson College, United States). Ann M. Fox is a Professor of English specialising in modern and contemporary drama, disability studies in literature and art, and graphic medicine. Her scholarship on disability, drama, and art has been published widely, and she has co-curated four disability-related visual arts exhibitions.

Gerard Goggin (University of Sydney, Australia). Gerard Goggin's research focuses on social, cultural, and political aspects of digital technologies, especially disability and accessibility. Key books include *Listening to Disability: Voices of Democracy* (2019), *The Routledge Companion to Disability and Media* (2019), *Disability and the Media* (2015), and *Digital Disability* (2003).

Shawn Goh (National University of Singapore, Singapore). Shawn's research interests are in issues relating to Singapore's arts and cultural policies, such as community arts and arts funding. He was also the rapporteur for the inaugural Arts and Disability International Conference 2018. His other research interests include online falsehoods and digital inclusion. In his free time, he also conducts ethnographic fieldwork in unofficial sacred spaces.

Bree Hadley (Queensland University of Technology, Australia). Bree Hadley is Associate Professor in Drama at Queensland University of Technology. Her research on representations of disability in contemporary, pop cultural, and public space performance, and spectators' responses to these representations, has appeared in *Theatre, Social Media and Meaning Making* (2017), *Disability, Public Space Performance and Spectatorship: Unconscious Performers* (2014), and numerous performance and media studies journals.

Contributors

Simon Hayhoe (University of Bath, United Kingdom). Simon Hayhoe is the author of *Blind Visitor Experiences at Art Museums, Grounded Theory and Disability Studies, Arts, Culture and Blindness* and *Philosophy as Disability and Exclusion*. His writing has been the topic of discussion on BBC Radio 4 in the UK and syndicated radio in the US, in magazine articles, and in a theatrical installation project in London by Extant and the Open University.

Susan Hogan (University of Derby, United Kingdom). Professor Susan Hogan has research interests in the history of medicine. She has written extensively on the relationship between the arts and insanity and the role of the arts in rehabilitation. She is also very interested in the treatment of women within psychiatry. Susan is currently conducting research with several partner institutions including Harvard University, The University of Nottingham, and The Royal College of Music. She is also a Professorial Fellow of the Institute of Mental Health, University of Nottingham.

Kirsty Johnston (University of British Columbia, Canada). Kirsty Johnston has published her research on disability theatre and performance in a range of theatre and performance journals as well as in *Disability Theatre and Modern Drama: Recasting Modernism* (2016) and *Stage Turns: Canadian Disability Theatre* (2012).

Sarah Kanake (University of the Sunshine Coast, Australia). Sarah is a lecturer in Creative Writing at the University of the Sunshine Coast. Her debut novel, *Sing Fox to Me*, was released in early 2016 to outstanding reviews, and her second novel *Lazarus* has already been accepted for publication. Her research interests include representations of Down syndrome and disability in narrative fiction, Australian gothic writing, and the Vietnam veteran in fiction.

Andy Kempe (University of Reading, United Kingdom). Andy Kempe was the first recipient of the University of Reading's Award for Teaching Excellence. His publications cover a wide spectrum of issues in drama education. His books include *Drama Education and Special Needs* (1996) and *Drama, Disability and Education* (2013).

Petra Kuppers (University of Michigan, United States). Petra Kuppers is a disability culture activist and a community performance artist. She is author of the queer/crip speculative short story collection *Ice Bar* (2018) and of award-winning academic books from *Disability and Contemporary Performance* (2003) to *Theatre & Disability* (2017).

Justin Lee (National University of Singapore, Singapore). Justin has research interests in disadvantaged groups and is running an open collaboration project to crowdsource social needs using a wiki platform. He is also Chairperson of ArtsWok Collaborative, a non-profit organisation engaged in arts-based community development in Singapore.

Sarah Meisch Lionetto (British Council Singapore, Singapore). Dr. Sarah Meisch Lionetto is Director of Arts and Creative Industries for the British Council Singapore. She is committed to positive social change and has led the British Council's Inclusive Arts Programme. Sarah has a PhD in Literature and a master's degree in Modern Art. Her research interests include multilingualism, identity, belonging, and translation in the context of cross-cultural studies.

xiii

Contributors

Brian Lobel (University of Chichester, United Kingdom). Brian Lobel is a performer, teacher, and curator who shows work internationally in a range of contexts, from Sydney Opera House to Lagos Theatre Festival to Harvard Medical School, blending provocative humour with insightful reflection. Brian is Reader in Theatre at University of Chichester, Co-Director of The Sick of the Fringe and a Wellcome Trust Public Engagement Fellow.

Alex Lubet (University of Minnesota, United States). Alex Lubet is the author of *Music, Disability, and Society* (2010) and dozens of articles and chapters on disability issues within and beyond music. His scholarship also includes the music of Bob Dylan, including disability perspectives. He is also a composer and multi-instrumentalist.

Lachlan MacDowall (University of Melbourne, Australia). Lachlan MacDowall is a researcher at the University of Melbourne, Australia. His research examines modes of urban informality such as graffiti and street art. He has published widely in this area and works closely with artists, local governments, heritage agencies, and galleries.

Tony McCaffrey (Ara Institute/Different Light Theatre, New Zealand). Tony McCaffrey has been researching theatre and 'intellectual disability' with members of Different Light Theatre for 14 years. His *Incapacity and Theatricality: Politics and Aesthetics in Theatre with Actors with Intellectual Disabilities* will appear in the Routledge series 'Advances in Theatre and Performance Studies' in 2018 now.

Donna McDonald (Griffith University, Australia). Donna McDonald is an Adjunct Senior Research Fellow with Griffith University, an art therapist, and an artist. Her publications include two books, *Jack's Story* (1991) and *The Art of Being Deaf: A Memoir* (2014), and chapters in several books including *Complicated Grief* (2013), *Deaf Epistemologies* (2012), *Literature and Sensation* (2009), and *A Revealed Life: Australian Writers and Their Journeys in Memoir* (2007). McDonald regularly exhibits her paintings and mixed-media works in art shows.

Ann Millett-Gallant (The University of North Carolina, United States). Ann Millett-Gallant is an Art Historian and Disability Studies scholar. Her scholarship includes *The Disabled Body in Contemporary Art* (2010), *Re-Membering: Putting Mind and Body Back Together Following Traumatic Brain Injury* (2017), and, with Dr. Elizabeth Howie, the co-edited book *Disability and Art History* (2017). She is also a painter. annmg.com.

Laura Misener (Western University, Canada). Dr. Misener's research focuses on how sport and events can be used as instruments of social change, with an emphasis on how events for persons with a disability can positively impact community accessibility and social inclusion. She also serves as a research and policy advisor to a number of disability sport organisations focused on broadening the role of sport in positive social outcomes.

Veronica Pardo (Arts Access Victoria, Australia). Veronica Pardo is the Executive Director of Arts Access Victoria. In this role, she has led an ambitious agenda of social and artistic transformation for people with a disability and the communities in which they live. With a passion for social justice and equity, she has spearheaded campaigns relating to the inclusion of people with a disability in arts and culture as audiences and cultural innovators.

Contributors

Eddie Paterson (University of Melbourne, Australia). Eddie Paterson is a senior lecturer in scriptwriting for theatre, contemporary performance, and new media. His research explores intersections between performance, politics, and everyday life – with a focus on monologue, experimental writing, and live art. His recent books are *The Contemporary American Monologue* (2015) and *redactor* (2017).

Bronwyn Preece (University of Huddersfield, Canada). Bronwyn Preece is honoured to be a guest on the Traditional Territory of the Coastal and Straits Salish Peoples. She is an improvisational, site-sensitive performance eARThist, author, editor, applied theatre practitioner, pioneer of earthBODYment, poetic pirate, and boundary-pushing renegade. She is currently completing a SSHRC-funded PhD through the University of Huddersfield, titled *Performing Embodiment: Improvisational Investigations into the Intersections of Ecology and Disability*. She recently guest-edited a themed issue for the Center for Sustainable Practice in the Arts Quarterly titled *dis/sustain/ability* (2017). www.bronwynpreece.com.

Nancy Quinn (Western University, Canada). Nancy Quinn is a PhD candidate and sport physiotherapist with extensive experience with Paralympic sport and culture. Utilising ethnographic methodology, her research examines assumptions held by medical professionals regarding disability sport and the medical encounter from the athlete's perspective.

Matthew Reason (York St John University, United Kingdom). Matthew Reason's research focuses on understanding audiences' experiential and affective responses to theatre and dance performance. He has published various books, including most recently *Experiencing Liveness in Contemporary Performance* (co-edited with Anja Mølle Lindelof, 2016) and *Applied Practice: Evidence and Impact Across Theatre, Music and Dance* (co-edited with Nick Rowe, 2017).

Janice Rieger (Queensland University of Technology, Australia). Janice Rieger's research in history, theory, and criticism looks at the relationships among disability, design, and material culture from a spatial perspective. This research is informed by her practice in inclusive design, museum and gallery studies, curatorial practice, and visual/material culture histories that spans across Australasia, North America, and Europe.

Megan Strickfaden (University of Alberta, Canada). Megan Strickfaden is a design anthropologist who looks into how places and things affect people with different abilities. Her scholarly outcomes include designed products, patents, publications, exhibitions, and films: for example, *Light in the Borderlands* (2013), and *Rethinking Disability: World Perspectives in Culture and Society* (co-editor, 2016).

Joanne Tay (British Council Singapore, Singapore). Joanne Tay is Senior Programme Manager at the British Council Singapore, where she delivers inclusive arts and cultural programmes. She has worked in the arts, entertainment, and public sector and advocates both the social and creative cases for inclusive arts.

Jess Thom (Touretteshero). Writer, artist, and part-time superhero, Jess Thom co-founded Touretteshero in 2010 as a creative response to her experience of living with Tourette syndrome. Her art and advocacy work tour internationally, and she is a regular contributor to media and television. Jess is committed to 'changing the world one tic at a time.'

Akhila Vimal C. (Jawaharlal Nehru University, India). Akhila Vimal C. is a PhD candidate at Jawaharlal Nehru University, New Delhi. Her research interests are disfiguration and staging of relationalities of disability, gender, and caste in textual and performance practices of India. Find her articles 'Prosthetic Rasa: Dance On Wheels And Challenged Kinesthetics' in Research in Drama Education (RiDE) and 'Performing Disfiguration: Construction of the 'Primitive' and the Ambiguities Of Representing Pain In Kathakaḻi' in *Journal of Emerging Dance Scholarship* (JEDS).

Sarah Whatley (Centre for Dance Research, Coventry University, United Kingdom). Sarah Whatley's research on dance and disability has been published in *Dance, Disability and Law: InVisible Difference* (2018), *Moving Matters* (2008), and in several edited collections and journals. Her funded research, *Resilience and Inclusion; Dancers as Agents of Change*, developed an online toolkit for dancers with disabilities.

Acknowledgements

Creating, analysing, and critiquing representations of d/Deafness and disability has been a passion of ours for decades, across the course of our work in the arts industry, government arts and culture agencies, and academia. Throughout that time, we have been inspired, emboldened, supported, and sometimes challenged by colleagues working in related areas throughout the world. Though they sometimes feel too rare, the presentations from our peers at industry and scholarly gatherings and, perhaps more importantly, the commentary around these work-in-progress presentations over the course of these gatherings are the things that most sustain our work.

Arts practices, media practices, and ubiquitous cultural practices are hugely impactful on the way disabled people are engaged, included, or not included in the many social situations and institutions we encounter in everyday life. The work of those who create, analyse, critique, and change these practices and the representations of disability they promote in the public sphere are vital contributors to efforts to address the exclusion of those with physical, sensory, intellectual, and other disabilities in so many spheres of social life. Their insights are useful not just to those producing or studying these types of practices but also to those working across community services, social services, health, medicine, education, and other industries which engage disabled people as part of their day-to-day business. The opportunity to bring some of the conversations occurring amongst artists, activists, and scholars with interests in the way disability experience is enacted in arts, culture, and media practices together in this collection and to make them readily accessible to a wide readership has been one of the most valuable and rewarding experiences of our career so far.

We are thankful to Claire Jarvis and Georgia Priestley at Routledge, and to the contributing authors, for the chance to bring these perspectives together in a handbook designed to introduce readers to some of the critical historical and contemporary debates about disability arts, culture, and media. We are grateful to the artists, activists, and scholars who have worked with us in the field over decades now – those included in this collection, and those cited so often in the chapters that come together in this collection – for the work they have done to bring the field to a point of maturity where we can engage in debates of the depth and richness seen here. We are grateful to our families, friends, and colleagues at Queensland University of Technology in Brisbane, Australia, for their support over the course of the year it has taken to bring this collection together and for embracing our efforts to bring issues of disability inclusion to the foreground of the equity, diversity, and innovation agendas in the academy, both locally and globally.

As some of our contributors note, entering the academy, and taking agency in the way we are researched and represented in the academia as much as in arts and media practices, remains a challenge for many people who identify as d/Deaf, disabled, or otherwise diverse.

Acknowledgements

Continuing shifts in culture, politics, economics, and technology can both help and hinder efforts to make a place for people with disabilities in the public sphere and the public imagination. The interest of so many in supporting, contributing to, collaborating on, and now reading this collection highlights how much goodwill there is to assist each other in navigating this sometimes difficult terrain. We are thus above all grateful to the readers who are interested in joining this community of goodwill to help navigate this field and the social practices it speaks to as we move into what will hopefully be a more inclusive future.

1

Introduction
Disability arts, culture, and media studies – mapping a maturing field

Bree Hadley and Donna McDonald

The way we see, speak, and think about disability – in real life, and in fictionalised representations of real life in the arts, the media, and popular entertainment – defines disabled identities, which in turn defines disabled people's access to agency, authority, and power in society. In this Introduction, we want to review historic and contemporary studies in disability arts, culture, and media studies, identify current challenges in the field, and set the scene for the chapters engaging these topics to come in this collection. Most critically, we want to highlight the benefits an understanding of this field – and the practical, philosophical, and at times provocative diversity of approaches, aesthetics, and politics discussed in this collection – can bring, not just for scholars of arts, culture, and media but for scholars across education, social services, science, health, and medicine, as they think about the way the rights of disabled people are reflected or not reflected in their own systems, institutions, and discourses.

Interest in the way arts and media representations shape the lives of disabled people sits at the intersection of two fields of study – disability studies and disability-focused arts, culture, and media studies. In the last 30 years, a distinctive intersection between disability law, service, advocacy, and activism studies and disability arts, culture, and media studies has developed. This, as Kirsty Johnston notes, is because the upsurge in interest in how disability is represented in drama, theatre, dance, film, television, literature, visual art, media, and entertainment from the 1980s forward is connected to the upsurge in advocacy, activism, and rights initiatives in the same period (Johnston 2012, 6). Both disability studies and disability arts, culture, and media studies are driven by the belief that disability is best understood not through the lens of a medical model, which sees disability as an individual problem to be controlled or cured, but through the lens of a social model, which sees disability as the product of social, institutional, architectural, and representational systems that preclude the full participation of those with corporeal and cognitive differences in society (Abberley 1987; Oliver 1992). Though pain and impairment may be embodied phenomena that we need to acknowledge, and are acknowledged in subsequent nuancing of the social model, the prejudices which disabled people encounter in their everyday lives are external social phenomena which are enacted, re-enacted, and re-envisaged in encounters across many media and in many contexts throughout the course of our lives. This social construction of disability is something which scholars, activists, and artists working in disability studies and in disability arts, culture, and media studies seek to investigate and intervene in. Disability studies examines the social structures that impact on disabled people's lives. Disability art, culture, and media studies engages with the socially constructed stories that drama, theatre, dance, film, television, literature, art, media, and entertainment tell about what it means to be disabled. These stories include provocative, parodic, and unconventional representations of disability as a minority experience marginalised by the images, discourses, and institutions of mainstream culture.

Over the course of the past 30 years, disability studies and disability arts, culture, and media studies have worked in parallel, and in productive conversation, as mutually committed contributors to the disability rights movement in the US, UK, Europe, Asia, Australasia, and elsewhere. The scholars working in the fields draw on each other's expertise and insight to provide compelling accounts of the way disability is defined in dominant cultural systems, institutions, and discourses. In disability arts, culture, and media studies, scholars also deliver insights into how arts and media workers are developing new accounts of what it means to be disabled and adapting, adopting, and imagining new production platforms, aesthetics, and audience engagement techniques to assist disabled people to speak back to the stereotyping they are subject to in the public sphere. For this reason, a working understanding of the practice and research taking place at the intersection of disability studies and disability arts, culture, and media studies is important for anyone seeking to understand how the disability movement is manifest in contemporary culture, and how it is pushing to change perceptions and create a society more inclusive of disabled people.

A historic overview of disability arts, culture, and media studies

At this critical stage of the field's development, the range of scholarly literature that attempts to identify, document, and describe art, culture, and media practice about, with, or by disabled and d/Deaf people is large. It ranges from theoretical analyses of disability signifiers in screen, stage, aesthetic, and social performance (Garland-Thomson 1996, 1997, 2009; Mitchell & Snyder 2000; Siebers 2010; Johnston 2016), to theoretical analyses of the part disabled people have been called on to play in fairs, sideshows, freak shows, and other popular media and culture phenomena (Bogdan 1988; Garland-Thomson 1996, 1997; Adams 2001; Chemers 2008), to accounts of contemporary disability arts practices (Kuppers 2003, 2011; Sandahl & Auslander 2005; Kochhar-Lindgren 2006; Lewis 2006; Davidson 2008; Hickey-Moody 2009; Henderson and Ostrander 2010; Johnston 2012), to accounts of spectators' relationships to such art forms and artists (Hadley 2014). Accounts of professional, experimental, and political arts and media practice by disabled people run parallel with accounts of arts, health, well-being, and therapy projects and practices with disabled people (Payne 1993; Cattanach 1999; Rubin 1999; Jones & Doktor 2009; Moon 2011; Malchiodi 2012; Bates, Bleakley & Goodman 2014; Clift & Camic 2016).

The earliest scholarly engagement with disability arts, culture, and media studies was through historical and theoretical analysis of fairs, sideshows, and freak shows. From Robert Bogdan's *Freak Show* (1988) to Rosemarie Garland-Thomson's *Freakery: Cultural Spectacles of the Extraordinary Body* (1996), Rachel Adams' *Sideshow USA* (2001), and Michael Chemers' *Staging Stigma: A Critical Examination of the American Freak Show* (2008), the literature in this field has consistently shown the pivotal role representations of the disabled body play in defining the bounds of the 'normal' and the 'abnormal' human body.

Analyses of freak shows as a specific form of popular entertainment have been followed by accounts of the way representational practices in drama, theatre, television, film, literature, and the visual arts more broadly have used the disabled body as what David T. Mitchell and Sharon Snyder (2000) call a "narrative prosthesis" – a figure of trauma, tragedy, pity, terror, or inspiration – to prop up dominant culture accounts of what it means to be human. Rosemarie Garland-Thomson's *Extraordinary Bodies: Figuring Physical Disability in American Culture and Literature* (1997) and *Staring: How We Look* (2009), Tobin Siebers' *Disability Aesthetics* (2010), and Kirsty Johnston's *Disability Theatre and Modern Drama: Recasting Modernism* (2016) all contribute to growing field of scholarship.

In the last 15 years, analyses of mainstream representations of disability have been joined by analyses of disabled artists' own self-representation practices, in books and articles that examine how disabled arts and media makers are challenging problematic legacies of representation, creating and co-creating their own aesthetics, and creating and co-creating their own communities of practice. This includes examination of the work of specific practitioners, companies, or practices, as well as examination of whole series of work in specific art forms such as performing arts, visual arts, or the media, in specific countries, or in other specific contexts. Amongst the most influential are Petra Kuppers' *Disability and Contemporary Performance: Bodies on Edge* (2003) and *Disability Culture and Community Performance: Find a Strange and Twisted Shape* (2011); Gerard Goggin and Christopher Newell's *Digital Disability: The Social Construction of Disability In New Media* (2003); Ann Millett Gallant's *The Disabled Body in Contemporary Art* (2010); Richard Sandell, Jocelyn Dodd, and Rosemarie Garland-Thomson's *Re-Presenting Disability: Activism and Agency in the Museum* (2010); Katie Ellis and Mike Kent's *Disability and New Media* (2011); and Kirsty Johnston's *Stage Turns: Canadian Disability Theater* (2012). The field has also begun to consider the question of how spectators respond to these practices more explicitly, beginning with Bree Hadley's *Disability, Public Space Performance, and Spectatorship: Unconscious Performers* (2014).

As the field has matured, understanding the work of specific practitioners, companies, and categories of work has become a focus. This includes, for instance, analysis of d/Deaf practices in Kanta Kochhar-Lindgren's *Hearing Difference: The Third Ear in Experimental, Deaf, and Multicultural Theater* (2006) and Michael Davidson's *Concerto for the Left Hand: Disability and the Defamiliar Body* (2008). It also includes analysis of intellectual or learning disability in theatre, such as in Anna Hickey-Moody's (2009) *Unimaginable Bodies: Intellectual Disability, Performance and Becomings*, and Matt Hargrave's (2015) *Theatres of Learning Disability: Good, Bad, or Plain Ugly?* The volume of interest in intellectual or learning disability theatre is also clearly flagged in a number of collections investigating responses to representations of intellectual disability or learning disability in theatre, including Helena Grehan and Peter Eckersall's (2013) *'We're People Who Do Shows': Back to Back Theatre – Performance Politics Visibility*, on the work of Back to Back Theatre (Australia), and Sandra Umathum and Benjamin Wihstutz's (2015) *Disabled Theater*, on Jérôme Bel's controversial work with Theater HORA (Switzerland) in the production *Disabled Theater*.

As the field has gained momentum, and interest from arts, culture, and media scholars more broadly, other collections have offered broad accounts of the field, albeit focused on either artmakers or media makers, but not both, in the way this collection does. This includes Susan Crutchfield and Marcy Epstein's *Points of Contact: Disability, Art, and Culture* (2000); Sheila Riddell and Nick Watson's *Disability, Culture, and Identity* (2003); Carrie Sandahl and Philip Auslander's *Bodies in Commotion: Disability & Performance* (2005); and Bruce Henderson and Noam Ostrander's *Understanding Disability Studies and Performance Studies* (2010). Though these collections are mainly dated to the early 2000s, and mainly US-, UK-, and Europe-focused in the practices their contributors discuss, they have provided a valuable point of introduction for the larger numbers of scholars acquiring interest in this field in the last decade.

Most recently – and appropriately for a field that has reached a point of maturity, where common understandings exist, central debates are known, and attention turns to how we do what we do and how we negotiate contestation amongst ourselves about pathways forward – attention has turned to how we teach and research and introduce others to this topic. Petra Kuppers has published a short *Theatre & Disability* resource text (2017) and a *Studying Disability Arts and Culture* (2014) textbook, each designed to assist scholars in introducing disability arts, culture, and media practices to students in the classroom from the earliest stages of their university studies.

Though accounts of arts, health, well-being, and therapy projects address arts practice with disabled people, as well as with other marginalised communities, it is interesting to note that these have tended to sit somewhat separately from accounts of professional, experimental, community, independent, and political practice about, with, and by disabled people to date. Introductions to arts therapy like Judith Rubin's (1999) *Art Therapy: An Introduction*; handbooks like Helen Payne's (1993) *Handbook of Inquiry in the Arts Therapies*, Cathy Malchiodi's (2012) *Handbook of Art Therapy*, and Stephen Clift and Paul Camic's (2016) *Oxford Textbook of Creative Arts, Health, and Wellbeing: International Perspectives on Practice, Policy, and Research*; analyses of issues like Susan Hogan's *Problems of Identity: Deconstructing Gender in Art Therapy* (1997); and 'how to' guides about processes, protocols, and media in this work like Ann Cattanach's (1999) *Process in the Arts Therapies*, Phil Jones and Ditty Dokter's (2009) *Supervision of Dramatherapy*, and Catherine Hyland Moon's (2011) *Materials and Media in Art Therapy* tend to be focused on advice for practitioners assisting people with their mental health, communication skills, and community engagement skills rather than on the issues of agency, power, and political impact in the public sphere foregrounded in other disability arts, culture, and media studies work. As a result, work on health, well-being, therapy, and outreach programmes in the past decade has tended to be by a different group of scholars, working on different issues, for different readers. A push towards emphasis on professional, political, or social artistic practices located outside a therapeutic paradigm in both disability arts industry practice and disability arts scholarship has amplified this sense of separation in the field (Murakami 2012, cited Austin et al. 2015). There has thus perhaps been less mutual identification and cross-fertilisation between the arm of the field in which scholars work on disability arts, culture, and representational politics and the arm of the field in which scholars work on disability arts, outreach, and therapy, and even some hesitancy around engagement based on ongoing desire to differentiate disability arts, culture, and media studies from medical models of disability.

Current issues in disability arts, culture, and media studies

With this sizeable legacy of scholarship to draw on, the disability arts, culture, and media studies field is no longer the under-researched sector it was a decade ago. It has reached a stage of maturity, moving past the stage of initial statements, summaries, and surveys that establish the value of studying the work, and past initial attempts to coin terminology and theory to suit analysis of the work. Those entering or expanding the field now can make use of foundational work by the aforementioned practitioners and scholars as a basis to articulate core principles succinctly and go on to exploration and at times contestation of specific issues in relation to the production, presentation, reception, or critique of work.

In line with the emphasis on professionalisation in the industry in the last ten years, most scholars working in this field at present acknowledge and attend to professional, pre-professional, community, and political practices, addressing disabled people as leaders with agency and authority in these practices. The cutting edge of debate in the field currently focuses on the way disability disrupts conventional representation, communication, or aesthetic models, the way the mainstage is co-opting this disruption as part of its innovation agenda, and the problems this co-option presents for the aesthetic, professional, and political agendas of disability arts (Hargrave 2015; Umathum & Wihstutz 2015). There is concern that artists and the scholars they study may be suffering from their own success in showing the ways in which the disabled body can destabilise the aesthetic and political impact of representational practices. There is suspicion that mainstage practitioners may be making use of the aesthetic possibilities of the disabled body without necessarily acknowledging the legacy of effort in establishing the need for disabled people to take leadership in exploring these aesthetic possibilities. The field today is also increasingly interested in analyses of the way artists and their publics are moving to new and more 'democratic' digital media platforms to communicate their aesthetic and political messages in a context where access to the mainstream remains challenging (Ellis & Goggin 2015; Ellis, Goggin & Kent 2015; Ellis & Goggin 2016; Hadley 2017b). Though analysis of how changes in the policy, industry, and production climate around these disability arts and media practices impact on the aesthetics, politics, and business models for the work have been less frequent – in disability arts and culture studies, if not in disability media studies – more work in this area is starting to emerge. The field includes one oft-cited chapter on different models of disability arts (Perring 2005) and one article on the way evolutions in policy lead to evolutions in practice in a particular country's context (Hadley 2017a). As some of the contributions to later sections of this book show, this is an area of interest for the future, and the question of how practitioners are becoming leaders, albeit accidental leaders, adapting practices, and finding ways to make these industries accommodate them is a valuable new path for future work. For practitioners and scholars alike, there is a desire to ensure that ebbs and flows in the funding, publication, and promotion of disability arts and media practices over time do not stall the continued evolution of the field or create a situation in which lack of visibility of past work leads new researchers entering the field now to reinvent rather than evolve the work.

Challenges in disability arts, culture, and media studies

As might be expected of a maturing field, scholars working in disability arts, culture, and media studies are highly conscious of the way the aims, approaches, and outcomes of their research are framed and the way terminology flags this framing. As initial analyses of representations of disability across mainstage arts, culture, and media practice demonstrated, disabled people have often been represented as figures of trauma, tragedy, pity, terror, or inspiration. Even today, cheats, charity cases, and inspirations constitute the vast majority of mainstream representations of disabled identities. Most mainstage representations are still embodied by non-disabled performers in 'crip drag' as it has been called (Mazzeo 2016). Those working in disability arts, culture, and media studies thus tend to be suspicious of any terminology, or any research aim, approach, or outcome, that positions disabled people as subject, spectator, or research participant rather than as producer of culture. The field, in parallel and in collaboration with the industry it investigates, has debated the relative merit of terms, aims, approaches, and outcomes designed to take the conversation beyond these limited and limiting terms. In some cases, terminology is drawn from disability studies – discussion of social models versus medical models, disabilities versus impairments, and people with disabilities versus disabled people is as frequent in scholarship as in the industry studied. In other cases, terminology is drawn from the industry – differentiation between art and disability, disability arts, and disabled artists, or between inclusive arts and integrated arts, for instance. The field typically acknowledges and expects strong differentiation between art and disability as a facilitated practice in which typically non-disabled artists work with disabled people, disability arts as a professional practice by disabled artists that addresses disability rights issues, and disabled artists whose work may or may not address such issues and who may or may not wish to be identified as disabled in accounts of their work (Perring 2005; Austin et al. 2015). The field also typically acknowledges and expects differentiation between inclusive arts, which brings disabled and non-disabled artists together to undertake work with a strong social inclusion agenda, and integrated arts, which attempts to bring people together without amplifying boundaries, binaries, and power relations between disabled and non-disabled arts involved (Fox 2010). Both practitioners and scholars tend to advocate for disability-led practice, in which agency lies with artists and media makers with lived experience of disability, though the meaning of the term can range from actual director or producer roles, to acting roles with input into direction and production, to consultation and advisory committees, and notions of lived experience can range from being disabled to being a parent, partner, or child of a person who is disabled (Hadley 2017a). Together, these nuances in terminology are designed to help the field define and describe the differences between mainstream work which 'normalises' disability in typically negative terms, therapeutic work that 'helps' disabled people with communication, expression, and community engagement skills, post-therapeutic work that 'facilitates' disabled people's efforts to express their own stories and engages with notions of professionalism, excellence, or political effect, and socially and politically subversive 'professional' work in which disabled people themselves challenge conventional notions of what it means to be disabled whether via direct reference or simply by presenting work as a disabled person without direct reference to disability as a topic (Perring 2005; Hadley 2017a). Though emphasis on disability-led practice, professional practice, and socially, politically, and aesthetically provocative practice is common in the field which this terminology helps define, there are also regional differences in the way terminology is deployed in different countries and contexts. In the UK, for example, scholars and practitioners will speak of 'learning disabled' practice to avoid use of 'intellectual disability' as a terminology they find problematic, whereas in the US and Australasia, 'learning disability' and 'intellectual disability' still mean different things, so scholars and practitioners will still speak of 'intellectual disability' in arts and media practice. As Anna Hickey-Moody (2009, 43) notes, despite continuing contestations, emphasis on language serves the same aim for most practitioners and scholars. Much of the day-to-day language used to describe disability arts, culture, and media practice can still be seen as holding the potential to fall back into the problematic power relations embedded in the dominant social system, a system designed to render those with corporeal or cognitive difference 'other' and limit practice to therapeutic rather than professional and political paradigms. As a result, shifts in language and contestation about language are part and parcel of efforts to establish new ways of seeing, speaking, and thinking about disability, embodied difference, and identity that move beyond the limited and limiting paradigms of the past.

The continuing challenge of coming to consensus about the terms, aims, and approaches that afford disabled people agency, avoid historical conceptions of disability as trauma, tragedy, pity, terror, or inspiration, and avoid binaries between disabled and non-disabled is a key priority for disability arts, culture, and media studies moving forward. This is perhaps why critiques of mainstage co-option of the disabled body for its aesthetic possibilities, critiques of mainstage practices too slow to adapt to include disabled people, and commentary about disabled people's use of more 'democratic' and accessible modes of practice feature so prominently in contemporary work – and, as it turns out, feature so strongly in this collection, in which scholars again and again critique practices that co-opt the disabled body in service of a dominant cultural agenda, celebrate disabled people's attempts to adapt practices, tools, and production platforms to their own agenda, and consider creative new ways of pushing people to imagine a future in which disability is figured differently in the fabric of our culture. These types of focal points capture continuing concern and commitment amongst disabled and non-disabled scholars and practitioners alike to increasing the agency, authority, and empowerment of disabled people through the work.

The growing body of work outlined earlier notwithstanding, and the growing emphasis on disability-led, professional, and politically charged practice that positions disability as an identity and culture worth celebrating rather than a condition to be cured notwithstanding, the ways in which respectful relationships are enacted in practice and in research still tend to be determined on a case-by-case basis. Practitioners, researchers, and practitioner-researchers consider these principles, common understandings of these principles, and examples of enactment of these principles in the field in the past and come up with an approach they can articulate and argue as defensible for the research project at hand. There are excellent examples scholars entering the field can draw on – most particularly the work of Petra Kuppers (2003, 2011, 2014, 2017), who works within a disability culture paradigm and draws on her artmaking methods to establish respectful learning, teaching, and research methods in which the agency of disabled people is undeniable. To date, these examples, these accounts of how a particular scholar has respectfully engaged a particular practice, practitioner, company, or collection of practice, and this advice on enacting respectful relationships in the classroom are the best guide available for those looking to form respectful relationships in disability arts, culture, and media research. The field as whole has not yet had an explicit debate, with explicit back-and-forth in journals, and explicit case-building in books to articulate common approaches to respectful and rigorous research with disabled artists and media makers in the way disability studies did with the 'emancipatory disability research' debate of the 1990s (Oliver 1992). For this reason, the contributors to this collection still show considerable diversity in their terminology, in their research aims, approaches, and outcomes, and in their manner of articulating these outcomes. This diversity of approach is as, if not more, evident than the diversity of art forms, representations, production, and reception processes the contributors address in the chapters to come. This diversity is particularly apparent when comparing the historical and textual analyses of representational practices early in this collection with accounts of health, therapy, well-being, and outreach practices later in the collection and the calls for creative new ways of thinking about disability toward the conclusion of the collection. This does have the potential to create slippages, clashes, and conflicts in terminology and perspective across the chapters gathered here. However, in a field where conversations about methodology are still to fully unfold at scale, and contributions from beyond the US and UK are still to receive the attention they deserve, embracing rather than editing out these issues has proven the most useful approach to sharing something of the questions, tensions, and differences in the field for the reader.

Overview of this collection

In this book, an internationally recognised collection of established and emerging scholars, artists, and activists from across the US, UK, Europe, Asia, and Australasia come together to trace the development of disability arts, culture, and media studies in recent decades, flag current interests, and forecast future concerns. The book is designed to provide scholars, students, and practitioners with a broad-based and accessible set of insights into the variety of voices, topics, and concerns that have informed the historical evolution of the field, as well as the issues that are most pressing for the field in the present and into the future. The contributors consider past, present, and potential future engagement with drama, theatre, dance, film, television, literature, art, media, entertainment, and everyday social self-performance through the lens of disability. This includes accounts of mainstream arts and media representations of disability and attempts to change mainstream arts and media representations of disability. It includes accounts of practices designed to provide platforms and opportunities for disabled people to present their own representations of their experiences in therapeutic, post-therapeutic, and politically subversive arts and media practices. Most critically, it includes creative works and commentaries that address the pressing present and future concerns for the field, as new industrial formations, new technologies, and new trends towards conservatism, austerity, and cutbacks to welfare and support services take hold across the US, UK, Europe, Australasia, and elsewhere. As the collection unfolds, the contributors' focus shifts across art, culture, and media – traditionally treated separately in collections attempting to capture the state of the field to date – displaying both the similarities and differences in how activists attempt to make everything from photography to performance art, classical Indian dance to contemporary integrated dance, toys to television representation of sporting events, and dozens more cultural phenomena and practices more inclusive of people with disabilities. Between the lines, these contributions show how different scholars, areas of scholarship, publications, and problems across the whole field of cultural practice broadly defined influence and inform each other.

In **Part I**, on ***Disability, identity, and representation***, contributors offer comment on the critiques of mainstream representations of disability in theatre, film, literature, visual arts, digital arts, and the media that disability scholars, activists, and artists have made over the last 30 years.

Kirsty Johnston opens this collection with a discussion of how disability and theatre have intersected in the past and the ways in which disability theatre practitioners have been innovating since the 1980s. As Johnston observes, the practical and scholarly fields are so active, robust, and rapid in their innovations at present that it is challenging to stay current with them.

In their chapters, Donna McDonald, Janice Rieger, and Megan Strickfaden turn their attention to the way images of disabled people – as monsters, medical specimens, cripples, charity cases, figures of pity, and inspirations – have been represented in museums and galleries. Donna McDonald reflects upon the power contemplation of historic visual arts images of disability and disablement has to disturb and reshape contemporary attitudes about the experiences of disabled people. Janice Rieger and Megan Strickfaden then present case studies of two national museums in Canada and Australia through the lens of remembering, forgetting, and silencing to reveal how disability can weave into conversations, interrupt, and even disrupt cultural norms and stereotypes in the museum context.

Sarah Kanake's investigation of the 'Down Syndrome novel' shows that while contemporary narratives in creative writing can have all the appearance of social inclusivity and empowerment, they can also remain problematic in the sense that they rarely give the disabled character any real power. Kanake challenges the reader into a deeper understanding of how deploying disability as a metaphor can be problematic, preventing the realisation of the authentic realities of human beings who have disabilities.

Laura Misener, Kerri Bodin, and Nancy Quinn pick up on this theme in their chapter about media representations of disability in sport and in large-scale sporting events and initiatives such as the Paralympic movement. They illustrate how most forms of media representation emphasise the 'heroism' and 'able-bodiedness' of athletes. In doing so, they argue, these media representations reinforce problematic representations of disability. They use a 'tragedy' narrative around acquired disability to reinforce hierarchies of disability, thereby doing little to advance equity and inclusion for people with disabilities.

Together these chapters highlight the way representation of disabled characters on stage, on screen, in the media, and in museums as innocent victims of tragedy, or inspirational overcomers succeeding in spite of challenging personal problems, continues to be a problem. In a great many contexts, the disabled person's plight is still positioned as an individual problem, and a pity, which, though tragic, fails to register as part of an identity politics agenda for the majority of the public. Their plight is at best a salutary example of how or how not to overcome problems or go on when problems cannot be controlled, cured, or overcome and at worst a metaphor with little relation to the lived reality of disability experience. This motivates many disabled people and their allies to turn to alternative modes or forms of art, entertainment, engagement, and media production practice to create opportunities and platforms where disabled people can experience arts and media in new ways, supplanting the mainstream's tendency to present natural, autobiographical, and 'heroic' narratives about diagnosis, crisis, overcoming, and cure with their own theatrical, comic, poetic, symbolic, and political narratives.

In **Part II**, on *Inclusion, well-being, and whole-of-life experience*, contributors examine inclusion of disabled people – across the lifespan from childhood, adolescence, and adulthood into old age – in art, culture, and media practices within well-being oriented and therapy programmes. In the US, UK, Europe, Australasia, and most welfare state countries in the latter part of the twentieth century, bringing disabled people out of institutions and integrating them into the community to a greater or lesser degree has become a recognisable part of policy frameworks – a result of success in the disability rights advocacy, activism, and law spheres. This shift in policy, programming, and funding provision – in health, education, social services, and the arts – has created new opportunities for disabled people to participate in primarily therapeutically oriented dance, drama, music, visual, and media arts programmes.

In the first chapter in this section, Andy Kempe discusses the provision of access to the theatre for children with autism through 'relaxed performance.' As Kempe demonstrates, the arts and disability sectors are increasingly working together to create more integrated cultural participation opportunities for disabled people. Significantly, Kempe highlights how such opportunities are beneficial, not only to the children's learning and the cause of social justice, but for the wider community.

In the next chapter, Justin Lee, Shawn Goh, Sarah Meisch Lionetto, Joanne Tay, and Alice Fox investigate the implications of the massive increase in charity, city council, and health service provider organised groups offering arts programmes with communication, socialisation, social connection, and well-being aims. They share the suspicions of some disability scholars, activists, and artists about some of these programmes, suggesting they offer diversion, rather than meaningful opportunities to train, produce, and present one's own work, and thus construct a paradigm with little connection to what professional scholars, activists, and artists mean when they speak of 'disability arts.' In their exploration of the evolution of the arts and disability beyond the 'art as service' paradigm in Singapore, they note that the evidenced-based evaluation of the therapeutic effects of these programmes suggests that they have been successful in enabling people with disabilities – including people with multiple, profound, and intellectual communities – to learn communication and social skills, connect with community, and experience joy, pride, and pleasure. However, they observe that a purely 'instrumental attitude' to the arts, which views arts only as a service and values arts only for evaluable outcomes, is risky and potentially problematic if it neglects the expressive force, aesthetic power, and emancipatory potential of arts practice.

In her reflective essay, Sue Cheesman examines precisely this question of the potency of creative expression opportunities for people with disabilities. She reviews her 15 years' involvement with integrated dance in the context of Encompass, an education and outreach arm of Touch Compass Dance Company in New Zealand. Her analysis and theorising of the journey of integrated dance and of her challenges, strategies, and successes – undertaken through a dynamic questioning lens – illustrates how integrated dance, especially in a community setting, has acted as a site for change not only in dance but also in disability culture.

Simon Hayhoe further advances the themes flagged in Part II, focusing on the importance of human values, inclusive capital, and the concept of cultural access in providing opportunities for disabled people to engage with all aspects of social life. Hayhoe illustrates how these principles can be applied in practice through a case study of Yosemite National Park's Deaf Service, which provides accessible communication to allow d/Deaf visitors to experience their nationally significant park and environs in meaningful ways.

While accepting that health workers, council workers, arts workers, parents, and communities may be well meaning, many of the contributors to Part II highlight the risk that their practices and programmes may unwittingly reinforce rather than challenge stereotypes and separations. In this context, Susan Hogan, an early forerunner in theorising the field of arts and health, in particular gender representation, power, and identity in arts therapy, reflects on the level of systemic change required to ensure that art therapy with women experiencing mental health issues does not reinforce problematic gender roles. Hogan reviews her 30 years of research and practice in the field of art psychotherapy and mental health, drawing on art theory, cultural theory, and feminist critiques of science to highlight problematic precepts practitioners need to break through to be effective working with women experiencing mental health problems. Hogan's contribution reminds readers of the importance of understanding disability identity as intersectional with gender, sexuality, race, class, and other components of identity, and the importance of continued engagement with other bodies of theory and other community-based programmes with marginalised participants – indigenous people, migrants, women, people experiencing mental health problems, or otherwise disenfranchised people – for disability scholars, activists, and artists.

In the final chapter in Part II, Morgan Batch argues for positioning dementia adjacent to current disability studies and describes how the medical narrative of dementia has stigmatised people with dementia. Like other contributors in this section, Batch notes common trends in the representation of disability, bodily difference, and mental difference – in this case, dementia – in the arts and in the media. The current focus on dementia and the arts is, Batch's research demonstrates, deeply rooted in therapy programmes with instrumentalised outcomes of the type Lee, Goh, Lionetto, Tay, and Fox describe. A broader look at the current landscape of representations of dementia in contemporary performance is worthwhile, Batch argues, because looking at therapy, outreach, and aesthetic representations in tandem shows how many performances strongly differentiate and demarcate between people with dementia and people without dementia in a binary way. Clinical affectations of language and memory, a generational discourse that juxtaposes age and cognitive decline with the potentiality of youth, and a distinctive selection of performance forms all contribute to this binarisation. Significantly, Batch notes that even creators with the best intentions can still fall into stereotyped representations that position people with dementia as 'Other' and somehow less than fully human. Her analysis highlights the ever-present challenge of developing practices that go beyond the normalising-therapeutic-countercultural spectrum Giles Perring (2005) proposed as a way of categorising approaches to disability theatre and that create more overlaps, synergies, and potentials for truly disability-led self-representation practices, to provide a more complex, nuanced, and sophisticated account of disability experience.

In **Part III**, on *Access, artistry, and audiences*, contributors consider contemporary and sometimes disruptive renderings of disability across the spectrum of the creative arts. In the chapters in this section, disability is seen as a perspective and a way of being in the world, which disabled people draw on to produce art, culture, and media work that differs from mainstream work not just in content but in form. When disabled people express the problems they encounter in daily life and their desire for a more inclusive society in their own ways, contributors to this section show, they often tend towards a distinctly postmodern aesthetic. This is because of their need to negotiate their consciousness of their positioning as other in the public sphere, along with a range of competing modes of thinking, speaking, and symbolising experience – and sometimes also a range of screens, devices, captioners, and translators, to ensure every participant's modes of performing and spectating are accommodated – to capture and convey disability experience in sophisticated, nuanced, and impactful ways. This makes the work innovative and aesthetically interesting but at times also challenging for spectators to perceive and interpret.

In his chapter, Matthew Reason takes the reader along a threefold journey of literature review, direct research, and reflection about what he identifies as the five aesthetics of learning disability theatre. He draws upon interviews with learning disabled performers and other practitioners working in the field, alongside research with audiences about their experience of learning disabled theatre, to examine the relationship between theatres of learning disability and the concept and practice of theatre spectatorship. He thus engages the reader with the dilemmas, swings, and turns within that sometimes complex journey of understanding the different ways of watching that audiences adopt in relation to learning disability theatre.

In the next chapter, Dave Calvert continues this examination of the issues and challenges of watching work by performers with learning disabilities. Calvert explores the relationships between learning disability and performance and offers a model of critical spectatorship that takes into account how people with learning disabilities have been historically situated. Calvert's chapter is emphatically embedded in integrated interdisciplinary scholarship, drawing from philosophy, disability studies, theatre, education, jurisprudence, history, music, and other fields. His skilful use of history and philosophy together with his respectful interrogation of the work of various scholars – for example, Matt Hargrave's (2015) analysis of Mind the Gap performer Jez Colborne – drives his arguments about the interrelationship between the status of people with learning disabilities in the social economy (historically and contemporaneously) and their place in theatre, both in their performance and how they are viewed.

In the following chapter, Tony McCaffrey's intensely reflective review and analysis of significant theatrical performances by actors with intellectual disabilities over the last 50 years is driven by a humanistic philosophy and infused with a deep understanding of disability history and disability studies as well as epistemology, and theatre theory, and practice. McCaffrey considers three influential groups working in the field of theatrical performance by people with intellectual disabilities – Back to Back Theatre, Theater HORA, and Mind the Gap Theatre – and delineates the aesthetics and politics of this form of theatre. His chapter reflects on the increased desire amongst non-disabled artists to collaborate with disabled people, including both fascinating and fraught examples of such collaborations. Concomitantly, he considers how the audience, whether intellectually disabled or not, come to perceive the disability and ability of the actors.

As becomes evident here, multidisciplinary, multi-discursive, and multichannel work, characterised by disruption and meta-level negotiation amongst different performers and spectators with different needs, interests, and desires, is increasingly not just tolerated but celebrated in contemporary aesthetic practice. The work, though sometimes challenging for artists and audiences in the way Calvert, Reason, and McCaffrey describe, has been celebrated for its ability to draw attention to different modes of existence, communication, and artistry and, in doing so, bring a range of benefits, including for the development of new aesthetics as well as for the inclusion of disabled people.

Amanda Cachia continues this section's exploration of the politics of creative expression and spectatorship in a visual art context in the next chapter. Drawing on her experience as a curator, Cachia notes the importance of multisensorial access – including touch – in museums and galleries. Her observations of curatorial and exhibition practices, her frank review of her successes and disappointments, and her recommendations and ideas for future exhibitions and practices are all supported by photographs which help the reader feel 'present' in her journey of ideas and exhibitions – in particular, her case study of *Sweet Gongs Vibrating*. In pursuing questions about how we should be touching in museums, and if there is a right way and a wrong way to touch, Cachia shows how the hierarchy of the senses might be realigned to allow more space for new knowledge to be generated through touch.

In the closing chapters of this section, Ann Millett-Gallant and Ann M. Fox take a more epistemological approach to analysis of the visual arts to conceptualise and reconceptualise the creative expression of disabled people. In their respective discussions of 'Crip Aesthetics' in the multimedia works and narratives by disabled feminist artist Persimmon Blackbridge and the portraiture by disability artist Riva Lehrer, they show how the multiple dimensions of access are critical in creating platforms for disabled people to present their own work, driven by their own personal, aesthetic, and political prerogatives and capabilities, in and beyond conventional art, culture, and media-making spaces and systems.

In **Part IV**, on *Practices, politics, and the public sphere*, contributors consider how disabled people are currently negotiating a public sphere, and a long-standing legacy of policy, industrial, production, and reception norms in professional arts, culture, and media practice, that can still be hostile to them. The chapters that come together in this section are each designed in different ways to allow disabled people and disabled practitioners creating their own aesthetically, politically, and socially subversive work to speak about their work in their own voices. Their work demonstrates as well as describes some of the distinctive disability aesthetic, or distinctive disability transformation of traditional arts, culture, and media aesthetics, and some of the distinctive blurring between art and activism or academics and activism, that is characteristic of many working in the sector.

In the first chapter, Brian Lobel and Jess Thom present a dialogue on artmaking, access, rights, and community as experienced by disabled artists who find themselves at the fringe of the Fringe festival. Jess Thom, who performs in collaboration with Matthew Pountney as Touretteshero, provides a brutally honest account of her experience bringing her show *Backstage in Biscuit Land* to the Edinburgh Fringe Festival in 2014. As Lobel and Thom show, Thom's work, and the effort and energy she put into making space for her work at the event, proved transformative for the long-standing conversations and commentary about access at the Edinburgh Fringe Festival. As an example of disabled artists' attempts to bring their work to a wider audience encounter, Lobel and Thom's conversation raises far-reaching issues – about rights, comfort, discomfort, and what it means to be part of a community – of relevance to disabled artists and activists around the world.

In the next chapter, Sarah Austin, Kath Duncan, Gerard Goggin, Lachlan MacDowall, Veronica Pardo, Eddie Paterson, and collaborators offer a collaboratively authored account of similar issues in an Australian context, and highlight the way factors such as funding help or hinder development of what is increasingly described as 'ground-breaking,' 'cutting edge,' 'postdramatic,' or even 'avant-garde' aesthetic experimentation in disability performance (Yinka Shonibare cited Bragg 2007). They note the impact that support, particularly support in the form of regular funding for the work, has had during critical stages in the evolution of the work and aesthetics of the Quippings performance troupe and the Rawcus theatre company, both innovators in the landscape of disability arts in Australia. Their analysis reveals that disability arts in Australia holds a precarious position and that the policy, funding, and industry climate cannot be separated from the ability of artists to make aesthetic advances.

In the following chapter, Jori De Coster retains the focus on the energy, effort, and precarity of trying to make space for disability in dominant systems, institutions, and discourses, but shifts the context from dramatic performance to daily social self-performance. De Coster places herself in dialogue with Danielle, a middle-aged Belgian Congolese woman who participated in De Coster's research into how people navigate intersectional disabled identities in their daily lives. Working and walking with Danielle as a vision-impaired black woman over a number of years provides De Coster with insight into the complex navigations, negotiations, and contestations that characterise Danielle's daily attempts to make a place for herself in social systems. For Danielle, as for many disabled people, there is a strong sense of being a social performer, playing a socially defined role, and pushing to expand the bounds of that role in everyday encounters with social systems, institutions, architectures, and stakeholders around her. The focus of the fragments of Danielle's story that De Coster takes the reader through in this chapter is on Danielle's search for a sense of belonging and how the interactions that unfold during that search impact on her sense of identity. Intertwined with De Coster's narrative as a fieldworker, and what De Coster has learnt about the frustrations Danielle experiences, the chapter shows the feelings raised by navigating inaccessible spaces, places, and systems in daily life can be as frustrating as navigating inaccessible systems in the arts and media industries.

While the early chapters in Part IV focus on dialogue between disabled arts and media makers, between disabled people and non-disabled researchers, or between disabled people and the policy, funding, and industry systems that impact on their lives and their careers, Petra Kuppers' chapter invites a collaborative dialogue between herself and her readers. For Kuppers, storytelling is an activist tool, a way of making change, and participatory, collaborative, and creative storytelling practices can be extremely useful in generating new knowledge and in imagining new worlds in which new roles, relationships, and rules start to prevail. By presenting her chapter as a story fragment, Kuppers invites the reader into this practice, asking the reader to consider where they see the characters, relationships, and scenarios in a science fiction story set in the future going next. The chapter demonstrates how embracing stories – whether of the fictional characters in this chapter or of real people in their real lives in some of the previous chapters – can help rehearse actions, reactions, and calls for change that become part of disability culture activism. The chapter performatively demonstrates and invites the reader to consider the way embracing the capacities of all humans to tell stories, and to rehearse actions and reactions in them, can form part of disability culture activism.

In the final chapter in this section, Bronwyn Preece also blurs the bounds between creative practice and scholarly practice. Preece offers reflections on the way we perform our 'ecological' selves in a style that captures something of the tone, character, and force of her own performance activism as well as a set of arguments about disability, environment, ecology, the interdependency of the human and the natural, and the way aligning disability with notions of nature, wilderness, the uncultured, and uncontrollable disables our performance of self. The chapter gives a sense of how Preece operates in her work, her scholarship, and her life and how her strategic choices go beyond live art, performance art, or social intervention as art into ways of living designed to embody her physically, environmentally and politically engaged self.

Throughout the chapters in Part IV, there is a strong sense of dialogue between disabled people and their environments, disabled people and their communities, and disabled people and their collaborators, in their efforts to provoke change through their art, culture, and media practice. There is a strong sense of dialogue between fact, fiction, and desired futures. Daily practice, scholarship, and performance are intertwined in these alternative format contributions. Personal work and productive collaboration, conversation, and co-creation are intertwined. In some cases, the practitioners put themselves in vulnerable positions in service of their desire to change public perceptions about disability, putting themselves at risk to help both disabled people and the non-disabled public at large see and commit themselves to paths to change. The approach gives insight into how disabled people build communities of practice, cultures, and critical forms – designed to support their distinctive practice rather than replicate, subvert, or reinvent mainstage practice and perceptions of quality – as part of their efforts to create a counter, alternative, or new public sphere more accommodating of their ways of being in the world.

In **Part V**, on *Activism, adaptation, and alternative futures*, contributors give accounts of the way disabled people take agency and leadership in fighting for adaptations, accommodations, and alternative futures, individually and in groups, in their arts, culture, and media practices. While their context and focus varies, what each of the chapters in this section demonstrates is the way disabled people adapt, adjust practice, and act as leaders – accidental or otherwise – in the face of new trends and challenges in the economic, social, cultural, technological, or political sphere.

The section starts with a chapter from Katie Ellis outlining the way in which depictions of disability in toys, merchandise associated with toys, and media associated with toys have evolved over the past century. She traces the social, cultural, and medical history of toys to ascertain what the toys and the culture created around the toys communicate in terms of social values with regard to disability, from ableist representations to social inclusion agendas. She then looks at the way advocates and activists have critiqued disability representation in toys, and called for more inclusive disability representation in toys, including through campaigns on social media designed to push toymakers to make more inclusive toys available.

In the next chapter, Alex Lubet looks at the adaptations and accommodations required to facilitate performance in music for many people with disabilities. He looks at medical model and social model perspectives on the best approach to such adaptations and at the differences between adaptations constructed by rehabilitation centres who work in this area and adaptations constructed by musicians themselves. In doing so, Lubet draws attention to the cost associated with adapting musical instruments to be accessible for disabled musicians, running into tens of thousands of dollars, and raises questions about the way economic access is related to disability access. If the power to push for adaptation and accommodation is restricted to those with the economic and social power – and thus restricted along gender, race, and class lines – then efforts at inclusion in fact risk further excluding certain categories of disabled people. There is thus, Lubet argues, a case for looking at the economics of class in the overall context of disability arts, culture, and media studies, as a clear factor in disabled people's ability to adapt cultural phenomena to make them more inclusive.

Career trajectories for dance artists with disabilities are the concern of Sarah Whatley's chapter. Despite initiatives in recent decades, dance training remains inaccessible for many students with disabilities, as a result of self-perception, self-doubt, and assumptions about inclusion and its compatibility with excellence amongst teachers, training organisations, and parents, amongst other factors. As a result, Whatley observes, dancers with disabilities often find themselves positioned as 'accidental leaders' responsible for their own training, their own careers, and advocacy around inclusion as an enriching feature of the field. Drawing on the work and experiences of disabled dance artists pursuing careers in the UK, and the steps they have taken to dismantle discriminatory attitudes rooted in a narrow dance aesthetic, Whatley captures both the positive features of this self-reliance, self-resourcing, and adaptability and the problematic features of this approach in that it flags persistent inequality of access in the field.

Together, these chapters point to continuing challenges in engagement with mainstream cultural and training institutions, mainstream media, and mainstream corporations, as well as the way disabled people work with, within, around, against, and in parallel to mainstream systems to achieve their goals.

In the next chapter, Akhila Vimal C. addresses the way practitioners are adapting classical Indian dance aesthetics and production practices to include performers with disabilities. In codified classical dance forms that trace their lineage back to the prescriptions about quality performance outlined in the *Nāṭyaśāstra*, Vimal shows, there is little room for representation of the disabled body, except in very defined roles. In India, as in some of the Western performance traditions described in earlier sections of the collection, contemporary practitioners have critiqued this legacy, and looked for ways to include the disabled body in classical dance. In case studies of the work of eminent Bharatanatyam performer Sudha Chandran, who has lived experience of disability, and Delhi-based Bharatanatyam performance troupe Ability Unlimited, led by choreographer Syed Sallauddin Pasha, who does not have lived experience of disability, Vimal finds two approaches to including disabled bodies in classical Indian dance performance. The attention and approval these practitioners have received in some quarters notwithstanding, Vimal raises concerns about the work, and the strong emphasis on overcoming disability to perform with aesthetic quality that equals or exceeds that of non-disabled artists in the work. She asks if practices based on passing, rather than on the distinctive aesthetic possibilities of different bodies, in fact overturn traditional power relationships in the performances and in the production processes that underlie the performances. In doing so, she demonstrates some of the perils of the increased fashionability and popularity of including disabled people in art, culture, and media representations in India and around the world. Vimal questions the value of non-disabled practitioners casting themselves as leaders in the field at the expense of disabled people wanting to act as leaders, and of adaptations that emphasise passing within a traditional aesthetic rather than expanding aesthetics. She highlights potential for these approaches to accommodating the disabled body to, in fact, further increase emphasis on traditional concepts of elite performance and increase challenges for disabled people attempting to adapt forms to their own needs, interests, and desires.

In the final chapter in this section, Bree Hadley considers how the current 'age of austerity' is impacting on art, culture, and media practices by and about people with disabilities, and, in particular, on art-based protest practices by people with disabilities. In recent years, much has been written about austerity as neo-liberal economic, political, social, and ideological agenda that has the potential to have adverse effects for many disabled people – the element of the population already most frequently affected by poverty, prejudice, and abuse. Though actioned in the name of sustainability, these new economic, political, social, and ideological agendas represent a threat to disabled people's ability to survive, thrive, and sustain themselves as integral actors in society in the way the United Nations' 2030 Agenda for Sustainable Development describes. This trend also risks leading to a new set of potentially problematic images, symbols, systems, and institutions that scholars, activists, and artists need to critique in new ways. Much has been written about the way groups affected by local and global governmental shifts towards austerity are protesting, presenting themselves, and being represented by others. The question of how disabled artists are adapting their practices to address these changing cultural circumstances has received less attention. For disabled arts, culture, and media makers, the impact of funding cuts is doubled, decreasing their access to day-to-day support as well as decreasing their access to art and media-making support. In this chapter, Hadley examines responses to austerity amongst disabled performing artists, particularly in the UK and Europe, where protest against this agenda has been most extreme and immediate. The results show a perhaps surprising return to accounts of pain and impairment in performance-based protest practices, an understandable but at the same time risky adaptation to current circumstances in a field that has so long fought to push beyond medical model accounts of disability.

For artists with disabilities, the need to take leadership, and to fight for inclusion and rights as emergent technologies and emergent economic, professional, cultural, or political trends change the landscape in which they work, is both a positive and a negative experience. As the chapters in this final section of the collection show, these practices have the potential to influence the evolution of art, culture, and media forms, and to allow those who follow easier access into art, culture, and media formats that have historically excluded them. At the same time, however, the need to fight for ad hoc accommodations, adaptations, and alternative practices time and time again can be complex, time-consuming, energy-consuming, economically prohibitive for some disabled people, and it can risk re-engaging the professions and the public at large in historically problematic concepts of disability. It can risk increasing the inclusion of some at the expense of increasing exclusion of others with specific intersectionalities of gender, sexual, racial, and disability identity. Tracing through issues in training, production, funding, and reception of current art and media practice by artists with disabilities, the chapters in this section frequently show how critical communities of practice, sharing, and supporting each other can be to disabled people's attempts to continue working in theatre, television, film, literature, visual arts, digital arts, and the media in the face of challenges. In some cases, they also show how critical calling on online communities to help support campaigns – whether for accessible toys, access to training, or access to funds required to continue making work – can be in contemporary disability arts, culture, and media practice.

In the conclusion, the editors take a cue from some of the collaborative and creative contributions to the collection, working together with some of the contributors to reflect on the research into disability arts, culture, and media practices represented in the collection. Collaboratively authored based on research currently underway in the work of many of the Australian contributors, and including reflections from the global contributors, the conclusion reflects on what the disability arts, culture, and media research of the future might look like, do, and achieve in the public sphere.

Rounding out, reflecting on, and contemplating future possibilities arising from the accounts of approaches, aesthetics, and politics gathered in the collection, the conclusion argues for the importance of interdependency, shared conversations about contested matters in multiple communicative modalities, and shared vulnerability in this field of research.

Though the disability arts, culture, and media field has learnt from debates about emancipatory research practice in disability studies more generally, examples of emancipatory approaches in the work of leading authors, disabled scholars, and their non-disabled allies focused on arts- and media-based issues more often turn to their own arsenal of creative tools in advancing the research methodologies operative in the field. Understanding the way these more accessible, collaborative, creative research methods can assist in making voices heard can be of immense value to anyone researching the way the rights of disabled people are reflected or not reflected in their own systems, institutions, and discourses. With strong legacies of collaborative art, culture, and media practice to draw on, the development of research methods that enable this interdependency is something scholars in creative fields can contribute to benefit themselves and the education, social services, science, health, and medicine fields that also research disability issues. In this collection, in which conventional scholarly work is combined with collaboratively authored work, conversation-based work, and creative work, authors take some initial steps in developing research methods and outputs that allow stakeholders to perform relations of interdependency, engagement, collaboration, conflict, and negotiation in which a variety of different voices can be heard. This includes the provision of a plain language summary, to invite the widest community possible into the conversations that unfold in the book. There is great potential to develop these approaches further in the future in continuing productive conversations between disability studies and disability arts, culture, and media studies, as scholars, activists, and artists continue to work together to achieve a greater level of inclusivity in society.

References

Abberley, Paul. 1987. "The Concept of Oppression and the Development of a Social Theory of Disability." *Disability, Handicap, and Society.* 2 (1):5–19.

Adams, Rachel. 2001. *Sideshow U.S.A.* Chicago: University of Chicago Press.

Austin, Sarah, Brophy, Chris, MacDowall, Lachlan, Paterson, Eddie, and Roberts, Winsome. 2015. *Beyond Access: The Creative Case for Inclusive Arts*, Melbourne: Arts Victoria. Accessed 1 June 2018. Available: www.artsaccess.com.au/beyond-access/.

Bates, Victoria, Bleakley, Alan, and Goodman, Sam ed. 2014. *Medicine, Health and the Arts: Approaches to the Medical Humanities.* London & New York: Routledge.

Bogdan, Robert. 1988. *Freak Show.* Chicago: University of Chicago Press.

Bragg, Melvyn. 2007. "The Last Remaining Avant-Garde Movement." *The Guardian*, 11 December 2007. Accessed 1 June 2018. Available www.theguardian.com/society/2007/dec/11/disability.arts.

Cattanach, Ann. 1999. *Process in the Arts Therapies.* London & Philadelphia: Jessica Kingsley Publishers.

Chemers, Michael. 2008. *Staging Stigma: A Critical Examination of the American Freak Show.* London & New York: Palgrave Macmillan.

Clift, Stephen, and Camic, Paul M. ed. 2016. *Oxford Textbook of Creative Arts, Health, and Wellbeing: International Perspectives on Practice, Policy, and Research.* Oxford: Oxford University Press.

Crutchfield, Susan, and Epstein, Marcy. 2000. *Points of Contact: Disability, Art, and Culture.* Ann Arbor: University of Michigan Press.

Davidson, Michael. 2008. *Concerto for the Left Hand: Disability and the Defamiliar Body.* Ann Arbor: University of Michigan Press.

Ellis, Katie, and Kent, Mike. 2011. *Disability and New Media.* London & New York: Routledge.

Garland-Thomson, Rosemarie. 2009. *Staring: How We Look.* Oxford & New York: Oxford University Press.

Garland-Thomson, Rosemarie. 1997. *Extraordinary Bodies: Figuring Physical Disability in American Culture and Literature.* New York: Columbia University Press.

Garland-Thomson, Rosemarie ed. 1996. *Freakery: Cultural Spectacles of the Extraordinary Body.* New York & London: New York University Press.

Goggin, Gerard, and Newell, Christopher. 2003. *Digital Disability: The Social Construction of Disability in New Media.* Lanham: Rowman & Littlefield.

Grehan, Helena, and Eckersall, Peter ed. 2013. *'We're People Who Do Shows': Back to Back Theatre – Performance Politics Visibility.* Wales: Performance Research Books.

Hadley, Bree. 2014. *Disability, Public Space Performance and Spectatorship: Unconscious Performers.* London & New York: Palgrave Macmillan.

Hadley, Bree. 2017a. "Disability Theatre in Australia: A Survey and a Sector Ecology." *Research in Drama Education: The Journal of Applied Theatre and Performance. 22*(3): 305–324.

Hadley, Bree. 2017b. *Theatre, Social Media, and Meaning Making.* London & New York: Palgrave Macmillan.

Hargrave, Matt. 2015. *Theatres of Learning Disability: Good, Bad, or Plain Ugly?* London & New York: Palgrave Macmillan.

Henderson, Brian, and Ostrander, Noam ed. 2010. *Understanding Disability Studies and Performance Studies.* London: Routledge.

Hickey-Moody, Anna. 2009. *Unimaginable Bodies: Intellectual Disability, Performance and Becomings.* Rotterdam: Sense Publishers.

Hogan, Susan. 1997. *Problems of Identity: Deconstructing Gender in Art Therapy.* London: Jessica Kingsley Press.

Johnston, Kirsty. 2016. *Disability Theatre and Modern Drama: Recasting Modernism.* London: Bloomsbury Methuen.

Johnston, Kirsty. 2012. *Stage Turns: Canadian Disability Theatre.* Montréal: McGill University Press.

Jones, Phil, and Dokter, Ditty ed. 2009. *Supervision of Dramatherapy.* London & New York: Routledge.

Kochhar-Lindgren, Kanta. 2006. *Hearing Difference: The Third Ear in Experimental, Deaf, and Multicultural Theater.* Washington: Gallaudet University Press.

Kuppers, Petra. 2017. *Theatre & Disability.* London: Palgrave Macmillan.

Kuppers, Petra. 2014. *Studying Disability Arts and Culture.* London & New York: Palgrave Macmillan.

Kuppers, Petra. 2011. *Disability Culture and Community Performance: Find a Strange and Twisted Shape.* Houndmills: Palgrave Macmillan.

Kuppers, Petra. 2003. *Disability and Contemporary Performance: Bodies on Edge.* New York: Routledge.

Lewis, Victoria. 2006. *Beyond Victims and Villains: Contemporary Plays by Disabled Playwrights.* New York: Theatre Communications Group.

Malchiodi, Cathy ed. 2012. *Handbook of Art Therapy.* New York & London: The Guildford Press.

Mazzeo, Esme. 2016. "Not a Costume: Disability and Authenticity in the Media." *Disability in Media.* 17 May 2016. Available: https://disabilityinmedia.wordpress.com/.

Millett-Gallant, Ann. 2010. *The Disabled Body in Contemporary Art.* New York: Palgrave Macmillan.

Mitchell, David T., and Snyder, Sharon L. 2000. *Narrative Prosthesis: Disability and the Dependencies of Discourse.* Ann Arbor: University of Michigan Press.

Moon, Catherine Hyland ed. 2011. *Materials and Media in Art Therapy: Critical Understandings of Diverse Artistic Vocabularies.* London & New York: Routledge.

Oliver, Michael. 1992. "Changing the Social Relations of Research Production?" *Disability, Handicap & Society.* 7 (2): 101–114.

Payne, Helen ed. 1993. *Handbook of Inquiry in the Arts Therapies: One River, Many Currents.* London & Philadelphia: Jessica Kingsley Publishers.

Perring, Giles. 2005. "The Facilitation of Learning-Disabled Arts: A Cultural Perspective." In Carrie Sandahl and Philip Auslander ed. *Bodies in Commotion: Disability and Performance.* Ann Arbor: University of Michigan Press, 175–179.

Riddell, Sheila, and Watson, Nick. 2003. *Disability, Culture and Identity.* London & New York: Routledge.

Rubin, Judith A. 1999. *Art Therapy: An Introduction.* London & Philadelphia: Brunner Mazel.

Sandahl, Carrie, and Auslander, Philip. 2005. *Bodies in Commotion: Disability and Performance.* Ann Arbor: University of Michigan Press.

Sandell, Richard, Dodd, Jocelyn, and Garland-Thomson, Rosemarie. 2010. *Re-Presenting Disability: Activism and Agency in the Museum.* New York: Routledge.

Siebers, Tobin. 2010. *Disability Aesthetics.* Ann Arbor: University of Michigan Press.

Umathum, Sandra, and Wihstutz, Benjamin. 2015. *Disabled Theater.* Chicago: University of Chicago Press.

Part I
Disability, identity, and representation

2

Great reckonings in more accessible rooms

The provocative reimaginings of disability theatre

Kirsty Johnston

In the context of a media relations workshop that my home university urged faculty to take, I was coached to explain my research on disability theatre in short, media-friendly ways. After several failed attempts which were rightly criticised for being too dense, meandering, or opaque, the experts and interdisciplinary workshop participants selected one story as their favourite 'hook.' It concerned the time I went to see a stage adaptation of Dostoevsky's famed 1898 novel *The Idiot* which used flashing lights to achieve its dramatic effects. Otherwise a compelling, award-winning, socially thoughtful, and artistically innovative production, the event nonetheless provided a clear example of theatre's frequently bewildering and antagonistic relationship with disabled people. Although it focused on one of the most famous fictional characters with epilepsy and drew on the work of one of the most celebrated Western literary authors whose life experiences included epilepsy, its design and directorial choices risked inaccessibility for patrons who experience epilepsy and photosensitivity.

Over the past two decades of my engagement with disability theatre artists, activists, and scholars, I have learnt of and witnessed many such bewildering and provocative theatre moments. In this same time period and in the media workshop, however, I have also discovered that this example has been among the most effective for introducing core impulses driving disability theatre and disability performance studies.

One reason that this example seems to have more traction than others is that the public space of its theatrical event pits the hyper-spectacularity of the flashing lights artistic choice against people with invisible disabilities – people who, until the threshold of the theatrical event, might have 'passed' as non-disabled and expected full inclusion. Instead, the event forced an outing and a public division along the line of disability at its very threshold. This particular line of exclusion was therefore more startling than those that disabled and non-disabled people routinely confront while theatre-going: inaccessible theatre architectures, absence of assistance and/or assistive technologies, ableist dramatic content, and either a total absence or paucity of disabled performers.

Kirsty Johnston

To demonstrate some of this inaccessibility, Petra Kuppers opens her book *Theatre and Disability* (2017) with a nuanced account of her visit to see *The Curious Incident of the Dog in the Night-Time* in London's West End, a play rich in disability themes and disabled characterisation. Taking readers through her negotiations with ticket-sellers and ushers to find legally acceptable space for her and her wheelchair, she shows theatre to be an apparatus or machine whose levers and pulleys, assumptions and exclusions, are laid bare by disability. Arguing that "There is nothing unmarked about my visit to the theatre," she notes that

> [d]isability as a lived category can hardly ever afford that distance from the realities of bodies and their fit or non-fit with social space. We have to think about how to get into the theatre, how to get into our seat, how to access the spectacle – these are core issues for disabled audiences.
>
> *(Kuppers 2017, 5)*

As Kuppers emphasises, the disabled theatre patron can anticipate many physical and sensory barriers in theatre-going, particularly in relation to the long established architectures and professional performance practices of these kinds of urban, commercial theatres. In contrast, my example of *The Idiot* gained traction with my media coaching group precisely because it played with less marked disabilities, happened in a newer theatre, and turned on the seemingly much more optional and remediable choice of a lighting effect. In this case it struck the interdisciplinary group of both regular and infrequent theatregoers that the spectatorial needs of people who experience epilepsy ought to have been a primary design concern in this particular production. Both Kuppers' example and mine also demonstrate the paradox of theatre's evident interest in showcasing disability narratives and characters in the public sphere but without involving disabled people as artists or audiences.

As many scholars have noted, disabled people have a long and complex history with spectacle in the public sphere. In their pioneering and award-winning collection *Bodies in Commotion: Disability & Performance*, Carrie Sandahl and Philip Auslander argued that "people with visible impairments almost always seem to 'cause a commotion' in public spaces," despite the "ubiquitous, even mundane" nature of their experience (2005, 2). In her compelling book *Disability, Public Space Performance and Spectatorship: Unconscious Performers*, Bree Hadley builds in part from these insights to argue that

> As soon as the disabled body enters the public sphere – on the street, in social institutions, in medical institutions or in popular theatre, television and film or literature – it becomes a spectacle. It becomes the focus of more or less furtive stares as passers-by attempt to make sense of its startling, unruly or strange corporeality.
>
> *(Hadley 2014, 2)*

Hadley helpfully locates theatre as one medium among an entangled many by which disabled bodies are seen, read, interpreted, and imagined.

In this chapter, I aim to tease out some of the more particular ways in which theatre has been, and might yet be, involved in this web. This involves attending to questions of both theatre production (for example, dramaturgy, casting, training, access aesthetics) and reception (for example, disabled patron access and inclusive critique), but I make no claim to an exhaustive account in either direction. As an art form with different global traditions stretching back millennia, it is not yet possible to account for every way that disability and theatre have intersected (though there are examples of this in other regions, such as in Akhila Vimal

C.'s discussion of the Indian context in Chapter 27). Instead, I will focus on one of the areas that has received the most scholarly attention: contemporary Anglo-Western disability theatre practices and the dramatic and theatrical traditions that they seek to disrupt.

Disability theatre and production

Beyond the issues raised for spectators, the example of *The Idiot* production and its indebtedness to Dostoevsky serves as a reminder of disabled people's profound and valuable artistic contributions over time. Remembering disabled people's artistry also prompts questions about the involvement of disabled people and people with epilepsy in the cast, crew, and artistic management. What roles did or could people who experience epileptic seizures perform in the production and how? Following the "Nothing about us without us" logic of so much disability activism, culture, and art (see Charlton 2000), is it appropriate for non-disabled people to continue to represent disability experience onstage without regard for accessibility, both at the level of production and reception? What protocols do disability artists, activists, scholars, and audiences invite theatre practitioners to consider or adopt?

I ask these questions in the wake of Jan Derbyshire's "Infrequently Asked Questions, or: How to Kickstart Conversations Around Inclusion and Accessibility in Canadian Theatre and Why it Might be Good for Everybody" (2016). Derbyshire, a playwright, director, dramaturge, performer, and disability inclusion activist, also asks many questions in this vein to foment the idea that

> as creators, innovators, and makers within arts and culture, we are all designers. We plan the processes and develop the practices by which we train or, create, produce, administrate, and disseminate our work; we choose the facilities and can encourage or fight for renovations.
>
> *(Derbyshire 2016, 263)*

Derbyshire's questions emphasise the multifaceted and highly social way that theatre as a medium is both produced and received. As performance theorist Shannon Jackson reminds us, even a solo performance typically involves a "run crew" of people, from lighting operator to performer, playwright to patron, stage manager to director, not to mention the social supports of training, audience development, granting bodies, artistic juries, and marketing.

Thinking about theatre and disability, Derbyshire's article and Jackson's book emphasise the ways in which so many current "run crews" have not yet been designed to support disabled people. For this reason, much disability theatre activism has been directed at creating equitable systems. For example, the Alliance for Inclusion in the Arts in the US advocates for several communities that have been "denied equitable professional opportunities," including those who are "Deaf and hard of hearing, blind and low vision, have mobility, physical, developmental or intellectual disabilities" (cited Derbyshire 2016, 263). It has broadened its activist scope over time to focus not just on casting more disabled actors but also on involving more disabled personnel at all levels of television, theatre, film, and media production. Theatre depends on a complex network of interrelated artistic, technical, community, and business decisions. Derbyshire concludes with an optimistic call for a more "virtuous cycle" and imagines a time ahead when disabled people are wholly involved at all levels, experiencing reciprocity and respect rather than sidelining and exploitation. Her call thus also gestures to Western theatre's far from virtuous history.

Kirsty Johnston

Dramaturgy

An important dimension of this history concerns dramatic representation. As Victoria Ann Lewis argues in her groundbreaking anthology *Beyond Victims and Villains: Contemporary Plays by Disabled Playwrights*, "our contemporary streets, our theaters and mass media are still haunted by the ghosts of a disability past" (2005, xv). Indeed, disabled characters have been mainstays in a wide array of theatre traditions over time.

They are evident in the mad characters of Japanese Noh *monogurui* plays and the contemporary uptake of these figures in such plays as Mishima Yukio's *Lady Aoi* and Kara Juro's *Two Women*. Yoruban popular performance traditions also feature the trickster figure Elegba Esu, a complex and powerful figure often depicted as 'crippled' that scholar Heather Hewett argues would gain from further analysis from a disability studies perspective (Hewett 2005). Disability is also evident in the visually and physically impaired characters of classical Greek drama, like Tiresias the blind seer and the eponymous heroes of Sophocles' *Oedipus Rex* and *Philoctetes*. Italian commedia dell'arte also regularly featured 'mad scenes' by such inamorata as Isabella Andreini, and these can be connected to Shakespeare's Ophelia, Hamlet, and Lear as well as the numerous other disabled characters in his oeuvre. Indeed, a growing Shakespeare and disability studies field re-examines how blindness, epilepsy, dementia, and other disabilities have been configured, performed, and interpreted in his work over time. Likewise, a growing scholarship investigates the significant number of modern plays that centre on disabled figures, from Buchner's *Woyzek* to Brecht's Kattrin in *Mother Courage*, from Treadwell's Young Woman in *Machinal* to Wole Soyinka's cognitively impaired Ifada in *The Road*. This is to say nothing of the many contemporary representations of disability in plays such as Sam Shepard's *Buried Child*, Maria Irene Fornes' *Mud*, August Wilson's *Fences*, Judith Thompson's *Lion in the Streets*, Sarah Kane's *4:48 Psychosis*, and Martin McDonagh's *Cripple of Inishmaan* or musicals like Andrew Lloyd Webber's *Phantom of the Opera*, Jonathan Larson's *Rent*, Stephen Schwartz and Winnie Holman's *Wicked*, Tom Kitt and Brian Yorkey's *Next to Normal*, and Benj Pasek, Justin Paul, and Stephen Levenson's *Dear Evan Hansen* (see Wallin 2012 for an extended discussion about the persistence of pathology in performances of disability). In short, scholars are demonstrating various ways in which Western drama routinely relies on disabled characters, themes, and tropes to achieve its ends.

Therefore, the concern among contemporary disability theatre artists, activists, or scholars has not been about a *lack* of representation. Rather, the focus of concern has been on the *kinds* of representations that have dominated theatre stages. As Sandahl (2005) has summarised,

> In Western dramatic and performance traditions, outward physicality is most often used as shorthand for the character's inner psychological or emotional state. Consider Oedipus's self-inflicted blindness, a bloody wound that signifies his denial of truth; Richard III's hunchback, a beacon of evil, justifying his antisocial behavior; or Laura Wingfield's limp, a mark of shame, explaining her depression and unrealized cravings for male companionship.
>
> *(Sandahl 2005, 255)*

Indeed, as Lewis (2005) notes in her anthology, anyone interested in bringing disability to the contemporary stage must contend with legacies of dramatic disabled figures cast as either evil villains or innocent victims. Performance traditions formed to serve the large public, pictorial stages and large auditoria in which nineteenth-century melodrama flourished, and created a visual lexicon which imbued prosthetics and other visible signs of disability with symbolic meaning (e.g. the use of hooks, peg legs, and eye patches), strategies that certainly carry over to other media as the many villains in Bond, Disney, or other melodramatic films could attest. The tradition of using disability as a shorthand or signal for something else in Western theatre, Lewis argues, has "been so successful in the imaginative arena that it now functions as real" (Lewis 2005, xxii).

Disability activists, artists, and scholars have challenged these inherited, all too often unexamined, misleading, and/or simplistic sign systems in a range of media. In relation to theatre, an especially powerful conversation was published in *American Theatre* in 2001. Featuring leading disability theatre artists, playwrights, and activists John Belluso, Brother Rick Curry, Mike Ervin, Victoria Ann Lewis, Joan Lipkin, Lynn Manning, Susan Nussbaum, Carrie Sandahl, and Cheryl Marie Wade, the conversation was moderated by Kathleen A. Tolan and published under the title "We Are Not a Metaphor." Together the group demonstrated the endurance and potential danger of old, stigmatising disability metaphors in relation to their own theatre practice. In her 2017 analysis of this influential conversation, Petra Kuppers juxtaposes Manning, Wade, and Sandahl's distinctive responses to disability as metaphor in theatre to suggest that

> All three of these theatre practitioners call in different ways for the full weight of a disabled life on stage, though not for metaphor and shorthand, and not for disability as a showcase for non-disabled ability. Creating compelling, in-depth characters in the heritage of the realist dramatic tradition has become one of the focal points of dramatic development around disability.
>
> *(Kuppers 2017, 22)*

Manning's play *Shoot!*, featured in Lewis' *Beyond Victims and Villains* anthology, was written in part as a response to the disability metaphors in *King Lear*. In the 2001 conversation, he explained that although his plays are not always populated by people with disabilities, when he does create a character with a disability,

> I try to make him or her a more fully rounded character and not a metaphor for something else. Let the story be about the grander aspect of the human condition, and let the disabled character be a real human being, for a change.
>
> *(Manning 2001, 20)*

Wade, by contrast, acknowledged the aesthetic pull of "crippled metaphors," particularly in the work of Tennessee Williams, but insisted that the challenge is rather to figure out their emotional power, tap it, and "make our characters so compelling, and their emotional journeys so rich and so full, that we demolish some of those metaphors, and those kind of simplistic and narrow views of what it means" (Wade cited Tolan 2001, 21).

Drawing the conversation in a different direction, Sandahl emphasised how "when people with disabilities are performing, they challenge the way that a lot of these metaphors work" (Sandahl et al. cited Johnston 2016, 20). In *Shattering the Glass Menagerie*, a play Sandahl cowrote and performed with Terry Galloway, M. Shane Grant, and Ben Gunter, scenes from *The Glass Menagerie* intersect with the performers' autobiographical, artistic, and critical responses to it. Early in the play, for example, Sandahl explains her love/hate relationship with the character of Laura Wingfield:

> This play pisses me off because I've always longed to play the part of Laura. After all, she was the only crippled girl who limped her way into the dramatic canon. I never got to

play the pretty girl. Even in my late teens and early twenties, I was cast as the old lady, the crazy inmate, the wacky servant, or as a man. As if my disability cancelled out my femininity. But Laura would give me the chance to play a pretty girl, crippled and all. I always believed that part belonged to me. She was the girl that I loved to hate. I hated her so much that I didn't trust anyone else to play her.

(Sandahl et al. cited Johnston 2016, 20)

This play clearly builds from invested autobiographical performances and pointed critique of past dramatic traditions. The challenges are direct, metatheatrical, playful, and generative.

Introducing her anthology, Lewis (2005) notes the significant power and number of autobiographical disability performances since the 1970s in the realms of stand-up/sit-down comedy, performance art, and theatre. In the 1980s, for example, Canadian playwright Lyle Victor Albert performed internationally his hilarious, multi-award-winning, autobiographical one-man play *Scraping the Surface*. Drawing on Albert's experiences growing up with cerebral palsy in rural Alberta, the production turns on his particular body bringing an intimate action, shaving, into the public sphere through performance. In his analysis of the performance for a special disability-focused issue of *Canadian Theatre Review* in 2005, Andrew Houston argued that by blending oratory, demonstration, and wit "within the first five minutes of the performance, Vic has fully established his skilled approach" (Houston 2005, 34). Mobilising the metaphor "scraping the surface," Albert skilfully takes advantage of theatre's ability to confront prejudice of disabled experience by bringing the actual bodies of disabled performers and audiences together into shared time and space. An international host of performers whose solo performances similarly involve autobiography and reference their own disability experience would include Mat Fraser, David Roche, Greg Labine, Jan Derbyshire, Siobhan McCarthy, Cheryl Marie Wade, Victoria Maxwell, Jess Thom, Lynn Manning, and many others.

Although Lewis (2005) acknowledges the powerful role these productions have had, particularly in galvanising disability art, culture, and activism, her stated goal for her anthology is

to encourage professional, academic and community-based theaters to produce the plays included, and to search out the work of other talented disabled playwrights, performers and theater artists not out of civic duty but because of the artistic return they will reap from such explorations.

(Lewis 2005, xvi)

For this reason, she favours multivoiced dramas with professional production histories that do not require the playwrights themselves to perform. In addition to building opportunities for other actors, her focus on multicharacter dramas aims to allow for the "complex presentation of social life" and do the important activist work of presenting "disability not as an individual condition, but as part of a social and historical process that takes shape between people and across divisions of race, class and gender" (Lewis 2005, xvi–xvii). In addition to the play *P.H.*reaks: the Hidden History of People with Disabilities*, a collaborative project she developed and adapted with Doris Baizley, Lewis includes the work of David Freeman, Lynn Manning, Mike Ervin, John Belluso, Susan Nussbaum, and Charles Mee Jr. Before his play *A Summer Evening in Des Moines*, the anthology also includes Mee's important and oft-quoted "Note on Casting" in which he underlines that while his plays do not take up race and disability as their primary subjects,

Great reckonings in more accessible rooms

> I want my plays to be the way my own life is: race and disability exist. They are not denied. ... There is not a single role in any one of my plays that must be played by a physically intact white person. And directors should go very far out of their way to avoid creating the bizarre, artificial world of all intact white people – a world that no longer exists where I live – in casting my plays.
>
> *(Lewis 2006, 233)*

Mee's comments point to a further primary disability theatre production concern beyond the content and authorship of drama: casting.

Casting

In a scene from Ricky Gervai's and Stephen Merchant's television comedy series *Extras*, actor Kate Winslet, deadpanning as herself in the role of a feature actor on set in a film about the Holocaust, is incongruously dressed in a nun's habit while taking a cigarette break with World War II German soldier 'extra' Andy Millman (Gervais). Pointing at a physically disabled woman walking past them, unaware of their attention, she coaches Millman on how to win an Oscar:

> That is another way you win an Oscar. Seriously, think about it. Daniel Day-Lewis in *My Left Foot* – Oscar. Dustin Hoffman in *Rain Man* – Oscar. John Mills in *Ryan's Daughter* – Oscar. Seriously, you are guaranteed an Oscar if you play a mental. See you later.

The scene satirises the long-standing and commonplace practice of non-disabled actors receiving accolades for their portrayal of disabled characters (and the kind of commonplace dehumanising and homogenising language used to describe disabled people). The most recent example of this practice is Eddie Redmayne's Oscar-winning portrayal of Stephen Hawking in *The Theory of Everything* (2014).

Theatre has an even longer history of this practice as the countless non-disabled performers of plays from *Oedipus Rex* to *The Curious Incident of the Dog in the Night-Time* attest. We can look, for example, at the dust jacket summary of the 2006 special twentieth-anniversary edition of Antony Sher's *Year of the King: An Actor's Diary and Sketchbook*, which highlights his much-lauded approach to performing Richard III in the Royal Shakespeare Company's 1984 production:

> From his brainstorm to use crutches to bring the king's deformity to life, to his research for the role, which included watching interviews with psychopaths, reading about mass murderers, and speaking with doctors and physically challenged individuals, to his visit to his homeland of South Africa, to his experiences in working with the Royal Shakespeare Company, the reader is given a front-row seat to Sher's physical and mental preparation or rather transformation for his landmark performance as "the bottled spider".
>
> *(Sher 2016, n.p.)*

By contrast, in May 2017, when well-known UK activist and disability film, television, theatre, and performance artist Mat Fraser took on the role, many reviewers responded to the unusual sight of a disabled performer playing Richard III. Writing for the *Daily Telegraph*, theatre reviewer Dominic Cavendish gave some sense of this interruption of performance tradition:

> The customary thought when watching the opening "Now is the winter of our discontent" soliloquy of Richard III is "How will they [usually he] do it?"...When Mat

Fraser steps forward in Northern Broadsides' new revival in Hull, you're confronted with something that hits you at a far more visceral level than usual: the humbling spectacle of real-life deformity.

(Cavendish 2017, n.p.)

While Cavendish emphasised his experience of the performance as viscerally new, Susannah Clapp, writing for *The Observer*, noted Fraser's casting as a "coup" for the production and began her review with an explanatory biography of Fraser:

Mat Fraser, who hosted the 2012 Paralympics opening ceremony, has been a stripper and played Seal Boy in the US TV show *American Horror Story*. His mother was given thalidomide when she was pregnant: as a consequence, his arms are short. When he delivers the opening speech of *Richard III*, and talks about being "curtailed," only "half made-up," he does not caper or smirk, but simply dips slightly towards the audience, challenging them to measure the words against his body.

(Cavendish 2017, n.p.)

A similar set of review responses emphasising the considerable break from tradition can be found about the 2017 production of *The Glass Menagerie* in which Madison Ferris made her Broadway debut playing Laura, alongside Sally Field as her mother Amanda, Joe Mantello as her brother Tom, and Finn Wittrock as Jim O'Connor. As the first ever actress in a wheelchair to play a leading role on Broadway, Ferris drew a lot of publicity. In a review entitled "Dismantling 'The Glass Menagerie'," *New York Times* critic Ben Brantley found the production to be "less a thought-through interpretation than a sustained scene-study class" (2017, n.p.). In a further article for the *New York Times* "A Wheelchair on Broadway Isn't Exploitation. It's Progress," Neil Genzlinger noted the abundance of attention and mixed reviews the production received:

Some leading critics have objected to the transformation of Williams's subtle play about a family enveloped in denial into something more strident. The kindest objections say that Mr. Gold's interpretation simply doesn't mesh well with the text; harsher ones on theater chat boards have called his use of Ms. Ferris exploitative.

(Gentzlinger 2017, n.p.)

Disability performance activists, artists, and scholars are far more likely to describe as exploitative the models of acting driving Winslet's satirical smoking and Oscar-seeking nun and Antony Sher's brainstormed crutches. In the UK, award-winning playwright Kaite O'Reilly has been a staunch critic of such practices, arguing in 2005 that "cripping up is the twenty-first century's answer to blacking up" (O'Reilly cited Komparály 2005, n.p.). As Sandahl explains further,

In the disability arts and activist communities, casting non-disabled actors as disabled characters is called pejoratively "cripping up," referencing the outdated practice of white actors "blacking up" to play African American characters. In "cripping up," … an actor is cast to play a character from a less dominant social position. Rarely is an actor of color, a woman, or a disabled person cast against type to play a character from a more dominant social position. Actors from marginalized groups must battle on two fronts, then: to be cast in roles that resemble their own identities and to be cast in roles that do not.

(Sandahl 2005, 236)

In the aforementioned "We are not a Metaphor" conversation amongst disabled artists, playwright and performer Cheryl Marie Wade argued that

> non-disabled actors think that disability *is* the character [*general assent*]. That's what they're busy paying attention to playing. So all of the attention and the emotion goes into having their head postured right, or their wrist lax, or whatever. It's playing a mannerism rather than playing a human being. To some extent, that's like a white guy putting on blackface. It's just as offensive.
>
> *(Wade cited Tolan 2001, 21)*

When I encounter productions that feature non-disabled actors playing disabled characters, mingled with the feelings Wade describes is my sense of profound missed opportunity. Instead of feeling engaged and alive to an innovative or compelling performance, I typically feel as if I am at a museum facing an antiquated object. Like Kuppers, I wonder at all the layers of decision-making and ableist infrastructures that brought this moment to the stage instead of others. In *Stage Turns: Canadian Disability Theatre* (2012), I wrote about a Vancouver production aimed at youth that was about the life of famed Canadian disability advocate Rick Hansen. It showed the character both before and after the accident through which he became paraplegic. Casting an excellent but nonetheless non-disabled actor in the role was a missed opportunity for the youth and student audience, non-disabled and disabled, to see a disabled theatre artist take the stage, particularly given the inclusion goals of the play's hero. With all the talent involved in that production, why was it not directed at imagining new ways to tell the "before and after" disability narrative in a way that privileged disabled artists? Exploring such creative possibilities would have been generative for the theatre, the upcoming audiences, future artists, and other future leaders this show aimed to reach.

While emphasising the problems of "cripping up" is one important line of critique regarding casting, in the "We are Not a Metaphor" (Tolan 2001) conversation, playwright Susan Nussbaum complicates the argument by reminding disability artists that theatre is about artifice. It is a medium fired by the artistic power of making one thing seem like something else: artificial lights painting a sunset, humans playing gods, puppets playing humans, costuming to create a sense of period, and so on. For this reason, some disability theatre artists and activists focus more on highlighting the overwhelming ways by which theatre training, production, and reception systems have thus far overwhelmingly favoured non-disabled people in their pursuit of and access to this artificial and transformative power. As O'Reilly noted in a 2016 interview with Joe Turnbull for *The Stage*, "Theatre is the site where we gather collectively to explore what it is to be human. We have to have the breadth, depth and diversity of experience, rather than a monoculture or just a segment of society talking to itself" (O'Reilly cited Turnbull 2016, n.p.). The challenge is to make sure that those who gather in the theatre have equal access to the various roles of the site both on and off stage.

Training

In response to the oft-used excuse that there are just not enough talented disabled performers available to change the kinds of ableist casting patterns discussed earlier, many disability theatre artists point to the need for more accessible training, auditioning, casting, and production protocols. Sandahl (2005) has written compellingly on the topic of ableist bias in standard actor training sites and models. Exploring more beyond the physical inaccessibility of so many theatre training venues, in "The Tyranny of Neutral: Disability and Actor Training," she provides an insightful analysis of the challenges that standard contemporary actor training poses for many disabled people. She demonstrates how the metaphors and assumptions at play in Western acting curricula entrench some of theatre's largest barriers. Chief among these is the training concept of "neutral," an idealised, foundational state:

> Whatever the acting style, the notion that actors' bodies should first be stripped of individuality and idiosyncrasy as a prerequisite to creating a role undergirds them all. Bodies are considered damaged physically and emotionally from the process of living, and those bodies capable of cure are suitable actors. Disabled bodies, though, cannot be cured. They may tremor, wobble, or be asymmetrical. Implicit in the various manifestations of the neutral metaphor is the assumption that a character cannot be built from a position of physical difference. The appropriate actor's body for any character, even a character that is literally disabled or symbolically struggling, is not only the able body, but also the extraordinarily able body.
>
> *(Sandahl 2005, 261–262)*

Sandahl's exploration of "The Tyranny of Neutral" resonates with the many further frustrations shared by artists who have struggled more with the attitudinal than the physical barriers they encountered in theatre school. Moreover, in addition to taking an inventory of accessibility of the training spaces, times, and resources, Victoria Ann Lewis (2010) argues that

> Without an awareness of the social and historical redefinition of disability that has occurred over the past twenty to thirty odd years, the theatre educator will be ill-equipped to resist the force of centuries of tradition assigning meaning to the disabled figure in dramatic texts and in performance. Educators are encouraged to become as familiar with the prevailing stereotypes of disabled characters (victims or villains) as they are with those of African American depiction (crooks or clowns) or those of women (Madonna or whore).
>
> *(Lewis 2010, 188)*

In a 2009 article entitled "Into the Scene and its impact on inclusive performance training," Kathy Dacre interviews disability playwright, performer, activist, and Into the Scene project coordinator Alex Bulmer about the team of artists she was leading in 2006 from renowned UK disabled-led theatre company Graeae. Dacre first notes how the project was instigated by the Arts Council of England as "a practical intervention designed to challenge and address institutional barriers in order to increase the quantity of disabled/deaf artists entering and graduating from accredited training courses and to increase the quality of that experience" (Dacre & Bulmer 2009, 133). Working with three institutions – Rose Bruford College, the Central School of Speech and Drama, and the Royal Academy of Dramatic Art – the initiative explored actor training, production, and auditioning, ultimately developing models and mentoring schemes and producing a resource guide and DVD. Bulmer explains the genesis of the project in the Arts Council's recognition that

> the professional profile or status of actors with disabilities is far more likely to be improved if educational opportunities are available. There is a real concern that disabled actors at the moment do not have the same access to skill development as non-disabled

performers and in order to compete in the industry with graduates from three-year programmes they need to be equally skilled.

(Dacre & Bulmer 2009, 134)

More recently, in Canada, Bulmer has again been involved in a series of large-scale events aimed at improving the opportunities for disabled theatre artists to develop artistically and professionally. Writing about the first of these held in Toronto in February 2015 under the title of The Republic of Inclusion, Bulmer (2016) argued that

> two of the essential ingredients in creating inclusion are desire and resilience – to not only create desire but also to protect it, and engender resilience. ... Shall we consider how we can structure activity to enliven desire while designing practice that better protects and enables the possibility of fulfillment?
>
> *(Bulmer 2016, 262)*

As Bulmer suggests, a critical part of building desire for theatre among disabled people and resilience in the face of so many barriers is to make theatre accessible to disabled artists and patrons. Bulmer's work with Graeae Theatre Company introduced her to a whole new range of accessibility practices and possibilities.

Access aesthetics

Although there is a strong and vibrant international community of prominent and renowned disability theatre companies, Graeae Theatre Company stands out for its originality and leadership. Formed in the UK in 1980 by Nabil Shaban and Richard Tomlinson as a means to confront social prejudice against disabled people as well as develop and showcase disabled artists, the company developed as a major hub of Deaf and disability artist training and disability theatre innovation. Although many of its productions and company members tour widely, the company has a permanent home in Hackney, East London. In promotional materials, the company describes the space as among the most accessible in the world:

> The award-winning building, the first of its kind in the UK, has creative access at the core of its design. From tactile flooring to sensitive heating systems, the Graeae offices and studio space are sophisticated and urban...a world away from the kind of institutional buildings often associated with access standards.
>
> *(Graeae 2016, 1)*

Jenny Sealey, the company's multi-award-winning artistic director since 1997, has recently published *Reasons to be Graeae: A Work in Progress*, which includes the reflections of the company's artists about their work. She has also shared many of her access ideals in public forums and interviews. For example, in a 2016 interview, she argued that

> Accessibility and inclusion are absolutely permeated within Graeae's DNA. So, it's not a question of understanding it, it's a question of feeling it and knowing that it's your right and responsibility to create accessible theatre. As a Deaf person, I want to go down to see more theatre, and I can't because there is such a lack of signed performances or caption performances. So, for me, making the work that I do at Graeae, it has to be accessible for me, for my Deaf actors on stage; it also has to be accessible for a Deaf audience. But

at the same time, it has to be accessible to blind and visually impaired people, and the set and everything has to be accessible for any wheelchair users or people with mobility issues in the play. We only perform in theatres where the backstage is accessible, and the auditorium has access for more than one wheel chair user, which sometimes is the case with some old theatres. Inclusion is, well, it's everything we do. Some of the mainstream theatres now are including at least one disabled person. I'm waiting for the day when they might include more than one. And I'm waiting for the day when they might include real accessibility in terms of sign language, captioning and audio-description into their main productions.

(Sealey 2016, n.p.)

For Sealey, "real accessibility" involves what she describes as access aesthetics whereby inclusive staging choices are imbricated into the production early in the process rather than tacked on later as an afterthought. Thus, instead of simply agreeing to have someone off to the side of the stage signing for Deaf and hard of hearing audience members or relying on independent audio-description services, the rehearsal and development process would seek creative, disabled artist-led signing, audio description, and other access means from the beginning of the process. Graeae is far from the only company to build creative access protocols into their work, but their long-standing commitment and innovative risk-taking in pursuit of access aesthetics stands out.

Graeae and other companies such as Stage Left Theatre and Theatre Terrific in Canada and Theatre Breaking Through Barriers in the US all seek to feature and serve a diverse complement of disabled people and artists. By contrast, a number of successful disability theatre companies focus more specifically on particular kinds of access. Extant in the UK, for example, is a theatre company that is run by and for visually impaired people. In different ways, the National Theatre for the Deaf and Deaf West Theatre in the US as well as FTH:K in South Africa involve and feature Deaf, hard of hearing, and hearing theatre artists and serve Deaf, hard of hearing, and hearing audiences. Matt Hargrave's 2017 book, *Theatres of Learning Disability*, charts the work of an international complement of theatres featuring learning disabled artists and serving disabled and non-disabled audiences. In another direction, some companies have focused their disability performance aims around specific themes, topics, and concerns. Sins Invalid in the US, for example, self-describes as a "performance project on disability and sexuality that incubates and celebrates artists with disabilities, centralising artists of color and queer and gender-variant artists as communities who have been historically marginalised from social discourse." As this brief and incomplete sampling of companies suggests, there have been and continue to be many ways in which disabled theatre artists have sought to take the stage and serve diverse audiences.

Disability theatre reception

As many of the previous examples suggest, it has been important for disability theatre artists to create accessible spaces, and they have pursued many avenues of opening theatre up to disabled patrons. For example, touch tours in advance of productions allow blind and vision-impaired audience members to feel the scenic space, key properties, and costumes in order to enhance their experience of the show and audio descriptions. Some companies provide visual stories in advance of their productions in order to prepare audiences for the broader theatre architecture and significant production features. Importantly, solicited among such patrons are critics, disabled and non-disabled. While the vast majority of the latter continue to exclude disabled people from their imagined readership, neglecting to assess access issues and failing to critique tired and disenfranchising disability-themed work, the field is gaining from a growing number of critics like Lyn Gardner and Jo Verrent in the UK who regularly attend disability theatre and demonstrate firm understanding of its precepts, possibilities, and pitfalls. Further, social media and other digital platforms have helped to forge valuable critical communities. See, for example, the archived and current posts concerning theatre at the BBC Ouch! Blog, a forum featuring disabled people's voices and critical cultural perspectives.

Disabled audiences have also actively demanded more inclusive modes of viewership. This has led to organisations such as Theatre Access NYC. A joint initiative of the Broadway League and the Theatre Development Fund, it has helped guide theatres towards greater access and regularly provides online services to help patrons find out how to access such production services as audio description, open captioning, sign language, wheelchair access, listening devices, touch tours, and autism-friendly performances. On Broadway and elsewhere, it is now commonplace for companies to schedule 'relaxed performances' in their runs (a practice described in fuller detail by Andy Kempe in Chapter 7). Writing for *Howlround* in 2016, Erica Nagel, director of education and engagement at McCarter Theatre Center, describes relaxed performances as "true judgement free zones" and summarises their key dimensions:

> A Relaxed Performance is a performance in which certain production elements such as light and sound cues are adjusted slightly to even out or soften the sensory experience of the show, or removed altogether. A relaxed performance may also offer accommodations outside of the show itself, such as a relaxation/quiet area, an activity area, family/non-gendered bathrooms, a live-feed of the show in the lobby, and online pre-show materials like a social story (a sort of story-book for individuals with autism about what to expect in seeing the show) and FAQs for parents and caregivers. Ushers for these performances receive some special training, and often autism specialist volunteers are on hand in the house and lobby to support families who need it. Audience members are welcome to bring snacks, toys, and fidgets (objects that can help soothe and focus individuals on the autism spectrum) into the theatre with them, and are welcome to exit and return to the theatre whenever they need to.
>
> *(Nagel 2016)*

Nagel's description helps to demonstrate the way in which theatre auditoria can be opened up to challenge tradition and create space where a broad range of disabled people can gather to build the critical desire and resilience that Bulmer cited earlier.

In this chapter I have touched on only some of the important ways in which disability and theatre have intersected in the past and the ways that disability theatre practitioners have been innovating since the 1980s. The practical and scholarly fields are active, robust, and innovating so quickly that it is challenging to stay current. I conclude, then, simply by noting that the festival and one of the companies involved in *The Idiot* example cited at the outset of this paper returned six years later in January 2018 to the theatre at which I encountered the show, this time providing relaxed performances akin to those Nagel describes and featuring four disabled actors. Each night I attended, it received great audience praise and had already toured to two other cities. It has also engendered criticism from some disabled artists who wonder at the balance of power in the creative process and the kinds of funding this non-disabled-led company received to produce the show in comparison with the kinds of funding disabled-led companies have typically received. These kinds of questions suggest the ongoing nature of the debates and the need for sustained critical engagement with the field as it develops.

References

Albert, Lyle Victor. 2000. *Scraping the Surface: Three Plays by Lyle Victor Albert*. Edmonton: NeWest Press.

Alliance for Inclusion in the Arts. 2015. *Promoting Full Diversity in Theatre, Film and Television*. Accessed 1 June 2018. Available: http://inclusioninthearts.org/.

Brantley, Ben. 2017. "Dismantling 'The Glass Menagerie'." *New York Times*, 3 September 2017. Accessed 1 June 2018. Available: www.nytimes.com/2017/03/09/theater/the-glass-menagerie-review.html.

Bulmer, Alex. 2016. "Inclusion: Building a Culture of Desire and Resilience." *Theatre Research in Canada*. 37 (2): 258–262.

Cavendish, Dominic. 2017. "A Brave Production with Some Powerful Moments – Richard III, Hull Truck Theatre." *The Telegraph*, 11 May 2017. Accessed 1 June 2018. Available: www.telegraph. co.uk/theatre/what-to-see/brave-production-power-richard-iii-hull-truck-theatre-review/.

Charlton, James I. 2000. *Nothing About Us Without Us: Disability Oppression and Empowerment*. Berkeley: University of California Press.

Clapp, Susannah. 2017. "Richard III Review – A Stark and Powerful Coup." *The Observer*, 14 May 2017. Accessed 1 June 2018. Available: www.theguardian.com/stage/2017/may/14/richard-iii-review-northern-broadsides-hull#comments.

Dacre, Kathy, and Bulmer, Alex. 2009. "Into the Scene and its Impact on Inclusive Performance Training." *Research in Drama Education: The Journal of Applied Theatre and Performance*. 14 (1): 133–139.

Derbyshire, Jan. 2016. "Infrequently Asked Questions, or: How to Kickstart Conversations Around Inclusion and Accessibility in Canadian Theatre and Why it Might be Good for Everybody." *Theatre Research in Canada*. 37 (2): 263–269.

Galloway, Terry, Grant, M. Shane, Gunter, Ben, and Sandahl, Carrie. 2016. "Shattering the Glass Menagerie." In Kirsty Johnston ed. *Recasting Modernism: Disability Theatre and Modern Drama*. London: Bloomsbury Methuen, 163–182.

Genzlinger, Neil. 2017. "A Wheelchair on Broadway Isn't Exploitation. It's Progress." *New York Times*, 24 March 2017. Accessed 1 June 2018. Available: www.nytimes.com/2017/03/24/theater/a-wheelchair-on-broadway-isnt-exploitation-its-progress.html.

Gervais, Ricky, and Merchant, Stephen. 2005. *Extras*. Season 1, Episode 3, UK.

Graeae Theatre Company. 2016. *Graeae Theatre Company: Who We Are*. Accessed 1 June 2018. Available: http://graeae.org/wp-content/uploads/2016/12/Graeae-who-we-are_Sept-2016-D2-HR.pdf.

Hadley, Bree. 2014. *Disability, Public Space, Performance and Spectatorship: Unconscious Performers*. London: Palgrave.

Hargrave, Matt. 2017. *The Theatres of Learning Disability: Good, Bad, or Plain Ugly?*. London: Palgrave.

Hewett, Heather. 2006. "At the Crossroads: Disability and Trauma in The Farming of Bones." *MELUS*. 31 (3): 123–145.

Jackson, Shannon. 2011. *Social Works: Performing Art, Supporting Publics*. New York: Routledge.

Johnston, Kirsty. 2016. *Recasting Modernism: Disability Theatre and Modern Drama*. London: Bloomsbury Publishing.

Johnston, Kirsty. 2012. *Stage Turns: Canadian Disability Theatre*. Montreal & Kingston: McGill-Queen's University Press.

Komparály, Jozefina. 2005. "Cripping Up is the Twenty-first Century's Answer to Blacking Up: Conversation with Kaite O'Reilly on Theatre, Feminism, and Disability." *Gender Forum: Illuminating Gender*, 6 June 2005, British Library, London. 12. 29 August 2007. Accessed 25 September 2015. Available: www.genderforum.uni-koeln.de/illuminating/interview_oreilly.html.

Kuppers, Petra. 2017. *Theatre & Disability*. London: Palgrave.

Lewis, Victoria Ann. 2010. "Disability and Access: A Manifesto for Actor Training." In Ellen Margolis and Lissa Tyler Renaud ed. *The Politics of American Actor Training*. New York: Routledge, 177–197.

Lewis, Victoria Ann. 2005. *Beyond Victims and Villains: Contemporary Plays by Disabled Playwrights*. New York: Theatre Communications Group.

Nagel, Erica. 2016. "Relaxed Performances: The Nuts and Bolts of Offering Sensory Friendly Experiences to Your Audience." *Howlround*, 29 September 2016. Accessed 1 June 2018. Available:

http://howlround.com/relaxed-performances-the-nuts-and-bolts-of-offering-sensory-friendly-experiences-to-your-audience.

Sandahl, Carrie. 2005. "The Tyranny of Neutral: Disability and Actor Training." In Carrie Sandahl and Philip Auslander ed. *Bodies in Commotion: Disability and Performance*. Ann Arbor: University of Michigan Press, 255–268.

Sandahl, Carrie, and Philip Auslander. 2005. "Introduction: Disability Studies in Commotion with Performance Studies." In Carrie Sandahl and Philip Auslander ed. *Bodies in Commotion: Disability and Performance*. Ann Arbor: University of Michigan Press, 1–12.

Sealey, Jenny. 2018. *Reasons to Be Graeae: A Work in Progress*. London: Oberon Books.

Sealey, Jenny. 2016. "Access Aesthetics and Modern Drama: An Interview with Jenny Sealey on Graeae Theatre Company's *The Threepenny Opera* and *Blood Wedding*." In *Recasting Modernism: Disability Theatre and Modern Drama*. London: Bloomsbury Methuen, 153–162.

Sealey, Jenny, and Lynch, Carissa Hope. 2012. "Graeae: An Aesthetic of Access: (De)Cluttering the Clutter." In Susan Broadhurst and Josephine Machon ed. *Identity, Performance and Technology: Practices of Empowerment, Embodiment and Technicity*. London: Palgrave Macmillan, 60–73.

Sher, Antony. 2006/1986. *Year of the King: An Actor's Diary and Sketchbook*. Twentieth Anniversary Edition. London: Limelight Editions.

Tolan, Kathleen. 2001. "We Are Not a Metaphor: A Conversation About Representation." *American Theatre*. 17 (21): 57–59.

Turnbull, Joe. 2016. "Kaite O'Reilly: 'I'm Challenging the Notion of Normality'." *The Stage*, 4 May 2016. Accessed 2 June 2018. Available: www.thestage.co.uk/features/interviews/2016/kaite-oreilly-im-challenging-the-notion-of-normality/.

Wallin, Scott. 2012. "Next to Normal and the Persistence of Pathology in Performances of Psychosocial Disability." *Disability Studies Quarterly*. 33 (1): Accessed 1 June 2018. Available: http://dsq-sds.org/article/view/3428/3202.

3

Visual narratives

Contemplating the storied images of disability and disablement

Donna McDonald

Visual narratology

Most of us intuitively understand that attentive listening to other people's stories is an act of empathy. We also understand that when we read stories, whether they are fiction, non-fiction, or memoir, we engage in not only our imagined worlds of drama, romance, adventure, and so on, but also the affective worlds of fear, joy, love, horror, curiosity, hope – indeed the whole gamut of human emotions. Narratology, the theory and study of narratives, is well established and helps us to understand the interactions between the writer, the written text, and the reader. It also serves as a companion to a certain kind of knowledge, that which results from a person's insider viewpoint of events or issues, either as a witness or as a participant who has the lived experience of those particular events or issues.

As an arts psychotherapist and disability policy/studies researcher, I embrace these approaches for understanding the lives and experiences of people with disabilities. I rely on historic and contemporary memoirs (including texts, oral histories, and documentaries and films) of people with disabilities as a counselling, research, and teaching resource, as a way of talking back to stereotypes, and to challenge cultural tropes of sentimentality, most often in stories of inspiration and triumph over adversity. In doing so, I have learnt much about the literary representations of disability from disability studies scholars David Mitchell and Sharon Snyder (2000) and others. My own memoir, *The Art of Being Deaf* (2014), was an act of pushing back against entrenched notions of what it means to be deaf.

In more recent times, and mindful of the argument by art philosophers Alain de Botton and John Armstrong (2013) that "the underlying mission of art [lies in] changing how we experience the world" (151), I have reflected upon the potency of visual arts narratives of disability. In this context, I am less interested in the aesthetics of those visual arts images and more concerned about how to build bridges of understanding between art psychotherapy, disability studies, art history, and art practice. In doing so, I have turned to critical discourses and teaching resources by disability studies scholars such as Ann Millett-Gallant, Rosemarie Garland-Thomson, Tobin Siebers, and Petra Kuppers; art historians such as Richard Sandell, Joceyln Dodd, Keri Watson, and Jon Mann; and art philosophers such as Alain de Botton and John Armstrong. Millett-Gallant's (2000) book *The Disabled Body in Contemporary Art* draws on art history and disability studies to analyse "contemporary artworks that feature visibly disabled bodies and [to] draw these images into longer visual traditions" (19). Garland-Thomson's (2009) book, *Staring: How We Look*, is a forensic examination of the act of staring at disability, disablement, and disfigurement as a "physical response, cultural phenomenon, social relationship, and knowledge gathering endeavor … [which] explores the history, social regulation and cultural contradictions of staring" (11). She draws on the visual imagery of photographs, paintings, films, and sculptures to illustrate her points. Siebers' (2010) *Disability Aesthetics* attempts "to theorize the representation of disability in modern art" (2), and he argues that "In the modern period, disability acquires aesthetic value because it represents for makers of art a critical resource for thinking about what a human being is" (3). Kuppers (2014), a disability culture activist and community performance artist, writes extensively about the interrelationships between disability and culture. Her book, *Studying Disability Arts and Culture: An Introduction*, is a textbook for scholars and artists, examining the work of disabled artists within a critical disability studies framework.

Art historians and museum curators Richard Sandell and Jocelyn Dodd concern themselves with the potential activist role of museums and galleries in advancing improved ways of understanding the lives and experiences of people with disabilities. In their book co-edited with Garland-Thomson, *Re-Presenting Disability: Activism and Agency in the Museum*, they consider creative and visual arts representations of disability in themes as diverse as the classical portraiture of disability, war, freakery, medicine and disability, mental illness, disability and sexuality, disfigurement, and human rights. Similarly, Watson and Mann's online art history teaching resource, *Disability in Art History* (n.d.), persuasively bridges the disciplines of art history and disability studies. In their work, they invite students to "look at examples of the disabled human body as it has been represented in art history" (Watson & Mann n.d., n.p.), and they provide 38 images of visual artworks to illustrate and demonstrate their three main themes: the historical representations of disability; freakshows, power, and privilege; and body, performance, and the post-human.

In this reflective commentary, I share my musings and speculate about the power – for a range of disciplines including art psychotherapy, research, and teaching, as well as self-awareness – arising from the exploratory contemplation of visual arts images of disability, disablement, and the experiences of disabled people. I am influenced in this task by Erwin Panofsky (1955) who reminds us not only that "we cannot analyze what we do not understand" (9) but also that "there is no such thing as the entirely 'naïve' beholder" (16). He suggests that we, as the viewers, have "something [or even] a good deal to forget, and something to learn" (16) before we can appreciate what we are viewing. Just as significantly, we may unconsciously bring our own contemporary cultural histories to our viewing responses without realising how our personal experiences influence our appraisal and interpretation of artworks of other cultures and from earlier times (Panofsky 1955).

Consequently, Panofsky expounds the iconographic-iconologic framework as an objective way of understanding and responding to what we are viewing. He explains that iconography concerns itself with the meaning of artworks rather than their form (26). Meaning is "manifested in images, stories and allegories" (29), while form is "manifested in artistic motifs" (29–30). Panofsky defines iconography as a process of describing and classifying images (31). He defines iconology as the process that finds meaning in the artwork by seeking to understand the principles "which reveal the basic attitude of a nation, a period, a class or religious or philosophical persuasion" (30). He warns that the artist may be unaware of these principles and, indeed, that they may even be contrary to the artist's intention.

Lenette (2016) has simplified and systematised Panofsky's principles in a four-step questioning process as a way of considering photographic images of refugees. I have adapted her process to my task of contemplating visual arts representations of disability. In addressing the form, subject, meaning, and purpose of a visual art image of disability and disablement, the four-step or four-question process consists of:

- Describing the image systematically (what can we see in the image?)
- Drawing inferences from the image (what fresh ways of understanding the social, political, and cultural experiences of disability and disabled people historically and/or contemporaneously can be obtained from this image?)
- Analysing the image (what meanings can be assigned to the artist's image of disability based on what we can see combined with what we think we know about the image?)
- Assuming the artist's intent and purpose in making the image (what was the artist's narrative intentions in portraying disability and the impacts of disablement?)

In short, I aim to explore the narratology of visual arts representation of disability, disablement, and the experiences of disabled people, i.e. the interactions between the artist, the artwork, and the viewer.

A glimpse back into history

But first, let us take a step back in time. Before the invention of the Gutenberg printing press in the fifteenth century, most Europeans' knowledge was gleaned from what they heard and what they directly witnessed. By 1499, more than 2,500 European cities had printing-press houses, and 15 million books had been produced, which in turn drove the costs of books down and expanded the readership (Gornall 2009). Literacy was thus democratised for the general population, liberating reading and writing from the stranglehold of the monasteries, and disseminating knowledge throughout Europe. This brings me to my pivotal questions: to what extent did drawings, paintings, and other visual art forms historically reflect and influence people's understanding of their culture, society, and politics? More specifically, how did the absence and/or presence of images of disability and disablement in the visual arts influence people's understanding of disability by whatever term was used historically, e.g. cripple, handicap, impairment, disablement, and disfigurement? And how might those historical responses pertain to contemporary visual narratives and concomitant 'readings' of disability and disablement?

My musings were heightened when I stumbled across a 2013 documentary, *The Portrait of a Disabled Man from the 16th Century*, available on YouTube (selbstbestimmt1 2013), about a 2005–2006 research project, *The Painting of a Disabled Man—Study on the Representation of Disability and its Relevance to the Present* (Schönwiese & Flieger 2007). According to Schönwiese and Flieger (2007), this sixteenth-century painting, exhibited in the Kunst- und Wunderkammer (Cabinet of Wonders) at Ambras Castle near the city of Innsbruck, had apparently gone unnoticed by the scholarly community. It shows a naked man lying on his stomach on a dark green cloth resting on a table or pedestal. His limp and misshapen body is painted realistically (that is naturalistically), and great technical care appears to have been given to the colour tones of his body and also to the light and shadows within the room. The man's arms are placed downwards by the sides of his body, and his legs are bent up from his knees and crossed over at the ankles, pushing up against his lower back. On his head – which is twisted towards the viewer in a direct gaze – is a dome-shaped red hat with a small floral motif; a white ruffle adorns his neck. Despite the man's evident physical vulnerability, his direct gaze out towards the viewer infuses him as a person, and the image as an object, with dignity. Indeed, forensic curatorial analysis of the work revealed that at that time, the image of this disabled man was decorously covered by a sheet of red paper; if a patron wished to see more, he or she could lift the sheet and look directly at the image (Schönwiese & Flieger 2007).

In their analysis of this painting, Schönwiese and Flieger were concerned with the visual representation of disability, and its relevance to everyday life and to science, from the past to the present. They suggested that this painting provides a historic perspective of 'the gaze,' bringing into sharp focus the deeply ambivalent gaze of the contemporary viewer, a gaze located between curiosity, fright, and detachment (Schönwiese & Flieger 2007). I was moved by this documentary, both professionally and personally. Professionally, I saw how this long-ago painting of a disabled man could teach us so much today about historic attitudes towards disability. Personally, I experienced, very powerfully, its lessons about the vulnerability of human dignity.

Separating the artist's work from the artist's biography

I pause now to explicate what I am *not* talking about. At the risk of contradicting my opening statements about my commitment to the 'insider perspective' of disability memoirs, I am not talking here about visual artworks exclusively produced by people with disabilities with the overtly deliberate and perhaps political intention of proselytising about disability, disability rights, and experiences of living with disability (Amanda Cachia in Chapter 16, Anne Millett-Gallant in Chapter 17, and Ann M. Fox in Chapter 18 of this collection will touch on more politically oriented work in the visual arts). Diane Kirkpatrick (1998), an American art historian, observes that through their artworks, disabled artists can "generate empathy for the hard and dazzling realities of life with disability" (439). De Botton and Armstrong (2013) observe that "Art builds up self-knowledge, and is an excellent way of communicating … to other people. Getting others to share our experiences is notoriously difficult; words can feel clumsy" (40). While important, these insights lead to an entirely different discussion, with a range of topic points including the perceived 'charity' and 'triumphal' status of disabled artists and their artworks. The focus on the artist's 'disability biography' can distract from or, more alarmingly, can be conflated with the artwork itself: the artists' disabilities become the default 'credential' for interpreting their artwork.

I am also mindful of Arnold Hauser's observation in his 1951 four-volume work, *The Social History of Art*, that "those who want to portray their own lives are social groups satisfied with their condition, not those who are still oppressed and would like a different life" (as cited by Eco 2007, 148). If we accept Hauser's proposition, then we need to acknowledge that the works of visual artists with disabilities as acts of protest and reclamation of their identity did not erupt into public attention until the disability rights movement of the 1960s–1970s. Artists such as Frida Kahlo and Chuck Close were early exceptions. This arguably means there is a gap in our understanding of the role of visual arts in telling the stories of people with disabilities prior to the rise of the disability rights movement.

Some visual artworks disclose something about disability either incidentally or to support the work's broader narrative theme. Other works with images of disability, disablement, or illness are comprehensively constructed as 'insider' manifestos calling out for disability rights, respect, or even just the simple acknowledgement of the existence and experiences of disabled people. This distinction matters for at least three reasons.

First, in my conversations about the representation of disability in the visual arts – how disability experiences are shown or 'recorded' in visual artworks and, by corollary, what the viewer can learn about the historic, cultural, social, and political contexts of people's experiences of disability — most listeners default to reframing this topic somewhat unctuously as a form of remedial therapy. Their focus deflects responsibility away from themselves, instead drilling down to the present-day clinical setting for the 'other,' that is the patient or client with a disability, and not on the self-knowledge they themselves might acquire from the precedent of many centuries of art history. The possibility that the historic visual narratives of disability might be a mainstream area for research and teaching across the fields of humanities and the social sciences as well as in health and medicine, or of interest and relevance for anyone other than a person with disability, seems to provoke benign incredulity at best and scepticism at worst.

Second, how we understand the interactions between the contemplative act of *viewing* images of disability and disablement in the visual arts, together with understanding the artist's motivation for *making* those images, seems to be an under-researched area, notwithstanding Rosemary Garland-Thomson's (2009) rigorously conceptual work, *Staring: How We Look*, along with her other similarly themed texts. Third, while contemporary art history explores the context and history of ideas such as Marxism, feminism, sexualities, queer theory, cultural studies, and postcolonial theory (see D'Alleva 2012), relatively little comparable work seems to have been done on the context and history of disability studies in art history. Ann Millett-Gallant's (2000) *The Disabled Body in Contemporary Art* and Tobin Siebers' (2010) *Disability Aesthetics* are the exemplary breakthrough texts in this latter field of study. The alliance between disability studies and art education also appears to be gaining traction (see Wexler 2009; Derby 2013; National Art Education Association 2017). Siebers' texts present perspectives on disability's cultural labour: how disability appears in art, architecture, literature; how its presence and relational web compels new insights into cultures, writing, and experience; and how criticism can offer readers tools for thinking anew about bodies in public space (Kuppers 2015).

Siebers' interest centred on the aesthetics of disability, rejecting the societal belief that disability cannot be beautiful (Levin 2010). My interest takes the next step, going beyond the question of beauty into the 'everyday,' 'ordinary' experiences of disability and disablement, and our responses to them.

A brief discussion of artworks across history, time, and place

I turn now to a small selection of artworks across history, time, and place: *The Beggars* (1568; also known as *The Cripples*) and *The Parable of the Blind Leading the Blind* (also 1568) by the Netherlands Renaissance artist Pieter Bruegel the Elder; *Christina's World*, painted in 1948 by American artist Andrew Wyeth; and the *Schoolgirls and Angels* and *Alice in Wonderland* series of paintings by Australian artist Charles Blackman, during the mid- to late twentieth century.

I apply Lenette's (2016) adaptation of Panofsky's (1955) iconographic-iconologic framework and draw upon socio-historical critique by art historians and other writers in my discussion of these works. I have elected to write specifically about a selection of paintings, rather than rely on the generic but vague term 'visual arts,' to anchor more firmly my premise that the narratives within art images can engender fresh ways of understanding disability and the experiences of disabled people.

Disability as a metaphor for spiritual concerns

First, I consider Pieter Bruegel the Elder's painting *The Beggars*, which is also discussed by Watson and Mann (n.d.) in their online art history resource. Adeline Collange (n.d.)

describes this image systematically (step one of the iconographic-iconologic enquiry process): "Five beggars and cripples are dragging themselves along painfully on their [stumpy, too-short] crutches in the sunny courtyard of a hospital built of red brick. They seem to be about to head off in different directions to beg, as is the woman in the background who is shown holding a begging bowl. On the back of the painting is an inscription in Flemish, "Cripples, take heart, and may your affairs prosper"" (n.d., n.p.). A contemporary viewer, such as myself, might regard this sixteenth-century image of disablement with dismay or revulsion.

In drawing inferences (step two of the iconographic-iconologic exploratory process), I initially made hasty judgements about social cruelty and even speculated upon Bruegel's contempt for these people, given his brutish, albeit detailed, portrayal of the impoverished beggars and their crudely carved crutches. A more objective and sustained analysis of this image (step three) required me to understand its historic context together with insights into Bruegel's narrative intent for his painting. Watson and Mann (n.d.) explain that the decline of the Catholic Church in the sixteenth century resulted in the concomitant decline of charitable services, which in turn led to the rise of homelessness among the poor. They also explain that Christianity had two responses to people with disabilities: they were either sinners who had incurred God's punishment or saints who had a divine purpose. Nevertheless, irrespective of their status as sinners or saints, they were excluded from mainstream society. On further reading about this artwork, I found that several hypotheses have been proposed by art historians to explain the meaning or purpose of this work (step four of the iconographic-iconologic exploratory process), including its "allusion to Koppermaandag, the beggars' feast day held annually on the Monday after Epiphany, when the beggars would sing as they begged for alms in the streets" (Collange n.d., paragraph 3).

We can seek further clues to Pieter Bruegel the Elder's intentions for this painting by looking at his other works, such as *The Parable of the Blind Leading the Blind* (1568), as recounted in the Gospel of Matthew 15:14. Blind beggars were a recurring concern for Bruegel, reflecting his pessimistic view of life and humanity, and perhaps also denoting his moral view that "spiritual blindness" results in people's unhappiness (Bordin & D'Ambrosio 2011). Other interpretations of Bruegel's artistic intentions speculate on his bitterness with the Catholic Church and its lack of care for the tragic lives of people so impoverished and disabled (Karcioglu & Marmor 2002).

Physicians have also long been interested in Bruegel's works, as his masterly detail has enabled them to critically analyse the medical conditions he portrays in his paintings (Karcioglu & Marmor 2002). In his painting of the six blind beggars, ophthalmologists have been able to identify several possible causes of blindness, including corneal leucoma, atrophy of globe (eyeball), removed eyes (enucleation), pemphigus (conjunctival scarring) or pemphigoid (blisters), and photophobia (Karcioglu & Marmor 2002). Thus, contrary to my first judgemental reactions, Bruegel's detailed intentionality seems to signify his concern for his subjects rather than contempt for their lowly status.

My brief excursion around Bruegel's paintings raises further questions for enquiry. For example, how did sixteenth-century viewers respond to this painting? What can we learn, if anything, about sixteenth-century cultural, medical, and political attitudes to blindness and blind people? How might contemporary responses and attitudes differ, and why?

Disability: sentiment versus historical reality

Next, I consider Andrew Wyeth's (1948) 1948 painting, *Christina's World* (The Museum of Modern Art, New York), which is claimed to be one of the best known images in twentieth-century American art (Hoptman 2012). First, we can see and describe the back of a young woman wearing a pale pink dress, with her dark hair tied back off her face (which is hidden from the viewer), sprawled across the bottom of a greenish-ochre-yellow grassy hill. The top half of her body looks lithe and supple, in contrast to her stretched out spindle-thin arms – one behind her, the other in front – in a posture of exertion and tension. The sway of her slim back leans away from the viewer, and her legs, which are mostly hidden at an awkward angle beneath the pink dress, seem inert. A farmhouse with outlying sheds or shacks sits distantly at the top of the hill, giving off an air of remoteness. The windows of the house and sheds are barely visible; the farmhouse door is shrouded in shadow. A pale grey sky hangs over the scene.

Second, we now try to draw inferences from this work. In the absence of prior knowledge, we might wonder at the young woman's twisted, almost prone, posture. Because the young woman's face is turned away from the viewer, she is infused with an anonymity that allows us to imaginatively fill in our own descriptive details. We are left to our own private contemplation of this scene; it looks and feels serene, if somewhat sentimental. Indeed, in the Museum of Modern Art's curatorial essay for this painting, the curator, Laura Hoptman (2012), is initially coy about Christina's personal history. She asks, "Who is this young woman, vulnerable but also somehow indomitable? What is she staring at, or waiting for? And why is she lying in a field?" (4).

However, our analysis – the third step of the iconographic-iconologic exploratory process – of "the meaning of *Christina's World* changes dramatically when we learn about the subject" (Griffin 2010, 32). On page 19 of Hoptman's (2012) curatorial essay, we find that "as a young girl, Christina [Olson] developed a degenerative muscle condition – possibly polio – that robbed her of the use of her legs by the time she was in her early thirties" (19). Christina refused to use a wheelchair, which would have been difficult to use in any case on those grassy slopes, and orthopaedic leather and steel leg braces were not invented until much later, in the 1940s. Instead, she crawled around the house and grounds. Wyeth was disturbed by Christina's half-paralysed body, and he reportedly "felt that when she dragged herself along, she looked 'like a crab on a New England shore'" (Griffin 2010, 35). *Apropos* Wyeth's comment, Griffin (2010) notes:

> As Rosemarie Garland-Thomson (1997) argues in her landmark study, *Extraordinary Bodies: Figuring Disability in American Culture and Literature*, that kind of comment is consistent with the ways in which the physically disabled have often been cast as subhuman.
> *(35)*

Unfortunately, "that kind of comment" made in 1948 is reprised in Hoptman's 2012 curatorial essay when she writes that Christina has a "rather startling combination of girlish beauty and grotesque disfigurement" (25). Siebers (2010) provides a "disability aesthetics" framework for understanding such a conflicted response to Christina's body. He writes, "The senses revolt against some bodies, while other bodies please them" (1). He then poses the question, "Since aesthetic feelings of pleasure and disgust are difficult to separate from political feelings of acceptance and rejection, what do objects representing disability tell us about the ideals of political community underlying works of art?" (2).

With this question in mind, when we proceed to step four in the iconographic-iconologic process, we see a glimpse of the "ideals of political community" in Wyeth's disclosure that he intended his painting "to do justice to [Christina's] extraordinary conquest of a life which most people would consider hopeless" (Hoptman 2012, 23). It is also useful to recall, as

Griffin (2010) does, that in 1948 "Wyeth did not have any visual templates of disabled women in art to emulate when he was painting 'Christina's World'" (39).

However, Wyeth's picture is significantly more than the story of one woman, Christina Olson. Contrary to Hoptman's sentimental assertion that the painting is "less a picture of a living individual than an allegorical figure of American womanhood" (21), the painting reflects the "era's heightened awareness of the vulnerability of the body. Christina's figure emerged from a society peopled with veterans who had recently returned from traumatic experiences in World War II and from widespread contemporaneous fears about polio" (Griffin 2010, 31). A medical history snapshot provides context to Griffin's claim: localised paralytic poliomyelitis epidemics appeared in Europe and the US around 1900, and then global epidemics occurred annually until about 1950 (Nathanson & Kew 2010). It was not until 1955 onwards, with the creation of poliovirus vaccines, such as the Salk vaccine, that the occurrence of polio declined and was eventually eliminated in the US by 1972.

Griffin (2010) concludes his essay by noting that "Christina's gesture of turning away from the viewer and the outside world distils the tyranny of the social norms that circumscribed and marginalised her, norms that can make the handicapped feel less than fully human" (47). Griffin's historically grounded insight contrasts searingly with Hoptman's sanguine conclusion that *Christina's World* embodies "the ideals of an America of Andrew Wyeth's creation and of countless viewers' imaginings" (41). What other interpretations or lessons might Wyeth's witness-perspective of Christina's life provoke about the medico-cultural legacy of polio in particular and the historical sociocultural responses to polio in general?

Deepening understanding of disability images over time

Finally, I consider a series of works by an Australian artist, Charles Blackman, acclaimed as having "drawn and painted some of the most brilliant images in Australia's modern art history" (Dickins & McGregor 2010, 9). I was a convent schoolgirl in 1970 when I first saw Charles Blackman's paintings, which is apposite given schoolgirls in hats and starchy uniforms figured so thematically in his work. Alice in Wonderland also dominated. Despite the schoolgirls' skipping postures and Alice's floral abundance, the vibrancy of those works was muted by an underscoring of loneliness, threat, and unease. At the time, and again now in recollection, Blackman's rendering of the girls' eyes was haunting. The girls' eyes – the schoolgirls' and Alice's – were rarely open. They were either cast in deep shadow (sometimes by the shade of their hats, sometimes by the turning aside of their faces, sometimes for no apparent reason at all) or shut tight in solitary meditation. Even when their eyes were open, they seemed sightless, as if they were staring into a middle distance without focus or attention.

When I was young, I did not draw informed inferences from this motif of sightlessness or question Blackman's artistic purpose. I liked Blackman's paintings for his expressionistic use of colour. I was a compliant and accepting viewer; I gazed and moved on. At most, I assumed Blackman's rendering of the schoolgirls' eyes was merely his artistic motif, his shtick, as it were. When I saw a painting of a girl – any girl – with closed eyes or eyes so deep in shadow that I could not see them, I recognised the painting as a Blackman.

Many years later, when I learnt that his wife, poet Barbara Patterson, was blind, I took Blackman's painterly portrayal of his wife's blindness for granted. It seemed a reasonable thing to do; I assumed he simply saw his wife's blindness and wanted to translate what he saw into those shadowy, haunting images. This shift in my responses to Blackman's paintings over time is consistent with the four-step questioning process in Panofsky's iconographic-iconologic framework. That is, I moved from the first step of a simple descriptive regard for Blackman's work, to the second step of drawing fresh inferences about his paintings based on my new knowledge about his wife's blindness together with my changed personal circumstances in that I was no longer a schoolgirl but a social worker specialising in disability policy.

More recently, I have undergone yet another change, involving a more contemplative regard for these paintings. This is consistent with Panofsky's third step in which we seek a deeper analysis and understanding of the visual arts image. My curiosity about the representation of disability in the visual arts has sent me squirrelling down many rabbit holes – much like Alice. One of those rabbit holes was the Queensland Art Gallery's exhibition of Charles Blackman's works, *Lure of the Sun*, 7 November 2015 to 31 January 2016. The Queensland Art Gallery's blog on 7 January 2016 (The Queensland Art Gallery 2016) states: "Barbara came to stand for Alice herself. Her struggle with her progressive blindness parallels Alice's efforts to conquer the mysterious circumstances in which she found herself."

It is worth reflecting upon this curatorial statement as it achieves a respectful balance between clarity about the artist's purpose ("Barbara came to stand for Alice herself") and explicitness of description ("Her struggle with her progressive blindness..."). In their chapter on activist practice in museums and galleries, Sandell et al. (2010) discuss the tensions and anxieties that museum staff can experience in their efforts to avoid causing offence "by inappropriately drawing attention to or stigmatising difference or by using language which might be judged disrespectful or outdated" (12). Some scholars advocate the social model of displaying and curating visual artworks, rejecting "individualist and medicalized ways of portraying disabled people" (16). However, Sandell et al. (2010) note that museums are well placed "to deploy diverse interpretative approaches" to understanding and learning (16).

Turning again to Panofsky's four-step framework for analysing visual arts images, we need to ask the fourth question: what were Charles Blackman's artistic intentions? What did he himself say or write about his painterly renderings of sight and blindness? In a 1967 interview, Blackman said he was influenced by Australian poet John Shaw Nielson's poems of schoolgirls:

> I thought them very beautiful, and very akin to what I felt myself, in some kind of way: the frailty of their image as such. And there was also the fact – though I did not realise it till much later – that he had very bad eyesight, and he used to write about these things using these emotional powerful throbbing colours ... I was [also] then getting into a kind of vague feeling about painting something about Barbara's personality, because she didn't see as well: all these things seemed to coalesce in a kind of way.
>
> *(Shapcott 1967, 17)*

The striking thing about Blackman's statement is that he is so attentive to the 'aesthetics'" (to use Siebers' term) of his wife's blindness. Blackman's artistic intentions were not political or dramatic; he did not set out to paint 'blindness' as a psycho-medical drama, with the laden stereotypes that both blindness in particular and disability in general carry: vulnerability, invalidity, tragedy, alienation, segregation, or triumph over adversity (see Oliver 1996; Barnes & Mercer 2003; Shakespeare 2006). Rather, Blackman saw his painterly challenge more simply and truly. He wanted to capture the essence of his wife's personality. He wanted to understand and show her completely, not simply as a vessel containing the darkness of lost vision.

However, in 1997, Barbara Blackman wrote dismissively of her (by then divorced) husband's "first-ever exhibition, that of the weird little schoolgirls" (Blackman 1997, 151):

My blindness is my secret, a locked chamber because nobody has the key. Nobody asks the right questions. They [turn the] key in their imagination of blindness, the fear, the exotic, the dark into which we all go. But my blindness is luminance ... Now the schoolgirls, the Alices, the family icons ... they all fade in memory, invaded by light.

(Blackman 1997, 321)

Barbara Blackman's words strike a tone of territoriality. She seems scornful that people do not understand her blindness because they (and it seems that she includes her former husband, Charles, in this group of people) do not ask her "the right questions." She describes her blindness as 'luminance' rather than 'the dark.' For someone who saw writing as her life's vocation, her words are cloyingly dense, hiding more than they reveal. Barbara Blackman goes on even more obliquely: "The schoolgirls are, after all, in transit between the home where they eat and sleep, and the school where they work and play. Transition is perilous. Falls the shadow" (321). How and why is the transition perilous? What shadow, what threat is she alluding to here? And how does this threat pertain to her life, if at all? Barbara Blackman's contrary responses to the schoolgirl paintings – and my questions about her responses – illustrate the wisdom of Panofsky's insight that none of us regards a visual arts image as an "entirely 'naïve' beholder" (16).

Conclusion

Pictures tell stories to viewers through visual elements and conventions, and they shape the way we understand each other (Garland-Thomson 2010). Visual arts narratives of disability and disablement offer us alternative means of understanding, contesting, and reconfiguring what we think we know about disability and the everyday life experiences of people with disability. The power of a single visual arts image, let alone a body of works over time, to illuminate a theme such as disability cannot be underestimated. Just as significantly but perhaps less well understood, the difficulty of accessing images in which people from historically marginalised groups in society can 'recognise' themselves demonstrably contributes to the continued marginalisation of those groups (Leavy 2015, 228). If people with disabilities are rendered 'invisible' or inaccessible both to themselves and to others, then the task of understanding their experiences becomes difficult, if not impossible.

In my discussion of a small selection of visual artworks across history, time, and place, I illustrate how artworks offer scope for critical reflective thinking about the experiences of people with disabilities. The iconographic-iconologic framework is a particularly useful process for contemplating visual arts narratives of disability. It can be applied as a single 'point in time' activity (as in my earlier discussion of the Pieter Bruegel and Andrew Wyeth paintings), or the process might unfold over several years (as in my discussion of Charles Blackman's paintings). It can also be undertaken either as a personal reflection or, for a practitioner, for teaching and research purposes in disciplines as diverse as psychotherapy, medicine, allied health, social sciences, and humanities.

Through this combination of reflection and analysis, we learn not only how "the art related to disability reflects the different ways people come to inhabit their bodies" (Sherwood 2006, 192), but also how artworks can signify the broader sociocultural contexts of disablement. In this way, the visual arts can move beyond merely reflecting the world as it once was, and now is, for disabled people. The visual arts can be an instrument of future disability reform and change. They can be used to contribute to informed discussions in the class-rooms, research domains, or even simply among friends and colleagues. Such discussions may yield nothing more than an occasional changed attitude or new insight about the prospects of better possibilities for people with disability. People's understanding about disability can be reformed by one painting at a time, one conversation at a time.

Acknowledgements

I am grateful for the insightful guidance of Dr Caroline Lenette, University of New South Wales, the encouragement of Dr Naomi Sunderland, Griffith University and Queensland Conservatorium Research Centre, in helping me think through my ideas for this article, and the assistance of Ms Therese Nolan-Brown, Visual Arts Librarian, Queensland College of Art Library, Griffith University, in helping me source useful literature for this article. I also thank Alice J. Wexler and John Derby, co-chairs of the Disability Studies in Art Education (DSAE) Association for their thoughtful editorial support in early drafts of this chapter.

References

Barnes, Colin, and Mercer, Geoff. 2003. *Disability.* Cambridge: Polity Press.
Blackman, Barbara. 1997. *Glass After Glass: Autobiographical Reflections.* Ringwood & Victoria: Penguin Books.
Bordin, Giorgio, and D'Ambrosio, Laura Polo. 2011. *Medicine in Art.* Los Angeles: The J. Paul Getty Museum.
Collange, Adeline. n.d. *The Beggars (1568).* Paris. Musee du Louvre. Carol-Ann. www.louvre.fr/en/oeuvre-notices/beggars.
D'Alleva, Anne. 2012. *Methods and Theories of Art History.* London: Laurence King Publishing.
De Botton, Alain, and Armstrong, John. 2013. *Art as Therapy.* London: Phaidon Press.
Derby, John. 2012. "Art Education and Disability Studies." *Disability Studies Quarterly.* 32 (10). Accessed 25 February 2016. Available: http://dsq-sds.org/article/view/3027/3054.
Dickins, Barry, and McGregor, Ken. 2010. *Charles Blackman. Mini-Art Book No.14.* South Yarra: Macmillan Art Publishing.
Eco, Umberto. 2007. *On Ugliness.* New York: Rizzoli.
Garland-Thomson, Rosemarie. 2010. "Picturing People with Disabilities: Classical Portraiture as Reconstructive Narrative." In Richard Sandell, Jocelyn Dodd, and Rosemarie Garland-Thomson ed. *Re-Presenting Disability: Activism and Agency in the Museum.* London: Routledge, 23–40.
Garland-Thomson, Rosemarie. 2009. *Staring: How We Look.* Oxford: Oxford University Press.
Garland-Thomson, Rosemarie. 1997. *Extraordinary Bodies: Figuring Disability in American Culture and Literature.* New York: Columbia University Press.
Gornall, Dael. 2009. *Dael Gornall Blog.* Accessed 25 February 2016. Available: http://daelgornall.blogspot.com.au/2009/10/gutenberg-caxton-and-origins-of.html.
Griffin, Randall C. 2010. "Andrew Wyeth's *Christina's World*: Normalizing the Abnormal Body." *American Art.* 24 (2): 30–49.
Hoptman, Laura. 2012. *Wyeth. Christina's World.* New York: The Museum of Modern Art.
Karcioglu, Zeynel A., and Marmor, Michael, ed. 2002. "Ocular Pathology in the Parable of the Blind Leading the Blind and Other Paintings by Pieter Bruegel." *Survey of Ophthalmology* 47 (1): 55.
Kirkpatrick, Diane. 1998. "Images of Disability." *Michigan Quarterly Review.* 37 (3): 426–440.
Kuppers, Petra. 2015. "Remembering Tobin Siebers, English Professor, Disability Studies Advocate." *The University Record.* Accessed 25 February 2016. Available: https://record.umich.edu/articles/tobin-siebers-english-professor-and-disability-studies-advocate-dies.
Kuppers, Petra. 2014. *Studying Disability Arts and Culture.* New York: Palgrave Macmillan.
Leavy, Patricia. 2015. *Method Meets Art: Arts Based Research Practice.* New York: The Guilford Press.
Lenette, Caroline. 2016. "Writing with Light: An Iconographic-Iconologic Approach to Refugee Photography." *Forum: Qualitative Social Research.* 19 (2). Accessed 25 February 2016. Available: http://nbn-resolving.de/urn:nbn:de:0114-fqs160287.

Levin, Mike. 2010. "The Art of Disability: An Interview with Tobin Siebers." *Disability Studies Quarterly*. 30 (2). Accessed 25 February 2016. Available: http://dsq-sds.org/article/view/1263/1272.

Millett-Gallant, Ann. 2000. *The Disabled Body in Contemporary Art*. New York: Palgrave Macmillan.

Mitchell, David, and Snyder, Sharon. 2000. *Narrative Prosthesis: Disability and the Dependencies of Discourse*. Ann Arbor: The University of Michigan Press.

Nathanson, Neal, and Kew, Olen M. 2010. "From Emergence to Eradication: The Epidemiology of Poliomyelitis Deconstructed." *American Journal of Epidemiology*. 172 (11): 1213–1229.

National Art Education Association. 2017. *Disability Studies in Art Education*. Accessed 25 February 2016. Available: www.arteducators.org/community/articles/295-disability-studies-in-art-education-dsae.

Oliver, Michael. 1996. *Understanding Disability: From Theory to Practice*. Basingstoke: Macmillan.

Panofsky, Erwin. 1955. *Meaning in the Visual Arts*. Chicago: University of Chicago Press.

Queensland Art Gallery. Exhibition of Charles Blackman's Works, *Lure of the Sun*, 7 November 2015 to 31 January 2016.

Queensland Art Gallery. 2016. Charles Blackman Exhibition. The Queensland Art Gallery – Blog, 7 January 2016. Accessed 1 June 2018. Available: http://blog.qagoma.qld.gov.au/charles-blackman-the-blue-alice/.

Sandell, Richard, Dodd, Jocelyn, and Garland-Thomson, Rosemarie. 2013. *Re-presenting Disability: Activism and Agency in the Museum*. London: Routledge.

Schönwiese, Volker, and Flieger, Petra. 2007. *The Painting of a Disabled Man—Study on the Representation of Disability and its Relevance to the Present*. Institute of Educational Sciences, University of Innsbruck. Presentation to University of California at Berkeley, USA. Accessed 25 February 2016. Available: http://bidok.uibk.ac.at/projekte/bildnis/bildnis-ambras/handout_san_francisco.pdf.

selbstbestimmt1. 2013. *The Portrait of a Disabled Man from the 16th Century*. YouTube. Accessed 1 June 2018. Available: www.youtube.com/watch?v=mIsyJMoVwVQ.

Shakespeare, Tom. 2006. *Disability Rights and Wrongs*. London: Routledge.

Shapcott, Thomas. 1967. *Focus on Charles Blackman*. St Lucia: University of Queensland Press.

Sherwood, Katherine. 2006. "Art, Medicine, and Disability." *Radical History Review*. 94: 191–196.

Siebers, Tobin. 2010. *Disability Aesthetics*. Ann Arbor: University of Michigan Press.

Watson, Keri, and Mann, Jon. n.d. *Disability in Art History*. Accessed 25 February 2016. Available: http://arthistoryteachingresources.org/lessons/disability-in-art-history/.

Wexler, Alice. 2009. *Art and Disability: The Social and Political Struggles Facing Education*. London: Palgrave MacMillan.

Wyeth, Andrew. 1948. *Christina's World*. Tempera on panel, 32 1/4 × 47 3/4 in. Museum of Modern Art, New York. Accessed 25 February 2016. Available: www.moma.org/collection/works/78455.

4

Dis/ordered assemblages of disability in museums

Janice Rieger and Megan Strickfaden

Introduction

Museums are spaces of power and care. They are institutions that present assemblages (Deleuze & Guattari 2002), which are reconstructions and representations of history and societal values, and thus are partial realities that curate human existence. These assemblages cannot ever represent the totality of human existence because it is never possible to do so, and yet these assemblages are embedded with power because choices are made about what ought or ought not be represented within museums (Ott 2013; Bennet 2017). The nature of partial realities is that, at their centre, these are still representations that tell stories of what one would imagine to be the most significant events related to a place (nation, city), with a particular focus on a societal event or issue (war, art, sports, nature, human rights, etc.) and peoples (e.g. immigrants, migrants, First Nations or Indigenous peoples, etc.).

Persons attending museums rely on the expertise of historians, curators, archivists, conservators, and exhibition designers to present materials within the museum that focus upon and represent societal values. Most museum visitors are not aware of the power that museums hold, although more and more museum visitors push against narratives which they do not feel to be adequate representations of the places, events, issues, and peoples of society (Hooper-Greenhill 1992, 2000; Anderson 2004; Janes 2009, 2010). Where there is power, there is also care. Historians, curators, archivists, conservators, and exhibition designers take great care in how they assemble materials within museums. Historians seek to find documented information that represents accurate narratives of interest to the societies and eras in which they work. Curators look for evidence of these narratives through artefacts and material things that aid towards showing the relations of things. Archivists and conservators work towards keeping objects of material culture organised and in good condition so that these pieces of human narratives can be used in storytelling. Exhibition designers work with historians, curators, archivists, and conservators to bring narratives together through visual imagery, spatial environments, text, lighting, and other means as an assemblage of meaning making. As such, a great deal of care is delivered through various experts who are acting to create value and meaning for society.

Dis/ordered assemblages in museums

Assemblages are a complex entanglement of relations among human and non-human things in museums (Kennedy et al. 2013). Here, all things are understood as relational, embodied, and vibrant. Bennet (2009) expands:

> While the smallest or simplest body or bit may indeed express a vital impetus, conatus or *clinamen*, an actant never really acts alone. Its efficacy or agency always depends on the collaboration, cooperation, or interactive interference of many bodies and forces. A lot happens to the concept of agency once nonhuman things are figured less as social constructions and more as actors, and once humans themselves are assessed not as autonomous but as vital materialities.
>
> *(Bennet 2009, 21)*

This idea of materialities becomes a relational force within the assemblage of a museum, and in this case, we consider and explore the notion of disability as part of the museum's assemblage.

When we look closely at how disability is often assembled within museums, it is elevated and focused upon as a unique phenomenon of spectacle or, conversely, it is treated as though it does not exist (Sandell 2002, 2003, 2007; Macleod 2005; Sandell et al. 2005; Church, Panitch & Frazee 2010; Sandell, Dodd & Garland-Thompson 2010; Sandell & Nightingale 2013; Cachia 2016; Frazee, Church & Panitch 2016; Boys 2017). This act of focusing on disability can be attributed to a kind of remembering of disability, while ignoring or pushing it away is a kind of forgetting. In his significant work on cultural forgetting and remembering, Connerton (2006) elaborates upon the way society remembers and forgets, particularly when issues or events within society have been horrific, terrifying, or inhuman. Connerton (2006) argues that often historians among other academics pay a great deal of attention to the role of memory in transmitting knowledge and forming identity, but little attention to what people forget, how they forget, and what they forget.

Forgetting is always entangled with remembering, and Assmann (2008) contends that people must forget in order to remember, and that "memory including cultural memory, is always permeated and shot through with forgetting. In order to remember anything, one has to forget; but what is forgotten is not necessarily lost forever" (105–106). Following along a similar line, Van Assche and collaborators (2009) explain:

> In order to remember, one must be able to forget, to release the capacities of memory. Remembering something necessarily entails the forgetting of other things. Although the crucial importance of forgetting for memorising is nowadays largely acknowledged, the common understanding of memory still tends to privilege remembering over forgetting.
>
> *(Van Assche et al. 2009, 212)*

To understand the assemblage of a museum, we need to explore the dominant narratives that are remembered and recognise those 'other' narratives that are forgotten. People with disabilities often become what Prince (2009) calls the "absent citizen," which is socially constructed, created, and reproduced through cultural beliefs, material relations, and everyday social practices. This "absent citizen" is often absent in museums and their discourse. If disability is present in the museum, it is often represented as an 'overcoming' of something challenging, and persons with disabilities often become worshipped as heroes in the museum (Sandell et al. 2005; Church, Panitch & Frazee 2010; Carden-Coyne 2013; Graham 2013;

Frazee, Church & Panitch 2016). Moreover, the stereotypes often associated with disability and represented in the museum are social outcast, hero, victim, noble symbol, and freak (Carden-Coyne 2013).

This chapter explores how assemblages of disability are created within museums by looking more holistically at how disability is represented, embodied, included (remembered), or excluded (forgotten or silenced) in two museum case studies. Furthermore, this chapter takes a post-humanist approach of enquiry where both human and non-human actors come together to create an assemblage within the museum (Tilley 1990; Olsen 2006). Two case studies, one from Canada and one from Australia are highlighted with the aim of providing details on how disability is remembered, forgotten, and silenced in explicit and implicit ways and how museum spaces embody power and care. We explore how disability is represented through the material culture of museums and the voices of historians, curators, archivists, conservators, and exhibition designers. This work reveals a complex assemblage of how disability is often hidden, how museums care for disability, and the sometimes inadvertent or overt power of museums to control narratives around disability. By exploring assemblages of disability in museums, we reveal deep-seated values and assumptions about disability and its relations.

Disability and museums: a tenuous relationship

Throughout history, museums have acted as places to guide society about events, issues, and peoples. Museums are places of knowledge that form understandings that are often attached to the places that they are embedded within. When visitors come to a new place, they often go to museums in order to understand the characteristics and history of that particular place. The very nature of a museum is to deliver knowledge that is relevant, interesting, and valued by the people who visit it, while also preserving objects, narratives, and histories. Strictly speaking, disability is not typically related to a specific place, and it is not an issue at the forefront of society. For instance, multiple museums in various locations represent war (e.g., Jewish Museum in Berlin, Germany; In Flanders Fields Museum in Ypres, Belgium), First Nations and Aboriginal cultures (e.g., Canadian Museum of History in Ottawa, Canada; Tjapukai Aboriginal Cultural Park, Cairns, Australia), and sports (e.g., Future of Sports Museum in Washington, DC, US; Canada's Sports Hall of Fame, Calgary, Canada), but there is only one known museum of disability, The Museum of disABILITY History in Buffalo, NY, US. Although there are not many museums dedicated to disability, it is interesting how museums with various themes or issues assemble and represent disability. This is because disability is part of the historical fabric of society and can be found within any given theme or issue such as war, sports, human rights, and art.

In all these different kinds of museums, the most common way that they represent disability is through the built environment and the objects that improve access. For example, in Canada at the Nickel Arts Museum, the extent of their "awareness of the needs of disabled people has been primarily limited to facilitating ease of access to the museum building, installing automatic doors and providing for the basic comforts of patrons in wheelchairs through accessible washroom facilities" (Russell-Chimirri 2013, 170). Access to museums (and other public institutions such as libraries, schools, medical centres, for that matter) is exemplified by dedicated parking for people with disabilities, elevators and ramps as alternatives to stairs, automated doors, and accessible amenities such as toilets, ticket counters, and more. However, these ways of representing disability through designed things is predominantly focused on physical mobility, and thus wheelchair access. Furthermore, access is often considered in relation to these services and amenities and not to the content of the museum.

When it comes to the content within museums, Connerton (2006) questions what the museum-going experience is and whether it is inclusive of marginalised narratives. He expands, "in exhibiting a master narrative, the museum's spatial script is overt in its acts of celebratory remembrance and covert in its acts of editing-out and erasure" (Connerton 2006, 321). For example, entering the Great Hall of the Metropolitan Museum in New York, the visitor stands at the intersection of the museum's principal axis: Greek and Roman art, the Egyptian collection, and European painting. A shaping of knowledge and an ordering of values based on the Western tradition are encountered as soon as the visitor enters the front door (Connerton 2006). The knowledge that a museum shapes has often been created outside of marginalised voices, and these marginalised narratives, if they are included within the master narrative, are often hidden from view (Connerton 2006).

Previous studies have been conducted on the relationship between disability and museums based predominantly in the UK, but these studies have not looked at the material manifestation of disability as being both physical access and content in the museum environment. Sandell (2007) suggests that "the museum is a potentially powerful site in which audience perceptions of an issue, a prejudicial view, or a socially accepted memory—even one that is deeply ingrained might be challenged and altered" (85). Candlin (2006) critiques the overly ocularcentric focus of museums and art galleries and emphasises the use of touch, by arguing that museums do not understand *how* people touch and how *sight* still structures tactile exhibits and museum education. Although Sandell and Candlin each acknowledge that museums are places of knowledge, they also push against the kinds of knowledge produced and encourage museums towards alternative ways of representing history, people, societal values, and abilities. This points to a rather tenuous relationship between disability and museums, which lends it to further exploration through our case studies.

Embodied and material case study research

Our case study research was framed by material culture and a more holistic embodied approach. A material culture approach is understood as the study through objects of the values, ideas, attitudes, and assumptions of a society or culture at a given time (Prown 1982; Miller 2010), whereas a more holistic embodied approach involves actively engaging the haptic body (sight, sound, touch, body) of the researchers and research participants including persons with disabilities. Rather than putting objects, artefacts, or things at the centre, like material culture studies, or people at the centre like humanist studies, our approach decentres both to bring them together to explore disability in museums.

As material culture is primarily based on the proposition that objects can be used actively as evidence rather than passively as illustrations (Prown 1982), this became the fulcrum of our research. Prown expands:

> The word *material* in material culture refers to a broad, but not unrestricted, range of objects. It embraces the class of objects known as artefacts—objects made by humans or modified by humans. Thus, the study of material culture might include a hammer, a plow, a microwave, a house, a painting, or a city.
>
> *(Prown 1982, 2, original emphasis)*

Thus, our research moves through material culture research to include other things, like people and their embodied knowledge and experiences in relation to museums and disability. Our research does not study a single object but rather an entanglement of things within the larger thing of the museum and takes it further yet by looking into a more holistic assemblage of two museums.

Our research design is a *following* in each museum as we allowed for the enactment of disability, by leaving our research open to discovery through spaces, text, artefacts, interviews, and through a multitude of differing and embodied encounters. We could have just studied the access of the built environment or the text and artefacts about disability in the museum, but instead our research design was to follow, wander, and encounter differing things to create an assemblage. By doing this, we allowed for black-boxed (Latour 1987; Jones 2014; Rieger & Strickfaden 2016) assumptions about disability to be revealed that would otherwise go unnoticed.

The two case studies featured in this chapter are part of a set of case studies at museums in Canada, Europe, and Australia. The ones examined in this chapter are the Canadian War Museum in Ottawa and the National Gallery of Australia in Canberra. The Canadian War Museum is located in the nation's capital and calls itself "Canada's national museum of military history and one of the world's most respected museums for the study and understanding of armed conflict" (Canadian War Museum n.d). The building and contents studied were opened in May 2005 and include "more than 3 million artefacts, specimens, works of art, written documentation, sound and visual recordings" (Canadian War Museum n.d). The authors spent seven full days studying the Canadian War Museum, which included eleven interviews with museum professionals, walk-along interviews with persons with disabilities, exterior and interior building analyses, deep content analyses (text panels, imagery, artefacts on display, exhibitions), and archival analyses. The National Gallery of Australia in Canberra opened in October 1982 with the aim of developing and maintaining "a national collection of works of art" (NGA n.d). The first author spent five days studying the National Gallery of Australia in Canberra including eight interviews with museum professionals, exterior and interior building analyses, and archival analyses. The resulting data for each case study include audio recordings of interviews with museum professionals, audio recordings of diarised notes created by the researchers, field notes and sketches from object analyses, photographs, audio recordings of acoustics and natural soundscapes within various spaces, information on archival materials related to disability, floor plans of the building and exhibition spaces, audio recordings of interviews with persons with disabilities, transcripts of all audio recordings, and emails documenting follow-up questions with interviewees. This material culture and more holistic embodied approach resulted in rich and detailed information about how disability is represented or not represented in museums.

Remembering, forgetting, and silencing in museums

In each of our case studies, disability is sometimes present; at other times, aspects of disability are barely present or even absent because these are related to cultural memories of silence, loss, and that which is hidden or forgotten. This remembering or forgetting of disability is performed through entangled representations through imagery, objects, text, and the built environment. In both museums, disability was forgotten, remembered, and silenced, and, more specifically, the majority of the narratives on disability are only implicitly present.

What is remembered, forgotten, and silenced can be described as sociocultural memories, those that are spoken and presented explicitly, those that are implicitly present, and those that are often intentionally left out. Many of the explicit aspects of disability were about empowerment, heroic acts, and creating explicit inclusion, whereas the silenced aspects of disability were historical events, peoples, and places that were thought to have messages more valuable than the ones disability could tell. It is important to note that the distinction between forgetting and remembering is not articulated as fixed in this research but as fluid and relational rather than being at two ends of a spectrum, but they are entangled. Remembering and forgetting are also entangled with silencing to create a dis/ordered assemblage in the museum.

Remembering at the Canadian War Museum (CWM)

Remembering disability at the CWM was primarily framed by a medical model of disability, war, and rehabilitation (Rieger, 2016). The CWM is abundant with signifiers of remembering disability, beginning with the ability for all people to enter the museum and navigate freely within it. At the CWM, visitors with disabilities can use all facilities, even though they may be slightly stigmatised by having to push buttons to open doors. The building has no stairs or overt barriers throughout it, and has dedicated toilets for disabled visitors and push buttons on the doors. Many different mobility aids (scooters, walkers, wheelchairs) are available for borrowing by visitors. For the exhibits, some experiences go beyond the typical *sight-focused* way of designing exhibitions, and some artefacts illustrate disability. Several paintings are of veterans who are disabled, veterans with shell shock, and paintings and photographs of wounded bodies and injured veterans. Exhibits included texts, medals, photographs, and sculptures that spoke to the individual stories of veterans who were wounded; for example, a prosthetic leg was displayed in a glass case. A small exhibit, *Rehabilitation: Industry*, displayed photographs and text that referred to the veterans who returned home disabled after the war and the kind of work that they were doing. Visitors also have opportunities to immerse themselves in experiences such as being in a trench or walking over mud fields. The museum mostly highlighted the experiences of soldiers with able bodies who returned from war, with the exception of a short film about shell shock that featured two soldiers from the First World War.

Remembering disability at the CWM was predominantly represented in the displays, a few specialised exhibitions that encouraged haptical engagement (for example, a full-scale trench, a mud field with bodies underneath that could be walked over), one artefact (a prosthetic leg), artefacts created by war veterans (paper poppies), and photographs of veterans creating objects after the war as a part of their rehabilitation (furniture). The most impactful representation of disability in the museum was the short film of 30 seconds that showed veterans from the First World War who had severe shell shock. The word disability was not used throughout all the displays and exhibitions at the museum.

When scouring the archives of the museum, we found additional artefacts representing disability that were not included in the exhibitions (these were both forgotten and remembered). These included paintings by war veterans who were disabled, posters about war veterans and those blinded by the war, letters from soldiers describing that they were wounded or injured, discharge papers, knitwear for veterans who had been disabled, furniture created by veterans who were disabled, artificial eyes used by the veterans, wound bars on the soldiers jackets, and tags that were placed on wounded soldiers that described their disability to doctors.

Remembering at the National Gallery of Australia (NGA)

Remembering disability at the NGA was primarily focused on access and programmes. The remembering was of the recent changes and renovations – accessible parking, lifts, wheelchairs for visitors, and ramps – that have been made to create a more physically accessible environment. Many different mobility aids (scooters and manual wheelchairs) are also available for borrowing by visitors. The NGA has additional ramps to enter into some of the exhibits and accessible toilets (but these do not have automatic push buttons on the doors for access). An audio induction loop has been installed in many areas and in the theatres; audio guides with Auslan are available for some of the special exhibits. The gift shop and café also have a lowered counter for accessibility. Accessible programmes such as the *Art and Dementia* programme and sign interpreted lectures are a feature of major exhibitions and tours. A Braille brochure for the Sculpture Garden and a Braille guide to the gallery are also available. The NGA also offers verbal description tours and touch tours on demand for people who are blind or vision-impaired and assisted-access events where times are reserved for individuals of all abilities to come at specific times that are not crowded or noisy (NGA n.d).

Forgetting at the CWM

Forgetting at the CWM was explored through a more holistic embodied process, wherein we walked, wheeled, touched, talked, looked, listened, climbed, and tasted in order to uncover the threads of forgetting disability. We found that visitors have to travel great distances to see the entire building. There was no logic to the placement of spatial transitions, which resulted in too many orientation issues in the museum. Signage was not tactile, and the museum has very little Braille. Little consideration was given to staff who may also have disabilities. For instance, the gift shop is too crowded for wheelchair access, most of the counters are not adapted, and the only access to the theatre projection booth for staff is by the stairs. Many walls within the museum were physically slanted, making it disorienting and confusing for some visitors. Additionally, the space was very large in scale and acoustically challenging at times.

The collections had diverse content and many things in relation to disability, but when the collections managers and specialists were asked, they were unable to identify and locate items or things about disability. We had to 'dig' and press for more disability-related content and to locate it in the collection. Only one artefact, an artificial limb, was on display that was explicitly related to disability. While a significant amount of content and things in relation to disability was present, these were not named/labelled as such and were not identifiable in the archival database. The word *disability* was almost completely absent from all didactics. The rhetoric of war was overlaid upon the experience of disability in that disability was not named explicitly but implicitly through words such as wounded, injured, and discharged. Most of the artefacts were behind glass and 'hands off' with exceptions to interpretive tables that were brought out periodically. (Amanda Cachia explores the politics of sensorial access in Chapter 16 of this collection, 'Sweet Gongs Vibrating').

These threads of forgetting disability were both implicit and explicit. As such, very little disability content was explicitly communicated; many design features were explicitly inaccessible; the staff did not have explicit training on the needs of visitors with disabilities; and the CWM access was explicitly for people with physical mobilities requiring wheelchair access. The implicit aspects of forgetting were more difficult to find in that we had to search for them and remember what we were looking for in order to identify what was forgotten. For example, when we asked the CWM archivists to retrieve all the things related to disability, they neatly laid out on the table (beside our white gloves) some letters from soldiers, discussing their wounds and injuries, and some textbooks picturing prosthetics.

Most of the things about disability retrieved for us at the CWM were grounded in a medical understanding of disability. And yet, when we dug and pulled, we found other, more sociocultural, items *about* disability. One such item was a knitting pattern for Amputation Covers by *Service Woolies by Beehive*. These were knitting patterns from the Second World War, specifically for soldiers who had become amputees. This pattern, this object in the archives from the CWM, represents a dis/ordered assemblage as it entangles memories of people, stories, objects, and embodied knowledge together, as knitting was much more than a hobby during the war. It was an act of care for the veterans and for many people, a significant feature of life. This forgotten object, when opened up to exploration and viewing, revealed new and entangled knowledge about disability in and out of the medical 'model and rhetoric of war.

Forgetting at the NGA

Forgetting disability at the NGA was illuminated through various discussions with museum professionals and through our analyses of the museum. When interviewed, a number of participants, acknowledged disability through a discussion of artists who had experienced mental illness – such as schizophrenia and depression. As an art museum, the NGA's archival documentation of artists with a disability prioritises biographical information as it relates to the works of art in the collection. The history, collection, and archives of these artists were remembered and documented, but the history of disability through artists with disabilities was limited in terms of its understanding and documentation, as considerations of disability are secondary to art historical narratives. What is remembered and forgotten in a museum or gallery matters, as that translates into knowledge that is, or is not, shared and communicated.

As with the CWM, visitors to the NGA have to travel significant distances to see the entire building, which can be extremely difficult to navigate. There are different elevators for different areas of the museum, which is also disorienting. Signage was not tactile, and the signage was on glass, which often created glare that made wayfinding difficult. Several museum staff advised that they regularly help people to find their way back to the main entrance, and a dedicated visitor experience team aids wayfinding and access for the public. The NGA building is somewhat restricted by the 1970s architectural fabric and its heritage status, which limits structural modifications. The new wing is substantially different from the older parts of the building, with a greater level of ease of orientation. Having said that, the design of spatial transitions in the building, has resulted in several orientation issues. The accessible toilets do not have automatic buttons, and the locks on the doors are extremely small and difficult to use, especially for those with dexterity and mobility issues. As such, some of the facilities at the NGA are below the minimum standards for access as defined in the Australian Government's *Disability (Access to Premises – Buildings) Standards 2010*, which in turn are subject to subsection 31 (4) of the *Disability Discrimination Act 1992*. In addition, the majority of artefacts were 'hands off' with signage indicating this protocol. Finally, there was little to no representation of disability made explicit through the permanent exhibits and artworks on display.

Silencing at the CWM

Silencing of or about disability occurs when knowledge of something very significant about disability is left out of a narrative, either deliberately or unintentionally. At the most basic level, disability was silenced at the CWM by avoiding the use of the very word 'disability.' This silencing was linked to the theme that highlights the glory of war and avoids the results of war. For example, the CWM had an exhibit about the Halifax Explosion of 1917, a maritime disaster in which a ship transporting war munitions exploded, killing 2,000 people and injuring 9,000 others. This is the largest human-made explosion before the development of the nuclear bomb and devastation resulted in the establishment of the Canadian National Institute for the Blind (CNIB) because it was also the largest single event in Canada that had caused the highest number of disabilities, most of which were blindness (CNIB 2012).

One of our research participants who is blind and who spent hours wandering the CWM with us said, "I would like to have them do a special exhibit for the CNIB's 100th birthday in 2018 to celebrate our beginnings and to emphasise those who lost their sight in the wars." We were all troubled that the CWM only represented the Halifax explosion with one painting, with little elaboration about the disaster and its subsequent impacts. This silence about one of Canada's largest disability organisations, the CNIB, and its entanglement with war and history is a significant shortfall in the museum's representation of war and disability. Indeed, blindness in general was silenced throughout the design of the CWM's physical environment (access is primarily around wheelchair access) and services, and through the staff, who seemed unaware of how to contend with visitors who have vision loss. Our research participant who is blind emphasised this silencing of disability around blindness when she commented,

> I don't think that they were necessarily thinking about vision loss when they designed the museum. I think that the nature of trying to create an experience for the participant simply resulted in a better experience for people with vision loss.

That is, while some of the exhibits are tactile and multisensorial, the wayfinding, architecture, and other aspects of the museum are not intentionally designed for people with vision loss. She expands further:

> This is where I would suggest it is lacking. There were many soldiers who were blinded in WW1 and other wars. This did not seem to be reflected at all in the museum. There was mention of those who lost their lives, as it should be, but there are so many who came home with disabilities and I don't think that this was mentioned enough.

Silencing of and about disability at the CWM flows through and from ableist discourse. This ableist discourse is around the design of the museum (its building, site, and exhibits) and around the fit, able-bodied soldiers and veterans. Expanding upon this thread at the CWM and through the stories and embodied experiences of soldiers and veterans, we found that the articulation of the disabled soldier and disabled veteran is silenced because it is overtaken by ableist discourse around the fit, young, and able-bodied soldier. The CWM has many exhibits which illuminate who went to war, who enlisted, and the kinds of measurements that were used (e.g. to assess if the soldier had flat feet) to enlist 'the physically fit and mentally alert' young men. These exhibits are participatory and allow for the visitor to 'test' out their abilities. Exhibits like these perpetuate ableist discourse without allowing for a criticality around war and ableism, and around the line that is and was drawn between the (perceived) 'heroism' of an enlisted able-bodied soldier and the (perceived) 'disgrace' of a discharged disabled veteran. The silencing around ableism was also evident through our archival explorations around disability. We found that as soon as a soldier was disabled (and a tank or vehicle was also disabled), they were no longer *in* the war; instead, their stories and the terms associated with their stories were about being discharged, wounded, injured, broken, and silenced. We are not asserting that the CWM does not include stories about wounded and injured soldiers who then become veterans, but rather that their stories are framed around rehabilitation, a medical model of disability, and above all, around a silencing of the concept of ableism.

Silencing at the NGA

Silencing of and about disability at the NGA is also entangled within ableism. In interviews with gallery staff, there were repeated statements about the desire and need for a culture of inclusion and a broader philosophical shift at an institutional level, rather than a reliance on a few champions. In a recent major exhibition, *Hyper Real*, the language used in the NGA's accompanying exhibition catalogue to describe one exhibit, Sun Yuan and Peng Yu's *Old people's home* (2007), about disability, was framed around ableist discourse and cultural stereotypes about disability:

> Thirteen decrepit old men sit slumped in battery-powered wheelchairs, gazing off into space, drooling from open mouths and hanging on to their positions of power, seemingly by a single breath ... One is missing a leg and clutching a can of beer.
>
> *(Babington 2017, 30)*

We fully support the content of the *Hyper Real* exhibition and its installation at the NGA to engage the public in contemporary issues around normalcy and able-bodiedness. However, we believe that the voices that shape and influence the physical access and inclusion to the installations in *Hyper Real*, could be broadened. While the specific focus on the representation of disability through art is an important inclusion for the NGA, we believe that a more fulsome discussion around disability stereotypes should be presented to engage the public to challenge narratives which they do not feel to be adequate representations of the places, events, issues, and peoples of society.

Power and care in museums

Our research has revealed that the remembering, forgetting, and silencing of disability in the museum is complicated, and sometimes stories and objects are threads that need to be pulled out. Pulled from the vaults, pulled from the databases, and pulled from the memories and stories of museums staff and visitors. Sometimes these threads are extremely difficult to find, unravel, and pull because they have been silenced along the way and so forgotten. Our research opened up a dialogue, an exploration of disability in the museum, as it is often hidden from view or forgotten. The nature of our case studies allowed for an exploration and analysis of the differences and similarities between disability in a war museum and disability in an art gallery. What our research revealed was that the similarities and differences between these two case studies were not based on culture or geography but rather the power and care of the rhetoric around the museum. War framed disability at the CWM, while the rhetoric and appreciation of art and artists framed disability at the NGA. Within these museums, stories, objects, and didactics are curated in relation to the rhetoric of the museum. The physical space and content are both manifestations of the rhetoric of these museums, and although these are easily written or mapped as separate things, they are not neatly separable because they are entwined with knots and relationships in an assemblage of power and care (Hillier & Tzortzi 2006).

This dis/ordered assemblage of disability entangled with power and care became evident from our exploration of museum case studies. It was not easy to disentangle what was the exercise of institutional power and what was the ethics of curatorial care when both were being articulated, and often with a temporal focus as well. For example, one art curator explained how sometimes care for the artist and how the contemporary (living) artist wants to be represented – in this case, a contemporary artist whose physical disability is a central theme of their work but who does not want to be labelled disabled – pushes the narrative away from an articulation of disability towards care for the artist. These choices, of what is told and not told, have the potential to determine future histories and, in turn, cultural memories.

Conceptualising the power of silence and its complex entanglement with remembering and forgetting became very important for this research. We found not just one kind of silence or silencing but many differing threads of silence. Some are articulated as silence in spaces or silences in process, whereas some are silences as oppressed discourse and silence as a boundary (not being able to access certain story lines) (Van Assche & Costaglioli 2011; Dauenhauer, 1980). Trouillot (1995) submits that in thinking about the powers at play affecting silences and the determination of which stories get told and which ones leave traces, it allows for a way of articulating silences (Zeitlyn, 2012).

In both institutions, the implications of the power in determining which stories got told and which stories did not get told became very apparent. Where power exists, tensions also exist. These tensions arise in communicating difficult knowledge, sharing difficult knowledge, and even acknowledging that differing knowledge exists. By this, we mean that when museums and museum staff can acknowledge ableist discourse, they can also begin to acknowledge differing knowledge and begin to share that differing knowledge.

Care at both museums is demonstrated through the built environment and the overt creation of access to get into each building. This care for accessibility is a response to government mandated policies that expect public buildings to support persons with disabilities to engage in activities deemed to be culturally and socially significant for all citizens of society. Interestingly, this care of the built environment so often defaults to accessible design, which does not translate to access for all persons with disabilities. Accessible design often involves larger spaces, which are not necessarily valued for persons who are blind or for people who are older, have dementia or autism.

Furthermore, tensions exist between the museum environment, the object (and care of the object), the visitor (and care of the visitor), the artist (and care for the artist) that weave together to create an assemblage in continual flux depending on the push and pull of these main forces. The CWM's remit includes caring for one of the largest collections of artefacts on war history in Canada and attending to the visitors, war veterans, and their families. The building itself is a response to the visitors' needs. It is designed cleverly with sloped floors to allow for visitors with limited abilities to move throughout the space easily. The visitors are further cared for at the CWM by being provided with wheelchairs and scooters to traverse through the vast space with assistance. The NGA shows great care through the design and dissemination of a variety of programming for all visitors. The research, time, and care that are put into the creation and support of the various public programmes offered at the NGA are exemplary. But as one interviewee explained it is a lot of work undertaken by a few champions and may not be broadly understood by all employees as important. It was explained that not all staff seemed to understand how the Disability Discrimination Act applied to decisions made in the day to day work of the gallery at all times.

The research at the NGA also revealed an interesting relationship between an ethics of care for the object and an ethics of care for the visitor and artist. After doing case study research of museums across three continents over the past five years, this was the first time that this relationship of care with the museum was disentangled. In some cases, more emphasis is put on the care of the object and artist than on the care of the visitor. A museum conservator explains the ethics of care of an object and that it is to be symmetrical and inclusive: "We're not to judge … we're meant to treat all the works of art the same." If this ethics of care and attention for the object was translated to the care and access of the environment and to the diverse needs of visitors, then the NGA would be one step closer to creating an inclusive museum/gallery.

Conclusion

Assemblages within museums are complex networks with rhizomatic paths where disability is remembered, forgotten, silenced, and embedded with power and care. By examining disability as relative to being human but represented through non-human materials, we are able to examine societal values around the notion of disability. Non-human materials are often bracketed off from humans and seen as passive (Callon & Law 1997). Yes, there are differences between objects, texts, environments, and bodies, but we should consider that all of these things have an active role to play in creating representations of disability (Callon & Law 1997).

According to Latour (2005), relationships among people and things are dependent on repeated performativity or the meaning will dissolve. All things are thus seen as constitutive elements and an embodiment of social relations. Objects, things, artefacts are not passive, in this sense, awaiting the curator, designer, or archivist to give them meaning. For instance, museum space as material culture is not the background for experience to happen but is an active agent in shaping knowledge and creating relations. Therefore, museums as an assemblage create multiple entryways and encounters for us to reveal the entanglements of museums with disability.

By researching museums from a more holistic perspective, and analysing them through the concept of an assemblage, it allows for new opportunities of knowledge to be opened up and shared. Our desire is not for an ordering of the assemblage or a pulling apart of the museum into discrete things, but rather for an acknowledgement of the complexity and dis/ordered threads of the assemblage. In this way, disability can weave into conversations, interrupt, and even disrupt cultural norms and stereotypes in the museum.

References

Anderson, Gail. 2004. *Reinventing the Museum: Historical and Contemporary Perspectives on the Paradigm Shift*. Lanham, MD: AltaMira Press.

Assmann, Aleida. 2008. "Canon and archive." In Astrid Erll and Ansgar Nünning ed. *Cultural Memory Studies: An International and Interdisciplinary Handbook*. Berlin: Walter de Gruter, 97–107.

Australian Government. 2010. *Disability (Access to Premises — Buildings) Standards 2010. Disability Discrimination Act 1992*. Accessed 1 June 2018. Available: www.legislation.gov.au/Details/F2010L00668

Babington, Jaklyn. 2017 "The Hyperreal Figure: From the Uncanny to the Cyborg." In Eric Meredith ed. *Hyper Real*. Canberra: NGA Publishing, 26–35.

Bennett, Jane. 2009. *Vibrant Matter: A Political Ecology of Things*. Durham: Duke University Press.

Bennett, Tony. 2017. *Museums, Power, Knowledge: Selected Essays*. Routledge.

Boys, Jos, 2017. *Disability, Space, Architecture: A Reader*. New York: Routledge.

Cachia, Amanda. 2016. "Along Disabled Lines: Claiming Spatial Agency Through Installation Art." In Jos Boys ed. *Disability, Space, Architecture: A Reader*. New York: Routledge, 247–260.

Callon, Michel, and Law, John. 1997. "After the Individual in Society: Lessons on Collectivity from Science, Technology and Society." *Canadian Journal of Sociology/Cahiers Canadiens de Sociologie*. 22 (2):165–182.

Canadian National Institute for the Blind (CNIB). 2012. Website. Accessed 1 June 2018. Available: www.cnib.ca/en/news/Pages/20121203_Remembering-the-Halifax-Explosion.aspx

Canadian Museum. 2014. Website. Accessed 10 July 2014. Available: www.warmuseum.ca/home/.

Canadian War Museum. n.d. Website. Accessed 1 June 2018. Available: www.warmuseum.ca/about/.

Candlin, Fiona. 2006. "The Dubious Inheritance of Touch: Art History and Museum Access." *Journal of Visual Culture*. 5 (2): 137–154.

Carden-Coyne, Ana. 2013. "Ghosts in the War Museum." In Richard Sandell, Jocelyn Dodd and Rosemarie Garland-Thomson ed. *Re-Presenting Disability: Activism and Agency in the Museum*. New York: Routledge, 64–78.

Church, Kathryn, Panitch, Melanie, and Frazee, Catherine. 2010. "Out from Under: A Brief History of Everything." In Richard Sandell, Jocelyn Dodd and Rosemarie Garland-Thomson ed. *Re-Presenting Disability: Activism and Agency in the Museum*. New York: Routledge, 197–292.

Connerton, Paul. 2006. "Cultural Memory." In Chris Tilley, Webb Keane, Susanne Küchler, Mike Rowlands, and Patricia Spyer ed. *Handbook of Material Culture*. London: Sage Publications, 316–324.

Dauenhauer, Bernard P. 1980. *Silence: The Phenomenon and Its Ontological Significance*. Indiana: Indiana University Press.

Deleuze, Gilles, and Guattari, Félix. 2002. *A Thousand Plateaus: Capitalism and Schizophrenia*. Translation by Brian Massumi. London: Continuum.

Frazee, Catherine, Church, Kathryn, and Panitch, Melanie. 2016. "Fixing: The Claiming and Reclaiming of Disability History" In Christine Kelly and Michael Orsini ed. *Mobilizing Metaphor: Art, Culture and Disability Activism in Canada*. Vancouver: UBC Press.

Graham, Helen. 2013. "To Label the Label? 'Learning Disability' and Exhibiting 'Critical Proximity'." In Richard Sandell, Jocelyn Dodd and Rosemarie Garland-Thomson ed. *Re-Presenting Disability: Activism and Agency in the Museum*. New York: Routledge, 115–129.

Hillier, Bill, and Tzortzi, Kali. 2006."Space Syntax: The Language of Museum Space." In Sharon Macdonald ed. *A Companion to Museum Studies*. Oxford: John Wiley & Sons, 282–301.

Hooper-Greenhill, Eilean. 2000. *Museums and the Interpretation of Visual Culture*. London & New York: Routledge.

Hooper-Greenhill, Eilean. 1992. "What is a Museum?" In Eilean Hooper-Greenhill ed. *Museums and the Shaping of Knowledge*. New York: Routledge, 1–22

Janes, Robert R. 2010. "The Mindful Museum." *Curator: The Museum Journal*. 53 (3): 325–338.

Janes, Robert R. 2009. *Museums in a Troubled World: Renewal, Irrelevance or Collapse?* New York: Routledge.

Jones, Paul. 2014. "Situating Universal Design Architecture: Designing with Whom?" *Disability Rehabilitation*. 36 (16): 1369–1374.

Kennedy, Rosanne, Zapasnik, Jonathon, McCann, Hannah, and Bruce, Miranda. 2013. "All Those Little Machines: Assemblage as Transformative Theory." *Australian Humanities Review*. 55: 45–66.

Latour, Bruno. 2005. *Reassembling the Social: An Introduction to Actor-Network-Theory*. London: Oxford University Press.

Latour, Bruno. 1987. *Science in Action: How to Follow Scientists and Engineers Through Society*. London: Harvard University Press.

Macleod, Suzanne. 2005. *Reshaping Museum Space: Architecture, Design, Exhibitions*. New York: Routledge.

Miller, Daniel. 2010. *Stuff*. Cambridge: Polity Press.

National Gallery of Australia, n.d. Website. Accessed 15 September 2017. Available: https://nga.gov.au/aboutus/building/history.cfm.

Olsen, Bjørnar. 2006. "Scenes from a Troubled Engagement: Post-Structuralism and Material culture studies." *Handbook of Material Culture*. London: Sage, 85–103.

Ott, Katherine. 2013. "Collective Bodies What Museums do for Disability Studies." In Richard Sandell, Jocelyn Dodd, and Rosemarie Garland-Thomson ed. *Re-Presenting Disability: Activism and Agency in the Museum*. London: Routledge, 269–279.

Prince, Michael J. 2009. *Absent Citizens: Disability Politics and Policy in Canada*. Toronto: University of Toronto Press.

Prown, Jules David. 1982. "Mind in Matter: An Introduction to Material Culture Theory and Method." *Winterthur Portfolio*. 17 (1): 1–19.

Rieger, Janice. 2016. *Doing Dis/Ordered Mapping/s: Embodying Disability in the Museum*. Unpublished PhD thesis, University of Alberta.

Rieger, Janice, and Strickfaden, Megan. 2016. "Taken for Granted: Material Relations Between Disability and Codes/Guidelines." *Societies*. 6 (1): 6.

Russell-Chimirri, Geraldine. 2013. "The Red Wheelchair in the White Snowdrift." In Richard Sandell, Jocelyn Dodd, and Rosemarie Garland-Thomson ed. *Re-Presenting Disability: Activism and Agency in the Museum*. London: Routledge, 168–178.

Sandell, Richard. 2007. *Museums, Prejudice and the Reframing of Difference.* London & New York: Routledge.

Sandell, Richard. 2003. "Social inclusion, the museum and the dynamics of sectoral change." *Museum & Society.* 191: 45–62.

Sandell, Richard. 2002. *Museums, Society, Inequality.* London: Routledge.

Sandell, Richard, Delin, Annie, Dodd, Jocelyn, and Gay, Jackie. 2005. "Beggars, Freaks and Heroes? Museum Collections and the Hidden History of Disability." *Museum Management and Curatorship.* 20 (1): 5–19.

Sandell, Richard, Dodd, Jocelyn, and Garland-Thomson, Rosemarie. 2010. *Re-Presenting Disability: Activism and Agency in the Muse*um. London: Routledge.

Sandell, Richard, and Nightingale, Eithne. 2013. *Museums, Equality and Social Justice.* London: Routledge.

Tilley, Christopher. 1990. *Reading Material Culture Structuralism, Hermeneutics and Post-Structuralism,* Oxford: Basil Blackwell.

Trouillot, Michel-Rolph. 1995. *Silencing the Past: Power and the Production of History.* Boston: Beacon Press.

Van Assche, Kristof, and Costaglioli, Felip. 2011. "Silent Places, Silent Plans: Silent Signification and the Study of Place Transformation." *Planning Theory.* 11 (2), 128–147.

Van Assche, Kristof, Devlieger, Patrick, Teampau, Petruta, and Verschraegen, Gert. 2009. "Forgetting and Remembering in the Margins: Constructing Past and Future in the Romanian Danube Delta." *Memory Studies.* 2 (2): 211–234.

Zeitlyn, David. 2012. "Anthropology in and of the Archives: Possible Futures and Contingent Pasts. Archives as Anthropological Surrogates." *Annual Review of Anthropology.* 41: 461–480.

5

The Down Syndrome novel

A microcosm for inclusion or parental trauma narrative

Sarah Kanake

In this chapter, I investigate recurrent themes and tropes in the 'Down Syndrome novel' and explore how they privilege mother/child relations to the exclusion of broader, more inclusive representations of Down syndrome. Significant narrative presence requires active agency by the characters, sophisticated representation of identity, and/or a primary narrative voice, but the Down Syndrome novel relies on Down syndrome being presented as an issue or trauma, generally experienced by the mother, and not the life of the disabled character themselves.

I will first define what the Down Syndrome (DS) novel is and briefly map the representation of Down syndrome in mainstream contemporary narrative fiction. I will then undertake textual analysis of DS novels which privilege the mother/disabled child relationship such as *The Memory Keeper's Daughter* (2005) by Kim Edwards and *Jewel* (1991) by Brett Lott. In doing so, I will examine the narrative limitations of characters with Down syndrome when they are viewed exclusively through the mother's point of view, particularly as they relate to agency, narrative inclusion, and adulthood. I will then show how the mother/child narrative functions as a social argument for inclusion without actually including disability as a natural part of our world. By using a close-reading analysis of two important hinging points within the narrative – the diagnosis or introduction of Down syndrome into the narrative, and the conclusion or concluding paragraphs of the narrative – I will show how the mother/disabled child narrative eclipses the experiences of people with Down syndrome in favour of foregrounding the mother's trauma and struggle to accept Down syndrome. Lastly, I will briefly discuss the reception of Down syndrome and Samson Fox in my own novel *Sing Fox to Me* (2016, see also Kanake 2014).

But before that...

I do not have Down syndrome and do not in any way mean for this chapter to remove voice or space from those practitioners, artists, writers, and thinkers with Down syndrome. This chapter offers a textual analysis of a specific style of narrative written by writers largely without an intellectual disability, but often with lived experience of Down syndrome. I fit this category. I am a fiction writer without an intellectual disability who has written a novel about a character with Down syndrome. I do not speak for people with Down syndrome, nor do I speak for anyone with an intellectual disability. However, I seek to understand how fiction writers have constructed the identity of intellectual disability through the use of Down syndrome within contemporary narrative design.

No story without a syndrome

The Down Syndrome novel, as a scholarly classification, describes a specific form of contemporary narrative where Down syndrome figures prominently within the narrative design and subsequently motivates the plot. The Down Syndrome novel builds plot from the inclusion of an intellectually disabled character and makes the acceptance of this character essential to the story. If you remove the character with Down syndrome, or more importantly, their disability, the plot caves in. There is no story without the syndrome.

It is crucial to refer to these narratives as Down Syndrome (DS) novels and not novels with characters who have Down syndrome to reflect the hierarchy of Down syndrome as 'Other' within these texts and acknowledge the way intellectual disability is used by the plot. In the term 'Down Syndrome novel,' the contemporary lower case 's' is eschewed and replaced with the more traditional and virtually obsolete upper case 'S' to immediately identify the power imbalance central to these novels. This is not to criticise Down Syndrome novels or the authors who write them but rather to present a line of difference between depictions of Down syndrome generally and those novels where the syndrome is crucial for the plot.

At first glance, DS narratives have all the appearance of social inclusivity and narrative empowerment. After all, a story that needs Down syndrome to exist is surely providing an inclusive space for a character with Down syndrome. However, these stories rarely give the disabled character any real power and instead often use the syndrome to underpin a moral theme which is not necessarily about disability at all. Indeed, the mother/disabled child genre novel uses Down syndrome as a lens through which to see motherhood without necessarily illuminating the disability experience. These novels include the very popular *The Memory Keeper's Daughter* by Kim Edwards (2005); *Jewel* by Bret Lott (1991); an Australian novel, *Water Under Water* by Peter Rix (2011); and *The Unfinished Child* by Theresa Shea (2013). These novels rely on depictions of intellectual disability and, more importantly, the assumed 'horror' of having a child with Down syndrome to build the plot. Without the syndrome, there would be no story.

There are also novels where Down syndrome is included to enrich, add to, or underpin the plot, but where the character with Down syndrome is not relied on by the narrative. If the syndrome is removed, these novels can still function. They include *Dreamcatcher* (2001) by American novelist Stephen King, *In One Skin* (2001) by Australian author Kristina Olsson, *Foal's Bread* (2011) by Australian author Gillian Mears, and my own novel, *Sing Fox to Me* (2016). Although they will not be discussed in this chapter, a third category of characters with Down syndrome is worth mentioning. These are characters with conditions that *could* be Down syndrome (or possibly Down syndrome plus something else) but go undiagnosed. These novels include *The Sound and the Fury* by William Faulkner (1929), *Barnaby Rudge* by Charles Dickens (1841), and perhaps even *To Kill a Mockingbird*, with its character of Boo Radley, by Harper Lee (1960). These novels cannot be called DS narratives because, in part, the disability is never diagnosed. One of the foundational building blocks of the DS novel is the diagnosis or naming of the syndrome. From the point of diagnosis, the DS novel shifts from whatever it has been and becomes about the inclusion, trauma of, and dealing with the syndrome. For this reason, it is crucial to pause and understand the power dynamics involved in diagnosing, or naming, Down syndrome in the DS novel.

Sarah Kanake

The Down Syndrome novel – diagnosis

The representation of Down syndrome within narrative fiction is dissimilar to many other intellectual disabilities because of its visibility. It is clear that the character has Down syndrome because of the 'stigmata' of the disability, and this visibility is often connected to the polarisation of the character within the story because the character with Down syndrome is never given the chance to introduce their own difference with any sense of ownership or place. How the author handles the immediacy of recognition defines what kind of story it will be. Will the character be born and have their Down syndrome revealed quickly and traumatically like Phoebe in *The Memory Keeper's Daughter* or gently as the angelic Brenda Kay of Bret Lott's *Jewel*? Or will they lumber out of nowhere like the monstrous Benjamin Compson in William Faulkner's *The Sound and the Fury*? The most common introduction for Down syndrome in the DS novel is diagnosis at birth, perhaps because these stories are most commonly told through the eyes or experiences of the mother or perhaps because it is the simplest narrative hinging point to manage.

When a character with Down syndrome arrives in the parental DS novel (most commonly at birth), the narrative must halt to inspect them and diagnose their disability. The moment of diagnosis significantly affects the narrative as a whole. It is the hinging point, or moment of change, from which the narrative cannot return. It signals to the reader that they are now reading a DS novel. But the connection between Down syndrome and plot does not stop there. The denouement is always significantly connected to the syndrome, and the story can only resolve or conclude once the narrator or protagonist has come to grips with the intellectual disability. However, the moment when the disabled character's stigmata is first seen and diagnosed is perhaps the most significant of the narrative.

In 1866, John Langdon Down diagnosed and categorised the classic features or 'stigmata' of Down syndrome. At the time, representations of disability within narrative fiction were reserved to lumbering ferocious giants, pitiable halfwits, madwomen, or the comedic fool. Disabled was as good as saying evil or not to be trusted: "Many literary villains are disabled, providing a metaphorical shortcut to ideas of deviance, bitterness or desire for revenge" (Barker & Murray 2018a, n.p., see also Barker & Murray 2018b). As the diagnosis of Down syndrome became more commonplace, and the stigmata recognisable to non-disabled people, the disability rights movement developed too and the health memoir became more and more popular. With this popularity, depictions of Down syndrome slowly begin to change. Even so, it took time for the portrayal of characters with Down syndrome to develop beyond broken or misshapen figures. Many of these early fictionalised characters are caricatures with pudding basin haircuts, toothless grins, large, lumbering bodies, shuffling gaits, and ill-fitting clothes. They are non-verbal or communicate in broken English, are institutionalised, pitiable, or criminal.

Narrative representation of intellectual disability is inherently troublesome because even when it is done badly, it argues for sameness, to be seen. Despite this threat, these characters are always figures to be pitied. This is seen in a variety of early contemporary texts including poet Anne Sexton's "December 12th" (1969), a narrative poem from a series entitled "Eighteen Days Without You" from the collection, *Love Poems*. In "December 12th," Sexton tells the story of a day spent at an institutionalised "State School where the retarded are locked up with the hospital techniques" (Sexton 1999, 214). She categorises the "invalids" she meets. There is the "five-year-old who sits all day and never speaks," "the two-headed baby," and her "favourite Mongoloid" Bobby. Of these people, she writes that they are a product of "nature, but nature works such crimes" (Sexton 1999, 215). This way of looking at groups of disabled people is backward and outdated to the modern reader, but it is still very much a part of the contemporary DS narrative. We see the horror of institutionalised care through the disabled body again in *The Memory Keeper's Daughter* when Caroline takes the then unnamed baby girl with Down syndrome to a nearby institution:

> The air was thick with cleaning fluid, steamed vegetables, and the faint yellow scent of urine... she passed several doors, glimpsing moments of people's lives, the images suspended like photographs; a man staring out a window, his face cast in shadows.
>
> *(Edwards 2005, 30)*

In addition to this way of seeing institutionalised disabled people, we see diagnosis used as an early hinging point for the plot in *The Memory Keeper's Daughter* when only hours before, Phoebe is delivered by her doctor father. He immediately recognises the stigmata of Down syndrome and is horrified by the child's imperfections. He asks his nurse, Caroline, to take the child to an institution. This was not an uncommon reaction (although the father's medical knowledge allows the author, Edwards, to speed up the process), and institutions appear frequently in both DS narratives and stories of lived experiences with Down syndrome:

> In not so distant days, the diagnosis of Down syndrome was so awful that parents were told to abandon all hope for a normal life with or for the child and to pass their Mongol [sic] straight into the hands of an institution.
>
> *(Gothard 2010, 31)*

What is unusual is what happens next in the novel: Caroline takes Phoebe and raises the child herself, and David, the doctor father, lies to his wife by telling her their baby has died. This one moment – the moment of seeing Down syndrome, calling it by its name, and being subsequently horrified or not horrified by it – is the point at which the narrative becomes about Down syndrome. Without the syndrome, this particular narrative could not exist.

In *Jewel*, this hinging moment comes when Jewel, the eponymous mother of the novel, learns that her intellectually disabled daughter Brenda Kay is diagnosed as a Mongoloid by a doctor some months after the child's birth. Unlike *The Memory Keeper's Daughter*, however, this movement towards diagnosis happens over three chapters. In Chapter 8, Jewel notices Brenda Kay is "a different child" (Lott 1991, 74), and later, "something was wrong... Brenda Kay was wrong somehow" (Lott 1991, 79). In Chapter 9, Jewel begins to notice specific things "wrong" [sic] with her child. She prays that her "baby would smile up at me... roll over...laugh... Nothing came. Now she was five months old" (Lott 1991, 80). Jewel lists the 'stigmata' and symptoms of Down syndrome without realising what they mean. There are several visits to doctors before finally, at the end of Chapter 10, one of these doctors tells the family that Brenda Kay has Down syndrome. Jewel's reaction to this diagnosis sets the tone for the entire narrative:

> "Don't you say those words [mongoloid] in front of me," I said. I'd stopped the rocker without knowing I had, felt myself holding Brenda-Kay even tighter to me. I whispered, "don't you dare."
>
> *(Lott 1991, 199)*

From this moment the narrative changes and becomes not about Jewel's family life or even Brenda Kay's disability, but about Jewel's determination to have her daughter be seen as normal, her struggle to come to terms with Brenda Kay's disability, and her adamant defence of her daughter's right to a good life. How, and by whom, Down syndrome is introduced within the narrative can also keep a narrative from becoming *about* Down syndrome, as we see in *Darcy's Utopia* (Weldon 1990).

Fay Weldon's novel *Darcy's Utopia* (1990) was one of the first contemporary novels to openly identify a character with Down syndrome. The narrative voice observes both mother and child from a distance, which is not unusual in a novel where Down syndrome is included but not essential for driving the narrative arc. This point of view is generally found in novels where the character is built into the periphery of the story, allowing the narrator's voice to freely describe the character with Down syndrome, not necessarily more realistically, but perhaps through a lens more familiar to society. In *Darcy's Utopia*, the character Eleanor Darcy introduces unpleasant but very common opinions regarding the right of someone with Down syndrome to life:

> We saw she was the only one of her family unit who couldn't bear not to see the fruit of her womb, however sour, ripen, drop and live. And that's how it turned out: the child, now twelve, is badly retarded. Erin is no more than its nurse… Left to us, friends and family, we would have said no, sorry Erin, sorry, not for you. This baby you insist on having keeps other babies out, ones, which won't cause this distress to you and yours. Just not this one; Erin, try again.
>
> *(Weldon 1990, 140)*

The view of the mother shifts with a change in narrative voice, and she is herself viewed from the outside by Eleanor, who dreams of a Utopia where the 'mindless child' has no place, and the mother is not heroic but pathetic. In her own narrative, the mother cannot be viewed this way, beyond occasionally doubting herself. She fights, protects, and demands acceptance from society for her child, thus making an argument for the space where Down syndrome can be included, even embraced in society. However, this fight is almost exclusively made by the mother and rarely, if ever, made by the person with Down syndrome, unless that person is directly resisting the parental figure. Often the character with Down syndrome is even depicted as passively accepting these limitations and therefore supporting lowered expectations of real people with Down syndrome. These lowered expectations permeate fictional narratives which have characters with Down syndrome, in part because many of these narratives are trying to understand Down syndrome by way of the struggles of the mother, but in part also because so many of them are set in the past.

Many parental DS novels are set within a single point of time in history, and so it is difficult to find narratives that provide varying perspectives of the moment of diagnosis across a historical time span. An interesting exception is *The Unfinished Child* by Theresa Shea (2013), which is set both in the 1940s and the early 2000s, and follows the stories of two mothers: one who gives birth to a daughter with Down syndrome and institutionalises her, and the other who is considering a termination. Shea shows the reader that little, besides perhaps medical technology, has changed in how society views the birth and value of a child with Down syndrome:

> In 2011, Denmark boasted that it would be "Down Syndrome Free" by 2030. By contrast, in March of 2013, North Dakota banned abortion based on the result of prenatal testing. These diametrically opposing views exist within the same cultural time frame; clearly, we are not united in our views on whether or not to bring people with Down syndrome into the world. On a certain level, the very fact that a test exists to pinpoint

the existence of Down syndrome suggests that this condition has been identified as being "wrong." In other words, the rhetoric is tipped in a certain direction that makes it difficult for people to think outside of that diagnosis.

(Shea 2013, n.p.)

It is easy to see why the moment of diagnosis has such power within parental DS narratives. They are largely told by mothers, and this moment still carries enormous power in life: "The birth of a child with Down syndrome still causes immense grief and untold anxiety for the family" (Gothard 2011, 30). This act of diagnosing the character with Down syndrome and setting them apart from others in expectation, ability, and appearance sets the plot into motion and defines what is and what is not a DS narrative. It also forms the tone of the novel and even, to some extent, the voice. The syndrome is central to virtually every aspect of the novel's construction including the conclusion.

The Down Syndrome novel – arriving at the conclusion

The DS novel not only revolves around the narrative themes of acceptance, tolerance, and inclusion, but also largely follows the same design: the character with Down syndrome is born, the character is diagnosed, the narrator or protagonist begins the struggle of living with and understanding the character with Down syndrome, and the end of the novel arrives only when the narrator or protagonist has achieved that understanding. The plot is the movement towards this conclusion, but how these endings unfold is important because most DS novels end with the disabled character being placed in a care situation, dead, or rejoined with a non-disabled counterpart. To understand how these conclusions function and what they say about the purported theme of acceptance, I turn now to explore texts that are not explicitly DS novels, but which include problematic conclusions for intellectually disabled characters, such as the death ending.

The death ending in the DS novel is difficult to unpack. There are many reasons – both social and narrative – for why the fictional character with Down syndrome 'must' die. In many ways, they are 'killed off' simply because they are the most vulnerable character and deemed to be the most poignant to kill. Their death creates the most sympathy with the reader:

> Disability has so often been represented in such metaphorical terms that it can seem almost invisible. Every... melodrama whose sentimentality relies on a "retarded" [sic] child, does not require an actual engagement with the details of such difference. Readers, well attuned to the details... understand that the lives of such characters are not as important as what they symbolise. As such, literature can mirror and perpetuate those social processes by which people with disabilities are marginalised and excluded.
>
> *(Barker & Murray 2018a, n.p.)*

Because of this, the death of the character can feel preordained, even natural. It protects the character from the scrutiny of the reader, but it also protects the reader from having their worldview destabilised. In death, the reader is no longer required to pity or worry about the character with Down syndrome. The burden is gone. The character with Down syndrome will not walk out of the novel and into the real world. They have been kept, like a fiction themselves, to the confines of the page. The reader does not have to deal with them:

> Tom from *Water Under Water* and Uncle Punky from *The Man Who Loved Clowns* both die at the end of their narratives. Tom dies a hero saving his friend Amit from

a snakebite while Uncle Punky dies in bed after a prolonged illness. Tellingly, after Punky's death, Aunt Queenie says: "Punky's not handicapped [sic] anymore. He's just like everyone else." (Wood 1995, 218). In death Punky is made safe. His disability melts away and the remaining image is a man who should have been. The baby they "dreamed of having."

(Gothard 2011, 28)

In Stephen King's novel, *Dreamcatcher* (2001), the character with Down syndrome, Duddits, suffers from leukaemia and also dies heroically towards the end of the novel. Duddits follows many of the narrative stereotypes of characters with Down syndrome. He lives with his mother into adulthood; he has a ridiculously simple or infantilised name; he has psychic ability which is central to the narrative plot; he has a limited vernacular; and he dies towards the end of the novel. However, Duddits does not *just* die. In fact, he dies in order to say something about someone else:

> Duddits saw him. Even through his bloody eyes, Duddits saw him. Henry more than felt this: For a moment he actually saw *himself* through Duddits's eyes. It was like looking into a magic mirror. He saw the Henry who had been....

(King 2001, 665)

Instead of being a character in his own right with his own history and his own final last words, Duddits is a narrative device, a mirror intended to bring the non-disabled characters into focus. We also see something more troublesome for the narrative: we see Duddits reflect Henry. Henry is inside Duddits. They are two halves, but only Henry is allowed to survive, and Duddits, in dying, gives Henry back to himself so that Henry can live wholly.

We see something similar in *Cloudstreet* by Tim Winton (1991), when Fish (who is intellectually disabled but does not have Down syndrome) must reunite himself with the man in the river – the man he should have become had be not almost drowned in a fishing accident at the start of the novel – by throwing himself into the river. In drowning, Fish rejoins his non-disabled half and is made whole.

In some DS novels, we see conclusions that imply the character with Down syndrome will either live at home forever, most commonly in the care of their mothers, or be institutionalised, or placed into a group home. In real life, each of these endings would likely have very different results for the person living with the disability. However, in the DS novel, they have much the same effect because, much like the death ending, something must be *done* with the character with Down syndrome. They are inherently subversive because they are not complete or whole, and therefore must be removed, or housed away from the mainstream of society. One DS novel, *Water Under Water*, ends a little differently. After Tom's death, another character remarks:

> Tom was Tom you see... I have never known anyone who was so strongly his own person. And I don't want to think... I *refuse* to think about him as anything else. There is nothing I can do for him now, but I can do that.

(Rix 2011, 257)

Rix leaves us with a clear moral conclusion: Tom, and by extension people with Down syndrome, are here and they are whole. This evolution of the death ending may be down to the narrator being Tom's father, Jim, who is free of the same expectations and limits as a female/

mother narrator. DS novels are most commonly narrated by mothers almost asphyxiated by maternal guilt.

In Bret Lott's novel, *Jewel*, we see this maternal guilt throughout the novel, but it is not until the final chapter that we encounter Jewel's deep maternal jealousy when she places her daughter, Brenda Kay, into a group home. She watches while Brenda Kay's carer helps Brenda Kay to develop a new cleaning ritual and stops Jewel from translating for her daughter. Jewel thinks, "I stood there feeling smaller, shrinking away from the world and everything I'd ever tried to do in it" (Lott 1991, 351). Caring for her daughter, Brenda Kay, is what Jewel has done with her entire life; the character of Brenda Kay is also what Bret Lott has done with virtually his entire narrative. Brenda Kay is only present to create a story for his novel, *Jewel*. Her Down syndrome is the scaffolding of the narrative. Without Down syndrome, the mother, Jewel, would have no hardship and there would be no story. On the surface, the story appears to show Brenda Kay's successful transition from childhood and adolescence into adulthood, but another reading of the novel suggests that Down syndrome is unnatural, not meant to be, and inherently traumatic.

We see something a little different from the conclusion to a typical realist DS novel in *The Memory Keeper's Daughter* when Phoebe's long-lost brother, Paul, takes her into his home (Edwards 2005, 401). Like Fish joining back together with the man in the river, or Punky becoming "like everyone else" in death, or Duddits giving his non-disabled friend back his childhood self, Paul rejoins with his sister and in so doing, he subsumes Phoebe. Until the last line of the novel, Phoebe has been a refreshingly rounded intellectually disabled character, resilient, stubborn, and sharp. Nevertheless, at the novel's end, Paul arrives to 'rescue' Phoebe, making her safe. Such an ending could be read as a 'happy' one, signifying Phoebe being acknowledged and accepted, becoming part of her biological family. Alternatively, and more problematically, this ending also shows Paul as Phoebe's 'better' half, her less subversive half, and, like Fish in *Cloudstreet*, Phoebe is deemed to be made whole and her disability disappears – as does she – into her non-disabled twin.

There are other popular exceptions to the care, death, or rejoining endings, and these are found in young adult narratives such as *Boss of the Pool* by Robin Klein (1986) or Mark Haddon's radio play *Coming Down the Mountain* (2007). In *Boss of the Pool*, the already institutionalised Ben moves from swimming student to teacher with the help of non-disabled protagonist, Shelley, and in *Coming Down the Mountain*, non-disabled David learns not just to accept his brother Ben but to really see him as human, as 'normal.' Haddon said he intended *Coming Down the Mountain* to be a truthful portrait of a multifaceted family, and he hoped to portray Ben as more than just a character with Down syndrome: "Making Ben's character realistic was just like making any other character realistic: does it feel real? Does it feel like a human being?" (Haddon in Rampton 2007). Both these narratives have one thing in common: the mothers are not the narrators.

In novels and films about Down syndrome siblings, the siblings (particularly if they are teenagers) are allowed to openly and often savagely express what parents must fight against or keep hidden. The sibling is the opposite of a mother. While a mother must be loving, stable, forgiving, and endlessly caring, a sibling can be resentful, angry, and jealous. A sibling-young adult narrative rarely builds Down syndrome into the plot because the teenage voice is inherently selfish; their narrative will always be about them. Young adult fiction is also the most acceptable place to tell stories free of parental influence. It is a trope of the genre to almost immediately remove the mother. In *Boss of the Pool*, Shelley's mother is busy working, and in *Coming Down the Mountain*, David separates his brother from their parents by taking him up the mountain to kill him.

Sarah Kanake

The freedoms found in sibling narratives suggest ways for the author to disengage with restrictive depictions of Down syndrome by untethering the character's disability from the plot. In unpacking the diagnosis and conclusions common to DS novels, we can see that the character with Down syndrome is not real, but is a device exploited to reach narrative extremity. The mother of the intellectually disabled character (and the most common point-of-view voice) is demonstrably similarly exploited.

Point of view – Down syndrome novel or mother trauma narrative?

The DS novel is arguably not about Down syndrome at all, but about mothers. The representation of intellectual disability is a narrative device used to reach some extremity in the depiction of motherhood and women. In *Jewel*, the trauma of Brenda Kay's birth is the challenge her mother must overcome. It is the driving force behind the narrative and shares a compellingly similar structure to women's trauma narratives as outlined by Andermahr and Pellicer-Ortin in *Trauma Narratives and Herstory* (2013). They write: "Women's trauma fiction presents women's grief as a complex response to loss and women's attempts to overcome it as significant and meaningful" (Andermahr & Pellicer-Ortin 2013). Ultimately, this attempt to overcome becomes so significant that it *becomes* the plot. Similarly, in splitting the point of view in her novel, Edwards is able to address three parental traumas: the trauma of giving away your child, the trauma of losing your child, and the trauma of keeping a child with Down syndrome. *The Memory Keeper's Daughter* gives

> readers the opportunity to ponder the question 'what if'; This 'what if' is further clarified in *Trauma Narratives*: 'What if I had a baby with Down syndrome? What if I had a test and could abort? If I kept the baby, how would it affect other members of my family… women's trauma fiction operates in a public sphere, working to focus discussion, highlighting issues, and facilitating a shared listening to the trauma of others.
>
> *(Andermahr & Pellicer-Ortin 2013)*

Here we see the strange dichotomy of the mother Down syndrome narrative. The mother struggles through the novel to include the child with Down syndrome in both her family life and society. She is represented as hero, saviour, martyr, and all that stands between her child with Down syndrome and a faceless peer group. However, once the mother has reached acceptance, the child is often no longer a child but an adult and ready to leave home. This is the narrative arc of the story: "The measure of a mother [in mother narratives] is her child" (Austin & Carpenter 2008, 379). We rarely, if ever, see narratives where the mother struggles to overcome the termination of a child with Down syndrome, in part because these narratives take a very traditional view of motherhood under the guise of creating an acceptance narrative about disability. Subsequently, the mother of a character with Down syndrome often has very little beyond her role as a mother, and in some ways, she is as trapped being the 'child's' mother as the character with Down syndrome is trapped by being translated through her. She is made just as safe as the character with Down syndrome is, but how the narrative is told and what society's expectations of women, mothers, and the disabled are: "The ultimate test of the salience of a disability representation is the various social and cultural contexts within which they might be thought to have a broader effect" (Quayson 2007, 25). The mother novel has benefits for depictions of Down syndrome. Significantly, the character with Down syndrome never becomes part of this

The Down Syndrome novel

faceless community, unlike stories where the narrator is viewing the character with Down syndrome from outside the family unit.

In *Tuesday's Child* (2007), writer Kathy Evans recognises her daughter's broader connection to her "community," but also articulates her distaste for this community when she says, "it served only as a reminder that my child was not just a member of my family, built from the atoms of generations of Celtic ancestors, but part of a distinctly recognisable breed like poodles or Siamese cats" (Evans 2007, 83). In attempting to make her daughter distinct within and perhaps even from "her community," Evans is articulating something important about how Down syndrome is viewed. *Your* child with Down syndrome is valuable, but *groups* of disabled people are subversive. Likewise, the mother is needed to protect the character with Down syndrome from the reader, and the reader from Down syndrome: "A character with an intellectual disability [is] a silent Rorschach ink blot onto which society projects its devices and desires" (Iyer 2007, 2).

I wrote my own disability narrative, *Sing Fox to Me*, in the Australian Gothic mode. I also removed the non-disabled parental voice not only to develop the character with Down syndrome, Samson Fox, but also to extend the storied possibilities for characters with Down syndrome beyond the usual limitations so evident in mainstream contemporary narrative. In doing so, I aimed to avoid five significant hinging points of the DS novel: to give Samson Fox the space to inhabit the narrative; the point-of-view voice of the mother; the act of diagnosis, classification of the stigmata to the exclusion of the character's actual features; the rejoining with a non-disabled twin or counterpart; and, finally, the death or care conclusion. All Gothic characters have some monstrousness. Being damaged is the currency of how the characters belong: "The Gothic is preoccupied with the hidden or monstrous side – particularly as it relates to human nature" (Turcotte 2009, 354). The Gothic novel invites mystery, cruelty, and deformity: "The Gothic knows the body. It knows about physical frailty, about vulnerability… The Gothic also knows about monstrosity and about people who seem to be dangerously unknowable" (Punter 2012, 3). In *Sing Fox to Me*, I could wrestle with ideas of deformity, strangeness, and disability without needing to protect Samson. He was let loose in a strange and uncertain place and, because of his own uncertainties and ultimately his act of accepting not just himself but his disability, he was able to thrive in an environment that swallowed his grandfather, grandmother, aunt, and brother. I believe I succeeded in forging a new path through an old narrative because of the opportunities I created for Samson's character in the Australian Gothic mode. "Kanake… treats with acuity and sympathy the weight on him of Samson's extra chromosome, his sensitivity to how outsiders perceive his condition, and the bonds that he is still able to forge" (Pierce 2016). But Samson is not without his critics: "I'm conflicted about this book. I struggled to accept the Down syndrome character – I think he was attributed a self-awareness far beyond the ability of someone with Down syndrome and I wanted to scream every time his 'heavy chromosome' was mentioned" (Goodreads 2016) (Matthew Reason in Chapter 13, Dave Calvert in Chapter 14, and Tony McCaffrey in Chapter 15 offer consideration of the way readers and spectators respond to representations of disability, in their case on theatrical stages).

Some of the criticisms of *Sing Fox to Me* focus on how Samson is drawn; other criticisms are about the perceived realities of Down syndrome. Questions about what a person with Down syndrome is capable of and where intellectually disabled people fit in society are the questions I am most often asked by readers. My answer is always the same: I can't tell you. I don't have Down syndrome. What I can tell you is that there continues to be a culture of low expectations around people with Down syndrome, and what are often seen as natural limits for people with Down syndrome are reinforced again and again by fictional representations of their lives and experiences. The Down Syndrome novel may be thematically driven by the principle of inclusion, but it does not necessarily provide a microcosm of inclusion. In diversifying novels around characters with Down syndrome, it is important to move into different narrative landscapes. In *Sing Fox to Me*, I found in the Australian Gothic mode a space ripe for invention and a microcosm where representations of Down syndrome need not bend to socially constructed limitations but where practitioners and readers might more meaningfully engage with the future of narratives including characters with Down syndrome. In *Sing Fox to Me*, I hope to have overcome some of these narrative limitations and raised some of the narrative expectations for characters with Down syndrome, even just a bit.

References

Andermahr, Sonya, and Pellicer-Ortin, Silvia. 2013. *Trauma Narratives and Herstory*. New York: Palgrave Macmillan.

Austin, Helena, and Carpenter, Lorelei. 2008. "Troubled, Troublesome, Troubling Mothers: The Dilemma of Difference in Women's Personal Motherhood Narrative." *Narrative Inquiry*. 18 (2): 378–392.

Barker, Clare, and Murray, Stuart. 2018a. "From Richard III to Captain Ahab: What Literature Reveals About How We Treat Disabilities". *The Guardian*, 12 January 2018. Accessed 12 January 2018. www.theguardian.com/books/2018/jan/12/disability-literature-point-of-view.

Barker, Clare, and Murray, Stuart. 2018b. *The Cambridge Companion to Literature and Disability*. Port Melbourne: Cambridge University Press.

Becker, Amy Julia. 2013. "The Unfinished Child, a Story of Down Syndrome, Love, and Choice." *Thin Places: Christianity Today*. Accessed January 2018. Available: www.christianitytoday.com/amyjuliabecker/2013/may/unfinished-child-story-of-down-syndrome-love-and-choice.html.

Dickens, Charles. (1841) 2003. *Barnaby Rudge; A Tale of the Riots of Eighty*. London: Penguin Publishing.

Edwards, Kim. 2005. *The Memory Keeper's Daughter*. Sydney: Penguin Books.

Evans, Kathy. 2007. *Tuesday's Child*. Sydney: Bantam.

Goodreads. 2016. "Sing Fox to Me by Sarah Kanake." Goodreads, 1 March 2016. Accessed 21 June 2018. Available: www.goodreads.com/book/show/28804484-sing-fox-to-me.

Gothard, Jan. 2010. *Greater Expectations: Living with Down syndrome in the 21st Century*. Fremantle: Fremantle Press.

Haddon, Mark. 2007. *Coming Down the Mountain*. Directed by Julie Anne Robertson. Produced by Sarah Brandist and Greg Brenman. Great Britain: BBC 1.

Iyer, Anuparma. 2007. "Depiction of Intellectual Disability in Fiction." *Advances in Psychiatric Treatment*. 18 (1): 127–133.

Kanake, Sarah. 2016. *Sing Fox to Me*. Melbourne: Affirm Press.

Kanake, Sarah. 2014. "Sing Fox to Me, a Novel." In *Sing Fox to Me: An Investigation into the "Use" of Down syndrome in both the Down Syndrome and Gothic Novel*. Brisbane: Queensland University Technology.

King, Stephen. 2001. *Dreamcatcher*. Great Britain: Hodder Publishing.

Klein, Robin. 1986. *Boss of the Pool*. New South Wales: Omnibus Books.

Lott, Bret. 1991. *Jewel*. New York: Washington Square Press.

Mears, Gillian. 2011. *Foal's Bread*. Sydney: Allen and Unwin.

Olsson, Kristina. 2001. *In One Skin*. Brisbane: UQP.

Pierce, Peter. 2016. Sing Fox to Me and Wildlight Review: Two Impressive Debuts in Wild Settings." *The Sydney Morning Herald*, 1 April 2016. Accessed 21 June 2018. Available: www.smh.com.au/entertainment/books/sing-fox-to-me-and-wildlight-review-two-impressive-debuts-in-wild-settings-20160331-gnvc53.html.

Punter, David. 2012. *Gothic Pathologies: The Text, the Body and the Law*. London: Palgrave Macmillan.

Quayson, Ato. 2007. *Aesthetic Nervousness: Disability and the Crisis of Representation*. New York: Columbia University Press.

Rampton, James. 2007. "Mark Haddon: First He Tackled Asperger's, Now the Writer is Putting Down's Syndrome in the Spotlight with a New Drama." *The Independent*, 30 August 2007.

Accessed 2 February 2012. Available: www.independent.co.uk/news/media/mark-haddon-first-he-tackled-aspergers-now-the-writer-is-putting-downs-syndrome-in-the-spotlight-with-a-new-drama-463565.html.

Rix, Peter. 2011. *Water Under Water.* Sydney: Random House.

Sexton, Anne. 1999. *The Complete Poems of Anne Sexton.* New York: Mariner Books.

Turcotte, Gerry. 2009. *Kangaroo Gargoyles: Footnotes to an Australian Gothic Script.* Notre Dame: University of Notre Dame.

Weldon, Fay. 1990. *Darcy's Utopia.* London: Collins Publishing.

Winton, Tim. 2007. *Cloudstreet.* Sydney: Penguin Publishing.

Wood, June Rae. 1995. *The Man Who Loved Clowns.* New York: Hyperion Books for Children.

6

Paralympics, para-sport bodies, and legacies of media representation

Laura Misener, Kerri Bodin, and Nancy Quinn

The Paralympic Games have grown in popularity and global reach since the inaugural games in Rome in 1960. With this growth in popularity, disability rights, accessibility, and inclusion have come to the forefront of many discussions in the sporting context. Large international para-sport events are often advertised as a way to meet social change objectives within host cities and countries. A number of international disability sport events, along with the Paralympic Games, are governed by the International Paralympic Committee (IPC). As such, they are subject to the IPC's guidelines as they pertain to accessibility and inclusion requirements, as well as justifying claims that the event will have lasting benefits on the host city and country. While these are certainly worthwhile objectives, challenges arise when discussing the impact that sporting events may have on broader social change initiatives in this realm.

In particular, the use of media to drive the narratives associated with the Games is directly connected to the accessibility and inclusion agenda. This frames the athletes and disability in a particular light to international audiences. Concerns have been raised over the years about the ways in which athletes with a disability are framed around inspirational narratives and the apparently transformative power of sport. Van Hilvoorde and Landeweerd (2008) have argued that "for many people in disability sport, the athlete is still a 'patient combating their limitations.' instead of an elite athlete with specific talents or virtuosity" (108). The media then frames para-athletes around two central narratives – the 'supercrip' narrative, where an athlete is celebrated as heroically overcoming their disability, or the 'invisible disability' narrative, where impairment is excluded from the references as this presents a contradictory vision of an athlete (Purdue & Howe 2012). Media and marketing efforts surrounding the Paralympic Games are aspects of such events that could alter public perceptions of disability (Misener 2013). While the volume of media coverage of the Paralympic Games has increased over the years, concerns regarding the trajectory of growth and the content of this coverage remain. The ways that para-sport and para-athletes are represented in the media often reinforce ableist understandings of sport and society, doing little to advance equity and inclusion of persons with a disability.

Sport presents a unique occasion to showcase opportunity, ability, and distinction. This is apparent in the way that the Paralympic movement showcases athletic talents. However, this approach can perpetuate negative stereotypes of disability, over-sexualisation of athletes, and an able-bodied understanding of sporting practices. Media emphasis on the "able-bodiedness" of athletes and the "tragedy" narratives of acquired disability serve to reinforce hierarchies of disability (Howe 2011). This emphasis often excludes athletes with congenital impairments and those with high support needs. Mediated high-performance sport often reinforces the stereotypes of disability. Research has shown that in countries where disability rights are entrenched in the policy agenda, there have been shifts in the ways that media emphasises the distinctions of disability (McGillivray et al. 2018). Other countries such as 2016 Paralympic Games host Brazil and upcoming hosts Korea, Japan, and China continue to draw heavily on the tragic and gendered narratives of disability. Consider the two 'superhero' mascots for the Tokyo 2020 Games that are gendered and distinct for the Paralympic Games. During the Rio 2016 Opening Ceremonies, former IPC President Sir Phillip Craven called the athletes the "Superhumans" as part of his address. Para-sport remains fettered by the media's emphasis on the 'heroic' narratives of athletes with disability.

Our chapter will consider these approaches as they reinforce marginal perspectives of disability but can also offer transgressive ways of conceptualising norms of ability. We explore media representations of disability in sport and how sport itself dictates the media's direction in relation to the inspirational narrative trajectories. To do so, we begin by examining how the various theoretical models of disability intersect with sport to frame societal understandings of the sporting body. Our intention is not to rehash the well-known work on models of disability, but to consider how these dominant understandings of the 'disabled' body shape the way that media frames narratives regarding athletes.

The medical model of disability

The medical model of disability and its relationship with disability sport is long-standing, significant, and contentious. This model is considered by contemporary scholars to be the dominant manner in which disability is understood and managed in Western society (Areheart 2008). The medical model relies on normative categories of 'disabled' and 'non-disabled' or 'abled' and assumes that bodily impairment is a personal problem and a medical problem. It is often viewed as a problem which requires a medical cure or a rehabilitative intervention to normalise, or to 'make like normal.' Disability is considered a physiological condition of the body whereby "the individual is the locus of disability" (Areheart 2008, 186). In the medical model of disability, the corporeal is dominant, the social experience of the body is excluded, and medical authority is sacrosanct.

An understanding of the origins of disability sport and its connection with the medical profession is necessary to appreciate the impact of the medical model of disability on para-sport. Organised Deaf sport for people who are d/Deaf or Hard of Hearing can be traced as far back as the 1900s as a by-product of the large-scale institutionalisation of d/Deaf people; many disability sport scholars and athletes consider the 1940s as the birth date of disability sport and Dr. Ludwig Guttman the "founding father" (Mason 2012). In 1943, Dr. Guttman, a German neurologist, established the Stoke Mandeville Hospital in Great Britain and embraced sport as an integral rehabilitation practice for ex-servicemen and women who had sustained spinal cord injury during World War II. Guttman considered sport a powerful tool in the post-injury recovery of these injured men and women, both physically and physiologically. The Stoke Mandeville Games, the predecessor of the modern Paralympic Games, were founded on medicalised notions of the impaired body

(Mason 2012). Dr. Guttman insisted that participants in the Stoke Mandeville Games be referred to as patients rather than athletes or competitors. Guttman also believed that the contribution of the games and disability sport in general was to provide opportunity for sporting participation rather than competition (Legg & Steadward 2011). Guttman's influence and authority were powerful, securing almost complete and uncontested medical control of disability sport. The entrenchment of Guttman's medicalised ideology with respect to para-sport is not surprising. Ideological assumptions about disability sport are reflected in the International Olympic Committee's (IOC) *Handbook of Sports Medicine* published in 1978. Dr. Sperryn, a sport medicine physician and author of the *Handbook of Sports Medicine*, reiterated the rehabilitative and recreational value of sport and exercise for "those suffering with permanent handicap" and cautioned that "rather than break the spirit of a disabled person, who simply cannot compete adequately, it may be that recreational pursuits are often preferable" (Malcolm & Safai 2012, 84). The repercussions of medicalised beliefs about disability and 'impaired' bodies have significantly influenced the development of sport classification systems of para-athletes and disability sport in general. (As they have influenced approaches to accommodating the disability body in other fields of human performance, for instance in musical performance, as discussed by Alex Lubet in Chapter 25.)

The social model of disability

The social model of disability offers an alternative theoretical framework for conceptualising disability. Conceived and constructed over four decades of activism in multiple global disability rights movements (Thomas 2002; Davis 2006), the social model asserts that disability is a product of social marginalisation within the dominant able-bodied or ableist culture, rather than a product of biological difference (Hahn 1985, 1999; Davis 1993; Goggin & Newell 2003; Barnes & Mercer 2005). Essential to the social model are unique and distinct meanings of impairment and disability which have significant implications within the context of sport.

In the medical model, disability is understood as an impairment of the body, in which biological differences alter how bodies with impairment function in the world. Impairment is personal and unique to the individual. In the social model, disability is conversely understood to be a consequence of how society is organised, and is distinguished from physiological impairment.

The social model of disability asserts that the dominant able-bodied culture is imbued with social practices, physical spaces, and shared attitudes which prevent the full social, economic, and cultural participation of people with impairment (Hahn 1996; Thomas 2002; Barnes & Mercer 2005; Davis 2006). Disability is constructed and compounded by access and opportunity (or lack of it) for impaired bodies to participate as full citizens in diverse and multiple social contexts: the local, the global, and the virtual worlds. So, in contrast to medicalised notions of disability that require the impaired body to be fixed or normalised in order to fit into society, the social model "shifts the locus of responsibility for the problems disabled people face from the individuals themselves to their inhospitable environments" (Areheart 2008, 190). The social model also contends that disability results in the persistent denial of the civil rights of people with impairment.

The disability studies community has long rejected the medical model of disability and embraced the social model of disability. However, the role of impairment within the social model of disability remains contentious for many people. Some members of the disability community argue that an undue focus on the biology of impairment poses a threat to the gains arising from the reconceptualisation of disability as a social construction and its application. At the same time, some proponents of the social model assert the importance of the concept of impairment (Thomas 2002). The personal experience of impairment is real and has impacts on the lived experience (Hughes 2012). It is through the embodied experience of impairment that the discrimination of disability is realised (Thomas 2002). Failure to explicitly recognise the role of biological body impairment denies the lived experience of people with impaired bodies, unnaturally separating the private from the social, the personal from the public (Morris 1993; Marks 1999; Thomas 2002; Titchkosky & Michalko 2009).

The growth of disability sport through the 1980s illustrates the evolutionary impact of the social model of disability in this sporting market. Sport for people with impaired bodies ceased to be exclusively a tool for rehabilitation, and the value of disability sport itself was recognised. Increased competitiveness, the commodification of para-sport, heightened media attention, and — for a small number of athletes — the achievement of elite athlete status placed tremendous pressure on para-sport to transition from a highly medicalised practice of sport (Howe & Jones 2006) and to consider the transformative power of disability sport. The vision statement of the IPC, founded in 1989, "To enable Para-athletes to achieve sporting excellence and inspire and excite the world" (International Paralympic Committee, 2015, 14) is a clarion call to integrate bodily high performance through disability sport with social empowerment and opportunity.

To achieve social opportunity through disability sport, an alternative theoretical framework by which to view disability sport remains essential. Medicalisation of disability ignores the social reality experienced by people with impaired bodies, while the social model advances the agenda of social exclusion at the expense of embodied experience of impairment and disability. DePauw (1997) recognised that the body was foundational to sport and physical activity. Her work acknowledged the dominance of biological essentialism in sport alongside the privilege allocated to bodies that are male, heterosexual, and able-bodied. Additionally, the medicalised body, a by-product of biological essentialism, affords little consideration of the many social criteria that act on the body. All bodies are fluid, everchanging, and shaped by myriad social identifiers and cultural influences; inclusive of gender, race, ethnicity, impairment, sexuality, and class, to name just a few. She called for a radical reconceptualisation of sporting bodies that rejected the medicalised hegemony and made space for the subjective bodily experience of sport: "sport culture (will mean) when we are able to 'see' sport and athlete with a disability without seeing any contraction, without assuming a physical liability, stigma or deformity, and without assuming an impaired athletic performance" (DePauw 1997, 428).

A biosocial model of sport and disability

Twenty years have passed since DePauw issued the challenge to reconceptualise notions of sporting bodies and sport itself and to seek a framework for disability sport that bridges the historical dichotomy of the medical and social models. Privileging the embodied experience of sport with impaired bodies is essential to the construction of a credible biosocial model. Feminist scholarship is credited with elevating the role of the body, reinforcing the experiences of the body as central to a person's identity, and "bringing the body back into sociological inquiry" (Zola 1991). Postmodernism's rejection of the duality of normal/abnormal creates opportunity to reimagine bodies and bodily ability as locations on a continuum. There is agreement within the disability community, sport and otherwise, that the centrality of the body is essential to the understanding of impairment and disability. A biosocial model of disability must be informed by the lived experiences of impaired sporting bodies.

Little research is available that examines the experience of the athlete with impairment as subject. Smith and Sparkes (2008) suggested that narrative as a methodology has the potential to capture the personal experience of impairment. Narrative provides the opportunity to tell personal stories, to provide structure for making sense of self, to authenticate the bodily experience of impairment and disability, and to teach others. Storytelling about the lived experience of impairment can forge connection, solidarity, and potentiate social action within the disability community and the broader social world. Narrative can affirm, resist, and transform dominant notions of impaired bodies in sport. Perhaps also, powerful institutions such as the media will conceptualise the impaired body differently and construct alternative representations of sport and disability when informed by personal stories of impairment and ability.

Malcolm and Safai (2012) date the long-standing relationship between sport and medicine back to Herodicus, a Greek physician of the fifth century BC regarded as the father of sports medicine and mentor of Hippocrates (Georgoulis et al. 2007). Contemporary medical and rehabilitation professions have retained authority to assert the 'naturalness' of differing abilities, to categorise bodies using physical characteristics including gender, height, weight, and body type, and to use these physical characteristics as indicators of ability. Disability sport classification relies on medical expertise to organise athletes with impairment "into smaller entities based on observable properties that they had in common" (Tweedy & Vanlandewijck 2011, 3). Today, bodily impairment remains foundational to contemporary classification in sport, even with the introduction and implementation of more functional disability sport classification systems. With a medical lens fixed on the impaired sporting body, the larger political, economic, and social forces at play in sport are ignored. Disability sport classification affords little consideration of the athlete experience of sport and myriad social determinants of ability, including access to financial resources and performance enhancing technology. If the intention of classification is to maximise athlete participation and equitable competition, reimagining disability sport classification and athleticism through a biosocial discourse of sport is necessary.

Sport medicine, a young, dynamic subset of conventional medicine, has been shaped by the practice of sport as much or more than the practice of medicine. Historically, that which did not alleviate suffering was not considered within the scope of medical practice (Malcolm & Safai 2012). Health maintenance of athletes/active people, establishment of ethics of fair play, organisation of sporting events, and optimisation of elite performance fall within the skill set of sport medicine professionals. This skill set has been shaped by the social and organisational demands of athletes, clubs, teams, sport organisations, and governmental bodies, perhaps more so than human physiology and anatomy. Because of this biosocial ideology, the sport medicine community may be well-positioned to contribute to the reconceptualisation of an embodied, athlete centred, biosocial model of disability and sport. The role of media in that reconceptualisation is integral.

Media and bodily narratives of sporting impairment

The study of media coverage of athletes with disabilities is in its infancy (Pappous, Marcellini & Léséleuc 2011; Bruce 2014). Little is known about how such coverage shapes public attitudes or influences the daily lives of people with impairment (Silva & Howe 2012). Some of the key contributions have focused on the construction of disability within the sport media during the Vancouver 2010 Paralympic Games (Misener 2013) and the London 2012 Paralympic Games (Bush et al. 2013; Jackson et al. 2015). For example, Pappous et al.

(2011) found in a longitudinal study of media images spanning an eight-year period, that few journalistic accounts of Paralympic sport used sporting photography or athletic imagery to support any of the stories about para-athletes and their successes at the Games. Such studies in turn raise important questions about the stereotypical mediation of para-sport athletes/bodies, the media's role in the construction of disability (Barnes & Mercer 2010; Claydon 2015; Hodges, Scullion & Jackson 2015), and its considerable authority to inform and shape attitudes (Goggin & Newell 2003; Ellis & Goggin 2015; Kamenetsky et al. 2016).

Early research in the area involved content analysis – evaluating the quantity of coverage across print media and television outlets during the para-sport events themselves. Unsurprisingly, coverage was significantly less than that of Olympic athletes and the Olympic Games. Aspects of evaluated media included the frequency of content, the size of images and text, the location of such content in newspapers, and the messages most often delivered (e.g. Schell & Duncan 1999; Schantz & Gilbert 2001). These early studies were critical for considering how and where media were perceiving the role of disability, athletes with a disability, and para-sport events in the context of the broader media mix. It is important to note that in this research, much of the media content around athletes with a disability or around the Paralympic Games did not make it to the sporting or main pages of news outlets. Rather, content was typically found in lifestyle sections of the news, demonstrating the marginal role of sport and disability in the media.

The most dominant narrative present in media representations of para-athletes has been framed around a medial model of disability, highlighting the athlete as heroic due to the 'ability' to overcome a medical impairment. This journalistic framework is referred to as the 'supercrip' narrative. The supercrip narrative depicts athletes as superhuman, achieving the impossible and downplaying the bodily experience of 'being different' in order to find athletic success. This narrative sets up a distance between athletes with disabilities as able to 'overcome' the impairment and those living with disability in everyday life. Further, this implied that 'if you just try harder, you can also overcome your disability.' The supercrip narrative creates a hierarchy of impairment and misrepresents the realities associated with the bodily experience of impairment and disability. Scholars have long critiqued this representation of para-athletes. Silva and Howe (2012) explained how the supercrip narrative distances the experiences of athletes on the field of play from the real, lived experiences of those with a disability. Further, this dominant narrative may render participation in athletic activities as seemingly unattainable for persons with disabilities (Silva & Howe 2012). The notion of Paralympians as supercrips has been present in the media from the outset of media coverage of para-sport and still exists in today's media. Entire marketing campaigns for the Paralympic Games have focused on depicting athletes with a disability as superhumans to sell the Games to a broad audience (e.g. Portugal's 2008 *Superatleta* campaign, and the UK's 2012 *We're Superhumans* campaign, Canada's 2016 #Paratough campaign). These representations further marginalise those in society who do not have the resources, the capacity, or the desire to achieve a similar status (Silva & Howe 2012). This is done by elevating athletes with disabilities above their peers, not due to athletic prowess *per se*, but instead because of their supposed success in 'overcoming' their physical impairments.

Scholars doing work in this area have also found that a hierarchy exists in the representation of disability (see Haller 2000; Quinn & Yoshida 2016). The hierarchy of disability extends to a number of spaces, including acquired versus congenital impairment, gender, equipment, and sporting adaptation. DePauw (1997) explained the hierarchy of disability in relation to the male wheelchair athlete demonstrating a number of these hierarchical elements. The thought is that the wheelchair offers a sort of replacement for lower body function while the athlete's upper body appears unaltered. The male wheelchair athlete does not challenge the socially constructed notion that sport is inherently masculine (DePauw 1997). In this way, male wheelchair athletes may be highlighted in para-sport media more often due to society's ableist understanding of sport as a space of masculinity and physicality (DePauw 1997). Further, because the sport itself aligns well with the able-bodied counterpart of basketball, it remains palatable and identifiable to the general public. On top of that, many of the athletes involved in sport have acquired disabilities; this enables the associated narratives to be wrought with tragedy and the overcoming of impairment. These narratives marginalise the bodily experience of other impairment groups and lesser known sports such as goalball or boccia. Unfortunately, when only certain athletes are represented in the media, individuals who do not fall within those 'categories' remain on the margins and a single perception of the impaired body in the sporting experience is perpetuated. Representing only those with less visible impairments does not reflect the diversity of the Paralympic and disability communities (Quinn & Yoshida 2016).

The Paralympic paradox has been used to explain tensions regarding the foregrounding and/or backgrounding of disability in the media (see Purdue & Howe 2012). Para-athletes can be role models within the disability community; therefore, bodily impairment needs to be at the forefront of media messaging. On the other hand, para-athletes can also be seen as elite athletes by the able-bodied audience, compelling media to background impairment. The Paralympic paradox may offer an explanation of the hierarchy that exists in disability sport media. Athletes who use a wheelchair or have an acquired visible impairment may be highlighted more often by the media because these images offer unspoken visual cues regarding impairment and disability (Hardin & Hardin 2003). The IPC has attempted to overcome some of these dominant media narratives by providing desired media and marketing frameworks in IPC guidelines. However, these guidelines apply only to official media, or those selected for IPC accreditation. Furthermore, the IPC itself continues to perpetuate the tragedy narrative. Consider the words of IPC President Sir Philip Craven during the Opening Ceremony of the 2016 Summer Paralympic Games in Rio: *"You are the Superhumans. You know that impossible is nothing."*

Gender is also a critical factor in the portrayal of para-athletes. Although this is by no means a new concept in sport media research, gender is particularly significant when exploring the multiple identities associated with a female para-sport athlete; athlete, woman, and person with a disability. Biological essentialism in sport which privileges bodies that are male, heterosexual, and able-bodied is pervasive and exacerbated in the domain of para-sport. Unlike media coverage of able-bodied sport, the quantity of media that represents female athletes with a disability may equal that of male athletes, given the higher number of men with disabilities in society. However, the manner in which female para-athletes are depicted varies greatly in contrast to male para-athletes. The 2014 Glasgow Commonwealth Games media demonstrated a surprisingly gendered representation of Paralympians, particularly in photographs accompanying text (McPherson et al. 2016). For example, coverage of one female Paralympian specifically highlighted the asexuality of this athlete, a challenging stereotype that is pervasive in mediated representations of women with impairment (Quinn & Yoshida 2016). Again, these trends are often described with reference to DePauw's (1997) work where the male hegemony of sporting representations dominate the media discourse. In this way, female athletes with a disability do not fit into the accepted 'physical' nature of sport, nor does the socially constructed masculine nature of sport. In contrast, media all too often situate men with disabilities in a manner that uses sport as a way to reinforce masculinity (Hardin 2007) and elevate the athlete above physical impairment. However, female para-athletes are still typically viewed in a one-dimensional, disembodied way. The dominant representation of the female figure is that of athlete or disabled person without a convergence of these perceptions. These ideas are perpetuated through media's continued use of either the medical model of disability which enhances the tragedy narrative, or the social model of disability which emphasises society's problems of inaccessibility or opportunity. This approach has been argued to be de-humanising by removing the individual experience from the frame of reference. For the most part, these narratives have predominated in the media.

In more recent years, there has been some move towards a greater consideration of the intersection between sport and the body in the way that athletes are portrayed. These narratives attempt to draw more heavily on the biosocial understanding of the impaired body. Quinn and Yoshida (2016) analysed Canadian coverage of the 2004 Athens Paralympic Games. The authors found that media representation of the male Paralympian highlighted in the coverage was quite progressive, embracing a more biosocial perspective that acknowledged the intersection between the embodied impairment and society. Quinn and Yoshida (2016) illustrated how the Canadian Broadcasting Company (CBC) constructed a male Paralympic athlete who competed at the track using a wheelchair, as a complex, multidimensional individual. Specifically, this athlete was constructed as an elite athlete, and as a member of a broad social circle – son, uncle, brother. Biological impairment was an integrated part of the media's representation of this athlete as were the many social roles he performed as a person living with impairment. Implementation of his biosocial model of disability was in sharp contrast to the less progressive, narrower representation of an equally capable female track athlete who also wheelchair raced. CBC chose to represent this athlete as athlete only, choosing to ignore her impairment and her broader social life beyond the athletic. The authors suggested that CBC was unable to reconcile the "double whammy" (Schell & Duncan 1999) of gender and disability, and incorporate a biosocial model of representation.

Paralympic media research has expanded to consider various theoretical frameworks of disability that influence the content and context of media messages. This has also led to research using critical discourse analysis that has ultimately shed light on the impact that media messages have on societal attitudes and the lives of persons with disabilities (e.g. Paradis et al. 2017). In McPherson et al.'s (2016) analysis of print media during the Glasgow 2014 Commonwealth Games, the authors found that journalists acknowledged the role that society plays in disabling people who live with impairment. However, journalists continued to focus on the stories of tragedy and loss, while overtly asexualising female athletes with a disability. The authors argue that this is likely due to the poor understanding of how to frame the societal role of the athlete and the role of athlete in the sporting context. All too often, media around para-sport events and athletes is undertaken by those with no experience of disability or disability sport. As Misener (2013) pointed out, reporters working at the Vancouver Paralympic Games in 2010 tended to be those with little to no Games experience, had worked primarily with hockey, and had no experience with disability and journalism.

This leads to further questions about the roles and responsibilities of media reporting in the sport and disability context. Fortunately, media outlets are attempting to reframe the conversation and perspectives around sport and disability. Some recent work examining a number of large-scale disability sport events has demonstrated some clear examples where media outlets are working to reframe the narrative of disability sport. In an analysis of print media for the Toronto 2015 Parapan American Games (TO2015), McPherson et al. (2017) showed that media reports often included discussion of human rights and local policy commitments to accessibility, demonstrating the progressive opportunity of such an event from a disability rights perspective. Similarly, media outlets during TO2015 offered education-based content, highlighting information about specific disciplines and the sport classification system, alongside the high-performance athlete potential for the 2016 Rio de Janeiro Paralympic Games. Coverage during TO2015 demonstrated a slight shift towards representing para-athletes with athletes-first language emphasising athletes' achievements. However, media coverage is still wrought with the 'supercrip' narrative, using language which frames stories of disability sport within the medical model of disability. Nevertheless, it is encouraging to see evidence that a move towards a broader perspective on the embodiment of disability in the sporting context has begun.

Countries such as Canada and the United Kingdom offer political climates conducive to working towards change in the media representations of sport and disability. As such, Games hosted in these countries have shown to be more progressive, working towards social change regarding persons with disabilities. In both countries, political priorities and public policy agendas supported legacy goals in the areas of accessibility and inclusion for persons with disabilities. In Canada, the Accessibility for Ontarians with a Disability Act (2005) and the political environment of the host country have demonstrated the opportunity for progressive action. In Glasgow, The Equalities Act (2005) demonstrates a similar political environment, emphasising the progressive opportunity of the event to bring about equality measures. These examples speak to how the political environment in which the Games are held influences media coverage of para-sport events as well, generating potential to influence the public's perceptions of persons with a disability.

Future of para-sport and media

According to the World Health Organisation (2011), the experiences of young people with disabilities are impacted by negative attitudes, beliefs, and prejudices about (dis)ability, resulting in the construction of barriers to education, employment, and community participation. The modes of media representation that maintain disability as a marginalised reality recognise journalistic frameworks that construct realistic and human representations of ability. It is therefore imperative to think creatively about how the media can be harnessed to enhance the positive social change potential through para-sport. Increased media coverage of para-sport events, specifically the Paralympic Games, has led to a hyper-visibility of particular types of para-sport bodies, particularly male, and athletes with an acquired disability. Representation of more 'able' bodied athletes perpetuates the dominant media narrative of the disabled body. In the disability studies literature, there is a long history regarding how the impaired body has been constructed as the 'other' in predominantly Western culture. Dovetailing this work has gained scholarly attention in the media studies realm and has demonstrated that these 'otherly' bodies (i.e. disabled bodies) have typically been marginalised by the media, particularly disabled bodies that do not conform to Western socially accepted understandings of disability.

Representation of para-athletes as elite athletes, the understanding of disability as a social issue, and the educational power of the media are beginning to gain traction. While certain progressive narratives are emerging in media content, much of the media released on para-sport, para-athletes, and the Paralympics continue to favour an able-bodied understanding of disability. Sport and the sporting body continue to be framed specifically in relation to DePauw's (1997) three aspects of marginality – masculinity, physicality, and sexuality. The supercrip narrative that emphasises a medicalised understanding of disability remains dominant in disability sport media despite critique of these representations and the marginalising impact on the broader disability community. Notably, there remains significant tension as to how to represent female Paralympians and how to negotiate the Paralympic paradox. Media emphasis on the 'able-bodiedness' of athletes and the tragic narrative of acquired disability continues to reinforce hierarchies of disability, contributing little to the advancement of equity and inclusion for persons with a disability.

In this chapter, we have examined the intersection of disability studies, media studies, and sport studies and attempted to analyse the contemporary meanings of disability representation within and without the para-sport community. There is significant potential to reveal how the hyper-visibility of media constructions of disability influences the lived experiences of people with disabilities and public attitudes towards people with impairments. Sport presents a unique occasion to showcase opportunity, ability, and distinction. The Paralympics in particular offer a global platform upon which to advance disability rights. Although sport can provide opportunities to change individual and public perceptions of individuals with impairment, challenges in capitalising on that opportunity remain. By involving more individuals with impairments in decision-making positions regarding para-sport, including event organising committees, sport organisations, and media providers, progress can be made to advance the overall agenda of disability rights.

References

Areheart, Bradley A. 2008. "When Disability Isn't Just Right: The Entrenchment of the Medical Model of Disability and the Goldilocks Dilemma." *Indiana Law Journal*. 83 (1): 181–232.

Barnes, Colin, and Mercer, Geoff. 2010. *Exploring Disability*. Cambridge: Polity Press.

Barnes, Colin, and Mercer, Geoff. 2005. "Disability, Work, and Welfare: Challenging the Social Exclusion of Disabled People." *Work, Employment and Society*. 19 (3): 527–545.

Bruce, Toni. 2014. "Us and Them: The Influence of Discourses of Nationalism on Media Coverage of the Paralympics." *Disability & Society*. 29 (9): 1443–1459.

Bush, Anthony, Silk, Michael, Porter, Jill, and Howe, P. David. 2013. "Disability [sport] and Discourse: Stories within the Paralympic Legacy." *Reflective Practice*. 14 (5): 632–647.

Claydon, E. Anna. 2015. "Framing the Difference(s): Analysing the Representation of the Body of the Athlete in the 2012 Olympics' and Paralympics' Official Programmes." In Daniel Jackson, Caroline E.M. Hodges, Mike Molesworth and Richard Scullion ed. *Reframing Disability?: Media, (Dis)Empowerment, and Voice in the 2012 Paralympics*. New York: Routledge, 79–93.

Davis, Laurel R. 1993. "Critical Analysis of the Popular Media and the Concept of Ideal Subject Position: Sports Illustrated as Case Study." *Quest*. 45 (2): 165–181.

Davis, Lennard. 2006. *The Disability Studies Reader*. New York: Routledge. Karen P. 1997. "The (in)Visibility of DisAbility: Cultural Contexts and Sporting Bodies." *Quest*. 49 (4): 416–430.

Ellis, Katie, and Goggin, Gerard 2015. *Disability and the Media*. London: Palgrave Macmillan.

Georgoulis, Anastasios D., Kiapidou, Irini-Sofia, Velogianni, Lamprini, Stergiou, Nicholas, and Boland, Arthur. 2007. "Herodicus, the Father of Sport Medicine." *Knee Surgery, Sports Traumatology, Arthroscopy*. 15 (3): 315–318.

Goggin, Gerard, and Newell, Christopher. 2003. *Digital Disability: The Social Construction of Disability in New Media*. Lanham: Rowman & Littlefield.

Hahn, Harlan. 1996. "Antidiscrimination Laws and Social Research on Disability: The Minority Group Perspective." *Behavioral Sciences & the Law*. 14 (1): 41–59.

Haller, Beth. 2000. "If They Limp They Lead? News Representations and the Hierarchy Disability Images." In Dawn Braithwaite and Teri Thompson ed. *Handbook of Communication and People with Disabilities*. Mahwah: Lawrence Erlbaum Associates, 273–288.

Hardin, Brent, and Hardin, Marie. 2003. "Conformity and Conflict: Wheelchair Athletes Discuss Sport Media." *Adapted Physical Activity Quarterly*. 20 (3): 246–259.

Hardin, Marie. 2007. "'I Consider Myself an Empowered Woman': The Interaction of Sport, Gender and Disability in the Lives of Wheelchair Basketball Players." *Women in Sport and Physical Activity Journal*. 16 (1): 39–52.

Hodges, Caroline E.M., Scullion, Richard, and Jackson, Daniel. 2015. "From Awww to Awe Factor: UK Audience Meaning-Making of the 2012 Paralympics as Mediated Spectacle." *Journal of Popular Television*. 3 (2): 195–211.

Howe, P. David. 2011. "Cyborg and Supercrip: The Paralympics Technology and the (Dis)empowerment of Disabled Athletes." *Sociology*. 45(5): 868–882.

Howe, P. David, and Jones, Carwyn. 2006. "Classification of Disabled Athletes: (Dis) Empowering the Paralympic Practice Community." *Sociology of Sport Journal*. 23 (1): 29–46.

Hughes, Bill. 2000. "Medicine and the Aesthetic Invalidation of Disabled People." *Disability and Society*. 15 (4): 555–568.

International Paralympic Committee 2015, *Strategic Plan 2015–2018*. International Paralympic Committee. Accessed 1 June 2018. Available: www.paralympic.org/sites/default/files/document/150916131143110_2015_09%2BIPC%2BStrategic%2BPlan%2B2015-2018_Digital_v2.pdf.

Jackson, Daniel, Hodges, Caroline E.M., Molesworth, Mike, and Scullion, Richard ed. 2015. *Reframing Disability? Media, (Dis)Empowerment, and Voice in the 2012 Paralympics*. New York: Routledge.

Kamenetsky, Stuart B., Dimakos, Christina, Aslemand, Asal, Saleh, Amani, and Ali-Mohammed, Saamiyah. 2016. "Eliciting Help Without Pity: The Effect of Changing Media Images on Perceptions of Disability." *Journal of Social Work in Disability & Rehabilitation*. 15 (1), 1–21.

Legg, David, and Steadward, Robert 2011. "The Paralympic Games and 60 Years of Change (1948–2008): Unification and Restructuring from a Disability and Medical Model to Sport-Based Competition." *Sport in Society*. 14 (9): 1099–1115.

Malcolm, Dominic, and Safai, Parissa, ed. 2012. *The Social Organization of Sports Medicine: Critical Sociocultural Perspectives*. New York: Routledge.

Marks, Deborah. 1999. "Dimensions of Oppression: Theorising the Embodied Subject." *Disability & Society*. 14 (5): 611–626.

Mason, Fred. 2012. "From Rehabilitation Patients to Rehabilitating Athletes: Searching for a History of Sport Medicine for Athletes with Disabilities." In Dominic Malcolm and Parissa Safai ed. *The Social Organization of Sports Medicine: Critical Socio-Cultural Perspectives*. London: Routledge, 77–103.

McGillivray, David, McPherson, Gayle, and Misener, Laura. 2018. "Major Sporting Events and Geographies of Disability." *Urban Geography* 39 (3): 329–344.

McPherson, Gayle, O'Donnell, Hugh, McGillivray, David, and Misener, Laura. 2016. "Elite Athletes or Superstars? Media Representation of Para-Athletes at the Glasgow 2014 Commonwealth Games." *Disability & Society*. 31 (5): 659–675.

McPherson, Gayle, Misener, Laura, McGillivray, David, and Legg, David. 2017. "Creating Public Value Through Parasport Events." *Event Management* 21(2): 185–199. doi: 10.3727/152599517X14878772869649.

Misener, Laura. 2013. "A Media Frames Analysis of the Legacy Discourse for the 2010 Winter Paralympic Games." *Communication & Sport*. 1 (4): 342–364.

Morris, Jenny. 1993. "Gender and Disability." In John Swain, Vic Finklestein, Sally French, and Mike Oliver ed. *Disabling Barriers- Enabling Environments*. London: Sage Publications, 85–92.

Pappous, Anthanasios, Marcellini, Anne, and Léséleuc, Eric de. 2011. "From Sydney to Beijing: The Evolution of the Photographic Coverage of Paralympic Games in Five European Countries." *Sport in Society*. 14 (3): 345–354.

Paradis, Kyle F., Misener, Laura, McPherson, Gayle, McGillivray, David and Legg, David. 2017. "Examining the Impact of Integrated and Non-integrated Parasport Events on Volunteer Attitudes Towards Disability." *Sport in Society*. 20 (11): 1724–1744.

Peers, Danielle. 2009. "(Dis)Empowering Paralympic Histories: Absent Athletes and Disabling Discourses." *Disability & Society*. 24 (5): 653–665.

Purdue, David E.J., and Howe, P. David. 2012. "See the Sport, Not the Disability: Exploring the Paralympic Paradox." *Qualitative Research in Sport, Exercise, and Health*. 4 (2): 189–205.

Quinn, Nancy, and Yoshida, Karen. 2016. "More than Sport: Representations of Ability and Gender by the Canadian Broadcasting Corporation (CBC) of the 2004 Summer Paralympic Games." *Canadian Journal of Disability Studies*. 5 (4): 103–129.

Schantz, Otto J., and Gilbert, Keith. 2001. "An Ideal Misconstrued: Newspaper Coverage of the Atlanta Paralympic Games in France and Germany." *Sociology of Sport Journal*. 18 (1): 69–94.

Schell, Lee-Ann Beez, and Duncan, Margaret C. 1999. "A Content Analysis of CBS's Coverage of the 1996 Paralympic Games." *Adapted Physical Activity Quarterly* 16 (1): 27–47.

Silva, Carla Filomena, and Howe, P. David. 2012. "The (In)validity of Supercrip Representation of Paralympian Athletes." *Journal of Sport and Social Issues*. 36 (2): 174–194.

Smith, Brett, and Sparkes, Andrew C. 2008. "Narrative and its Potential Contribution to Disability Studies." *Disability & Society*. 23 (1): 17–28.

Thomas, Carol. 2002. "Disability Theory: Key Ideas, Issues and Thinkers." In Colin Barnes, Mike Oliver and Len Barton ed. *Disability Studies Today*. Cambridge: Polity Press, 38–57.

Titchkosky, Tanya, and Michalko, Rod. 2009. *Rethinking Normalcy: A Disability Studies Reader*. Toronto: Canadian Scholars Press.

Tweedy, Sean M., and Vanlandewijck, Yves. 2011. "International Paralympic Committee Position Stand-background and Scientific Principles of Classification in Paralympic Sport." *British Journal of Sports Medicine*. 45 (4): 259–269. Accessed 1 June 2018. Available: doi:10.1136/bjsm.2009.065060.

Van Hilvoorde, Ivo, and Landeweerd, Laurens. 2008. "Disability or Extraordinary Talent – Franscesco Lentini (Three Legs) versus Oscar Pistorius (No Legs)." *Sports Ethics and Philosophy*. 2 (2): 97–111.

Zola, Irving Kenneth. 1991. "Bringing Our Bodies and Ourselves Back In: Reflections on a Past, Present, and Future Medical Sociology." *Journal of Health and Social Behaviour*. 32 (1): 1–16. Accessed 1 June 2018. Available: doi:10.2307/2136796.

Part II

Inclusion, well-being, and whole-of-life experience

7

Beauty and the Beast

Providing access to the theatre for children with autism

Andy Kempe

Introduction

Corn Exchange Newbury (CEN) is a medium-sized theatre venue in the south of England. Like many such venues, it has a tradition of staging a pantomime for the Christmas season. In 2017–2018, it offered *Beauty and the Beast*. First published in France in 1740 as *La Belle et la Bête*, the tale reflects the myth of Cupid and Psyche, though da Silva and Tehrani (2016) argue that its roots may go back at least 4,000 years. Indeed, as Celine Dion and Peabo Bryson sing in their pop duet, *Beauty and the Beast*, it's a "Tale as old as time, True as it can be" (Wikipedia n.d). As a parallel, the 'story' of autism and Asperger syndrome may be attributed to the work of Leo Kanner and Hans Asperger in the early 1940s (Silberman 2015), though one may assume that autistic spectrum disorders (ASD) are also 'as old as time.'

In the 2013–2014 season, CEN was the first venue of its kind to offer a 'relaxed performance' (RP) of a pantomime, that is, one which had been adapted to make it accessible to children with ASD. Five years later, offering at least one RP in the Christmas programme has become standard practice for most theatres. This paper examines how the RP initiative first came about, the effect it has had on families living with autism, and its potential for a bigger shift in attitudes towards social inclusion.

The emergence of RPs

While some UK theatre companies have long pioneered work aimed at widening participation, mainstream theatres have woken up to the need to provide for such audiences more recently. Following an incident in which the family of a boy with an ASD felt discriminated against at a performance in London's West End in 2011 (London Evening Standard 2011), a theatre industry day was organised in conjunction with the National Autistic Society. From this emerged a project involving eight leading theatres across the UK aimed at sharing best practice (Relaxed Performance Project 2013). The project engaged with almost 5,000 audience members. Forty-two per cent of those surveyed were families living with autism; 30 per cent had never previously been to the theatre. These figures reflect Shah and Priestley's (2011) assertion that people with a disability have significantly lower rates of participation in the arts than those without a disability, while family members of children with a disability are also less likely to take part in cultural activities.

RPs adjust the performance and the organisation of the front of house to reduce anxiety and stress for children and their families (and, as noted by Kirsty Johnson in Chapter 2, have started to appear in theatre culture in many countries around the world). In this way, RPs provide "a new example of how theatres – and their programmes – might impact those critical social issues of access, inclusion, tolerance and understanding" (Relaxed Performance Project 2013, 5). Heather Wildsmith of the National Autistic Society notes that a particular challenge for people with autism is facing up to new experiences; RPs could help them to "adjust to the theatre – with hopefully as few changes to the plot and story as possible – in a neutral environment, before they consider attending a mainstream theatre show" (*The Independent* 22 December 2014). The overwhelmingly positive response to the Relaxed Performance Project suggests that this is not an unrealistic aim.

Some theatres make a specific point of using the term "autism friendly" rather than "relaxed performance" (for example, the Disney Corporation's *The Lion King*). However, 'autism friendly' is problematic in that it suggests a very specific target audience which may exclude people with other needs. Conversely, 'relaxed performance' may be interpreted as suggesting that the professional integrity of the performance has in some way been compromised. Rupert Rowbotham, currently Learning and Participation Manager at Nuffield Theatre, Southampton, notes that whatever appellation is chosen, "a theatre is effectively signalling that this is an occasion when the people who want to shout out in the middle of a performance can, and that, in some sense, limits other people from coming" (Interview 3 January 2014). In attempting to be inclusive, theatres may inadvertently be excluding some people. Nonetheless, the promotion of such performances can be instrumental in raising public awareness and facilitating an increased understanding of autism and other learning disabilities as members of the public, staff, and volunteers engage with this sector of the community.

If theatre is to contribute to the development of an inclusive society, then events such as RPs must have some transferability. This is recognised by Sarah Gregson, currently Learning and Participation Manager at CEN, who reported that training for the RP of *Jack and the Beanstalk* in 2013 heightened the front of house team's awareness of autism and their capacity to cope with different audience reactions (Interview 3 January 2014). In preparing for the RP of *Beauty and the Beast*, CEN's fifth, she noted that the management team felt they now knew what was needed. Nonetheless, faced with many staff changes, it could not be assumed that new colleagues would know how to deal with the various issues that might arise nor was there room for complacency. Because systems have worked, it cannot be assumed they will again. What has been recorded is that people who booked for a RP subsequently booked for other shows, especially those targeted at children. Additionally, the demographic of those attending RPs has widened, with more children with learning disabilities other than autism now attending. Reflecting on this, Gregson commented that NEC has realised that several things they were doing anyway fitted the criteria for RPs, though they never spoke of them in these terms. This suggests the need to reflect on how any audiences to any event are treated. She recounted how her husband had taken their child to a performance aimed at young children at another local venue. The child had been frightened at one point and needed to be taken out to be calmed down. In the foyer, they were castigated by an usher for making a disturbance. Rather than returning to the auditorium once the child was calm, they left the theatre and went home. This raises a question about what needs to be learnt about how to deal with an audience's difficulties whether they are on the autistic spectrum or simply parents managing upset children.

Interviews with adults attending the RP of *Beauty and the Beast* suggested that far from excluding potential audiences in the way Rowbotham feared, the opposite has occurred. A grandmother present with her six grandchildren told me she deliberately chose the RP because "I've got some real fidget bums here and didn't want to have to keep telling them off for disturbing people," while a mother with a babe in arms said, "This little fella is only 11 weeks old but I wanted to see the show. I read about the relaxed performance on the website and it seemed the obvious one to come to." At the other end of the age spectrum, a care home had brought a group of its residents to the RP. Some had dementia. Another was non-ambulant. Their carer told me that they "had a wonderful time and coped well with the other visitors. I don't believe they would have coped at all with a regular performance."

Notwithstanding the special name, RPs offer effective prospects for socialisation just as any other social event might. A father who had brought his two young sons noted how they had been totally engaged, though when he had taken them to a football game a couple of weeks before they had "been a nightmare, so I thought if they fidgeted today it wouldn't be so bad but everyone seems pretty chilled actually and they've been fine."

Autism as a case in point

The community and medical profession's understanding of ASD continues to develop, though the implications of its definition in the most recent edition of the *Diagnostic and Statistical Manual of Mental Disorders* (APA 2013) have attracted considerable controversy, not least because of the problem of homogenising a set of people whose individual differences fall within a broad spectrum (Shore & Rastelli 2006). The National Autistic Society (n.d.) defines autism as "a lifelong developmental disability that affects how a person communicates with, and relates to, other people." Regarding ASD or indeed any special educational need as a predominantly medical condition of the individual in effect absolves society from interacting with that individual. Conversely, the social model of disability regards disability as a product of the way society is organised and so attends to ways of removing barriers that restrict life choices for disabled people (Oliver 1990). If communication is commonly regarded as a two-way process, the same must hold true for people with autism; the onus is thus not solely on those with ASD to communicate and relate to other people, but for other 'neurotypical' people to play their part in the process.

Some children with ASD may not have developed as complete an awareness of the thoughts and feelings of those around them as others of their age. However, their awareness of others may be awakened when their behaviour causes those others to react negatively. Ball (2013) claims that for many people theatres represent a degree of challenge and alienation; to avoid the embarrassment of contravening unknown or misunderstood codes, they simply do not go, even if they would like to. To what extent is the fear of embarrassment exacerbated for families aware that their children's responses or even their very presence may interfere with another audience member's enjoyment? The evaluation of the Relaxed Performance Project provides evidence that RPs help remove the fear of negative judgement, because if children start to scream, nobody cares because they all understand (Relaxed Performance Project 2013).

People with ASD may experience over- or under-sensitivity to sounds, touch, tastes, smells, light, or colours. This is not exclusive to ASD, and so represents a challenge for theatres about what adjustments should be made to any performances aimed at greater inclusivity. Hurley (2010) argues that theatre sets out to provoke internal and external feelings by offering "super-stimuli" that "concentrates and amplifies the world's natural sensory effects" (23).

RPs must therefore determine the extent to which effects should be amplified or muted and, perhaps more importantly, what facilities will be available to either help avoid or ameliorate any adverse responses to over- or under-sensitivity.

Towards an inclusive audience

Current estimates suggest that 1 in 88 of the population in the UK may be on the autistic spectrum (Centres for Disease Control and Prevention 2012). This translates to over 680,000 people (Office of National Statistics 2015). Attempting to include more of this considerable number of individuals into the theatre audience makes sense economically as well as morally.

In any theatre event, there may be "several distinct, co-existing audiences to be found among those gathered together to watch a show and that each individual within this group may choose to adopt a range of 'viewing positions'" (Freshwater 2009, 9). Not all these positions will necessarily be directed at the performance. For example, while keeping one eye on the show, adults may be watching their children while the children may be watching other members of the audience. Bundy's research (2013) into young people's first encounters with theatre records that some "indicated that they experience pleasure when their own responses were affirmed by other people's apparently similar reactions" (156). The relevance of this to RPs is that they may represent a self-affirming social experience. If the response of some audience members disturbs others, then what may be learnt is that somehow, confusingly, engagement leads them to experiencing the negative feelings of others. In an RP, however, all members of the audience are invited to engage with the action however they wish. That other members of the audience are doing likewise ideally leads to the recognition that theatre is a good space in which feelings can be physically and verbally expressed.

Grandin and Barron (2005) insist that children with ASD need direct experience and live interaction for social skills to become "hard-wired" in their brains. The social dynamic that can be fostered in the theatre may help develop social and communication skills. A central element of the Social Communication Emotional Regulation Transactional Support Model (SCERTS), which aims to address deficits in social and communication skills, is the notion of "joint attention" whereby the child follows what a partner is very deliberately pointing to or gazing at while using "exaggerated facial and verbal responses to an unexpected or anticipated event" to emphasise appropriate social reactions (Shore & Rastelli 2006, 173). An integral facet of pantomime is the actors' use of exaggerated facial and verbal responses and an active encouragement of the audience to make their responses visible and audible. If the actors are successful in this, then an attending child will not have just one partner to refer to in terms of "joint attention" and associated response, but the entire population of the auditorium! Thus, the act of jointly attending with a group and the object of that attention may be seen as efficacious in the development of social skills while also representing a rich aesthetic, cultural, and communal experience. Asked if he thought there was a danger that bringing children to RPs would prevent them from learning the usual accepted codes of theatre behaviour, the father of two boys attending *Beauty and the Beast* didn't think so: "They can see that the majority of the audience are sitting still and paying attention... They're learning through watching and being a part of the audience rather than from me telling them off all the time."

The way in which certain behaviour may become infectious in an audience is illustrated by in anecdote related by the mother of Ella, a ten-year-old with autism. Ella attended the first RP at CEN, and in addition to attending every one since, she has enjoyed going to

RPs at other venues including Shakespeare's Globe. In a production of *Alice in Wonderland* at a theatre offering an RP for the first time, one child began to repeat what Alice said. As Alice went on, more voices started to call back her words. At first Ella's mother thought this was a part of the show designed to create a sense of disorientation before realising it was students from the local school for autistic children. Later, Ella voiced her delight with the Cheshire Cat by calling out, "Oh my God, look at that ridiculous cat!" and cried out, "It's that stupid cat again!" every time it appeared, which made the rest of the audience laugh. In this instance, much to everyone's delight, joint attention developed into joint theatrical enterprise! Asked if Ella actively looks forward to going to the theatre, her mother replied, "She absolutely loves it. She loves to pretend, and to act, and to dress up so she loves to go and see shows." Such evidence flies in the face of now discredited notions that children with autism have no imagination. Ella had been taken to see a special production of *The Tempest* mounted by Flute Theatre in 2016 (Kempe 2017). Because of a subsequent visit, director Kelly Hunter invited Ella to be a part of the rehearsal process for *A Midsummer Night's Dream* and spent an afternoon "just being herself and playing with the actors." What began as one visit to the RP at CEN has not only become a major factor in Ella's life but is also informing the work of at least one theatre company dedicated to further exploring the artistic and social possibilities of inclusive practice.

Vital preparations

RPs require theatres to be well informed about the target audience and organise their operation accordingly. This includes being actively involved in preparing that audience for the visit. One strategy for this is to provide a 'visual story' that may be sent out in advance. The idea of the visual story derives from the Social Story™, a term coined by Carol Gray (n.d), a consultant on children with ASD.

By way of encouraging families to attend the RP, CEN prepares a visual story to show what a visit would entail. This resource is available on their website at https://cornexchangenew.com/ and freely sent to all those enquiring after, or booking tickets for, the performance. Pictures show the front of the building, the foyer, smiling assistants in the box office and the auditorium, and offer guidance and encouragement regarding behaviour. For example,

> You can wear what you are comfortable in.
> You can bring ear defenders or noise filtering headphones if you like.
> During the show, some people might make some noise. People will clap at the end to show they have enjoyed the show.
> You can join in if you like.

The resource gives specific information regarding the special arrangements put in place for the RP, noting, for example, that there is a quiet area available should they want to leave the show for a while.

The traditional English pantomime, or 'panto,' is colourful and vibrant. Considerable use is made of stage technology, special effects, make-up, and costume. There is also a considerable amount of lively interaction with the audience who are encouraged to cheer for the hero, boo the villain, and call out stock phrases such as "He's behind you!" or catchphrases introduced by certain characters. Sometimes the action moves from the stage into the auditorium, or audience members are invited onto the stage for comic sequences and competitions that have been integrated into show. The panto is often the only piece of theatre many children will ever see, and their memories of this can be profound. However, due to the high levels of light, noise, and audience participation and the unsettling effect that this may have on children with autism, it was considered by the Relaxed Performance Project (2013) that pantomime was not the most appropriate genre to include in future phases of the RP initiative. Notwithstanding these reservations, CEN decided to offer an RP of *Jack and the Beanstalk* as a part of their 2013–2014 programme. An evaluation of their pilot concluded that

> there are no reasons why, given the appropriate preparations and adjustments, RPs of pantomime can't be as successful as any other show and perhaps even more so given the nature of the form and its traditional standing as an annual family/school event.
>
> *(Kempe 2014, 13)*

A question arising from this initial research concerned the longer-term impact the CEN's initiative might have on the children who had attended. To investigate this further, interviews were conducted following the RP of *Aladdin* in the 2014–2015 season (Kempe 2015a).

The RP of *Jack and the Beanstalk* was regarded by CEN and the parents interviewed as a success that could and should be replicated. The project received a good deal of coverage in the local press, which led to enquiries about future RPs. In preparation for *Aladdin*, parents from a local support group for families living with autism and a representative of the National Autistic Society were once again invited to advise CEN regarding adjustments to the production and front of house arrangement, and contribute to staff and volunteer autism awareness training. The theatre's database of families, which included children with special educational needs, was used to advertise the performance and draw attention to the website which included a preview of the production and an invitation to attend a 45-minute-long familiarisation tour of the theatre and stage. A visual story pertaining specifically to the production was sent out electronically as both PDF and Word documents so that parents/carers could edit them and print out only those parts they felt their children would benefit from. A "list of surprises" was also supplied so that parents/carers had the option of whether to share these in advance. The story contained pictures and details of the different characters and outlined the story in words and photographs. For example, the caption attached to a photograph of the Dame read:

This is Widow Twankey. She is Aladdin's mother and she does all the laundry for the residents of Old Peeking.
THINGS TO KNOW – It is a Pantomime tradition that this role is played by a man, dressed as a woman. This is supposed to be funny!

Advice from parents and guidance from the National Autistic Society suggested that the visual story should explain where the lights would come from in the show and why; give a warning that the chairs flipped back; and state that pantomimes make a lot of noise and that dry ice would be used, which might have a slight odour to it. Very importantly, it should emphasise that it is "OK" to call out because in a panto this "is NOT being rude." Sometimes, the story explained, the cast would come into the audience. Each child attending the RP would have a green card and by holding it up they would be signalling that they didn't mind being talked to (an initiative that many adults would no doubt appreciate stand-up comedians employing!).

On the day of the RP, hand dryers in the toilets are turned off, and additional volunteer stewards are drafted in and briefed that the house will only be 75 per cent full, so if anyone wishes to move from their allocated seat to a different area, this should be possible. During the performance itself, lights are dimmed but not blacked out entirely in the auditorium, the use of strobes and pyrotechnics is either eliminated or reduced, and the volume generally lowered. CEN's reflections on their experiences with *Jack* and continued commitment to training staff and volunteers in the light of this paid dividends, as is evident in this comment from the mother of six-year-old Fay:

> We did more of the visual story this year. Last year she didn't want anything to do with it but this year she asked lots of questions like, "will there be people putting dresses on?" I said, "yes, it will be like last year" and she remembered that so well so she had something to look forward to.
>
> *(Interview 28 January 2015)*

The impact of RPs

Responses from parents I personally interviewed in Newbury mirrored those of the Relaxed Performance Project in several ways, not least the effect on the behaviour of the children. In part this was seen as resulting from the adults being more relaxed. Nine-year-old Jay had not attended an RP before, but his mother had brought him to *Aladdin*, having heard about the success of *Jack* from contacts in the local support network:

> I came along to the relaxed performance knowing about the way they worked so felt more relaxed about the whole thing and I think this made him more relaxed. I thought "it's going to be OK because I won't have to keep telling him to sit down" and I didn't.

Ella's mother noted that one year on from her first experience of an RP, Ella, then aged six, had "tolerated" looking at the visual story of *Aladdin*, whereas she had completely rejected the one offered for *Jack*. During the performance she had asked why Widow Twanky was a man dressed as a woman, and this had led to a string of subsequent "whys":

> One of the lovely things about a relaxed performance is that you can do a little bit of talking. On the other side, is that teaching them that they can do that in any performance? There's a tension between how you're preparing the child for the real world as opposed to giving them an amazing experience that there's no way would they be able to access otherwise. Last year we were thinking with Ella that there's no way could we have this experience if it wasn't like this (i.e. a relaxed performance). There's still no way could Ella not talk so what we're doing is getting her used to talking quietly!

Such opportunities for socialisation are similarly recognised in this comment:

> I see my job as a parent to help my son learn to self-regulate his traits. If part of that is going to the theatre and understanding that he is sensitive to sound, he's learnt now that if he uses his headphones then he can control that.

In an interview following the performance of *Jack*, the mother of six-year-old Harry associated Grandin and Barron's (2005) philosophy with "the school of hard knocks" which she saw as a necessary factor in bringing up all children. She had some reservations about RPs serving to unnecessarily mollycoddle children like Harry but shared the view that they were a safe place to find out more about the child's responses to different sensory and social experiences. One aspect of the theatre experience that certainly caught Harry's attention was the technical side, with him being rather more fascinated with what the man operating the lighting board was doing than the show itself. This is something that has been noted by CEN, who now offers familiarisation visits prior to the RP. Pantos generally employ a good deal of technical wizardry. Familiarisation visits are thus important on two levels in that they prepare children so that they are not alarmed in the performance itself while offering insights into the backstage and technical aspects of the theatre.

Children's memories of visiting the theatre can last an entire lifetime. A primary aim of theatre, and most especially panto, is to generate experience and sensation. This can be for no other reason than the aesthetic and celebratory pleasure of it, but that does not negate the possibility of valuable social and cultural development arising from the experience. One measure of the impact *Aladdin* had was in the talk of the children following the visit. One mother reported how her normally reticent son Jay had talked so enthusiastically about the show to others, quoting key catchphrases employed by the main characters.

Novelist David Mitchell argues that it is a misconception to believe that all children with ASD lack imagination and therefore struggle to differentiate fact from fiction or empathise with either real or fictitious characters. Rather, distinction needs to be made between imagination and social imagination, that is, the ability to recognise what others may be thinking and feeling if it is not expressed explicitly (Mitchell 2007). All the parents interviewed for in my study of RPs at Corn Exchange Newbury strongly refuted that this equated to the lack of ability to engage in drama and dramatic play (Kempe 2015b). Nonetheless, a persistent trait of ASD is to take things literally and see things as they are on the surface. An example of this was Jay's insistence that Widow Twanky was a woman. While his mother had explained that it was a man dressed up, he continued to "sees things as they are. What he sees is what it is." Ella's mother similarly noted that Ella would routinely cover her face when she encountered someone out of the context in which she is used to seeing them, for example, a teacher in the high street. Pretending to be someone you are not lies at the heart of acting just as suspension of disbelief lies at the heart of the art form of drama. Exposing children with ASD to the possibilities of this aspect of human behaviour through inclusion in the theatre may represent an important step forward in their socialisation. Interestingly, a number of the parents I met reported that despite being diagnosed as being on the autistic spectrum, their children loved dressing up and pretending to be someone or something else. (A personal friend of mine who is diagnosed as having Asperger syndrome is something of a local character. He delivers the local 'freebie' newspaper, usually in the guise of a steam train!)

A notable effect of RPs on Ella has been the opportunity the events give for another aspect of socialisation that was not being offered in her formal educational provision, as indicted in this comment by her mother:

> She put her feet on the seat in front so I asked her how she thought the person there may feel about her doing that and she said "sad." So I said, "well it's probably best if you don't put your feet there then," and she took them down. Now the opportunity for me to say that to her wouldn't necessarily come up in another situation. The biggest thing she needs now is to be in social environments, but her situation in education means she's just in a bubble with a few adults.

A similar incident was reported by Jay's mother:

> A boy sitting behind him was given some keys to keep his hands busy but then he kept hitting Jay on the head with them. A steward saw this and said we could move but Jay said it was OK and not to worry. Another boy was making quite a lot of noise but he accepted it for what it was. It's like he saw that this behaviour was a sort of the norm in this social situation. It makes you realise how hard he has to try in other social situations and I think this is what makes his behaviour worse because he gets anxious about it. But here you learn to get used to it and just accept it.

Fay's mother also saw the social experience as one that could help Fay "be herself" without fearing the consequences of not conforming to expected norms. The RP allowed Fay to see a reflection of herself in others with important side effects:

> Having other people joining in like she was helped her. There was a boy behind us who was quite vocal. She asked me "why is that boy making noises?" So I said, "the same reason you are – he's enjoying himself," which she accepted. It allows her to be herself and this makes me feel more relaxed because you're with like-minded people.

The magic created by RPs does not stop when the show finishes, as this further comment from Fay's mother illustrates:

> Fay was fidgety and talkative but responsive and really involved with what was going on. At the end she said, "Hooray! It's over!…. Oh no! It's finished!" She was really relaxed afterwards. We went for a pizza. We don't get to do things like that. Ever. But she was really calm, talking about the performance. Maybe it's because we were all chilled out. It was good. That doesn't often happen. It was lovely to do something as a family. I can't remember the last time we went out to somewhere where you had to wait for a meal. So yes, it's had a massive impact.

Such social learning is not confined to children with ASD or other complex individual needs. Reflecting the notion that RPs could play a part in raising awareness and understanding in the broader community, a Scout leader attending *Aladdin* with his troupe of Cub Scouts stated that:

> We came along to this performance because this was the date that suited us best. I knew it was a special performance but that's fine. If the dates suit next year we'd probably choose to come to the relaxed performance again.

The devil in the detail

Following the RP of *Jack and the Beanstalk*, several interviewees expressed some regret that the visual and sound effects had been tempered to such an extent. Harry, who had seen *Jack* with his school, had enjoyed the explosions in the mainstream performance, while for Ella, "the more crash, bang, the higher the sensation, the better…she would like to be tickled with a stick and have people come down and chuck things at her – it's that level of interaction she craves." Teachers at a special school for autistic children who had seen the mainstream performance of *Jack* with some of their classes were similarly disappointed that some effects had been cut, as they considered that the highly sensory children who attended the RP would have enjoyed it. However, there was general agreement among those interviewed that if adaptations are to be made, it is best to tone effects down because of the serious distress overstimulation can cause. A case in point involved five-year-old Fay's visit to *Jack and the Beanstalk*. Arriving at the theatre in need of the toilet, she immediately became anxious because of her previous bad experiences with the noise of the hand dryers. On this occasion, she could read the sign which said that the dryers were turned off and visibly relaxed. According to her mother, the memory of this contributed to her going to subsequent RPs in a more relaxed manner.

Getting everything absolutely right for every child is an unrealistic expectation. There are no guarantees that all children will like the event or find it a turning point in their lives any more than children involved in drama as a part of their mainstream education will find it a catalyst for the development of their confidence or interest in the theatre. Nonetheless, theatres can still learn from parents how best to tailor their provision, just as parents may learn more about their children by giving them new social experiences. For example, Ella's mother noted that Ella had spotted a little model of Peppa Pig, a popular children's television character, in the visual story picture of the quiet space. Ella was excited by this and was upset when she discovered the toy was not actually in the quiet space when she visited:

> If you take a picture of what a space is like it really needs to be like that because if it's not there can be a real problem! The visual sense is so strong it has to be that exact.

Conclusion

This anecdote illustrates that tiny details which may appear inconsequential to many people can have a profound significance for children with ASD. The need to attend to such details clearly represents a challenge to theatres wishing to make their programmes more inclusive by offering RPs. However, the challenge is not insuperable and an increasing number of theatres are taking it up. For the 2014–2015 pantomime season in the United Kingdom, 47 theatres followed CEN's 2013 lead and offered an RP of their panto. An admittedly unscientific Google search of regional theatre websites in the weeks leading up to Christmas 2017 suggested that offering an RP of the annual Christmas show has since become more a rule than an exception.

Autism is not, in itself, a beast, though dealing with it can feel beastly when the attitudes of others towards those with disabilities and complex needs are beastly. Recalling Ella's visit to *Alice in Wonderland*, her mother tells how Ella wanted to move closer to the stage. The show had a sensory element to it, and Ella sat on the edge of the stage and started playing with some sand there. An usher came forward and sensitively asked Ella's mother to get her off the stage. Ella has pathological demand avoidance, so her mother knew that trying to get her off the stage was likely to have the opposite effect. Sure enough, Ella got onto the stage and, said her mother,

> it ended up with me joining her and there we all were dancing the lobster quadrille. The audience were laughing their heads off and Ella very much became part of the performance. We spoke to the actors afterwards and they thought Ella had been hilarious. It was the most beautiful, beautiful thing. One of those things that was better because of the interaction. It was just priceless. Total theatre anarchy!

The RP initiative in the UK started as a response to an incident involving one family living with one specific condition. The subsequent ripple that occurred seems now to have swelled into an enduring tide of change in attitude and action that increasingly sees beauty where once it saw just a beast.

References

American Psychological Association. 2013. *Diagnostic and Statistical Manual of Mental Disorders* (DSM 5), Washington: APA.

Ball, Stephen. 2013. "Regional Theatre as Learning Resources." In Anthony Jackson and Chris Vine ed. *Learning Through Theatre*. London: Routledge, 155–164.

Bundy, Penny, Ewing, Robyn, and Fleming, Josephine. 2013. "Drama and the Audience: Transformative Encounters in TheatreSpace." In Michael Anderson and Julie Dunn ed. *How Drama Activates Learning*. London: Bloomsbury, 145–158.

Centres for Disease Control and Prevention. 2012. "Prevalence of Autism Spectrum Disorders – Autism and Developmental Disabilities Monitoring Network, 14 sites, United States." *MMWR Surveillance Summaries*. 61 (3): 1–21.

da Silva, Sara Graca, and Tehrani, Jamshid J. 2016. "Comparative Phylogenetic Analyses Uncover the Ancient Roots of Indo-European Folktales." *Royal Society Open Science*. 3 (1): 1–11; 20 January 2016.

Freshwater, Helen. 2009. *Theatre and Audience*. Basingstoke: Palgrave Macmillan.

Grandin, Temple, and Barron, Sean. 2005. *The Unwritten Rules of Social Relationships: Decoding Social Mysteries through the Unique Perspectives of Autism*. Arlington, Texas: Future Horizons.

Gray, Carol. n.d. *Carol Gray Social Stories*. Accessed March 2018. Available: https://carolgraysocialstories.com/social-stories/.

Hurley, Erin. 2010. *Theatre and Feeling*. Basingstoke: Palgrave Macmillan.

Kempe, Andy. 2017. "The Tempest." *Drama: One Forum Many Voices*. 23 (1): 42–43.

Kempe, Andy. 2015a "'Open Sesame!' How Panto Can Pave the Way for Inclusion in Theatre." *Drama Research*. 6 (1): 2–21.

Kempe, Andy. 2015b. "Widening Participation in Theatre through 'Relaxed Performances'." *New Theatre Quarterly*. XXXI (1): 121.

Kempe, Andy. 2014. "Developing Social Skills in Autistic Children through 'Relaxed Performances'." *Support for Learning*. 29(3). Accessed 21 June 2018. Available: www.researchgate.net/publication/266025693_Developing_social_skills_in_autistic_children_through_%27Relaxed_Performances%27.

London Evening Standard. 2011. "Theatre Accused of 'Outrageous Discrimination' Against Autistic Boy." *London Evening Standard*, 2 August 2011. Accessed 21 June 2018. Available: www.standard.co.uk/news/theatre-accused-of-outrageous-discrimination-against-autistic-boy-6428576.html.

Mitchell, David. 2007. "Introduction." In Naoki Higashida ed. *The Reason I Jump*. London: Sceptre, 3–26.

National Autistic Society. n.d. *What is Autism?* Accessed November 2013. Available: www.autism.org.uk/about-autism/autism-and-asperger-syndrome-an-introduction/what-is-autism.aspx.

Office of National Statistics. 2015. *Compendium of UK Statistics*. Accessed January 2015. Available: www.ons.gov.uk/ons/guide-method/compendiums/compendium-of-uk-statistics/population-and-migration/index.html.

Oliver, Michael. 1990. *The Politics of Disablement*. London: MacMillan.

Relaxed Performance Project. 2013. Conference Evaluation. Accessed November 2013. Available: www.childrenandarts.org.uk/our-projects/evaluation-reports/relaxed-performance-project-201213.

Shah, Sonali, and Priestley, Mark. 2011. *Disability and Social Change: Private Lives and Public Policies*. The Policy Press: Bristol: The Policy Press.

Shore, Steven M., and Rastelli, Linda G. 2006. *Understanding Autism for Dummies*. Hoboken: Wiley Publishing.

Silberman, Steve. 2015. *Neurotribes: The Legacy of Autism and How to Think Smarter About People Who Think Differently*. London: Allen & Unwin.

Wikipedia. n.d. "Beauty and the Beast (Disney Song)." Accessed 16 June 2018. Available: https://en.wikipedia.org/wiki/Beauty_and_the_Beast_ (Disney_song).

8

Moving beyond the art-as-service paradigm

The evolution of arts and disability in Singapore

Justin Lee, Shawn Goh, Sarah Meisch Lionetto, Joanne Tay, and Alice Fox

Introduction

A substantial part of the arts done *for*, *with*, and *by* people with disabilities has largely been framed in terms of its therapeutic goals. This chapter examines how the field of arts and disability has evolved in Singapore, investigates the structural reasons for this change, and highlights some of its consequences. We also discuss new possibilities and the potential for moving beyond this 'art-as-service' paradigm and the value of a 'disability arts' that has expressive, aesthetic, and political agendas.

The terms 'arts and disability' and 'disability arts' have been used relatively loosely and sometimes interchangeably. We regard 'arts and disability' as a broad umbrella term that includes community arts done *for* or *with* people with disabilities. This constitutes one end of a spectrum, where typically non-disabled artists produce art that is accessible to the disability community, or co-create art with varying degrees of participation by people with disabilities. Some examples include offering painting lessons for people with muscular dystrophy, poetry for people with intellectual disabilities, or music lessons for youths with special needs. When professional artists get involved, more serious artworks may be produced, such as a play about deaf issues staged by non-disabled professional playwrights and actors, an orchestra that includes musicians with disabilities, or creative productions where the artistic strategising is done by people with disabilities. Such work starts to shade into what is known as 'disability arts,' especially when they include disabled performers.

Here, Sandahl's (2006) definition of disability arts is useful – "artwork by people with disabilities that reflects a disability experience, either in content or form" (Sandahl 2006, 406). 'Disability arts' often connotes professional work because it is often done by full-time artists with disabilities who create artwork about the disability experience. However, not all artists with disabilities are professionals, since some may do these activities as a hobby. Furthermore, 'disability arts' often has implicit or explicit political messages since "its themes and aesthetics run counter to prevailing notions of disability…[and] can explicitly expose the marginalisation and societal mistreatment of disabled people" (Sandahl 2006, 406). Borrowing from Decottignes (2016), we regard artworks by disabled artists that possess such moral or political agenda as 'disability-identified arts,' to distinguish them from disabled artists whose work has no bearing on the disability experience nor any disability agenda. For example, some musicians or painters prefer their work to be appreciated in itself and may even intentionally hide their disability from the audience (so their work is not conflated with their biography in the way Donna McDonald discussed in Chapter 3). Disability-identified arts on the other hand disrupts social misperceptions through the development and dissemination of artworks that invert the position of people with disabilities in society as "lesser than," and affirm impairment as a source of diversity and pride (Decottignies 2016, 44). As Decottignes (2006, 46) explains,

> disability-identified art prioritises the politics of inversion and affirmation over inclusion. It inverts authority over disability arts by putting disabled artists firmly in control of both artistic production and product ... a significant aspect of disability-identified art is that it is non-normalising.
>
> *(46)*

Certain examples may fall clearly as 'community arts' for people with disabilities or clearly as 'disability-identified arts.' However, there is wide range of artists and artworks that cannot be clearly defined and fall along the blurred boundaries between 'arts and disability' and 'disability arts.' Figure 8.1 illustrates the spectrum of artistic work in this space. We do not see any special analytic advantage in devising precise terminology to clarify such differences, but seek only to characterise the range of artworks and artists that fall variously along this spectrum (see Figure 8.1).

Criticisms of 'art as therapy'

Policymakers have been keen to experiment with the role of the arts and culture in facilitating the inclusion of people with disabilities, supporting programmes that utilise dance, drama, music, or visual arts to improve social and communication skills, or to enhance psychological well-being by improving self-esteem or confidence (for a discussion of art therapy, see Susan Hogan in Chapter 11). However, some disability scholars are suspicious and critical of these programmes. For example:

> The problem is that you will almost never see any actual disability art in a theatre, museum, gallery or even at a disability arts festival. Even if you do, it is there because it has been mis- or re-interpreted. Mostly, though, what you will see is pseudo-therapy

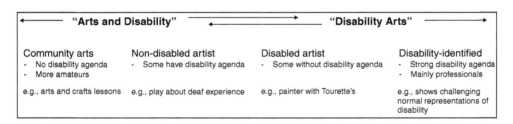

Figure 8.1 Characterising the spectrum of arts

> workshop products or impairment-orientated works. Usually, it will be from a craft basis or developed in an empowerment course, superficially structured within the social model of disability but actually impairment-specific. This might be described as low level community arts... such art "activities" have nothing to do with disability art, but they are to do with traditional preconceptions of art or therapy or, worse, as some form of inspirational role modelling.
>
> *(Riddell & Watson 2003, 133)*

The argument is that some forms of community and participatory arts tend to work within an 'impairment' framework, often in partnership with the education, health, and social care sectors (Newsinger & Green 2016). For instance, Geoffrey Lord's (1981) *The Arts and Disabilities: A Creative Response to Social Handicap* gives an anthology of the therapeutic aspects of arts, such as using movement as a form of physical education and drama therapy or using music to teach listening skills. The evidence-based movement in health and social care sectors has also produced research to evaluate the therapeutic effects of artistic work, demonstrating how it creates meaning and structure in life for people with disabilities, facilitates social exchange with others, and increases self-confidence (Boeltzig, Sulewski, & Hasnain 2009; Hall & Wilton 2011).

However, critics lament that it is unfortunate that such forms of community arts tend to be the most prominent forms of cultural participation available for people with disabilities, when the arts in fact has greater communicative, transformative, and socially empowering potential (Newsinger & Green 2016). Furthermore, they argue that disability-identified arts "ha[ve] continuously been threatened by arts institutions and charitable organizations that seek to promote disability arts while dismissing its political base" (Decottignies 2016, 16). These criticisms echo those levelled at the 'medical model' of disability, where disability is considered a pathological defect of the body and curative interventions are used to ameliorate the physical or mental disabilities of a person. This model of understanding disability is further perpetuated if the arts are seen merely as an alternative form of therapy. Instead, the 'social model' of disability more adequately understands disability as the result of how normative prejudices and social institutions have failed to be inclusive of a class of persons and that disabilities are in fact perpetuated by societal structures and attitudes.

Background: emergence of arts and disability in Singapore

Recent improvements in access to the arts and culture for people with disabilities in Singapore can be broadly classified into two areas – improvements in physical access to cultural institutions, and more inclusive programming that accommodates the needs of different groups of people with disabilities.

Accessible infrastructure

One example of Singapore's efforts in improving the physical accessibility for people with disabilities to arts and cultural facilities is by adopting the principles of Universal Design. Singapore's Building and Construction Authority (BCA)'s Code of Accessibility in the Built Environment was revised in 2013 to encourage the construction of more accessible buildings for people with disabilities, as well as for seniors and families with young children. Important changes in the code include having wider corridors, installing hearing enhancement systems in venues used for performances, and having braille and tactile warning indicators to benefit people who are visually impaired (Audrey Tan 2013).

The BCA also created an Accessibility Fund that co-funds up to 80 per cent of upgrading costs for private, commercial, and institutional building owners to improve accessibility to their buildings via retrofitting of basic accessibility features such as ramps, lifts, and accessible toilets (Ariffin 2016). Many of Singapore's cultural institutions such as the National Gallery Singapore, the Art Science Museum, and the Asian Civilisations Museum include such features. Furthermore, the Ministry of Culture, Community and Youth provides subsidised entrance fees to all museums and heritage institutions for people with disabilities. For instance, people with disabilities and their caregivers are either granted free entry or given special concession rates when they visit exhibitions at public museums such as the Singapore Art Museum and the Peranakan Museum (Zaccheus 2016).

Inclusive programming

Besides improving physical access, efforts to improve accessibility to the arts and culture are also done through more inclusive programming. For instance, the National Gallery Singapore offers sign language interpretation tours of the Gallery's collection, which are led by a docent and sign language interpreter from the Singapore Association of the Deaf. Others like theatre company W!LD RICE have also worked with the Singapore Association of the Deaf to stage its first sign language interpreted performance of its popular hit, *Grandmother Tongue* ("Sold-Out Smash Grandmother" 2016). Sensory-friendly theatre like *Koko the Great* – a play for children aged two to four, staged with bright lights and no sudden changes in the sound – made it accessible to audiences with cognitive or sensory disabilities. Audiences were also allowed to enter and leave the theatre studio at any time (Nanda 2017). Lastly, the Asian Civilisations Museum and the Peranakan Museum have also started a *Quiet Mondays* programme, where soundscape volume and house lights are reduced in order to encourage people with disabilities to visit the museums on Monday mornings (Enabling Village n.d.).

Apart from institutional efforts, ground-up efforts have also played a role in providing inclusive arts and cultural programmes for people with disabilities. One example is *Superhero Me*, a values-based community arts movement started in 2014, which focused on children with special needs in its 2016 iteration. Funded by the Lien Foundation and the National Arts Council, the 2016 programme brought together children with and without special needs to participate in an experiential art show put together by the children themselves. The process saw meaningful interactions between the two groups of children where participants learnt more about the disability experience as well as the interests and ambitions of the artists (Goy 2016). Another example is *Unseen: Constellations* by artist Alecia Neo, which provided a platform for students with visual impairments and sighted persons to work on a myriad of creative projects together ("Young artist award recipients" 2016).

Inclusive programming also includes bringing disability issues to the forefront of mainstream arts through disability-themed arts performances and festivals. One example is *Disabled Theatre*, an item featured in the 2014 Singapore International Festival of the Arts, which challenged conventions of performance and explored ideas about the representation of people with disabilities (Cheng 2014). More recently, Very Special Arts Singapore (VSA, a voluntary organisation that supports and promotes artists with disabilities in Singapore) hosted the *True Colours Festival* for artistes with disabilities in March 2018. The four-day festival included an indoor concert and free outdoor performances, with both local and international artistes with disabilities showcasing their artistic talents (Tan 2017).

Crystallisation of an 'arts and disability' field

While the inclusive programming was well covered by the media, many of them were once-off events. VSA is one of the few voluntary organisations that has consistently supported and promoted disabled artists in Singapore. Their core focus is to provide people with disabilities with the opportunities to access the arts for rehabilitation and social integration, as well as for avenues for creativity and expression. Some of its programmes include *Welcome to My World: A Concert by People with Disabilities*, which is a national-level platform that showcases the performing talents of individuals and groups from the special needs community in Singapore, and *Voices: Expressions of Young VSA Artists*.

The National Arts Council (NAC), the British Council (BC), and the Singapore International Foundation (SIF) are also pivotal to the crystallisation of an 'arts and disability' field. Since 2015, they have organised *Arts and Disability Forums* that brought in international and regional influences to local artists and Voluntary Welfare Organisations (VWOs). These forums have grown from a half-day programme with a focus on bringing together healthcare professionals, artists, and policymakers to raise awareness about the gaps between the arts and disability sectors, to the current two-day programme that includes insights from keynote speakers with local, regional, and international perspectives on a variety of topics around the theme of inclusiveness, empowerment, and collaboration.

Their efforts have not only brought in an international pool of scholars and arts practitioners, but also provided training and arts mentorship to local practitioners. For example, NAC and BC have offered artists and teachers workshops with Bamboozle Theatre Company from Britain, which specialises in creating multi-sensory art for children with autism and other complex disabilities. Another example is NAC's artist-in-school scheme, which has helped nearly 800 students in ten special education schools learn dance or other art forms from practising artists (Nanda 2017).

Structural reasons for the instrumentalisation of art in Singapore

In this section, we examine the broader structural reasons underlying why the arts have largely been used as a service in the disability sector. We look at how VWOs that deliver social services in the disability sector focus on the arts as an alternative form of social intervention, and how Singapore's arts and culture policies encourage this way of framing the arts. We also investigate the consequences of such policies on the nature of community arts in the disability sector. In other words, we examine how the policy context has informed agency behaviour, resulting in certain consequences for the artworks produced.

Arts funding policy

Concerted state involvement has played a critical role in the direction and significance of the arts in Singapore. In the 1960s and 1970s, the focus of the Singapore government was on economic development, defence, housing, healthcare, and education. Following Singapore's independence in 1965 and faced with the immediate challenges of poverty, unemployment, and housing shortage, policymakers focused on developing infrastructure and the economy. Policies pertaining to the arts and culture therefore took a backseat (Kong 2012). It was only in the late 1980s and 1990s that policymakers began to turn their attention to the arts and culture, and even then, only as a sector with economic potential. Scholars have highlighted the overwhelming economic ethos inherent in the various arts and cultural policies (Kwok & Low 2002; Chong 2005; Tan 2007).

Arts and culture have also been used by the state as a stand-in for racial harmony and multicultural integration. In the immediate post-independent years, arts and cultural policies were oriented towards nation-building and creating interracial understanding and tolerance through displays and performances by local cultural groups. This reflected a concern among policymakers that globalisation and the flow of migrants may introduce societal tension. The role of the arts in community participation and engagement became better articulated in more recent arts and cultural policies, in which the arts were seen as a tool for community bonding through broad-based participation in art activities. Besides creating and promoting local works, efforts were also made to grow future audiences by bringing the arts to the heartlands, and by providing access to the arts and culture for low-income families and people with special needs. Over time, Singapore's arts and culture scene also progressed from one that was largely public sector-organised to one that saw increasing contribution from the people sector. Community arts received further attention in the Arts and Culture Strategic Review (ACSR), which was initiated in 2010 to chart the course of Singapore's cultural development until 2025. This gave an extra push to the arts and the work of NAC, where one of the strategic thrusts was to "bring arts and culture to everyone, everywhere, every day." To cultivate a bustling cultural scene, the ACSR found it necessary to permeate the arts and culture throughout all levels of society. "The key challenge facing all arts and culture professionals, advocates and policymakers is this: how may all Singaporeans, regardless of origin, race, age and social standing, be encouraged to appreciate, participate and engage in arts and culture?" ("The Report of the" 2012, 12).

In short, Singapore's arts and culture policies evolved from treating the arts as an instrument of economic development and nation building, towards one that emphasises on community participation. Generally, the arts are seen as a means to achieve economic and social goals defined by the state. While the move towards community arts has created greater access and participation by a broader audience base, it has also created an instrumentalist paradigm that considers the arts as useful only when it achieves these objectives.

Central planning and voluntary sector implementation in the disability sector

The Singapore government's approach to welfare provision has been shared responsibility with VWOs. In the early years, the government focused on providing services that the voluntary sector could not. Then Acting Minister for Social Affairs said in a conference on voluntary social services in 1992,

> In those early years of the existence of the Social Welfare Department, there was a clear understanding of the respective roles of the government and the voluntary organisations in the field of social welfare. The Social Welfare Department, it was clearly understood, *entered the field only to operate such residual institutions or services as are not, or cannot conveniently be, established and maintained by voluntary effort alone.*
>
> *(Jurong Junior College 1992, emphasis added)*

While the government understood the benefit of sharing welfare responsibilities, it also recognised the importance of coordinating the multitudes of VWOs in a growing sector. It has increasingly taken the lead in many aspects of social welfare provision and sector development, much of which was to create more consolidation and control. For instance, federated fundraising through the Community Chest was created to address fundraising challenges faced by individual VWOs; the Social Service Institute was set up to provide skills and capabilities upgrading; the SunRay Scheme of the National Council of Social Services provided centralised manpower planning and hiring to address manpower shortage in the sector.

Having positioned itself as the antithesis of a welfare state and priding itself on the ethos of hard work and self-reliance, Singapore's disability policies emphasised getting people with disabilities to reduce their dependence on the state through employment (Zhuang 2016). Centralising tendencies also mark the developments in Singapore's disability sector. One key initiative for this sector is the *Enabling Masterplan*, a national roadmap that details recommendations across the life course that covers early intervention, education, and employment. First conceived in 2007, it is currently into its third five-year plan. In general, state attitude towards disability has gradually shifted away from viewing people with disabilities as "economic liabilities on society and state, to viewing them as human beings deserving of dignity and state support" (Wong & Wong 2015, 147).

VWOs pursue therapeutic outcomes, so artists follow suit

Given that government funding for social services constitute their key concerns, many VWOs naturally regard the arts as a 'good to have' that complements the work done by social workers and therapists, and assess any potential partnership based on promised client outcomes. Even private funders of the social sector find it hard to recognise the value of arts beyond their social or therapeutic outcomes. They typically see the arts as an 'intervention,' one out of many possible interventions they can choose from, and are inclined to use it if it demonstrates better efficacy than traditional social interventions.

This therapeutic focus is augmented by the pressures of New Public Management, which have brought private sector principles of accountability and management to public sector organisations. As a result, VWOs are increasingly scrutinised and required to demonstrate effectiveness and efficiency, and to focus on delivering outcomes rather than outputs (Norman 2011). In Singapore, VWOs receiving government funds are subject to a performance management regime that sets quantifiable targets based on outcomes for clients.

In this context, artists who want to work with VWOs feel compelled to offer the arts as a service, and subordinate artistic goals to therapeutic or social outcomes. Community artists in Singapore have used the arts – including the *Yellow Ribbon Project* and *Superhero Me* – to engage with various vulnerable client types ranging from migrant workers, inmates and ex-offenders, children from impoverished families, seniors in nursing homes, and of course, people with disabilities. Artists typically go through social service agencies to gain access to their client groups, so artists scope projects that are aligned with the social agency's objectives for their clients. As a result, many of the community arts efforts in Singapore are not so much for a *community* as they are for a *client type* – members of who share a similar condition or experience, and who may or may not form part of a community. Arts focused on therapeutic outcomes are the most common form of community-based arts in Singapore because these are aligned to the objectives of many community and social service agencies. Artists are further disadvantaged because evaluation methodology is less well distributed in the arts sector in Singapore compared to the health, education, and social sectors, and also because artistic outcomes tend to be less tangible and harder to measure. Thus, artists are often unable to negotiate meaningful evaluation approaches with funders who may not understand the artistic process and outcomes (Tan, Goh, & Samsudin 2017).

It is telling that there is an Art Therapists' Association of Singapore (ATAS) that was established in 2008 when there is currently no such association for community artists. The number of therapists registered under ATAS has tripled to 30 since it first began in 2008 with local hospitals such as Singapore General Hospital beginning to use art therapy more (Rachel Tan 2013). Even relatively small and informal arts projects face such pressures especially when they need to convince funders and VWOs for continual support. For example, a group of volunteers who were teaching poetry to people with intellectual disabilities faced pressures to conduct evaluations of their project in order to be able to demonstrate gains in clients' communication or cognitive skills.

Consequences of 'art as a service'

Thus far, we have demonstrated that arts and disability in Singapore is largely shaped by three factors – 1) state funding that instrumentalises and co-opts the arts for key state concerns; 2) pressures faced by social service delivery systems to deliver client level outcomes; and 3) a relatively unorganised community arts sector that is compelled to 'speak the language' of social service agencies as a result.

Arts and crafts – for diversion, recreation or product sales

Prevalent among VWOs is the use of arts and craft to engage clients. In its most devalued form, this is merely using recreation as a form of diversion, no different if the clients were to visit a park or the zoo. Some do focus on the clients acquiring skills and artistic technique, and the result could be the sale of products or a performance, where clients become art producers. Sales of products or tickets are often used to fundraise for the VWOs.

Art as 'therapy in a different form' – to overcome personal challenges

As mentioned earlier, many VWOs also use the arts for therapeutic purposes. For example, the Muscular Dystrophy Association of Singapore (MDAS) "encourages its members to take up art and crafts as a therapeutic activity" because "when [its clients] are doing art, they are exercising their fingers at the same time without realising it … such activities also boost their self-esteem when they see the art they are capable of [making]" ("Poems inspired by special" 2008). MDAS also sells the keychains, photo frames, and greeting cards made by its clients to raise funds.

In such cases, the arts are used as an instrument for addressing social service needs. Disabled artists may see the arts as a tool for overcoming barriers to academic achievement, communication barriers, and as coping mechanism (see Boeltzig, Sulewski & Hasnain 2009). Thus, disabled artists are engaging in the arts to overcome personal challenges, and not necessarily for artistic excellence. The subheading of a *Straits Times* article reveals the way the arts are considered in terms of their instrumental value – "Art therapy gains popularity as way to help patients *deal with disabilities*" (Rachel Tan 2013, emphasis added). The framing of the arts as a way to 'deal with disabilities' treats the arts as an intervention for a 'problem,' similar to a 'cure' in the medical model of disability.

Typical of the marketing discourse used in these art forms, participants report gains in self-esteem or other forms of psychological attributes as benefits to justify the validity of the art. As a member of a band called Cactus Rose, whose seven members have disabilities ranging from intellectual challenges to visual impairment, playing music gave Ken Wong confidence and a chance to mentor others (Nanda 2017). For such work, therapeutic goals are also more important than aesthetic goals or the artistic process. This point is driven home by an art therapist who pointed out that, for them, "aesthetic results are secondary" (Rachel Tan 2013).

Justin Lee et al.

Disability agenda by non-disabled artists – who benefits more?

Ironically, disability arts in Singapore are championed mostly by non-disabled artists. For example, theatre company Pangdemonium's production *Tribes* portrayed the experience of deafness in an authentic way by performing portions of a theatre play in sign language, featured sign language interpreters on stage to translate the dialogue for deaf audiences, and provided members of the Singapore Association for the Deaf subsidised tickets (Tan 2015). However, these are mostly once-off initiatives that may not even include disabled artists.

While some of this arts as advocacy work can be helpful to the disability community, others can become more self-serving than truly benefitting the community. For example, a student's poetry anthology seemed like it benefitted the students more than it did anything for the disabled artists. They viewed more than 3,000 paintings, eventually choosing works by 21 disabled artists, and wrote poems based on them. They had interviewed physically disabled artists, looking over their work and scribbling snatches of rhymes and metres. These students are part of an enrichment programme for highly talented and gifted learners, so when the chance for a project came up, they decided to apply their poetry skills towards "changing the world around them." Such projects may benefit themselves more than the disability community (Cheong 2008).

Normalising disabled artists – downplaying disability
as irrelevant and de-politicised

People with disabilities already have limited training opportunities and pathways to become professional artists. Yet, when they do end up with viable careers, professional disabled artists themselves often downplay the relevance of disability issues in their art. They often disregard their disabilities as significant to the art and, in that way, normalise themselves to fit into the criteria and norms of the specific art world they have chosen. For instance, theatre actor Ramesh Meyyappan also only reveals his disability after his performances, and audience members are usually surprised to discover that he is deaf. The Singapore-born, Scotland-based artist explained that he wants people to focus on the quality of his art first and recognise him as a person with disability second ("Drop the labels, recognise" 2017). Others such as hearing impaired pianist Azariah Tan also works very hard to overcome the challenges his disability poses for conforming to the standards of playing –

> A lot of people just play the piano for the sake of playing it but they don't put enough emphasis on listening to what sounds are coming out. While I can't hear everything, it makes me strive to listen to everything. It makes me listen more closely and respond to it.
>
> *(Wong 2016)*

Describing the pianist's playing as "genuinely distinctive," Dean of Yong Siew Toh Conservatory and Professor Bernard Lanskey adds:

> The issue of control in the softest playing is one all pianists face, whether or not you can hear the result, but there is no doubt he is overcoming most of the challenges naturally faced to make music which is communicative, passionate and beautiful. I am sure his music-making will be valued intrinsically and not just because of the hurdles overcome.
>
> *(Wong, 2016)*

When disabled artists overcome barriers to conform to mainstream aesthetic practice and standards, this often adds to the appreciation of their ability to overcome personal odds. However, this is not disability-identified arts, but instead art that happens to be done by a person with disability. As a result, it is not necessarily fulfilling the aesthetic or political potential of disability arts. Decottignes (2016) points out that people with disabilities spend their entire lives striving to become as normal as possible, and similarly for disabled artists. However, "encouraging disabled artists to satisfy traditional aesthetics, through processes of adaption that seek to normalise impairment, is consequently considered by disability-identified artists to be a form of cultural imposition" (Decottignes 2016, 46).

Expressive, aesthetic, and emancipatory potential of disability arts

Expressive: disability art supports the creation of disability identity and culture

Artists with disabilities are producers of disability culture when they shape and create disability values and identities. As Sandhal (2006) puts it,

> Disability art … forms the base of support for the emergence of disability culture. Disability art events provide an occasion for disabled people to gather and define themselves as a subcultural community…Disability art often fosters disability pride by embracing a politicised disability identity, celebrating bodily difference, and consciously participating in the building of a distinct disability community.
>
> *(Sandahl 2006, 405)*

A clear example of this is Deaf culture.

> Deaf people across different cultural contexts consider their deafness not as an impairment but as a linguistic difference from phonocentric language norms (i.e., language that relies on sounds rather than gestures). Deaf people who consider their deafness as a linguistic difference, rather than an impairment or even a disability, have self-identified as a linguistic minority and have developed a Deaf culture they consider distinct from disability culture or majority culture. Their notion of culture is primarily built on their distinctive language and associated sociocultural practices and beliefs, rather than that of a dominant or majority (mainstream) culture. As a result, deaf people who embrace a Deaf culture claim their inalienable right to exist apart from 'mainstream' society.
>
> *(Peters 2006)*

In this way, deaf-identified art valourises Deaf culture.

Disability arts also contribute to a sense of identity and solidarity. Colin Barnes (2008) expresses the full potential of what disability arts can do this way:

> Disability arts … is not simply about disabled people obtaining access to the mainstream of artistic consumption and production. Nor is it about simply expressing the individual experiences of living with or coming to terms with an accredited impairment. Disability art is the development of shared cultural meanings and collective expression of the experience of disability and struggle. It entails using art to expose the discrimination and prejudice disabled people face, and to generate group consciousness and solidarity.
>
> *(Barnes 2008, 4)*

Justin Lee et al.

Aesthetics: disability-informed standards of beauty and art

Disabled artists may not realise the potential of their work when they are mired in the normalising force of conventional aesthetic standards. Disabled artists in Singapore have constantly innovated their artistic practice, and this has the potential to inform or elevate aesthetic standards. For instance, an accomplished painter with Tourette's previously tried to control his ticks, especially during the process of painting, but has come to accept that the ticks are part of who he is. At times, he lets his ticks dictate the kind of brush strokes he takes. Lily Goh, a deaf performer, has created a genre of art of her own in the signing of songs, which requires a visual and sign language that aptly coveys the emotional tenor of the music. In some of these cases, artists are starting to see that disability can actually be an advantage instead of a barrier to making art.

Such artworks then educate and expand horizons of audience. Sandhal (2006) astutely observes,

> The particularities of these bodies transform the media in which they work. Disability artists that are most successful take advantage of the transformative potential of difference rather than trying to fit their non-standard bodies into standardised conventions. The sometimes startling and innovative results of these artistic experimentations are known as disability aesthetics.
>
> *(Sandahl 2006, 406)*

Letting the disability experience inform aesthetics expands the range of aesthetic criteria and standards, and the horizons of what counts as beauty and art. While this poses a dilemma for professional artists because such alternative standards may limit broader public recognition, it breaks free from traditional constraints that have limited artistic possibilities and pathways.

Emancipatory: unique qualities of art that make it suitable for broader political and social goals

As a vehicle for promoting inclusion, "disability arts has the potential to succeed where other forms of ideological critique fail because of the way in which difference is deployed, playfully and pragmatically, in order to make a political difference" (Allan 2005, 31). When it works, audiences are forced to recognise their own role in discrimination and exclusion which creates self-consciousness. An uncomfortable space for audiences is created in which they are forced to pause and contemplate. As an approach which forces able-bodied people to confront their own banality, to laugh at their stupidity, and to recognise how they contribute to disablement and exclusion, it does appear to be more spirited and possibly more productive than other approaches which have been tried (Allan 2005).

Arts-based approaches to enquiry and research have the ability to go beyond conventional approaches to understanding social issues (Simons & McCormack 2007; Barone & Eisner 2011). Arts-based approaches not only facilitate deeper forms of interpretation and understanding, but are often better at evocation than scientific modes of enquiry. Proponents argue that they enhance understanding through the communication of subjective realities or personal truths that can occur only through works of art (Barone & Eisner 2011). Therefore, they constitute a powerful means of *understanding*, *documenting*, and *representing* disability experience. As Simons and McCormack (2007, 296) put it, "when participants have the opportunity to portray their experience through different art forms, they often reveal insights

110

that they cannot articulate in words." Given these strengths, it is no surprise that arts-based approaches have often been used as a tool for social justice (Magee & Kochhar-Bryant 2013; Osei-Kofi 2013).

Conclusion

When VWOs regard the arts as a kind of service that achieves therapeutic outcomes for clients, they regard the arts as merely one community asset out of many others that they can mobilise to serve their target beneficiaries. Government agencies may support disability arts projects to increase community bonding. However, taking the arts as merely an instrument towards other goals may neglect its expressive value, aesthetic power, and emancipatory potential.

Even when participants engage in arts and craft, there is virtue in taking the arts and crafts-making techniques seriously, so that people with disabilities can participate in cultural life of society as producers instead of just consumers. When aesthetic quality is considered secondary, or even irrelevant, an important dimension of the process of artistic creation is lost. Even if there are therapeutic effects, it should not mean the aesthetic value gets neglected. Some community arts programmes do this very well by taking the arts seriously. For example, a certain day activity centre provides artistic training and commissions projects that provide a sense of dignity and allow its members to participate in the cultural life of their society, which contrasts to other centres that treat them merely as recipients of services (Knutes Nyqvist & Stjerna 2017). Participants at that day activity centre reported that their art is taken seriously with the projects being planned to offer different ways of expression and development of techniques and skills:

> This project is really taken seriously. Our supervisors don't exactly say, 'Okay, everyone, let's paint clouds.' 'Take a seat and get busy with your stuff'. No, it's been all about making field trips, having people come and give talks, about our exhibitions, and it has all been really in-depth.
>
> *(Focus group participant cited Knutes Nyqvist & Stjerna 2017, 974)*

Another respondent pointed out that the centre is not just a "place to keep people safe during the day" (Focus group participant cited Knutes Nyqvist & Stjerna 2017, 974), but as a workplace which offers its participants opportunities to develop both personally and as artists.

The argument here is not that disability-informed arts are better than arts as therapy. They both have their merits, but the *worth* of disability-informed arts is harder to appreciate in a context where the arts are seen merely as a means of achieving therapeutic outcomes for individual clients. That said, not everyone wants to be a professional artist or engage in understanding, documenting or representing disability experience for social and political change. There is indeed much value in simply engaging in the pleasures of arts and crafts, even as a form of recreation. Therefore, policy should create choice instead of limit them, and one of the areas that is underdeveloped is disability-informed arts in the Singapore context. Just as artists should focus on their strengths and tap into the potential of arts-based approaches for advocacy and social change, with more support for disability-informed arts, disabled artists can focus on their disability experience as a relevant and powerful way of exploring meaningful and authentic social inclusion of people with disabilities, an important force for advocacy and social change.

Justin Lee et al.

References

Allan, Julie. 2005. "Encounters with Exclusion through Disability Arts." *Journal of Research in Special Educational Needs.* 5 (1): 31–36.

Ariffin, Afifah. 2016. "Existing Buildings to Meet New Accessibility Requirements from 2017." *Channel NewsAsia,* Accessed 1 June 2018. Available: www.channelnewsasia.com/news/singapore/existing-buildings-to-meet-new-accessibility-requirements-from-2-7929208.

Barnes, Colin. 2008. "Generating Change: Disability, Culture and Art." *Journal of Disability and International Development.* 1: 4–13.

Barone, Tom, and Eisner, Elliot W. 2011. *Arts Based Research.* London: Sage Publications.

Boeltzig, Heike, Sulewski, Jennifer Sullivan, and Hasnain, Rooshey. 2009. "Career Development Among Young Disabled Artists." *Disability & Society.* 24 (6): 753–769.

Cheng, Gloria. 2014. "Dance Review: Complex, Spunky Portraits that put the 'able' in Disability." *The Straits Times,* Accessed 1 June 2018. Available: www.straitstimes.com/lifestyle/entertainment/dance-review-complex-spunky-portraits-that-put-the-able-in-disability.

Chong, Terence. 2005. "Singapore's Cultural Policy and Its Consequences: From Global to Local." *Critical Asian Studies.* 37 (4): 553–568.

Decottignies, Michele. 2016. "Disability Arts and Equity in Canada." *Canadian Theatre Review.* 165: 43–47.

"Drop the Labels, Recognise the Work" (no author byline). 2017. *The Straits Times,* 29 August 2017. Accessed 1 June 2018. Available: www.straitstimes.com/lifestyle/arts/drop-the-labels-recognise-the-work.

Enabling Village. n.d. "5 Activities for Kids with Disabilities this June Holidays (and beyond)." Accessed 1 June 2017. Available: https://enablingvillage.sg/2017/06/19/5-activities-for-kids-with-disabilities-this-june-holidays-and-beyond/.

Goy, Priscilla. 2016. "Art Brings Together Kids with Special Needs, Those Without." *The Straits Times,* 11 July 2016. Accessed 1 June 2018. Available: www.straitstimes.com/singapore/art-brings-together-kids-with-special-needs-those-without.

Hall, Edward, and Wilton, Robert. 2011. "Alternative Spaces of 'Work' and Inclusion for Disabled People." *Disability & Society.* 26 (7): 867–880.

Jurong Junior College. 1992. Voluntary Social Services in Singapore Seminar.

Knutes Nyqvist, Helen, and Stjerna, Marie-Louise. 2017. "Artistry and Disability – Doing Art for Real? Affordances at a Day Activity Centre with an Artistic Profile." *Disability & Society.* 32 (7): 966–985.

Kong, Lily. 2012. "Ambitions of a Global City: Arts, Culture and Creative Economy in 'Post-Crisis' Singapore." *International Journal of Cultural Policy.* 18 (3): 279–294.

Kwok, Kian-Woon, and Low, Kee-Hong. 2002. "Cultural Policy and the City-State." In Diana Crane, Nobuko Kawashima, Ken'ichi Kawasaki ed. *Global Culture: Media, Arts, Policy, and Globalization.* London & New York: Routledge, 149–168.

Lord, Geoffrey ed. 1981. *The Arts and Disabilities: A Creative Response to Social Handicap.* London: Little and Brown Co.

Magee, Christine Morano, and Kochhar-Bryant, Carol A. 2013. "The Studio: An Environment for the Development of Social Justice in Teaching and Learning." In Mary Stone Hanley, Gilda L Sheppard, George W. Noblit, and Thomas Barone ed. *Culturally Relevant Arts Education for Social Justice: A Way Out of No Way.* New York: Routledge, 205–215.

Nanda, Akshita. 2017. "Greater Push for Arts to Engage Audiences, Art-Makers of All Abilities." *The Straits Times,* 29 August 2017. Accessed 1 June 2018. Available: www.straitstimes.com/lifestyle/arts/arts-embraces-all.

Newsinger, Jack, and Green, William. 2016. "Arts Policy and Practice for Disabled Children and Young People: Towards a 'Practice Spectrum' Approach." *Disability & Society.* 31 (3): 357–372.

Norman, Richard. 2011. "NPM Ideas and Social Welfare Administration." In Tom Christensen and Per Lægreid ed. *The Ashgate Research Companion to New Public Management.* London: Ashgate Publishing, 177–192.

Osei-Kofi, Nana. 2013. "Exploring Arts-Based Inquiry for Social Justice in Graduate Education." In Mary Stone Hanley, Gilda L Sheppard, George W. Noblit, and Thomas Barone ed. *Culturally Relevant Arts Education for Social Justice: A Way Out of No Way.* London & New York: Routledge, 1–11.

Cheong, June 2008. "Poems Inspired by Special Paintings; Four RI Students Compile a Poetry Anthology Written after Viewing more than 3,000 Paintings by Disabled Artists." *The Straits Times*, 24 January 2008.

Riddell, Sheila, and Watson, Nick. 2003. "Disability, Culture and Identity: Introduction." In Sheila Riddell and Nick Watson ed. *Disability, Culture and Identity*. London & New York: Routledge, 1–18.

Sandahl, Carrie. 2006. "Disability Arts." *Encyclopedia of Disability*. 1: 405–406.

Simons, Helen, and McCormack, Brendan. 2007. "Integrating Arts-Based Inquiry in Evaluation Methodology: Opportunities and Challenges." *Qualitative Inquiry*. 13 (2): 292–311.

"Sold-Out Smash Grandmother Tongue Returns by Popular Demand!" 2017. *Wild Rice*, 3 July 2017. Accessed 1 June 2018. Available: www.wildrice.com.sg/images/production/17GMT/Grandmother_Tongue_Press_Release_final.pdf.

Tan, Audrey. 2013. "New Code to Improve Access for Families, Elderly and the Disabled." *The Straits Times*, 30 August 2013. Accessed 1 June 2018. Available: www.straitstimes.com/singapore/new-code-to-improve-access-for-families-elderly-and-the-disabled.

Tan, Kenneth Paul ed. 2007. *Renaissance Singapore? Economy, Culture, and Politics: Economy, Culture, and Politics*. Singapore: NUS Press.

Tan, Rachel. 2015. "Reaching Out in a Silent World." *The Straits Times*, 19 May 2015. Accessed 1 June 2017. Available: www.straitstimes.com/lifestyle/reaching-out-in-a-silent-world.

Tan, Rachel. 2013. "Art Therapy Gains Popularity as Way to Help Patients Deal with Disabilities." *The Straits Times*, 27 November 2013. Accessed 1 June 2018. Available: www.straitstimes.com/singapore/art-therapy-gains-popularity-as-way-to-help-patients-deal-with-disabilities.

Tan, Tarn How, Goh Ze Song, Shawn, and Nadzirah Binte Samsudin, Siti. 2017. *Beyond Happy People for Happy Arts: Full Report on the Roundtable on the Development of Community Arts in Singapore*. Institute of Policy Studies. Available: http://lkyspp2.nus.edu.sg/ips/event/ips-sam-spotlight-on-cultural-policy-series-three-roundtable-on-development-of-community-arts-in-singapore.

Tan, Winnie. 2017. "Singapore's First Festival for Artistes with Disabilities to be Held Next March." *The Straits Times*, 18 April 2017. Accessed 1 June 2018. Available: www.straitstimes.com/singapore/spores-first-festival-for-artistes-with-disabilities-to-be-held-next-march.

The National Arts Council. 2012. "The Report of the Arts and Culture Strategic Review." Accessed 1 June 2018. Available: www.nac.gov.sg/dam/jcr:1b1765f3-ff95-48f0-bbf9-f98288eb7082.

Wong, Kim Hoh. 2016. "Hearing-Impaired Pianist Hears the Music in His Mind." *The Straits Times*, 16 October 2016. Accessed 1 June 2018. Available: www.straitstimes.com/singapore/i-hear-the-music-in-my-mind.

Wong, Reuben, and Wong, Meng Ee. 2015. "Social Impact of Policies for the Disabled in Singapore." In David Chan ed. *50 Years of Social Issues in Singapore*. Singapore: World Scientific, 147–166.

"Young Artist Award Recipients" (no author byline). 2016. *The Straits Times*, 4 October 2016. Accessed 1 June 2018. Available: www.straitstimes.com/lifestyle/arts/young-artist-award-recipients.

Zaccheus, Melody. 2016. "Free Entry for People with Disabilities." *The Straits Times*, 15 April 2016. Accessed 1 June 2018. Available: www.straitstimes.com/singapore/free-entry-for-people-with-disabilities.

Zhuang, Kuansong. 2016. "Inclusion in Singapore: A Social Model Analysis of Disability Policy." *Disability & Society*. 31 (5): 622–640.

9

Ten years of Touch Compass Dance Company's integrated education programme under the spotlight

A reflective essay

Sue Cheesman

Introduction

In this chapter, I review the kinds of opportunities that have emerged for integrated dance over the last 20 years, specifically within the context of Encompass, an education and outreach arm of Touch Compass Dance Company based in Auckland, New Zealand. In doing so, I identify and discuss practices and influences that have opened up creative opportunities and synergies in the work I have been involved with as a part of Touch Compass for over 15 years. I analyse challenges, strategies, and successes through a dynamic questioning lens, showing commitment to negotiation while also theorising the journey of integrated dance specifically within the Encompass context.

Integrated dance

There are tensions and complexities in embracing difference within the frameworks of integrated dance, both in practice and echoed in the literature of integrated/inclusive dance practice (Cooper Albright 1997; Shapiro 1998; Sandahl & Auslander 2005; Kuppers 2007, 2014; Whatley 2007; Amans 2008; Benjamin 2010). While I analyse this journey from a variety of standpoints, I also acknowledge what has been achieved so far in heading towards the realisation of a fully disability-led dance practice.

"While the Inclusion Movement was spear-headed by the disability community, the Civil Rights and Social Justice movements of the 1960s expanded the philosophy and broadened the focus to encompass all people" (Bevan-Brown 2013). These movements paved the way for the development of community arts programmes in the late 1970s, 1980s, and 1990s, championing far greater access and opportunities for all, but particularly for people who were being restricted by societal barriers. Disability activists worldwide were advocating for change. For example, in Britain in 1976,

> Shape was founded by [non-disabled dancer] Gina Levete MBE, with the purpose of introducing creative opportunities for pockets of the community where there was little

or no opportunity to participate in the artistic life of the country. Shape acted as a network connecting individual artists from all disciplines, and established performing groups to environments where people were isolated through illness, disability or social disadvantage.

(Shape Arts n.d.)

Furthermore, within dance specifically, Gina Levete observed that the idea that young disabled people could seriously learn to dance was a new concept, as were many of the workshops and activities which Shape introduced at that time. Over the subsequent years, criticism has been levelled at this kind of approach with a preponderance of non-disabled people in a variety of roles. Shape responded, "[we are] recruiting disabled people, both at a planning and production level and as artists and facilitators in order to see through this vision" (Perring 2005, 176).

Some 20 years later, Arts Access Aotearoa in New Zealand was founded in 1995. Its purpose is to advocate "for all people in New Zealand to have access to the arts by supporting people who experience barriers to participation in the arts or whose access to the arts is limited" (Arts Access Aotearoa n.d.). In 2001, a partnership between government and disability activists in New Zealand resulted in a social model based *Disability Strategy*. However, it was not until 2010 that the national organisation for dance in New Zealand, DANZ, developed the *Disability and Dance Strategy*.

In the last two decades worldwide, there has been an increase in integrated community dance opportunities within the outreach programmes of dance companies and/or as part of a community-based arts programmes (Kuppers 2006; Amans 2008; Benjamin 2008; Zitomer 2013). Outreach work has been embedded in the aims and objectives of many integrated dance companies such as Dancing Wheels (USA 1980), Amici Dance Theatre (Britain 1981), Touch Compass (New Zealand 1995), Axis (USA 1987), Candoco (Britain 1991), DanceAbility International (USA 1987), Restless Dance Theatre (Australia 1991), Jolt (New Zealand 2001), and Common Ground Stopgap (Britain 1995) through their education work. An early exponent of this work, Alito Alessi, began exploring mixed ability dance in 1987 (mixed ability dance is synonymous with integrated dance). Alessi's Youth Outreach programme was established in 1995 to educate youth about art and the potential of people with disabilities. Subsequently, in 1997, Alessi developed international DanceAbility Teacher Training (DanceAbility International 2008).

Much of this education outreach work comes under the umbrella of "community dance," defined by scholar Petra Kuppers (2007) as "a movement that facilitates creative expression of a diverse group of people, for the aims of self-expression and political change" (2). Adam Benjamin (2008) agrees that "its role in nurturing creativity and contributing to the cultural life of its locale, aware of its potential for education and enlivening the imagination [supports] opening up channels of communication between strangers" (105). Both definitions are useful and have much to offer those who work in this field. "Through dance, the body can move with passionate commitment to one's life and responsibility to others and the larger world" (Shapiro 1998, 19). However, there are debates as to what counts as community dance in comparison to professional dance, and this often has ramifications in terms of funding and status.

Within the so-called high art forms, there is still a very rigid concept of what a body would or should look like in order to dance (as discussed by Sarah Whatley in Chapter 26). This has shifted somewhat in contemporary dance practice, with more allowance made for difference than is seen in ballet (Cheesman 2017b). How much power and control are exerted by the professional dance world and the ramifications of this for community integrated dance? Kuppers (2014) points to the reliance of dance on physical presence and expressivity. She develops this argument further by talking about "normate bodies, hyper visible, operating at the extremes of functionality and strength" (114). Briggs, Kolb, and Miyahara (2012) expand this point by observing that "dancers with disabilities not only struggle against societal prejudice, but also against the strictly confined body image in much western theatre dance" (Briggs, Kolb & Miyahara 2012, 1). In the pursuit to reproduce the same kinds of disciplined bodies and disciplined aesthetic, this 'ideal dancing body' does act as a potential gatekeeper for diverse bodies making diverse movements challenging what dance can look like. I agree with Whatley and Marsh (2017) who note that "differently abled dancers show how no bodies are static; we are all unique and in transition gaining and losing functions, and capacity for movement" (Whatley & Marsh 2017, 4). This opens up a range of possibilities for dancing differently.

Many debates also arise around language use, its tensions, binaries, and complexities. It is important to recognise the exclusions, the contested and challenges that result: "words are relational, are wielded at different times, and by different people, for different reasons" (Kuppers 2014, 12). Disability is a deeply contested term. The medical model places disability at the centre and regards it as abnormal and in need of fixing. Perring (2005) argues that this perception of disability as a deficit condition has limited learning-disabled people's opportunities to make informed artistic choices (178). Much is to be gained from this idea of moving beyond the fixed positioning of 'other' and finding new possibilities for the body. "Disability is a disjuncture between the body and the environment" (Sandahl & Auslander 2005, 8), as Sandahl and Auslander have put it – between a physical or psychological configuration and a world that does not accommodate it – and this disjunction has rich potential to show new possibilities in terms of how people think, speak, move, relate to each other, and relate to the world at large.

Oliver (2013) attributes his development of the social model of disability to the "Fundamental Principles of Disability document first published in the mid-1970s which argued we are not disabled by our impairments but by the disabling barriers we face in society" (1024). From a social model's perspective of disability, we live in an ableist society with many gatekeepers, and in which people create barriers by designing a world for their way of living. Morris, Baldeon, and Scheuneman (2015) state, "[t]here is no universal agreement on the type of language to use regarding disability" (123). Language and terminology morph and change over time with the continuing evolving of discourses centred on disability culture and community.

So, to define integrated dance as both able-bodied and disabled dancers performing together might be contentious and double-edged, suggestive of a binary or collaboration. Furthermore, the defining of integrated dance raises further questions: how do we account for an invisible disability? Are we required to have equal numbers of disabled dancers to able-bodied? What happens if we have more of one group than another? This kind of thinking can lead to value judgements being made around the yardstick created by these questions. Benjamin (2010) refers to a resistance to using integration. Although there is resistance to using the word 'integration' (because of its association to the medical models of rehabilitation), he says, "its etymology refers to 'being in touch' and of not only playing an integral part in a larger picture, but of changing that picture" (115). Irving and Giles (2011) warn that "[i]t may only be, however, through the acceptance of dominant discourses that integrated dance groups will gain recognition by the mainstream dance community" (378). I prefer the notion that "integrated dance can be defined as people with different forms of embodiment, including disability" (Kuppers 2011, private communication). This way of thinking about integrated dance seems to suggest inclusivity of diversity and difference without setting up a binary or privileging a single view of a dancing body.

It was not until post-1990s that an increasing body of written work started to be published about integrated dance, contesting what dance is, who can dance, and challenging notions of representation, embodiment, and access (Albright 1997; Sandahl & Auslander 2005; Kuppers 2007, 2014; Whatley 2007; Benjamin 2008). Dance companies over time saw the need to produce their own resource packs to support people working in this area. Others have written about how to teach integrated dance in a variety of settings with useful information on the practicalities of teaching and specific content for a range of dance learning experiences (Levete 1993; Hills 2003; Kaufmann 2006; Cheesman 2011a, 2011b; Cone and Cone 2011; Zitomer 2013). Of note is that none of these authors uses specific codified techniques but instead come from an improvisation, problem-solving base through unpacking the elements of dance such as body awareness, action, space, time, and energy dynamics and relationships. Adam Benjamin's extremely useful and groundbreaking book, *Making An Entrance: Theory and Practice for Disabled and Non-Disabled Dancers* (2002), contains a more extended guide to the challenges and creative opportunities in teaching integrated dance. He embraces respect for individual difference and encourages freedom of choice through improvisation-based content (Benjamin 2002). Kuppers, who through her actions and writings champions the disability cultural movement, recently wrote *Studying Disability Arts and Culture* (2014), a handbook that foregrounds problematic concepts in the study of disability arts and culture within this diverse world.

Touch Compass and the Encompass education and outreach programme

This body of work in the field has informed practice, including for companies like Touch Compass, though their Encompass programme. Encompass is an education and outreach arm set up in 2006 for the purpose of creating an umbrella for community engagement under Touch Compass Dance Trust in Auckland, New Zealand, founded in 1995. Encompass aims to:

- Provide inclusive dance programmes that are open to anyone who wants to dance through workshops and community dance classes
- Enable dancers to discover their own creativity, expression, and self-confidence
- Build the skills of practitioners necessary for sustainable employment
- Offer professional development for teachers of inclusive and mainstream dance
- Raise society's awareness and understanding of inclusive dance
- Present stage performances that are enjoyable, challenging, and memorable (Touch Compass Dance Company 2017a).

The journey to sustain a variety of provision and opportunities for integrated community dance under this umbrella has not always been easy, with many obstacles to dance around, under, or through. In her book celebrating the first ten years of Touch Compass, Michelle Powers (2007) wrote "[i]n New Zealand there was no one working in integrated dance in 1995. In fact, the term and concept was generally unknown" (17). Similar to the beginnings of other integrated dance companies, from the outset Touch Compass provided workshops, classes, and lecture demonstrations to a variety of groups to increase their visibility, educate, and build capacity. Catherine Chappell, artistic director and founder of Touch Compass, attended the first Alito Alessi DanceAbility International Teacher Training in 1995 to increase her knowledge of integrated dance. This content became a staple from which she drew upon extensively to teach workshops, subsequently building on the course content to fit differing needs (Powers 2007).

Contact improvisation (CI) and structured improvisation were the foundation corner-stones of the Touch Compass work from its inception and remain so today. It is interesting to note here that DanceAbility training is based in CI, which has roots in the work of Steve Paxton and others in the dance activist movement of the 1960s. CI "radicalism lay in its accessibility to all, regardless of background or experience and in that advanced or professional dancers could dance with beginners and 'non dancers'" (Benjamin 2002, 32). This revolution paved the way for integrated dance to develop, challenging traditional and modernist perspectives by opening up avenues "for dancers with and without disabilities to create and embody alternative discourses of ability, validity and professionalism in dance and beyond" (Irving & Giles 2011, 377). Catherine Chappell (2000) talks about being excited to work in contact improvisation combined with integrated dance and felt that this com-bination offered the following: depth of communication, elements of surprise, connection, beauty, risk, and reality. In implementing Touch Compass' education philosophy, the aim is for all class participants to be challenged, which can be demanding in large classes with a diverse range of participants. Some of the early approaches were definitely based on trial and error and required on-the-spot thinking to adapt to the situation to promote more inclusion and positive dance learning. I would argue that this still happens today and keeps the work alive. I also agree with Adam Benjamin (2002), who asserts that "for every solution he has found to problems encountered there have been others who have found different but equally satisfying ones" (10).

My own teaching philosophy aligns with feminist pedagogical practices and is built around my strong belief that everyone can dance and deserves the opportunity to explore the full range of human capabilities and potential through the moving thinking body (Cheesman 2011b). My approach does not put the teacher on a pedestal as the fountain of all knowl-edge and emphasises that all involved have much to give in reciprocal learning encouraging multiple voices to be heard. I have taught the Touch Compass community dance class for over ten years.

Teaching the community dance class and trying to facilitate everyone's development is, at times, a complex struggle, and I am acutely aware of my imperfections. I believe it is important to rigorously resist the acceptance of mediocrity or total exclusion of certain type of participants from the task. My intent is to extend the skills and learning of all members of the class including non-disabled students, with the expectation that everyone works ac-cording to their own capabilities and beyond, stretching the boundaries of what is possible (Cheesman 2011a). These challenges provided the opportunity for teachers such as myself to adapt content as well as extend and hone teaching skills, while also being aware of privilege we may hold. Cone (2007) illuminates how teaching and learning are neither fixed nor finite processes but are dynamic, expansive, and shaped by the moment. In this way, the dance-teaching experience becomes a nurturing one, by fostering different possibilities of making sense of and accepting other ways of knowing. Multiple voices are encouraged and recog-nition of one's lived experiences is valued (4). Reciprocity in the exchange of knowledge between teacher and student is maximised, and teacher imposition is minimised in these in-tegrated dance contexts. In the class, it is very important for all students to have a voice and be able to express themselves in different ways that value their diversity. The students are involved in classroom demonstrations of movements, and they have their movement ideas accepted and applied within class situations. These values are identifiable within the class members' evaluative comments, namely, being accepted for who we are, not being judged, allowance for diverse responses, and a freedom to explore our own movement possibilities (Cheesman 2017b).

Relationships within Touch Compass' Encompass programme

Touch Compass' broader aim is to provide pathways for people associated with the company, whether in a community or professional capacity. Over the years, members of the community class have been involved in a range of opportunities, such as youth intensives, leading to one-off performances within Tempo Dance Festival Auckland 2011, 2012, and 2013, YouDance 2014, photo shoots, DanceBox films, the Matariki Night parade, Heidi Latsky's on-display site-specific project, and InterACT's yearly disability arts festival.

Right from the outset, a governance structure was set up to enable and encourage company dancers to take on the roles of tutor supports and dancer-helpers in the community dance classes. Over time, considerable consistency in performance skill has emerged among those company dancers who have taken on the roles with the effect that the community dance class has developed its own sense of being a committed community within a larger organisation. Both positions – tutor supports and dancer-helpers – lead to community dance class participants being exposed to positive role models, generating a strong sense of connection with the professional dancers. This interchange of experiences provides a rich platform for all participants to collaborate, learn, engage, and journey, as well as helping to sustain consistency in the teaching and supporting of this class and its vision. Strong relationships are evident within this group and have been sustained over time. We also encourage volunteer dancers to come to the class and receive mentoring within the framework of the class. From my experience, this strategy has been successful to a certain extent, but students in full-time dance training have so many demands on their time that it is hard for them to be consistent in keeping their commitment to a regular time slot.

In response to a perceived need expressed by the wider dance community, Touch Compass has created opportunities to learn skills in facilitating this work. Over the years, a group of individuals involved in integrated dance and with expertise in differing perspectives in the field have lead, planned, contributed to, and delivered several tutor training three- to four-day intensives. The group includes Janice Florence (Australia), Marc Brew (UK), Catherine Chappell (NZ), Suzanne Cowan (company member, Touch Compass, NZ), Rodney Bell (company member, Touch Compass, NZ), and me (NZ). In keeping with the aims of being an integrated company, every project has a mixture of experts with and without a disability. Within these intensives, there have been opportunities for the community dance class to be involved, which has resulted in a rich interchange of ideas and experiences for all involved. These intensives are written up and make very useful resource packs for that particular intensive.

The Saturday community dance class is taught through a problem-solving improvisational approach, with various dance and music scores, and tasks having a close connection to contact improvisation in which the participants are constantly making decisions in the moment. Participants work in solo, duet, and class groupings, and are given open-ended questions and problems to explore and solve in multiple ways (Cheesman 2011a). Benjamin (2002) points out that "Borrowing and reintroducing movement material, echoing and developing it through a course of improvisation is one way of adding texture and depth to improvisations and giving coherent structure to choreographed works" (58). In the community dance class, we celebrate and embrace diversity of movement responses. Lucy Bennett, artistic director of the inclusive Stopgap Dance Company in the United Kingdom (2012), describes inclusive dance as responsive practice as coming "from being flexible creative and patient with participants and having a sense of playfulness in developing bespoke dance skills for individuals" (Bennett 2012, 1; Caines 2014). Bennett's insight resonates with me, as I have found that sometimes able-bodied individuals come to the Saturday community dance class and discover that their own sense of insecurities about dance and dancing seemed to be heightened as they witness other class participants demonstrating high skill levels in improvisation. I wonder why they did not return. Was it that they felt inadequate, while experiencing their own vulnerabilities coming to the fore during this class, and could not surmount these differences, making them uncomfortable? Were they comparing their ability to do the task against other class participants? Did they place this Saturday class in the 'dance therapy' box and so deduced this was not for them? Were the dance tasks so hard that they could not find a way to continue? In questioning these students afterwards about their experience of the first class, they replied that they wanted a class that taught routines delivered in a step-by-note transmission (teacher does and the student-participant copies; a model and primary mode of delivery akin to private dance school teaching). The inclusive, Saturday community dance class is certainly not delivered in this way, and the main objective is not to teach routines.

Understandably, these participants do not return to the Saturday dance class, although it does reasonably raise the point that one size does not fit all. However, I argue that New Zealand has a considerable dominance of routine-based dance classes run in community settings. There are tensions here, and although the aim is to make the class as accessible as possible in a myriad of ways, this class is running counter to what might be considered an ableist aesthetic agenda. I rationalise this by considering that it is important to have a variety of classes to choose from, and not everyone wants to participate in a class which is heavily based in on improvisation. Nevertheless, it does raise the point of what is valued and what is not. It also highlights the difficulty of encouraging individuals without a disability to come to class as participants.

The sympathy attitude, although well meaning, still raises its head today and is often because of a lack of understanding or exposure to people with diverse movement ranges in dancing. Furthermore, how does this filter through to community dance practice? Is it possible to have a range of aesthetics operating which celebrates both diversity and diverse bodies dancing? When the community dance group performs in public, there are always responses congratulating them saying how great they are, but rarely, if ever, is there any critical feedback. Is this because the same yardstick to other community dance performances is not being used? How does seeing diverse bodies dancing affect feedback? And in community integrated dance performance, what form does critical feedback take, if any, and through what lenses are judgements being made? Allan (2014) argues that "the arts have inclusive potential both as a force that draws people into participation and as a political vehicle for seeking out normally silenced and disenfranchised voices" (518).

Performance opportunities within Touch Compass' Encompass programme

Performance opportunities have always been a part of the class' yearly schedule; for example, this could be in the form of showing a dance created by the community class for parents, support workers, and community and to perform yearly at InterACT Disability Arts Festival in Auckland. Performance opportunities contribute to the class ethos by inviting their input into the choreography during the process and working together towards a specific outcome. All performance opportunities provide a vehicle for the class over the proceeding few months to collaborate through structured improvisation to build a piece that we are all invested in performing. For example, in 2017, we performed in Touch Compass' 20-year celebration at the viaduct basin in Auckland. For this performance, we used LED-lighted poi as our prop (the Māori term poi refers to a ball on the end of a string used in movement in dancing). Much excitement, engagement, and risk-taking was generated from the building of a dance piece to be shown during this night-time InMotion parade. During this parade, a large audience congregated and watched the community class perform *Dancing Colours* accompanied by a marimba band. They were very proud of their achievements, and this dance has been subsequently performed at InterACT Festival in October 2017.

Logistics are a big part of the planning for any such event. They include organising transport for class members to the outdoor performance space, negotiating the issues around access to one disability toilet for all 18 performers near the performing site, organising food, and arranging rehearsals at the site before the performance. Transportation is an ongoing negotiation issue for some people; for example, several class members rely on a small number of disability taxis or support workers to get to class. Overcrowded congestion is frequently a factor with Auckland traffic, and/or limited availability of accessible taxis means that participants may be late or early to class. Loading and unloading of equipment also takes time. These multiple logistical concerns signify the need to be flexible with activities and to develop accommodating strategies without making people feel 'othered.'

The company continues to create performance opportunities through these types of events, but, at the same time, has taken advantage of the huge explosion and growth of online media such as YouTube. The emergence of these new media and platforms has seen dance artists and companies take up new social media opportunities to offer their work – and filmed versions of their work – as open source, free for anyone to view, and gives the potential for far greater exposure of their performance work.

Touch Compass began its foray into making short films in 2003, before the emergence of social media. One of these films, *Union*, depicted a pivotal moment with the meeting of Tim Turner and his dog, Boiski, who between them have four legs, each having lost a limb in road accidents. The film included a poem written by Tim, and there was a version of the film which includes a sign language interpretation. Following on from the initial films, Catherine Chappell's idea for more films was for the Touch Compass company community to share their stories (Powers 2007). The company embarked on producing the *DanceBox* collection of short films portraying significant moments in dancers' lives. The works are choreographed and devised by Touch Compass and its community, and all filmed within the confines of a 2 × 2 × 2 m plywood box. Workshops were held with many of the community class participants to find the pivotal moments in their lives that could be made into a film. The footage was then crafted by artistic film director Alex Duncan. The success of the first films has meant that eight dance box films have been made to date. These have been disseminated widely, through film festivals, YouTube, conferences, schools, and with one being played on an international airline in-flight entertainment. These developments have opened up far more possibilities to freely view a range of dance performances, including performers with different embodiments.

In 2016, I expanded on this engagement with film and embraced the possibilities of social media technology by making my first foray into digital storytelling with three members of the community class. Digital stories are short, 2–5 minutes in duration, moments in time.

Bliss and Fisher (2014) define digital storytelling as person-driven, self-created, audiovisual ethnographic narrative. The digital storytelling model that was used for this research project has been adapted from the practice that was developed at the Center for Digital Storytelling (CDS) in Berkeley, California, predominantly by Joe Lambert. The philosophy underpinning CDS practice emerged out of social justice movements in the United States in the 1960s and 1970s. Furthermore, Lambert (2009) asserts that he is absolutely committed to freedom of expression: most important is that the work is participant-centred, and people are encouraged to find their own path in their story. Benmayor (2008) claims that both product and process in digital storytelling empower participants to find their voice and to speak out, especially those marginalised by racism, educational disadvantage, or language. Therefore, it may be argued that digital story is strongly aligned with principles of social justice through embracing new perspectives on different forms of embodiment and opening up spaces for a range of representations that disrupt outdated constructs of youth and difference (Cheesman 2017a). In my 2016 engagement with digital storytelling, I asked three of the community dance class members, all in their 20s, why they danced, and the responses were recorded, edited, and shared online.

Although both the earlier films and the subsequent digital stories started with the same premise of telling a story, I contend that the films' final artistic product was paramount, whereas in the digital stories the process was more significant. This is not to promote one as more important or valued than the other, as both forms are valid and did much to champion integrated dance, simply to note the different results. Both forms gave community dance class members a raft of different opportunities and experiences, ranging from being the main character or dancer to having support roles. As Bliss and Fisher (2014) argue, the stories we tell about ourselves influence our sense of self and agency. In producing the digital stories, the process was as important as the product in influencing sense of self and agency.

Conclusion

The class culture within Encompass is not about prescription, but, rather, it emphasises curiosity and individual/collective achievement, which will confidently fulfil everyone's potential. The lack of a syllabus, lack of adherence to technical dance virtuosity, allowing for a range of creative endeavours and varied movement possibilities to occur, and embracing divergent thinking as opposed to convergent, are critical to this culture. The embracing of new developments and opportunities – presenting solo work, contributing to the facilitation of work in the beginning phases of the class, exploring new media to share dance and relationships to dancing – has consistently been welcomed by the community class. The feedback suggests these opportunities are valued for the following reasons: that of affirmation and acceptance from their peers, opportunities to perform for the class, and to take risks knowing that their dancing will be celebrated in all its diversity. "What is distinctive" in integrated dance, Allan says, "is a shifting space of participation to encompass knowing together with sensing feeling and perceiving that engagement with the aesthetic enables and indeed provokes" (Allan 2014, 520). Commenting on the opportunities they have had through the community class, members say they value being accepted for who they are, not being judged, the welcoming of diverse responses, and the freedom to explore their own movement possibilities without being judged. Barr (2013) states that in integrated dance the "participants find a sense of self while taking ownership of their dancing" (116). Barr (2013) suggests that through sharing, learning, and creating, a unique relationship evolves among all present in the class. I would also argue that within the Encompass community dance classes, a sense of agency is seen in the capacity of individuals to act independently and to make their own free choices.

Through my involvement in this work, I have found it is important to be aware of multiple privileges facilitators may hold and to consistently check my own facilitator agendas and prejudices, which may or may not be in conflict with what is transpiring in terms of the choices the class wants to make at that point in time. Having a sense of humour and being open to laugh with the class at my own foibles seems to slice through hierarchies that may exist. Still, lingering questions and challenges do remain: how do we further sustain and build these classes? Is there a place for the teaching of dance styles? How do we encourage more individuals with a disability into more leadership roles? How do we maintain and develop diverse performance opportunities? With the increase in groups doing this work, how can funding sources be increased to allow for this growth as opposed to all groups competing for the same small pool of money?

In closing, I argue that integrated dance, especially in a community setting, has acted as a site for change and growth from the initial forays in the late 1970s and 1980s spearheaded by the activisms of the 1960s in disability culture and dance. It is possible to trace how a web of international connections and interchange of ideas from dancers, teachers, and artists working in this field has certainly influenced the growth and development of integrated community dance in New Zealand. Touch Compass has been at the forefront of these developments in heading towards achieving the realisation of a fully disability-led practice. It is important to remain committed to advocating for meaningful and respectful dialogue, opening up the spaces of vulnerability and honesty on the journey towards fully integrative dancing. This includes opportunities for all to take charge, to have input and leadership roles, and to have their voice and ideas valued in integrated dance.

References

Allan, Julie. 2014. "Inclusive Education and the Arts." *Cambridge Journal of Education*. 44 (4): 511–523.

Amans, Diane ed. 2008. *An Introduction to Community Dance Practice*. Hampshire: Palgrave Macmillan, 99–108.

Barr, Sherrie. 2013. "Learning to Learn: A Hidden Dimension within Community Dance Practice." *Journal of Dance Education*. 13 (4): 115–121.

Benjamin, Adam. 2010. "Cabbages and Kings: Dance, Disability and Some Timely Considerations." In Alexandra Carter and Janet O'Shea ed. *The Routledge Dance Studies Reader*. London: Routledge, 111–121.

Benjamin, Adam. 2008. "Meetings and Strangers." In Diane Amans ed. *An Introduction to Community Dance Practice*. Hampshire: Palgrave Macmillan, 99–108.

Benjamin, Adam. 2002. *Making an Entrance: Theory and Practice for Disabled and Non-Disabled Dancers*. London: Routledge.

Benmayor, Rina. 2008. "Digital Storytelling as a Signature Pedagogy for the New Humanities." *Arts and Humanities in Higher Education*. 7 (2): 188–204.

Bennett, Lucy. 2012. *Introduction to Stopgap Dance Company*. Accessed June 2018. Available: http://stopgapdance.com/media/files/Intro_Inc.pdf.

Bevan-Brown, Jill. 2013. "Including People with Disabilities: An Indigenous Perspective." *International Journal of Inclusive Education*. 17 (6): 571–583.

Bliss, Elaine, and Fisher, Janice. 2014. "The Journey to a Good Life: Exploring Personal and Organisational Transformation Through Digital Storytelling." In Robert E. Rinehart, Karen N. Barbour and Clive C. Pope ed. *Ethnographic Worldviews. Transformations and Social Justice*. Dordrecht, The Netherlands: Springer, 93–109.

Briggs, Hahna, Kolb, Alexandra, and Miyahara, Motohide. 2012. "Able as Anything: Integrated Dance in New Zealand." *Brolga: An Australian Journal About Dance*. 37. Accessed 1 June 2018. Available: https://ausdance.org.au/articles/details/able-as-anything-integrated-dance-in-new-zealand.

Caines, Matthew. 2014. "Arts Head: Lucy Bennett, Artistic Director, Stopgap Dance Company." *The Guardian*, 8 April 2014. Accessed 1 June 2018. Available: www.theguardian.com/culture-professionals-network/2014/apr/08/stopgap-dance-company-disabled-artists.

Cheesman, Sue. 2017a. "Digital Stories: Three Young People's Experience in a Community Class." In Stephanie Burridge and Charlotte Svendler Nielsen ed. *Dance, Access and Inclusion*. Oxon: Routledge, 122–131.

Cheesman, Sue. 2017b. "Issues and Challenges around the Fostering of a Productive Respectful Community Ethos within an Integrated/Inclusive Class Context." *Dance Research Aotearoa*. 5: 99–112.

Cheesman, Sue. 2011a. "Facilitating Dance Making from a Teacher's Perspective within a Community Integrated Dance Class." *Research in Dance Education*. 12 (1): 29–40.

Cheesman, Sue. 2011b. "A Dance Teacher's Dialogue on Working within Disabled/Non-Disabled Engagement in Dance." *The International Journal of the Arts in Society*. 6 (3): 321–330.

Cone, Theresa, and Cone, Stephan. 2011. "Strategies for Teaching Dancers of All Abilities." *Journal of Physical Education, Recreation & Dance*. 82 (2): 24–32.

Cone, Theresa Purcell. 2007. "In the Moment: Honoring the Teaching and Learning Lived Experience." *Journal of Physical Education, Recreation & Dance. Reston* 78 (4): 35–42.

Cooper Albright, Ann. 1997. *Choreographing Difference*. London: Wesleyan University Press.

DanceAbility International. 2008. *About Us: History*. Accessed May 2018. Available: www.danceability.com/history.php.

Dunphy, Kim, and Scott, Jenny. 2003. *Freedom to Move: Movement and Dance for People with Intellectual Disabilities*. Sydney: MacLennan and Petty.

Hills, Peppy. 2003. *It's Your Move!* Birmingham: The Questions Publishing Company Limited.

Irving, Hannah, and Giles, Audrey. 2011. "A Dance Revolution? Responding to Dominant Discourses in Contemporary Integrated Dance." *Leisure/Loisir*. 35 (4): 371–389.

Kaufmann, Karen A. 2006. *Inclusive Creative Movement and Dance*. Champaign: Human Kinetics.

Kuppers, Petra. 2014. *Studying Disability Arts and Culture*. New York: Palgrave Macmillan.

Kuppers, Petra. 2007. *Community Performance: An Introduction*. London & New York: Routledge.

Kuppers, Petra. 2006. "Vibrant Agencies: Dance, Disability Embodiment and Phenomenology of Communication." *Discourses in Dance*. 3 (2): 21–31.

Lambert, Joe. 2009. *Digital Storytelling: Capturing Lives, Creating Community*, 3rd edn. Berkeley: Digital Diner Press.

Levete, Gina. 1993. *No Handicap to Dance: Creative Improvisation for People with and without Disabilities*. London: Human Horizons.

Morris, Merry Lynn, Baldeon, Marion, and Scheuneman, Dwayne. 2015. "Developing and Sustaining an Inclusive Dance Program: Strategic Tools and Methods." *Journal of Dance Education*. Special issue on Teaching Dance to Students with Disabilities. 15 (3): 122–129.

Oliver, Mike. 2013. "The Social Model of Disability: 30 Years On." *Disability and Society*. 28 (7): 1024–1026.

Powers, Michelle. 2007. *Touch Compass*. Auckland: David Ling.

Sandahl, Carrie, and Auslander, Philip. 2005. *Bodies in Commotion: Disability and Performance*. Ann Arbor: University of Michigan Press.

Shape Arts. n.d. *Shape at 40: Founder Gina Levete on Shape's Beginnings*. Accessed 1 May 2018. Available: www.shapearts.org.uk/news/gina-levete.

Shapiro, Sherry. 1998. *Dance, Power and Difference*. Champaign: Human Kinetics.

Touch Compass Dance Company. 2017. *About the Company*. Accessed 1 April 2018. Available: www.touchcompass.org.nz/what-we-do.

Touch Compass Dance Company. 2017a. *Encompass Education Programme*. Accessed 1 April 2018. Available: https://www.touchcompass.org.nz/encompass.

Whatley, Sarah. 2007. "Dance and Disability: The Dancer, the Viewer and the Presumption of Difference." *Research in Dance Education*. 8 (1): 5–25.

Zitomer, Michelle. 2013. "Creating Space for Every-body in Dance Education." *Physical & Health Education Journal*. 79 (1): 18–21.

10

Inclusive capital, human value and cultural access

A case study of disability access at Yosemite National Park

Simon Hayhoe

Introduction

I have two aims for this chapter. My first aim is to contribute to the debate about how best to provide services for people with disabilities in cultural heritage sites by providing an example of best practice. My second aim is to provide a model that can be used by professionals to design access provision in cultural heritage sites. To meet these aims, I discuss inclusive capital, which is a model of developing access in institutions in five stages, and an analysis of these stages in Yosemite National Park's Deaf Service.

My observations about how we develop inclusive capital evolved out of a survey of previous philosophies of human value, the ideas they shared, and their description of the value of capital. In common with those previous philosophies, I was interested in the ways human value influenced identity and behaviour, and ways of thinking about motives and desires. Human value also seemed to be an effective way of understanding our personal knowledge, activity and skills, and how these elements shape our personality, memory, and character traits.

For instance, the informal and intangible knowledge which we discover outside formal learning develops value for us as individuals. This value might be the skills we learn in the school yard, such as who is popular or who should be avoided and why. Or this knowledge can be about what clothes we need to wear to make ourselves valued by our peers. Alternatively, we can learn when to use certain types of language, such as slang and swearing, and with whom this language is socially valuable.

Our moral and immoral knowledge, such as the rules of bullying and how to exclude others who don't fit our rules of social acceptability, can also hold a form of value, *albeit* a socially negative value. Hierarchies of power in the schoolroom or school yard, or the development of sexual and romantic relationships, can be said to value your place in a social or cultural hierarchy of popularity. What is more, certain moral values which we may not align ourselves with may nevertheless hold value to others who do hold those moral beliefs.

For instance, a knowledge of how to steal, what is acceptable to steal, and who the most vulnerable members of society are to be stolen from, can be said to have a pernicious form of value to some people.

As shown in this case study, knowledge of our interactions in museums and national parks can also be valuable and hold values. These values can be the measurement of our knowledge and our motivation for visiting museums and national parks that for us hold a cultural value of what we feel is our heritage. Values can also be said to be the subconscious habits that dictate the way we learn about accessing museums. Our understanding of the importance of museums and national parks is also a value. The outcome of this knowledge and practice can also be a *sense of inclusion* and a feeling of well-being that visiting cultural institutions brings, as it makes us feel valued. Value does not have good or bad qualities, as morals themselves are appreciated according to our own individual values.

In this chapter, I develop this theory of inclusive capital by arguing practical skills needed for inclusion are developed by different forms of values of non-economic capital. I also argue different types of identity demand different forms of access strategies, from technical and educational access to access based on spaces and places. In this chapter, I argue that the most widely used models of disability, such as the medical and the social models of disability, as described by Barnes and Mercer (2005), have done little to emphasise the elements of access in ensuring inclusive capital.

I start my discussion by outlining a survey of philosophy on human values that evolved into theories of non-economic capital, and by describing how the philosophical history of human capital as value evolved.

Inclusive capital

Philosophies of human value have evolved chronologically since the Enlightenment, from Adam Smith (1776) to Karl Marx (1867) to Pierre Bourdieu (2010) to Sarita Yardi (2009, 2010). Human value, referred to as intangible forms of capital by Bourdieu and Yardi, is an effective way of understanding our personal knowledge, activities, and skills and how these elements shape our personality, memory, and character traits. According to Smith, Marx, Bourdieu, and Yardi, human values shape individual identity and behaviour, and our ways of thinking about motives and desires. Human value can also be applied to informal knowledge.

These previous philosophies of human values have a common theme: they value a *sense of inclusion* for a category of people as part of our human condition to feel part of a network. That is, they hypothesise the value of family, friends, social class, religion, and ethnicity as a community. Subsequently, these philosophies agree it is important, if not instinctive, for people to network and to learn through others. To put it another way, although there are better and worse ways of networking and learning and we might be encouraged to use one way over another, because we are not specifically taught to network and learn, we simply network and learn. Networking and learning are therefore arguably part of our human condition. Yardi's model of technical capital (2009, 2010) also shows us that not only is it important to get information and to use it to feel included, but it is a large part of our human history to develop and use technology, just as it can also be said to be part of our history to seek out our heritage and the heritage of others.

Cultural capital, such as that described by Bourdieu (1990, 2010), can also be knowing when to use certain types of language, such as slang and swearing, and with whom certain language is socially acceptable. More controversially, human capital is our moral and immoral knowledge, such as our rules about how to exclude others who don't fit our rules of social acceptability. It could also be said that it is part of our human character to seek out inclusion as a value to feel our *sense of inclusion,* and this inclusion fosters our *sense of value.* It can be said that throughout history, people have fought wars, crossed continents, hidden, or fled from oppressors to form new communities, to feel secure, and to feel a *sense of value.* Consequently, to develop inclusive capital can also then be central to our human history, as it provides us with a *sense of value.*

I argue that acquiring inclusive capital is especially important if you are a disabled or an older person. This difficulty is caused because people with disabilities are more likely to find barriers to accessing the first steps of inclusive capital. This leads to a lessening of their sense of inclusion in mainstream society, and to a growing sense of social exclusion and isolation. For instance, disabled people often find it harder to access technologies they can interact with, or to access the environments of cultural institutions (as discussed by Alex Lubet in Chapter 25 and Sarah Whatley in Chapter 26). They are less likely to have their needs understood, or be thought of as needing access to the learning of non-disabled people. They are often thought to want separate cultural institutions, such as schools or classes, or separate museum entrances or exhibitions in museums.

The physical nature of some disabilities or infirmities caused by old age can also lessen our access to acquiring inclusive capital. For instance, acquiring deafness and/or blindness later in life can make it harder to join group discussions that are an essential part of networking for gaining information or using technology; for example, some people who have late disabilities often do not learn sign language or Braille or identify themselves as being disabled (Hayhoe 2018). Physical disabilities may also make it harder to find transport or access cultural institutions or physical networks. Late acquired learning disabilities can similarly be thought to restrict access to mainstream learning, and the spaces and places of cultural institutions that people once enjoyed. Therefore, it is another task of this chapter to illustrate the need for cultural institutions and teachers to recognise the need for inclusive capital, to foster a *sense of inclusion.* Cultural institutions and teachers do not just need to understand this *sense of inclusion* intellectually and academically; they need to feel empathy with this sense of inclusion.

Practically, cultural institutions and teachers must also understand and study ways in which they can adapt their spaces and places – both their physical and virtual environments. These institutions and teachers also need to adapt their own behaviour to develop habits and practices that recognise a sense of inclusion in others. To develop this argument and to understand the evidence for cultural inclusion in the case study, I start by developing the academic background developing inclusive capital from human values (Hayhoe 2018). The process of developing this background will structure the model of inclusive capital as a framework of different stages of development.

Five stages of developing inclusive capital

As with other forms of capital, it can be said inclusive capital is not born in us, it is acquired. It can also be said that a single cycle of acquiring inclusive capital takes place in five stages.

The first stage in this cycle is connecting and bonding with a network of people – that is to say, to acquire bonds from our human necessity to bond. These groups are largely seen as a family or a group of friends, classmates, or workmates, or, as Yardi (2009, 2010) observed, connecting and bonding with a group developed through social media. Without connecting and bonding to this social or cultural network, there is no *sense of inclusion*. Consequently, our *sense of inclusion* is premised on a social and cultural process of feeling valued in these bonds and connections.

The second stage in this cycle is learning inclusive capital through our networks – that is to say, we use our human condition to learn to develop and acquire human capital. Thus, learning inclusive capital consists of acquiring habits, knowledge, and practices that can lead to a *sense of inclusion*. In common with the writing of Marx, part of this learning of inclusive capital is also about seeing ourselves as equally included as others are, in order to humanise our skills. However, unlike Marx's understanding of morals, this is also where we develop a further sense, the moral *sense of justice*, which can also be described as a form of moral knowledge. In this respect, justice is also connected to a process of bonding, connecting, and feeling included, and being included could be said to be an important part of our moral understanding.

The third stage in this cycle is collecting information that points to or later leads to knowledge. This collection of information can include finding out about our surroundings, making judgements about their worth, or planning to travel within our surroundings. For example, this information could be directions from maps. Yardi and Bourdieu suggest such forms of cultural capital can also be acquired through the use of technology or gaining information. In the modern era, this third stage can also mean accessing digital networks or learning, and access to these networks and this learning can help develop a *sense of inclusion*. Information is consequently a vital part of planning and designing inclusive capital, and its subsequent habits and practice. It can be described as the raw material or the atomic level of inclusive capital.

The fourth stage in this cycle is physical or virtual access to spaces and places, such as visiting or attending cultural institutions or reading about their collections and history. These institutions can include places such as schools, parks, universities, museums, or, as Yardi suggests, surfing websites.

The fifth stage in this cycle is a form of capital that weaves its way through all the others. This capital is physical and virtual mobility, which allows for navigation through spaces and places, networks, information, and learning – for instance, this can include the skills needed to surf the Web for information, move around or between institutional environments, or navigate technologies like telephones. Conversely, lacking mobility can lead to exclusion, to being unable to attend an institution as a place, to being unable to find information, or to being unable to move between networks. Subsequently, mobility is the essential catalyst of inclusive capital.

As the philosophies in my survey observe, although our networks do not have to be in a single place, we need an area – either physical or virtual – where we can access them. This access is important for connecting and bonding within or between networks. We also need access to cultural environments, objects, or performances that connect and bond us to our networks, or allow us to see our networks in relation to 'others.' These five stages are represented in Figure 10.1.

So, how can these five stages of developing inclusive capital be implemented in a cultural institution? What follows is a case study of the evolution of the Deaf Service at Yosemite National Park, California, which illustrates how inclusive capital was implemented through this service.

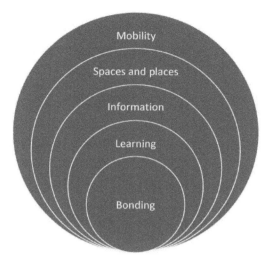

Figure 10.1 The development of inclusive capital and a *sense of inclusion*

The research process used in the Yosemite National Park Deaf Service case study

This case study comes from a broader pilot study of museums and national parks in the US and UK, which started in 2011 with consultations with nine professionals in access to cultural heritage and education, and 12 people with disabilities who participated in cultural heritage activities in London, Boston, New York, and San Francisco (Hayhoe 2018). The sampling of these participants was mostly through personal contacts and took little account of factors such as age, gender, or ethnicity.

My consultations with the study participants ranged between half an hour and an hour and all started with a simple question: what makes a cultural space accessible? These discussions then developed into explorations of what the participants considered to be examples of good practice – the professionals worked for institutions such as national museums, small and large regional museums, and schools for students with disabilities; the participants with disabilities had many years' experience of visiting museums, monuments, and national parks. From these discussions, I identified six criteria that were considered to provide effective accessibility: (1) access was more successful when spaces were easy to find out about and book; (2) spaces were more accessible when they could be reached and entered easily from car, bus, subway, or rail; (3) spaces were more accessible when they made cultural objects accessible, preferably physically, and provided accessible information about these objects; (4) spaces were more accessible when they provided other accessible services such as bathrooms, cafes, classrooms, and shops; (5) spaces were more accessible when they had classes and activities for all; (6) access was at its best when the space was open and mobility was easy.

After drawing up these criteria, I searched for institutions which met these criteria through online searches of documents describing their history, buildings and restoration, and access services. I also researched their locations for ease of accessibility through Google Maps/Street View and their collection of objects through their online databases. This search

Simon Hayhoe

resulted in a list of 23 national parks and museums. A further search was then conducted through these institutions' websites for access information, information about transport, education, and policies, and any other information, which the study participants with disabilities had told me was useful.

From this list of 23 cultural heritage sites, data was analysed to choose suitable institutions, which could provide useful case studies using the following four criteria: (1) whether their location was in the same state as the locations of the case studies I was developing; (2) the diversity of the sites, with a blend of physically large sites and small sites and large visitor numbers and relatively small visitor numbers; (3) the diversity of access issues at the sites, from sites displaying untouchable art, to sites with natural barriers, to monuments where the building was the attraction and couldn't be changed; and (4) the sites had personnel who agreed to participate in the study.

This second search identified six sites to choose from: four in the US and two in the UK. Eventually, I only chose sites in the US and emphasised the National Park Service for two practical reasons: (1) the National Park Service had a national policy of accessibility; and (2) all US sites adhered to the same laws defining inclusion for people with disabilities, most particularly the Architectural Barriers Act, which governs the actions of the federal government, and the Americans with Disabilities Act, which directs non-governmental actions. This preference for the US meant I could make direct comparisons among the four cultural heritage sites in the country. Although the UK has its own legislation, the 2010 Equalities Act, its legal philosophy is different, as disability is just one of several protected characteristics under this legislation, including age, gender, ethnicity, religion or belief, sexuality.

Subsequently, I arranged telephone discussions or online questions with the professionals responsible for inclusion and access at the four chosen sites. Each professional was sent the same questions and an informed consent ahead of time by email, and I requested they either send their answers by emails or post or arranged a telephone discussion. I carried out the last of these interviews in fall 2017. In some cases, participants sent me additional policies that were reviewed during our discussions or email correspondence.

I started my survey of the Yosemite National Park through its website and the website of the National Park Service in California, which includes several other national parks in California. After analysing its public policies and other public information, I contacted personnel at the National Park Service and was put in touch with their relevant officers in Yosemite. My contact at Yosemite was an assistant superintendent I called "Rosamunde," and my contact at the National Park Service central office was an officer whom I called "Alfred." Before questioning Rosamunde and Alfred, I sent them an informed consent letter and my list of questions via email. Both Alfred and Rosamunde provided extended answers in reply via email, and numerous links to management and access policies, as well as laws that informed their practice in late 2017. After writing up the case study of Yosemite, I sent the case that follows to Rosamunde at Yosemite for verification and incorporated her suggestions.

Access and inclusion at Yosemite National Park

Yosemite is over 1,100 square miles, more than 3,000 square kilometres, of mountains, meadows, rivers, glaciers, and sequoia forests. Around 95 per cent of the park is designated as wilderness by the US government. At just over 5 square miles, around 15 square kilometres, the heart of the national park is Yosemite Valley, which gave Yosemite its name. This relatively small valley was incorporated as a national park by Abraham Lincoln in 1864 and was the first part of Yosemite to be designated as national park. The rest of Yosemite was later designated a national park in sections, after it was observed that its natural heritage was under threat from those using its natural resources without respecting its unique environment. In the present era, and being so vast, Yosemite has a vast range of natural and cultural heritage. San Francisco is more than 165 miles by road, Los Angeles is almost 280 miles by road, and Las Vegas, Nevada, is over 455 miles by road.

Historically, national parks in the US supported individual visitors with disabilities informally until the early 1970s – i.e. there was no official policy or guideline to follow, and so support was provided ad hoc. Alfred and Rosamunde explained that the National Park Service first considered accessibility as a national issue following the passing of Section 504 of the Rehabilitation Act in 1973. This law required federal agencies to ensure their programmes and facilities were accessible to individuals with disabilities:

> No otherwise qualified individual with a disability in the United States ... shall, solely by reason of his or her disability, be excluded from the participation in, be denied the benefits of, or be subjected to discrimination under any program or activity receiving Federal financial assistance or under any program or activity conducted by any Executive agency or by the United States Postal Service.
>
> *(US Department of Labor 2017: Para 1)*

In common with other government-funded institutions, the Rehabilitation Act applied to the environments of national parks. Later in the twentieth century, the Americans with Disabilities Act (ADA) of 1990 effected the management of private concessions within national parks. Rosamunde noted that the ADA did not directly change the Rehabilitation Act, although in practice they work in tandem; the ADA, which is much more detailed, is used to understand and provide examples for the Rehabilitation Act's intent. Alfred observed, "Between the two laws, all government funded programs are covered. Of course, there are many programs, such as school districts which receive federal, state and local funds, and are therefore covered by both laws at the same time."

The National Park Service now tackles and develops its access strategies through the National Accessibility Branch (NAB), a separate national office with responsibility for inclusion. As Alfred explained, operationally NAB sits within the Parks Facilities Management Division, under the Associate Director for Parks Planning, Facilities, and Land, as physical access is a key issue. NAB's role is primarily to collaborate with others across the National Park Service, such as the in-house specialists on accessible media and exhibits. In addition, NAB also leads the National Park Service's Accessibility Coordinating Committee (ACC) to discuss broader issues and policy. All of NAB's activities are designed to bring together stakeholders in accessibility from across the US national parks on a regular basis. This network of expertise provides something akin to a community-of-practice model of cooperation and information sharing (Wenger & Snyder 2000). To incentivise good practice across the US national parks, every year NAB presents awards to individual parks that complete outstanding projects related to accessibility. As Alfred explained, these awards are for national park teams who "have shown sustained commitment to accessibility over a long time."

The original system of accessibility was originally set out in an order by the director of the National Park Service in November 2000, which crystallised the looser system that had been in place since 1979. The director is the highest ranked administrative officer in the

Simon Hayhoe

National Park Service and defines issues such as policy and visitor support. The order was written as follows:

> In 1979, the National Park Service (NPS) decided to approach the issue of accessibility in a comprehensive, organized way, rather than on a project-by-project basis. The primary goal of the program was to develop and coordinate a System-wide, comprehensive approach to achieving the highest level of accessibility that is reasonable, while ensuring consistency with the other legal mandates of conservation and protection of the resources we manage.
>
> *(National Park Service 2000: Para 1)*

However, during my correspondence with Alfred and Rosamunde in September 2017, the National Park Service was finishing the third year of a five-year strategic plan to introduce an updated system of accessibility. This plan was to take into account contemporary issues such as new legal mandates, technological development, and updates in practice by other services. It would also incorporate the original five objectives of its Director's Orders:

1 Incorporate the long-range goal of providing the highest level of accessibility that is reasonable for people of all abilities in all facilities, programmes, and services, instead of providing "separate" or "special" programmes.

2 Implement this goal within the daily operation of the NPS, its policies, organisational relationships, and implementation strategies.

3 Provide further guidance and direction regarding the NPS interpretation of laws and policies.

4 Establish a framework for the effective implementation of actions necessary to achieve the highest level of accessibility that is reasonable.

5 Ensure the implementation of "universal design" principles within the national park system (National Park Service 2000: Objectives).

Of all its services, Yosemite is perhaps best known for its Deaf Services, and this service is no more apparent in its policy of inclusive learning and information. I write about this latter element more below. This access provision is largely made up of American Sign Language (ASL) interpreters and has been provided in-house by Yosemite for almost 40 years. The history of this service is so important that it has become significant to the story of the National Park itself. Rosamunde said,

> Our Deaf Services program began with a summer seasonal position in 1979 and that position became permanent and year-round in 2016. Yosemite has the first year-round, permanent Deaf Services Coordinator/ASL interpreter-ranger in the NPS ... [And] Yosemite won the US Department of the Interior National Park Service Park Planning, Facilities and Lands 2008 National Programmatic Accessibility Achievement Award for the Deaf Services Program.

The Deaf Service was first established through the agreement of the head of Interpreting Services, the Disabled Access coordinator, and the Valley District interpreter. This led to Maureen Fitzgerald, a local ASL interpreter, being sponsored by Yosemite Natural History Association to be based in Yosemite Valley in 1979, where the service is still based.

According to Jennifer Jacob's 1990 article for *Courier*, the journal of the National Park Service, Fitzgerald was first noticed by those informally providing translation at Yosemite when she attended a tour with an ASL signing friend provided by the head of interpreting service in 1978. By coincidence, Fitzgerald then attended Yosemite with the Berkeley

132

Outreach Recreation Program to participate in disability awareness training. About this time, she was approached by the Disabled Access Coordinator to discuss the embryonic Deaf Service, something the coordinator had considered previously. So how does the Deaf Service at Yosemite develop practice and inclusive capital at Yosemite?

Developing inclusive capital through the Deaf Service at Yosemite

Bonding

Both Rosamunde and Alfred advised that it is very rare for national parks in general to offer tours specifically for Deaf people, preferring instead to include all visitors in their regular tour schedules. This being said, Yosemite can accommodate an advance request from groups of individuals travelling together who need bespoke tours. These bespoke tours are particularly important, as schools or associations for the Deaf can make provision for a specific visit according to their particular needs. Alfred noted,

> For example, if a large group of individuals who are Deaf wanted a tour with a sign language interpreter, a unit would arrange it. In other cases, there are park units that have areas that have been designed to be more accessible.

Importantly, and in common with other national parks, Yosemite is not allowed to provide services that charge Deaf people extra because their services cost more to provide. This equal charging also goes for concessions and businesses that run within Yosemite, although if this extra cost makes a business loss-making, the National Park Service makes up the difference. For instance, Yosemite provides visitors who are Deaf or hard of hearing with free services prior to arrival and during visits, such as trip planning and assisted listening devices. Yosemite also installed a public videophone at Yosemite Lodge for signing and lip-reading visitors and offers a free access pass to the park. This access pass is common to all US national parks.

Yosemite's regular tours can also include an ASL interpreter on request at no extra cost, so that ASL signers can join in tours with hearing groups. According to its Deaf Service documentation, ASL signers can also be made available at visitor centres, Yosemite's hotels, and in its medical services.

Learning

Yosemite's Deaf Service offers proactive and inclusive learning provision within its Interpretation Services rather than Access Services; the coordinator reports to the chief of Interpretation as a means of more easily coordinating with all interpretive branches and other divisions. Important in this process, Yosemite did not previously employ staff specifically because they are language interpreters, although this was a skill sometimes held by park staff. As Rosamunde stated, the hiring of a permanent ASL interpreter was largely for four reasons: (1) to comply with the Rehabilitation Act; (2) to support the large number of Deaf visitors; (3) Yosemite's history of having a Deaf Services programme; and (4) Yosemite's commitment to being a leader in the National Park Service in this field. Yosemite also has the capacity to develop bespoke specialist classes for Deaf people. For instance, the Deaf Service can develop lessons and learning tours if contacted by the group in advance; as the Deaf Service is based in Yosemite Valley, this can be arranged relatively quickly. Rosamunde said, "Deaf Services frequently offers specialty talks or walks for large Deaf groups ... We wouldn't normally hire outside contractors. Our staff can provide this service upon request."

Simon Hayhoe

Information

Yosemite expends a great deal of effort developing its information provision for Deaf people and develops access to information through three main strategies: (1) technologies in Yosemite, which provide alternative communication through technologies; (2) human interpretation; (3) the website, which is becoming an increasingly important access tool for Yosemite, as it is for the National Park Service as a whole.

According to Alfred, information is a core theme to all the access services provided by the parks – specific information about physical access to the environments, tourism information about the parks, and learning-oriented information. For instance, Yosemite provides captioned videos and captioned interactive technologies such as computerised guides for visitors with mixed sensory impairments. Rosamunde also explained that Yosemite proactively develops its own information services, including its specialist Deaf Services webpage; its social media presence, such as the Deaf Service's Facebook page; its Accessibility webpage, with accessible information for visitors with travel, accommodation, and other information; and its downloadable accessibility guide, with more detailed information about access needs and what visitors can expect to be legally provided.

At the time of our correspondence, Yosemite's Deaf Service was developing new documentation for visitors. This form of review is regular, and the service's provision is guided by updates to the Rehabilitation Act, the ADA, and the US Department of the Interior's Accessibility Statement and the first statistics about the take-up of the Deaf Service, although, as Rosamunde pointed out, it is notoriously difficult to gather accurate user figures. She reported that

> Summer, 2017, brought 3–5 Deaf groups through the Deaf Service program per week. December, 2017, Yosemite will compile the first year-round statistics on the Deaf Service program, but those statistics will not represent all of Deaf visitorship. There are probably still more visitors who are Deaf who do not contact Deaf Services than those that do.

Space and place

In common with other similarly large national parks which are known for their natural features and whose primary purpose is conservation, Yosemite makes its website space and place physically accessible to Deaf people, by using accessible standards. For the National Park Service as a whole, proactive physical accessibility to national parks is a priority, and this is outlined in its Director's Orders. Typically, accessible spaces and places in Yosemite are legally mandated as part of a general accessibility programme. Again, this development of physical accessibility is typically aimed at Yosemite's lodges, visitor centres, and museums, but can also refer to its monuments, such as its cemetery, which are harder to change.

Accessibility for Deaf people at Yosemite is also developed with help from the National Park Service itself. Logistically, Yosemite's most accessible space and place is the Yosemite Valley, and in this provision the most significant changes are made to publicly accessible buildings.

Conclusion

By developing an image of capital as a non-economic, psychological, and cultural value, we immediately broaden the ways we develop inclusion. Inclusion is no longer merely the opposite of exclusion, and particularly, the opposite of social exclusion. Instead, it becomes a recognised human need.

Seeing inclusion as a form of capital also allows us to go about developing it as a process, one in which the person with a disability controls its development according to their needs. It also allows people from different backgrounds to develop their own capitals, their backgrounds, and their own cultural heritage according to their needs. Seeing inclusion as a capital also allows us to develop institutional strategies targeted at not just overcoming social injustice and singling out institutions that do not provide inclusive spaces and places. In addition, it allows us to emphasise inclusion as a practical means of education, which needs different practical learning strategies as a process of partnership with people deserving access and value.

In this respect, inclusive capital is a tool for people with disabilities to gain access to cultural institutions. Perhaps of all cultural communities, people with disabilities need more practical support to access and feel a sense of inclusion.

Yosemite's Deaf Service came about when the head of Interpretation observed the needs of visitors using ASL in the late 1970s. Yosemite then reacted to this new situation by housing Deaf Services in Interpretation, and this provision evolved into an alternative language provision as well as an access need. However, developing a site with inclusive capital for Deaf people was challenging. Although it is a uniquely beautiful national park, Yosemite's vastness and its many isolated natural features make access difficult to develop. This issue seems to be common in traditional national parks in the US, forcing the National Park Service to develop an evolving strategy of access and inclusion.

The legal implications of being designated a US National Park can both enhance and complicate strategies of inclusion, with no single policy covering all eventualities. For instance, as it is largely wilderness, Yosemite itself cannot be changed or adapted, but its lodges, visitor centres, and museums have to be fully accessible. Subsequently, Yosemite's superintendents and wardens often walk a fine line between developing creative solutions to a lack of access and managing Deaf people's expectations.

At the same time, Yosemite's wilderness is also its main attraction for visitors who are disabled and non-disabled alike, as to conquer many of Yosemite's trails is to develop inclusive capital. This means access to Yosemite's various environments has to be differentiated, and access to its human environments needs to be managed differently from its natural environments.

Consequently, much of Yosemite's Deaf Service's strategies leading to inclusive capital are centred on the Yosemite Valley, where the greater majority of its visitors stay and where the activities are less dangerous. Of these strategies, Yosemite particularly relies on accessible communication through guided tours and information technology to guide people around its environments. Lodges in Yosemite Valley have video phones; visitor centres have close captioning; Yosemite's website has accessible information and educational material guiding visitors; Yosemite's websites also point the way to access facilities. Because it has a partially devolved approach to managing access, Yosemite has been able to develop its Deaf Service using proactive strategies, which are themselves originally inspired by creative approaches to reactive situations.

The redefinition of ASL users as a language group has meant such services are seen as a core issue of communication and education, as well as an issue of social justice in the round. More importantly, this practical redefinition of ASL also allows Yosemite to employ a full-time ASL interpreter, developing a further layer of inclusion. Consequently, the development of inclusive capital in Yosemite has not always followed a simple pattern of policy development through the National Park Service. Instead, access has evolved organically to serve the inclusion rights of Deaf people as and when they arise.

References

Barnes, Colin, and Mercer, Geoff. 2005. *The Social Model of Disability: Europe and the Majority World.* Leeds: The Disability Press.

Bourdieu, Pierre. 2010. *Distinction.* London: Routledge Classics.

Bourdieu, Pierre. 1990. *The Logic of Practice.* Stanford: Stanford University Press.

Hayhoe, Simon. 2018. *Ageing, Disability, Identity and Cultural Heritage.* Abbingdon: Routledge.

Marx, Karl. 1867 (1986 edition). *Capital - A Critique of Political Economy: The Process of Production of Capital.* vol. 1. Moscow USSR: Progress Publishers.

National Park Service. 2000. "Director's Orders." Accessed December 2017. Available: www.nps.gov/applications/npspolicy/DOrders.cfm.

Smith, Adam. 1776/2005. *Wealth of Nations.* Chicago: University of Chicago Press.

US Department of Labor. 2017. "Section 504 of the Rehabilitation Act." Accessed December 2017. Available: www.dol.gov/oasam/regs/statutes/sec504.htm.

Wenger, Etienne C., and Snyder, William M. 2000. "Communities of Practice: The Organizational Frontier." *Harvard Business Review.* 781: 139–146.

Yardi, Sarita. 2010. *A Theory of Technical Capital.* Paper delivered to the TMSP Workshop, Georgia Institute of Technology, Georgia, 11–12 February 2010.

Yardi, Sarita. 2009. "Social Learning and Technical Capital on the Social Web." *ACM Crossroads.* 162: 9–11.

11

Gender representation, power, and identity in mental health and art therapy

Susan Hogan

When I wrote *Problems of Identity: Deconstructing Gender Issues in Art Therapy* in 1997, it was the first investigation of the topic in the arts-and-health literature. In that essay, I set out my rationale, explaining why awareness of representations of gender is an important topic for mental health practitioners and art psychotherapists in their practice. In this chapter, I survey and critically appraise my research and practice in this field since then. My appraisal includes an exploration of key concepts and contributions, especially about the usefulness of a focus on gender representation, power, and identity, and its importance for mental health. This work falls into an area that Facer and Enright (2016, 84) have called "cognitive justice" which concerns new forms of theory emerging from and reflecting previously marginalised views and perspectives. They note that such perspectives are often explicitly political, and they question the dominance of hegemonic forms of knowledge and produce reflective epistemological critiques of disciplinary norms. Detailed critiques are difficult to summarise, because they are meticulous and rely on the use of examples to drive points through, though some of the essays take a polemical stance (Hogan 2013). *Problems of Identity: Deconstructing Gender Issues in Art Therapy* (1997) was a courageous essay because it created a fundamental critique of disciplinary theory within British art therapy by offering a different conceptual framework and applying it to the discipline. It allowed a paradigm shift to take place by offering cultural rather than purely psychological explanations for states of being, particularly about women's experience of mental illness. It drew on art theory and cultural theory and feminist critiques of science. I shall focus some attention now on that 1997 essay as it began my research trajectory of looking at gender issues in mental health, a trajectory that has continued for 30 years.

I will set the scene a little here. The French philosopher Michel Foucault was important in decentring the subject in relation to mental health. What I mean by 'decentring' is that institutional processes are viewed as important in shaping human subjectivity, moving the focus away from biologically or psychologically determined explanatory frameworks. Meanwhile, feminist scholars such as Elizabeth Cowie (1977) and Tessa de Laurentis (1986), for example, pointed a finger towards representational systems as important in creating constructions of gender. In brief, we are regulated by systems and processes, of which we may not be fully aware. Foucault draws on the work of Althusser (1971) who postulated that ideological

Susan Hogan

processes can be hidden, creating a hegemony of taken-for-granted or seemingly "natural" systems, processes, and norms which are hard to see, let alone challenge (Foucault 1980a, 1980b). Foucault's notion of *dispositive apparatus* can be seen as a more complex elaboration of Althusser's earlier work, which highlights how oppressive social processes can become predominant and seemingly unchallengeable. I take up this theme directly in later work in which I look at *iatrogenic illness* (illness created by hospital treatments), which I shall discuss further in this chapter. Regulatory frameworks have been called *dispositive apparatus*, defined by Foucault as

> thoroughly heterogeneous ensemble consisting of discourses, institutions, architectural forms, regulatory decisions, laws, administrative measures, scientific statements, philosophical, moral and philanthropic propositions—in short, the said as much as the unsaid. Such are the elements of the apparatus. The apparatus itself is the system of relations that can be established between these elements.
>
> *(1977, 194)*

Another way of conceptualising this might be to think of a web of intersecting meaning-making elements including discourses, institutions, and so forth.

The field of arts in health as a whole was under-theorised, but British art therapy practice in the 1990s was becoming increasingly dominated by a rather dogmatic application of psychoanalytic theory, and also a reductive application of object-relations theory, both of which I strongly critiqued in *Problems of Identity* (1997). These conceptual frameworks tended to see the locus of illness as situated firmly within the psychopathology of the individual, though the way that this is understood is different in these two frameworks. In psychoanalytic theory, the aetiology of pathology is the result of repressed instinctual material, particularly from childhood. The psychoanalytic theory of symbolism has particular implications for how images are understood within art therapy. I shall briefly elaborate the psychoanalytic theory of symbolism, as this was the predominant theoretical framework in the period, having gained ground over the hitherto significant Jungian model, which had been very influential in the UK in the post-war period, as I explored in my historical monograph (Hogan 2001). The Jungian approach worked with a concept of psychological homeostasis and saw the artmaking as fundamentally therapeutic (hence the term 'art therapy'), and as having a balancing effect by revealing necessary aspects of being to the subject. However, a very brief explication of the psychoanalytic theory of symbolism is important for an understanding of the mainstream conceptual model of art therapeutic processes in this period and consequent modes of treatment.

In psychoanalytically orientated art therapy, symbolism is seen as arising out of an inter-psychic conflict between the repressing tendencies of the unconscious mind and the repressed content – only what is repressed is understood to need to be symbolised. The material repressed is of a basic instinctual nature, especially related to infantile sexual life. Through a process of *displacement*, it becomes transformed into symbolic material. The symbol is the result of intra-psychic conflict. The word 'symbolic' is therefore used in this very specific way by those psychoanalytically inclined (Hogan 2016a).

Object-relations theory is a theory of development from psychoanalysis, which places great emphasis on interpersonal relations and especially the relationship between the infant and mother for the infant's psychological well-being and psychic development. It is based on the idea that we internalise aspects of our parents, or parts of them (*object relations*), *that become internal objects* continuing to influence our behaviours unwittingly. Many of the discourses

138

about mothering place great emphasis on the mother-baby dyad and ignore more diffuse relations of extended networks of caregivers. From the 1940s, these ideas became very influential in social psychology and social policy. The notion of 'separation anxiety' became popularised in the 1960s in Britain. Riley notes of Bowlby, "He knew that a theory which claimed that to separate children from their mothers might do violence to 'human nature' also embodied a powerful sentiment" (Riley 1983, 108). Applied to art-therapy practice, internal representations acquired in childhood are seen as playing out in later life through relationships. There is usually an emphasis on exploring how such representations are projected outwards, particularly to the art therapist as part of their therapeutic relationship; hence, the main focus of art therapy becomes an exploration of this 'transference' relationship, with potentially problematic consequences.

These theories were the predominant conceptual schema for framing art therapeutic practice in the 1990s. In *Problems of Identity*, I sought to challenge these orthodoxies, and suggested that art therapists look about themselves at representations of women as expressions of cultural practices, conventions, and codes, which constitute our subjectivity. I observed that art therapy can serve as a tool, potentially, to produce images that might challenge dominant or hegemonic representations. The essay points out that people often give expression to their experience by using metaphors, which can better conceptualise and articulate their situation. In ideological struggles, metaphors are commonly used around a disputed site of meaning, which can take the form of pictorial or linguistic strategies to establish one meaning rather than another (Hogan 1997c, 2012a).

Problems of Identity elucidates biological determinism and gives historical examples of the limitation of women's political rights on evolutionary grounds, drawing on feminist critiques of how psychiatrists suggested, for example, that women might become infertile through too much study as an argument against allowing women to enter universities (My PhD was in cultural history, so I always like to add sociopolitical historical context). The main point being made through the examples given, some of which are quite shocking to the modern reader, is that medical practice embodies and perpetuates beliefs and norms linked to institutional arrangements, which are historically specific and subject to change. In *Problems of Identity*, I urge art therapists towards greater recognition of historically specific intuitional orthodoxies (especially a plethora of theories about female instability and inferiority) and their effects upon individuals, and to develop a more critically aware viewpoint.

The human rights dimension of *Problems of Identity* deserves elaboration. It contains a trenchant and detailed critique of those psychiatric practices, which may be viewed as oppressive or abusive, and which were beginning to influence art therapeutic practice. It looks at aspects of identity (colour, class, etc.) intersecting with gender too, before the term intersectional analysis was well established (see Hogan 2015c).

Underpinning theories are important. As I point out in my later work, different theories represent different understandings of what mental illness is and how it should be treated, and so are by no means insignificant:

> Whilst art processes are at the core of art therapy, there are different conceptualisations of the process, based on varied theories. These theories are not inconsequential, *since they posit different views about what a human being is*. Consequently there are different opinions about the role of the art therapist. How the use of art materials is advocated can vary, as well as the way the art materials may be used and the language chosen to explain the engagement.
>
> *(Hogan 2016a, 2)*

Problems of Identity includes a trenchant critique of some of the more reductive and crude applications of these theories, especially when they result in interpretations of the art, or dialogues about images based on *a priori* theoretical formulations. These interpretations are described as 'seductive fictions' posing as scientific writing, which claim to tell us what is *really* going on in the client's mind through their art work. Here is a child's narrative:

> The child didn't know what a key was, but put the bright thing in her bag, and when they came home her mother couldn't find the key, but a big dog came and knocked her down and the key fell out and the door was opened.

A psychiatrist interprets this story to reveal:

> A complex system of conflicts, including resistance at the phallic level against her father's sexuality, which is expressed in the fantasy that the little girl did not know a key. This is a defence by unconscious denial. It is coupled, however, with the wish to rob the mother of the father's penis by putting the unknown bright object into her own bag or womb and guilt over the wish. The dog is the punitive super ego.
>
> *(cited Hogan 1997, 40)*

Several such examples of this sort of excessive interpretation are given. Here is a Kleinian art therapist working with her idea of transference in the therapy room:

> it came from her perception of a split-off bad part of her "internal object" ... Paddy shot a fearful glance at me, as if she had just recognised me as the bad witch, and as if she was experiencing me in the same way that the infant part of herself had experienced the persecuting mother. When I put this to her she became quite frightened and moved away to a table at the far end of the room ... the witch mother image had been made real. In order to escape these feelings of persecution Paddy's ego attempted to transfer her projected sadism from something of her own making.
>
> *(cited Hogan 1997, 41)*

An alternative hypothesis is that Paddy's fear was due to the strange intensity and interpretation of the therapist, who seemed not to be interested in what she was *really* trying to express. I also wonder about the ethics of a therapist making comparisons between the child's mother and the witch in the drawing. In my essay, I allow that "the art therapist became convinced of her own interpretation though 'empathy' with her client is evidence of possible veracity," but go on to warn of the great dangers inherent in working with fixed theoretical models and in offering interpretations (Hogan 1997, 41). I suggest that therapists who interpret work without hearing what their clients have to say about it are committing a form of psychic abuse.

My work moves on to question the notion of madness itself, particularly in an era of reductive bio-medical accounts of symptoms. I suggest that a feminist art therapy practice is one that is mindful of representations of gender norms, and that these are in flux and contested. I was grappling with the idea that certain psychiatric beliefs are more than unhelpful to women's mental health and that these beliefs are 'live' both in texts and in images. As Fausto-Sterling (1992) put it, "there is no such thing as apolitical science" (Fausto-Sterling 1992, 207).

My criticism of *Problems of Identity* is that the women are rather passive, or only active in an inchoate way. Women are objects of the male clinical gaze, and the point is underlined by Andre Brouillet's famous picture of Charcot demonstrating a hysteric at Pitié-Salpêtrière – the swooning woman is propped up by men in front of an audience of men. Culture continues to be imprinted upon women, rendering the female body as contested terrain, e.g. Barbara Kruger's infamous 1989 *Your Body is a Battleground* billboard is shown next to a 'pro-life' anti-abortion billboard poster, the disputed terrain of the body emphasised by the illustration. I also discuss how the body is by no means a *tabula rasa* and further emphasise heterogeneity of cultural experience. However, in 1997, the body was seen as the 'ground' on which sociopolitical determinants took hold and were realised. This shows the body as a contested site, and overlooks, or perhaps even negates, agency and acts of resistance. Cultural theory is still grappling with this problem of acknowledging both dominant cultural processes and human agency in this period. The philosopher Judith Butler's influence was yet to permeate through the field of cultural studies, offering as she does a more sophisticated perspective that emphasises active agency in the construction of gender, albeit a reiteration of gender performance which renders the perception of gendered behaviours as immanent. In *Inscribed on the Body*, I produce a more sophisticated discussion of the body as contextually produced with cross-cultural examples (Hogan 2018a). However, the notion of the body as a contested terrain also gives rise to the notion of instability of meaning of the body (and instability of meaning potentially *felt* by subjects, creating 'dis-ease'), helping to generate more cultural explanations of mental distress rather than determinist ones based on the notion of individual acquired or inherited psychopathology).

Finally, femininity as encouraging 'self-enfeeblement' and dependency on the part of women as 'normal' is criticised in *Problems of Identity*. Though I think most of the essay is still pertinent and well argued, I'm not sure if I entirely agree with my statement that,

> More than this, violence against women can be seen as a natural result of certain aspects of feminine and masculine behaviour. These aspects of femininity include passivity, inability to assert and defend oneself and women as objects for the gratification of the male gaze which is considered to be part of normal socialisation.
>
> *(Hogan 1997, 42)*

Social norms around female passivity have shifted since the 1990s. I would query my use of the words "natural result" here, if only because it might appear to exonerate sexual violence as inevitable, though the essay does build on a developing body of theory that discusses the objectification of women in popular culture and the detrimental psychological consequences of this.

Pregnancy and motherhood

Problems of Identity appears in a book of essays which I edited called *Feminist Approaches to Art Therapy*, the first book in the field on the subject. It contains the first essay on internalised racism and is still well known and referred to in the literature and used in art therapy training. (I edited *Revisiting Feminist Approaches to Art Therapy* in 2012 and reproduced the essay there). It is also contained the first essay published in Britain on art therapy and new motherhood; when this essay was published, there were no other essays on the subject of the use of art therapy with pregnant women or new mothers published in the UK. I found only one US paper published prior to 1997 on this topic. This was an entirely neglected area of clinical practice and theory. After publishing numerous papers and book chapters on this subject, there is now lively interest in the field, which I recently summarised with colleagues as *The Value of Art Therapy in Antenatal and Postnatal Care: A Brief Literature Review* (Hogan, Sheffield, & Woodward 2017).

The way that motherhood is contested and conceptualised is complex and potentially destabilising for women's mental health, and so it is a subject which has continued to preoccupy me (Hogan 2003, 2007, 2008a, 2008b, 2013, 2015a, 2015b, 2016, 2017c; Hogan et al. 2015). *Post-modernist but not Post-feminist! A Feminist Post-modernist Approach to Working with New Mothers* (2012), in a somewhat polemical tone, critiques some of the 'mother blaming' language embedded in psychological theories, which underpins attachment theory, which in turn underpins many ideas about how women should behave and how their behaviour is defined. In that essay, I argue that many women are worried about the possibility of their baby experiencing emotional distress during their absence. They are left feeling guilty, indeed wretched, about leaving their babies, even with a most trusted friend or relative, and, of course, this also leads some women to spend too much time with their children. That women should then end up feeling constrained, resentful, and angry is not surprising. But of course such feelings are unmaternal and cannot be articulated or admitted; hence women suffer unnecessarily.

I bring anthropological research to the defence of women and cite Blaffer Hrdy, who illustrates that in many societies, babies and young children form "viable attachments" with many carers and gives examples of societies in which as many as "*fourteen minders are involved in an infant's care in any one day*" (Blaffer Hrdy 1999, 500, emphasis added). Such anthropological investigation undermines the idea that what is needed is one carer, ideally the mother, for the psychological stability of the infant. Unfortunately, the strong and permeating influence of attachment theory in its most reductive form (only Mum will do) is evident after even just a cursory reading of much modern child-development literature. The essay seeks to puncture universalising notions about 'maternal instinct' and to illustrate the societal pressures pregnant women and new mothers are under.

But it seems women *can't* get it right. One body of theory, which informs art therapy clinical practice, is that which comes from psychotherapy. Hopkins (1996) in the *Journal of Child Psychotherapy* describes how a "mother's devoted and sensitive care effectively deprived her [the baby being observed] of the development of some aspects of the sense of self and of possibilities for negotiation, concern and reparation" (Hopkins 1996, 407). The author explores how some "sensitive, responsive parents may inadvertently ''worse than castrate' their children" (her use of the word "parents" is anomalous as the paper is about the role of the mother). "Too good mothers" are condemned for their "empathy, sensitivity and skill" in sparing their babies frustration. They are also condemned for their aim to be "their babies' sole source of goodness" (Hopkins 1996, 407). The article goes on to critique a Mrs L, whose baby "was never left to cry for a moment and Mrs L was always devotedly on hand to comfort, feed or talk to her, alertly sensitive to all her moods." Indeed, mother and baby seemed to be "in perfect harmony," a crime of mothering leading to the baby developing a "paranoid" orientation (Hopkins 1996, 411)! The essay, with further examples, illustrates that there is no such thing as "*a good enough mother*" and points out that outdated, misogynistic theories continue to blight women's lives. New mothers are condemned no matter how empathetic their mothering skills, so perhaps they are right to feel angry and bewildered (Hogan 2008a, 2012b).

In compassionate art therapy groups, women can give each other vital support and realise that their experience is not isolated. It is a crucially important opportunity to articulate feelings which are not socially acceptable and feel shameful. Making art can feel empowering, after the disempowerment that so many women feel during childbirth (Hogan 2018b).

In two seminal essays, *The Tyranny of the Maternal Body: Maternity and Madness* (2006) and *The Beestings: Rethinking Breast-Feeding Practices, Maternity Rituals, and Maternal Attachment in Britain and Ireland* (2008), I explore a subject to which I have frequently returned. In my first essay, I critically interrogate the meaning of maternity in the Victorian and Edwardian periods. I explore the theories of heredity which held sway, noting Charles Darwin's views on maternal instinct, especially his belief that it distracted women from activities such as fashioning tools or hunting, which he erroneously believed to be more stimulating to mental development. I also examine ideas about puerperal insanity ('puerperal' relating to childbirth or the period immediately after) in relation to heredity and femininity, distinguishing between mania and melancholia, and citing prominent psychiatrists of the period. My essay illustrates how parturition was regarded as the fulcrum of women's instability by many psychiatrists. 'Puerperal insanity' was a catch-all phrase used to describe a wide variety of reactions to pregnancy and childbirth. These ranged from the (understandable) despair of a young girl experiencing an illegitimate pregnancy, to the mother of ten infants who experienced hallucinations because she was breastfeeding whilst malnourished. My essay illustrates that some women clearly suffering from postpartum microbial infections were defined as having puerperal mania; the cause of their feverish delirium was mistakenly assumed to be mental instability brought about by childbirth.

In the second essay, I explore the wider collective rituals of childbirth as liminal experiences, a concept helpful in helping to understand the highly contested nature of many cultural practices. I explore a wide range of childbirth rituals, from the medieval period onwards, especially with respect to processes of symbolisation. Childbirth has been a contested site with regards to male/female power relations, and the application of rituals. The essay explores how every aspect of the management of the event has been potentially highly inflammatory and subject to rival proscriptions. The essay also explores arguments which support the idea that it was to the advantage of women to maintain a wide range of pre- and post-partum rituals.

Finally, in my essay, *The Tyranny of Expectations of Post-Natal Delight: Gendering Happiness* (2016), I draw together a number of themes including the importance of the liminal and contested nature of childbirth. I debunk the idea that maternal competence comes naturally, and further theorise the destabilising nature of the event and critique some of the ways that post-natal depression is discussed (for example 'predisposing factors' being like little seeds implanted within the individual awaiting activation). I expand further upon childbirth itself as a professionally contested domain, as this has consequences for women's experience, caught as they are between different models of doing birth. The political and ideological nature of birth is also touched upon, as many potentially contradictory cultural ideals are involved and evoked. I also examine iatrogenic illness. Practices which can be counter-productive and illness-inducing form part of professional repertoires of behaviour; such practices with potential iatrogenic outcomes have been, and continue to be, embedded in hospital regimes. They are insidious, widespread, and 'normalised.' They are hard for women to resist. The most blatant example of a widespread illness-inducing practice is the tendency of hospitals to put women into beds, when mobility often helps with managing pain and hastens childbirth. My essay explores mobility in childbirth in different historical periods. Women may intuitively feel uncomfortable with the practices they encounter in hospital environments but feel unable to challenge them (McCourt 2009) or may only manage to marshal small acts of resistance (Martin 2001).

Susan Hogan

I acknowledge the heterogeneous nature of motherhood. However, as Toril Moi suggests, "there can be no 'identity' divorced from the world the subject is experiencing" (Moi 1999, 81). Hence, to discuss women's experience of childbirth purely as a pathological response, such as post-natal depression, for example, is to reify a complex set of experiences to which women are subject in a deterministic, reductive, and oppressive manner. Drawing on field theory, in my essay I ask the reader to think about the field as highly contested and to think further about what this might mean for women. I suggest that breaking off any one aspect of women's birth experience is unsatisfactory and that it is the *combination of a myriad of factors, which renders childbirth and new motherhood as uniquely disorientating and potentially distressing.* My essay concludes that pregnant women and new mothers are caught in a web of intersecting and conflicting discourses, practices, and expectancies which render the experience unstable. It is not women per se who are 'unstable;' it is the very terrain, or field, itself. This has profound implications for how post-natal distress can be understood.

Art groups are a valuable resource for women to make sense of, and understand their birthing experiences, as they potentially build self-awareness and self-confidence through the sharing of experience in the process of artmaking. Talking about and interrogating their experiences allows women to develop enhanced self-acceptance and self-compassion. Whilst verbal support groups might work well for some women, inchoate emotions can be captured in art in ways that are fundamentally different to that of a language-based approach. The transformational quality of artmaking was emphasised by a number of participants in *The Birth Project*, as well as their increased sense of volition: their capacity to make a creative act happen and to take risks in the process was liberating, exciting, and life-enhancing. Making time and space for personal reflection in a moment of transition was also noted as enriching (Hogan 2018b).

I have suggested through this body of work, that the contested nature of childbirth and new motherhood, coupled with a myriad of conflicting ideals inherent in discourses and images that surround us, combined with medically disempowering and iatrogenic practices and discrimination, as well as the visceral nature of the event itself, make for a destabilising and toxic mix which is unhelpful to women's mental health. I suggest it is profoundly important not to classify this as an individual's problem, as women's experiences are more helpfully understood as culturally produced.

I have also explored ageing, especially in relation to Sontag's famous idea of the "double-standard of ageing," which suggests that men and women are perceived differently as they age, and women more negatively, and that this affects women's self-esteem and mental health, as they are increasingly devalued. In *"Age is Just a Number, Init? Interrogating Perceptions of Age and Women within Social Gerontology"* (2016) I survey the literature in relation to women's experiences of ageing and critique some of the dominant ideas as inadequate, such as the 'mask of ageing' and the idea of a 'spoiled identity' emphasising the idea that we have embodied social relations.

In that essay, I challenge a reductive essentialism permeating some British theory within social gerontological discourse and illustrate a plurality of ways in which women respond to older age, especially in relation to women's late-in-life sexuality. In other papers, I explore images of ageing women as well as dominant discourses and think deeply about how inequality is gendered and perpetuated (Hogan & Warren 2012, 2013). Hogan (with Warren 2013) looks at more global aspects of women's inequality, and the use of participatory arts in enabling women to think about ageing and processes of inequality more generally and in current work. Hogan (2018b) explores processes of inequality more broadly in an international context. Images of gender part determine what it is possible to conceptualise, as part of the *dispositive apparatus*, so giving research subjects, or those in therapy, opportunities to think about themselves in relation to represented social processes is important and enriching for art therapy practice.

For 30 years, I have argued that it is essential not to view women with mental distress in reductive ways that further compound their suffering and help to consolidate social processes that are fundamentally toxic and illness-inducing. I have given pregnancy and motherhood as an example of an arena that is much contested (and therefore is a field which is unstable and destabilising), but gender is itself contested. Braithwaite and Orr suggest that "gender nonconformity is often viewed as threatening to social institutions" (Braithwaite & Orr 2017, 181). Ambiguity can be disconcerting. Ostentatious difference may be particularly threatening, but I suggest that gender is always going to be negotiated and subject to variable tensions, because it is subject to variable pressures and constraints through different gender styles being operational. Gendered subjects are constituted through social relations. The regulation of gender is always going to be an important aspect of our human flourishing or floundering (Hogan 2018a, 2018b).

In my recent film-research work, *Mothers Make Contemporary Art* (2017), I chart the progress of a group of women learning to make contemporary art, with their birth experiences and the transition to motherhood as the subject matter under exploration. This film is short-listed for the Arts and Humanities Research Council Research in Film Awards, for the Innovation Award 2017 (see Hogan 2017d). An important aspect of this film and the group work itself is that it is interested in iatrogenic aspects of hospital experience, whilst not overlooking the genuinely traumatic experiences of women.

Conclusion

In this essay, I have highlighted my contribution to art therapy taking a more cultural turn, which I have argued is more conducive to women not being further abused by mental health providers, who can unwittingly consolidate the effects of toxic social processes. My work as a whole (as a corpus) explores women's experiences, from their reception into a world where inequality greets them (Hogan 2018a) to motherhood to older age. There has been an increase in interest in representations of gender and their significance in generating scripts for us to live by which are potentially constraining, but also of potential significance in challenging entrenched ways of seeing (Hogan 1997). This also has implications for how mental distress may be viewed and conceptualised. There has also been a burgeoning of interest in the kind of experiential knowledge, which can be conveyed by images, and the use of images as routes to ways of knowing which may not be immediately accessible through conventional text-based research methods (Hogan & Pink 2011). The rich ways of knowing generated by art and art therapy techniques are now being considered and used in arts-based research as well as in arts and health practices (Hogan & Pink 2010, 2011; Hogan 2010, 2011, 2012c, 2013).

References

Althusser, Louis. 1971. *Ideology and Ideological State Apparatuses*. Translated from the French by Ben Brewster. London & New York: Verso.

Blaffer Hrdy, Sarah. 1999. *Mother Nature: A History of Mothers and Natural Selection*. New York: Pantheon Books.

Braithwaite, Ann, and Orr, Catherine. A. 2017. *Everyday Women's and Gender Studies. Introductory Concepts*. Oxon: Routledge.

Facer, Keri, and Enright, Bryony. 2016. *Creating Living Knowledge: The Connected Communities Programme, Community University Relationships and the Participatory Turn in the Production of Knowledge.* Bristol: University of Bristol/AHRC Connected Communities. Report. 1–168.

Fausto-Sterling, Anne. 1992. *Myths of Gender: Biological Theories about Men and Women.* New York: Basic Books.

Foucault, Michel. 1980a. "The Confession of the Flesh." In Colin Gordon ed. *Power/Knowledge Selected Interviews and Other Writings 1971–1977.* New York: Pantheon Books, 194–228.

Foucault, Michel. 1980b. "Body/Power." In Colin Gordon ed. *Power/Knowledge Selected Interviews and Other Writings 1971–1977.* New York: Pantheon Books.

Hogan, Susan, ed. 2018a. *Inscribed on the Body: Gender and Difference in the Arts Therapies.* Oxon: Routledge.

Hogan, Susan ed. 2018b. *Gender Issues in International Arts Therapies Research.* Oxon: Routledge.

Hogan, Susan. 2017a. "Birth Professionals Make Art. Using Participatory Arts to Think About Being a Birthing Professional." *5th International Health Humanities Conference, Seville. Creative Practices as Care. Conference Proceedings.* Seville: University of Seville. 115–125.

Hogan, Susan. 2017b. "Community Arts and Health in Britain." In Stickley, T. ed. *Arts Health and Wellbeing: A Theoretical Enquiry.* Newcastle: Cambridge Scholars Publishing, 219–235.

Hogan Susan. 2017c. "Working Across Disciplines: Using Visual Methods in Participatory Frameworks. In Sarah Pink, Vaike Fors, and Tom O'Dell eds. *Theoretical Scholarship and Applied Practice.* London: Berghahn, 142–166.

Hogan, Susan. 2017d. *Mothers Make Contemporary Art.* YouTube. Accessed 21 June 2018. Available: www.youtube.com/watch?v=GnU6zJARVqY.

Hogan, Susan. 2016a. *Art Therapy Theories: A Critical Introduction.* London: Routledge.

Hogan, Susan. 2016b. "The Tyranny of Expectations of Post-Natal Delight: Gendering Happiness." *Journal of Gender Studies.* Special Issue: Gendering Happiness. 26 (1): 45–55.

Hogan, Susan. 2016c. "Age is Just a Number Init? Interrogating Perceptions of Ageing Women within Social Gerontology." *Women's Studies. An Interdisciplinary Journal.* 45 (1): 57–77.

Hogan, Susan. 2015a. "Interrogating Women's Experience of Ageing—Reinforcing or Challenging Clichés?" *The International Journal of the Arts in Society: Annual Review.* 9: 1–18.

Hogan, Susan. 2015b. Mothers Make Art: Using Participatory Art to Explore the Transition to Motherhood. *Journal of Applied Arts & Health.* 6 (1): 23–32.

Hogan, Susan. 2015c. Lost in Translation? Inter-Cultural Exchange." In Charles E. Myers and Stephanie L. Brooke eds. *Therapists Creating a Cultural Tapestry Using the Creative Therapies Across Cultures.* Springfield: Charles C. Thomas, 11–25.

Hogan, Susan. 2013a. "Peripheries & Borders. Pushing the Boundaries of Visual Research." *Inscape: International Journal of Art Therapy.* 18 (2): 67–74.

Hogan, Susan. 2013b. "Your Body is a Battleground: Women and Art Therapy." *The Arts in Psychotherapy.* Special Issue: Gender & the Creative Arts Therapies. 40 (4): 415–419.

Hogan, Susan ed. 2012a. *Revisiting Feminist Approaches to Art Therapy.* London: Berghahn.

Hogan, Susan. 2012b. "Post-Modernist but Not Post-feminist! A Feminist Post-Modernist Approach to Working with New Mothers." In Helene Burt ed. *Creative Healing Through a Prism. Art Therapy and Postmodernism.* London: Jessica Kingsley, 70–82.

Hogan, Susan. 2012c. "Ways in which Photographic & Other Images Are Used in Research: An Introductory Overview." *Inscape: International Journal of Art Therapy.* 17 (2): 54–62.

Hogan, Susan. 2011. "Feminist Art Therapy"; "Reductive Interpretation" and "Post-Modernism." In Chris Wood ed. *Navigating Art Therapy. A Therapist's Companion.* London: Routledge.

Hogan, Susan. 2008a. "The Beestings: Rethinking Breast-Feeding Practices, Maternity Rituals, & Maternal Attachment in Britain & Ireland." *Journal of International Women's Studies (JIWS).* 10 (2): 141–160.

Hogan, Susan. 2008b. "Angry Mothers." In Marian Liebmann ed. *Art Therapy & Anger.* London: Jessica Kingsley Press.

Hogan. Susan. 2007. "Rage and Motherhood Interrogated and Expressed Through Art Therapy." *Journal of the Australian and New Zealand Art Therapy Association.* 2 (1): 58–66.

Hogan, Susan. 2006. "The Tyranny of the Maternal Body: Maternity and Madness." *Women's History Magazine.* 54:21–30.

Hogan, Susan ed. 2003. *Gender Issues in Art Therapy.* London: Jessica Kingsley Press.

Hogan, Susan. 2001. *Healing Arts.* London: Routledge.

Hogan, Susan ed. 1997a. *Feminist Approaches to Art Therapy*. London: Routledge, 21–48.

Hogan, Susan. 1997b. "A Tasty Drop of Dragon's Blood: Self Identity, Sexuality and Motherhood." In Susan Hogan ed. *Feminist Approaches to Art Therapy*. London: Routledge, 237–270.

Hogan, Susan. 1997c. *Problems of Identity: Deconstructing Gender in Art Therapy*. London: Jessica Kingsley Press.

Hogan, Susan, Baker, C., Cornish, Sheila, McCloskey, Paula, and Watts, Lisa. 2015. "Birth Shock: Exploring Pregnancy, Birth and the Transition to Motherhood Using Participatory Arts." In Nadya Burton ed. *Natal Signs: Representations of Pregnancy, Childbirth and Parenthood*. Canada: Demeter Press, 272–269.

Hogan, Susan, Sheffield, David, and Woodward, Amelia. 2017. "The Value of Art Therapy in Antenatal and Postnatal Care: A Brief Literature Review." *International Journal of Art Therapy (IJAT, formerly Inscape)*. 22 (4): 169–179.

Hogan, Susan, and Pink, Sarah. 2011. "Visualising Interior Worlds: Interdisciplinary Routes to Knowing." In Sarah Pink ed. *Advances in Visual Methodology*. London: Sage, 230–248.

Hogan, Susan, and Pink, Sarah. 2010. "Routes to Interiorities: Art Therapy, Anthropology & Knowing in Anthropology." *Visual Anthropology*. 23 (2): 158–174.

Hogan, Susan, and Warren, Lorna. 2013. "Women's Inequality: A Global Problem Explored in Participatory Arts." *Community-Based Arts in Health*. Special Issue: UNESCO Observatory International Perspectives on Research-Guided Practice. 3(2): 1–27.

Hogan, Susan, and Warren, Lorna. 2012. "Dealing with Complexity in Research Findings: How do Older Women Negotiate & Challenge Images of Ageing?" *Journal of Women & Ageing*. 24 (4): 329–350.

Hopkins, Juliet. 1996. "The Dangers and Deprivations of Too-good Mothering." *Journal of Psychotherapy*. 22 (3): 407–422.

Martin, Emily. 2001. *The Woman in the Body: A Cultural Analysis of Reproduction*. Boston: Beacon Press.

McCourt, Chris ed. 2009. *Childbirth, Midwifery and Concepts of Time*. New York and Oxford: Berghahn.

Moi, Toril. 1999. *What is a Woman?* Oxford: Oxford University Press.

12

Demarcating dementia on the contemporary stage

Morgan Batch

Dimensions of dementia

Statistics consistently report that dementia is on the rise (Innes 2009; Johnstone 2013; Lock 2013; Zeilig 2014). It is fast becoming a shared issue globally. This rise drives a social anxiety about dementia and ageing and also indicates the need for scholarship about dementia in multiple sectors. Despite a wealth of literature about dementia in various areas, the examination of dementia as it appears in contemporary theatre performance is underdeveloped. In this chapter, I consider this gap, introduce several emerging trends in this area, and demonstrate that the narrativisation of dementia tends towards a demarcation of the person with dementia from other subjects in the work. I first argue for positioning dementia adjacent to current disability studies and describe how the medical narrative of dementia has driven the stigma against people with dementia. I note trends of representation of the condition in media and arts and demonstrate how the current focus on dementia and the arts is rooted in therapy. I then give an overview of the current landscape of dementia in contemporary performance and centre on how the demarcation between people with dementia and people without manifests in several performances.

Defining dementia in a succinct manner is difficult, because of its historically changing meaning and application and the now epic proportions that the very *idea* of dementia has amassed. Moreover, the word has been the subject of "subtly changing psychiatric, biomedical, and socio/cultural stories" (Zeilig 2014, 260). Dementia symptomology is complex and varied, but generally speaking, "the dementia syndrome is characterised by progressive decline in cognition of sufficient severity to interfere with activities of daily living" (Zeilig 2015, 12). Affectations of cognition involve "thinking, judgement, talking, remembering, or decision making" (Cohen & Eisdorfer 2001, 39). On the whole, Mandell and Green (2011, 5) associate dementia with phrases such as "progressive deterioration, incurability, and irreversibility," evidence of the doom-laden tone of the medical narrative. This discourse also permeates the lay media and therefore social attitudes. Medical narratives are dictated by taxonomies of deficit, difficulty, damage, deterioration (Mandell & Green 2011, 5), and deviations from normal or "successful ageing" (Rowe & Kahn 1997). The imagery evoked by the dementia neuropathology – a brain in atrophy – is part of the daunting social illustration of dementia, and is exaggerated in the Western psyche because of the weight ascribed to cognition and intellect. Naturally, many theorists of dementia in cultural and social studies are pushing back against the medicalisation of dementia. They oppose it because of the dehumanisation that it evokes, the arbitrary taxonomies of health, and the negative connotations attributed to old age (McColgan 2004; Innes 2009; Kalbermatten 2009; Lock 2013). Dementia and old age seem intrinsically tied in the cultural psyche, and this drives the stigma against people with dementia further. Many theorists recognise that dementia is both subconsciously and discursively tied to ageing (Innes 2009; Robinson 2009; George & Whitehouse 2010; Zeilig 2015). Innes (2009, 10) observes that "the conceptualization of dementia used within Western societies binds dementia to old age, and the fear of ageing, disease and death that is associated with an ageing body." Crucially, the aged and ageing encounter a great variety of experiences that exist outside of ill health. And not all dementia is age-related. Yet, due to the pervasive cultural entanglement of ageing and dementia, critical discourses on ageing and society, and on ageing and the humanities, have a notable intersectional relationship with the enquiry into dementia and the arts.

Adjacent to ageism and the stigma of dementia, Thomas and Milligan (2018, 116) observe that "the connection between disability and ageing is a well-established arena for activism and research." I recognise the problematic nature of including a chapter about dementia in a book about disability. Dementia is often related to a disease – for example, Alzheimer's disease – or acquired damage and deterioration – for example, as a result of a stroke. However, "disability is inherent to the diagnosis of dementia" (Heinik 2004, 259). Furthermore, some scholars "have applied the social model of disability to individuals living with dementia" (Thomas & Milligan 2018, 115). The inclination towards discussing dementia in association with disability is "fuelled by the expansion of dementia-related activism and research" (Thomas & Milligan 2018, 116). To draw parallels, dementia is subject of stigma, medicalisation, and an often tragedised narrativisation in news, media, and art. As such, despite dissimilar causality and lived experiences, dementia – as it manifests in social contexts – could be described as disability.

Medically speaking, dementia usually results from a disease in the brain, most frequently Alzheimer's disease (AD) or vascular disease (Pollitt 1996; Elton 2008; Zeilig 2015). It is characterised by chronic deterioration, and a diagnosis is commonly accompanied by a prognosis of death within ten years (Mandell & Green 2011, 14). These clinical factors lead to the tendency to describe people with dementia as being dead – or lost – before their death. For example, Downs, Small, and Froggatt (2006, 194) identify several troubling descriptions of people with advanced dementia: "the death that leaves the body behind," "social death," and "the funeral that never ends." Elton's article, titled "Preventing a Fate Worse than Death," includes comments from Dr. Cheryl Sadowski, saying: "Did you know that individuals diagnosed with a dementia may eventually lose up to 1/3 of their brain mass? … The individual is lost but still present" (Sadowski cited Elton 2008, 271). Congruously, Behuniak (2011, 70) identifies ways in which a zombie metaphor is used to describe people with dementia "in both the scholarly and popular literature on [Alzheimer's disease]." These uses of language exhibit how medical conceptualisations of dementia can be transmitted into a societal expectation of people with dementia.

The medical model of disability reflects the belief that the disability is "lodged within a person" (Kuppers 2014, 23), while the social model argues that "disability appears in the interaction between the impaired person and the social environment" (Kuppers 2014, 27). Kuppers observes that the "person has an impairment, [and t]hese impairments become a disability when these particular forms of being human encounter a society" (27) which does not mediate the impacts or consequences of that person's impairment.

In the case of a person with dementia, as a result of cognitive decline, they experience "ruptures that threaten the continuity and familiarity of assumptions that enable us all to live day-to-day" (Mitchell, Dupuis, & Jonas-Simpson 2011, 23). For example, the person will forget "names, errands, or items on shopping lists" and subsequently becomes disorientated and lost in their own neighbourhood (Haberlandt 1997, 265). Significantly, a person with dementia loses the capacity for coherent speech. The expectation of adults to have a certain level of cognitive power and fluent spoken language disables a person with dementia. More severely, the condition can be seen to instigate a loss of self. In Behuniak's view, "[a]lthough the blame for negative perceptions of people with AD has been placed on the biomedical understanding of dementia ... strong negative emotional responses to AD are also buttressed by the social construction of people with AD as zombies" (2011, 70).

Behuniak (2011) also recognises that the euthanasia movement, or the Death with Dignity Movement, implies that a person with AD cannot live with dignity. An active debate exists around euthanasia, also known as "physician assisted suicide," for people with dementia. Johnstone (2013) and Cooley (2007) discuss arguments for and against euthanasia for people with dementia, touching on notions of brain death and burden, among others. Johnstone (2013) describes the "Alzheimerization" of the euthanasia debate as the way in which both sides of the debate have been coloured by representations of and discussions about AD. Although Johnstone takes neither a pro- nor anti-euthanasia stance, she reports on the "use and misuse of Alzheimer's disease in public policy debate on the legalization of euthanasia" (Johnstone 2013, 6). Cooley is more forthright in his application of the Kantian paradigm that "those who will lose their moral identity as moral agents have an obligation to themselves to end their physical lives prior to losing their dignity as persons" (2007, 37). He asserts that suicide committed by a person with dementia is both moral and ethical. This Kantian principle has previously been applied to paedophiles, rapists, and murderers, and Cooley proposes that people with dementia are similarly condemned. This judgement assumes a harsh delineation between the person before dementia and the person with/since dementia. Representations of people with dementia in popular media and art may not rule as harshly, but a demarcation is often present that splits the person into two. In addition to a changed self, people with dementia may be considered to experience a loss of self. This self-lessness may also be demarcated, as the person is positioned as being in some way *other* from those without dementia.

Overall, McColgan (2004, 169) maintains that "[d]espite a definitive research focus on finding the social meaning of dementia developed over the last decade, lack of understanding and negative popular representations of dementia persist." Zeilig (2015, 13) states that academics have acknowledged the significance of "exploring stories about dementia," adding that when "these narratives are scrutinised they can help to uncover truths about how a society imagines, and most importantly, how it engages with the people who live with a dementia." McColgan's and Zeilig's comments indicate the need for the examination of dementia representations.

Dementia narrativised as metaphor, stereotype, and 'other'

Across art forms and media, dementia tends to be presented via stereotyped criteria. First, dementia is most often tied to ageing and exaggerates fears of ageing, disease, and disability. In contrast, depictions of early-onset dementia in theatre are sometimes made more tragic by descriptions of the affected character as brilliant or intelligent, a doctor, an engineer, or an academic. Across various media, metaphors are employed to communicate dementia experiences. Zeilig (2015, 15) recognises that "we turn to metaphor when attempting to explain difficult concepts – like love." Johnstone (2013, 24) recognises that the use of metaphor to describe AD is significant in that "it encompasses much more than the mere use if everyday language to describe" the condition. The "metaphors persistently used to explain dementia shape our consciousness about the condition" (Zeilig 2014, 258). Thus, this criterion is worth further investigation. In stories about dementia, the affected person is often portrayed as lost or in isolation, even when living in the family home or a long-term residential care facility. Overall, the strong association to ageing (or the heightened devastation attributed to cases of brilliant sufferers of early-onset dementias), the tendency to position people with dementia as lost or isolated, and the pervasive analogising of the condition all contribute a narrative of general tragedy. While it may be difficult to argue against emotional and negative perceptions of the condition, these stereotypes veil and even dehumanise persons with dementia.

Hsu's (2014) discussion of photography and portraiture demonstrates this. The practice of photography and portraiture of people with dementia is limited; examples include painter Jeff Bowering and photographer Nicholas Nixon (Hsu 2014). Hsu (2014) finds the identified work largely fails to capture the person in the work and falls into the stereotypical rendering of the person as empty.

A more comprehensive list can be compiled of novels and memoires that depict dementia. These writings can similarly fall into stereotyped depictions and often describe dementia with metaphor and imagery-laden language. To generalise, books fall into several categories. They include non-fiction texts for carers and families, books for individuals with dementia – these are far less common than reading material for the former audience – and fictional depictions that either centre on dementia or use the condition as a minor story arc. Non-fictional, personal accounts are also a popular medium, written predominantly by family members of people with dementia. Significantly, McColgan (2004, 170) recognises that "[o]ddly, these personal accounts, like the fictional ones, also characterise people with dementia and use stereotypical images." This indicates the pervasiveness of the aforementioned dementia narrative criteria, so much that this construction of dementia has become the way we instinctively talk about dementia. Some narratives are characterised by decline and loss (most likely informed by dementia's clinical narrative), illustrating the 'demented' as "vulnerable and unable to cope" (McColgan 2004, 170). Even the titles of books can be a clear indication of the author's positioning of dementia. McGowin allegories her AD as a labyrinthine maze by way of her book's title, *Living in the Labyrinth: A Personal Journey Through the Maze of Alzheimer's* (McGowin, 1993). McColgan (2004, 170) observes that "titles of personal accounts suggest journeys into dementia, being engulfed and lost, and longing to go home." In these instances, the disorientation characteristic of dementia pathology is translated into a symptom that is all-encompassing of the experience of dementia. Some non-fiction books marketed to aid in the understanding of dementia also lead with a clichéd image of the condition by way of their title (Innes 2009, 24), for instance, *Alzheimer's Disease: Coping with a Living Death* (Woods, 1989) and *The Loss of Self* (Cohen & Eisdorfer 2001). Descriptions of dementia as a state of living death or self loss dehumanise people with dementia and echo the zombie metaphor that Behuniak (2011) identifies. Among these examples, an exception should be noted in Kate Swaffer's *What the Hell Happened to My Brain? Living Beyond Dementia* (2016), which challenges the usual themes. Swaffer is a well-known activist in Australia.

I turn now to examine the application of these criteria of the typical dementia narrative and to also consider whether those creating content should be bound by an ethical imperative when representing the condition. Several notable films have been produced that depict dementia. Novels such as neuroscientist Lisa Genova's *Still Alice* (2009) and Nicholas Sparks' *The Notebook* (1996) were adapted for cinema in 2014 and 2004, respectively, and *The Iron Lady* (2011) – marketed as a biopic about Margaret Thatcher's political career – presents a portrait of the former prime minister's dementia. The latter drew criticism from those who found it unethical to illustrate Thatcher's dementia while she was still alive and unable to give consent for her condition being depicted publically. *The Notebook* is also ethically problematic, but for different reasons. Clinically speaking, dementia is not authentically portrayed in the film. Moreover, the character with dementia, Allie, is told her children are not her own and her visiting husband is referred to by a different name. And yet Allie's inability to recognise her family members is lamented, and her husband is told by his doctor and his children alike that he should no longer visit his wife. *The Notebook* exploits dementia as subject matter for its capacity to evoke emotional responses from an audience, without taking any responsibility for the accurate depiction of the condition, those affected by it, or familial experiences of dementia. In contrast, *Still Alice* (2014) is generally regarded as an example of authentic representation that does not tragedize or dehumanise the person with dementia. The differences between *The Notebook* and *Still Alice* – aside from the Genova's expertise – may indicate the increased awareness of, and advocacy for, people with dementia in the decade between their releases. However, as a final cinematic example, M. Night Shyamalan's *The Visit* (2015) disputes this semblance of progress. *The Visit* was originally titled *Sundowning* in reference to sundown syndrome, a condition where the symptoms of a person's dementia may worsen at night (Robinson 2009). In the film – described as a horror – two children visit their grandparents who demonstrate very odd behaviour, which is attributed to dementia. Casting older people as movie monsters and using dementia as a premise for murderous madness, *The Visit* has been called "a prime candidate for the most gerontophobic film ever made" (Robey 2015). The potential reach of film as an artistic medium affords the ability to propagate inauthentic or unethical constructions of dementia.

Film media is a popular artistic platform on which to discuss major social concerns. Its combination of the visual and the auditory – including cinematography, costume and makeup, language, speech, sound mixing, and musical score – fosters fertile ground for layered representations. Theatre performance is differentiated from film in a significant way: its liveness. The immediacy of live performance "depends, in its essence, on the dialogical creation and exchange of meanings; it is a performative art that engages and integrates voice, body and imagination" (Bernard et al. 2015, 1141). Moreover, theatre presents greater possibilities for participation and proximity. This exchange of meanings testifies to the capacity for live performance to influence understandings of dementia via its use of the human body and voice, as well as theatre technologies.

Dementia as drama

Currently, drama and dementia are intertwined in several capacities: drama therapy, drama for understanding which is designed for audiences of family members and care staff, and the creative portrayal of dementia on the stage. Additionally, examples can be seen in contemporary literature attributing a dementia discourse to theatre that has not historically been about dementia, indicating that dementia is an issue at the forefront of cultural thought. Despite dementia's high cultural currency, academic study at the intersection of dementia and drama is currently leaning towards the applied, where there is an emphasis on drama therapy and dramas representing dementia to promote new understanding of the condition.

Research into arts-based interventions for people with dementia is a growing area of literature. The related programmes and studies are concerned with the management of behavioural and psychological symptoms of dementia, and take place in long-term care settings. While therapeutic practices are of significance to broader medical humanities research into dementia, this chapter considers theatre outside the realm of the applied and the therapeutic to examine the representation of dementia in contemporary performance.

While the literature at the intersection of drama and dementia is chiefly focused on therapeutic application, how dementia is represented in performance is largely uncharted territory. Literature on the representation of dementia on stage is scarce and appears as the description of works in isolation, for example, in reviews. No literature found investigates a substantive body of performances. As the cultural awareness of dementia is raised, drama theorists and practitioners have begun to attribute a potential dementia diagnosis or discourse to characters in landmark plays. As an example, the lead actor of Sam Mendes' 2014 production of Shakespeare's *King Lear* (ca. 1606) sought information on dementia with Lewy bodies, which involves "hallucinations, delusions, sleep disorders, agitation, aggression, and mobility problems" (Furness 2014, 11). Williamson (2012) notes that Willy Loman of Arthur Miller's *Death of a Salesman* (1949) can be performed as though affected with dementia.

In contemporary theatre, dementia appears on the stage more deliberately. Many works have emerged from Australia, New Zealand, and the US. However, the push for greater public awareness of dementia, and funding for performances that stage it, is strongest in the UK. "Dementia is a national health priority in the United Kingdom, which has led to a groundswell of national and local policies aimed at improving quality of life and care for those affected by the condition" (Heward, Palfreman-Kay, & Innes 2015, 230).

Emerging trends are the tendency towards a generational discourse, the prevalence of women with dementia in the works, domestic and/or care settings, and the use of physical or object theatre forms. Amid these tendencies, the demarcation of people with dementia is often produced through clinical affectations of language and memory, a generational discourse that juxtaposes age and cognitive decline with the potentiality of youth, and performance forms such as dance, song, or puppetry that dramaturgically delineate people with dementia from those without it.

Some works position dementia as a subplot or, at least, draw focus to the story of the affected family members around the person with dementia. In works of this kind, dementia may appear as a minor narrative strand, a stressor for the central protagonist or the family as a whole, or an additional quirk to an already dysfunctional family. As such, the character with dementia can be positioned more as an object of the drama than a subject. Common themes in these performances include family relationships, institutionalisation, burden, isolation, and the medical taxonomies of distortion, decline, and deficit. These plays typically draw on the symptomology of memory loss and communicative difficulty and can, therefore, easily disregard character development and authority from that character's arc. Familial relationships are the most significant in dementia narratives, particularly parent-child relationships. As such, the generational discourse has emerged as a common theme. These family dramas tend to be set in the family home, a private, domestic space. This proves an apt setting for staging the breakdown – or transformation – of familial relationships that results from dementia. In particular, the relationship between parent and adultchild is a dominant theme. When adult children are not carers, the care relationship then exists between the character with dementia and their spouse/partner or professional staff in an institutional care setting. Overall, performances of dementia show a tendency towards women with dementia. Moreover, adult child carers tend to be female.

Elinor Fuchs' (2017a, 2017b) two articles in *The Theatre Times* – the first of which declares dementia "the theatre season's 'in' disease" – discuss four plays, one of which is *The Father* (2014). In her view, "a standard dementia plot is emerging: Older Daughter ... is sacrificing her life to caregiving" (Fuchs 2017a). *The Father* – Christopher Hampton's English translation of Florian Zeller's *Le Père* (2012) – is arguably the most extensively reviewed play about dementia in English-speaking theatre. This play is about a man with dementia and his relationship with his daughter and son-in-law. *The Father* is frequently used as a point of reference in the sphere of dementia performances, to the extent that it is cited in reviews of other plays about dementia, positioning it as a kind of exemplar. Currently, most literature on dementia in live theatre is in the form of critic reviews, and so outputs such as Fuchs' are invaluable resources.

The standard dementia plot that Fuchs theorises (2017a) to be of the daughter as caregiver is part of the broader propensity towards a generational discourse. The generational discourse refers to the inclusion of, and sometimes the focus on the experiences of, child and grandchildren of the character with dementia. This theme can be attributed to several factors. First, the direct dementia experience presents a greater challenge for representation than the family experience of illness. Second, the process of memory loss has implications on the relationships between the person with dementia and their family members. Third, the parent-child role reversal is recognised as a significant disruption to familial relationships (Rau 1991; Jarvik 2007; Zimmermann 2013). In addition to the expected theme of familial burden, the generational discourse easily facilitates comparisons between old and young, and the demarcation of those with dementia and those without. Further, family dramas are often set in a domestic place where a blurring of familiar and unfamiliar can play out. In this space, an additional phenomenon emerges: there are more mothers than fathers with dementia onstage. Some research does demonstrate that age-related dementia affects more women than it does men (Nepal, Brown, & Ranmuthugala 2008). However, women's longer life expectancy is recognised as the driving factor (Nepal, Brown, & Ranmuthugala 2008). Despite the observed female prevalence in dementia statistics, the number of females affected by dementia in contemporary performances compared to male representations is surprising. Naturally, the women affected with dementia in the performances tend to be wives, mothers, and/or grandmothers, and these relationships are often foregrounded in the narratives. Note the centuries-old emphasis on women as both the bearers and carers of children (Clatterbaugh 1990; Gustafson 2005a; Connell 2009). The physical act of childbearing is a considerable factor because "biological ties are presumed to bind together mother and child emotionally, socially, and morally" (Gustafson 2005b, 26, for further discussion of the way mothers are figured, see Sarah Kanake in Chapter 5 and Susan Hogan in Chapter 11 of this book).

Many works also contain a discourse of motherhood and the breakdown of parent-child relationships, if not a child-parent role reversal. These stories tend to shift the focus from the person with the dementia onto their child, hinging the tension and resolution of the plot on the experience of the adult child. As Gustafson (2005b, 29) observes, "we learn from popular representations of mothers and maternal absence tends to be from the perspective of those, particularly children, who are left behind rather than from perspectives of mothers who leave." In this way, dementia narratives can be focussed on the familial ripple as opposed to the experience of the character with dementia.

Connell (2009) recognises that fathers are traditionally positioned to be the family's representative outside the home. The corollary is that motherhood is contextualised as a domestic role, and thus mothers are culturally connected to the domestic space (Blunt & Dowling

2006). Blunt and Dowling note that "domestic relations are critically gendered" (2006, 15). In this way, the prevalence of women with dementia and the inclination to stage these stories in a domestic space may not be pure coincidence.

Two settings dominate the landscape of staged dementia narratives: the home and institutional care facilities. Blunt and Dowling comment that the familiar/family home as a hospice "becomes coded as both good and bad – a familiar, non-institutional setting, but also a site of unresolved family tensions" (2006, 100). On the other hand, Blunt and Dowling state that in long-term care institutions, "[h]ome becomes much more public, a space entered and sometimes controlled by health professionals, as they care for the residents' needs every day" (2006, 100). These settings are also called – sometimes euphemistically – homes, nursing homes, long-term care, dementia wards, and care facilities. Either setting may position characters with dementia as demarcated from others. In the family home, the person with dementia is in flux in a place characterised by constancy. They represent the unpredictable and unfamiliar in a place of familiarity. In an institutional care setting, characters with dementia are cut off from the outside world, sheltered but also quarantined. Care relationships may be staged in either setting. In this dynamic, a demarcation naturally emerges, not to mention the potential infantilisation of the character with dementia. In line with a care discourse, clinical presentations of dementia in language and demonstrations of memory loss delineate the affected in two ways. First, a line may be drawn between their past, fluent self, and their presently 'dementing' self. Second, they are positioned as being different from others in the performance in the lack of coherency. *The Lion's Face* (2010) is a work by the Mahogany Opera Group. In the performance, the character with dementia is positioned as separate from everyone else in the story. The whole cast sings except for the man with dementia who speaks throughout the opera. This dramaturgical choice implies his lack of fluency and alienates him from the other characters. Few performances present detailed medical or clinical portraits of dementia. Instead, many use easily recognisable clinical markers to signpost dementia. Overall, the narrative of decline characteristic of dementia appears to be rooted to these private and isolated spaces. No matter how these settings are conjured in the physical set of the performance, the demarcation of the person with dementia from those without is communicated, either through spoken references to place or with visual emblems of the domestic/care space.

The physical composition of a performance is particularly significant in works of puppetry theatre that stage dementia. Often the forms and technologies used are incidental. For instance, performances that use puppets in their dramaturgy tend to come from companies whose work is grounded in puppetry. Likewise, dance theatre performances have emerged from dance theatre companies. Nevertheless, the evocations of such dramaturgies have significant implications for the representation and positioning of characters with dementia.

In *D-Generation: An Exaltation of Larks* (Sandglass Theater, 2013, US), *Risking Happiness* (Reckless Kettle, 2015, UK), and *State of Grace* (Reckless Kettle, 2015, UK), only those with dementia are represented as puppets. The co-presence of puppets and live actors playing characters without dementia is particularly noteworthy. Gross states,

> The curious law is that the liveliness of a puppet onstage, in movement and voice, must incorporate something of the puppet's lack of life, or its belonging to a different kind of life. The very stories that the puppets are invited to tell, or the characters they imitate, must be fitted to their puppet-ness and yet transfigure it.
>
> *(Gross 2011, 69)*

That puppets may belong to a different kind of life echoes descriptions of dementia as 'social death' or 'living death,' as well as the label of zombie attributed to those affected. Bearing in mind these references to a state straddling life and death, the use of the puppet in dementia theatre takes on additional significance. Further, the use of "created actors" (Blumenthal 1997) alongside human actors represents a patent demarcation between the live and those perceived to be at its edge. Piris (2014) considers puppets to be ontologically ambiguous; they "share the same existence as subject with the puppeteer but nonetheless [remain objects]" (Piris 2014, 38). When a live actor interacts with the puppet subject, not just as a puppeteer, their "[c]o-presence stresses this ontological ambiguity by confronting the puppet with a human protagonist" (Piris 2014, 30). This is because their presence has significance within the story world of the performance. This dramaturgical relationship is remarkable "because it establishes a relation of self to Other between the two beings that are ontologically different: one is a subject (in other words, a being endowed with consciousness) and the other one an object (in other words, a thing)" (Piris 2014, 30).

D-Generation: An Exaltation of Larks is the creation of Sandglass Theater Company, whose performances are based in puppetry. The performance is set in a care facility, and its story was developed out of TimeSlips sessions carried out in a nursing home, a process in which the residents contribute to a script for verbatim performance. In the work, live actors play carers and facilitators of the TimeSlips method, while also manipulating and voicing the puppets who represent five residents of the long-term care facility. The "puppet's lack of life, or its belonging to a different kind of life" (Gross 2011, 69) dehumanises the characters with dementia in relation to the live human actors. And where a person with dementia is portrayed via a puppet, the person's voice also becomes ontologically unstable. Gross comments that a puppet's voice is always disembodied, or "alien" (Gross 2011, 66). Consequently, characters represented through puppetry are brought to life physically and verbally by their puppeteers. And, in co-presence with their operator, their object status is heightened. Notably, it is expressly stated in marketing material that "the play focusses on five inhabitants of a care-facility (the puppets) and their caregivers (the puppeteers)" (Figuren Theater Festival 2017). This description of the work illuminates a further distinction between the two groups. In the performance, the residents have little agency and are essentially manoeuvred by the carers. The ontological ambiguity that Piris describes is made explicit in this dialogical distinction between the two groups.

At times, the live actors break the fourth wall and deliver a sort monologue, directly addressing the audience. These speeches express the point of view of a carer or visitor to the home and report on the experience of collecting the stories. These instances of direct address are performed further downstage and closer to the audience than the rest of the action in the work. This shift enhances the meta-theatricality of the act. The perspectives presented in these addresses are significant and do shed light on experiences that may in the past have been or may remain taboo. Yet, these moments of direct address embody a layer of reality from which the residents appear to be excluded or incapable of joining. The act of stepping forward, in front of the space in which their interactions with dementia have taken place, while still in character, physically exempts them from this diegesis (in which the narrator tells the story) and gives them an additional power over the narrative. Their ability to assume the homodiegetic role of both narrator and character, albeit briefly, affords them influence over the audience's interpretation of the performance and their place in it. In this performance, the use of puppetry in co-presence with live actors is problematic, as it echoes the dehumanising language used to describe people with dementia. And, this direct address enhances the demarcation between those with dementia and those without that is already established by the use of puppetry to represent people with dementia.

The puppeteers enable the puppets to perform in ways that live actors cannot. In one scene, a character's recollection of dancing is embodied on stage as she is lifted by the puppeteers to perform a dance through the air. As Blumenthal notes, "human actors remain inherently limited. They come in a paltry range of sizes and shapes" (1997, 16). In this way, created actors are less bound than live actors and have the capacity to transcend humanness. This transcendence may alleviate some of their dehumanisation. The puppets in *D-Generation* are especially easy to manipulate due to their size. They are roughly the size of an average doll. The reduced scale of the characters with dementia advances the demarcation between those with dementia and those without. It also has the capacity to infantilise the characters with dementia. The infantilisation is heightened when the puppets are passed to audience members in the front row and their characters become spectators; for a time, they are no longer part of the action on stage, but continue to be a performative element of the work. The transition from created actor to spec-actor anthropomorphises the puppets. The action of handing over the puppets is carried out carefully, sharing with the audience the nurturing relationship between live and created actor, the carer and cared for. Yet the act of handing a character to an audience member embodies infantilisation nonetheless. Because of the downscaled size of the puppets, they sit in the laps of the audience members and become more like small toddlers or dolls. The infantilisation of older people with dementia is a concern in institutionalised care, and studies demonstrate that the residents of long-term care dislike this treatment (Andrew 2006; Marson & Powell 2014). In light of infantilisation in residential care and the issues therein, the diminutive stature of the puppets – and the way they are handled – undermine the characters, despite the efforts towards giving people with dementia a voice. The creators of this performance of *D-Generation: An Exaltation of Larks* earnestly aimed to give people with dementia a voice and to honour their stories in performance. Nevertheless, despite their genuine efforts, through their particular use of puppetry, the work inadvertently echoes negative constructions of dementia and people with dementia that dehumanise and demarcate.

The creative team from the puppetry company Reckless Kettle fell into a similar construction in their performances of *State of Grace* and *Risking Happiness*. The former is about dementia specifically, and the latter is about caring for an aged parent more generally. Both feature a father-daughter relationship and tend to focus on the experience – and frustration – of the adult-child carer. The Reckless Kettle performances are similar to *D-Generation* in that the character with dementia is depicted as puppet and live actors play characters without dementia. In contrast, both *State of Grace* and *Risking Happiness* are set in a domestic space, the home of the aged father. Nevertheless, care dynamics exist in this setting. In these works, the "familiar, non-institutional setting" of home is, as Blunt and Dowling describe, "a site of unresolved family tensions" (Blunt & Dowling 2006, 100). The presence of a family member – particularly one who plays out a generational discourse – in lieu of residential care staff, is a contrast between these plays and *D-Generation*. Additionally, in Reckless Kettle's two creations, the live and dramaturgically significant actor does not double as puppeteer. Because the puppet appears autonomous from the performer with whom it interacts, the co-presence evoked between the two is deepened.

The co-presence of the puppet and the live actor emphasises the former's "belonging to a different kind of life" (Gross 2011, 69) and demonstrably demarcates the one from the other. The delineation between the two is heightened by the puppet's lacking a voice. In *State of Grace*, the puppet is, naturally, voiceless, but also not lent a voice by a puppeteer.

The live actors perform one-sided conversations throughout. These conversations imply that the person with dementia *is* speaking, and yet the audience is witness to the puppet's movement and behaviour only. The presentation of the puppet is much the same in *Risking Happiness*, except towards the end of the work, the puppet writes down "listen to me" and then a voiceover projects a compilation of statements from older people naming something they can still do for themselves. This part of the performance grants the man with dementia some autonomy. It is worth noting that the puppets in both Reckless Kettle works are closer to life-size than those in *D-Generation* which serves to create better balance between them and the live actors. However, the demarcation and dehumanisation persist. These cases demonstrate the instability of the character with dementia when played by a created actor, particularly in light of the dehumanisation and infantilisation of real people with dementia. Evoking a co-presence between puppet and puppeteer especially emphasises the ontological ambiguity of the puppet by demarcating it in its object status from live actors.

The challenge of reframing dementia

While demarcation occurs in most performances of dementia, staged in various ways, works that more successfully reframe dementia do exist, but this is a matter for another study and another publication. As this chapter has shown, even creators with the best intentions can fall into stereotyped criteria. Additionally, despite efforts made to reframe, or shine new light on, dementia and people with dementia, reviews of performances (and sometimes even marketing materials) step back into dominant representations of the condition. Many articles introducing the shows use phrases such as 'tragic' and 'heart-wrenching' to describe the content of the performance, and fall into patterns of describing the caregiver 'battle' and the grieving of the 'fading' loved one. Salter (2007, 230) may call these the "accepted touchstones of contemporary cultural significance" within the dementia conversation. Such reviews also emphasise the experience of family members, the child or spouse 'left behind.' This discussion of dementia narratives positions the character with dementia as an object in the performance, not its subject. This predisposition to overlook the experience of the character with dementia is rooted in the assumption that people with dementia lose their selves. The investigation of dementia narratives in contemporary theatre performance is yet to be developed in a significant and authentically meaningful way.

In this chapter, I have considered this gap and made note of several representative trends, including the generational discourse, domestic and/or care settings, and the use of puppetry, all of which have the capacity to demarcate the subject with dementia from those without. The demarcation of people with dementia dialogically quarantines the person and renders them other. The perceived difficulty of genuinely accessing the stories of people with dementia can make them an object of the drama. Currently, the representation of dementia in various media and art forms exhibit stereotyped criteria. These criteria can also disqualify the person with dementia from attaining subject status and effectively dehumanises those affected. In this way, McColgan's (2004, 169) comment rings true that "[d]espite a definitive research focus on finding the social meaning of dementia developed over the last decade, lack of understanding and negative popular representations of dementia persist." Certainly, the increasingly frequent incidence of dementia on stage suggests that performance makers are ready to tackle the stigma associated with the condition. However, more needs to be done to achieve the staging of dementia narratives and experiences which retain the humanity and selfhood of people with dementia.

References

Andrew, Alexa. 2006. "The Ethics of Using Dolls and Soft Toys in Dementia Care." *Nursing and Residential Care.* 8 (9): 419–421.

Behuniak, Susan M. 2011. "The Living Dead? The Construction of People with Alzheimer's Disease as Zombies." *Ageing and Society.* 31 (1): 70–92.

Bernard, Miriam, Rickett, Michelle, Amigoni, David, Munro, Lucy, Murray, Michael, and Rezzano, Jill. 2015. "Ages and Stages: The Place of Theatre in the Lives of Older People." *Ageing & Society.* 35 (6): 1119–1145.

Blumenthal, Eileen. 1997. "The Life and Death of Puppets." *American Theatre.* 14 (1): 16–19.

Blunt, Alison, and Dowling, Robyn. 2006. *Home.* London & New York: Routledge.

Clatterbaugh, Kenneth. 1990. *Contemporary Perspectives on Masculinity: Men, Women, and Politics in Modern Society.* Colorado & Oxford: Westview Press.

Cohen, Donna, and Carl, Eisdorfer. 2001. *The Loss of Self: A Family Resource for the Care of Alzheimer's Disease and Related Disorders,* 2nd edn. New York & London: W.W. Norton & Company.

Connell, Raewyn. 2009. *Gender: In World Perspective,* 2nd edn. Cambridge & Malden: Polity Press.

Cooley, Dennis. 2007. "A Kantian Moral Duty for the Soon-to-be Demented to Commit Suicide." *The American Journal of Bioethics.* 7 (6): 37–44.

Downs, Murna, Small, Neil, and Froggatt, Katherine. 2006. "Person-Centred Care for People with Severe Dementia." In Alistair Burns and Bengt Winblad ed. *Severe Dementia.* West Sussex: John Wiley & Sons, 193–204.

Elton, Trevor. 2008. "Preventing a Fate Worse than Death: Dementia Prevention in 2008." *Canadian Pharmacists Journal.* 141 (5): 271–272.

Figuren Theater Festival. 2017. Erlangen: Festival programme.

Fuchs, Elinor. 2017a. "Dementia: The Theater Season's 'In' Disease Part 1." *The Theatre Times,* 16 January 2017. Accessed 21 June 2018. Available: https://thetheatretimes.com/dementia-theater-seasons-disease-part-1/.

Fuchs, Elinor. 2017b. "Last Spring, Dementia Made It to Broadway! Part 2." *The Theatre Times,* 4 February 2017. Accessed 21 June 2018. Available: https://thetheatretimes.com/last-spring-dementia-made-broadway/.

Furness, Hannah. 2014. "Russell Beale: King Lear may have had Dementia." *The Daily Telegraph,* 7 February 2014. Accessed 4 April 2015. Available: http://search.proquest.com/docview/1495379049?accountid=13380.

Genova, Lisa. 2009. *Still Alice.* New York: Gallery Books.

George, Danny, and Whitehouse, Peter. 2010. "Dementia and Mild Cognitive Impairment in Social and Cultural Context." In Dale Dannefer and Chris Philipson ed. *The Sage Handbook of Social Gerontology.* London: Sage, 343–356.

Gross, Kenneth. 2011. *Puppet: An Essay on Uncanny Life.* Chicago & London: University of Chicago Press.

Gustafson, Diana L. 2005a. "Framing the Discussion." In Diana L. Gustafson ed. *Unbecoming Mothers: The Social Production of Maternal Absence.* New York: The Haworth Clinical Practice Press, 1–20.

Gustafson, Diana L. 2005b. "The Social Construction of Maternal Absence." In *Unbecoming Mothers: The Social Production of Maternal Absence.* New York: The Haworth Clinical Practice Press, 23–50.

Haberlandt, Karl. 1997. *Cognitive Psychology,* 2nd edn. Boston, MA: Allyn and Bacon.

Heinik, Jeremia. 2004. "Dementia and Disability in Old-age: A Clinical Perspective." *The Israel Journal of Psychiatry and Related Sciences.* 41 (4): 259–267.

Heward, Michelle, Palfreman-Kay, James, and Innes, Anthea. 2015. "In Their Words: How Television and Visual Media Can Raise Awareness of Dementia and Other Health Conditions that Carry Stigma, Including Disabilities." *Journal of Popular Television.* 3 (2): 229–242.

Hsu, Xi. 2014. *A Portrait of Dementia: The Symptoms of Dementia as a Model for Exploring Complex and Fluid Subjectivity in Portrait-Painting.* Unpublished Doctor of Creative Arts thesis, University of Wollongong.

Innes, Anthea. 2009. *Dementia Studies: A Social Science Perspective.* London: Sage.

Jarvik, Elaine. 2007. "Dealing with Dementia." *Deseret News,* September 5. Accessed 3 April 2015. Available: http://gateway.library.qut.edu.au/login?url=http://search.proquest.com.ezp01.library.qut.edu.au/docview/351583872?accountid=13380.

Johnstone, Megan-Jane. 2013. *Alzheimer's Disease, Media Representations and the Politics of Euthanasia: Constructing Risk and Selling Death in an Ageing Society.* Farnham: Ashgate.

Kalbermatten, Urs. 2009. "Aspects of Ageing: Consequences for Dementia." In Sabine Bährer-Kohler ed. *Self-management and Chronic Disease: Alzheimer's Disease*. Heidelberg: Springer Medizin Verlag, 20–27.

Kuppers, Petra. 2014. *Studying Disability Arts and Culture: An Introduction*. Hampshire & New York: Palgrave Macmillan.

Lock, Margaret. 2013. *The Alzheimer Conundrum: Entanglements of Dementia and Ageing*. Oxfordshire: Princeton University Press.

Mandell, Alan M., and Green, Robert C. 2011. "Alzheimer's Disease." In Andrew E. Budson and Neil W. Kowall ed. *The Handbook of Alzheimer's Disease and Other Dementias*. Oxford: Wiley-Blackwell, 3–91.

Marson, Stephen M., and Powell, Rasby M. 2014. "Goffman and the Infantilization of Elderly Persons: A Theory in Development." *Journal of Sociology & Social Welfare*. 41 (4): 143–158.

McColgan, Gillian. 2004. "Images, Constructs, Theory and Method: Including the Narrative of Dementia." In Anthea Innes, Carole Archibald and Charlie Murphy ed. *Dementia and Social Inclusion: Marginalised Groups and Marginalised Areas of Dementia Research, Care and Practice*. London and Philadelphia: Jessica Kingsley Publishers, 169–183.

McGowin, Diane Friel. 1993. *Living in the Labyrinth: A Personal Journey Through the Maze of Alzheimer's*. New York: Dell Publishing.

Mitchell, Gail J., Dupuis, Sherry, and Jonas-Simpson, Christine. 2011. "Countering Stigma with Understanding: The Role of Theatre in Social Change and Transformation." *Canadian Theatre Review*. (146): 22–27.

Nepal, Binod, Brown, Laurie, and Ranmuthugala, Geetha. 2008. "Years of Life Lived with and without Dementia in Australia, 2004–2006: A Population Health Measure." *Australian and New Zealand Journal of Public Health*. 32 (6): 565–568.

Piris, Paul. 2014. "The Co-presence and Ontological Ambiguity of the Puppet." In Dassia N. Posner, Claudia Orenstein, and John Bell ed. *The Routledge Companion to Puppetry and Material Performance*. Oxon & New York: Taylor and Francis, 30–42.

Pollitt, P. A. 1996. "Dementia in Old Age: An Anthropological Perspective." *Psychological Medicine*. 26 (5): 1061–1074.

Rau, Marie T. 1991. "Impact on Families." In Rosemary Lubinski ed. *Dementia and Communication*. Ontario & Pennsylvania: B.C. Decker, 152–167.

Robey, Tim. 2015. "The Visit Review: 'The Most Gerontophobic Film Ever Made'." *The Telegraph*, September 9. Accessed 22 February 2016. Available: www.telegraph.co.uk/film/the-visit/review/.

Robinson, Sarah. 2009. *Alzheimer's: The Difficult Transition*. Unpublished PhD thesis, Pacifica Graduate Institute. Accessed 21 June 2018. Available: http://search.proquest.com.ezp01.library.qut.edu.au/docview/276252061.

Rowe, John W., and Kahn, Robert L. 1997. "Successful Aging." *Gerontologist*. 37 (4): 433–440.

Salter, David. 2007. *The Media We Deserve*. Carlton: Melbourne University Press.

Sparks, Nicholas. 1996. *The Notebook*. New York: Warner Books.

Swaffer, Kate. 2016. *What the Hell Happened to My Brain? Living Beyond Dementia*. London: Jessica Kingsley Publishers.

Thomas, Carol, and Milligan, Christine. 2018. "Dementia, Disability Rights and Disablism: Understanding the Social Position of People Living with Dementia." *Disability & Society*. 33 (1): 115–131. Accessed 21 June 2018. doi:10.1080/09687599.2017.1379952.

Williamson, Kevin D. 2012. "Resurrection of a Salesman," *The New Criterion*. 30 (10): 37–41.

Woods, Robert T. 1989. *Alzheimer's Disease: Coping with a Living Death*. London: Souvenir Press.

Zeilig, Hannah. 2015. "What do We Mean When We Talk about Dementia? Exploring Cultural Representations of 'Dementia'." *Working with Older People*. 19 (1): 12–20. Accessed 26 February 2015. doi:10.1108/WWOP-10-2014-0032.

Zeilig, Hannah. 2014. "Dementia as a Cultural Metaphor." *The Gerontologist*. 54 (2): 258–267. Accessed 26 February 2015. doi:10.1093/geront/gns203.

Zimmermann, Martina. 2013. "'Journeys' in the Life-writing of Adult-Child Dementia Caregivers." *Journal of Medical Humanities*. 34 (3): 385–397. Accessed 19 April 2015. doi:10.1007/s10912-013-9233-9.

Part III
Access, artistry, and audiences

13

Ways of watching

Five aesthetics of learning disability theatre

Matthew Reason

Over the last two decades, following in the footsteps of pioneering companies such as Mind the Gap (UK) and Back to Back Theatre (Australia), theatre by performers with learning disabilities has progressively moved from the domains of the therapeutic or community orientated to that of art. While the boundaries between these categories are far from absolute, this movement is marked by a shift in venues (from private facilities or community halls to 'mainstream' theatres), funders (from health or community provision to arts funders), and audiences (from friends and family to a wider public). All these factors combine to entail a transformation in the ways that audiences are invited to watch. From a history in which people with learning disabilities have attracted a predominately medicalised or fearful gaze, learning disability theatre now invites a different kind of aesthetic attention. This chapter examines the particular ways of watching that this constructs.

For theatre academic Dave Calvert, performance has a particular potency for its ability to "establish a communicative space where people with learning disabilities and non-disabled people can meet on something approaching equal terms" (2010, 513; and also in Calvert's contribution to this collection in Chapter 14). Indeed, learning disability theatre represents one of the few spaces, even within contemporary society, where individuals with learning disabilities are actively regarded at all, let alone given respect (literally given an 'audience') within the public sphere. This presence of learning disabled voices in public discourse is one of the significant political propositions of the form. Yet, at the same time, there is concern about the nature of this regard, whether it is voyeuristic, or offered with either prejudice or condescending favour.

My thinking for this chapter has developed through three entwined processes. First, I conducted empirical research with audiences in collaboration with Mind the Gap, along with interviews with learning disabled performers from Mind the Gap, Dark Horse, and Hijinx Theatre (all UK). Secondly, I reviewed existing literature and discussion on learning disability theatre and conducted personal interviews with practitioners working in the field. Finally, and just as importantly, I draw on self-reflective engagement with my own experience of watching theatre by actors with learning disabilities and awareness of my position as a non-disabled spectator. Not all this material appears directly in this discussion, but from this mix of sources the objective of this chapter is to propose an embryonic typology of the aesthetic positions – or ways of watching – that audiences adopt in relation to learning disability theatre.

Matthew Reason

Aesthetics of watching learning disabled theatre

My starting point, based not least on my own experiences as an audience member, is that there is *something* about the intersection of audiences / aesthetics / learning disabilities / theatres that does *something* or asks *something* about the nature of spectatorship and our experiences of art. The plurals are deliberate: there is no single or homogenous audience; no single, essential, or uniform manifestation of learning disability; no singular manifestation of theatre that results. Most particularly for this chapter, there is no singular aesthetic of learning disabled theatre. Yet there is *something* here that produces aesthetic questions. The implications of looking are of course a recurring motif in discussions of disability arts and culture, eloquently explored by Rosemarie Garland-Thomson (2009), who writes of the histories and practices of looking in relation to disability. Elsewhere, this is a key observation of Helena Grehan and Peter Eckersall's book on Back to Back Theatre, where they suggest that the company's work "disturbs the very idea of theatre [and] it also disturbs the act of spectatorship" (2013, 17).

In exploring the 'disturbed' act of watching that learning disability theatre provokes, this chapter will propose a series of typologies or aesthetics of watching. For the purposes of this chapter 'aesthetics' is taken to mean nothing more or less than the impossibly complex question of how we critically and experientially engage with art. Aesthetics describes the nature of our relationship with the frame that art puts around the world, and how experiencing something as art invites us to experience in particular ways. This proposal that there is an aesthetic "way of knowing" is present in Raymond Williams' entry for aesthetic in *Keywords*, where he describes its potential "to express a human dimension which the dominant version of society appears to exclude" (1983, 32). Elsewhere, John Dewey argues that artistic experiences prompt a particular relationship with the world, one of "heightened vitality" and of being in "active and alert commerce with the world" (1934, 19).

In developing any typology, one question is how many categories are needed to imperfectly contain the indefinite complexity of a real world phenomenon? Too few and it is meaningless; too many and it is useless. Here I am not, for example, going to explore two common relationships with learning disability – one of 'caring,' the other of 'disregard.' The first is marked by an uncritical stance, often exhibited by friends, family, and others motivated by a desire to support, but in the context of disability arts easily shades into attitudes of uncritical condensation. The second is underpinned by prejudice, a lack of desire to engage, and a lack of understanding and sometimes fear. Neither are ways of watching informed or influenced by the aesthetic frame.

The following discussion suggests five ways of watching: (1) aesthetics of no difference; (2) aesthetics of radical difference; (3) aesthetics of identification; (4) aesthetics of authenticity and presence; and (5) post-dramatic aesthetics. These are proposed to group together the kinds of aesthetic framings that are constructed around learning disability theatre in the desire to make these ways of watching more visible and knowable (Figure 13.1).

Aesthetics of no difference (or aesthetics of universal humanity)

If aesthetics describes our ways of knowing art, then this first aesthetic approach to learning disability theatre is directed by the a priori adoption of a moral, politicalised standpoint. That is the belief that what people share through our common humanity overrides any other differences, and that learning disability theatre offers an opportunity to engage with and across this universal humanity. Vanessa Brooks, former artistic director of Dark Horse, talks

164

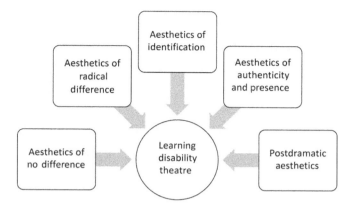

Figure 13.1 Typology of five aesthetics of learning disability theatre

about how as a theatre director she seeks to work with what she terms the human "givens": "We all eat, we all hate people, we all love people, and we all try and solve problems" (2017). Maria Oller, artistic director of Lung Ha, articulates something similar when she talks of her process of working with learning disabled actors, declaring, "The thing is I don't think about my actors as disabled. I don't see the disabilities anymore. I see the actors behind the disability" (2017). Both these directors are interested in theatre's ability to tell personal stories within a fundamentally shared experience.

Neither Oller nor Brooks make this step, but the slippage from such focus on shared experience to the erasure of all difference haunts this standpoint. Time and again during interviews practitioners would report audience members saying to them that they had entirely forgotten that the performers had disabilities at all. Moreover, spectators often said this *as if it were a marker of the purest or greatest form of praise*. Whether genuine or wilfully adopted, this describes the aesthetics of no difference.

The political ideology behind this position is the assertion of difference blindness – I don't see race, I don't see disability, I don't see sexuality – often motivated by the belief that it is the act of seeing difference that itself produces prejudice. bell hooks describes this as a "myth of sameness" constructed through a "liberal conviction that it is the assertion of university subjectivity" that will make all prejudice disappear (1997, 167). In the context of learning disability theatre, the attitude of not seeing difference asserts the ethical credentials of the spectator (I'm so enlightened I forgot about the disability) and has an additional motivation relating to the perceived quality and value of the work (it was so good I forgot about the disability).

Within disability arts 'quality' is a touchstone issue, with the desire to be recognised for creating work of quality, to be judged by the same standards as any other artist, and to not be patronised all much repeated and well-appreciable values (for an extended discussion of this, see Hargrave 2015, 79–111). In discussions with audiences, actors, and practitioners, even attempting to broach the question as to whether we watch or judge learning disability performance by the same or different criteria as any other performance can produce vitriolic responses. The very asking of the question is seen as a denial of the aspirational erasure of difference. It produces a tangible awkwardness and an almost instinctive desire to assert "no!" – because to say otherwise would "sound like you're making allowances sort of thing" (Audience Focus Group 2017). Theatre director Lucy Campbell articulates this desire as part of a simultaneous push and pull that produces an anxiety of spectating. During an interview, Campbell commented, "I wanted the audience to forget almost, whether they had a learning disability or not, because the fact was it was an actor up there who just made them laugh, end of story," before revising this almost immediately to state that "I don't want people to forget they're learning disabled [… my] drive was to avoid any type of aaaah factor. I didn't want anyone coming in and laughing because they felt they should" (2017).

This simultaneous push and pull is also present when talking to actors with learning disabilities, who strongly assert their desire to be seen and treated as any other actor. In part, this is to avoid the kind of "aaaah" factor Campbell describes – "I really get annoyed because people will come up to you and say, oh wow for a disabled person you've got a lot of lines to learn" (Jez Colborne. Actors Focus Group 1 2017) – or because they do not want to be narrowly defined – "I don't want to be seen as the disabled actor. I don't want to be seen as that. Because it pigeonholes you" (Paul Wilshaw. Actors Focus Group 1 2017). Yet, at the same time, they recognise that their status as learning disabled actors does have an impact on the work, talking about its "uniqueness" and acknowledging that the experience of watching learning disabled performers is part of what spectators are looking for: "if you take the disability side away from it," asked one actor, "who's going to care?" (Jez Colborne. Actors Focus Group 1 2017).

More broadly, it is vital to stress that there are both political and aesthetic limitations to an aesthetics of no difference. Ignoring difference depoliticises difference, allowing the real inequalities and injustices that *do* exist to become hidden beneath a feel-good veneer of universality. Social injustices consequently become depowered and perceived as problems concerning individuals, rather than society as a whole. It is for this reason, as Jim Ferris notes, that the disability arts often refuses to allow audiences to overlook disability, because this can allow non-disabled people the ways that society oppresses people with disabilities (2005, 66).

Ignoring difference also disavows the particular experiences that result from difference, which in an unequal society become flattened, universalised, and largely ignored in favour of the normative. It is only by recognising that difference exists, and that it is important, that it becomes possible to agitate for space to tell stories and allow voices to be heard from the margins. This is eloquently articulated by disability activist Simi Linton, who writes, "I'm not willing or interested in erasing the line between disabled and nondisabled people, as long as disabled people are devalued and discriminated against, and as long as naming the category serves to call attention to that treatment" (cited Carlson 2009, 193).

Finally, difference exists. Whatever well-meaning spectators might assert, whatever aspiring learning disabled actors might desire, we certainly do see and notice difference. As Garland-Thomson writes:

> When we do see the usually conceal sight of disability writ bodily on others, we stare in fascinated disbelief and uneasy identification. Why, we ask with our eyes, does that person with dwarfism, that amputee, that drooler, look so much like and yet so different from me? Such confusing sights both affirm our shared humanity and challenge our complacent understandings.
>
> *(2009, 20)*

Shared humanity doesn't disallow recognition of difference. Indeed, perhaps shared humanity is *defined* by human variation. Moreover, difference is amongst the elements that stimulate, affect, and move us in performance. Disentangled from prejudice, difference itself becomes an aesthetic.

Aesthetics of radical difference

The counterpoint of attempts to elide difference – we are all just people – is the observation of the multiple ways by which, as Licia Carlson writes, people with learning disabilities "have been portrayed as profoundly other" (2009, 189). Constructions of Otherness describe not just a passing or superficial kind of difference that might be ignored by claims to universality, but a more radical difference that implies an unknowability in which the Other is striped of fundamental rights, powers, and shared humanity.

Constructions of Otherness have fundamentally discriminatory histories of exclusion and oppression, and it is impossible to rule out that, for some contemporary spectators, the experience of watching learning disability theatre produces associations of superiority and disgust. The conflation of different with prejudice, however, is not the focus of this section. Partly this is because I have not come across such responses within my research – this is perhaps inevitable, as those who might hold such perspectives would not engage in the research or indeed attend learning disability theatre in the first place – but also because it represents a moral and intellectual dead end. Instead, I am interested in how perceptions of learning disability as a profound Otherness have been articulated as a politically *progressive* and aesthetically *generative* position: difference not as lesser than or lacking or wrong, and equally not difference reduced to the same through some universal humanity, but difference as an active, positive, and radical way of being and seeing.

There are interweaving strands to an aesthetics of radical difference, starting with Tobin Siebers' observation in *Disability Aesthetics* that modern art has long embraced "disability as a distinct version of the beautiful" (2010, 9). This is also the focus of Anita Silvers' article "The Crooked Timber of Humanity," which pointedly asks why disability, which is often hidden or reviled in everyday society, is such a prominently recurring feature of artistic representations: "the history of art shows again and again that aesthetic representations of people with disabilities make for beautiful art ... what accounts for the eagerness and enjoyment elicited by aesthetic imitations of people whose actual appearance is commonly impugned" (2002, 230). Silvers examines a variety of possible answers to her question, including the role of disability in art as quasi-therapeutic for non-disabled audiences, enabling them to assuage social guilt and congratulate themselves on their own empathy. Crucially, however, she argues that while society works rigorously to police and maintain standards of the norm in everyday life, where the anomalous is rejected as deviant, in art the reverse is often the case: in art, "normalcy is seldom prized" (238). Aestheticising disability, Silvers suggests, elevates Otherness to originality in a manner that potentially advances our understanding of humanity. Again there is a similarity with Siebers' articulation of an active disability aesthetic that asserts how "disability enlarges our vision of human variation" (2010, 3).

The framing of diversity as a state of radical and generative potential is a defining feature of contemporary identity politics. In the context of learning disability, this assigning of positive value to difference is the ideological underpinning for celebrations of alternative, non-normative, or neuro-divergent ways of being. Rather than being marked by lack or inferiority, difference becomes a site for radical creative and social diversity.

Indicative of this, both Silvers and Siebers suggest that disability aesthetics describes an engagement with Otherness, with "human variation" (a phrased used by both writers), with the potential to open (even to break) normalised acts of perception. Within the arts, the construction of the valuable, creative, and impactful potential of the outsider has exactly this currency in the form of Outsider Art. This is present in how Back to Back Theatre frames their work, as "uniquely placed to comment on the social, cultural, ethical and value-based

Matthew Reason

structures that define the institution known as 'the majority.'" It is the status of the performers as learning disabled outsiders – possessing a radical difference – that enables this act of perception. Helena Grehan writes,

> Members of the ensemble exist on the fringes of society. They are often objectified and at times rendered invisible. They mobilise this experience as a sort of camouflage that allows them to watch, or eavesdrop on, and reflect back the workings of mainstream society.
>
> *(2013, 105)*

For Bryoni Trezise and Caroline Wake, the consequence is that audience "startle themselves into a moment of self-conscious insight" (2013, 120).

Tim Wheeler, co-founder and former artistic director of Mind the Gap, draws upon similar ideas when describing what for him is the impact of watching a performer with learning disabilities:

> There's a sense of Otherness and there's a sense of wanting to see into and understand the world of others, and yourself through others. And your difference, your sense of difference: that I identify that as me or that resembles me but it's not me, that's definitely not me. There's a sense of reflection and reflexivity in terms of who we are.
>
> *(Wheeler 2017)*

Carlson describes this sense of reflection and reflexivity as "the face of the mirror"; that is, how "the intellectual disabled function as a mirror for the non-disabled" (2009, 190). In his discussion of theatres of learning disability, Matt Hargrave elaborates on this notion to describe the existence of a persistent notion "that cognitive impairment ... has something to teach 'us' about who 'we' are" (2015, 120). The aesthetic impact of the learning disabled performer, therefore, is as an outsider to 'mainstream' society whose radical difference invites the non-disabled spectator to a point of reflective self-consciousness.

In a powerful reversal of normalisation and the denial of difference, the radical potential of radical difference is to step outside normative forms and patterns of thinking and saying or doing or making. Again, however, there are limitations with this perspective, the most significant being that the metaphor of the mirror is an act of projection – the non-disabled viewer projecting their own fears and beliefs *onto* an objectified and largely imaginary figure. There is evident danger here, concerning what happens to the learning disabled identity and voice. As Carlson writes,

> When the intellectually disabled simply performs this mirror function, there is the potential for a double distortion to occur. Not only do I see myself in some disturbing, alien form, but I simultaneously run the risk of distorting the reality of the other precisely because she becomes a manifestation of my own fears as I imagine myself in this condition.
>
> *(2009, 191)*

Arguably, companies such as Mind the Gap, Back to Back Theatre, and others seek to do something far more radical than this – not least through reading agency back into this relationship. This is one of the strengths of Garland-Thomson's exploration of staring, as she describes how the recipient of the stare need not always be passive, or manipulated, or purely objectified. Particularly within the context of the aesthetic frame, and the particular ways of looking this provokes, Garland-Thomson reads agency back into the object of the look describing how the "accomplished starees" can assert their agency through the active return of the gaze. As Yoni Prior writes, again of the work of Back to Back, "This work glares back, remorselessly demanding an apologia from its audience, asking 'What are you looking at?'" (2013, 217).

Nonetheless, perhaps the idea that we aestheticise difference should cause pause. Is this another form of objectification, treating people as material? Does it problematically maintain difference, which is also accompanied by social-political marginalisation and division? Does it entail a narrowing of disability, seeking a singular aesthetic that not only ignores but actively flattens disability and reinforces Otherness? Finally, an aesthetics of radical difference presumes not only that the audience are non-disabled and experience the performance through the lens of difference, but also implies that validity and meaning are found specifically in the non-disabled audience and society. Scott Wallin usefully critiques this in his close reading of Jérôme Bel's *Disabled Theater*, examining how the work was "created from a normate perspective and resonates with non-disabled spectators who feel an unnatural, painful chasm between themselves and disabled people" (2015, 64). This reflects how the particular 'communicative space' that learning disability theatre constructs for the non-disabled spectator is one of cognitive dissonance: an active disruption of engrained forms of watching and experiencing art. While this is part of the political and aesthetic power of learning disability theatre, there is limitation in a relationship that at its worse becomes a form of introspective therapy for the non-disabled spectator. Moreover, it entirely neglects learning disability theatre in its relationship to learning disabled spectatorship, and the possibilities this offers in the form of an aesthetics of identification.

Aesthetics of identification

Implicit within most discussions of learning disability theatre is the presumption that the audience is non-disabled, a view underpinned by the non-disabled status of the vast majority of academic writers and reviewers. This does two things. First, perceived as an encounter between learning disabled performer and non-disabled audience, it is precisely *difference* – whether as radical potential or source of prejudice to be overcome – that is the primary relationship between the work and the audience. Second, it implies that the meaning and value of the work is as constituted for and by this audience. What, however, if rather than defined by radical difference, the audience experience was defined by radical identification? Radical because it is an identification largely denied elsewhere in society and is therefore revolutionary in overturning normalised relationships? The illustration of this aesthetics of identification comes from the responses of a group of learning disabled spectators after watching *Mia* by Mind the Gap.

Mia is a devised performance exploring questions of parenthood and disability, incorporating comedy, multimedia, and pastiche, with the four learning disabled actors presenting variously characters and elements of themselves. In post-show focus groups, the majority of the spectators, both learning disabled and non-learning disabled, engaged with the work powerfully and emotionally. However, responses from the learning disabled spectators were significantly distinctive, with an immediate and very visceral sense that they had been watching a version of their life being presented on stage. In talking about the production, these spectators constructed almost zero experiential or emotional gap between the work and their own memories and experiences. Conversations often took a very direct structure: the production showed this; that also happened to me. The details of this were frequently painful, personal, and dramatic: stories of being in care, being physically, sexually, or verbally abused, of domestic violence, of being judged, of having their right or ability to be a parent questioned. The specifics of these personal stories are not necessary to include here, but the nature of the relationship to the work can be communicated by phrases such as the following:

PARTICIPANT 3: I can relate to that.
PARTICIPANT 2: When I saw it tonight it was, like, you know, brings back memories, you know, of what happened years ago.
PARTICIPANT 6: I've been through it in the past, and it brought back memories.

(Audience Focus Group 1 2017)

In contrast to discussions that construct difference as the core audience experience of learning disability theatre, these responses display a profound degree of empathetic identification. Moreover, while the responses did not exhibit pleasure as such – indeed, for one participant the level of identification was such that the performance made her "quiet, really upset, and I just wanted to get out of the show … I felt like I just wanted to get out. I didn't really want to stay in there" – there was an implicit political and personal satisfaction in seeing lives like their own represented on stage. That is a sense of rightness – of justness and justice – in the representations.

The issues here might seem to be political rather than aesthetic – the right of a minority group to visibility, the right to see representations of oneself on stage, screen, and media. Theron Schmidt, however, usefully asserts the "strong connection between political distributions of visibility and aesthetic practices" (2013, 191). Schmidt's essay, however, is focused resolutely on the disruption that learning disability theatre causes to *non-disabled* perceptions of the self, of theatre, of spectatorship, of politics. In other words, the focus is once again on the politics and aesthetics of difference, with value, interpretation, and critique again from a non-disabled perspective. The audience perspectives in this section overthrow this presumption, asserting the importance of also acknowledging a learning disabled spectatorship, which represents a radical disruption to an otherwise dominant aesthetics of difference. Indeed, perhaps this is the *most* radical way of watching of all, for it resituates meaning, value, and perspective away from the normative non-learning disabled centre and places it with the learning disabled outsider.

Aesthetics of authenticity and presence

This section interrogates the familiar and recurring perspective that learning disabled performers possess – or inhabit, or transmit – an innate, natural *authenticity* and an absolute, undiluted *presence*. In contrast to the previous discussion, these ideas emerge very fundamentally from a non-disabled perspective and therefore say more about the desires and prejudices of the non-disabled spectator, than learning disability itself. Either ironically or inevitably, it is precisely because of this that they are recurring tropes within ideas of an aesthetics of learning disability theatre.

Both of these concepts have a considerably and contested analytical history in their own right, even before being interwoven with the history and discourses of learning disability, much of which is far beyond the scope of this discussion. Instead, I will focus exclusively on ideas of authenticity and presence within the context of learning disability theatre, where the

Ways of watching

nexus of the issue is located in the nature of the learning disabled performer's presence on stage. This can be illustrated through a series of discursive examples, such as when Matt Hargrave cites dramaturg Bridget Foreman commenting that learning disabled performers "will only ever be themselves on stage," and "there is no affected performance" (2015, 105), or Theron Schmidt's description of the popular perception (which he goes on to critique) that

> animals, children, and intellectually disabled actors might all be useful because (we might think) they apparently can't act, and so when we encounter these beings on stage we encounter them for themselves rather than for whom they appear to be.
>
> *(2013, 191)*

Or Yoni Prior describing how Back to Back Theatre's work often involves "playing the reality line," commenting, "We who watch don't know what is fiction and what not" (2013, 216).

The recurring perspective is that performers with learning disabilities are presumed to be not-acting but *being*, exhibiting perhaps an extreme of Michael Kirby's Acting/Not-Acting Continuum. There is a double-edged quality to this perception: on one hand often celebrating the authenticity (the realness) of the performance, but also denying any agency, intentionality, or craft. To illustrate this, Hargrave contrasts the extensive praise given to non-disabled actors portraying disability (Dustin Hoffman in *Rain Man*, for example) where the "sheer amount of acting ... is evidence of a 'special' talent" (2015, 178) with concern from audiences to autistic actors portraying autistic characters that "the actors were performing themselves" (198). The latter is deeply authentic perhaps, but denied intentionality and respect, limiting learning disabled performers to *merely* presenting themselves.

From the perspective of actors with learning disabilities, the assertion that they have a particular kind of stage presence might assert their eminent watchability but also discredits their craft, talent, and extensive training. Learning disabled actors themselves frequently talk of presenting characters on stage, stressing their training and their investment in particular roles. For one actor with Hijinx Theatre, this is the very pleasure of performing, declaring

> When I go into a role, I imagine myself as a different character in a different story as it were. I feel like I'm no longer Richard Newman I'm this character and this character now has to go through this journey, whatever the story may be, whatever the character may be, and it's just nice: the enjoyment of playing characters.
>
> *(Richard Newman. Actors Focus Group 1 2017)*

Meanwhile, an actor with Mind the Gap demonstrates the clear ambition to engage with the transformative challenge of acting, saying, "I try my best not to put too much of myself in it ... I try to erase as much of myself as I can out of it" (Daniel Foulds. Actors Focus Group 2017).

A second thread locates the authenticity of the learning disabled performer slightly differently, although ultimately no less problematically, not in the lack of acting but in the innate possession of a particular kind of authentic presence. Giles Perring, for example, cites non-disabled artists talking about how they find an exciting and rewarding spontaneity in working with learning disabled people: "there's the different quality they bring to performing that's informed by learning disability that I find really interesting." Or, from the point of view of the audience, "What I enjoy about watching people with learning disabilities perform — their aesthetic — is the sense of raw energy" (cited Perring 2005, 184).

Hargrave examines how Jon Palmer and Richard Hayhow, two non-disabled directors with extensive experience working in learning disabled theatre (with The Shysters and Full Body and the Voice, respectively), construct the notion of the "authentic performer," who "due to their lack of sophistication in social terms, is more 'naturally authentic' and that they bring this quality into the rehearsal room" (2015, 92). There is, of course, a set of problematic stereotypes emerging here, which deny people with learning disabilities full agency and intentionality, replacing it with a kind of unreflective creative power or transcendent presence. It can become, as Perring suggests, "new labels of specialness" (2005, 185). The slippage from authenticity and presence to other kinds of motifs (of innate innocence, naivety, spirituality) is all too easy. Hargrave also critiques the "authentic model," partly for how it positions learning disabled performers as *only* able to make certain kinds of work, but also for reconstituting a particular kind of Othering (2015: 227). Here he draws on Zizek's observation that "the power to position the Other as 'authentic' is only made possible by assuming a 'privileged empty point of universality'" (2015, 109).

For the non-disabled spectator, however, there remains an awkward reluctance to entirely surrender these perspectives, for while the labels of authenticity and presence are problematic, they do begin to describe something of the affective experience of watching a learning disabled performer. For a number of informed practitioner-spectators, they evoke something of the qualities that actors with learning disabilities seem to bring to a performance. Again, some discursive examples are useful. Tim Wheeler, for instance, describes learning disabled performers having a "different sort of sensibility on stage, an interesting way of working" (Wheeler 2017). The exact nature of this "different sort" is left floating, and is similarly tangible yet ineffable for Jesper Michelsen, who describes both the experience of watching learning performers and the struggle to account for this experience:

> There is a certain aesthetic, if you will, or a certain way of being there, being on stage, and it's tough and I'm pretty sure you can't really generalise about the aesthetic of disability performance, but there is definitely that ... It's definitely there.
>
> *(Michelsen 2017)*

Meanwhile Joyce Lee, director of Mind the Gap's *Mia*, talks about still being in the process of searching for an aesthetics or poetics to watching a learning disabled performer with the twin ideas of sincerity and disarmament surfacing in her mind:

> It is the intention, how they want to share with other people who are watching. ... they're so disarmed ... It's a form, a way of being which is really, yes, which is just honest and genuine I think.
>
> *(Lee 2017)*

Each of these practitioners seeks to resist generalisations, are acutely cautious of formulating 'new labels of specialness,' but are aware that they do experience particular and different affective experiences – and want to acknowledge and begin to understand these. The challenge is to do so without essentialising, without reducing the learning disabled performer to what Hargrave and Schmidt both describe as an "iconic function." The final aesthetic way of watching seeks to resolve this by shifting attention away from the figure of the learning disabled performer to the form of learning disability theatre.

Post-dramatic aesthetics

For many of the writers cited in this discussion, one impact of learning disability theatre is to disrupt the very fundamentals of theatre. The disruption rests in two connected features, both of which have been exposed and explored in this chapter. First is the nature of the learning disabled actor, whose presence blurs the boundaries of acting and being, challenges the relationship between the real and the fictional, and disrupts our sense of intention and authorship. Second is the relationship with the audience, whose gaze is turned back on themselves, provoking awareness of and reflection on their own act of perception. In both these factors, learning disability theatre resonates with a wider contemporary aesthetic impulse that finds strength in the spaces where the real and the representational overlap. If, as Hans-Thies Lehmann articulates it, post-dramatic theatre is characterised as a "palette of stylistic traits" such as "parataxis, simultaneity, play with the density of signs, musicalization, visual dramaturgy, irruption of the real, situation/event" (2006, 86), then this resonates strongly with the aesthetics of learning disability theatre.

I can see this in four pieces of otherwise very different examples of learning disabled theatre I saw in 2017 – *You Have Been Watching* (Dark Horse), *Mia* and *Contained* (both Mind the Gap), and *Meet Fred* (Hijinx) – which variously engage with metatheatrical devices (such as the play within the play), direct address of the audience, explicit reference of other genres, the inclusion of music/song/dance, and parallel performance texts/screens/media. In *Meet Fred*, for example, the director of the play appears as himself, while the main character is a puppet who has to decide which of his puppeteers to sack as his disability allowance is reduced. In *Mia*, one scene involves a faux game show titled "Don't Drop the Baby," while throughout, TV monitors, projection screens, and live relay cameras are used to provide different frames within the already explicitly referenced frame of theatre itself. Even the most conventional, narrative-based of these pieces, Dark Horse's *You Have Been Watching*, which was very consciously aimed at a broad, accessible audience, incorporates a looping feature as the leading character addresses the audience about his desire to gain a part within the fictional sitcom that is taking place within the production itself. And layered across all of these is the fundamental "irruption of the real" in which the learning disabled actor performs the learning disabled identity. (And, conversely but perhaps less recognised, the non-disabled spectator is required to become increasingly, critically aware of their non-disabled identity.)

What is interesting, however, is whether the predilection towards post-dramatic forms in learning disability theatre is the result of it being a contemporary form operating within contemporary environment and tastes, or if there is there something aesthetic, something relating to form or content, that propels learning disability theatre in this direction? The value and potential of reading learning disability theatre through the lens of the post-dramatic is articulated most explicitly by Schmidt (2013), in relation to Back to Back Theatre's *Food Court*. For Schmidt, the particular value of Lehmann's intervention is the positive value it places on the theatrical, in distinction to the dramatic, proposing that *Food Court* utilises post-dramatic motifs through an emphasis on the surface of theatricality and appearances in order to open up the representational space of learning disability. It is, he argues, not about being disabled (which isn't political) but about *appearing* disabled (which is). Bree Hadley also sees a political alignment between disability performance and the post-dramatic, particularly in the relationship between the spectator and the work. She notes the use of multiple, sometimes simultaneous, frames within post-dramatic theatre and suggests that "To open an event to dual framing ... draws spectators into a liminal space in which attempts to apply habitual, ready-made responses are deferred, delayed or thwarted" (2014, 69).

Matthew Reason

For both Schmidt and Hadley, one of the values of the post-dramatic in the context of disability performance is how it enables practitioners (and perhaps *requires* audiences) to disrupt and reframe traditional hierarchical relationships and established representational forms. In other words, post-dramatic forms – intrinsically interested in edges, margins, the texts between the texts – have a particular affinity to the voicing of perspectives from the margins and the edges.

In their introduction to *Postdramatic Theatre and the Political*, Jerome Carroll, Karen Júrs-Munby, and Steve Giles suggest that post-dramatic theatre's distinct approach to the political is centred on the "reality-status" of the performance in which the audience "encounter 'real' people, who bring aspects of their real world identity into the theatre, unadorned with fiction or character" (2013, 3). This enables performers (and again requires spectators) to construct new, inherently political, relationships between performance and audience. The alignment of this reality status with the discourses described earlier in this chapter should be apparent, present, for example, in Bruce Gladwin's description of how a spectator might ask themselves, "There's a guy with Down's syndrome. I wonder if he's playing a person with Down's syndrome?" (cited Schmidt 2013, 197).

As with all the ways of watching I have been presenting here, there are hesitations and gaps within this discourse. We might wonder, for example, who makes the choice about whether post-dramatic devices are employed. It would also be possible to ask whether an emphasis on the 'reality-status' of the learning disabled actor presenting the learning disabled identity simply loops discussion back to ideas of authenticity. Alternatively, the learning disabled actor might ask, what about my desire to present a character? Perhaps the lens of the post-dramatic represents a narrowing of the form of learning disability theatre to only one particular kind of representation and particular way of watching.

Conclusion

The five aesthetics of watching that I have presented in this chapter are far from exhaustive, but aim to facilitate conversation and analysis, and bring habits of watching to the surface. Each has a seductive political or aesthetic appeal; each also has flaws and limitations. My conclusion, therefore, is to propose that learning disability theatre should *actively* seek to maintain all these aesthetic frames wilfully, deliberately, and simultaneously in play. Rather than competing ideological lens through which we might read learning disability theatre, in practice, audiences might more productively cycle through positions of difference and identification, of reflecting on ourselves and on others, of engaging with a different kind of sensibility that results from the diversity of human variation.

Acknowledgements

I thank all the actors, practitioners, and audience members who have given their time in interviews and focus groups actors; their knowledge and experiences underpin this discussion. Thanks also to Catherine Heinemeyer and Matt Harper for co-facilitating audience research workshops.

References

Actors Focus Group 1. 2017. 1 July 2017.
Audience Focus Group 1. 2017. 21 July 2017.
Calvert, Dave. 2010. "Loaded Pistols: The Interplay of Social Intervention and Anti-Aesthetic Tradition in Learning Disabled Performance." *Research in Drama Education: The Journal of Applied Theatre and Performance*. 15 (4): 513–528.

Campbell. Lucy. 2017. Interview taken on 6/11/17.

Carlson, Licia. 2009. *Faces of Intellectual Disability: Philosophical Reflections*. Bloomington: Indiana University Press.

Carroll, Jerome, Júrs-Munby, Karen, and Giles, Steve. 2013. "Introduction." In Karen Júrs-Munby, Steve Giles and Jerome Carroll ed. *Postdramatic Theatre and the Political*. London: Bloomsbury, 1–30.

Dewey, John. 1934. *Art as Experience*. New York: Minton, Blach, and Co.

Ferris, Jim. 2005. "Aesthetic Distance and the Fiction of Disability." In Carrie Sandahl and Philip Auslander ed. *Bodies in Commotion: Disability & Performance*. Ann Arbor: University of Michigan Press, 56–68.

Garland-Thomson, Rosemarie. 2009. *Staring: How We Look*. Oxford: Oxford University Press.

Grehan, Helena. 2013. "Responding to the 'Unspoken' in *Food Court*." In Helena Grehan and Peter Eckersall ed. *"We're People Who Do Shows": Back to Back Theatre. Performance, Politics, Visibility*. Aberystwyth: Performance Research Books, 105–114.

Grehan, Helena, and Eckersall, Peter. 2013. "The Existential Antagonists: Back to Back, Dramaturgy and Spectatorship." In Helena Grehan and Peter Eckersall ed. *"We're People Who Do Shows": Back to Back Theatre. Performance, Politics, Visibility*. Aberystwyth: Performance Research Books, 15–20.

Hadley, Bree. 2014. *Disability, Public Space Performance and Spectatorship: Unconscious Performers*. Basingstoke: Palgrave.

Hargrave, Matt. 2015. *Theatres of Learning Disability: Good, Bad, or Plain Ugly*. Basingstoke: Palgrave.

hooks, bell. 1997. "Representing Whiteness in the Black Imagination." In Ruth Frankenberg ed. *Displacing Whiteness*. Durham: Duke University Press, 165–179.

Lee, Joyce. 2017. Interview taken on 18/7/17.

Lehmann, Hans-Thies. 2006. *Postdramatic Theatre*. London: Routledge.

Michelsen, Jesper. 2017. Interview taken on 1/3/17.

Oller, Maria. 2017. Interview taken on 4/4/17.

Perring, Giles. 2005. "The Facilitation of Learning Disabled Arts." In Carrie Sandahl and Philip Auslander ed. *Bodies in Commotion: Disability and Performance*. Ann Arbor: University of Michigan Press, 175–189.

Prior, Yoni. 2013. "'Scott's Aired a Couple of Things', Back to Back Theatre rehearse *Ganesh Versus the Third Reich*." In Helena Grehan and Peter Eckersall ed. *'We're People Who Do Shows': Back to Back Theatre. Performance, Politics, Visibility*. Aberystwyth: Performance Research Books, 209–217.

Schmidt, Theron. 2013. "Acting, Disabled: Back to Back Theatre and the Politics of Appearance." In Karen Júrs-Munby, Steve Giles, and Jerome Carroll ed. *Postdramatic Theatre and the Political*. London. Bloomsbury, 189–207.

Siebers, Tobin. 2010. *Disability Aesthetics*. Ann Arbor: University of Michigan Press.

Silvers, Anita. 2002. "The Crooked Timber of Humanity: Disability, Ideology and the Aesthetic." In Marian Corker and Tom Shakespeare ed. *Disability/Postmodernity: Embodying Disability Theory*. London: Continuum, 228–244.

Trezise, Bryoni, and Wake, Caroline. 2013. "Disabling Spectacle: Curiosity, Contempt and Collapse in Performance Theatre." In Helena Grehan and Peter Eckersall ed. *'We're People Who Do Shows': Back to Back Theatre. Performance, Politics, Visibility*. Aberystwyth: Performance Research Books, 119–130.

Wallin, Scott. 2015. "Come Together: Discomfort and Longing in Jérôme Bel's *Disabled Theater*." In Sandra Umathum and Benjamin Wihstutz ed. *Disabled Theatre*. Zurich: Diaphanes, 61–80.

Wheeler, Tim. 2017. Interview taken on 27/11/17.

Williams, Raymond. 1983. *Keywords: A Vocabulary of Culture and Society*. New York: Fourth Estate.

14
History, performativity, and dialectics
Critical spectatorship in learning disabled performance

Dave Calvert

Introduction: escaping from history

In her analytical exploration of the Australian dance company Restless, Anna Catherine Hickey-Moody follows Deleuze and Guattari in noting that her "experiences of dancers 'with' intellectual disability challenging staid psychological limits which are often imposed upon them, are a local instance of 'turning away' from history" (Hickey-Moody 2009, xix). During the collaborative encounter between non-disabled and learning disabled dancers, new ways of understanding each other emerge through physical and sensory connections that cannot yet be articulated: they escape history because they have not been fixed in place by its narrative. The imposition of psychological limits on the dancers is itself effected by historical narratives since such limits are "generally constructed through majoritarian cultural understandings of intellectual disability" (Hickey-Moody 2009, xix). As an identity, learning disability has been shaped by a dominant non-disabled perception which views it as a state of being defined by inherent limitations, a self-contained identity that cannot be, or become, other than itself. During collaborative acts of creative experiment and performance, the dancers appear beyond history by exceeding, and contesting, such presumed limitations.

Petra Kuppers has also adopted a Deleuzoguattarian approach to exploring disabled performance, centred on "the concept of the haptic, the touch, as a way of thinking through different positions and bringing them in contact with one another" (Kuppers 2011, 92). Such tactile experience is indicative of the research of both Kuppers and Hickey-Moody, whose valuable insights into performance are opened up from their intimate involvement with the work. As Kuppers elaborates, this model requires a "smooth space of close vision ... [O]ne never sees from a distance in a space of this kind" (Kuppers 2011, 91).

Licia Carlson, however, observes a principle within traditional philosophy which carries an important consideration for a Deleuzoguattarian analysis: "the intellectually disabled are discussed in a way that is ahistorical; references to the history of this classification are either absent or considered irrelevant" (Carlson 2010, 11). Anne Digby has noted a similar lack of recognition of learning disability within historical studies, observing that even "when the 'new social history' … made visible a number of social groups previously neglected by historians, people with learning disabilities at first did not come into view" (Digby 1996, 1). There are two significant implications of this ahistorical perception of learning disability: first, that learning disability is proposed as an unchanging condition that transcends historical developments, one which is therefore natural and immutable rather than socially determined; and second, that it becomes largely absent from recorded history. The consequence of both of these claims is that intellectual disability has, for centuries, been situated outside of history, having neither a history of its own nor a substantive place within historical narratives. As such, a contradiction exists within Deleuzoguattarian explorations of learning disabled performance, since claiming such encounters as a turning away from history paradoxically reinstates the traditional situation of people with intellectual disabilities as ahistorical.

Carlson has noted the recent emergence of an alternative "critical disability approach" in philosophical considerations of learning disability, which counteracts the traditional approach in several ways:

> First, the very nature and status of disability as a category is being challenged by philosophers who refuse to accept it as a self-evident and unproblematic "natural kind." Second, in response to the ahistorical approach to disability found in so much philosophical literature, some philosophers are exploring the social, political, and historical foundations of the oppression of persons with disabilities. Finally, critical disability theorists are exposing the discriminatory and erroneous assumptions that underlie certain philosophical treatments of disability.
>
> *(Carlson 2010, 12)*

In this chapter, I will follow a similar critical approach to the understanding of learning disability within performance studies, to consider how social and historical perceptions of intellectual disability in relation to performance continue to shape and delimit the possibilities for reading such performance. My analysis will differ from, and hopefully add to, the insights of Hickey-Moody and Kuppers by employing a more distanced perspective than their haptic, intimate modes of engagement. It will open up a model of critical spectatorship that takes into account how people with learning disabilities have been historically situated.

This approach draws on the theories of Theodor Adorno, who proposes that in order to fully recognise how an object – such as the learning disabled performer – evades history, one must be "mindful of the historic positional value of the object in its relation to other objects" and also recognise that this value is "stored in the object" (Adorno 2007, 163). In effect, the conceptual framing of the object that emerges from history both overdetermines our perception of the object and shapes the material reality of the object in itself and in its social relations. This forms a "sedimented history" which "is in the individual thing and outside it; it is something encompassing in which the individual has its place" (Adorno 2007, 163).

Adorno also recognises that material objects are never identical to this sedimented history, advising that, when encountering them in reality, we must be alert to their specific individual differences. Like Deleuze and Guattari, then, Adornian theory proposes that our experience of learning disabled performers can exist outside of given historical narratives, but adds that in order to recognise this, we must know the sedimented history that already exists in and around the performance object. This chapter will set out how learning disability has been historically constructed as an identity which is not performative and, by extension, non-dialectical. It will also explore how this sedimented history can inform a critical reading of Peter Bowker's film *Marvellous* (2014). Before turning to that overview and analysis, it is worth reflecting on an existing conundrum for spectatorship in this field.

Critical spectatorship: an impasse

A recurring observation in critical analyses of learning disabled performance is a moment of anxiety or uncertainty which presents difficulties for non-disabled spectators in knowing how to engage. In their analysis of the opening sequence of Back to Back Theatre's *Food Court*, Bryoni Tresize and Caroline Wake observe that actor Mark Deans' first appearance: "holds the audience in a state of flux, unsure of who or what they are seeing and when or how they should be responding" (Tresize & Wake 2013, 119). Scott Wallin similarly comments that the spectators of *Disabled Theater* by Swiss company Theater HORA often retreat into conventional responses to the actors:

> Neurotypical audiences who desperately want to connect with disabled people but don't know how end up settling for rather mawkish sentiments, which they erroneously understand as deriving from a significant, honest encounter with disability.
>
> *(Wallin 2015, 73–74)*

Matt Hargrave's extensive analysis of theatres of learning disability includes a detailed account of Mind the Gap's *On the Verge*, a solo show performed by Jez Colborne whose idiosyncratic style exposes the mechanics of the performance, and consequently "complicates spectatorship" (Hargrave 2015, 163).

The aesthetics of learning disability in performance therefore strain the limits of non-disabled spectatorship. It is, as Hargrave notes, "as though the 'surplus' sign of disability overshadows other signs at the actor's disposal" (Hargrave 2015, 200, a concept Matthew Reason in Chapter 13 and Tony McCaffrey in Chapter 15 of this book also discuss). Such overshadowing obscures the aesthetic, either by denying non-disabled audiences a secure capacity for reading the work on its own terms, or drawing them, as Wallin perceives, into conventional social attitudes to the performers. For Hargrave, learning disabled theatre is always troubled by a persistent tension between the social and aesthetic value of the work, with the former prioritising the well-being and political concerns of the performers and the latter prioritising artistic merit and quality. These conflicting positions, he suggests, cannot be reconciled "because the aesthetic and the social cannot be collapsed or synthesised" (Hargrave 2015, 81).

The inability to synthesise these realms leads Hargrave to propose that they are separated by a parallax gap "which cannot be mediated or reconciled through the dialectic" (Hargrave 2015, 80). Having rejected dialectics, Hargrave advocates instead for a disciplined shift in perspective in order to concentrate on the aesthetic at the exclusion of the social, which would ultimately reveal the political realities of intellectual impairment underlying the performance situation.

In my analysis of the integrated British punk band Heavy Load (Calvert 2010), I alternatively argue that the band does dialectically overcome the impasse between the social and the aesthetic within non-disabled spectatorship. Footage of its performances in Jerry Rothwell's documentary, *Heavy Load* (2008), repeatedly presents audiences as initially confused by the learning disabled members of the band before relaxing into a more familiar recognition and appreciation of the act. I offer a dialectical explanation of this audience reaction, noting that the performances work through a contradiction in the original punk form between the social perception of punk identity as violently destructive and its aesthetic self-perception as fun. In its original form, punk also experienced an impasse between its aesthetic intentions and its mainstream social reception.

Heavy Load resolves this tension, allowing for the punk form to contest social values while appearing aesthetically engaging, rather than alienating. The movement from non-disabled punk to the integrated form of Heavy Load is reflective of the form of dialectical progression theorised by the German philosopher Georg Friedrich Hegel, a deeply influential idea which John Grant identifies as "the ground zero of dialectics … [I]t is impossible today to think about dialectics without first going through Hegel" (Grant 2011, 14). Dialectical progression for Hegel begins with an internal contradiction that demands resolution, between an originating idea (the thesis) and its confounding opposite (the antithesis). Translating this into punk form, the thesis is the desire to liberate people from social repression, which is the source of its aesthetic energy. The antithesis is that this liberation must proceed through an aggressive confrontation with dominant social ideas, giving rise to the perceived violence which is in turn repressive rather than liberatory.

Heavy Load, by contrast, produces punk performances that both contest dominant social attitudes and engage audiences aesthetically. In doing so, they achieve a Hegelian synthesis by overcoming the tension between thesis and antithesis. What facilitates this is Heavy Load's refinement of a key element of the original punk movement which is the cultivation of intellectual impairment as an aesthetic and social tactic. Playing with stereotypical tropes of the "moronic" and the "vacant" (Calvert 2010), the Sex Pistols in particular assumed learning disabled personas in order to register their incomprehension of dominant ideas and values.

The appearance of actual, rather than feigned, learning disability in Heavy Load reorders these elements. The inclusion of learning disabled musicians in itself enacts a new social vision, embodying a positive form of liberation which makes the aesthetics more productive than destructive. Because this form already contains the impression of intellectual impairment as an aesthetic and political trope, non-disabled spectators do not struggle with the same impasse that is observed in other learning disabled performances, since the sign of learning disability is here intrinsic rather than surplus. Learning disability is therefore the agent for a Hegelian dialectical progression that resolves the contradictions in the original form and also overcomes the usual tensions between the social and the aesthetic in learning disabled performance.

This is, perhaps, a unique situation given the inclusion of an intellectually impaired caricature in the original punk form. How might such dialectics resolve the performance situations discussed earlier, where no existing referent of learning disability can assist the spectator? Grant adds an important caveat to Hegel's originating and powerful influence in the field of dialectics, noting that "to say that the importance of Hegel to dialectics is irreducible is not the same as saying that dialectics is reducible to Hegel" (Grant 2011, 14). Adorno offers an alternative approach which he titles Negative Dialectics. He rejects the Hegelian progression from thesis and antithesis to synthesis, and does not focus on the contradictory tensions within or between ideas, but between objects in the real world and our conceptual understanding. In this critical approach, objects contain more than our understanding of them, and so there is always a remainder beyond existing knowledge. Therefore, we must pay attention to what appears new in the objects we encounter. In this way, Adorno's dialectics resonate with Deleuzoguattarian thinking, as the remainder in the object is that element which escapes its sedimented history.

The key difference is, from a position of critical distance, we must first go through that history to identify what exists outside it. In order to move beyond the impasse between the social and the aesthetic in learning disabled performance, therefore, we must begin critically and dialectically by understanding the history of the social, the aesthetic, and the performative in relation to learning disability. The example from punk is useful again here. In appropriating an image of intellectual impairment, punk recalls the tradition of the artificial fool, a performer who impersonates learning disability for dialectical effect, in order to expose the contradictory incoherence of a worldview, just as punk employed it as a metaphor for incomprehension. The sedimented history of learning disability is therefore already bound up with the interplay between the social and the aesthetic, the performative and the dialectical.

Learning disability, performativity, and dialectics: a sedimented history of 'idiocy'

Rosemarie Garland-Thomson proposes that performativity is central to the social understanding of disability, with "staring" as a particular way of looking which "marks bodies by enacting dynamic visual exchange between a spectator and a spectacle. Staring, then, enacts a drama about the people involved" (Garland-Thomson 2005, 31). It is through such staring encounters that cultural ideas about disability are constructed. Her project to "bring forward the generative rather than the oppressive aspects of staring ... leans more toward Erving Goffman than Michel Foucault" (Garland-Thomson 2009, 10).

At the heart of Goffman's notion of performance as a feature of everyday public interactions is the negotiation between performer and spectator about the meaning of the encounter as

> a kind of interactional *modus vivendi*. Together the participants contribute to a single overall definition of the situation which involves not so much a real agreement as to what exists but rather a real agreement as to whose claims concerning what issues will be temporarily honoured.
>
> *(Goffman 1959, 136)*

For Garland-Thomson, where the non-disabled starer determines the meaning of the everyday drama, the encounter is oppressive; where the disabled staree does so, it is generative.

Staring encounters with people with learning disabilities, infused by performance and spectacle, extend to official contexts as well as everyday settings and performance events. Patrick McDonagh traces the emergence of legal conceptions of learning disability in England to the thirteenth-century document *Prerogitiva Regis*, in which the "need to define certain parameters of mental aptitude is directly linked to the social and political parameters defining land occupancy and ownership" (McDonagh 2008, 81). This was concerned with preventing weaknesses in the gentry's management of estates, which fed into the royal revenue. Three legal categories of inaptitude existed: minors, who would be placed under supervision until they came of age; lunatics, who might be cognitively incapacitated on a temporary basis and so, like minors, would be temporarily absolved of their managerial duties; and idiots, the ancestral category of contemporary learning disability, whose mental incapacity was deemed permanent and irrevocable.

Suspected idiots were brought before the Court of Chancery, and public 'inquisitions' took place in which government officials tested the defendant before a jury. Richard Neugebauer details that the ability to recognise coins, and to perform simple numerical functions in relation to these coins or in the abstract, was particularly common … Knowing one's own age or kin, for example, also formed part of these tests. Comments on the physical appearance and health of the individual were also introduced as the basis for arriving at a diagnosis.

(Neugebauer 1996, 29)

These tests were not designed to examine abstract notions of intelligence but the practical abilities required of landowners. Additionally, the emphasis on physical appearance and health is also significant. C.F. Goodey comments that

[t]he key to a courtier's professional knowledge (*scienza*) was knowing how to imitate natural grace. He had the ability to *perform* as a member of the honour society, and only as a result to *be* one.

(Goodey 2011, 85, original emphasis)

Idiocy is therefore identified as a functional and mimetic failure to perform the required role of an aristocratic landowner. Those subsequently declared idiots would have the management of their lands reclaimed by the Crown until their death, at which point the title and lands would revert to their heirs.

The mechanism for determining idiocy is a formal staring encounter in which a staree appears as a spectacle before starers in order to determine whether the former is to be legally designated an idiot. In Goffman's terms, "there will usually be some reason for [the staree] to mobilize his activity so that it will convey an impression to others which it is in his interests to convey" (Goffman 1959, 115). This, for Goffman, is the dramaturgical motivation of everyday performance. Being designated an idiot by the Court of Chancery, however, is unlikely to be in the interests of the defendant. An unsuccessful appearance is therefore not the straightforward failure to perform an aristocratic role but, in its inability to define the situation beneficially, is indicative of a deeper failure to perform at all. It is not merely that the staring encounter here is oppressive rather than generative, but that the oppressive verdict itself provides vital evidence: idiocy is the fundamental inability to define oneself to others. As such, at its foundation, learning disability becomes recognised as socially non-performative.

At the same time, the generative potential of idiocy becomes appropriated by non-disabled theatre performers, culminating in Elizabethan performance when, William Willeford notes, "a distinction came to be expressed between the 'natural' and the 'artificial' fool, the latter being the person who 'professionally counterfeits folly'" (Willeford 1969, 10). The current irreconcilable tension between the social and aesthetic dimensions of intellectual disability has its roots in this historical separation between the natural fool in society and the artificial fool of the playhouse.

In one sense, it is the idiot's perceived failure to perform a given role that is being pressed into aesthetic service by the artificial fool, or clown. These comedic actors, as Tim Prentki notes, are distinct from tragedians such as Richard Burbage who "in some sense disguised himself to play Othello or Hamlet, but Will Kempe was always himself whether he played Bottom or Dogberry" (Prentki 2012, 19). This is not a mere inversion in which the clown's personality – or the surplus sign of disability, in Hargrave's terms – obscures the character, however. Rather, the performer appears alongside and in a relationship with the character, as suggested in Prentki's later discussion of Kempe's performance as Jack Cade in Shakespeare's *Henry VI Part 2*: "here there is both Cade [the character] and Kempe [the actor]; within Cade both the clothier and the pretender to the throne; within Kempe both the actor performing the role of Cade and the *extempore* stand-up comedian" (Prentki 2012, 41; original emphasis). The artificial fool in performance, therefore, always appears doubled, subject to a visible separation between the self and the performance object. While the non-performative idiot in the social realm is positioned as inescapably singular, through the incapacity to enact the social role of landowning aristocrat, Kempe's doubling defines the artificial fool as fundamentally performative, necessarily appearing as both itself and other-than-itself.

If this artificial folly is generative in the performance encounter, however, it is not by means of determining the meaning of the event but by exploring it dialectically. Such doubling allows the performative fool to operate both inside and outside of the playwright's dramatic landscape, opening a productive gap in which the consistency of this world can be critically observed. Idiocy is aestheticised as a performance strategy for exposing the incoherence of the play and its world, exactly as punk would appropriate the image centuries later. Prentki accordingly sees the fool as drawing on a Socratic and Pauline intellectual tradition in pursuing "some kind of dialectical relationship where folly is an indication of wisdom lurking within and the only language that wisdom can speak through is that of foolishness" (Prentki 2012, 15). Accordingly, Prentki concludes that Will Kempe maintains "a consistent function as the purveyor of contradictions between the ideal and the real" (Prentki 2012, 81). The artificial fool's performativity therefore functions dialectically; by contrast, the natural fools' singular non-performativity renders them non-dialectical, implying that their identity is self-contained and internally coherent. While the artificial fool is abandoned as a theatrical trope in Restoration drama, however, the cultural perception of the natural idiot as socially non-performative continues to exert a profound influence.

Goodey proposes John Locke's *An Essay Concerning Human Understanding*, published in the post-Restoration context of 1689, as establishing the dominant modern conception of learning disability. Locke bases his political argument that human beings are worthy of liberty on the grounds of the rational faculties gifted to all human beings, as opposed to specific forms of knowledge: "It is not the actual *content* of the common ideas, [Locke] says, but the *operations leading there* that are innate and can be known with certainty" (Goodey 2011, 346; original emphasis). If idiocy in medieval society was recognised as the failure to perform the specific role of landowner, the Lockean conception of idiocy focuses on a more general failure to perform universal intellectual operations in any given context.

Locke's philosophical ideas come into significant practical effect in the scientific and liberal social order of the nineteenth century. The empirical explorations and classifications of learning disability by educationalists such as Eduard Seguin, and physicians such as John Langdon Down, establish idiocy as an essential and identifiable state of being, rather than a fluid identity relative to social values. While the substance of the concept may change with historical and social circumstances, the mechanism, now shifted from a legal framework to medical and educational assessment, remains consistent. Learning disability is still identified through a double failure to perform: an explicit failure to perform according to particular normative criteria, and an implicit performative failure to determine the meaning of the assessment situation.

This sedimented history of people with learning disabilities goes some way to explaining the impasse in non-disabled reception of their performances, since the social construction of non-performativity implicitly undercuts the aesthetic potential of the work, not least by conceiving of learning disabled actors as always already incapable of determining the situation. The Adornian approach that I propose as a model of critical spectatorship begins with a knowledge of this historical positioning in order to draw attention to what contradicts it within learning disabled performance. It also recognises where the performers' actions may be generative in Garland-Thomson's terms, and where the performance engages dialectically with the contradictions in and around the performance event. Peter Bowker's television drama *Marvellous* (2014), which itself understands learning disability as both performative and dialectical, is worth critically examining in relation to these ideas.

Marvellous and performativity

Marvellous is a biopic of Neil Baldwin, a protagonist with learning disabilities from Staffordshire in England. The drama covers Baldwin's improbable successes, from minor achievements (persuading a vicar to give him a lift across Scotland, having tea with a Member of Parliament in the House of Commons) to more substantial goals (being awarded an honorary master's degree by Keele University, becoming the kit-man for Stoke City football club). The film also documents his accumulated friendships with senior clergy, famous entertainers, renowned footballers, and high-profile politicians.

Writer Peter Bowker has explored cognitive impairment elsewhere in his work, including the 2002 television film *Flesh and Blood*, in which an adopted man discovers his birth parents have intellectual disabilities, and the series *The A Word*, centred on autistic characters, which began in 2016. *Marvellous* differs from these by taking Baldwin's non-fiction biography as its starting point. Where the other dramas examine the impact of impairment on non-disabled family members, *Marvellous* treats Baldwin's learning disability, and its representation, as key themes in themselves.

The opening of the drama sees Baldwin performing in the circus as his alter ego, Nello the Clown. After a dispute over pay with the ringmaster, Baldwin is abandoned in Scotland and returns home, where he begins his self-appointed role welcoming students to Keele University, before joining the staff at Stoke City. There are several relevant points of dramatic licence, even within this brief synopsis. The chronology of Baldwin's life is substantially reordered and condensed, and there is little historical clarity or consistency in the representation. The events depicted took place in reality between 1960 and 2013, but appear in the film only to cover a few years given the limited extent to which the key characters age. There are also difficulties in dating the action. Lou Macari's first tenure as Stoke City manager, which is central to the story, ran from 1991 to 1993, and the car registration plates indicate a similar time period. At the same time, well-known figures from football such as player-turned-commentator Gary Lineker and referee Uriah Rennie appear in the drama as themselves, with their current ages making the action seem contemporaneous.

Such playful inconsistencies suggest that Bowker is not concerned with documentary standards of realism, and the omitted details also reflect a lack of concern with the social and political realities of impairment. In Baldwin's autobiography, also titled *Marvellous* (Baldwin and Clarke 2015, 987), co-author and long-time friend Malcolm Clarke notes that he was surprised to discover Baldwin was not paid as Stoke City's kit-man. He raises practical concerns about this situation regarding insurance, while such an arrangement is also questionable in terms of ethics and exploitation. This is a complex issue, not only with regard to the employment approach of the football club, but also to the wider infrastructure surrounding disability benefits and the British welfare state. The film, however, obscures such issues. It suggests that Baldwin first sought out the Stoke City role in order to pay an unexpectedly high electricity bill, strongly implying that he is being paid.

The distortion of the social and political realities of Baldwin's life is neither wishful idealism nor accidental oversight, and the film does acknowledge the economic vulnerability of people with learning disabilities. In the aforementioned pay dispute at the circus, the ringmaster deliberately underpays Baldwin in an effort to exploit him. Baldwin retaliates by embarrassing the ringmaster during the performance, which leads ultimately to his abandonment. The key difference between the acknowledged exploitation here and the ignored exploitation at Stoke City is that the former, as cash-in-hand employment, operates within Baldwin's sphere of influence. He has the capacity to tackle the ringmaster as the source of injustice, unlike the invisible powers and complex bureaucracies of the football club and the welfare state. By focussing on spheres of immediate influence, Bowker is able to align Baldwin with Goffman's definition of performance as "all the activity of a given participant on a given occasion which serves to influence in any way any of the other participants" (Goffman 1959, 234). His construction of Baldwin therefore runs against the dominant historical conceptualisation of learning disability as fundamentally non-performative.

The reordering of the chronology further emphasises this understanding of Baldwin as performatively astute. Although the film presents the loss of his circus job as the motivation for assuming a self-appointed role at Keele University, in reality, Baldwin had been active at the university since 1960 and only joined the circus two decades later. By introducing Baldwin to the audience as Nello the clown, Bowker emphasises his performativity from the outset. Discussing Baldwin's unofficial role greeting new students at Keele University, Bowker "asked him how he managed to pass himself off as someone who worked there and he said 'I may have been wearing a dog collar'" (Jeffries 2014).

Baldwin's use of costume is, then, another performative tactic for influencing the situation. The dog collar lends him authority and credibility and, in a later scene, Baldwin similarly, and successfully, dresses as Nello to attract attention while hitch-hiking to London. Fancy dress also becomes part of his role at Stoke City, appearing at matches dressed as a chicken, or in top hat and tails. While this is irregular for a kit-man, it is intrinsic to Baldwin's core function at the club, which exploits his performativity more than his ability to launder football kits. Macari notes that Baldwin's

> real value was in helping the players relax before games. No chemist ever produced a drug that could reduce stress levels like Nello. I was convinced that this gave us an edge in matches.
>
> *(Macari cited Baldwin & Clarke 2015, 952)*

Baldwin's use of costume is a performative tactic for productively defining the pre-match situation as comical and relaxed.

The representation of Baldwin thus contradicts the sedimented history of learning disability as non-performative. This opens up a dialectical approach, in Adornian terms, with Bowker attending to tensions between the conception and the reality of impairment. He develops this further by including sequences in which Neil Baldwin himself – titled Real Neil in the script – appears in the film in a series of brief conversations with Toby Jones, the non-disabled actor who plays him. Jones remains in character for these sequences, an Artificial Neil appearing alongside, and in comparison with, Real Neil. This is another Adornian dialectical device, as the audience's encounter with the real Baldwin exposes them to the differences between his actual identity and Jones' interpretation of that identity, lending Real Neil the dialectical potential to contradict the version of learning disability operating in and around the film.

Real and Artificial Neil appearing alongside each other also employs a form of doubling in the tradition of the artificial fool, an observable separation of the self and represented object through which the biographical central character appears both in the dramatic universe and outside it. Their conversations accordingly offer a commentary on the biopic's veracity, with Real Neil corroborating, elaborating, or contradicting the dramatic representation. The film itself also presents Baldwin as fundamentally doubled, in the distinction between Neil and Nello, his theatrical alter ego. These gaps between Real and Artificial Neil, Neil and Nello, allow for further dialectical explorations of learning disability within the film.

Marvellous **and the dialectic of vulnerability**

The focus on Baldwin's performativity, as a generative capacity to influence a situation in his own interests, not only offers a dialectical contradiction to the historical conception of learning disability as non-performative, but also undermines conventional dramatic tropes of disability representation. By celebrating Baldwin's successes in achieving improbable goals, the film engages with a standard disability narrative which Jenny Morris (1997, 27) calls the "'overcoming all odds' model of disability." Under this model, disability is not socially constructed but equates to a set of individual limitations that the disabled character contends with and, in doing so successfully, "exhibits the personal strength and will-power to achieve 'against all odds'" (Morris 1997, 27).

Marvellous, however, does not frame Baldwin in this way. His achievements are mostly quirky personal adventures or ambitions rather than substantive feats in themselves, and the film emphasises the comic manner in which Baldwin achieves them. Baldwin's success is impressive because it is improbable, but this improbability is intrinsic to the goals themselves rather than a consequence of impairment. The odds of inveigling one's way on to the Cambridge launch at the University Boat Race, or of persuading a vicar to give one a lift from Scotland to England, or inspiring a famous football manager to give one a significant – if voluntary – role would test anyone's performative skills. What is being celebrated is the ease, rather than the difficulty, with which Baldwin achieves such unlikely goals through his unique combination of optimism and opportunism.

The doubling of Real Neil and Artificial Neil allows for a further dialectical probing of Baldwin's performativity through the contrast between the two performers. They differ in physicality and vocality, key resources for a performer. Jones is shorter and slighter than Baldwin, and his voice is softer and gentler compared with Baldwin's richer, more sonorous tone. These differences shape their performative tactics. Real Neil's presence is more commanding, and the impression he cultivates in the conversational sequences is one of self-assurance and self-belief, making his optimism explicit. In the dramatic scenes, Jones' representation of Baldwin, while no less effectively charming, is more hopeful than optimistic, in that he wishes for, rather than presumes, success. His self-presentation is less assured, characterised by a stammer and observable relief or gratitude when he succeeds.

Jones' representation of Baldwin's performative tactics deploys another traditional understanding of disability which Carlson (2010, 195) describes as "the quantitative portrait, where the intellectually disabled may have certain qualities that are more pronounced or evident, for example, vulnerability, dependence, neediness." These three characteristics are all intrinsic to Jones' presentation of Baldwin, and the film interrogates them dialectically in several ways.

First, in a direct comparison between the two Neils, it seems unlikely that Real Neil, exuding self-assurance, would appear vulnerable in this way. The evidence in our encounter with Real Neil therefore unsettles the easy equation of learning disability and vulnerability, emphasised through the contrast with Jones. Second, the connection between performativity and vulnerability qualifies the dominant perception of intellectual impairment as intrinsically needy and dependent. Artificial Neil feigns heightened, rather than genuine, vulnerability in order to achieve his favoured outcome, a point underlined in its tactical adoption by Jones, the non-disabled actor, rather than Real Neil.

Third, in dialectically testing the extent of Baldwin's vulnerability, the drama does not present him as invulnerable. As noted earlier, he is susceptible to the exploitation of the circus ringmaster, and the later scenes demonstrate private – and therefore non-performative – grief and depression following his mother's death. Vulnerability therefore becomes a more complex concept, which is not intrinsic to, or inevitable in, people with learning disabilities, but may be genuine in some situations, deployed for generative effect in others, and absent elsewhere. Fourth, and finally, the film significantly refuses to associate vulnerability exclusively with people with learning disabilities, reversing the expected dependency relations throughout. In one scene, Baldwin explains to Macari how he talked a Keele University student out of suicide, and towards the end of the film, Mary, Baldwin's mother, is in a care home and dependent on her son for material and emotional support. The learning disabled protagonist therefore operates within a fluid and reciprocal network of vulnerabilities, responding to the vulnerabilities of others while attending to his own.

Carlson notes that the exaggeration of the extent to which people with learning disabilities are vulnerable, needy, or dependent informs a perception that people with learning disabilities are non-human. She adds, however, that such characteristics are actually "part of what makes us human animals. And the post-modern call to recognise disability as the paradigmatic unstable identity places disability at the center, rather than at the margins, of a conception of human subjectivity" (Carlson 2010, 195). The acknowledgement and exploration of the performativity of learning disability in *Marvellous* opens up its dialectical potential, allowing for this fluid exploration of learning disability which ultimately contradicts traditional perceptions of cognitive impairment as non-performative, non-dialectical, and non-human through recognising the dialectical complexity of vulnerability as an element of human experience.

Conclusion

Like the performances by Heavy Load, *Marvellous* is not subject to the same kind of impasse in spectatorship that is observed in other performances by learning disabled artists. For Heavy Load, this is a consequence of the dialectical interplay with the original punk form, rendering it fundamentally familiar. In *Marvellous*, alternatively, it is perhaps connected to the relatively marginal inclusion of Real Neil in sequences that are distinct from the dramatic narrative itself. The presence of learning disability on the sidelines does not in itself arrest the spectators' engagement with the aesthetic form. Yet it is this sideline position that draws attention to the dialectical operations in our encounter with Real Neil. In theatrical terms, it connects with the *platea* of the medieval mystery plays which, as Prentki explains, is

> a space less firmly demarcated for the stage fiction where interventions from the real world of the audience, scripted or improvised, can be launched. It is the domain of the fool, servant or vice; figures who operate both in and out of the fiction.
>
> *(Prentki 2012, 38)*

Positioning Real Neil in such a space establishes an opportunity for negative dialectics, as his material presence in the film contradicts both the fictional account and the sedimented history of learning disability.

Such dialectical operations may be more pronounced by the structure of *Marvellous*, therefore allowing for the contesting of dominant perceptions of learning disability as non-performative and non-dialectical. Where learning disabled performers are more central to the aesthetics of performance, and where their presence destabilises formal conventions, spectators may struggle to read the performance. Hargrave proposes that the route through this impasse involves a parallax shift from the social to the aesthetic dimensions of learning disability, but the historical proposition of learning disability as socially non-performative inhibits such a shift in perspective. It is the social which overdetermines the aesthetic, denying the performative and dialectical qualities of performers with intellectual disabilities, and consequently restraining their aesthetic potential.

It is, therefore, by attending to the performative qualities of the actors – noting the generative possibilities of their actions, in Garland-Thomson's terms – and by engaging dialectically with the performance that the social and the aesthetic can both be connected. This may in itself draw on the dialectics operating within the performance structure, or it may require the spectator to be active in nurturing such dialectical reflection through acts of critical spectatorship. Whether or not this is the case, and whether or not the performance provokes an aesthetic impasse, acts of critical spectatorship depend on a knowledge of the sedimented history of learning disability in order to recognise the ways in which such performances are themselves a form of escape from that history.

References

Adorno, Theodor W. 2007. *Negative Dialectics*. New York: Continuum International.
Baldwin, Neil and Clarke, Malcolm. 2015. *Marvellous*. Kindle edition. Accessed 8 February 2018. Available: www.amazon.co.uk.
Calvert, Dave. 2010. "Loaded Pistols: The Interplay of Social Intervention and Anti-Aesthetic Tradition in Learning Disabled Performance." *Research in Drama Education: The Journal of Applied Theatre and Performance*. 15 (4): 513–528.
Carlson, Licia. 2010. *The Faces of Intellectual Disability: Philosophical Reflections*. Bloomington: Indiana University Press.
Digby, Anne. 1996. "Contexts and Perspectives." In David Wright and Anne Digby ed. *From Idiocy to Mental Deficiency*. London & New York: Routledge, 1–21.
Garland-Thomson, Rosemarie. 2009. *Staring: How We Look*. Oxford & New York: Oxford University Press.
Garland-Thomson, Rosemarie. 2005. "Disabled Women Performance Artists & the Dynamics of Staring." In Carrie Sandahl and Philip Auslander ed. *Bodies in Commotion: Disability & Performance*. Ann Arbor: University of Michigan Press, 30–41.
Goffman, Erving. 1959. *The Presentation of Self in Everyday Life*. Middlesex: Penguin Books.
Goodey, C.F. 2011. *A History of Intelligence and "Intellectual Disability."* Farnham: Ashgate Publishing.
Grant, John. 2011. *Dialectics and Contemporary Politics: Critique and Transformation from Hegel through Post-Marxism*. Oxon: Routledge.
Hargrave, Matt. 2015. *Theatres of Learning Disability: Good, Bad or Plain Ugly?* Basingstoke: Palgrave Macmillan.
Heavy Load. 2008. Directed by Jerry Rothwell. UK, APT Films [Video: DVD].
Hickey-Moody, Anna Catherine. 2009. *Unimaginable Bodies: Intellectual Disability, Performance and Becomings*. Rotterdam: Sense Publishers.
Jeffries, Stuart. 2014. "Toby Jones: Totally Stoked." *The Guardian*, 21 September 2014. Accessed 11 February 2018. Available: https://unilearn.hud.ac.uk/bbcswebdav/pid-2266550-dt-content-rid-3535208_1/orgs/AE1200/Harvard-referencing.pdf.
Kuppers, Petra. 2011. *Disability Culture and Community Performance: Find a Strange and Twisted Shape*. Houndmills: Palgrave Macmillan.
Marvellous. 2014. Directed by Julian Farino. UK, Tiger Aspect Productions [Video: DVD].
McDonagh, Patrick. 2008. *Idiocy: A Cultural History*. Liverpool: Liverpool University Press.

Morris, Jenny. 1997. "A Feminist Perspective." In Ann Pointon ed. *Framed: Interrogating Disability in the Media*. London: British Film Institute, 21–30.

Neugebauer, Richard. 1996. "Mental Handicap in Medieval and Early Modern England: Criteria, Measurement and Care." In David Wright and Anne Digby ed. *From Idiocy to Mental Deficiency*. London & New York: Routledge, 22–43.

Prentki, Tim. 2012. *The Fool in European Theatre*. Basingstoke: Palgrave Macmillan.

Tresize, Bryoni, and Wake, Caroline. 2013. "Disabling Spectacle: Curiosity, Contempt and Collapse in Performance Theatre." In Helena Grehan and Peter Eckersall ed. *"We're People Who Do Shows": Back to Back Theatre. Performance, Politics, Visibility*. Aberystwyth: Performance Research Books, 119–130.

Wallin, Scott. 2015. "Come Together: Discomfort and Longing in Jérôme Bel's *Disabled Theater*." In Sandra Umathum and Benjamin Wihstutz ed. *Disabled Theater*. Zurich-Berlin: Diaphanes, 61–80.

Willeford, William. 1969. *The Fool and His Scepter*. Evanston: Northwestern University Press.

15

Institution, care, and emancipation in contemporary theatre involving actors with intellectual disabilities

Tony McCaffrey

It would appear that theatre involving people with intellectual disabilities is a theatre whose time has come. From origins in institutions and therapeutic environments in a number of countries over the last 50 years, theatrical performance by people with intellectual disabilities has started to take centre stage. In 2017, Back to Back Theatre, founded in Geelong, Australia, in 1987, performed *Lady Eats Apple* at the Theater der Welt in Hamburg, the Wiener Festwochen in Vienna, and the Holland Festival in Amsterdam, and the company released its first feature film *Oddlands*. In 2017, Theater HORA, founded in Zurich in 1993, performed *Disabled Theater*, their collaboration with Jérôme Bel, at the Festival d'Automne in Paris, having been touring with the production since 2012, during which time actress Julia Häusermann won the Alfred Kerr Acting Prize at the 2013 Theatertreffen Festival in Berlin and a Bessie Award for Outstanding Performer in New York. In 2016, HORA was awarded the Schweizer Grand Prix/Hans-Reinhart-Ring, the most important Swiss theatre prize. In January 2017, "Crossing the Line," a showcase festival, took place in Roubaix, northern France, bringing together three European theatre companies employing people with intellectual disabilities: Mind the Gap from Bradford, UK (founded in 1988), Compagnie de l'Oiseau Mouche from Roubaix (founded in 1978), and Moomsteatern from Malmö in Sweden (founded in 1987). This was part of a two-year small-scale cooperation project funded by a 200,000-euro grant from the European Union to allow the three companies to collaborate and produce three separate productions (Mind the Gap n.d.).

As these companies and others seek to explore further paths of development, it is important to take stock of the recent history of this form of performance, although this is in many ways an impossible history, as it has, as yet, never been written by those people whom it most directly concerns. In fact, all contemporary theatre involving people with intellectual disabilities has emerged from performance practices that up until now have been generated through the facilitation of people without such disabilities. This has meant that this theatre has been caught up in the agendas, ideologies, and desires of people without intellectual disabilities. Over the past 50 years, this has included a 'charity' model of theatre within institutions, based on ideals of usefulness and gainful occupation, as a form of therapy that might, if not cure, then at least ameliorate 'intellectual disability.' This included a particular form of theatre that Erving Goffman called "institutional theatricals" (1961, 99–100). This

Tony McCaffrey

theatre has at times been motivated by religious or spiritual practices that favour narratives of triumph over adversity and of inspiration. It has included models seeking to cast people with intellectual disabilities as embodiments and "enmindments" (Kuppers 2014, 44) of alterity or unknowability, as enabling *others* or politically resistant *others*. There are models of this type of theatre that are practically motivated to seek inclusion for people with intellectual disabilities in paid, creative, and collaborative work. There are also models that seek a new aesthetics and politics of theatre that challenge current hegemonies and the very mechanisms of representation and construction of the self.

If we consider three of the most influential groups working in this area, Back to Back Theatre, Theater HORA, and Mind the Gap Theatre, it is possible to delineate the following points of comparison in the aesthetics and politics of this form of theatre. Each group has

1   been founded by and is, in most instances, facilitated and administered by people without intellectual disabilities
2   its origins in community projects and theatrical performance emerging from institutions and therapeutic environments, but all three are now touring internationally and remunerating their professional performers
3   a process of devising and rehearsing that draws extensively upon the particular life experiences of members of the ensemble and seeks to accommodate their particular physical or cognitive challenges
4   generated critical and audience response to their work which includes a fundamental questioning of the terms of the participation and agency of people with intellectual disabilities within performance and the group processes
5   generated an increasing body of academic analysis, and includes academics embedded within the company analysing the processes of devising, rehearsal, performance, and the reception of performance.

And now, after a number of years of working together, each group is exploring different paths of development that seek to democratise or shift the power relationships of the means of production, of the processes of making theatre, from non-disabled directors and facilitators to those members with intellectual disabilities.

To assess the possible future of this socially engaged art form, especially the development of the presence, participation, and agency of people with intellectual disabilities, it is necessary to look at the epistemology, or grounds of knowledge and practice, on which this theatre is based. Any possible future developments will need to deal with the legacies of past thinking that continue to inform both the place and treatment of people with intellectual disabilities and the shifting meanings of theatricality and performance. In many ways, I am attempting to unearth "cripistemologies" of contemporary theatre involving people with intellectual disabilities. The term "cripistemologies" was developed by Johnson and McRuer (2014) to explore

> ways of knowing and unknowing disability, making and unmaking disability epistemologies and the importance of challenging subjects who confidently "know" about "disability" as though it could be a thoroughly comprehended object of knowledge.
>
> *(130)*

There is, of course, a danger in overthinking and over-theorising this form of theatre and thereby reiterating the very exclusion of those people with intellectual disabilities that such theatre claims to represent. Whilst acknowledging this danger, my response to this problem is that theatre involving people with intellectual disabilities is deserving of all manner of critical analysis. This includes "high" theory, "low" theory, more aligned with urgent political activism (Halberstam 2011, 16), no theory, and *theatre* as *theory*, as both words share an etymology in "ways of looking" at the world (Fortier 1997). In the same way, people with intellectual disabilities deserve the fullest attention, consideration, and thoughtfulness of all others with whom they come in contact. Writing about theatre involving people with intellectual disabilities is not the same as practising or experiencing such theatre, but it is important. What can be understood, and misunderstood, conceptually within a theoretical discourse may also be experienced perceptually, affectively, and somatically within theatrical performance by both performers and audience. Moreover, it is often in the interaction or the gaps between these different discourses that conceptual, perceptual, and practical change may be generated.

While I do not self-identify as a person with intellectual disability, I have worked alongside, devised performance with, been in dialogue with, developed friendships with, and made theatre with, people with intellectual disabilities for some 13 years. This does not necessarily give me any special authority to speak for, or on behalf of, such people; I could have been engaged in this activity for any number of years and learnt nothing. However, I believe that my experiences and contact with the particular people with whom I have worked and played have generated in me an even deeper desire to undermine and trouble the concept of 'intellectual disability.'

In the 'cripistemologies' which inform theatrical performance involving people with intellectual disabilities, I pay particular attention to the meanings of *institution*, which include not only the asylum and post-deinstitutionalisation reiterations of institution but also the institution of theatre and of other media. I consider *care* as a practice generally understood as something given by people without intellectual disabilities to people with intellectual disabilities, but which, due to its presumption of inequality, is so often open to abuse. I also consider care as an urge to sympathy or empathy and as a provision of support. Finally, I consider the idea of *emancipation* for people with intellectual disabilities, as a movement towards both aesthetic and political freedom, and how this can or cannot be reconciled with institutions and systems of care.

The first example of theatre I consider here is the 300-seat proscenium arch theatre constructed at the Normansfield Hospital in 1897 by John Haydon Langdon Down after he left the Earlswood Asylum for Idiots and Imbeciles in London. Down gave his name to the syndrome that characterises the symptomology of Trisomy 21. My reason for considering this theatre is because its location as an institution within an institution presents a paradigm that has been extremely influential in the subsequent development of theatre involving people with intellectual disabilities. In his "Observations on an Ethnic Classification of Idiots," Down (1866) noted of the "Mongolian type of idiocy":

> They have considerable power of imitation, even bordering on being mimics. They are humorous, and a lively sense of the ridiculous often colours their mimicry. This faculty of imitation may be cultivated to a very great extent, and a practical direction given to the results obtained.
>
> *(262)*

In Down's institution, knowledge as symptomology and taxonomy intersects with power to produce the regimen of moral treatment imposed upon inmates in their lifelong and involuntary segregation. By the time of Earlswood's founding in 1847, the meaning of asylum had shifted from the seventeenth-century associations with a refuge or protection, and the fifteenth-century meaning of sanctuary or inviolable place, to "a benevolent institution affording shelter and support to some class of the afflicted, the unfortunate or destitute" (OED, n.p.).

In a place apart, dedicated to refuge and benevolent care, Down established another space apart, an aesthetic space. This was, however, an aesthetic space with a specific social purpose: the cultivation of the faculty of imitation that might be turned to a practical direction, in which both theatre and people with intellectual disabilities might be rendered socially useful or valuable. As Down notes elsewhere of "the Mongolian type of idiot": "They are cases which very much repay judicious treatment" (1866, 262). Here the "judicious treatment" of the person with intellectual disabilities proves to be well worth it: they *repay* this care, proving the treatment's moral *and* economic value. This generation of repayment or redemption proves at once the moral, economic, and spiritual efficacies of such theatre.

Earlswood and Normansfield were institutions based on very clear systems of hierarchy and exchange. Asylum was given to people with intellectual disabilities in exchange for lifelong, involuntary segregation. Asylum was given in exchange for submission to the strict hierarchy separating staff and inmates and in exchange for being classified according to capacity: idiots, possessing a mental age of three or younger, imbeciles, three to seven (Ronell 59). The Victorian benevolent institution, the charity model of disability, was often merely the other side of the coin of what Eunjung Kim (2017) has termed "curative violence," a violence that was likely to be of an indefinite temporality given the assumption of the *incurability* of idiots and imbeciles.

Within the asylum, the theatre operated as a licensed relaxation of institutional power that served only to confirm that power. The control of bodies in space and time was so regimented that the theatre could be no more than a temporary exception to, and a strange mirror of, the daily regime of treatment and care. The theatre allowed the institution to show its benevolent and caring face while also cultivating such faculty of imitation as could be given a practical direction. This latter objective aligns with Aristotle's defence of theatrical mimesis as akin to the efficacy of imitation in teaching children how to perform the tasks of good citizenship.

Contemporary theatre involving people with intellectual disabilities is still trying to deal with the legacy of this institutional paradigm. Theatre itself is an institution: of representation, expression, and communication, often in the service of normalisation or celebration of what is held in common. Like other institutions, it has historically operated according to certain hierarchical structures which have now become sedimented: these include the hierarchy of director over actors, of visible labour over hidden (or backstage) labour, of presumed active performers over presumed passive audience, of the sacred space of performance over the *theatron* or place of looking. It is also, since Aristotle, the place of the hierarchy of prioritising *muthos* or plot over *opsis* or spectacle, of the requiring of a *synopsis* in which dramatic narrative governs all that is seen and heard as relevant to arcs of character and narrative that become subjected to the moral judgement of spectators (see Weber 2004).

Theatre involving people with intellectual disabilities, therefore, is subject to an epistemological basis which has enshrined the sedimented, hierarchical structures of both the 'benevolent' institution and of dramatic or Aristotelian theatre as an institution. To take one example, a characteristic of the institution of dramatic theatre is the validation of the actor's ability to learn lines of text and to 'own' in performance a complex score of motivated verbal and movement text. This functionality is likely to be challenging for some people with intellectual disabilities. Much recent theory and practice of such theatre seeks to respond to this epistemological bias by exploring how to provide systems of support suitable to actors with intellectual disabilities, whose 'disability' may be determined by lack of access to education, training, or opportunity.

In *Theatres of Learning Disabilities*, Matt Hargrave (2015) refers to Shannon Jackson's (2011) idea of a usually hidden "support" that is foregrounded in contemporary theatrical performance. In the case of theatres of learning disability, such support strategies attempt to deal with "a continuing gap between non-disabled expectations of theatrical performance and the technical impacts of impairment on the performer" (Calvert 2017, 8). As Yvonne Schmidt (2017) points out, these "technical impacts" may require support such as "a performer with a learning disability ... using ... a script on stage because she is unable to memorise the text" (448). This echoes Hargrave's analysis: "a physically disabled performer may reveal the supportive infrastructure of prostheses, chairs or crutches ... a learning-disabled actor may depend on *invisible* support structures such as the extended time required to memorise script" (100). These analyses of practice are, however, based on a binary notion of the capacity/incapacity of the actor and how the (assumed abled) audience will view this. The possibility of dialectical perceptions of capacity in the aesthetics of a particular theatrical production is not explored.

Such a possibility is offered in singular moments in Back to Back Theatre's *Super Discount*, in the representation of the distinctive actions of Sarah Mainwaring, an actress with an acquired brain injury, removing and placing a microphone in a stand, actions which frame or bookend the whole performance. In the context of the performance, this becomes an intense presentation and contemplation of what is different, fascinating, infuriating, but ultimately compelling in her shaky and almost incapacitated performance of the supposedly simple action (see McCaffrey 2018).

In his discussion of support in theatre involving people with intellectual disabilities, Hargrave notes the paradox that "the offer of unconditional support is perhaps the highest human offer, but aesthetically represents a low order of merit" (2015, 100), but perhaps a more complex dialectical consideration is desirable than this perceived contrast between care and performance. Unconditional support may be merely reiterating the care of the benevolent institution, a smothering and coddling treatment that is exemplified in some of the less-developed theatrical practices involving people with intellectual disabilities. It is possible to offer support more rigorously and with a motivating degree of expectation. Support for actors with intellectual disabilities might include, for example, either working in ways that do not demand the rote learning of lines, or of allowing more time for the learning of lines, dependent on the actor and the situation. Including actors with intellectual disabilities requires a variety of different strategies and a complex and careful negotiation of support.

Support based on certain kinds of benevolence and care may too easily become inflected with the religious, moral, and economic values of institutions of intellectual disability, such as Earlswood Asylum. These values that persist to the present deny the agency of people with intellectual disabilities and foreclose the possibility of more nuanced and dialectical or dialogic relationships between people with and without intellectual disabilities. How then might emancipation from such structures be achieved for people with intellectual disabilities? Theatre groups with a longstanding commitment to developing the aesthetic form and the social efficacy of such performance are now asking such deeply political questions of self-determination. Can freedom or emancipation ever be *given*? If people with intellectual disabilities are to be emancipated, what state is it that they are being emancipated *from* and *to*?

Emancipation is a term that locates the oppression of people with intellectual disabilities within a similar trajectory of resistance to the historical movements for civil rights, women's rights, gay rights, and disability rights. Intellectual disability, long seen as the poor cousin of (physical) disability rights, has only recently emerged into various fields of activism, academic study, and theatrical performance. Disability studies has developed analyses based on the social model of disability, disability equity and justice, and more recently, on an awareness of intersectionality: that systems of oppression operate – and should, therefore, be resisted – across diverse classifications of race, gender, gender preference, and ability. Mitchell and Snyder (2017), Goodley et al. (2017) and others have drawn from the work of Jasbir Puar (2017) the use of the term "debility" as a prompt to situate disability studies within more intersectional analyses:

> I mobilize the term "debility" as a needed disruption (but also expose it as a collaborator) of the category of disability and as a triangulation of the ability/disability binary.
>
> *(Puar 2017, 166)*

This analysis is overdue and urgent given that according to a recent Ruderman Foundation report (Hause & Melber 20166), over half the people who died at the hands of US police in the period 2013–2015 had some kind of disability, often some form of learning disability or psychiatric history. In many cases, the intersectionality of blackness and intellectual disability marks people down for what Puar in the title of her recent book has termed the state's "right to maim" (2017). Puar is highly critical of disability studies and disability rights frameworks that:

> recognize(s) some disabilities at the expense of other disabilities that do not fit the respectability and empowerment models of disability progress – what David Mitchell and Sharon Snyder term the "biopolitics of disability."
>
> *(2017, 2)*

This intersectional perspective becomes particularly important to take into account when looking at the contemporary theatrical performance of people with intellectual disabilities. It stands as a corrective to viewing the history of this form as one of progress and development and also highlights the danger of theatrical performance being appropriated by neoliberal agendas of "ablenationalism" (Mitchell & Snyder 2015). These include successful performers with intellectual disability being appropriated into narratives of inspiration porn and promoted as exceptional contributors from a section of the population normally marked for debility.

'Intellectual disability' as a signifying term is awkward in that it does not easily lend itself to claims or reclamations of self- or group identification in the way that people have appropriated 'queer,' 'crip,' "crip-queer" (McRuer 2006), or 'Mad Pride' to reclaim historically pejorative terms as badges that assert pride in liminal or minoritarian identity. (While the term learning disability is used in the UK context, Matthew Reason and Dave Calvert discuss in Chapters 13 and 14, the term intellectual disability is still in use in other contexts, such as in Australasia). In *Authoring Autism*, Melanie Yergeau (2018) advocates embracing the terms "neurodivergent" to contrast with "neurotypical," and "autism" with "allism" (15). She cites Duffy and Dorner (2011) who assert that "autism is a narrative condition" (1) which for too long has been controlled by non-autistic people. She argues that non-autistic people are not able to "rhetorically listen" to how autistic people employ narrative and rhetoric, or

Institution, care, and emancipation

to how they may be employing their own rhetorical devices, such as the use of silences or gestural behaviour delineated in discourses of pathology as stereotypy. Identifying as autistic herself, Yergeau opposes her own sense of rhetoric to a scientific discourse that erases her: "Description cannot contain my hands. And yet, my former neuropsychologist described my movement as autistic stereotypy" (2018, 13). Medical and other dominant narratives efface the personhood of autistic people: "autism is medically construed as a series of involuntarities-of thought, mode action and being" (Yergeau 2018, 7). This presumption of involuntarity determines that "to author autistically is to author queerly and contrarily" (Yergeau 2018, 6). I ask the question whether this growing body of autistic writing and autistic-centred theory might be applied to other people who are generally referred to as 'intellectually disabled.' What similar rhetorics of intellectual disability and practices of 'rhetorical listening' can be developed to allow the rhetorics and poetics of intellectual disability to flourish?

Such investigations of identity and autonomy continue to be explored in the very practical, embodied processes of making theatre involving people with intellectual disabilities as this has developed in a number of countries over the last 50 years or so. In a recent overview of the field in *Theatre and Disability*, Petra Kuppers (2017) refers to "*third generation work*, no longer interested in pride or entry into mainstream aesthetics" (54; emphasis added). The substantial development of theatre practices of groups like Back to Back, Theater HORA, and Mind the Gap is part of a wider wave of inclusion in which people with intellectual disabilities are coming to prominence as actors, designers, educators, activists, photographers, and, in some cases, film directors.

Recent developments by these three specific theatre companies have sought to reassign power to people with intellectual disabilities in the means of production of theatre and to reconfigure the power relationships between people with and without disabilities. In "Towards a new directional turn? Directors with cognitive disabilities," Yvonne Schmidt (2017) tackles one of the key issues that has emerged in the development of such theatre. She states that "despite the many recent positive developments, artists with cognitive disabilities have yet to achieve full autonomy" (446). She points to how actors with intellectual disabilities are increasingly participating in contemporary performance, often in processes in which the devising and dramaturgical processes draw from their own lived experiences, yet for Schmidt, despite the potential aesthetic and political innovations of this form of performance,

> the question remains as to who is acting as a mouthpiece for whom, and who gets the final word during the creative process, which is too often "shaped" or "filtered" by non-disabled company directors.
>
> *(446)*

She then goes on to give an account of the project *Freie Republik HORA*, an attempt by Theater HORA – a company she has been investigating as an 'embedded researcher' since 2013 – to foster the creative autonomy of the disabled members of the group. To give some context, Theater HORA is the leading company of actors with intellectual disabilities in Switzerland. They had been devising productions, collaborating with other artists, and running a two-year training course for actors with intellectual disabilities for some 20 years before they were drawn into the international spotlight by collaboration with renowned French anti-choreographer Jérôme Bel on *Disabled Theater*. This production has been touring internationally for the last four years and has generated a lot of critical and academic debate around the issue of the agency of the performers. This arose because of the deliberate anti-theatricality of the piece, the apparent abnegation of many of the conventional

195

responsibilities of a director or choreographer by Bel, a dissension over what exactly was being dis-abled in this performance: the performers, the audience, the audience's expectations of theatrical performance or representative, dramatic 'theatre' itself. *Freie Republik HORA* is in many ways the company's own response to *Disabled Theater*: a radical attempt to restage the questioning of the agency of the performers with intellectual disabilities.

As Schmidt recounts elsewhere (2015), the project started with the performers chosen to participate as directors being given a simple instruction "Do what you want to- just the way you like it!" and a suitcase filled with 1,000 Swiss francs. This was an attempt to give the performers freedom – except it later became apparent that other guidelines were necessary: these included assistance with scheduling, meeting deadlines of tryouts in front of an audience, and an instruction not to damage other people's property or cause physical injury or sexual assault on stage. As the project progressed, it became increasingly a negotiation "between autonomy and supporting structures" (Schmidt 2017, 447).

Different members of the group reacted in different ways to being given leadership. Matthias Brücker provoked his performers; he wanted to create chaos, and his performers got more and more annoyed by rehearsal methods to the point that Elber, one of the non-disabled directors of the company, had to step in – although he later regretted doing so. Gianni Blumer's performers struggled with the amount of written text he expected them to learn for his Hunger Games re-enactment, but then again, as Schmidt points out, the time allotted for the performance tryouts was a lot less than a conventional theatre company would allow, let alone making any allowance for 'crip time.' The intention of the non-disabled directors to step back and to give control to the performers with disabilities became fraught with the terms on which that freedom to create and to control was given.

Schmidt cites Carlson and Kittay (2009) on a crucial paradox in the development of theatre involving people with intellectual disabilities: "the more people with significant cognitive disabilities obtain a greater degree of agency, the more assistance is required" (447). Those of us working in this area of performance are still encountering the spectres of the institution that Calvert referred to in his 2009 article, "Re-claiming authority: the past and future of theatre and learning disability": "Long-term incarceration … is not, of course, a fertile training ground for aspiring artists" (76).

Schmidt articulates how the *Freie Republik HORA* project sought to reverse the expected relationships between facilitators without disabilities and performers with disabilities in the practices of applied theatre as exemplified by Prendergast and Saxton (2016): "Key to applied theatre facilitation is the recognition that the community participants – both actors and spectators – hold the knowledge of the subject under investigation, *whereas the facilitator holds the knowledge of the theatre form*" (cited Schmidt 2017, 450, emphasis added). HORA's methodology assumed a knowledge of theatrical form by the actors with intellectual disabilities, actors who had undergone a two-year training period with the company and many of whom had many years' experience of theatrical performance: "The knowledge of the theatre form is not given or guaranteed by the facilitator's role. The HORA ensemble members, however, are the experts – as artists" (cited in Schmidt 2017, 450).

Prendergast and Saxton's model does not take into account that *holding* the knowledge is very different from *expressing* that knowledge. Much applied theatre assumes that the disadvantaged people with whom the facilitators are working are the experts on their own experience, on themselves. Although in many ways admirable, this assumption ignores the problem of how *anybody* can be an expert on themselves when the self is constructed within and by so many different discursive formations, languages, and rhetorics. Similarly, HORA's attempt to treat the actors as expert artists needs to take into account that the role of director requires

Institution, care, and emancipation

a very different set of skills than those demanded of the actor. Elsewhere, Schmidt outlines HORA's intention to facilitate "those with cognitive disabilities to be able to obtain artistic leadership," but is the creation of theatre, one of the most collaborative and dialogic of art forms, necessarily about *leadership*? HORA's experiment in democracy and freedom focuses on the individual member as director and centre of power, overseeing eye and sensibility. Is it not then inherently caught up in a very hierarchical model of the creation of theatre? As Schmidt perceptively observes, within this experimentation new models of collaborative work emerged immanently:

> Interestingly, new divisions of work are developed during the rehearsal weeks among the ensemble. Noha Badir, an ensemble member with Down syndrome, serves as a light technician in one of the projects. Remo Beuggert, another performer with a learning disability, takes over responsibility for the music in several projects, and assists Sara Hess as a dramaturge.
>
> *(Schmidt 2017, 457)*

In the history of theatre with actors with intellectual disabilities, strategies had been developed previously that sought to reconfigure relationships of power. These included the attempt at a direct reversal of the expected power relationship by Robert Wilson in his collaboration with Christopher Knowles, the 'autistic poet,' on *Einstein on the Beach* (1976). Stefan Brecht, one of the actors on the project, describes Wilson's methodology in *The Theatre of Visions: Robert Wilson*: "Wilson's idea … seemed to be that we, the performers, were to learn from Chris, by talking to and being with him, and by imitation of him" (1978, 271). In the production season, the actors attempted to imitate Knowles' stereotypy or autistic rhetoric:

> the entire cast's movements on stage reflected Knowles' mannerisms such as hand flapping, spinning, rocking, sudden marching across the stage, and other movements that, today, would be considered signatures of autism spectrum behavior.
>
> *(19)*

But as Telory Davies (2003) observes, Wilson's intention in requiring mimesis from the non-disabled actors may have been heuristic: "Knowles' performance/presence appeared more live, more full than any other performer's affect leaving the others to appear as automata [sic]" (cited McCaffrey 2015, 139). Wilson in his aesthetic sought to suggest a much more dialectical relationship between the capacity of the trained actors and the supposed incapacity of Knowles. By imitating Knowles, the actors failed and therefore appeared more disabled as performers than Knowles, diagnosed as disabled. Wilson's instructions to the actors to imitate Knowles were, however, complicated by the fact that Wilson found in Knowles a kind of *enfant sauvage*, a *tabula rasa* upon which he could project his own sense of artistic autism and his own self-perceived intellectual disability that fuelled his artistic vision (Absolute Wilson 2006).

The danger in this approach is that the 'intellectual disability' of the person with intellectual disabilities is both reified and romanticised, caught up in tropes and projections of 'intellectual disability.' I would trace a connection between this approach and the strategy of "reverse integration," which Anna Hickey-Moody (2009) refers to in the practice of Restless Dance Company in *Unimaginable Bodies: Intellectual Disability, Performance and Becomings*. This is a methodology of improvisation and devising in which dancers with intellectual disabilities initiate and lead the aesthetic direction and "those 'without'

197

impairment fit in with the styles of people 'with' intellectual disability" (Hickey-Moody 2009, xvi.). While this may be a valid approach, it leaves unasked the important question of how the performers with intellectual disability have developed their 'styles.' The danger is in thinking of the person with intellectual disabilities as some kind of latter-day *enfant sauvage* or outsider come to reinvigorate contemporary artistic and aesthetic practices with their 'authenticity.'

This is similar to Palmer and Hayhow's approach in *Learning Disability and Contemporary Theatre: Devised Theatre, Physical Theatre, Radical Theatre* (2008) Here, the two artistic directors of UK companies employing people with intellectual disabilities, Full Body and The Voice and The Shysters, outline their methodology as the development of a performance aesthetics founded on "learning disability." They argue that people subject to this diagnosis are likely to be a lot less integrated and included socially, and therefore, will approach performance more freely and openly, without the "blocks" to spontaneity of social conditioning. Such performers are able, by being disabled, to exhibit "a lack of self-consciousness on the performer's part, a lack of overt technique; a sense of being truly in the moment" (Palmer & Hayhow 2008, 41). The assumptions inherent in this model of theatre conflate the social construction of intellectual disability with some kind of transcendent idea of authentic self. They also posit theatre as an unproblematic and transparent medium of communication in which one may give an account of one's self.

This tension is also apparent in the 'Method' devised by Dark Horse Theatre (formerly Full Body and the Voice) as outlined on their website. The mission statement of the company's method is to "train learning disabled actors at the highest level." The training consists of two approaches: first, the "silent approach" in which "whole days can pass in the rehearsal room without the need for words," an approach which can be characterised as "accessible, physical, emotional and honest"; and second, "a competency based system for actor training ... used to develop and evaluate key skills in Stanislavsky based method." The website states that these two approaches go "hand in hand" and they may well do so. However, they also suggest tensions between exploring spontaneity through improvisation and vocational theatre training capable of producing employable working actors. At the same time, they imply that these are really ultimately the same thing: a faculty for imitation that may be put to practical use.

There is no authentic self – neither of intellectual disability nor of its opposite, normalcy – to be explored, merely "a kind of imitation for which there is no original," to borrow from Judith Butler on gender (Butler 2004, 127). Theatrical performance intersects with the performative self and the performance principle (see McKenzie 2001), and an awkward constellation emerges. It is within such an awkward constellation that the most interesting and empowering contemporary theatrical performance involving people with intellectual disabilities has emerged.

In "Disability, Care and Debility: Radically Reframing the Collaboration between Non-Disabled and Learning Disabled Theatre Makers," Dave Calvert (2016) offers a comparative analysis of Jérôme Bel and Theater HORA's *Disabled Theater* and Mind the Gap's *Contained*. He makes a direct comparison between the use of an onstage non-disabled presence in each performance. In *Disabled Theater*, this is the 'translator,' ostensibly there to facilitate the translation of the Swiss German of the performers to the language of the audience, but who also functions as a proxy for the choreographer. As Calvert argues, "the translator figure is not just setting up space and time for the actors, but is controlling the temporal rhythm of the action in particular" (2016, 3), thus revealing the presence of Bel the auteur in the apparent freedom to act and dance given to the 11 HORA actors in the production. In the case of *Contained*, the onstage presence is Charli Ward, who "performs a version of the directorial role as though in rehearsal. She speaks directly to the actors rather than the audience, and gives instructions in the present tense" (Calvert 2016, 2). In contrast to *Disabled Theater*, here it looks as if the onstage non-disabled presence is in control, whereas Calvert argues

> What Ward is doing, as an intermediary between the director Alan Lyddiard and the performers, is establishing the conditions in which the performers can have agency, in performance, over the form. Agency here is not completely independent autonomy to do as one pleases … but the freedom to make professional judgments in performance about the form as negotiated in the process.
>
> *(4)*

The theatrical moment he cites that exemplifies this freedom in performance is one in which Charli Ward herself takes centre stage in the testimonial or confessional style of so much learning-disabled theatre practice and tells her own autobiographical story. In her case, this is about the recent breakdown of a relationship, a story that prompts the breakdown of her composure as both storyteller and onstage facilitator of the actors with intellectual disabilities. Calvert describes the moments that follow:

> As she struggles to regain control, the performers move caringly towards her, an act of care which itself establishes the foundation that allows Ward to recover agency within the aesthetic. This nonetheless requires the performers to make a choice: not about performance, but between performance and care.
>
> *(5)*

These moments represent a complex constellation of care and performance. They are mediated or 'contained' within the frame of a theatricality that is a mixture of the liveness and presence of performance and the restored behaviour of theatre. The relationship breakdown is itself retold at each performance during the season. It is emotionally raw and also performed, immediate, and mediated. A narrative has been produced that aids emotional coping, couched in the rhetoric of regret. This whole experience is then mediatised theatrically. Similarly, the response of the performers with disabilities is an awkward mix of genuine, affective response and the mediatisation of that response in the gesture and citation (and recitation) of acting. These moments offer something like a role reversal of the expected roles of people with and without disabilities in the giving and receiving of care. They are also caught up in the complexity of agency and performance around acts of care and 'acting' care. Is acting required to recreate each night the original care? By acting as if they care on any given night, do the performers actually end up caring?

I turn now to connect these moments in the recent work of Mind the Gap to equally complex and affectively powerful moments in *Lady Eats Apple* by Back to Back Theatre. In the final moments of the production, a group of performers with intellectual disabilities dressed as the cleaning staff of a theatre speak to another performer who is not disabled but who is lying prone on the stage as if he were unconscious as the result of a fit. The performers repeat the phrase "We will look after you." As with the performers' approach to Charli Ward in Mind the Gap's *Contained*, the offer, or the promise, of care is made in a reversal of the 'expected' relationship between people with and without disabilities. These words in *Lady Eats Apple* are spoken as the lights are fading to indicate the end of the performance so they may well be interpreted as also addressed to the audience. "We will look after you" is a speech act, a promise, and to promise is generally accepted to mean to have the capacity to do something, to perform an action. This speech act, however, occurs in a theatre. J.L. Austin, who coined the term "speech act" as a performative utterance in *How To Do Things With Words*, was heavily dismissive of such a speech act: "A performative utterance will, for example, be in a peculiar way hollow or void if said by an actor on a stage" (cited Weber 2004, 9). The actors of Back to Back are quite clearly in a theatrical world, and so their offer of care to another non-disabled actor and by extension to the audience is surely not to be taken with the seriousness of an act (of care) as it is just *acting.* Yet the speech act needs to be taken in the context of the particular theatrical world of *Lady Eats Apple.*

When the words – "We will look after you" – are spoken, the audience is aware of another role reversal. Due to a *coup de théâtre* that has taken place earlier, they have been revealed as sitting onstage and the performers in the auditorium. This is not the only disorientation of audience expectations and perceptions. The voices of the actors are directly transmitted to the ears of the audience through individualised headsets in a kind of mediatised immediacy. The second section of the performance is a 20-minute sequence without words at an extremely low level of light, low enough for the eyes to play tricks on themselves, and is accompanied by loud music through the headphones. By the time the audience experiences the quieter third section of the production, both ears and eyes have been resonating, throbbing, and flickering in a kind of disconcerted synesthesia. This visual and aural 'noise' or interference exposes the gaps in perception necessary for sensory perception to take place.

Conclusion

In these gaps, we the audience, whether intellectually disabled or not, come to perceive the disability and ability of the actors. We likewise see and feel debility, feigned or actual, through acts of care and the acting of care. By accepting the terms of theatricality as *medium*, as that which gets in the way as much as that which communicates, the promise "We will look after you" attains its full force. *Lady Eats Apple* and other contemporary practices of theatre involving actors with intellectual disabilities have emerged out of institutions of segregation and representation to make radical promises of emancipation. It is not enough merely for the inmates to take over the asylum, for the freaks to take over the freakshow, for the cared for to become the caregivers. These institutions, with their sedimented hierarchical relationships and their concomitant economies, need to be dismantled – but they may well be best dismantled, with care, and careful cooperation, from within.

References

Absolute Wilson. 2006. *Dir. Katherina Otto-Bernstein.* New York: Alba Film Productions. DVD.
Aristotle. 1999. *Poetics.* Translation by Kenneth McLeish. London: Nick Hern Books.
Austin, John Langshaw. 1980. *How to Do Things with Words: The William James Lectures delivered at Harvard University in 1955.* Edited by J.O. Urmson and Marina Sbisa. Oxford: Oxford University Press.
Back to Back Theatre. 2016. *Lady Eats Apple.* Directed by Bruce Gladwin. Hamer Hall, Melbourne, 9 Oct, 2016.
Back to Back Theatre. 2013. *Super Discount.* Directed by Bruce Gladwin. Wharf Theatre, Sydney. 20 Sept–19 Oct 2013.
Brecht, Stefan. 1978. *The Theatre of Visions: Robert Wilson.* London: Methuen.

Butler, Judith. 2004. "Imitation and Gender Insubordination." In Sara Salih and Judith Butler ed. *The Judith Butler Reader*. Malden: Blackwell Publishing, 119–137.

Calvert, Dave. 2017. *Performance, Learning Disability and the Priority of the Object*. Unpublished PhD thesis, University of Warwick.

Calvert, Dave. 2016. *Disability, Care and Debility: Radically Reframing the Collaboration between Non-disabled and Learning Disabled Theatre Makers*. Paper given at Disability, Arts and Health Conference, Bergen, Norway.Calvert, Dave. 2009. "Re-claiming Authority: The Past and Future of Theatre and Learning Disability." *Research in Drama Education*. 14 (1): 75–78.

Carlson, Licia, and Kittay, Eva Feder. 2009. "Introduction: Rethinking Philosophical Presumptions in Light of Cognitive Disability." *Metaphilosophy*. 40: 307–330.

Dark Horse Theatre. 2017. *Actions Speak Louder Than Words*. Accessed 1 June 2018. Available: www.darkhorsetheatre.co.uk/method/.

Davies, Telory Williamson. 2003. *Performing Disability: Representations of Disability and Illness in Contemporary American Performance*. Unpublished PhD thesis, Stanford University.

Disabled Theater. Directed by Jérôme Bel. Vimeo file. Password Provided by Theater HORA. Recording of performance at Hebbel Am Ufer, HAU1, 11 March 2012.

Down, John Langdon Haydon. 1866. "Observations on an Ethnic Classification of Idiots." *London Hospital Reports*. 3: 259–262.

Duffy, John, and Dorner, Rebecca. 2011. "The Pathos of 'Mindblindness:' Autism, Science, and Sadness in 'Theory of Mind' Narratives." *Journal of Literary and Cultural Disability Studies*. 5 (2): 201.

Fortier, Mark ed. 1997. *Theory/Theatre: An Introduction*. London: Routledge.

Goffman, Erving. 1961. *Asylums: Essays on the Social Situation of Mental Patients and Other Inmates*. Chicago: Aldine Publishing Company.

Goodley, Dan, Liddiard, Kirsty and Runswick-Cole, Katherine. 2017. "Feeling Disability: Theories of Affect and Critical Disability Studies." *Disability and Society* (33) 2: 197–217

Halberstam, Judith. 2011. *The Queer Art of Failure*. Durham & London: Duke University Press.

Hargrave, Matt. 2015. *Theatres of Learning Disability: Good, Bad or Plain Ugly?* New York: Palgrave Macmillan.

Hause, Marti, and Melber, Ari. 2016. "Half of People Killed by Police Have a Disability." *NBC News*. Accessed 1 December 2017. Available: www.nbcnews.com/news/us-news/half-people-killed-police-suffer-mental-disability-report-n538371.

Hickey-Moody, Anna. 2009. *Unimaginable Bodies: Intellectual Disability, Performance and Becomings*. Rotterdam: Sense Publishers.

Jackson, Shannon. 2011. Social Works: *Performing Art, Supporting Publics*. New York & London: Routledge.

Johnson, Merri Lisa, and McRuer, Robert. 2014. "Cripistemologies: An Introduction." *Journal of Literary and Cultural Disability Studies*. 8 (2): 127–147.

Kim, Eunjung. 2017. *Curative Violence: Rehabilitating Disability, Gender and Sexuality in Modern Korea*. Durham & London: Duke University Press.

Kuppers, Petra. 2017. *Theatre and Disability*. London: Palgrave Macmillan.

Kuppers, Petra. 2014. *Studying Disability Arts and Culture: An Introduction*. London: Palgrave Macmillan.

McCaffrey, Tony. 2018. "'A Dance That Draws You to The Edge of Your Seat': Acting and Disability Faced with Technology." *L'Archée: cyberart et cyberculture*. Online journal July 2018 http://archee.qc.ca/images/edito-2018-06/Archee_2018_06_Tony.php.

McCaffrey, Tony. 2015. *Incapacity and Theatricality: Politics and Aesthetics in Theatre Involving Actors with Intellectual Disabilities*. Unpublished PhD thesis, University of Canterbury.

McKenzie, Jon. 2001. *Perform – or Else: From Discipline to Performance*. London & New York: Routledge.

McRuer, Robert. 2006. *Crip Theory: Cultural Signs of Queerness and Disability*. New York: New York University Press.

Mind the Gap Theatre. n.d. *Crossing the Line*. Accessed 1 December 2017. Available: www.mind-the-gap.org.uk/projects/crossing-the-line/.

Mitchell, David T., and Snyder, Sharon L. 2015. *The Biopolitics of Disability: Neoliberalism, Ablenationalism, and Peripheral Embodiment*. Ann Arbor: University of Michigan Press.

Oxford English Dictionary. "asylum, n." Oxford University Press.

Palmer, Jon, and Hayhow, Richard. 2008. *Learning Disability and Contemporary Theatre: Devised Theatre, Physical Theatre, Radical Theatre*. Huddersfield: Full Body and the Voice.

Prendergast, Monika, and Saxton, Juliana, ed. 2016. *Applied Theatre. International Case Studies and Challenges for Practice*. Bristol: Intellect.

Ronell, Avital. 2003. *Stupidity*. Urbana & Chicago: University of Illinois Press.

Puar, Jasbir. 2017. *The Right to Maim: Debility, Capacity, Disability*. Durham & London: Duke University Press.

Schmidt, Yvonne. 2017. "Towards a New Directional Turn? Directors with Cognitive Disabilities." *Research in Drama Education: The Journal of Applied Theatre and Performance*. 22 (3): 446–459.

Schmidt, Yvonne. 2015. "After Disabled Theater: Authorship, Creative Responsibility and Autonomy in Freie Republik HORA." In Sandra Umathum and Benjamin Wihstutz ed. *Disabled Theater*. Zurich & Berlin: Diaphanes, 227–240.

Weber, Samuel. 2004. *Theatricality as Medium* New York: Fordham University Press.

Yergeau, Melanie. 2018. *Authoring Autism: On Rhetoric and Neurological Queerness*. Durham & London: Duke University Press.

16

Sweet Gongs Vibrating
The politics of sensorial access

Amanda Cachia

Introduction

In March 2016, my group exhibition, *Sweet Gongs Vibrating*, opened at the San Diego Art Institute in California as the culmination of a four-month curatorial residency. *Sweet Gongs Vibrating* was a multimedia, multisensory exhibition that broke with ocularcentrism – that is, the privileging of vision over the other senses – by embracing myriad modes of perception. This project aspired to activate the multisensorial qualities of objects to illustrate alternative narratives regarding access, place, and space for the benefit of a more diverse audience, especially for people with visual impairments and/or blindness. I was especially interested in challenging the ocularcentric modality of curating exhibitions, and the tendency to rely on the convention that objects must be exclusively experienced through vision alone. It was my attempt at curatorial "haptic activism," a term introduced to me by the Australian artist Fayen d'Evie (see Haug 2016), as I aimed to have the visitor directly touch all works in the exhibition as much as possible.

The challenge I posed throughout this exhibition centred on the role of the sensorium: imagine learning new information about a body, a material, or a place through the sweet taste of ice cream, the gong of a sculpture, or the vibration in a wall. The exhibition included the works of 20 local, national, and international artists, including one collaboration. These artists explored the multimodal possibilities of sculpture, site-specific installation, video, and works on paper, constituting an exciting and accessible template for how one might glean untold accounts of everyday surroundings. Each artist was invited to either contribute extant or create new site-specific work. Each piece encouraged multisensorial engagement to greater and lesser extents (touching, hearing, smelling, looking), provoking thoughtful critique on the methods by which sensorium can be activated through modes of creative and conceptual access.

Historically, the limited preoccupation with the concept of access in museums and art galleries has obscured the possibility of more generative sensorial-related content within exhibitions, displays, and other curatorial practices. In *Sweet Gongs Vibrating*, I wanted to exhibit critical works showing their full range of sensorial and experiential possibilities as they pertain to the material, affective, and physical engagement with a wide variety of bodies. In doing so, I aimed to persuade institutions to avoid reproducing existing biases about bodies. My idea was to move beyond the usual understanding of access and rethink what the phrase 'visual culture' means in our society, and how our museums and galleries are arbiters for this culture. What would happen if the museum began to rethink of itself as an institution for sensorial culture rather than purely visual culture? For example, "haptic activism" suggests that the navigation of space can be experienced through tactility and need not rely on the typically predominant sense of vision. Many scholars (see Spence & Spence 2008; Candlin 2010, 2017) have demonstrated that a tactile and multisensorial engagement with works of art and objects in a museum has many benefits, as it contributes to the visitors learning about its material qualities, and even offers clues about the maker of the work, in addition to offering pleasure and all-round enjoyment. While access provision is provided by larger museums around the world for visitors who are blind and visually impaired through monitored touch tours, such offerings are sporadic and inconsistent.

Part of the challenge is that a 'lexicon of touch' still does not exist. Spence and Gallace (2008) state that we "do not have a recognized set of terms to describe the tactile sensations elicited by various material properties, although there have been sporadic attempts over the years to educate people's sense of touch…" (30). Touch is a much under-theorised and underutilised pragmatic and sensorial modality in the 'visual' arts.

In this chapter, I aim to show how the hierarchy of the senses might be realigned to allow more space for new knowledge to be generated through touch. I am candid in revealing some of the challenges and ultimately some of the failures of *Sweet Gongs Vibrating*. A lexicon of touch to *describe* tactile sensations is missing and so is a lexicon that describes *how* to touch. Most people are familiar with the general rule of no touching in an art museum, but when this rule is overturned, confusion can ensue in how to execute this engagement within the museum environment, with sometimes disastrous outcomes. Indeed, one might even go as far as to say that how to touch is more about art politics than art lexicon, because providing particulars on how to touch prompts more questions, such as how should we be touching in museums anyway? Is there a right way and a wrong way to touch? While a gallery or an artist may have a defined method for approaching tactile engagement, I believe these methods should be unpacked to push conventional access standards even further towards radical new pathways. This chapter reveals both the potential and the challenges to curating multisensorial contemporary art exhibitions by using *Sweet Gongs Vibrating* as a case study.

The exhibition at large

Many examples of artwork in the show stimulated a number of sensory functions in the human body: Cooper Baker's *Giant Spectrum* (2016) is an interactive audiovisual wall piece that displayed a live, moving spectral representation of the sounds it 'hears' through the flashing of lights. Much like light, sound comprises many different frequencies, and different sounds contain different frequencies with varying amplitudes. As sounds occur, the piece shows these changing parts as a moving visual spectral display. Patrons may interact with the piece simply by making sound, and any background sound present in the gallery will also appear on the display. As the visitor talks, yells, sings, claps, whistles, stamps their feet on the ground, or plays music, the piece displays the audio spectrum of the sound they are making (see Figure 16.1a and b).

The piece was effective insofar as the visitor was able to witness how movement, sound, and vision could function together in an artwork. However, it also operated as an inclusive object in the way that its flashing lights could give d/Deaf or hearing impaired people visual cues that announce sounds in the immediate environment, sensorial components to this piece that they may not otherwise have fully or partially experienced.

The politics of sensorial access

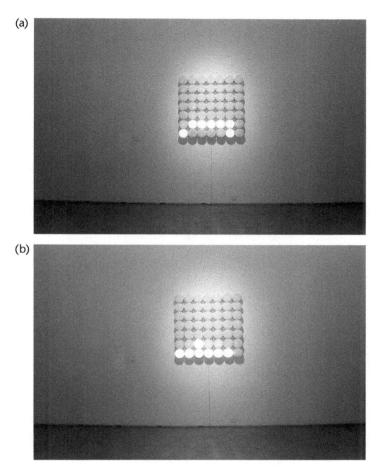

Figure 16.1 (a and b) Cooper Baker, *Giant Spectrum* (2016) in *Sweet Gongs Vibrating*, San Diego Art Institute, 2016, curated by Amanda Cachia

Another example is the work of Wendy Jacob, where she inserted the vibrational purr of a friend's cat into a drywall section of the gallery, creating a sound object that you can sense with your body in *Three threads an a thrum (for D.B.)* (2016). In 1993, Jacob animated a wall in the then new Museum of Contemporary Art San Diego to expand and contract with the steady pace of breathing, an action inspired by the artist's experience of sitting with her father while he was in a coma. *Three threads an a thrum (for D.B.)* is an echo of her earlier wall and addresses comfort in the face of a recent loss. This work did not rely on vision or hearing. Jacob launched her first vibration project in 2008 in Washington, DC at Gallaudet University, a private university for the education of d/Deaf and hard of hearing people in the US. She had taken a group of students from Massachusetts Institute of Technology (MIT), where she was teaching at the time, to map out the aural shape of the space to engage the d/Deaf students in the school. She wanted to have both her MIT students and the Gallaudet students consider looking at deafness spatially as opposed to lack of audition. The students attempted to map the conversation between two deaf and two hearing individuals. This experience proved to be a very rich one for the artist, and vibration has been a key tool in the artist's work since that time (see Figure 16.2a and b).

Figure 16.2 (a and b) Wendy Jacob, installation shots of visitors engaged with *Three threads an a thrum (for D.B.)*, (2016) at the opening reception of *Sweet Gongs Vibrating*, San Diego Art Institute, 2016, curated by Amanda Cachia

British artist Aaron McPeake, who identifies as visually impaired, created a series of bronze gongs suspended from the ceiling with black string. Each gong elicited rich timbres and tones upon contact with a handheld swinging mallet, which again elicited a rich conversation between movement, sound, and vision. McPeake provided titles for each of the gongs, along with creative description of the sounds each one would make as follows: *Eileen's Palette* (2008) history and creative intent; *Once I Saw It All* (2008), hum of a transformer, hiding; *I Broke Her 78 Records* (2007), guilt, regret, solemnity; *Breast Cancer Radiation Mask* (2008), fear, irritation; *Tainted Wedding Ring* (2007), a long reflection; *Family Photograph*

The politics of sensorial access

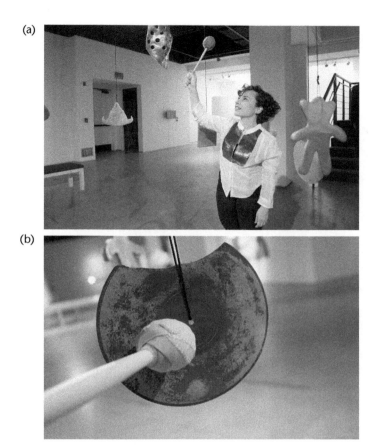

Figure 16.3 (a and b) Curator Amanda Cachia using the mallet to hit the gongs in Aaron McPeake's selection of gongs (2007–2010) in *Sweet Gongs Vibrating*, San Diego Art Institute, 2016, curated by Amanda Cachia

(2007), confused nostalgia; *Meditation Gong – After Derrick* (2009), seeking answers; *My Teddy Brownie* (2008), valuable friend; and *Wooden Spatula* (2010), uncertain of the recipe.

A visitor would be able to engage with the chain reaction of sensorial stimuli that the work offered, where they could start with haptically directing the mallet into contact with the gongs, which would then elicit sounds, which would then emit visual movement of the gongs as they swayed under the pressure of the mallet. This work was especially powerful in the effect that it, in turn, had on other multisensorial works in the show, for the sounds that the gongs emitted had an immediate impact on Cooper Baker's *Giant Spectrum*. When the gong clanged, the lights would flash vibrantly and energetically across the back wall of the gallery space, providing visitors with both a visual and sonic outcome of their tactile engagement between mallet and gong. It brought the entire gallery space to life and became the beating pulse of the exhibition (see Figure 16.3a and b).

I also included Raphaëlle de Groot's video, *Study 5, A New Place* (2015), which she originally created for an earlier online virtual exhibition I curated entitled *Marking Blind*. In the video, De Groot engages in a performance in which she fashions found materials collected in Florianópolis, Brazil (during an artist residency), on her head. They gradually obstruct her

Figure 16.4 (a and b) Raphaëlle de Groot, installation shots of *Study 5, A New Place* (2015) in *Sweet Gongs Vibrating*, San Diego Art Institute, 2016, curated by Amanda Cachia

sight completely as she creates a blind mask over her head. The video was a powerful work to include in this exhibition as an installation, but to fully activate the modality of touch for the audience with whom I was seeking to engage in de Groot's work, I asked her if I could include the original found materials she used to create her makeshift head mask. de Groot allowed me to place the materials as a disorderly bundle on top of a pedestal in front of the accompanying video (see Figure 16.4a and b).

In this way, we could not only see the physical detritus of what the artist was experimenting with on her face and head, but the viewer could also, importantly, touch those materials. As gallery visitors touched the bundle of scraps, I wanted them to explore the varied surfaces of de Groot's papers, ropes, roughly formed pieces of charcoal, plastic, and other materials. If they were sighted, they could visually observe how their touching actions mirrored the touching

(a)

(b)

Figure 16.5 (a and b) Darrin Martin, installation shots of *Objects Unknown: Sounds Familiar* (2016) in *Sweet Gongs Vibrating*, San Diego Art Institute, 2016, curated by Amanda Cachia. Photos by Emily Corkery

of the same materials taking place by de Groot in the video as she covered her head, and/or if they were hearing, they could hear how the crinkle, crinkle, crunch, crunch noise to emerge as a result of hands making impact with crumpled paper were echoed in the sounds emanated from de Groot's same haptics. Extending de Groot's work in this way was a bid to achieve a heightened level of tactile engagement; these types of access interventions need to be encouraged as we consider the expansion of the sensorial and haptic activism within our museums and galleries.

I also negotiated for the same method of access with another artist in the exhibition. San Francisco-based artist Darrin Martin included a video entitled *Objects Unknown: Sounds Familiar* (2016), where fragmented, layered, abstract forms were projected onto a wall, moving up and down in a long, thin, vertical strip similar in shape and function to a film strip. I had asked the artist to produce a three-dimensional version of these abstract shapes so that they could be accessible to the touch (see Figure 16.5a and b).

The artist used 3D printing technology to create scans of the objects from collaged foam packing material. These objects were animated digitally and then merged via analogue video tools, which further abstracted the image and produced sound through the manipulation of electronic frequencies. Mounted on pedestals that also served as speakers, the printed objects vibrated with the same sounds emanating from their projected counterparts.

All of these objects proved very successful as modes of multisensorial engagement in the gallery according to my observations, which were captured during my time sitting in the gallery for two days a week over a period of eight weeks to witness audience reactions first-hand. However, while the engagement was certainly successful in terms of motivating people to touch, I also observed that people did not always know how to touch, or at least, how to 'appropriately' touch. In the next section, I discuss the complexities of touching despite its many benefits.

Please Do Not Touch (after all)

During the opening reception of the exhibition on 26 March 2016, many different visitors attended to explore and engage with the show, including adults of various ages and young children. If the opening was anything to judge by, it seemed that the show was going to be a great hit with the audience, as people were quick to pick up mallets in order to make contact with the gongs, and all the other many interactive devices in the exhibition. Visitors young and old were equally captivated by the lights, sounds, and images in the space and enjoyed the new-found freedom to touch the work in a space that typically prohibits such behaviour (see Figure 16.6).

However, after the first week the show had been opened to the public, the objects had already been placed under a great deal of duress after some rough handling. It seemed that once we had provided the public with permission to touch, they were indeed overzealous in their eagerness to engage. It was not too long before serious damage was incurred. As one would expect, the gallery has much higher attendances when it provides free admission, making it

Figure 16.6 Visitors engaging with Aaron McPeake's selection of gongs (2007–2010) at the opening reception of *Sweet Gongs Vibrating*, San Diego Art Institute, 26 March 2016, curated by Amanda Cachia

more accessible to a more diverse public from various socio-economic backgrounds. This increase in attendance during free admission time means that the gallery staff may not always be able to spend time with each visitor, nor are they able to keep a close watch on each individual. During a particularly busy period, some teenagers were immediately drawn to the tactile objects in the show, especially the gongs. One individual decided to swing from the gongs in Tarzan-like fashion, gripping onto the bronze for support as the thin black rope swayed back and forth suspended from the ceiling. While bronze is a strong material, it wasn't strong enough to support the weight of an adult, and within minutes of this activity, the bronze gong snapped in half. The gallery notified me of the damage, and I informed the artist of the unfortunate news.

The gallery took further action by placing up new signs on the walls providing instruction for how people should engage with the work from now on. Even though I had taken great trouble to prepare labels that also included Braille versions, it seems my participatory directives were not clear enough. In my extended label, I stated: "The bronze bells each have their own clappers (labelled to correspond) and you are welcome to engage with them – please hit, touch and gong!" The San Diego Art Institute created two new labels with very large print in uppercase letters (as if shouting), which stated "DELICATE. PLEASE BE GENTLE" and "DO NOT SWING FROM THE GONGS." These labels got to the point of telling people both what they *should* do (to be gentle) and what they should *not* do (swing from the gongs, as individuals had done before) (see Figure 16.7a and b).

While these new labels were important to protect the gallery, as it did not want to be liable for any further damage to the work, they came across as patronising and less than welcoming to visitors, which was the antithesis of my curatorial vision and objective of the show. In fact, the new labels were quite comical, but also very embarrassing and unprofessional. The gallery was now also providing decidedly mixed messages to its visitors, because while they were encouraged to engage on the one hand, they were also being told to be careful. In some other instances, based on the circumstances and materials of other works in the show, the gallery's visitors were being told not to touch at all.

For example, the gallery informed me that several small works made of bone china intermingled with found and natural materials had been destroyed. Anne Gibbs, from Wales, had provided an installation entitled *Crossing Boundaries* that was a second version based on her original series from 2015. Given that the work was so fragile, I had asked her to create a second iteration of the piece in order for the work to be handled by the public. This was the first time that the artist had allowed her work to be touched by the audience, and so, indeed, the title of her work had a double meaning in that it also crossed a new sensorial threshold. Gibbs' work begged to be touched, as there were many fantastic sensorial qualities embedded into her bone china pieces, ranging from wire to charred pins, coral, coloured threads, and glaze. Unfortunately, during this first week of free admission to the gallery, several people who picked up Gibbs' various pieces accidentally dropped them onto the floor, cracking the delicate forms immediately as they splintered into several pieces. The gallery responded in the same way and put up signage amidst the installation, stating the all-too-familiar, upper-case "PLEASE DO NOT TOUCH" directive (see Figure 16.8a and b).

Again, the gallery made this decision as protection and because they did not want to keep deploying their insurance policy. While some artists were happy to accept the risks of having their works in my show be touched, others were not so flexible and wanted reimbursement for the damage incurred to their work. We had no written contracts with the artists, and so we left ourselves vulnerable to this very unpredictable situation. That was our

Amanda Cachia

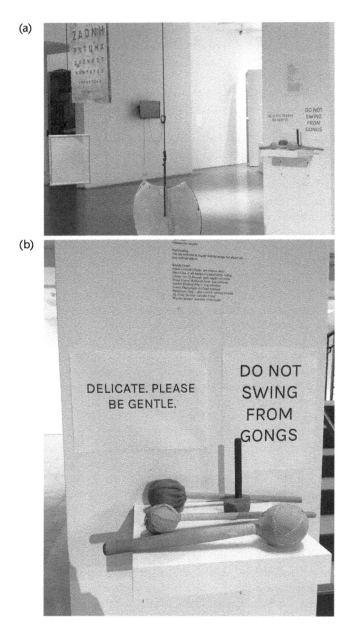

Figure 16.7 (a and b) Installation shots of the signage that accompanied Aaron McPeake's gong installation in *Sweet Gongs Vibrating*, San Diego Art Institute, 2016, curated by Amanda Cachia

first mistake. Signs were then put up throughout the entire exhibition to ward off people's irresponsible touching. A sign was even placed at the front desk to the entrance of the gallery space, stating "PLEASE HANDLE ALL OBJECTS CAREFULLY" (see Figure 16.9).

In her article, "Rehabilitating unauthorised touch, *or* why museum visitors touch the exhibits," Fiona Candlin (2017) writes about how touch authorised and sanctioned by a museum is very different to unauthorised touch. Authorised touch is, of course, much more

The politics of sensorial access

(a)

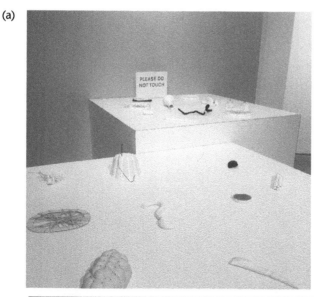

(b)

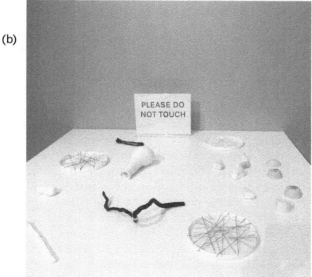

Figure 16.8 (a and b) Installation shots of the "Please Do Not Touch" signage to accompany Anne Gibbs' work, *Crossing Boundaries* (2016), in *Sweet Gongs Vibrating*, San Diego Art Institute, 2016, curated by Amanda Cachia

regulated – for example, through touch tours, which have defined parameters for tactile engagement. On the other hand, as Candlin notes, unauthorised touch is "much less predetermined" (255). Candlin states that "attending to unauthorised touch therefore widens the scope of enquiry, potentially encompasses sensory experiences that fall outside or exceed the institution's aims or intentions, and thereby attends to visitors' choices and agency" (255). Candlin is interested in learning from unauthorised touch as opposed to regulated touch. In the same article, she provides a brief history of touch in the museum, noting that museums

213

Amanda Cachia

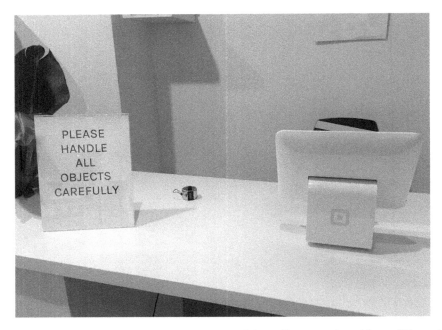

Figure 16.9 Signage at the front entrance of the gallery warning visitors, "Please Handle All Objects Carefully" in *Sweet Gongs Vibrating*, San Diego Art Institute, 2016, curated by Amanda Cachia

used to provide cabinets of curiosity that could, in fact, be touched. However, with the massive growth of museums, tactile engagement became unsustainable owing to an inability to maintain a controlled environment to keep a watchful eye over greasy hands and clumsy fingers. Candlin's observations of all the unauthorised touch that she witnessed at the British Museum in London convinced her of the power of touch and how touch provides a richer and even more imaginative experience with an object, but I suggest that unauthorised touch requires a different modality of touch. In other words, when one is unauthorised to touch, that touch is administered through surreptitious means; it must be brief and tentative so as not to draw the attention of a possible nearby security guard and to avoid any damage (although many highly publicised incidents show that this is not always the case when touching work on the sly). In contrast, when given full permission to touch, the execution of touch is flipped into reverse and becomes forceful, purposeful, and uninhibited.

In her book, *Art, Museums, and Touch*, Candlin (2010) explains why touch became a prohibited activity in the gallery. Touching was once a class-based activity because it was only the elite, wealthy classes who were not only given the privilege to touch objects in a museum, but who were also viewed by the museum staff as having the common sense to touch "rationally." Touching by the aristocrat's "social inferiors" was considered "unruly and destructive" (76). Candlin (2010) therefore argues that the "museum's sensory transition was partly a consequence of class difference and an elite perception of working-class touch" (77). Museum conservation protocols also entered into this sensorial restriction, along with the idea that curators were the only experts in object handling. Indeed, Candlin suggests that this superior attitude also translated into the visual realm, where it was assumed that the working class was no better in soliciting rational knowledge from simply looking at a work, let alone touching it. Candlin (2010) states that "once the working class (whose touch had always been denigrated) gained admittance, touching became associated with damage, a lack of common sense and an absence of justice" (85).

Such claims become very problematic because in the pursuit of justice and access for all – especially in the interests of disabled audiences and people who are blind and/or visually impaired – I suggest that other minority groups can be implicated in relation to class bias. At this intersection of disability and class, the museum must find a means to offer unrestricted and yet authorised access for all these groups, where learning about how to touch is achieved in tandem with developing a lexicon of the experience of touch itself.

Indeed, Candlin's research on unauthorised touching yielded useful results. Security attendants at the British Museum who were interviewed for their opinions on why so much illicit touching took place, suggested that most visitors did not set out to purposely damage work. Candlin (2010) states, "on the contrary they thought that it was related to poor signage, gallery design, staffing levels, and above all, confusion as to whether the objects were original" (85). This feedback is useful for it also relates to some of the problems evident in *Sweet Gongs Vibrating*. Gallery staff and I belatedly recognised after the exhibition had opened and destruction had already taken place that we had failed to include invigilators in the gallery at all times. These invigilators could keep a watchful eye on visitors and also have conversations with the audience, talking them about how to engage 'appropriately' with an artwork. The participatory notes, or as deaf artist and scholar Joseph Grigely (2010) likes to call them, "exhibition prosthetics" (3), that I had incorporated into my exhibition labels were not enough, as people either could not see them or they were not placed well within the overall exhibition design.

Once we recognised the need to have invigilators in the space, the gallery also realised it did not have the resources to maintain an active presence, and so I volunteered to be an invigilator in the gallery two days a week for the duration of the exhibition. I also wanted to experience first-hand how people were engaging with the work, and so I used this as a valuable opportunity to learn more about tactile interaction in a contemporary art gallery. I noticed that people often did not read any of the labels and just intuitively tried to interact with the work. Most of the time, people seemed to understand what was expected of them. At other times, there was some rough handling, and I stepped in and chatted with them about the best way to engage with the work to reap an anticipated response intended by the artist. While some works in the show could withstand rough handling, others needed to be treated much more carefully. Consequently, some visitors failed to exercise dexterity in their handling, as the exhibition demanded that the visitors switch from gentle-to-rough-to-gentle as they circled the room with their exploratory fingers. Based on my observations, I understood the need for more education on the practice of touch within an exhibition space, and saw that people can behave in all kinds of unexpected ways when we give them full permission to touch.

During my time observing the public, I began to call into question the very nature of so-called appropriate touching in a gallery. While Candlin (2010) explained that the historic context for the nature of touching was based on class distinctions, I began to ask other questions about touch. How should we be touching in museums anyway? Is the right way to touch only dictated by the museum, the artist, and/or the materials of the work? Can any way to touch become the right way? Can the contemporary art gallery ever exist in a space where damage is of no concern? While these utopian questions may be very difficult to entertain in a museum containing older works in its permanent collection, I believe that a contemporary art gallery space has more potential and flexibility for experimentation with these ideas.

It is true that some works are simply just more amenable and ideal for rough handling than others, and that it would surely be logical for the curator to include only those works and steer

Amanda Cachia

clear of all fragile pieces so as to avoid risky confusion. However, this would exclude a huge portion of frail objects from tactile interaction with the visitor, and this seems a great shame. What is critical within this field of questions is that touch, however implemented, must be deployed in a way in order for the visitor to gain maximum benefit of the work itself. Ostensible 'right' or 'wrong' modes of touching work are perhaps not how the lexicon or even the politics should be approached. Instead, it seems more important to think about the object first for its radical potential to educate, translate, and promote understanding. This, however, is tricky as it means that the curator and the artist must undertake more meaningful conversations to ensure that the artist's work is not being compromised while at the same time serving the needs of an audience who wish to revel in the potential of multisensorial engagement.

These mixed outcomes from *Sweet Gongs Vibrating* gave me the opportunity to develop a working list of criteria or guidelines that I would implement for future exhibitions of this nature. To begin, clearly it is important for the curator, artist(s), and venue to work collaboratively on all access components from the ground up. Other criteria include the importance of timing: for instance, all accessible components should be implemented well in advance of an exhibition opening – three months is ideal. Museums and galleries should also incorporate sufficient funds in the budget for all appropriate access components as a critical part of the overall enterprise, including funds for the education of tactile engagement, even if that means a panel on questioning what so-called 'appropriate' engagement means in each and every context. These funds could include payment of invigilators, or if funds are sparse, then perhaps touch tours can be arranged for a designated time each day under staff supervision. The curator should also have in-depth conversations with the artists about the level of tactile engagement in the exhibition and ensure that these specifics are laid out in contract form.

I am convinced that the labels or 'exhibition prosthetics' I developed, which provided dialogical directives on how to engage with the exhibition such as how to engage with the gongs, should not be abandoned completely. While they proved insufficient on their own as a means to successfully elicit the intended (or even unintended) response to a work through tactile means, I believe they are an important mode for the artist and curator to have a partial conversation with the visitor in their physical absence, particularly if the artists contribute to the text on the labels. In future, I would also think about how these directives can be offered in alternative formats so that they are made more obvious but also just as importantly, more accessible beyond merely the written format. If these labels as 'exhibition prosthetics' are meant to be dialogical in nature, then surely this dialogue can be viewed and heard in multiple formats as well.

Conclusion

In this chapter, I have suggested that a fuller spectrum of audience members can access objects in a museum or gallery that may not have been available to them previously, owing to conventional "PLEASE DO NOT TOUCH" policies. Being able to engage in encounters of tactility in a museum gives the disabled and non-disabled visitors a new advantage, where they are empowered through haptic aesthetics and do need not to rely on discursive or representational regimes in art history to validate or sanction either their presence or experience in the museum. Importantly, the tactile realm, while empowering and benefitting a disabled audience, is also equally accessible to non-disabled visitors as well, including visitors from various socio-economic backgrounds and class categories. In sum, touch has the potential to become a powerful egalitarian modality if museums provide the resources to educate its public on how tactility can effectively be utilised.

Despite my temporary disappointment that emerged as a result of poor planning and unanticipated reactions from the audience that led to restrictions on tactile engagement, *Sweet Gongs Vibrating* proved generative in how to consider intersectional axes of difference within a multisensorial contemporary gallery environment. How does class and/or disability impact multisensorial exhibition engagement? What is required of the museum and the artist in order to meet the demands of a diverse audience from multiple axes of differences when touch is involved? How should we educate on the lexicon of touch and what are the politics of sensorial access? The museum and its staff can do much to develop these lines of enquiry further so that museums and galleries can ultimately shift the sensorial regime once again into the next century and beyond. If the artist and curator are prepared to imaginatively engage with the work of access, then conditions of narrow standardisation will eventually not only be disrupted as they transform curatorial practice and the museum and gallery experience for the visitor, but vital new approaches to art-making and thinking will thrive.

References

Candlin, Fiona. 2017. "Rehabilitating Unauthorised Touch, or Why Museum Visitors Touch the Exhibits." *Senses and Society.* 12 (3): 251–266.

Candlin, Fiona. 2010. "Museum Visitors and a Changing Sensory Regime." In Fiona Candlin ed. *Art, Museums, and Touch.* Manchester: Manchester University Press, 58–90.

Grigely, Joseph. 2010. *Exhibition Prosthetics: Conversation with Hans Ulrich Obrist and Zak Kyes.* London: Bedford Press and Sternberg Press.

Haug, Kate. 2016. *Touching to See: Haptic Description and 21st Century Visuality.* Accessed 1 March 2018. Available: http://sfaq.us/tag/fayen-devie/.

Spence, Charles, and Spence, Alberto. 2008. "Making Sense of Touch." In Helen J. Chatterjee ed. *Touch in Museums: Policy and Practice in Object Handling.* Oxford & New York: Berg, 21–40.

17
Crip aesthetics in the work of Persimmon Blackbridge

Ann Millett-Gallant

Introduction

Persimmon Blackbridge is a disabled, female artist whose multimedia work exhibits what I call 'Crip Aesthetics.' In this chapter, I will describe 'Crip Aesthetics' as visual and conceptual elements that constitute a style Blackbridge shares with other contemporary disabled artists, specifically in artworks that manifest a 'crip' identity of the artists and/or of the subject depicted. My notion of 'Crip Aesthetics' draws from theories surrounding the term 'crip,' and more specifically, the use of this term to analyse visual culture, specifically in Carrie Sandahl (2003), Robert McRuer (2006), and Alison Kafer (2013), as well as from Tobin Siebers' *Disability Aesthetics* (2010). 'Crip,' as a noun and a verb, has been developed by theorists who draw from queer theory and terminology. Like queer, crip escapes binary definitions of disabled/non-disabled and reclaims and empowers the derogatory term 'cripple,' a one-dimensional epithet of disability, largely signifying misfortune and pity. First, I will summarise these scholars' arguments and discuss what my use of the term 'Crip Aesthetics' derives from them. Then I analyse works by Blackbridge. The crip aesthetics I see operating in her works may be characterised as acknowledgement and incorporation of the viewer's response to artworks; representations of the connections between impairment and disability; visible correlations drawn between the social and political status of disability with other markers of identity, such as gender, race, nationality, sexuality, and class; and visual expressions of pride. Many of Blackbridge's works hyperbolise and celebrate the corporeal and social experiences of being different from the so-called 'norm,' or the majority, and they conceptualise camaraderie between disabled people.

Cripping Aesthetics

In her essay "Queering the Crip or Cripping the Queer?: Intersections of Queer and Crip Identities in Solo Autobiographical Performances" (2003), disability studies and performance scholar Carrie Sandahl analyses the work of solo autobiographical performance artists who identify as crip and queer: Greg Walloch (in "White Disabled Talent"), Robert DeFelice (in "Crippled, Queer, and Legally Blond(e)"), and the work of Julia Trahan and Terry Galloway

("Out All Night and Lost My Shoes"). Sandahl points to crip and queer elements in their work in the forms of "theory, practice and representation" (Sandahl 2003, 25). She discusses how disability studies has drawn from queer theory in part to dismantle distinctions between disabled/non-disabled. She articulates that the term crip includes all kinds of impairments, crossing tradition divides between those with physical and mental and sensory impairments. Further, she argues that both crips and queers are diverse in other elements of identity and adamantly oppose concepts of normality. The performances she focuses on express multiple identities and showcase the performers' bodies and experiences, mediated in the artists own terms. These performers visually and vocally refuse and reject pity. Sandahl draws parallels between "coming out" as both crip and queer, in the actions and language the performers use to express their resistance to notions of normal and to underscore their self-pride. These performers also reclaim and celebrate their non-normative sexuality. Blackbridge's two-dimensional work shares with these performers the crip elements of addressing impairment and disability, identifying as disabled and as lesbian, and consciously incorporating the perceptions of a viewer.

Disability studies scholar Robert McRuer elaborates further the notions of "crip" in *Crip Theory: Cultural Signs of Queerness and Disability* (2006). McRuer theorises about and draws parallels between the construction of compulsory heterosexuality and compulsory able-bodiedness in mainstream culture, arguing that both systems work to construct the disabled and homosexual body as "Other" (McRuer 2006, 31). He focuses on examples drawn from the 1970s onwards, a time period he characterises by the development of new social movements, such as feminism, gay liberation, and the disability rights movement, as well as the economic crisis of the 1970s. McRuer states "Throughout the 1960s and 1970s, increasingly vocal liberation movements made disability and homosexuality spectacular in new ways; LGBT people, people with disabilities, and their allies attempted to define sexuality and bodily and mental difference on their own terms" (McRuer 2006, 12). This period was one of "coming out" for disabled people and the LGBTQ community, as well as for cultural representations of these groups. McRuer analyses various examples, including literature, laws, acts of public protest, television and film representations, and the performance work of disabled artists Cheryl Marie Wade (McRuer 2006, 39–41) and Bob Flanagan (McRuer 2006, 181–194), as well as the work of queer theorists such as Gloria Anzaldua and Judith Butler. Similarly, Blackbridge's projects advocate for the rights of women and lesbians, while referencing the development of her own social identity.

In *Feminist Queer Crip* (2013), feminist and disability studies theorist Alison Kafer joins crip, queer, and feminist theory to make disability understood as "political, as valuable, as integral" (Kafer 2013, 3). Kafer describes her methodology as positioning disability in a political/relational model, to complicate distinctions between impairment and disability. She uses the term "crip" as an identity shared by those with physical, mental, and sensorial impairments, as well as those with chronic illness. Quoting Disability Rights activist and writer Nancy Mairs' use of the term crip, Kafer underscores that it is meant to be jarring and to make people wince (Kafer 2013, 15). Kafer states that the term is meant to be "contested and contestable" (Kafer 2013, 18). Crip, for Kafer, is a term meant to destabilise categories of identity, as well as to politicise disability. Kafer also asserts that crip refuses to be static and defined; it is meant to recognise intersections of identity, such that people with impairments are also part of, and informed by, other social and political identities. Kafer's project is to make disability more dimensional, as well as desirable. Her chapters focus on various forms of contemporary culture including notions of time, medical interventions, intersections between disability and technology, the figure of the cyborg, and representations of disability in relation to nature and environment. In the final chapter, "Bodies of Nature," she analyses artworks by disabled artists Amanda Baggs and Riva Lehrer, particularly Lehrer's portrait of Eli Clare (Kafer 2013, 144–148). In comparison, Blackbridge's work represents a variety of impairments, draws connections between her identities as homosexual and as disabled, and makes disability political.

In *Disability Aesthetics* (2010), disability studies scholar Tobin Siebers theorises the portrayal of the body in modern art and visual culture, tracing the presence of the disabled body in modern aesthetic representation. He states that visions of the disabled body are traditionally met with disgust or dis-ease. In contradiction, he argues that disability is an aesthetic value, yet one that previously has not been recognised as such (Siebers 2010, 139). Siebers states: "In fact, so strong is the modern equation between art and disability that we cannot help but begin to view past works of art in terms of the irrepressible image of disability given by the modern world" (Siebers 2010, 135). The image of disability as "irrepressible" is not only defiantly present, but elicits powerful emotions.

Defining his use of the term "aesthetics," Siebers writes "[a]esthetics tracks the sensations that some bodies feel in the presence of other bodies" (Siebers 2010, 1). His study interrogates the embodied perceptions of viewers in the face of disability imagery. The term 'aesthetics' refers to historical philosophies on beauty, as well as visual elements of a work of or a movement in art. My use of the term 'Crip Aesthetics' designates visible details, imagery, and sentiments in the work of contemporary disabled artists. Siebers does not invoke the term crip, yet by unleashing the disabled body where it has not been previously noticed and theorising the presence of disability where it has been hidden, he effectively 'crips' aesthetics and aesthetic objects. Blackbridge directly addresses the viewer's embodied perceptions and even incorporates viewers' comments into her exhibits and books.

The work of Persimmon Blackbridge

Persimmon Blackbridge was born in 1951 in Philadelphia, PA, and moved to Canada as a teenager. From childhood, she was diagnosed with learning and psychiatric impairments, especially depression. Blackbridge has worked as a visual artist (primarily in sculpture), writer of fiction and non-fiction, curator, model, actor, and performer, as well as a "cleaning lady and very bad waitress" (Constructed Identities n.d.). Her artwork explores her and others' identities as disabled, as well as her own social and political affiliations as a feminist and a lesbian. She holds the 1991 VIVA award for visual arts, a 1995 Lambda Award, the 1997 Ferro Grumley Fiction Prize, the 1998 Van City Book Award, and a 2000 Emily Carr Distinguished Alumni Award. Blackbridge's artwork has been shown across Canada and the US, as well as in Europe, Australia, and Hong Kong. She has also published two novels, *Sunnybrook: A True Story with Lies* (1996) and *Prozac Highway* (1997).

Much of Blackbridge's work is feminist, with her focus on female bodies and experiences, as well as her inclusion of groups of women in its construction (See Queer Media n.d.). In the 1980s, Blackbridge created a sculpture exhibition for the Women in Focus Gallery in Vancouver, based on Sheila Gilhooly's three-year incarceration in a psychiatric institution in the 1970s and constructed with Gilhooly's help. Photos of the sculptures were featured in a collaborative exhibition catalogue-book, *Still Sane* (Blackbridge & Gilhooly 1985), and show that they were made from plaster casts of Gilhooly's body and painted clay, and found objects such as metal, glass, and wire mesh. The sculptures appear eerie in the photographs, like disembodied skin attached to armature. Some of the figures are paired with text blocks of Gilhooly's writing about her personal (and terrible) experiences of institutionalisation, and others have such script printed directly on their flesh. Their poses look worn out and worn down, and their eyes are always closed. Some of the figures seem attached to, and confined by, their surroundings. Blackbridge painted many of them with oil paints and rubbed graphite over them for metallic shine.

The sculptures explore the effects on Gilhooly of various psychiatric treatments, including isolation, confinement, intense drugs, and shock treatments. In addition, the works address mental, physical, and sexual abuse suffered by many female residents in mental institutions. They also materialise self-abuse. In "The Royal Hospital: Unladylike Behaviour" (c. 1980), Blackbridge has created a sculpture of Gilhooly's torso and head, made from clay with plaster casts, showing her standing defiantly with hands on her hips and a smirking grin on her face. On either side of her closed eyes are blocks of texts that tell her story of being shamed in the institution for her hairy legs, in reaction to which Gilhooly got a razor and attacked herself:

> I remember the rush of blood as I slashed myself as hard as I could, sort of not looking and then looking, seeing the skin all white and puffy-like, spitting, and then blood welled up and I sat there and let it run in the bath.

Later in the passage, she says her wounds were stitched up by medics at the institution, without the use of an anaesthetic. Other figures also feature scars and wounds in the flesh.

Several of the sculptural works refer to and incriminate shock treatment procedures, which have destructive physical and mental consequences. In the exhibition catalogue, *Still Sane* (Blackbridge & Gilhooly 1985), many quotes are drawn from popular and medical contexts, describing shock treatments which cause long-term effects, such as severe headaches, memory loss, brain damage, loss of sense of self, and inability to concentrate and learn. Some of Blackbridge's figures have electrodes on the sides of their heads, to replicate this procedure. In "Birchwood: Shock #2," a series of very thin and mangled bodies are laid out on the floor and hung on the wall in horizontal positions, to resemble the convalescence of the body following shock treatments. These victims resemble strips of fried bacon with little human detail.

Blackbridge and Gilhooly also reveal the effects that Gilhooly's institutionalisation had on her life once she left. "Outpatient: Suicide" (c. 1980) features an image of Gilhooly's partial body, without arms, legs, and most of her head, lying on her side with feeding tubes leading from a large gash in her stomach and up to her nose. A narrative about Gilhooly's attempted suicide, after her release from the institution, lays perpendicular to her body, creating a cross shape that reminds me of martyr images. In this sense, Gilhooly presents herself as a survivor of a violent past, one shared with a number of minority groups.

In *Still Sane* (1985), Gilhooly observes that her life changed for the better when she met a group of feminists and lesbians who identified with her and helped ease her pain. Blackbridge's sculpture, "Coming Out: In the Closet" (c. 1980), portrays a hopeful image of five women, most with their hands on their hips and defiant, and yet with satisfied smiles on their faces. They are warmed by red paint, out, proud, and joined together, providing one another with support. Here, Blackbridge's application of crip aesthetics expresses both her own and Gilhooly's social identities as feminist lesbians.

Still Sane also includes essays by feminist writers and critics of the mental healthcare system, all with lesbian perspectives, such as Dorothy Elias, Barbara Kuhne, Nancy Pollak, and Barbara Pulling. In one essay, "Coming Out Crazy" (74–79), Gilhooly and Blackbridge discuss their processes, inspirations, and shared experiences of being institutionalised. Identifying with Gilhooly's scars, Blackbridge references her own self-cutting in the book, as she commiserates with Gilhooly. Many heart-wrenching comments from viewers of the exhibition about their own suffering are also included in *Still Sane*, reflecting how the images resonate with the viewers and advocate for the rights of residents in mental health facilities. In this way, *Still Sane* displays crip aesthetics by including comments from viewers of the exhibition.

Still Sane concludes with essays by lesbian activist Nym Hughes, writer Nora D. Randall, and 'mad' activist Dee dee NiHera. Hughes (1985, 82–84) discusses psychiatry's role as a mechanism of social control. She charges psychiatry with racism, ableism, sexism, and homophobia. Randall (1985, 85–89) continues this discussion of how psychiatry has historically medicalised and discriminated against the LBGTQ community, and it has continued to do so even after 1973, when the American Psychiatry Association removed homosexuality from the official list of psychiatric disorders. She focuses on a specific case in which a lesbian and her partner were discriminated against by the staff, as well as by the other residents, of a psychiatric institution, an example which Randall laments is all too common. NiHera (1985, 90–94) describes the "mad" movement as a group of people who "recognise the existence of multiple realities, ecstasy, pain, and confusion" (91). Also critiquing the psychiatric institution, mad activists politicise the role of psychiatry and work to end the "torture" (90) of psychiatric procedures. They advocate for the power of the individuals to make choices about their lives and sexualities. The images and voices of multiple women compose a crip text as a collaborative, political, feminist work.

Continuing these themes, Blackridge joined with photographer and scholar Susan Stewart and artist and writer Lizard Jones in the 1990s performance group "Kiss and Tell." Blackridge modelled with Jones in a series of black and white photographs showing images of sexual practices that ranged from kissing and embracing to whipping and bondage. Stewart shot the photographs and consulted with her subjects on how the poses would be staged and what objects would be included. Blackbridge contributed to the composition of the scenes as well as posing for them. Her invisible (learning) disability is not alluded to in the photographs, as these are not biographical portraits. The photographs were displayed first at the Women in Focus gallery in Vancouver, where Blackbridge also showed her work with Gilhooly. These photographs were surrounded by paper on which viewers could write about their reactions and beliefs about sexuality. The exhibition travelled across the US and Canada, and it was also shown in Australia and the Netherlands. The photographs, all untitled, were subsequently published as a series of postcard-sized images with viewers' comments about them on the back (2002). "Kiss and Tell" worked together for ten years.

One photograph features the two women embracing and kissing against a rocky and lush background. On the left side of the image, a waterfall flows downward. The woman whose back is to the camera wears a button-down shirt and a pair of leggings, which are wrinkled from her straddled pose, as well as from the hands of her passionate lover. Comments on the back of the image include "I love sex and nature. Too bad I have allergies," "Feels dangerous – kissing outside – but maybe that's sexy too," and "I love outdoor sex, but I've had some close calls. It angers me that we're not safe to do this." These comments express the danger and resulting excitement involved in performing this act outside, although there are also certainly risks in two women showing such ardour and desire for each other in any setting. The untamed environment in which they are set in the photograph echoes the wildness of their act of love, as well as framing their relationship as natural. In this way, through crip aesthetics, Blackbridge's work advocates for human rights for the LGBTQ community as well as for disabled people.

An exhibition titled "From the Inside Out" came out of connections Blackbridge made while working at a public psychiatric institution called Sunnybrook. That exhibition was a large collaborative project involving visual art and narratives by people who had lived in British Columbia's major institutions for people with intellectual disabilities. First shown in 1998, the work led to the publication of Blackbridge's semi-autobiographical, graphic novel, *Sunnybrook: A True Story with Lies*. The story centres on Diane (whose other name is Persimmon), a young lesbian woman without any professional training who gets a job in such an institution. Diane identifies with the residents who have varying communication and intellectual impairments as well as quirky, mostly antisocial, and often humorous behaviours. Diane narrates her interactions with and perceptions of the residents, as well as her critiques of the staff and psychiatrists at the facility.

Blackbridge also illustrates these actions and characters. While her book does not identify the media used in these images, they appear as mainly two-dimensional, layered compositions of different textures and colours of paper, over which pastel and graphite drawings are placed. These graphics range from humorous to haunting. A portrait of the psychiatrist, Dr Carlson, includes a colour drawing of a young doctor standing rigidly in a white coat and tie beside a rendition of a self-portrait by Vincent Van Gogh in a winter hat and jacket (4). Van Gogh is a well-known modern artist who was also institutionalised and whose psychiatric impairments have been romanticised in analyses of his colourful, passionate works. Here, Van Gogh appears to be staring at Dr Carlson incredulously, who seems unaware of the painting.

A portrait of a resident named Stuart, who loved the outdoors, features another pastel drawing of a tall, rigid man, extending arms from his sides that are almost as long as his legs (7). He stands in front of a row of wood pieces that look like weeds or leafless trees and against a light yellow backdrop with silver images of nondescript figures in chairs. His round head, above a long, thick neck, appears to be angled upward, and his face bears a big smile. His triumphant expression, with closed eyes, gives the impression that Stuart is here captured in a moment of reverence or meditation. This image frames Diane's perception of Stuart as a complicated, colourful individual, rather than the sick, crazy person he is known to be in the institution. Another portrait of a semi-mute resident, Janey (45), whom Diane has been assigned to teach how to talk, features Janey from above the shoulders in muddy green, white, and yellow hues. Janey's neck is tilted upwards in a humanly impossible 90-degree angle, as her wide eyes attempt to view and understand a metal tray on the wall that contains small beads. The wall ornament is indeterminate and could resemble a switchboard or some other complicated information system. Her facial expression is one of strain and confusion, as her wide, flat lips are slightly open, and her hair is shown as untamed sections coming out of her head. The viewer can feel Janey's irritation and understand Diane's frustration in trying to teach her an almost foreign language of expression.

Page 40 features text and image that express Diane's identification with the residents. The text reads,

> Janey, your arms are scar on scar. Toothmarks track you layer on layer year on year. I've seen you tear your skin to blood and skin is strong. How can someone bite that hard? I guess you use what you can get. I use a razor.

> *(40)*

The accompanying image is another portrait of Janey from above the waist. Here, her mouth extends beyond her face in bright red and white and is angled like a blade, as it cuts her left arm, which is raised above her head. The narrator, Diane, as well as the author, Persimmon, relate to Janey because of their shared experiences of self-cutting. Crip aesthetics emerge as Diane identifies with and likens herself to many of the residents of Sunnybrook, as does the author, Blackbridge.

Throughout this novel, short sections centre on a soap opera that Diane imagines, based on the relationships between the nurses and doctors of the institution. The text for these fantasies is in a romantic script font, and colour images of a pretty, pensive woman and of a heterosexual couple embracing appear on the page like film stills. Diane's imagination is captured in these sections, as she finds herself, like the residents, escaping her strict and stressful environment through fantasy. Comments on and details about the narrative exist in notes printed in the margins, in a different font than the book, as if Diane is editing her own manuscript. For example, on page 30, text in the margins reads: "The reason she called me Persimmon was because it was my other name, the name my friends called me. Only shrinks and landlords and people at work called me Diane" (30). The collection of different kinds of texts, depictions of different emotional states, and mixed media images create the layered, colourful, and overwhelming nature of the subject matter. In the end of the novel, Diane leaves the institution for another job, yet still thinks about and even imagines seeing the residents at different public places. By applying crip aesthetics in her novel, Blackbridge erases the distinctions between healthy and sick, normal and abnormal, and disabled and non-disabled.

Blackbridge's crip collaboration projects continued. She helped assemble and edit the memoir by her friend, filmmaker Bonnie Sherr Klein (1998), about experiencing two strokes and her consequential rehabilitation. Blackbridge became one of five disabled artists and performers featured in Klein's documentary film, *Shameless: The Art of Disability* (2006), in which Blackbridge discusses her experiences as a learning disabled woman, a lesbian, and an artist. The group of five friends discuss their shared social and medical experiences and express comradery. The film briefly shows examples of Blackbridge's works, and especially a three-dimensional portrait she made of and for Klein. Blackbridge had asked all of the artists in the documentary to send her photographs and other materials that were mean-ingful to and autobiographical of them. This sculptural assemblage, or diorama, features a centred photograph of Klein, holding a phone to her left ear, leaning on a cane in her right hand, and smiling broadly, with her back seemingly adhered to a conch shell. This image stands in front of a beach and is flanked by other mounted personal photographs. In the film, Blackbridge says Klein sent her "a bunch of photographs and a bunch of items" (2006). The item that struck her the most was a shell, which reminded her of the canonical Renaissance painting by Sandro Botticelli, *The Birth of Venus* (c. 1485), a pairing that de-picts the moment the Roman goddess of love emerged from the sea. With crip aesthetics, Blackbridge's diorama pays tribute to Klein and serves as a visual symbol of the two women's friendship and collaborations.

In 2013, Blackbridge was one of 12 artists whose works were featured in Magic/ Realism Art Exhibit for Kickstart 5, a venue sponsored by a disability arts and activ-ist collaborative. Included in this exhibit were Blackbridge's "Liminal Barbie" series of figures, which stage female bodies in various states of contortion and with different amputations. The listed materials for the works include multiple forms of wood, metal, brass rods, bones, and "doll parts" (Blackbridge 2013). These Barbie-sized, disjointed fig-ures lie above and within wooden structures that resemble closets or dressing tables, filled with accessories that include weapon-looking objects and body parts. The traditional "Barbie" is a symbol of feminine ideal, and here her body exists in pieces. Blackbridge points out that "liminal" means a state of transition, such that everyone will become disabled as they age. With crip aesthetics, and like much of Blackbridge's work, these pieces demonstrate that 'disabled' and 'nondisabled' are not opposite states of being, but both are parts of human transitions. The work also draws parallels between identity with clothing and body changes.

In addition to the "Liminal Barbie" series, Blackbridge also exhibited works from her series "Five Diagnoses" and "Mistaken Identities," which also feature doll-sized female figures. An example from "Five Diagnoses" is another assembled figure, with arms raised overhead, standing in a sort of wooden doorway. The shelves above the threshold are stocked with found objects and doll parts that relate to the many mental diagnoses Blackbridge has received over the years. The assembled figure's pose suggests that she is overwhelmed by the symbols displayed beyond her reach, as well as by her own desire to view and understand them. In "Four Diagnoses," a figure composed of a variety of woods, scrap plastic, scrap metal, brass rod, bone, and a doll's head, leans farther to the right side on one leg, while the other leg made from bone, extends to the left. The figure looks so unbalanced that she seems to be in the process of toppling over. Below the figure is a shelf that showcases items similar to the ones in "Five Diagnoses." In her artist's statement, Blackbridge writes that these works refer to the "all too common experience of having a flock of labels that follow you about" (2013). She discusses the many diagnoses she has received about her learning disability and depression, and how they have placed her in "boxes." She goes on to write that the many medications she has been prescribed have caused mental changes, as well as kidney failure. Her "treatments" have had adverse results. The title "Mistaken Identities" likewise refers to multiple diagnoses, as well as the loss of a sense of self. The figure in "Mistaken Identity 1," composed of driftwood, padauk, fir, bone, and brass rod, leans to her left side, with her skinny arms extended out. She looks unbalanced on her legs; one is a piece of wood with cuts that only touches the floor at one thin point. Her other leg, made from a curved bone, is the primary support and seems to overpower the rest of the body.

In a similar vein, Blackbridge had a solo show in 2016 at the Tangled Arts and Disability Gallery in Toronto, titled "Constructed Identities." The exhibit consisted of mixed media and wood carving figures, many with fractured anatomies or missing limbs, which were meant to question how disability is constructed by society and visual culture as abnormal and broken. The 28 figures, vibrantly posed, poignantly project themes of disability, diversity, and sexuality; the title refers to "both the way the figures are built and to the ways that identities are inscribed on our bodies" (Ahsan 2016). The title, "Constructed Identities" refers to the social construction of identities, as well as the processes which resulted in the exuberant figures; human bodies are here assembled from scavenged forms and materials. They are asymmetrical and disjointed, and yet they extend their appendages and project their forms into surrounding space. Many of the figures commemorate Blackbridge's friends and family members who have died and incorporate materials that have personal significance for the artist. Like the "Liminal Barbie," "Five Diagnoses," and "Mistaken Identity" series, these figures display crip aesthetics by showing impairments and disability. They feature one of the most visible impairments, the amputations of limbs, and many of the figures struggle to balance and move freely. The bodies look like they have endured a lot of strain in their rough, fractured materials, and yet they are in dynamic poses, showing disability as active. As figures on the wall in a gallery space, they also show off their corporeal differences from what viewers might usually expect to see exhibited in a gallery – conventional, passive poses of women.

Conclusion

Blackbridge's work showcases what I designate as 'crip' aesthetics. Her works in a gallery space invite viewers to express their reactions to them and incorporate those perceptions in book forms. Her figures address her and others' impairment, as well as their social construction as disabled. They are materially constructed from found objects and, in pose, defy what viewers may assume their bodies can do. Her many group projects reflect and forge new connections between Blackbridge and other minorities, in particular, survivors of the mental health care system, feminists, and lesbians. These identities overlap and inform one another in visual forms in Blackbridge's work. Throughout her oeuvres, Blackbridge features multi-dimensional bodies in physical and/or political acts that celebrate their differences from the so-called norm and exhibit corporeal pride.

References

Ahsan, Sadaf. 2016. "Tangled, Toronto's First Accessible Art Gallery for Disabled Artists, Is Bringing the Outsiders In." *National Post.* 21 June 2016. Accessed 1 August 2017. Available: http://nationalpost.com/entertainment/tangled-torontos-first-accessible-art-gallery-for-disabled-artists-is-bringing-the-outsiders-in.

Blackbridge, Persimmon. 2013. "Liminal Barbie." In Kickstart 5 *Magic/Realism Juried Art Exhibit.* Accessed 1 August 2017. Available: https://magicrealism-art.weebly.com/persimmon-blackbridge.html.

Blackbridge, Persimmon. 1998. *Sunnybrook: A True Story with Lies.* Vancouver: Press Gang Publishers.

Blackbridge, Persimmon, and Gilhooly, Sheila. 1985. *Still Sane.* Vancouver: Press Gang Publishers.

Constructed Identities. n.d. *Tangled Art and Disability.* Accessed 1 August 2017. Available: http://tangledarts.org/gallery/season-2015-2016/constructed-identities.

Hughes, Nym. 1985. "Because She Was a Lesbian." In Persimmon Blackbridge and Sheila Gilhooly ed. *Still Sane.* Vancouver: Press Gang Publishers, 82–84.

Kafer, Alison. 2013. *Feminist Queer Crip.* Bloomington: Indiana University Press.

Klein, Bonnie Sher in collaboration with Persimmon Blackbridge. 1998. *Out of the Blue: One Woman's Story of Stroke, Love, and Survival.* Berkeley: Wildcat Canyon Press.

McRuer, Robert. 2006. *Crip Theory: Cultural Signs of Queerness and Disability.* New York: New York University Press.

NiHera, Dee dee. 1985. "Still Mad." In Persimmon Blackbridge and Sheila Gilhooly ed. *Still Sane.* Vancouver: Press Gang Publishers, 90–94.

Queer Media Database Quebec/Canada. n.d. *Persimmon Blackbridge.* Accessed 1 August 2017. Available: www.mediaqueer.ca/artist/persimmon-blackbridge.

Randall, Nora D. 1985. "Still Happening." In Persimmon Blackbridge and Sheila Gilhooly ed. *Still Sane.* Vancouver: Press Gang Publishers, 85–89.

Sandahl, Carrie. 2003. "Queering the Crip or Cripping the Queer? Intersections of Queer and Crip Identities in Solo Autobiographical Performance." *GLQ: A Journal of Lesbian and Gay Studies.* 9 (1–2): 25–56.

Siebers, Tobin. 2010. *Disability Aesthetics.* Ann Arbor: The University of Michigan Press.

Stewart, Susan, Blackbridge, Persimmon, and Jones, Lizard. 2002. *Drawing the Lines: Sexual Politics on the Wall.* Vancouver: Press Gang Publishers.

18

Exquisite model

Riva Lehrer, portraiture, and risk

Ann M. Fox

It is an exciting time to be engaged with disability arts, particularly where the visual arts are concerned. Again and again, artists are taking up the critical question: how can we continue to enhance inclusivity for disabled people through the arts, and in a way that values disability as an identity, aesthetic, and epistemology? Access within the arts, for example, has been deployed as a rallying point and as a generative conceit, taken up with verve by disabled artists. Wheelchair user and artist Park McArthur (2014), in her installation *Ramps*, offered a pointed commentary on the limited accessibility of downtown New York City galleries by presenting in one place a collection of the actual catch-as-catch-can portable ramps that galleries used to provide her access. Carmen Papalia (2018) has privileged non-visual learning in his blind field shuttle walks and developed tenets for open access derived from disability experience that result in inclusion for all people. The concepts outlined in his "Accessibility Manifesto" reimagine "normalcy as a continuum of embodiments, identities, realities and learning styles, and [operate] under the tenet that interdependence is central to a radical restructuring of power" (Papalia 1998). Georgina Kleege (2018) argues for the transformation of audio description into its own kind of aesthetic, "elevated from its current status as a segregated accommodation outside the general public's awareness and launched into the new media—a literary/interpretive form with infinite possibilities" (108).

However, we cannot discuss this contemporary and more public performative work around access and visibility without acknowledging the foundational work of Riva Lehrer, a Chicago-based disabled artist who has advanced the purposeful and progressive inclusion of disabled people as the subjects of portraiture. She has been drawing and painting disabled subjects who are imagined quite differently from their aesthetic forbears since 1995. For example, with her well-known early series *Circle Stories* (1997–2004), Lehrer created a kind of disability hagiography. In these portraits, Lehrer ennobled significant figures in disability arts and activism, evoking visual rhetorics of portraiture that, as Rosemarie Garland-Thomson (2010) has pointed out, are more typically used to depict social and cultural elites. In situating these subjects in the pantheon of portraiture, Lehrer places them front and centre as worthy of being revered and remembered. So, for example, the series includes images of playwright and novelist Susan Nussbaum, genderqueer eco-critic Eli Clare, disability rights activists Mike Ervin and Anna Stonum, and performance artist Tekki Lomnicki. As portraits

Ann M. Fox

of so-called disability royalty, the images create a radical intervention into cultural history, art history, and historiography. Yet they do not purport to serve as a canon. Instead, their presence prompts a viewer to wonder: who else is not here? Who else has been summarily erased by the history of portraiture, and who else belongs in an ongoing visual history of disability rights and culture, and of citizenship more generally?

Lehrer's work in *Circle Stories* also creates familiarity with a more diverse range of embodiments, in effect defamiliarising viewers' sense of the normate while underscoring a variety that better reflects the human condition than monolithic sameness; as Lehrer (2000) writes:

> I hope, by painting the people who move me, who attract me, that I can create a space for looking and thinking, to have a preliminary way of being comfortable in the face of the unfamiliar. If we have an intimate and non-judgmental forum to look at people with disabilities, perhaps a more mutual recognition may arise.
>
> *(381)*

She uncouples disabled bodies from the traditional metaphorical meanings and imagined lives of tragedy or malfeasance that have been thrust upon them. In her essay for *The New York Times* "Disability" series, entitled "Where All Bodies Are Exquisite," Lehrer (2017c) further elaborated on this ethos:

> These portraits do not ask for sympathy, or empathy, or even that viewers agree that the subjects are beautiful. I simply want viewers to daydream the life of the person before them. To stretch ourselves toward a world where all bodies are exquisite, as they flow between all possible forms of what it is to be human.

In her work, Lehrer therefore implicitly invites us to contemplate what Alison Kafer (2013) calls crip futurity, or the idea that disabled bodies will remain an enduring and important part of human existence as time goes forward. Disabled people have been, and will continue to be, a meaningful part of how the future of humanity unfolds, valued rather than erased through cure or genetic engineering. The portraits suggest subjects who are resilient, adaptable, enduring, and ubiquitous.

It is possible to see inspiration in several of the *Circle Stories* images, but of a kind quite different from what activists and scholars have labelled 'inspiration porn' (that is images in which disability, held up as motivational, is actually effaced, since its presence exists only to create a sentimental response in non-disabled viewers). Rather, disability studies scholars have seen in Lehrer's work the catalyst for and embodiment of theoretical arguments they themselves have developed. Kafer (2013) describes the *Circle Stories* portrait of Eli Clare, for instance, as the model for a significant kind of critical intersectionality around ecocriticism, gender studies, and disability studies, calling it "breathtaking in its conjuring of an entire ecosystem, one that recognises humans as inextricably part of nature. Its power also lies in its mythology, in its blending together of environmental, disability, and gender politics" (147). Kafer (2013) observes that Lehrer "presents a model of embodied environmentalism, of a concern with how we can get on together, earth, bone, and body" (148). In her consideration of the visual relations between starers and starees, Rosemarie Garland-Thomson (2009) holds up Lehrer's portrait of solo performer Tekki Lomnicki as an example of how disabled people subversively negotiate the stare:

> Interrupted in media res, she smiles out engagingly as if to the paparazzi. Comfortable with such exposure, she greets her starers dressed in a sexy and sweet white slip, black

Riva Lehrer, portraiture, and risk

Mary Janes, and one arm crutch, its partner tossed amongst a pile of outfits. Buxom, lipsticked, coiffed, feminine, and substantial, Tekki Lomnicki is mistress not victim of the stares she draws and the world in which she lives.

(176)

Linda Ware (2008) has discussed using Lehrer's art as a pedagogic tool to teach future educators how to consider disability as a lived and embodied identity. Ware (2011) points out that Lehrer's portraits can be used efficaciously by teachers:

Children and youth—with or without disabilities—must be provided both the encouragement and the opportunity to understand disability as another aspect of human diversity through explicit instruction within the curriculum. Reclaiming disability as a meaningful identity with productive value in the arts promises one such starting point for educators.

(197)

It is clear that Lehrer's work speaks powerfully across disciplines to underscore, again and again, the dignity of visibility and the richness of disability both as an identity and as a way of knowing.

Over time, since first creating *Circle Stories*, Lehrer has recreated the disabled body in portraiture with even more complexity, ranging from her own self-portraits to a more symbol-laden series like *Totems and Familiars*. Lehrer's most recent work, however, has unfolded in two projects that mark a decided turn, given the ways in which they invigorate and extend out a theorisation of disability in the visual. The first is a series of portraits entitled *The Risk Pictures* (2014–2017). This time, Lehrer approached possible subjects on the basis of their being virtuosic in their fields; some had an obvious connection to disability, some less so or not at all. Not all of the portraits foreground disability, and we cannot fully know the disability identity, if any, of their subjects. The second project is Lehrer's most recent collaborative project, first shown in August 2017, an installation entitled *Portrait of Carrie Sandahl: A Project in Four Parts*, created in collaboration with disability arts and culture scholar Carrie Sandahl and sound artist Christophe Preissing. In the gallery, a portrait Lehrer has painted of Sandahl is contextualised with sound recordings of discussions and ambient noises from the sessions in which Sandahl posed; the chair on which she sat, and the pillows and throws with which Lehrer made her comfortable; and sheets of handmade paper on which Lehrer and Sandahl have written responses to each other and reflections on embodiment, pain, and their process.

I am intrigued in the shift relative to thinking about what disability can do for visual art and beyond which *The Risk Pictures* and *Portrait of Carrie Sandahl: A Project in Four Parts* represent. Like *Circle Stories*, these works depended heavily on collaboration between artist and subject. They differ from *Circle Stories*, however, in that not all *The Risk Pictures* necessarily depict apparent disability, while *Portrait of Carrie Sandahl: A Project in Four Parts* engages with visible and invisible disability. Yet whether disability is apparent or not, all the images from these more recent series of images are 'cripped' in ways that privilege different facets of disability experience through representation. The traditionally authoritative position of the portraitist is made precarious; the work that results is a mutually constituted and more nuanced representation of disability, both individually and generally. In doing so, Lehrer's recent works underscore the notion, also advanced by disability studies scholars such as Tobin Siebers (2010) and Michael Bérubé (2016), that the study of disability representation and aesthetics need not, indeed cannot, rest with mimetic representation alone. Instead, the risks she takes in her latest work provide an exquisite model for how we might recognise how artworks evoke disability as an identity that is embodied and relational. In this essay, I will briefly discuss how a representative image from *The Risk Pictures* initiates this model, and how *Portrait of Carrie Sandahl: A Project in Four Parts* brings it to a full fruition. I will then close by suggesting how embracing Lehrer's example of exquisite risk can be a powerful means toward promoting further inclusion for all contingent bodies through the arts.

The Risk Pictures

The Risk Pictures were not the first time Lehrer grounded her work in collaboration. Such mutuality was first at the heart of *Circle Stories*:

> The portraiture method is a circular one, involving extensive interviews with each participant. We talk about their lives, work, and experience of disability. We suggest possible imagery, seeking imagery that accurately reflects their experience. In this way, we arrive at a collaborative composition.
>
> *(Lehrer 2000, 382)*

To upend the traditional hierarchical relationship between portraitist and subject, and to enhance her own vulnerability, Lehrer's collaborative process with *The Risk Pictures* became more extensive and material. Her method consisted of this: after creating the initial drawing of her subject, Lehrer then turned her home studio over to them, leaving them alone with both the image and her space. They could explore her apartment to their heart's content; most significantly, they were asked to make any changes they wanted to the image, adding or deleting things, even damaging it (or effectively 'disabling' the artwork). Lehrer neither limited nor defined the changes and even responded to them; she also shared a percentage of the proceeds from the portrait's sale with her subject. It did not always go as planned. Lehrer found that many of the subjects, chosen because they were virtuosic in their own fields, found themselves apprehensive when working outside their areas of expertise and tentative about making marks of any kind. Perhaps not unexpectedly, being highly accomplished in one's own field often seemed concomitant with a hesitation to travel into an area of more unfamiliarity and discomfort. And sometimes, too, the changes which subjects made deeply challenged Lehrer's own vision of the work.

Her subjects have included A. Finn Enke, a founder of the field of transgender studies, who added small figures from their comics-making to the portrait; filmmaker and writer Chase Joynt who chose the source photos for the images against which Joynt is posed; disability dance artist Alice Sheppard, who added dancing feet and small markings on her stomach; graphic novel scholar Hillary Chute, who added images from the comics she loves most; disability studies scholar Lennard Davis, behind whom Lehrer pencilled in "CODA" (standing for "child of Deaf adult") again and again; and novelist David Mitchell, who inscribed a journal entry of his last day visiting Chicago on his portrait. The choice of subjects was important not simply because they were experts; their pursuits all, in one way or another, subvert convention and reflect a broader understanding of embodied identity. Davis, for example, is a foundational scholar in disability studies whose book *Enforcing Normalcy* analyses normalcy as a social and historical construct; Joynt's and Enke's artistic and scholarly work interrogates gender; Chute works on the graphic novel, a genre at the intersection of visual art and textual narrative; Mitchell has fictionalised his own stuttering and (as the father of an autistic son) translated works by young autistic author Naoki Higashida; and Alice Sheppard, a wheelchair dancer, is an innovator in dance with her company, Kinetic Light.

Riva Lehrer, portraiture, and risk

The risk Lehrer and her subjects took was a critical one, not as simple as inverting positions of power and rendering someone who is highly competent in one area suddenly 'incompetent.' Rather, what resulted was mutuality, tentativeness, and the challenge of shaping a work together across different experiences of embodiment in a medium typically insisting on the individuated vision of the artist and a hierarchical relationship to the model.

For example, consider Lennard Davis' portrait (Figure 18.1; see description below portrait). Davis' picture on its very surface upends convention; the vividly and richly patterned couch on which he sits threatens to engulf him and become the focus of the image.

Indeed, Davis literally recedes into the furniture as his outfit grows less distinct, particularly as a viewer's gaze moves from the top of the portrait to the bottom. The spectacle of the couch turns our attention to the rather nondescript body sitting on it. Davis' slightly dishevelled appearance is humanising and refutes the notion that a body must be garbed

Figure 18.1 Riva Lehrer, *The Risk Pictures: Lennard Davis*. Mixed media and collage on paper, 2016

Description: This portrait shows a white, middle-aged man with short white hair and a closely trimmed beard. He is drawn in pencil and shades of grey; he is wearing a crew-neck sweatshirt and white pants; there are multiple creases in each. His right arm and hand are in his lap; his left arm and hand rest on the arm of the couch on which he sits. He gazes calmly at the spectator. The couch is vividly coloured; the cushions are red and gold, while the arm and edge of the cushions are in royal and aqua blues. The patterns are vivid and contemporary: alternating red and gold circles on the back cushions and alternating red and gold flowers on the seat cushions. On the outer edges of the arm and cushions are flowers in white and varying blues. The flowers appear to be daisy-like and chrysanthemum-like. The effect is vivid, contemporary, and striking, especially in comparison to Davis' paler appearance. Behind Davis, written over and over again in small letters in yellow pencil on line after line is CODA [child of Deaf adults]. Davis has written lines himself over these lines: quotes from literature, prayer, and popular song that reference hearing, variants of the word "deaf," and huge versions of the words "NOISE" and "SILENCE."

regally or formally to be worth portraying. Davis' written additions to the image further particularise it, making his own personal history, including his disability history as the child of Deaf adults, more visible. On either side of his head, he has written two columns of words:

space	between
drear	healing
dear	hearing
deaf	heading
dead	

Davis sets deafness and hearing in literal conversation around him through these columns and with other words he places on the drawing, as when he juxtaposes the oversized words "noise" and "silence." As his two lists suggest, between the positions "deaf" and "hearing" are many points in the "space between." For example, the space between dear/deaf, drear/deaf, and deaf/dead is literally a letter, a verbal slippage that underscores the constructed nature of language as well as the multi-varied nature of embodied experience (are you dear? deaf? dead?).

Davis' specific textual additions to the picture Lehrer has drawn of him reminds us that Deafness is also a relational identity. In the different snippets of text he has pencilled in on either side of his head and on the margins of the portrait, he evokes the social interactions that happen around hearing, and the contrast between not hearing at all and hearing all too well ("What were you saying?" "Can you keep it down?"). The quotes he has inscribed echo his Jewish heritage ("Hear O Israel the Lord Our God is One") and life as a literary scholar (with verses from William Shakespeare's *King Lear* and Samuel Taylor Coleridge's *The Rime of the Ancient Mariner*). But they also suggest the dread the non-disabled have around disabled bodies as monstrous (the line from Coleridge, "Like one that on a lonesome road doth walk in fear and dread," was requoted in Mary Shelley's *Frankenstein*) and animalistic (Lear's "Reason not the need" speech, quoted by Davis, asserts his own humanity in the face of his family's disdain for his comfort as an old man). As Davis' passages here wryly suggest, ableism/audism is ubiquitous, from sacred prayer ("Hear O Israel") to James Taylor songs ("All you have to do is call and I'll be there").

The eraser marks and crossings-out Davis creates suggest the intense labour of revision and scrutiny as he settles on which texts he finally wants to inscribe around his image. This process echoes the ways in which Lehrer is trying to render visible the collaboration between herself and her subject. The labour of Lehrer and her artist's assistant in writing "CODA" over and over and over honours Davis' invocation of his own history, and links the careful, repetitive labour of both portraiture and disability studies work. His own effort and experience as a child of Deaf adults is ultimately represented as a boon and not a burden by Davis when he writes, "Dear mom and dad thanks for the gift." This exchange between Davis and Lehrer results in more than a contribution from the subject to make the work more 'real' by enhancing personal biography. The interchange between Davis and Lehrer, in its mutuality and mutual agency, results in a depiction that moves past individual biography and gives substance to disability as a variable, and valuable, physical and socially constructed identity.

Portrait of Carrie Sandahl: A Project in Four Parts

Portrait of Carrie Sandahl: A Project in Four Parts (2017) further extends Lehrer's attention to and representation of disability as an embodied and relational experience. This can only happen, however, through the particular form of Lehrer's process. As Lehrer (2017a) points out in one of the wall texts of the installation, "Portraiture is, at base, an encounter between two people. The comfort of one or both significantly affects the final image/object." As she writes in her artist's statement, when we confront the portrait-as-object, we are "encouraged to think that the portrait object is the main – and only – point of the encounter between artist and subject." She continues,

> *I do not believe that to be true.* Portraiture is at base an encounter between two people. I propose that the real product of a portrait is the relationship between artist and subject, and the extent to which either or both are changed by the act of mutual looking. A painting or drawing can take weeks or months; it's a long time to spend together.

And so, in the project, Lehrer (2017a) worked to continue the objective she initiated in *Circle Stories* and *The Risk Pictures*: to demystify the conditions under which a portrait is created, and to "encourage viewers to imagine and question the circumstances under which all other portraiture takes place." In the course of *Carrie Sandahl: A Project in Four Parts*, something else happens: the installation in its different facets creates a rich understanding of disability as an embodied and a relational experience. It is not that these two aspects of disability have been underrepresented in culture. Rather, they have been ubiquitous to destructive effect: disability embodiment has been equated to misery, individuated suffering, and as something which non-disabled spectators assume they understand thoroughly. Similarly, disability's relational qualities have all been directed hierarchically in representation: disabled people must be the grateful recipients of attention from charitable and medical quarters. In contrast, through the collaboration of Lehrer, Sandahl, and Preissing, these two aspects of disability identity, embodiment, and interrelation are given new representational possibility. In its turn, the installation becomes a model for the way those of us who work with textual and visual representations, as well as disability in other contexts, might understand extant representations of disability in art with more complexity, and as a means to promote inclusion in the future.

I will discuss its broader meanings in a moment, but first let me describe the installation, which was rich with detail. Coming into it, a viewer passed around a tall white screen made of white cloth and framed by white plastic pipe that blocked it from the view of the larger gallery. The screen was added by the Evanston Art Center over concerns about having a nude portrait so near to where children's art classes were being held. The debatable merits of that decision aside, it turned out to be a happy accident that had a couple of salutary effects for me as a viewer. To begin with, the white screen suggested a medical setting, an intriguing irony given that this installation serves as a counter to the diagnostic gaze. Given that the installation was about conveying a sense of the process of collaboration between portraitist and subject, the screen also drew the spectator into that sense of intimacy. Rounding the corner of the screen, a spectator saw the portrait of Sandahl (Figure 18.2, described below) on the left far wall; the portrait is a nude which shows Sandahl holding herself up by bondage straps, toys for sexual play that also function to support her standing pose. A series of 23 texts written on handmade paper by both Lehrer and Sandahl covered most of the right far wall.

At the far end of the wall with the texts sat a furniture arrangement recreating the conditions under which Sandahl posed. Before the spectator was the actual grey, padded office swivel chair, with a striped throw pillow, heating pad, and soft blanket on the seat. There was a step-stool with a pizza box on it adding just a shade more height, making it perfectly poised to support Sandahl's feet; off to the right side of the chair sat a small side table with a batik scarf covering it, a china plate covered with cookies, and a small teapot, ready to provide sustenance. (At the opening, the cookies were available to anyone to eat, but the audience hesitated to break the fourth wall in this way until urged on by Lehrer.) The chair and its

Ann M. Fox

Figure 18.2 Riva Lehrer, *Carrie Sandahl*, Acrylic on cradled wood panel, 2017

Description: This picture is a full-length nude of a middle-aged white woman with chin-length, straight blonde hair. She is standing facing forward, looking off past the spectator slightly to the right. She appears to have a curvature to her spine, since her right shoulder is slightly higher than her left; there are visible scars running from her belly button to her pubic area. She holds herself up with black bondage straps; each wrist is cuffed, and the strap that attaches to the cuff is passed behind her back and grasped by the opposite hand. The remnants of the leather straps dangle from each hand; the length of leather on the right is longer than that on the left. She wears a necklace and nipple clamps draped on a chain around her neck. She stands against a white, weathered wall from which the plaster appears to be peeling and crumbling in parts. There is the shadow of a windowpane, and she casts two shadows. She stands on a blonde wood floor, and the baseboard where the wall meets the floor is damaged and missing in places; it also has a triangle-shaped opening through which sea glass tumbles. There are pieces of sea glass on the floor to Sandahl's right, and pieces of plaster on the floor to the left.

artefacts supported Lehrer's goal to recreate the experience of collaboration; as disability historian Katherine Ott (2014) writes:

> Objects give a tactile, sensory dimension to the past. They provide access to lived experience and nonverbal aspects of relationships. For historians, one of the most difficult

modalities of peoples' lives to retrieve from the past is how bodies move…Objects can help restore that lost knowledge.

(120)

If, as Ott (2014) proposes, "People come back into the story when attention is given to objects" (120), the items here from sitting for a portrait give us several things: a sense of the dimensions of Sandahl's body, and the workarounds she and Lehrer made so she could sit comfortably. It is important to note that the installation also pays careful attention to Lehrer's embodiment. We read in some of the wall texts, for example, how Lehrer manipulates her studio to make the labour-intensive work of painting manageable for her disabled body.

This emphasis on the materiality of the bodies of portraitist and subject was reinforced aurally as well. Speakers on both walls played a sound installation made by Christophe Preissing, who recorded the sessions during which Sandahl posed for Lehrer over several months. Lehrer described wanting to give the viewer the sense of being in a restaurant and overhearing snippets of conversation; there is no clear narrative line discernible, but over the course of the 30-minute loop, several ambient sounds and snippets of conversation (echoing topics addressed by the women in their textual conversation) compete for our attention. We hear, for example, the sounds of Lehrer painting, wiping the wood panel with rags, and spraying water on the portrait. This reminds us that if it is laborious to sit for a portrait, the work of creating one is also meticulous and demanding for the portraitist.

One aspect that is particularly emphasised by Lehrer's process and its product here is the embodied nature of disability. This may seem obvious or simple, but given that disabled bodies time and again have been compelled to carry metaphorical or symbolic weight, this is no small thing. At a basic level, the very number of wall texts − 23 − suggests the number of chromosome pairs on any given cell, upon which things can go differently and result in disability. One of Sandahl's (Lehrer, Sandahl & Preissing 2017) texts underscores the leap spectators too often make from difference to defect: "Ableism in the arts means that we aren't anything but metaphors for other people's—for nondisabled people's—angst or sense of alienation. That we are the other that defines the norm, instead of being anything unto ourselves." But the installation tackles this notion head-on, rejecting, for example, the notion that pain should be discounted or erased. Sandahl (Lehrer, Sandahl & Preissing 2017) wryly notes that when it comes to pain, "There's always this urge to say you're more than your pain, return to your life, your pain's ruining your life." She resists the notion that this is an either/or; instead, she insists,

> You are not your pain? That doesn't make sense to me. And I feel like I am my pain. My pain is me. My body is responding. That's me. That's who I am. There's the urge for people to say 'you're more than your pain. The pain has ruined your life.' And that doesn't make sense for us, I'd say.
>
> *(Lehrer, Sandahl & Preissing 2017)*

Instead, Sandahl's (Lehrer, Sandahl & Preissing 2017) texts try to give a sense of how she experiences pain:

> So there's always this narrative that you get rid of, if there's a flare, you tame it, or you deal with it, but it's kind of…I feel like it's more of a spiral. A spiral or some sort of a sine wave. Spiral <u>on</u> a sine wave? There's always multiple twistings in and out. And then no way to talk about pain having value except for listening to your body to tell you how to get out of it. But what is it we learn? What do we know? How does pain empower?

Lehrer's portrait of Sandahl plays with this pain paradox; Sandahl is pictured with nipple clamps draped on a chain around her neck, and bondage straps with which she holds herself. Why is some pain, the image seems to ask, regarded as pleasure, while the only way disabled people are imagined is as having a kind of pain both torturous and separate from their identities? The portrait retorts against this idea, given that the straps causing pain also support Sandahl. In the moulding near Sandahl's right foot, there is a wide gap through which stones and sea glass pour; these seem to reference Sandahl's Oregon upbringing, but also the beauty that emerges from fragmentation. Waves of pain are repetitive, as are breakers; here, the glass is buffeted into beauty by submitting to the unceasing, pounding action of the ocean.

Her wall texts work to give voice to Sandahl's embodied experience with pain, refusing to categorise it simplistically. For example, she describes for Riva the mental experience of what she calls "revving," a kind of disconnection from her pain, and its results:

> I disassociate. That's my problem. Maybe I like to be tortured. That's part of my problem. Ha Ha! That's how I've dealt with my pain, just turn it in to [sic] something. Ok. Ok. I'm going to stretch my neck. I think our bodies are more fragile just structurally. You and me, Riva. So I have good body awareness, I've learned that. When my mind stops running and my mind clears, that's when I feel my pain. I become aware of things. My problem is I'm an over-achiever, and they are trying to get me to pace myself.
>
> *(Lehrer, Sandahl & Preissing 2017)*

Other passages, rather than describing the "revving," directly perform it; they have the quality of stream-of-conscious arias and help make manifest what is in Sandahl's mind, itself also "multiple twistings in and out," as words dip, swoop, repeat, and double back on themselves:

> I won't break. I won't break. I won't. Break. I break won't break. Break. Won't. I. I. I. Won't break. I won't won't break. I won't break. Break. I won't break. Won't won't won't. Break. I won't break. I won't break. Won't I.
>
> *(Lehrer, Sandahl & Preissing 2017)*

Sandahl's bodymind is ever in flux, and her pain and "revvings" are part of that. It is a contingency that is, of course, shared by all bodies, but one which disability makes particularly visible. Lehrer and Sandahl make sure to emphasise this notion of the multiplicity of the body, rather than its being in one, fixed state permanently captured by the portraitist. That Sandahl as subject some days ate, some days rested, some days posed for extended times, suggests this. The draft drawings of the painting that bracket either end of the texts themselves thwart linear narratives of cohesive progress; if we read from left to right, the progress of the drawings actually regresses. At one point, one of Sandahl's wall texts reads, "Am I casting a shadow?" That seemingly innocuous comment points us toward the painting itself, in which Sandahl casts multiple shadows (Lehrer, Sandahl & Preissing 2017). The backdrop against which she is imagined is not a beautiful or cohesive whiteness, but a plaster wall with peeling and fragmented bits. In her turn, Sandahl (Lehrer, Sandahl & Preissing 2017) finds in the painting new ways to celebrate her disabled body; one text, for example, exclaims to Lehrer in response to the painting,

> I have square palms? Who knew? Nobody's going to mess with me now. Those hands. Just the grip. That's my shining glory. Because no one else could grip anything or open a jar. I'm like, 'Allow me!' 'Hand it over!'

That grip, emerging from years of crutch use, is a point of pride and strength.

Disability is also revealed to be relational in Lehrer's work with Sandahl. Most immediately, in the descriptions of caregiving, we are not only reminded of embodiment, but also that caregiving can be rewritten by disabled people themselves. Feminist critiques of caregiving have pointed to race, class, and gender as key aspects in considering the power dynamics of the caregiving relationship, but they have left largely unexamined the individuality and agency of disabled people. In *Carrie Sandahl: A Project in Four Parts*, disabled people have agency to engage in important and mutual care for one another. This is most obviously manifest in the physical caregiving detailed in the installation. The presence of the chair in which Sandahl sat and all its attendant ephemera remind us of this. The china plate next to the right arm rest suggests the importance of sustaining the energy of the subject's body; it, and the blanket are artefacts of a tender caregiving. The texts on the wall next to the chair reinforce this: they document these and other things Lehrer did to give Sandahl comfort:

> I loaned her my disabled parking space in front of my house so that she would not need to walk far.
> I met her at the gate and worked the doors of the birdcage elevator up to the 6th floor.
> Posing sessions were divided between standing full length poses and seated close-up sessions.
> We made sure there were plenty of breaks, not just for Carrie, but for my own needs as well.
> I made sure that BOTH our seating was supportive and comfortable.
>
> *(Lehrer, Sandahl & Preissing 2017)*

Further down the wall, there is also a list of the food Lehrer fed Sandahl, tender in its specificity and detail ("Chicken + mushroom pie. Pita Pizza. Hummous + Baba Ganoush…Brandy Toddys. IBUPROPHEN. [sic]") (Lehrer, Sandahl & Preissing 2017). All this suggests a kind of need for bodily sustenance and tending that suggests a mutual recognition of the disability experience, and careful care of members of the disability community for one another.

That relational mutuality, however, extends past caregiving to being oriented toward the community. Disability art is not just for a presumably non-disabled audience; as Sandahl notes about the disability community, "we are in relation to each other. We figure out our own thing." The installation also documents the give-and-take of the process of creating this work within the disability community, for the community. This is figured most particularly in Sandahl's submitting to the process of being seen by Lehrer. Sandahl is in the presence of someone who takes her pain seriously; she is also in the presence of someone who takes her personhood seriously. Here, the community turns to its own members for a better understanding of embodiment. As Lehrer writes in one of her wall texts,

> However, a positive and TRUTHFUL image might be the first time the subject sees themselves as acceptable. Even beautiful. Most of my collaborators have been people with disabilities and/or from feminist/LGBTQ/racial/ethnic communities. Most have dealt with continuous stigma.—When I first began this portrait work, about 30 years ago, I could barely tolerate being a person with disabilities. My collaborators have shown me other, better ways to live in my body. Without them I doubt I would have survived so long.
>
> *(Lehrer, Sandahl & Preissing 2017)*

And so Sandahl's (Lehrer, Sandahl & Preissing 2017) wall texts document her own process of submitting to how Lehrer looks at her: "Hey Riva, I'm tired of cropping my photos. Don't crop me. I want you to look. Ok? Riva? Carrie." The paradox, of course, is that in

Ann M. Fox

granting such permission, Sandahl must submit to Lehrer's gaze, a paradox Sandahl (Lehrer, Sandahl & Preissing 2017) acknowledges in one of the wall texts:

So I guess I'm reconciling things I'm learning and experiencing with what I'm seeing that you're seeing. I'm having a "mindfulness" moment—looking without judgement. And I'm learning from it. That's an important thing. I feel like we talked a lot and we looked at a lot of pictures. I like the painting much better than I like the photo. Well, the painting is more nuanced and the photo makes me feel naked. And the painting feels...um...I don't know. It's not naked. It's a subjective idea of your body. And there's a way you can own it and distance yourself at the same time...You know...a part of what happens in these pieces...I'm producing your body through my body.

As the subject of the portrait, Sandahl (Lehrer, Sandahl & Preissing 2017) relinquishes control to Lehrer; her nudity becomes both subject and symbol as she makes herself vulnerable:

I don't want to have to decide anything. Unless you want me to. I'm tired. I'm cold. Want to be seen and at the same time I want to hide conceal. Edit. Crop. Tell me what to do. I hide. I'm marked. Secret marks. Marks someone might see if they looked.

On another sign, she writes a boldface command to Lehrer: **Break Me. I Feel Safe** (Lehrer, Sandahl & Preissing 2017).

Submission has been fraught for disabled people. And yet, to submit to a member of her community as a subject is to see her body in a new way and claim the rightness of that view:

To lead like this. I have to submit. I have to submit to being a leader. I submit to my community. So I must submit to lead. To stand up for myself is to submit. And that confuses me. To submit is to lead. To stand up for cripples is to submit.

(Lehrer, Sandahl & Preissing 2017)

It is a radical way of understanding and explaining her pain. But theirs is ultimately a mutually constituted image; as Lehrer (Lehrer, Sandahl & Preissing 2017) writes, "I won't speak for Carrie." The community created in microcosm between them, as we listen to them gently laugh and talk to each other in the sound installation about their pain, bodies, and what their muscles are trying to do, stands in for the macrocosm for the larger crip community. They decide who looks and how they look at one another; written in pencil, dotting the wall around the texts, are notations by Sandahl and Lehrer (Lehrer, Sandahl & Preissing 2017) that echo the conversation they have had and the journey they have taken together:

Consent. Submit. Consent.
I break
You are your body
It's like waltzing
Break me. I won't break.
You are/are not your body
CRIP
Submit. Consent.
break me. break me. break me.
Consent
Body

Secret marks
We figure things

Lehrer and Sandahl do, indeed, "figure things" – Sandahl's figure, in Lehrer's view, becomes a way to figure out crip relationships and refigure disability representation.

Going forward: the lessons of risk

The process and products Lehrer builds across *The Risk Pictures* and *Carrie Sandahl: A Portrait* model a new way in which the relational and embodied qualities of disability simultaneously shape and emerge in representations that refigure our understanding of disability itself. Lehrer rejects a conventional, individuated sense of herself as an artist, and by extension, the paternalism to which disabled people are far too often subject. Instead, she has brought forward aspects of disability, such as an attention to interdependence and embodiment, that inform and enhance the work she creates to make it a more nuanced and genuine portrayal of the individual and communal experience of disability. The question for us viewers is: how can we use disability understanding to inform the work we engage, whether it is in a health-related field or an arts practice? How might our work foreground or even draw on disability knowledge in ways we might not have imagined, particularly when this means we risk giving up privilege or power accruing to (real or seeming) non-disabled status or privilege? Might we then risk engaging disability in new ways beyond simple diagnosis, with ourselves as the final and only arbiters of knowledge? What might then be more fully revealed about disability history, embodiment, and community?

Let me use my own work as an example. In my scholarly writing, I have focused on rereading characters in dramatic literature, and Lehrer's work provides a lesson for how to approach that work slant. More specifically, her process invites me to find a new way to define inclusion in representation through a critical re-evaluation of characters in some of our most canonical dramas, looking both forward and back. Think, for example, of how the speeches about Mary Tyrone's twisted hands or midnight ramblings in Eugene O'Neill's *Long Day's Journey into Night* might be seen as a way not just to diagnose her addiction but to invite us into her experience of it as meaningful and sometimes even important escape from a family that oppressively dismisses her as an older, arthritic woman, under the guise of love. Lillian Hellman's *The Little Foxes* shows a terminally ill man, a woman with anxiety and depression, a woman of colour, and a young girl forming a community necessary to fight the avarice of profiteers within their own family. What might seem like dependence and tragedy when the characters are individuated becomes coalition and strength when the characters band together in a new kind of community in which they give each other agency. Tony Kushner's *Angels in America* has addressed embodiment and community; Prior Walter moves in his life with AIDS from seeing himself as "polluted" to deserving of "more life," a life that is made meaningful and possible by the community of others who support him, and who he in his turn cares for.

During one part of the soundscape accompanying the installation in which her painting features, Sandahl describes showing a medical practitioner an image of the painting; the doctor literally cannot see the cuffs and bondage straps, thinking, instead, that they are ribbons, only seeing what they expect to see. Sandahl (Lehrer, Sandahl & Preissing 2017) recalls: "I told her that to me doing this painting was like an act of submission. She's like, well nobody's ever talked about it that way before. And I was like, well, I'm talking about it this way, now." Too often, when we are looking at disability representation, we see what we want to see instead of what might actually be there. If we risk following the exquisite model of this work, we might find that attending to cues in the work, especially when they run counter to what we might expect vis-à-vis disability, lets us be open to meanings that challenge those around which we have been conditioned to perceive disability. If we can interrogate our own spectatorship, we move toward a kind of mutuality and understanding through which inclusion becomes more meaningfully and capaciously embodied. That's worth the risk.

References

Bérubé, Michael. 2016. *The Secret Life of Stories: From Don Quixote to Harry Potter, How Understanding Intellectual Disability Transforms the Way We Read*. New York & London: New York University.

Garland-Thomson, Rosemarie. 2010. "Picturing People with Disabilities: Classical Portraiture as Reconstructive Narrative." In Richard Sandell, Josephine Todd, and Rosemarie Garland-Thomson ed. *Re-presenting Disability: Activism and Agency in the Museum*. London & New York: Routledge, 23–40.

Garland-Thomson, Rosemarie. 2009. *Staring: How We Look*. Oxford & New York: Oxford University Press.

Kafer, Alison. 2013. *Feminist, Queer, Crip*. Bloomington & Indianapolis: Indiana University Press.

Kleege, Georgia. 2018. *More Than Meets the Eye: What Blindness Brings to Art*. New York: Oxford University Press.

Lehrer, Riva. 2017a. "Artist's Statement." In Riva Lehrer, Carrie Sandahl, and Christophe Preissing. *Carrie Sandahl: A Project in Four Parts*.

Lehrer, Riva. 2017b. *Carrie Sandahl* [Acrylic on cradled wood panel].

Lehrer, Riva. 2017c. "Where All Bodies Are Exquisite." *The New York Times*, 9 August 2017. Accessed 9 November 2017. Available: www.nytimes.com/2017/08/09/opinion/where-all-bodies-are-exquisite.html.

Lehrer, Riva. 2016. *The Risk Pictures: Lennard Davis* [Mixed media and collage on paper].

Lehrer, Riva. 2014–2017. *The Risk Pictures*. Accessed 21 November 2017. Available: www.rivalehrerart.com/risk-pictures.

Lehrer, Riva. 2000. "*Circle Stories*: A Collaborative Project." *Feminist Studies*. 26 (2): 380–390.

Lehrer, Riva. 1997–2004. *Circle Stories*. Accessed 8 March 2018. Available: www.rivalehrerart.com/.

Lehrer, Riva, Sandahl, Carrie, and Preissing, Christophe. 2017. *Carrie Sandahl: A Project in Four Parts* [Acrylic on wood panel, pen on paper, graphite on wall, digital recording, furniture arrangement].

McArthur, Park. 2014. *Ramps* [wheelchair ramps (laminated chipboard, aluminum, a cabinet door, plywood, steel, two-by-fours, and other objects intended and not for this purpose)].

Ott, Katherine. 2014. "Disability Things: Material Culture and American Disability History, 1700–2000." In Susan Burch and Michael Rembis ed. *Disability Histories*. Urbana, Chicago & Springfield: University of Illinois Press, 119–135.

Papalia, Carmen. 2018. "An Accessibility Manifesto for the Arts." *Canadian Art*, 2 January 2018. Accessed 13 March 2018. Available: https://canadianart.ca/features/access-revived/.

Siebers, Tobin. 2010. *Disability Aesthetics*. Ann Arbor: University of Michigan Press.

Ware, Linda. 2011. "When Art Informs: Inviting Ways to See the Unexpected." *Learning Disability Quarterly*. 34 (3): 194–202.

Ware, Linda. 2008. "Worlds Remade: Inclusion through Engagement with Disability Art." *International Journal of Inclusive Education*. 12 (5–6): 563–583.

Part IV
Practices, politics, and the public sphere

19

On the fringe of the Fringe
Artmaking, access, rights, and community

Brian Lobel and Jess Thom

The Edinburgh Fringe is a particular beast. Every year, thousands of hopeful artists make their way to the world's largest open access festival to try to become the 'next big thing.' They come with their flyers, sleep in their eight-to-a-room overpriced August sublet, draw on all their enthusiasm to see as many shows as they can… and some even make a buck or two. There are any number of think pieces and Twitter conversations about the inaccessibility of the world's largest open access festival from an economic perspective – the horribly imbalanced deals between artists and venues, the increased price of housing in Edinburgh in August, the sheer number of shows that are demanding for limited media and audience (Youngs 2013; Gardner 2017; Mulholland 2017). However, as we hope the following interview will reveal, a conversation about accessibility – from a disability perspective – at the Fringe may start as a conversation about artmaking, but may seemingly and inevitably become a much more far-reaching conversation about rights, comfort, discomfort, and what it means to be part of a community.

While disabled and otherwise marginalised artists have been present at the Fringe for years, in the past few years, a number of concerted efforts have been made to address the festival's chronic and shameful lack of overall accessibility and to find new ways to showcase disabled artists and connect new audiences to their work. Platforms such as Unlimited and StopGap's iF have featured and supported the work of disabled performers through commissioning and co-marketing events, The Sick of the Fringe has attempted to provide more resource for artists sharing work on marginalised (and often hard-to-discuss) issues of health and well-being, and stand-up collective Abnormally Funny People continues to be a vanguard for disability-led comedy (Unlimited n.d.; iF n.d.; The Sick of the Fringe n.d.; Abnormally Funny People n.d.). In recent years, the prominence of work on mental illness and invisible disabilities has added further richness to this these conversations (Ellis-Petersen 2015; Mental Health Foundation 2017).

While the commercial appeal of the Edinburgh Fringe – and its promise of meteoric ascensions to fame – keeps the Fringe attractive and a useful tool for artists making radical work on the body and otherness, the problems which plague open access platforms and festivals generally (e.g. astronomic expense, inaccessible pop-up or temporary venues, press and marketing strategies which lack nuance or thoughtfully engaged language) may

243

disproportionately challenge artists whose lives and bodies are not often seen or discussed in public spheres.

What does it mean to be on the fringe of the Fringe?

The following transcript was an interview with Jess Thom – who performs as Touretteshero (a collaboration with Matthew Pountney) – whose show *Backstage in Biscuit Land* (2014) was transformative for the conversation about access at the Fringe. The goal of Touretteshero in 2014 was to bring *Biscuit Land* to a theatre audience, an audience who Thom had very rarely been a part of, due to (as she discusses in the show) the fact that theatre audience had often shunned her for her tics, provided unequal access to shows, or – disturbingly – asked her to sit behind soundproof glass so as to not disturb others. The enormous success of *Biscuit Land* led to a significant world tour, a larger platform for Touretteshero's advocacy and promotion of relaxed performances, and a returning to Edinburgh in 2017 with a performance of Beckett's *Not I*, considered to be one of the world's most challenging theatrical texts, which Thom reclaims as a disabled voice and performs in her own particular way. Beyond making an impassioned case for open access festivals in the promotion of disability arts and disabled artists, and drawing on the successful legacies of Fringe pioneers like Mat Fraser and Liz Carr, we also hope that we provide accurate reflections on how radical social justice, and disability justice-informed performance, can puncture the bubble of commercialism and Broadway-bound dreams of Fringe culture.

BRIAN LOBEL (BL): Hello Jess.

JESS THOM (JT): Hello Brian.

BL: Great to see you.

JT: And you.

BL: Oh, and before we start, when I type this up, do you record your tics when you are getting transcribed?

JT: I tend to, in writing up, leave them out.

BL: Okay, cool.

JT: In any other context, in terms of audio or whatever, I don't want people to go through the effort of taking it out.

BL: Yeah.

JT: Because that's editing out my disability or my impairment – but like this, they are not necessarily relevant.

BL: Great. So my first question I wanted to ask you is, "Why does any artist bring their work to the Fringe?"

JT: I don't know whether I can speak for any artist, but I know why I took work to the Fringe, and I can make guesses at why other artists take their work to the Fringe. But the reason that I took a show to the Fringe, in the first instance, was because I wanted to reach a theatre audience. I wanted to reach directors and makers and performers and people who are interested in theatre. I wanted *that* audience, I wanted to be visible to them, and I wanted my experiences to be visible to them, and so it felt important to take a show.

I had never been to Edinburgh before, and it had never been on my radar as something to do. But my colleague, Matthew, had been the year before, and he looked out for work relating to disability and realised there wasn't very much there, and he felt like there was a real opportunity for us to take something and speak to that audience and make visible some of the difficult experiences I've had accessing performance.

BL: Particularly because the content of that work (*Backstage in Biscuit Land*) was specifically about not being able to access theatre.

JT: Exactly, and so it definitely felt important to me to take that to theatre audiences. At that point, Edinburgh was the goal. We made a show to take to Edinburgh – the fact that then people liked it, and we toured it, none of that had even occurred to me. I hadn't understood it in that context. The point had been to take up some fucking space there and make people listen, and that's where they were, so we were going to go to them and make them hear.

But what I hadn't been prepared for was people's responses. In the end, *Biscuit Land* turned out to be a really good example of how art can be a catalyst of change, because we took it to Edinburgh, lots of performers saw it, lots of main theatre makers saw it and then wanted to make their work more accessible as a result and embraced the idea of or were intrigued by relaxed performance, which was discussed within that piece.

Jenny Sealey from Graeae Theatre Company said to me that "It's going to be as interesting, you being in Edinburgh in audiences, as it will be for people coming to see your show." I had not thought about that. Just by going and seeing work, I was also challenging some of the conventions of those spaces. So it wasn't just within the show; it was also by being an artist going to see shows.Why I would take work now is probably different. It's similar because we still want to make points and challenge people's thinking in particular ways, because that's the kind of artists that we are. But we're probably also much more conventional in that we take work because we want people to book it and take it in other places.

BL: That sounds very clear.

JT: Rambly, sorry.

BL: No, not at all. I just think for me, personally, you remind me that it's totally ridiculous, the Fringe, in many ways. Why does anyone do that thing?? But actually, at its core, it's about talking to the audience that's there, and there is a big "there" there.

JT: It's like a trade show in lots of ways.

BL: Yes!

JT: I had never been, but I went with three people who had. Hearing them talk about it ahead of time, I had a really bizarre mental image of what it was, and it was like part medieval fairy-tale realm. I just couldn't understand how it could possibly fit together in a real context, and I think it does have elements of that that is really interesting. But for me, the opportunity there is that there is an amazing congregation of artists and people focused on thinking about theatre or performance, and getting them to think about people for whom that wasn't an easy space to be in.

BL: We've spoken in the past about a "lost generation" of disabled young people and artists – people who have never had lives unaffected by austerity and the monstrous cuts to disability services and benefits in the UK, people for whom being an artist or creative (when day-to-day having to fight for basic services/dignity) seems an impossible ambition. And there is something about the possibility to even envision the Fringe which seems to be a huge privilege. If you've never been there, then you can't make work for there. And if artists, so many artists in the UK and internationally define around having gone, at some point, to the Fringe to do work.

JT: Yes…

BL: It's almost a rite of passage in many ways. And if you haven't done it, and you don't know about it, if you haven't gone to the parties, if you haven't lost some money at the Fringe, if you haven't handed out thousands of flyers…

JT: Yeah, all of that was totally alien to me. It was no part of any rite of passage for me. It wasn't even like, "Oh, this is a journey that I have to go on." As far as I was concerned,

I had a great career in a totally different area, I had no interest in being a performer straightforwardly, but I was interested in is being able to access public spaces and not be discriminated against.

Even being familiar with Edinburgh now, there's still a load of assumptions that people, particularly in the theatre industry, make around what being in Edinburgh "means" which aren't true for me. For example, people always talk about going to see seven or eight shows a day. There's no way that I have the capacity for that. Even as someone who is reasonably well known and is very confident articulating my access requirements – despite this, seeing any more than one show a day is impossible. I need to physically go through the process of contacting the company – there are a number of artists that I've contacted from shows I've wanted to see where I tried to make those adjustments and it just didn't happen because they didn't respond. Often I'm able to go and see things that are made by the people I know. There is so much effort and energy for me that goes into making a small number of adjustments. There is obviously the Access Team at the Fringe, and there's a legal requirement to make reasonable adjustments... but as a disabled person, knowing how to ask for them is a totally different ball game, and it puts the onus on you, so that you have to do all the work in that situation.

BL: All of that work...

JT: I've had experiences of going to see a West End show where the work I had to do took six hours. Which was longer than the show.

BL: And what's perhaps different for a West End show than at the Fringe is that the artist on the other end of the Fringe show may or may not have capacity to help you make those adjustments, because they're in a position, disabled or not disabled, which is disempowered at best, downright fucked up at the worst, given the expense of venues, their strict rules and inflexibility in many cases. It's a challenging scene for anyone, financially and energy-wise.

And the notable thing about everyone seeing seven or eight shows a day is, both, there's the physical inaccessibility of that for you, and then the technical inaccessibility, in that you need to make a billion phone calls in order to do that, so you can only do it for one show.

JT: And the emotional effort of all of that.

BL: Yes, the emotional effort for that. And I don't know why I keep banging on about this kind of idea of identity, but the identity of the Fringe is so built around a person's capacity, so it's not that they were seeing seven or eight shows and you couldn't able to do it, but in order to have a *true* Fringe experience, you had to see so many.

JT: Or you're wasting the experience of Edinburgh by not seeing loads of work.

BL: It's a dick-measuring competition in some ways, you know, "Oh, I saw 12 shows today, how many did you see??"

JT: And this year I knew that and thought, "That's not for me," I can't access the Fringe in that way. The first year I went up – because I had no concept of that and because I was with performers who had been lots of times before – there was an expectation.

I had a really difficult experience on the first night I was in Edinburgh when I went to see a show without having spoken to the venue, without having spoken to the comedian, can become going in with my performer's pass, and then being singled out for 15 minutes. I was asked, challenged, why I was in a wheelchair and various things in a really public setting. I have subsequently addressed all this with that artist but was reminded of all the normal rules that I follow in my cultural life in terms of going to

On the fringe of the Fringe

see stuff totally still apply. That being said, I still saw more theatre in that first week in Edinburgh in 2014 than I had seen in my life up until that point.

BL: Are there challenges that disabled artists face at the Fringe, aside from physical access to the space?

JT: Yeah absolutely. This year I was in a really fortunate position, in that we were taking a co-production that was really well supported, that sold out before we got there, for which we got some high-profile media attention, and we weren't carrying any financial risk. So that's an incredibly privileged position to be in. But I was incredibly aware of a responsibility as a disabled artist, not just about whether people liked or didn't like the show, it was about what that said about disability arts more broadly. I felt a huge pressure as a disabled artist that I do not think a non-disabled artist would feel. I felt like I wasn't just representing myself and my work, but I was representing a community of people. And I thought, "I don't want to fuck this up," because I don't want somebody to be able to say, "That was a shit show – disability arts are shit. It was a shit show because she was a disabled artist and therefore I'm not going to see work by a disabled artist again."

And so I definitely felt that pressure, much more than when we took *Biscuit Land*, where I had no idea what to expect and I felt no pressure because "we're just going to do this thing."

BL: And in some ways because the goal of the first show was actually just to take up space.

JT: Exactly, whereas with that is was like, it felt like I didn't have room to fail. I've definitely spoken to other disabled artists who expressed not having room to fail. As an artist, this can be potentially really restricting in terms of the risks that you feel able to make with your practise.

BL: My next question was going to be, "With a limited amount of disabled artists working at the Fringe, how much pressure is there relating to representation?"

JT: Loads.

BL: I mean, I think you just addressed that.

JT: There is shedloads, absolutely shedloads, and part of me thinks I can be quite reasonably resilient to that. I would rather take that pressure on than someone earlier on in their career. Twenty per cent of the population identify as disabled, and that's not just visible impairment, you know, lots of that is unseen impairments… but I am fairly confident that 20 per cent of artists taking work to the Fringe are not disabled, don't identify as disabled people.

BL: I often feel very similar in regards to the amount of stories around cancer and illness that I think of. One in three people has cancer, but everyone still jokingly says, "Oh it's so stereotypical that like someone gets cancer, and then they write a show." Actually it's not stereotypical, because they really don't. Five people go to the Fringe with a cancer story out of 3,000 stories in a year. There might be three that are about cancer or illness or fragility. And the sheer amount of shows about someone's first fucking girlfriend or, you know, their heartbreak, or war – or actually things that actually a lot of people don't experience or don't know anything about – reminds me of the shame in creating work about an embodied political experience that is stigmatised or marginalised. I think that you see the stigmatisation or the marginalisation of those experiences by the amount of shows that are about these experiences. You wouldn't bring a show up if you didn't think there was an audience that wants to see it, so this becomes cyclical logic. So for me, I'm always upset that there's only three cancer shows, or the year that was the "Big Year for Mental Health," there were four shows about it.

247

JT: One in four people can expect to experience a mental health condition. Visibility is really important, and I think visibility of disabled people in cultural spaces is important. I think that lots of exclusion doesn't happen as a deliberate attack – some does – but a lot of it doesn't. It happens because of a lack of thought because it never occurs to somebody. If you are able to easily follow the rule that you need to be quiet in the theatre, why would you think about someone who can't? So I think the visibility of different experiences within cultural spaces and within cultural communities is essential. I am always visible; that's how my body works. I can't turn that off, and so it's like, I am visible when I am onstage in Edinburgh, but I'm also visible when I'm going down the street or when I'm buying a coffee in Edinburgh. That is my day-to-day experience.

BL: Exactly.

JT: Within Edinburgh that can feel wearing, but it also has its benefits. If I'm in a show making a load of noise, and that needs to be acknowledged as part of the reasonable adjustment I request, then actually what was interesting is that lots of other artists were very generously talking about the fact I was a performer there with a show... the Fringe benefit...

BL: ...some free extra marketing.

JT: Yes, some extra marketing. There's this really confusing relationship with the fact you are invisible within lots of cultural spaces but also totally visible and fair game on a day-to-day basis – particularly on what people feel they have a right to know about you or right to comment on. An intelligent, thoughtful, experienced comedian feels it's acceptable to ask me why I'm in a wheelchair in front of several hundred people. He said within his show, "Oh, you prepare for lots of things as a comedian: you prepare for hecklers, you prepare for this, you prepare for that." He listed all these things that as an artists you prepare for, but you don't prepare for an audience member with Tourette's, and it's like, "Why not?"

BL: Here you are.

JT: 300,000 people in the UK have Tourette's, but many more have learning disabilities or neurological conditions or other conditions that might mean they might make noise or movement. Why do we expect go to the theatre and expect not to be sitting next to a learning disabled person. Why is that the assumption?

BL: Yes, yes, yes, yes.

JT: I want to watch theatre. I want to be part of an inclusive community. I don't want to sit in an audience where everybody is exactly the same as me or watch things about people who are exactly the same as me. The reason why I'm attracted to live performance is that it's live. I haven't been to the cinema in fifteen years because it's a much harder space for me to negotiate than theatre. Theatre is responsive, it's live. It's about a group of people watching stuff together – why then would you want to negate its liveness, like pretend it wasn't live?

BL: Has there ever been a theatre built or a space built that is accessible to you from the central audience point?

JT: Well, I very rarely have control on where I sit. That's done for me, be that within a theatre, or on a train. For most of my life, I have a designated space. And if that designated space is taken by someone else who has a similar access requirement to me, then there's not another option, other than do something that doesn't work well for your body, do something that is less safe, or you don't see the show.

BL: Or fight with a person with a baby carriage.

JT: Yeah, yeah yeah. Confront people, put them in situations of confrontation where people are made to weigh up their right to be in a space based on poor design. For *Biscuit Land*,

On the fringe of the Fringe

it was really important that that felt like a theatre space because of where that show was coming from, but for *Not I*, it didn't, and our references were much more gig-like. We deliberately do that in a space where there is no rake and where we can create space where everyone can choose where they sit and where you can lie down, or where you can stand or where you can sit. So you have much more autonomy over how to be.

For me in Edinburgh this year – experiencing chronic pain – actually just made the act of sitting upright for an hour physically really fucking uncomfortable. There was a show where I was like, "This is now too excruciating to do this, and I will have to get out of my chair and essentially lay out into the aisle." Now, I have the confidence to do that, and I'm a performer; I'm not worried about what people think about me lying down at the side. To a certain extent I do still feel nervous, and I'm really protective over my confidence because it's still really fragile when it comes to seeing work, and it can still go wrong really, really quickly. We were touring *Backstage in Biscuit Land*, and, you know, we had been touring for months as a company and very experienced in that, and we took the show to a comedy festival in Wales, and then because we were at this comedy festival, we wanted to stay the night and see some comedy. I did some of the work: I talked to the front of house manager, who I had seen all day and who had seen *Biscuit Land*, and I said, "Please, can you let the comedians know?" But I hadn't done that fully, and though Matthew said that this could go wrong, I was quite blasé about it. And then it was fucking awful. I was singled out over and over again. One comedian did seven minutes of Tourette's material, in which he asked the audience to consider what it may be like to have no control of your subconscious. I got called Tourette's Girl by a different comedian. And then Matthew was furious with me afterwards because my confidence was broken.

BL: Yeah, and the implications of that are so strong. You, Jess, are *the* most confident person to deal with a world that is not made for you and your inclusion. And you just think about anyone who doesn't have that confidence who has any access requirements that are less than or more than yours or more specific or more niche. It's horrifying to think about that intensity.

JT: One of the blog posts I wrote during this Edinburgh Fringe was literally about me and about what I do to ensure my access and comfort. It hadn't occurred to me before, but I do all of this work. I thought it might be useful for me to share in a public forum what I do, what I ask for and how I do it. As a part of your rights, you can ask for these adjustments; you do not have to put yourself through pain, through agony. You have a right to be in these spaces. This post was about how I go about making that possible. Sometimes it works, and sometimes it doesn't, but these are the tools I use. It was interesting to see how many people came back and was like "I had not known I could do that…" We have these principles ingrained in the law, but there's no teaching around how, as a disabled person, you do that or how, as an artist, you are providing a service and, therefore, to be lawful and to be compliant, you have to be ready to adjust.

And I think one of the things I have spoken about, more this year, is that adjustment, the power of adjustment, and how transformative that has been in my life – in knowing that I can change my environment to meet my needs, and the importance of making adjustments to ensure people can access culture. At the start of last year, I experienced a hate crime, a really intense experience, where I made no changes to that situation. The adjustment I made was to minimise it and accept it as it was happening, and not to challenge it, and not to ask for anything, and to internalise all of that. And then to feel frustrated with myself afterwards that I hadn't acted in a different way. But I realise as

249

a disabled person, you're so used to adjusting to situations and to having to be flexible that it's very easy to adjust to inequality, to adjust to a shit situation rather than to make sure the adjustments happen, to make sure there is equality, and to make sure people are written in. For me, that was an important reminder that adjustment can be negative as well a positive, and we have a real responsibility that we don't adjust to inequality, that we make the adjustments that are essential so that people can participate.

BL: You are on fucking point.

The situation described here is not unique to the UK context (for a discussion of similar issues in an Australia context, for example, see Austin, Duncan, Goggin, Macdowell, Pardo, and Paterson in Chapter 20). Moreover, the point made in such blunt and passionate terms here clearly resonates with the point that has been made so often by disability studies scholars over the years. Whilst reasonable adjustments and accommodations are a goal, and a step along the way to a hopefully more accessible world in the future, they also often highlight the dominant culture's continued attempts to allow access only on its own terms and to the extent that it does not disrupt systems overall and to train disabled people to be grateful for minimal accommodations. Oftentimes, a win in terms of accommodations in one area can paradoxically result in a perception that further attention to the matter is no longer required and thus paradoxically result in withdrawal of accommodations in other areas (as noted by Hadley in Chapter 28). It is a situation that still all too often places the burden to be flexible, accommodate, or come up with creative solutions to the problems on disabled artists themselves (see, for example, Lubet on creative adaptations of music artists in Chapter 25). For disabled artists, having to step up and fight for access can be physically, professionally, and emotionally exhausting. But, in the context of the Fringe festival, as in so many disability arts, culture, and media production contexts, this remains a necessity.

References

Abnormally Funny People. n.d. *Abnormally Funny People* website. Accessed 1 May 2018. Available: www.abnormallyfunnypeople.com/.

Ellis-Petersen, Hannah. 2015. "'I Want This to Be Joyous:' Edinburgh Fringe's Startling Shows about Depression." *The Guardian*, 9 August 2015. Accessed 1 May 2018. Available: www.theguardian.com/stage/2015/aug/09/edinburgh-festival-fringe-mental-health-stigma-depression.

Gardner, Lyn. 2017. "We Haven't Made a Profit for Five Years:' Risky Business at Edinburgh Fringe." *The Guardian*, 9 July 2017. Accessed 1 May 2018. Available: www.theguardian.com/stage/2017/jul/19/risky-business-edinburgh-fringe-hidden-costs-of-theatres.

iF Platform. n.d. *iF Platform* website. Accessed 1 May 2018. Available: http://stopgapdance.com/news/if-platform-launches.

Mental Health Foundation. 2017. "Winner Announced for First Mental Health Fringe Award at Edinburgh Festival." *Mental Health Foundation* website. Accessed 1 May 2018. Available: www.mentalhealth.org.uk/news/winner-announced-first-mental-health-fringe-award-edinburgh-festival.

Mulholland, Rob. 2017. "The Working Class Has Been Forced out of Comedy." *Chortle*, 16 August 2017. Accessed 1 May 2018. Available: www.chortle.co.uk/correspondents/2017/08/16/37528/the_working_class_has_been_forced_out_of_comedy.

The Sick of the Fringe. n.d. *The Sick of the Fringe* website. Accessed 1 May 2018. Available: http://thesickofthefringe.com.

Unlimited. n.d. *Unlimited* website. Accessed 1 May 2018. Available: http://weareunlimited.org.uk/unlimited-at-the-edinburgh-fringe/.

Youngs, Ian. 2013. "The Cost of Performing at the Edinburgh Fringe." *BBC News*, 26 August 2013. Accessed 1 May 2018. Available: www.bbc.co.uk/news/entertainment-arts-23778487.

20

The last avant garde?

Sarah Austin, Kath Duncan, Gerard Goggin, Lachlan MacDowall, Veronica Pardo, Eddie Paterson, and collaborators Jax Jacki Brown, Morwenna Collett, Fiona Cook, Bree Hadley, Kate Hood, Jess Kapuscinski-Evans, Donna McDonald, Julie McNamara, Gaelle Mellis, Eva Sifis, and Kate Sulan

Introduction

Disability … is not merely a theme. It is not only a personal or autobiographical response embedded in an artwork. It is not solely a political act. It is all of these things, but it is more. It is more because disability is properly speaking an aesthetic value, which is to say, it participates in a system of knowledge that provides materials for and increases critical consciousness about the way that some bodies make other bodies feel. The idea of disability aesthetics affirms that disability operates both as a critical framework for questioning aesthetic presuppositions in the history of art and as a value in its own right important to future conceptions of what art is.

(Siebers 2010, 20)

The Australian Research Council project *Disability and the Performing Arts in Australia: Beyond the Social Model* – known to collaborators as *the last avant garde* – is mapping disability performing arts in Australia. We open up this chapter, and our ongoing research project, with the words of the late Tobin Siebers. In researching disability and performance here in Australia, we also acknowledge that since Siebers' 2010 text, we have seen new experiments and emerging companies pushing the bounds of *how bodies feel* – in a sector which embraces differences in bodies, but also in thinking, in neurodiversities, in being, in articulating, in appearing, in sensing, in intersectionalities, and in the experiences for audiences. As such, this chapter aims to explore 'disability aesthetics' not as a set of specific techniques, themes, or politics, but in order to position disability at the centre of 'future conceptions of what art is' and what it can be.

In keeping with models that invite people with disability to become agents or co-producers in a "responsive" methodology with "a cyclical and emergent design" (Nierse & Abma 2011, 411), rather than subjects of research (Macpherson & Fox 2016, 373; Lenakakis & Koltsida 2017, 254), this collaborative chapter draws on multiple perspectives from artists and scholars perceived to have disability and not, and takes its lead from contributions by Jax Jacki Brown, Morwenna Collett, Fiona Cook, Bree Hadley, Kate Hood, Jess Kapuscinski-Evans, Donna McDonald, Julie McNamara, Gaelle Mellis, Eva Sifis, and Kate Sulan. As such, we are led by

Sarah Austin et al.

the diversity of disability experience, while also acknowledging that it is almost impossible to do justice to the range of lived experience from within our communities.[1]

In investigating 'the last avant garde,' we respond to Hannah Macpherson and Alice Fox's recent analysis of ways to "disrupt traditional research power hierarchies and facilitate multisensory modes of research dialogue" (2016, 373). Our commitment to a collaborative method of research and writing, then, is also led by an awareness that one reason current practices and experiences do not operate within conventional aesthetic criteria is because these same aesthetic criteria have historically served to exclude d/Deaf, disabled, and divergent performers from dominant arts practices and arts training, institutional and funding frameworks, and cultural and critical commentary – including academic research – about the arts. In contrast, Siebers' disability aesthetics places disability as the "critical framework for questioning [historical] aesthetic presuppositions" now and into the future (2010, 20).

This chapter responds to some International Day of Persons With Disability 2017 events: two recent performances in Melbourne – *Risky Business*, from the disability-led queer cabaret troupe Quippings, and *Song for a Weary Throat* by the Rawcus ensemble of performers "with and without disability" (Rawcus 2018) – and the workshop "Research in Action" (RiA), generated by the authors and led by Irish UK-based Vital Xposure artistic director and activist Julie McNamara (also known as Julie Mc). Altogether, these diverse events represent an opportunity to situate disability performance in Australia within what Paul Makeham, Bree Hadley, and Joon-Yee Kwok aptly describe as an "ecology" of the performing arts (2012), that is the shifting and sometimes unpredictable relationships between "aesthetic prerogatives, production infrastructure, people, relationships, and ideologies" (Hadley 2017, 307). In response to these multiple perspectives, this chapter is organised around two key questions that were central to our analyses of the events described above, amid current debates on the aesthetic values of disability performance practice:

1   How do disability innovations and creative thinking challenge aesthetics models?
2   How are aesthetics informed by process, practice, and infrastructure?

We discuss these questions in relation to recent works from Quippings and Rawcus – by inviting key artists to reflect on their modes of practice, production infrastructures, and the process of developing new work. In doing so, our collaborative process responds to a provocation made by Julie Mc that "The room we choose dictates what kinds of bodies and minds can find their way in. When rehearsal rooms look different, the work looks different" (RiA Workshop 2017, see Figure 20.1). In this chapter, then, we are interested in how disability, both as everyday lived experience and in the performance *process*, also impacts on the development of *aesthetics* (see Sandahl & Auslander 2005). Our discussion draws on contributions from the RiA workshop and the research team to explore the idea of the last avant garde and artists' views on how disability intersects with creative innovation.

This chapter does not aim to answer these two questions in any definitive way, but instead seeks to engage in a reflexive and ongoing conversation in which artists with disability are invited to reflect upon their own views on aesthetic value and performance practice. In doing so, we are alive to moments of engagement between artists and scholars – and spectators, advocates, and allies – that have the potential to animate what Hadley calls a "dialogics of difference," or "productive, unpredictable, improvisatory encounters," with the potential to alter the public sphere (2014, 186).

Figure 20.1 *Last Avant Garde* Inclusive Creative Workshop, Sydney, 4 May 2018. From left, foreground: lead facilitator Sarah-Vyne Vassallo, Mel Tyquin, Chris Bunton, James Penny, Holly Craig. Obscured on left: Riana Head-Toussaint. Image by Sue Wright

Disability innovations and new aesthetics models

In 2007, during a debate on the future of disability and deaf arts in the UK, British artist and Turner Prize nominee Yinka Shonibare argued that disability arts could be considered the last remaining avant garde movement (Bragg 2007). Shonibare's comment, which situates disability arts as a cultural and political movement in relation to the radical politics and aesthetics of the twentieth-century notion of the avant garde, remains a provocative one.

The concept of a 'last avant garde' is provocative because it has the potential to overturn presumptions about disability art. It inverts the often marginal position of disability art in terms of critical attention, experimental capacity, and aesthetic and cultural value. Instead, artists with disabilities are positioned as creative leaders whose value is to lead both aesthetic and social change.

The notion of the last avant garde suggests disruptive cultural practices that will challenge the status quo but also serve the people in driving social and political reform. For Shonibare, disability arts can be compared to "the early days of feminism and black arts" (Bragg 2007), implying it is a powerful cultural force that is yet to be fully recognised but will eventually force widespread change. Moreover, as 'the last remaining' movement, disability arts is compelling, positioned as temporally out of place (but overdue rather than out-of-date) and as the inheritor of the historical avant garde movements, once marginal groups that are now valued as among the most important artists of the nineteenth and twentieth century. Finally, it also implies that recognition of disability arts is like the 'last remaining' piece of a puzzle, the pinnacle of a longer social struggle for rights and acceptance.

Many questions flow from Shonibare's phrase. Are the collective energy and opportunities for disabled arts in the UK reflected in other countries and settings? Though being associated with the avant garde offers a powerful way of making a case for artists

Sarah Austin et al.

with disabilities, what are its drawbacks? Does an insistence on avant garde experimentation contribute to new forms of marginality?

Such questions are particularly important in the context of our project, which recognises increasing interest in the aesthetics and practices of disability arts practitioners in Australia and elsewhere, arising at a time when communities are facing the pressures of austerity politics and changing social policies (Hadley 2017, 305).

In Australia, the political, social, and aesthetic values of disability arts are yet to be widely publicly and culturally considered or recognised. Disability is not seen as a cultural experience, even though there is increasing awareness and interest in the diverse practices of disability performance (Austin et al. 2015; Hadley 2017). The management of the arts and disability sector is deeply political and deeply affected by wider societal norms that position disability and impairment as aberrant, and disabled people as incompetent and in need of help (Campbell 2009, 197). While approximately 20 per cent of Australians identify as disabled, only four per cent of characters on stage and screen are disabled, and of those, even fewer are played by genuinely disabled performers (Dow 2016). It is notable that the Australian disability rights movement has had only limited impact in making inroads on recruitment and traineeships for disabled artists, performers, arts workers, and arts administrators within the arts industries. Disabled Australians are more likely to live in poverty, with among the lowest employment statistics compared to similar nations (Goggin & Newell 2005, 18–22; Price Waterhouse 2011).

As Petra Kuppers argues, it is the power of disability as cultural force that engenders a diverse political aesthetic critique. While resistance to the norm may be only available to a few disabled people because of barriers to the arts, finances, and education, disability as a cultural force nonetheless situates disability-led performance as a site to "reject conventional art practice, certain kinds of irony and the aesthetic demands of the art market" (2011, 4). Importantly, the drive for creative self-determination among disabled, d/Deaf, and divergent performers in Australia is palpable. Ideal would be an independent sector where disabled performers manage and develop our arts practices ourselves (as author Kath says: HEY, I WOULD HAVE A REAL JOB!!!).

Two contrasting examples of how the links between process and experience might intersect in practice can be found in the recent stagings of Quippings' *Risky Business*, and *Song for a Weary Throat* by the Rawcus ensemble.

Quippings

> There's not a lot of space for all kinds of complicated representations of disability. Definitely not a lot of room for people who live with a disability to talk about themselves beyond 'oh, this is my disability and therefore I'm defined by it'.[2]
>
> *(Creatrix Tiara cited Morgan 2017)*

Quippings started as a small activist group who wanted to lobby private and public venues and companies about social and sexual access to premises and events, for queer men and women in Melbourne (Brown & Duncan 2016).[3] The development of Quippings into a performance troupe came about within a fortuitous combination of location, access, and the desire to build community.

The venue, Hares and Hyenas Bookshop Café, where initial discussions took place was physically and emotionally accessible: it had ramps and staff who were trained to embrace people of all descriptions, including gender variant people, people with unconventional lifestyles, D/deaf and disabled people, and queer and non-queer folk. The space includes a small stage, and the venue has a history of showcasing experimental performers.

Throughout its seven-year history, Quippings has produced over 20 shows to over 1,000 people and worked with over 100 emerging and established artists. The key imperatives are disability pride in practice, sustaining the disability-led troupe, and making disability rights and sexuality performative, as well as accessible to performers and audience. Always at issue is the longevity of Quippings, but for their seven-year run, the group has echoed the thoughts of UK actor Mat Fraser: "You've got to declare yourself disabled and beautiful" (1998: 83).

The live shows developed because the founders realised that fun and public expression of private taboos were powerful; they recognised that the spoken word, the show, and the performance are important advocacy tools – just as vital as any number of letters or phone calls to organisations – in shifting public and private views and practices. At stake was the critical mass needed to press for all disabled people to be sexually liberated, loud, and proud. In this way, the Quippings project echoes Caitlin Wood's argument that

> Using song, film, dance, visual arts, fashion and writing, uppity crips are defying mainstream culture's insistence on our subordination and doing it with style and humour. We don't shy away from the realities of our nonconformist minds and bodies – we flaunt them. And in this daring space of shameless flaunting, we find fellow crips who affirm and reflect our originality and beauty back at us, just as we affirm and reflect back to them. It's here where internalized ableism begins to crumble.
>
> *(Wood 2014, 2)*

Indeed, Quippings provides a diverse and nurturing space for the expression of performers' possibly unexpressed desires, to feature works written and workshopped by the performers themselves. From the beginning, Quippings' producers also recognised the need to define themselves as professionals by dividing income among the performers so that no one worked for free. Yet, without ongoing funding or meeting space, the troupe scatters and reforms with new members for every show, as the opportunity to perform stays open to all people who identify as D/deaf, disabled, divergent, and queer/queer friendly. This is rarity in performing arts companies within Australia, where most companies have a fixed or permanent cast (not to mention far less diverse). Quippings also provides Auslan (Australian Sign Language) interpreting services at all shows, or a feature show per season, and as with other accessible theatre events that integrate Auslan interpretation as a key feature, this element is simultaneously practical and theatrical. In this way, Quippings reflects the ways in which Crip performance space can also be seen to transform conventional performance spaces, both in terms of physical access but also economic access and through various levels of interpretation, translation, description, and even haptic experience (see Sandahl 2002).

The year 2017 was a standout year for Quippings, as the troupe received state government funding (Creative Victoria) for three shows, including writing development and rehearsal space. This extra support meant the troupe was able to engage outside directors and dramaturgs and hire significant venues for the first time, allowing the group to build towards their final show of 2017, *Risky Business*.

Risky Business

On 1 December, Quippings staged *Risky Business*. This cabaret-style work featured spoken word, comedy, and burlesque dance performance by ten performers – Kath Duncan, Rachel High, Anthony Julian, Jess Kapuscinski-Evans, Kochava Lilit, Gem Mahadeo, Julie McNamara, Sonia Marcon, Imogen Newhouse, and Creatrix Tiara – with a specific focus on individual stories about their riskiest experiences (see Figure 20.2).

Figure 20.2 Images of Quippings production of *Risky Business*, Melba Spiegeltent, Melbourne, Australia, 1 December 2017. From left: Julie McNamara, Rachel High. Image by Angel Leggas, 3FatesMedia

The stories and the telling of them were based around the central concept of an Oppression Olympics game show, featuring short, mainly individual, acts. The performances explored differences acquired and congenital, and the mysteries and treatments and varieties of body and 'invisible disabilities' – emotional, neurological, and psychological perspectives –as sites of political resistance.

Some *Risky Business* performers explicitly engaged with the political meanings of the disabled body. Creatrix Tiara's striptease dance to different versions of the same pop song, *You Spin Me Round*, was a homage in which the agony of an impairment, premenstrual dysphoric disorder, becomes art, influencing the performance while battling fear and emotional upheavals. Julie McNamara and Rachel High's comedy sketch, set in a tattoo parlour, exposed the 'flawed' female body as a social contract. Kochava Lilit's ode to the power imbalance inherent in relationships with non-disabled 'allies' spoke from a neurodivergent, physically impaired, and gender variant resistance and subversion to dominant ableist ideologies.

Quippings producers Duncan and Brown are inspired by Carrie Sandahl's assertion:

> Perhaps the most significant similarity between [disability and queerness] … is their radical stance toward concepts of normalcy; both argue adamantly against the compulsion to observe norms of all kinds (corporeal, mental, sexual, social, cultural, subcultural, etc.).
>
> *(Sandahl 2003, 26)*

While rejecting 'normalcy' is pleasurable for Quippings performers, nevertheless, the whole troupe is aware that they are readily 'Othered' by audiences, even by sympathetic and diversity-aware audiences.

As such, the live experience of *Risky Business* feels raw. This is partly because of the experimental process of coming together as a new troupe for the performance, but also because the cast are willing to explore tensions between radical and risky ideas of politics, otherness, identity, and disability. Pardo describes this strength, present in different ways in all Quippings works:

There appears to be almost limitless room for breaking the rules. As an audience member, the subsequent work is sometimes deeply satisfying, sometime less so, but it is innovative in that it feels risky and like rules are being broken. They're broken because of a desire for disability access and equality, which maybe gives people permission to break other rules.

(Pardo 2017, Personal Communication)

For the Quipping producers and many performers, this 'rule breaking' is a deliberate aesthetic strategy, as part of the process upholding difference in defiance to a dominant non-disabled performance aesthetic. Kuppers, whose creative contribution to this collection can also be found in Part IV, describes the possibilities of difference in a disability-focused environment.

To me, disability culture is not a thing, but a process. Boundaries, norms, belongings: disability cultural environments can suspend a whole slew of rules, try to undo the history of exclusions that many of its members have experienced when they have heard or felt 'you shouldn't be like this.' At the same time, disability cultural environments have to safeguard against perpetuating or erecting other exclusions (based on racial stereotypes, class, gender, economic access, internalized ableism, etc.).

(Kuppers 2011, 9)

However, the exclusions Kuppers refers to are also problematic for Quippings as well. Quippings producers have struggled with engaging key communities like disabled people of colour, Aboriginal disabled people, people who require certain levels of access beyond the reach of Quippings budgets (for example captioning), comfortable beanbags for audience members, a quiet space contained within the performance for neurodiverse performers and audiences, and so on. *Risky Business* was more successful than previous shows in responding to these calls for cultural diversity and impairment diversity. It featured two new performers who identify as people of colour, one new performer from interstate who identifies as learning disabled, as well as our largest ever (five) cast of non-binary gender diverse performers and crew, along with Julie Mc joining the troupe for her second *Quippings* show of 2017. Additionally, the state government funding opened up opportunities for documentation and publicity, as well as a level of cultural capital. Finally, the funding enabled meals for the Quippings artists and performers, who frequently could not afford to eat out during the production schedule.

Central to Quippings work is the desire to complicate representations of people with disabilities and challenge stereotypes. Use of a cabaret form and the different modes of storytelling it enables (comedy, dance, spoken work, poetry, satire, physical theatre) gives performers capacity to explore their individual difference in a range of ways. Combined with the Quippings performers identifying as culturally and gender diverse, the performance mode provides a direct challenge to the dominant narrative of people with a disability as both white and heteronormative. Yet, as their struggle for financial sustainability makes clear, it is often difficult to separate the Quippings artists' opportunity for aesthetic experimentation from the security, or lack thereof, that a stable funding and policy landscape can provide.

Rawcus

Rawcus ensemble is a Melbourne-based theatre company that has been creating new work in a range of mainstream and independent platforms for 17 years. The ensemble consists of 15 performers with and without disability: Clement Baade, Hannah Bradsworth, Michael Buxton, Harriet Devlin, Rachel Edwards, Nilgun Guven, Joshua Lynzaat, Paul Matley,

Mike McEvoy, Ryan New, Kerryn Poke, Leisa Prowd, Louise Riisik, Prue Stevenson, John Tonso, and Danielle von der Borch. The ensembles meet once a week for three hours, with a core team of artists led by founding Artistic Director Kate Sulan. The company devises new contemporary performance works that express the imaginative world of the ensemble.

Rawcus creates original contemporary performance works, devised by the ensemble and the artistic team, usually in response to thematic provocations from director Kate Sulan. Sulan explains how the traditional understanding of 'the director' does not necessarily reflect her role in the company when it comes to making new work. She has described her responsibility in the rehearsal process as working to create the right conditions for 'play,' finding the right 'playground' for the performers, and then crafting and editing the material offered (Sulan 2017, Personal Communication). Central to this process is the proposition that the work is crafted and shaped from the creative offers the ensemble make during the rehearsal process.

> There's no showing. There's no acting, there's just being.
>
> *(Prue Stevenson cited Bailey 2017)*

These offers are sometimes responses from the provocation provided by Sulan, or another ensemble member, and at other times are reflections the ensemble provides about something that has happened to them, or that they felt or experienced in response to the content of rehearsal.

> All our work evolves from the personal experiences and imaginations of the ensemble but by the time it gets to the performance it's gone through so many variations that it's not like telling our own stories. But they're all really richly and deeply in the work.
>
> *(Sulan cited Bailey 2017)*

This process of devising material is familiar to much contemporary arts practice. However, Rawcus brings a specific physical theatre and movement focus to generating material, and the ensemble members work kinaesthetically, actualising their imaginative or lived experience responses through a physical language that distils and distorts meaning into something more abstract and imagistic. As Sulan reflects, "We try to find a scene that is specific about an experience, but open so it can have multiple access points for people" (Personal Communication 2017).

Many disability arts contexts refer to embodied and engaged practice as a hallmark of their work. Embedded in Rawcus' practice is the idea of the body as a political symbol that is both coded and marked and invested in by power relations and is capable of disrupting, subverting, and expressing ideas. The fact that the bodies in the ensemble are diverse and disabled means that there is a range of possible meanings operating in each performance image.

Song for a Weary Throat

Song for a Weary Throat was performed at Theatre Works in St Kilda from 29 November to 20 December 2017, and marks Rawcus' twelfth major work as a company. Generated through a process of research, discussion, and improvisation, the development of the work happened over three years. As Sulan notes,

> *Song for a Weary Throat* began with a whole pile of text generated through improvisational exercises. The finished work is without words. That's typical of a Rawcus piece, which kneads and folds its raw materials until it might bear no resemblance to what was first laid out on the bench.
>
> *(cited Bailey 2017)*

The work is also a collaboration between the ensemble and the Invenio Singers, a trio of vocalists who provide live music throughout. Similar to Quippings, there is an attention to integrating accessible strategies into the work, such as signed interpretation. However, as the performance is largely wordless, the interpreter was given the provocation of creating a signed score that evoked the music without using any Auslan. Such aesthetic strategies were both innovative and accessible and commented upon favourably by deaf audience members, but other aspects, such as intense flashes of light and booming sounds, could also be overwhelming for neurodiverse spectators and inaccessible for people with photosensitivity (Q&A 2017).

Dance functions as a poetic metaphor in *Song for a Weary Throat*, which takes as its starting point ideas of hope and resilience in the face of great adversity (Program Notes). This focus on dance is a literal scoring and composition of the physical rehearsal language of the ensemble, who primarily communicate through the body and are asked to respond to ideas and intent through physical expression. In the words of ensemble member Hannah Bradsworth, "You have to use your body to dance, you have to use your body to communicate with other people" (Q&A 2017). As each ensemble member has idiosyncratic and particular ways of moving in their body, part of the ensemble's creative work is a negotiation of each other's physical differences as aesthetic opportunities.

Importantly, dance is also explored in *Song for A Weary Throat* as a potent symbol of connection, desire, resilience, hope, sadness, and loneliness. A particular illustrative moment occurs when Bradsworth, who is a performer with Down syndrome, requests other performers to dance with her. As each performer fails to respond, what is played out in this moment encapsulates a life of rejection and exclusion in all its forms. It does not point directly to a specific experience of rejection, but it resonates with Bradsworth's desire for acceptance and connection and her tenacity and spirit. It is pertinent that the request from Bradsworth is to dance, as it is can be understood as about meeting someone in an equal space. As this scene progresses and she continues to request the other performers to dance, she engages various strategies of play, persuasion, and demand. All attempts go nowhere, and the spectator might experience this scene both as a witness to an individual's experience and as a remembrance of a personal experience.

At tension in Rawcus' work is an aesthetic characterised by intense physicality, visual imagery, visible and invisible disability, and the level to which the work can be read as a comment on the lived experiences of disability. For a company composed of artists with and without disability, of which Rawcus is but one prominent Australian example, the notion of disability aesthetics and the last avant garde is particularly complicated. It raises questions about how inclusive processes (in the rehearsal room) become profoundly connected to how the work is read, the ways in which disability is foregrounded in the work (or not), the work's impact on audiences, its level of funding, and its relationship with the formation of new ecologies of disability performing arts in the future. Our reading of *Song for a Weary Throat* suggests that the question of how aesthetics develop – from rehearsal to production to presentation – needs to be considered from within the landscape of disability arts in Australia, in which funding is rarely sustainable, and its impacts on practice and process.

Process, practice, funding, and infrastructure

During a recent workshop, Julie Mc argued that people with a disability are "creative innovators and problem solvers" (RiA Workshop 2017). In doing so, Julie Mc explicitly made the link between how the practice of artists with disability is fundamentally connected with lived experience of disability: artists are innovators, not simply because of a desire for the 'new' or 'radical,' but because the lived experience of having to negotiate barriers in normative society *requires* innovation and problem-solving skills (RiA Workshop 2017). Such innovations, which are increasingly being recognised as distinctive to the practice of disability arts, situate the development of aesthetic advances not only in relation to access aesthetics or inclusive practice, but in direct connection with how the wider culture – including industry, policy, and funding settings – impacts on aesthetics developments (see Sandahl & Auslander 2005).

Throughout the following conversation, Kate Hood and Kath Duncan drew attention to the relationship between aesthetics and the unequal funding, training, and production models that exist in Australia and elsewhere. Similarly, when asked what conditions would enable them to more meaningfully engage with research and performance practice, many contributors highlighted that their work is overwhelmingly voluntary or poorly paid, with a lack of employment, or even unpaid internships, impacting on their art (RiA Workshop 2017). These ongoing economic and social inequalities may also be seen in the wider arts community, yet such factors contribute to what Duncan calls an "aesthetics of poverty and marginal art" (Duncan 2017, Personal Communication) that necessarily shapes many approaches to disability performance practice.

However, while it is important to recognise that aesthetic innovations frequently arise from lived experiences of problem-solving (on stage or in everyday life), the recognition of disability aesthetics as a possible future conception of what art is also points to the ways in which a desire for access, inclusion, and equality can be animated by radical approaches to politics and arts practice. In the words of outgoing Executive Director of Arts Access Victoria and member of the LAG research team Veronica Pardo,

> Perhaps it is when artists with disability are empowered to change processes and practices, whether it be through forces such as curiosity, accidental or purposeful experimentation, permission to fail, desire for equality and inclusion, as well as actively searching for new processes, that innovations in practice emerge.
>
> *(Pardo 2017, Personal Communication)*

In this way, Pardo not only highlights the profound barriers to access and equality that exist, but also the more exploratory terms of "curiosity [and] accidental or purposeful experimentation" that can coexist, perhaps with a sense of productive tension, within the concept of disability performance as the last remaining avant garde. This tension – embodied, conceptual, and experimental – can be seen in *Risky Business* and *Song for a Weary Throat*. These distinct performances bring into focus the complexity of diverse representations and lived experiences of disability in a range of ways, showcasing some of the emergent practices arising from the field of disability arts in Australia.

Conclusion

In a volume on the controversial work *Disabled Theatre* by choreographer Jérôme Bel, the editors Sandra Umathum and Benjamin Wihstutz write,

> Is there such a thing as an aesthetics of disability and, if so, to what extent could it be understood as a political aesthetics, or an aesthetics of resistance? Under what circumstances can the stage serve as a place of emancipation for socially marginalized people?
>
> *(Umathum & Wihstutz 2015, 8)*

Throughout the development of this chapter, the project's researchers, including those that identify as disabled performers, considered how we might collaborate best with disability arts performers, to make and shape our research while being both reflexive and critical. This process continues, but we suggest that the notion of a 'last avant garde' is a powerful place to locate our discussion of contemporary disability performance precisely because the concept may refer to both the political and historical aspects of disability arts. It allows us to consider how disability is visible in the public sphere of societies and cultures, and how disability is linked to new approaches to aesthetics of art produced by people with disabilities.

Our aim is to counter the prevailing paradigm of 'normative' aesthetics and research, which has historically seen disabled people disenfranchised by those 'normative' aesthetic criteria as well as by 'normative' research methods and agents. We want to stage performances and collaborative methods of research that engage in dialogic exchanges, which are open to contingency, (heated) debate, alteration, and celebration of disability aesthetics. These radical acts arise because disabled, d/Deaf, and divergent people conceive and develop performances differently, and, as some of us aver, better, than our non-disabled peers (Davis 1997, 2). As Pardo suggests,

> In my experience of watching/supporting hundreds of works made by artists with disability, when works are disability led, they are deeply personal, radical (rule breaking), subjective, unexpected, uncomfortable, joyous, disorganised, uneven, compelling, distinctive, fraught with conflict, celebratory. Often all at the same time.
> *(Pardo 2017, Personal Communication)*

As such, underlying our exploration of the last avant garde is that self-determination and sustainable funding for the sector also has a direct impact on aesthetics. What our analysis of recent work from Quippings and Rawcus reveals is that disability arts in Australia holds a precarious position in which the policy, funding, and industry climate cannot be separated from the ability of artists to make aesthetic advances. Yet, in many ways, the aesthetic advances of this work appear to have also arisen because of the drive and verve to innovate despite a lack of funding stability, and in the face of indifference, barriers, and hardships. Finally, then, at the core of our examination of disability performance as the last avant garde, is our awareness that we may need to keep thinking *radically* – to keep tearing things up, or moving forward in different ways, as disability aesthetics is not simply a theme, ideology, or politics, but a way of conceptualising the future as much through thinking and talking about performance as through enacting it.

Notes

1 The team at the core of producing this article are two non-identifying researchers, Sarah Austin and Eddie Paterson, and one disabled-identifying researcher, Kath Duncan. We consulted with our project researchers, project steering committee, and artist/performers in developing this article.
2 Creatrix Tiara joined the Quippings troupe in late 2017 and is co-producing with Jax Jacki Brown the first 2018 Quippings show.
3 Founded by Greg Axtens, Kath Duncan, and Crusader Hillis, and managed by Rowland Thomson, Hares and Hyenas Bookshop Café began as a bookshop, then developed into an accessible performance space and nightspot, over the course of a nearly 30-year queer cultural community development project.

References

Austin, Sarah, Brophy, Chris, MacDowall, Lachlan, Paterson, Eddie, and Roberts, Winsome. 2015. *Beyond Access: The Creative Case for Inclusive Arts.* Melbourne: Arts Victoria. Accessed 1 June 2018. Available: www.artsaccess.com.au/beyond-access/.
Bragg, Melvyn. 2007. "The Last Remaining Avant-Garde Movement." *The Guardian*, 11 December 2007. Accessed 1 June 2018. Available www.theguardian.com/society/2007/dec/11/disability.arts.

Brown, Jax Jacki, and Duncan, Kath. 2016. "Quippings Mission Statement." *Quippings Website*. Accessed 1 June 2018. Available: www.quippingstroupe.com/mission-statement/.

Campbell, Fiona Kumari. 2009. *Contours of Ableism: The Production of Disability and Abledness*. London: Palgrave MacMillan.

David, Lennard J. ed. 1997. *The Disability Studies Reader*. London and New York: Routledge.

Dow, Steve. 2016. "Disability and the 'New Normal': Why Australia Needs to Ramp Up Access to Stage and Screen." *The Guardian Australia*, 24 September 2016. Accessed 1 June 2018. Available: www.theguardian.com/society/2016/sep/24/disability-and-the-new-normal-why-australia-needs-to-ramp-up-access-to-stage-and-screen.

Fraser, Mat. 1998. *Dazed and Confused Magazine*, September 1998, 78–83.

Goggin, Gerard, and Newell, Christopher. 2005. *Disability in Australia: Exposing a Social Apartheid*. Sydney: UNSW Press.

Hadley, Bree. 2017. "Disability Theatre in Australia: A Survey and a Sector Ecology." *Research in Drama Education: The Journal of Applied Theatre and Performance*. 22 (3): 305–324.

Hadley, Bree. 2014. *Disability, Public Space Performance and Spectatorship: Unconscious Performers*. London & New York: Palgrave MacMillan.

Kuppers, Petra. 2011. *Disability Culture and Community Performance: Find a Strange and Twisted Shape*. London: Palgrave MacMillan.

Lemon, Alex. 2011. "And Now I See." In Jennifer Bartlett, Sheila Black, and Michael Northen ed. *Beauty is a Verb: The New Poetry of Disability*. El Paso: Cinco Puntos Press, 167–168.

Lenakakis, Antonis, and Koltsida, Maria. 2017. "Disabled and Non-Disabled Actors Working in Partnership for a Theatrical Performance: A Research on Theatrical Partnerships As Enablers of Social and Behavioural Skills for Persons with Disabilities." *Research in Drama Education: The Journal of Applied Theatre and Performance*. 22 (3): 251–269.

Macpherson, Hannah, and Fox, Alice. 2016. "Listening Space: Lessons from Artists with and without Learning Disabilities." *Environment and Planning D: Society and Space*. 34 (2): 371–389.

Makeham, Paul, Hadley, Bree, and Kwok, Joon-Yee. 2012. "A 'Value Ecology' Approach to the Performing Arts." *M/C Journal*. 15 (3). Accessed 1 June 2018. Available: http://journal.media-culture.org.au/index.php/mcjournal/article/view/490.

Morgan, Michaela. 2017. "Risky Business: The Queer Performance Group Challenging Disability Stereotypes." *SBS Online Sexuality*, 29 November 2017. Accessed 1 June 2018. Available: www.sbs.com.au/topics/sexuality/fast-lane/article/2017/11/21/risky-business-queer-performance-group-challenging-disability-stereotypes.

Nierse, C.J., and Abma, T.A. 2011. "Developing Voice and Empowerment: The First Step towards a Broad Consultation in Research Agenda Setting." *Journal of Intellectual Disability Research*. 55 (4), 411–421.Price Waterhouse. 2011. "Disability Expectations: Investing in a better life, a stronger Australia." www.pwc.com.au/industry/government/assets/disability-in-australia.pdf.

Q&A. 2017. Q&A Hosted by Sarah Austin for *Song For a Weary Throat*, Theatre Works, Melbourne, Australia, 3 December 2017.

Quippings. 2017. *Risky Business*. Melbourne: Melba Spiegeltent, Collingwood.

Rawcus. 2017. *Song for a Weary Throat*, Theatre Works, St. Kilda: Melbourne.

Rawcus. 2018. *Song for a Weary Throat at Melbourne Festival*. 10–14 August 2018. Accessed 1 June 2018. Available: http://rawcus.org.au/2018/08/song-for-a-weary-throat-at-melbourne-festival/.

Sandahl, Carrie. 2003. "Queering the Crip or Cripping the Queer? Intersections of Queer and Crip Identities in Solo Autobiographical Performance." *GLQ: A Journal of Lesbian and Gay Studies*. 9 (1–2): 25–56.

Sandahl, Carrie. 2002. "Considering Disability: Disability Phenomenology's Role in Revolutionizing Theatrical Space." *Journal of Dramatic Theory & Criticism*. 2 (XVI): 17–32.

Sandahl, Carrie, and Auslander, Philip ed. 2005 *Bodies in Commotion: Disability and Performance*. Ann Arbor: University of Michigan Press.

Siebers, Tobin. 2010. *Disability Aesthetics*. Ann Arbor: University of Michigan Press.

Umathum, Sandra, and Wihstutz, Benjamin ed. 2015. *Disabled Theatre*. Zurich: Diaphanes.

Wood, Caitlyn ed. 2014. *Criptiques*. Middletown, DE: May Day Publishing.

21

Seeing things differently
Danielle's place making

Jori De Coster

Various authors (for example, Hall & Kearns 2001) describe the central role that place and spatial expression play in identity formation and social marginalisation. People with a disability are often described as people who are "relegated to sites of exclusion" where they are kept "in their place" and "know their place" (Kitchin 1998). However, people can also use specific strategies in their performance of daily life to transcend the limitations of place and dis/ability as a place-bounded identity. While other authors in this book focus on specific practices, such as art or art-based political activism that blur boundaries between aesthetic performance and social performance, I reflect upon these performances during daily life, where boundaries are continuously encountered and can be crossed.

To understand disability in terms of being and becoming, my PhD research (2012–2017) examined a number of 'places' in which differences appear in relations of interdependence through feelings of otherness and the idea of being different. Who we are as human beings is bound to the places that we inhabit (Ingold 2000). Ingold describes movement as integrated knowledge or "the passage from place to place and the changing horizons along the way" (Ingold 2000, 227).

While I am interested in 'culture,' as an anthropologist, others have rejected the idea of culture as something that is fixed and bounded, tied to a static place or locality. Culture is performed, and for anthropologists such as Fisher,

> Culture is not a variable; culture is relational, it is elsewhere or in passage, it is where meaning is woven and renewed, often through gaps and silences, and forces beyond the conscious control of individuals, and yet serves as the space where individual and institutional social responsibility and ethical struggle take place.
>
> *(Fisher 2007, 39)*

In what follows, I offer some fragments from my fieldwork with Danielle, a middle-aged black woman with a visual impairment. Although she grew up in the francophone part of Belgium, she lived in Flanders (the Flemish region) during my research phase. If we want to ask the question of how 'society' creates a place in which people with a significant difference can participate and human beings can become, we need to start with people with

Jori De Coster

disabilities' experience of everyday life through interactions. In her encounters with others, Danielle presents herself, reflects, learns from interactions, and further becomes. While the fieldwork methodology used a multi-method approach, including ethnography, participant observation, and storytelling, this writing intertwines my own narrative as a fieldworker with Danielle's voice and her reflections about notions such as place, identity, performance of self, and belonging.

Our search

"At this moment, I am searching … trying to understand why my life is the way it is now," Danielle tells me. For my own part, I am also trying to find Danielle in the pile of documents on my desk as I go through her different scraps of A3-format paper with big letters in thick black marker. Poetic reflections fuse with complaints and observations in Dutch and French and the unexpected and unintended presence of waffle recipes and shopping lists. The writing, but especially the rereading, of all this takes Danielle a long time. This is time that she, as a single mother of three, does not often have. But with the children at home a lot and with all of her other appointments, keeping a diary about things that otherwise would be left unspoken between us became part of the methodology. Moreover, Danielle loves words and language in general.

Movements across places

"Ah la Congolaise," Danielle opens the door with a smile. I smile too after being greeted like that and step into the corridor of her by now familiar house. "Boni?" I ask, and she answers in Lingala that all is well and smiles again. Both of us enjoy the sudden opportunity to practise the little Lingala we know. She learnt some words from her parents and I while visiting Kinshasa during fieldwork. Danielle's parents met in Belgium, but they and their families originate from both Congo's; The Democratic Republic of the Congo and The Republic of the Congo are two neighbouring countries in Central Africa. During the Mobutu era, an uncle abroad invited her mother to study in Belgium. Eventually, her mother arrived in Belgium and became a nurse. Her father had difficulties finding a job ("my mother said that nothing he did ever worked") and travelled a lot between Belgium and DR Congo for business and another woman. Both parents and their four children led a turbulent existence in a village in Wallonia due to poverty and a life organised between different countries and realities. Danielle remembers how relatives who stayed over for some time often overcrowded the small family house. One of her brothers was diagnosed through "white psychology," with what appeared to be ADHD, which according to Danielle only brought further problems. After a while, this brother started travelling to DR Congo with their father. Some years ago, her father died during one of these trips abroad. Danielle never really understood what had happened during these journeys, what kind of "business" the men were involved in.

> He (her brother) told me, "You are not Belgian." What he meant to say was that "we are Africans."

Our visit together to the town in Wallonia, on this day, 26 August 2015, became a walk down memory lane. As we made our way along playing fields, former social housing projects, and small streets in between the graveyard and the church, Danielle recalled her life as a child here and smiled. Casey writes how

Moving in or through a given place, the body imports its own emplaced past into its present experience: its local history is literally a history of locales. This very importation of past places occurs simultaneously with the body's ongoing establishment of directionality, level and distance, and indeed influences these in myriad ways.

(Casey 1987, 194)

At secondary school, Danielle's eyesight diminished – it started with not being able to see the ball in sports class anymore – as did her learning capacities and self-esteem. She considered herself timid and stressed. Although she changed schools and finished her schooling, she still has trouble finding work.

> I thought, "Oh la la, I am here in Belgium – *allez*, the organisation is fine – but how are people in Africa doing?" It was so difficult ... with my *handicap*. With papers here that tell companies they'll be subsidised if they give a job to a person with a disability - I was thinking like that - I was convinced I could find a job ... I have my degree from secondary school ... It turned out to be not that evident. *Ik begon te twijfelen.* [I started to doubt] ... I do not have a job. My children are my job. (...) At that moment I was already going to music school, and I was learning braille. I started to think about people in Africa ... Perhaps I can do something for them?

She only found out what was wrong with her eyesight in 2005. A nurse who had a son with the same kind of eye disorder accidentally introduced the word 'impairment' and encouraged her to discuss it with a doctor. So, for the first time Danielle thought "ah ... an impairment!" and she called her mother.

> And I have had so many medical exams before that! In the States, I would have taken them to court! I still had my driver's license and could have killed someone. I was so angry! People just don't care!
>
> They never asked me any questions! They just saw a black girl, from social housing. "She doesn't like to work." It disgusts me!

Danielle has not been able to find a doctor in Belgium who can define her bodily difference. She has received different diagnoses from different people. Her eyesight is reduced to the faint light flares in her environment. Her uncle in the US has invited her to look for medical treatment there several times. The impairment is not very common in her immediate family – except for her brother who has "blue eyes," which indicated a health problem to the family – but she heard that it was common in a region in DR Congo.

In her 20s, Danielle followed her Congolese boyfriend, who never wanted to marry her, to a Flemish town, and they raised three children. The little money they had from her mother and his salary allowed them to buy the same house in which she lives today. To save money on electricity, her partner simply cut the electric wires in the house. The newly bought kitchen from IKEA was there to be viewed and shown to visitors, not to be used without great care.

> I looked at myself and I saw that I was black so I told myself that I would live my life with another black person. It was like that.
>
> Even the kitchen here that I did not choose, I could not use. "Yes, because I am Danielle. I am *handicapée*." He insulted me like that. I have not bought anything because I did not work.

Jori De Coster

> You eat breakfast or you don't, but simple things … cornflakes, bread, jam. It was not *semoule* (that I made him for breakfast).
>
> (him:) "Yes, but the other women make it!"

Danielle's partner often travelled between Belgium and DR Congo, like her brother and father. According to Danielle, he was seeing other women there. The relationship did not last. Reinterpreting her own sense of religion as a Christian, instead of as a Catholic, finally made her leave him. They separated, and she became a single mother of three. "Belief is something between my God and myself," Danielle says.

At the beginning of 2015, Danielle's former partner wanted to sell their house and Danielle went to court to resolve the matter. Together with her lawyer, we spent an entire morning waiting for the hearing. Her partner never showed up. That year many of our conversations concerned Danielle's fear of losing the house, the neighbourhood she had mastered with her cane, her children's schools around the corner, the bus schedules she knew so well. The event made clear the extent to which she was habituated, entangled, and how difficult it would be for her to move away.

In 2016, the matter was pleaded again, but this time in front of a notary between both partners and their lawyers. Her former partner and his male lawyer had asked for more money because he had renovated most of the house while maintaining a job. Danielle had been jobless the whole time they were together. She was not happy with the final agreement. After the meeting with the notary, Danielle, her female lawyer, and I started a discussion. While standing on the street in front of the notary's office we discussed the meaning of the word "work." It was Danielle who had taken care of the household and their three children before, during, and after their separation.

Finding your 'self' in everyday life's disorder

On 29 May 2015, I am sitting alone at Danielle's kitchen table. It is early Friday morning. Upstairs, Danielle tries to get her daughter dressed and her other son out of bed. Danielle's eldest son is at boarding school. After finding her way through organised piles of clothing, Danielle returns downstairs to prepare breakfast. "Where's the knife? Everything needs to be in place." Her children, however, do not stay in one place and fill the small living room and kitchen with overlapping sounds, movements, and stuff. Meanwhile I watch the clock, one of the few things hanging on the wall. It is almost time to leave for our trip. The bus will be waiting at the station. In between everything else, Danielle goes to her desk with the télélamp to enlarge the letters of the Braille Liga's invitation to take part in today's trip. The time of departure is only now properly revealed to me and confirmed to Danielle.

After bringing the children to school, Danielle and I make our own ways through other pedestrians, children running around, traffic lights, cyclists, and traffic signs. I choose to go through a park instead of walking next to the big road. This confuses Danielle until she finds some landmarks to orient herself again.

In one of our first conversations, Danielle told me that her disability made her lose direction in life.

> This is where I wanted to be going; studying, having a job, making a life … Then the disability came (…) *"Avec l'handicap ça m'a bouffé … pourquoi le me sort pas …"* [With the handicap … it has 'eaten' me … why does it not leave me?] My future was vague.

266

In the disorder of everyday life, Danielle also tries to find her 'self.' Sites of racism, sexism, memory, and struggle appear in our conversations where she often tries to situate herself in relation to others. She often thinks about 'the Other,' and the other tells her who she is. However, the many intersections that make up her life sometimes make her feel lost in a chaotic in-betweenness.

> I wait for the other first. How the other will present himself.
> *Le mélange est en moi, je peux pas me situer.* [I'm blended. I cannot situate my self.]
> When you can really observe life with your eyes ... when you cannot observe life well ... I believe you are lost and it is not easy.

When asked, she refers to herself as Belgian or Afro-Belgian because of her Belgian birthplace. Her family history and the colour of her skin become other markers. The disorder in her life comes from, among others, "the weight of our history," establishing the connection between her situation in Belgium and Africa's history.

> I know the history of these Empires (The Romans, Napoleon) but about Congo I do not know this very well.
> I am unable to situate myself ... Bon, through our skin ... There are things that are really difficult because ... There are things in the United States that are very unpleasant and unjust with all these people that are getting themselves killed ... and at the same time I always tell myself ... *whew* ... This is not America here ...
> My disability is my report to my position in the world ... because I have the weight of our past ... our past with colonisation ... enslavement and the fact that our parents came here, all this jostling with all these different movements that are going on.
> Sometime soon they will attack me too because I am *handicapée*. Hitler has done so.
> We Africans, we break things and we never ask why. Yes, our lives are sometimes broken too. Perhaps I'm wrong but I have seen many broken things.
> I love to write and I love things from African origin. White stories are not the same as black realities. Basically, there were four of us, but when we were little my mother adopted two of my cousins. This is really the African spirit. When I was little I told myself that I would love to adopt too, but when these children from the family came to visit our house they broke everything and created disorder. There was no stability.

In *All Our Kin* (1974), Carol Stack describes her research with an Afro-American family in an area with the fictitious name 'the Flats.' Her study shows how family members, despite poverty's harsh conditions, develop strategies to continue everyday life, for example through domestic networks and practices such as child keeping. Danielle's impairment often became an obstruction to enable these kinds of relations and practices through which people eventually still get by. This happened so often that she no longer dared to ask for further help.

> Now ... at 8 pm they phone me and come dropping off their children here. I told them I had to meet someone ... With my disability, I want the children to eat there (at the table). They (the visiting children) eat everywhere. It's really disorder. There is no stability.

She orientates herself in the world as a person with a visual impairment as: "*moi, une personne handicapée*," and in the world of people with a bodily difference in between seeing and being blind.

> When I walk the streets, I hear people talking about me: "Mama, she is *blind*." I don't say anything but I am not '*blind*'. I have a very low vision, it's not the same thing.

267

In this excerpt, Danielle narrates that she is not 'blind.' In the situation that she describes, she bumps into a Dutch word that makes her into something that she is not. Stockall (2001) describes a woman named Betty and her journey of self-reconstruction and how one's identity relates to the space that society creates for that person. She takes language into account in her discussion about identity construction. Stockall considers language from a postmodern perspective, as "a form of relatedness where meaningful communication is constructed through coordinated effort between participants" (Stockall 2001, 130). She further describes the situation of a mother and her child who – through their language use – expand their interactional boundaries and transform each other. In Danielle's story, boundaries of opportunity are often not extended in interactions.

In Danielle's daily self-performance, other people often become spectators and sometimes even test Danielle because of her particular impairment. She feels their gaze upon her, searching for signs that she really is 'blind.' For example, during a visit to a federal agency, the man behind the desk was attentively observing the way she walked into the room. He asked Danielle what kind of shirt he was wearing and if she could see any details on it.

> Because *voilà* my eyes, they move and they cannot believe because in the streets, when people see us we are with our cane, but they say … They are never sure … but what is annoying in my case is that it is emphasised because I am black.
>
> Me, with my handicap, when I have to go to ask for help … It is like passing a real school exam.

Overall, her entire situation makes her constantly question her identity, especially her identity as a woman. More than anything else, she considers herself a mother.

> Me, a woman … I ask myself … am I really a woman? Yes, I have given birth, it's true … that shows that I am a woman (cynically).

Danielle tries to find her way through all these constructions of difference. However, all of our discussions ended up involving our very humanity or being considered a human being.

> More than anything else I am a human being. I will end up being muted. That frightens me.

Belonging

For Danielle, defining who she is comes with a sense of belonging, "a sense of accord with the various physical and social contexts in which our lives are lived out" (Miller 2003, 220). Whether people belong to a place relates to relationships, local and global simultaneously, and the communities that characterise their lives. As individuals, people are simultaneously members of various groups that construct their sense of identity (family, work, church, village, etc.). Belonging is entangled with the (im)material environments humans dwell in and their sensorial and embodied experience of these environments. These complex senses of belonging shape people's multiple identities and performances of the self.

> The earth is my home. I believe I can go everywhere.
>
> I don't like to limit myself. Anyway, I do not feel like a stranger, like I am living in a foreign country. I really loved something a boy in my class once said: "*l'étranger, c'est*

l'autre. C'est celui qui mets le désordre." [The Other is *the Absolute Unknown*. It is the other who creates disorder.]

Her relationship with the neighbourhood can be very complex. She often stays at home because she is afraid of getting lost, of taking the wrong bus or turning the wrong corner. She is afraid to bump into people, to fall down, and she is afraid that people will laugh at her, especially teenagers.

> I have the impression that the streets are not big enough for me. I feel enormous. I have the impression that I am not walking straight ahead ... so I doubt ... I don't know if people see this when I walk ... I doubt a lot ... at the big square for instance with that kind of ground. I never walk with confidence, I never feel comfortable in the streets, on the sidewalks ... I want to go fast ... I just do what I need to do and then I come back ... so that's it; so that people see the least possible of me.

The state's regimes of belonging make Danielle acutely aware of her identity as an unemployed, black, disabled woman. Her story shows how situations are created "in which individuals are entrapped within discourses and regimes." Lakoff and Collier (2004) talk about 'regimes of living' or "congeries of moral reasoning and practice that emerge in situations that present ethical problems – that is, situations in which the question of how to live is at stake" (Lakoff & Collier 2004, 420). Hodder uses the notion of entanglement which focuses on "the practical messes, the everyday constraints and restrictions that people find themselves caught into" (Hodder 2016, 66). People with a disability, such as Danielle, often emphasise these constraints by the presence of several (state) services (and the norm they embody) in the home.

Danielle often repeats how the presence of the state in her home makes her feel that her house is her disability, how it feels like a prison, and that leaving is not an option. Her spatial exclusion pushes her into certain places and types of relationships that lack any sense of humanity, she says. Help is only on weekdays between nine o'clock and five o'clock. Social services make her feel poor, stupid, and infantile. Every expense needs to be negotiated with the social worker, and paying for school trips, clothes, a second-hand laptop becomes a battle. Danielle herself feels devalorised as the social service worker thinks she is not able to estimate the value of things. Her 'leefloon' (welfare allowance) does not allow her to live, and every social contact organised by the state feels fruitless. Instead of feeling integrated, all of the different services that visit her house often complicate things and make her feel blocked. Danielle depends on collaboration between social services and an organisation for people with impairment to access new communication technologies. All reciprocity in social work is superficial and hypocritical, she says when they tell her "it's her money, and that she is the boss who decides what happens to the money." Danielle often narrates feelings of being immobilised or stuck to a place, performing the recipient while others perform on her.

> It's true I need people to help me. But they are not there to help me! I need them for certain activities, but then they are not there! Social service starts at 8:30 am and ends at 12:30 pm or starts at 12:30 pm and ends at 4:30 pm. At that time, the children are not here but at school! Who is here during the weekend? Nobody! During the weekends, I have to take care of everything myself, alone! When they have finished their work, afterwards, they return to their homes, they close the files. They should think about why I feel pain everywhere!

> Me, I do not have money, because they told me to stay at home ... And then they come through the back door taking even more through all kinds of money! It makes me furious!
>
> They take money from our backs. Bon, it is true that it is not 'our' money. I have to be kind. It is true that this money comes from the entire Belgian community, who has kindly given this to me. *Merci à vous.* [Thank you] (We laugh) It's money from my mother. It's money from my nephews and nieces. From you. So, that's true. But really, stop wasting your money. It's sad, really. I am thrown in the garbage like that. Let's stop.
>
> I have another appointment to discuss my living allowance. I need it. I have my children so ... I have no choice ... It is very little this money but ... If I would not have my children I would say "*héla*! I'm off! I am going ... I don't like the States but that's a place where I could go ... to realise my dreams ... to dream ... Here? No, everybody's vision here is: "you have a disability? Just stay over there ... If you want to work ... take care of yourself!"
>
> They always connect us with '*le regard*', "There you go, you are a visually impaired person, go sit next to the other who is visually impaired or who is blind and who is unhappy."
>
> They come here to perform. They give their time and take much of my time. When they leave I am very tired. And I want to see through their work ... but I do not see exactly ... I do not see any results.

Moreover, after having an official meeting with a medical service she was told that they could not help her, as she did not fit their vision, and so one day they referred her to a psychiatrist:

> "We do not know how to help you. We think you will have to move into a more psychiatric direction because we have tried and we have gotten nowhere. We know it's hard, but perhaps the psychiatrist will succeed." (...) "But no, Danielle, you are tired. Your heart hurts." What's that all about? I do everything on foot! Everything on foot!

Danielle was given an old computer that stood in the corridor of her house for a while. It stood there, unused, until someone finally repaired it. It was not of any use to Danielle – she needs to connect it to another piece of adaptive technology equipment to be able to read the screen and the words and language she loves– but the children loved it. However, as Alex Lubet argues in Chapter 25 of this book, access to these kinds of technology "matters" (Miller 1998). After some months, Danielle's second-hand computer broke and she went without again. Her children's school, official instances, even the Braille Liga, all communicate by email and websites. She is always asked to look up information on the Internet – road descriptions and school announcements, for instance.

> When I didn't have Internet, I felt different too. It's like everybody is dressed and you're naked. Not everybody has a computer ...

Danielle also finds a strong sense of belonging in her religion as a Christian. She gets her sense of belonging less from going to Protestant Church, but by listening to her Bible.

> But in the end, you go there and you feel just like in society, completely different, completely excluded, because the people there ... they are nicely dressed, they are ... but I think a Church needs some kind of function. You arrive, there's prayer, we sing, the

priest preaches. But the women, for instance, could organise themselves. "Ah, there is a woman with that kind of problem, we have to help her, do something for the children, food, the household … we are going to try to help … and that could be a force. I can't find my place here either. It's really a pity because when you read the Bible you'll see that, yes, Jesus did miraculous work with paralyzed people, blind people, and who knows who else which shows that Churches are also here for us, but the reality when you go to Church.

Puzzling life

According to Giddens (1991), (late) modern social conditions provide individuals with more freedom to design and mould their place in society. Identity is about self-reflexivity and individual choice. I would comment here that it is not simply about individual choice, as people can also be caught in a double bind (Hodder 2016). People continuously search for new ways to locate and reposition themselves in a changing society. This is what Danielle does. She tries to order her life, and these actions are reflective for her. She gets feedback from her environment through her cane, her ears, and her memory. All of these give her a sense of place, an identity, a sense of belonging. She figures things out, reorientates herself, and continues her navigation. Through self-reflexivity, all of these events – such as our day trip – become internalised or part of her story. Danielle also organises her knowledge, performs based on that knowledge, and changes.

> *Formater mon esprit.* [Format my spirit]
> It is a war against everyone … you have to be alert.

The first time I visited Danielle at her place, she greeted me with surprise. How did I find her? Then again, other people often visit her because she is a person with a disability. While I got ready for our first formal interview, she got ready too. My voice recorder lay next to her Milestone recorder. She too wanted to register our conversation. This happened only during my first visit. However, Danielle frequently uses this technology and listens to her many recordings again afterwards. It improves her access to important practical information, conversations with unfamiliar people like me – when she feels brave enough to record – church prayers, and readings from the Bible, as well as poetry, music played at Braille Liga's events, feedback from her music school teacher, and her own flute music.

Whereas Danielle associates the presence of her mother and social services with disorder, she acknowledges that they also help sometimes. Other people can help her bring order to her life: one of the mothers at her children's school sometimes helps out; there is a pharmacist who knows that she cannot pay for her medication but plays along when she comes to the pharmacy. There is also her music teacher who also has a visual impairment and teaches her how to play the flute. Her eldest son helps her to manage the two other children's activities.

One service that enters her house occasionally specialises in helping children living in poverty. The organisation is present during some of my visits in the form of Hanne, a staff member assigned to Danielle's family. After a while, we recognise and greet each other on the street. I start receiving phone calls and emails to join them for meetings. We suddenly become a team that sometimes sits together at Danielle's kitchen table together with a girl from yet another organisation. Here, the family's everyday life is discussed.

Part of Hanne's job is to create order and structure, to build relationships between the family and their neighbourhood. Halfway through 2015, Hanne decided that the children's life could become more organised if we could just get some order in the house. During that time, Danielle did not feel well. She could not sleep. She spoke a lot about (material) leftovers from the past that she was unable to get rid of. When Hanne asked Danielle whether we could visit her bedroom, just to take a look at the quality of the mattress, we were taken by surprise. Danielle did not seem to be aware of us — intruding (staring) visitors — sharing a dazzled look when confronted with a bedroom stuffed with so much stuff and a mattress unworthy of the name.

Hanne decided Danielle needs a new mattress, and a new IKEA closet perhaps, to organise all of the children's belongings then spread throughout the house. In preparation for this purchase, we also decided that we could help Danielle to create more space in her house generally. We throw away all of the broken furniture, the huge old television that her mother was keeping to send to Kinshasa, piles of papers, dust, parts of pots, toys, and packaging. Over the next few months, the four of us organised ourselves to deal with the broken things, the fragments, the dirt, the past. Danielle also asked other friends to help her get rid of all the clutter. We finally succeeded in getting the new closet and, one morning in December, we put it together. It was a nice surprise for the children when they came home from school.

The radio and television create a different kind of order because they can give Danielle a sense of time and place. Jo Tacchi (1998) describes how radio sounds, for instance, add to the material culture of everyday life and co-create social selves. She paraphrases one of her informants who says that "radio stimulates the imagination, and imagination gives substance to sound. And sound can be seen to give substance, in its materiality, to relations between self and others" (Tacchi 1998, 43). Danielle smiles when she talks about all these voices that reach her from all over the world via the radio and television to tell her about literature, bad news. She connects her story to stories that come from elsewhere: violence in Syria and France, racism in the US, but also music and poetry.

Danielle also connects her story to her children's future. She tries to order her life through an understanding of her past so that she can improve her children's future. Because of the turbulent family history, Danielle spends much of her time trying to understand what went wrong and how she can prevent her children from such a dreadful heritage. According to authors such as Richards, "these entanglements of disability, immigration, space and place continue into the present" (Richards 2004, n.p.).

> They think one of my sons has autism. He did not feel well in his class being the only black child. "You have to act normal," they say. What is normal? Now he is in fourth grade and the teacher does not like to have him in class.
>
> Now I understand my mistake. But I must understand more. For my children. I have a little girl and two boys, but boys are stronger anyway (in theory). Sometimes I think that perhaps I should try to understand my life, my family tree, and my history so I can transmit these stories to my children. To look at this together to understand the pitfalls, so they can be careful, because I don't know if what I am doing now is ok?
>
> Jonah (eldest son) is a teenager so we often have a fight. He does not want to do this (accompany his little sister to after school activities). Normally a father would help out but the father is absent. And people ask me why I keep doing this and I tell them that my children have talent and that it needs to be developed.

Religion – "that means Christianity not the Church," according to Danielle – also gives her a sense of order. "For we are all susceptible to the uneasy sense "that there is *something wrong about us* as we naturally stand," and what we call religion is a set of ideas and practices for getting in touch with an "elsewhere," an "otherness," or a "wider self" that lies beyond the horizons of one's immediate life world, especially at times when our "lower being has gone to pieces in the wreck'" (James 1958 cited Jackson & Piette 2015).

> There is no order but nevertheless God has order ... he is organised.
>
> Me, personally, I work with my Bible alone. Me, I believe in God, I am Christian ... It's a powerful spirit. My mother is Catholic but always tells me: "At the base we are animist. The whites came to impose their (hi)stories." I said, "That's true, but when we read the Bible ... God is Law ... There are spirits who are fighting each other. *C'est parole contre parole via le comportment.* [It's discourse against discourse through conduct] ... My mother says: "But God ... look what he has done for you! Do you think it is just what he has done to you ...?" ... Of course, what he has done is just, because there is something that needs to be unveiled. There is something that needs to be said. If I am like this it is because there is something. Another accent that needs to be put in place because there is something that I need to discover ... I know that my God is working for me. I believe in God and there is a forceful malicious spirit there, against me. I belief it is a really strong spirit ... But because the world has never seen an African committing suicide, I don't like doing that ... (Laughs). I have cried a lot.
>
> Integration is not a word in the Bible.
>
> Jesus' work is not about nationalism, fundamentalism or integration.

Danielle's own interpretation of language and her bodily difference also bring order or a sense of understanding the world.

> *L'handicap*, it's the others, the others of the social world. *L'handicap* is a mysterious dame ... mysterious because *voilà* I am already nowhere ... my handicap is already a mystery. When they tell you in a meeting they don't know how to help you ... They do not know where I am ..." And she (*l'handicap*) is a liar and a thief because she comes, and she steals from me... It's a dame that lives in me, who has taken my eyes ... I call her a liar, but perhaps she is not a liar. Perhaps she is only showing me something, perhaps it's that too!

As it created order, religion often created disorder in Danielle's family and was often a topic of discussion between her and her mother. According to Danielle, there are bad forces that manifest themselves through money and alcohol. After some time, she quit the Flemish church in her neighbourhood and started frequenting an Evangelical Church in another town.

Danielle also invited me to a prayer session at her house. The children's toys and school material that lay around at the house now bulged out of the closet. One of Danielle's friends started reading from a book. The text was discussed and linked to the Bible after each passage. Meanwhile, Danielle recorded everything to listen to it again afterwards.

In these discussions with Danielle and one of her friends, Audrey, God was described as love, truth, life, harmony. They explained that God was "like a father," "a giver" who stands for conception. When a person takes the bread during Mass, it means that this person takes "*la parole de Dieu*" (God's Word). "Satan" stands for bad things in life, fears: "on television there are movements like that."

Belief is about making associations, Audrey explained. There is a source and then there are the spirit, the soul, and the body. Danielle and Audrey discussed how things were going wrong on the level of the spirit's connection to the human body. When one is blocked it means that energy can no longer circulate. Human beings develop systems that are contrary to nature and block "*la demande existentiel*" ("the existential demand"). When people are together as a community, they can augment the amount of energy to unblock a person. For this reason, it is better to pray in-group. A relation is always a dialogue; there is never simple dependence. Nowadays, people are often disconnected from the spiritual. During these conversations in Danielle's tiny living room, the universe came into existence and became ordered.

Making a life, not a living

According to Biehl and Locke, "becoming" refers to those individual and collective struggles to come to terms with events and intolerable conditions and to shake loose, to whatever degree possible, from determinants and definitions. It refers to the primacy of desire, claims to rights over power, to openness, and the flux of social fields. Becoming has a transformative potential. In his work, Deleuze emphasises the powers and potentials of desire, the ways in which social fields ceaselessly leak and transform, and the in-between, plastic, and ever-unfinished nature of life (Biehl & Locke 2010, 317).

In her search for help, Danielle has encountered different services and spent a lot of time talking about her problems. Some people addressed her about this and told her she had confidence because she was able to talk about her problems a lot:

> I told them: no. This has nothing to do with confidence. I talk because I am a human being. And human beings talk to each other. You express yourself. I am sorry. And what's more, I am really talkative.

In some of our conversations, Danielle reflected about the strength of her impairment: how it became a kind of internship, an education even. Titchkosky (2003) describes disability as a 'teacher' about our 'temporally abled' society. Due to its in-betweenness, disability can teach us alternative possibilities of being and knowing, of new meanings and beginnings. However, people have to open up to such engagements. Danielle's own processes of (dis) entanglement have changed her attitude towards her visual impairment:

> I am really living a true internship. It is really a big internship because I understand human relationships; I understand ways of talking.

Danielle is involved in problem-solving practices daily, but she finds strength in many things: in her children, her Bible, but also in small meaningful gestures from people around her. While we sit in her living room, Danielle dreams of visiting the States again, visiting her uncle, and perhaps finding some opportunities there. Danielle dreams about starting up a project for people in Congo and perhaps visiting that place one day. She talks about God and the universe with friends. She wants to improve her language and writing skills, and she continues to play the flute. Thus, as Danielle performs through and reflects upon daily encounters with others, she is continuously crossing multiple boundaries and she is making a life of her own.

> At the moment I am here, but one day I hope to go there (Congo), put my feet there, because I have the right ... when you look at the earth there are no thresholds, frontiers.

References

Biehl, João, and Locke, Peter. 2010. "Deleuze and the Anthropology of Becoming." *Current Anthropology*. 51 (3): 317–351. Accessed 20 April 2018. Available: doi:10.1086/651466.

Casey, Edward S. 1987. *Remembering: A Phenomenological Study*. Bloomington: Indiana University Press.

Fisher, Michael M.J. 2007. "Culture and Cultural Analysis as Experimental Systems." *Cultural Anthropology*. 22 (1): 1–65. Accessed 20 April 2018. Available: doi:10.1525/can.2007.22.1.1.

Giddens, Anthony. 1991. *Modernity and Self-Identity: Self and Society in the Late Modern Age*. Stanford: Stanford University Press.

Hall, Edward, and Kearns, Robin. 2001. "Making Space for the 'Intellectual' in Geographies of Disability." *Health & Place*. 7 (3): 237–246. Accessed 20 April 2018. Available: www.ncbi.nlm.nih.gov/pubmed/11439258.

Hodder, Ian. 2016. *Studies in Human-Thing Entanglement* . Accessed 28 September 2018. Available: http://www.ian-hodder.com/books/studies-human-thing-entanglement.

Ingold, Tim. 2000. *The Perception of the Environment: Essays on Livelihood, Dwelling and Skill*. London: Routledge.

Jackson, Michael, and Piette, Albert. 2015. *What is Existential Anthropology?* New Oxford & New York: Berghahn Books.

James, William. 1958. *The Varieties of Religious Experience: A Study in Human Nature*. New York: Signet.

22

ADAPT in space! Science fiction and disability

Storying interdependence

Petra Kuppers

The lug nut was stuck. Ham tried to find better leverage. He reached across the corridor and rammed one end of his pike into the soft pleather. Now he tried again, and the lug came loose with ease, allowing the wheelchair wheel to detach from its axle. Ham carefully sprinkled oil into the elderly screw housing, careful not to let any of the precious fluid lift off into the air. Reassembling it all, he patted Daniel's shoulder. Daniel had been patiently watching. Daniel engaged the electromagnet that kept him attached to an arbitrary 'down' in the corridor and pressed the joystick forward. He rolled.

"Yay! Thanks, Ham. I think we are good for now."

Ham smiled, shyly, and carefully tucked away the tools with his living hand. He never spoke with his mouth, but the fingers of his one hand were delicate apparatuses, ready-to-be-augmented flower stamens to insert and twist in the smallest spaces. All shipmates appreciated his skill. They let him know with eyes and caressing touch when he had saved them again from immobility.

Daniel rolled down the corridor, reengaged the magnet on a different level at the next juncture, and continued on his journey at a 45-degree angle from his previous path.

At the end of the corridor lay the sustainment bay, equipped for long-term space travel, rigged up by non-standard hands and with rations scavenged from both military and long-range ore exploration surplus. The three other travellers had already assembled around the round table. Most of the factory-standard fixed chairs had long been replaced by smooth anchor units to lock wheelchairs in place, or other modules jury-rigged for particular travellers.

When Daniel slotted himself in, he joined Clara, also a powerchair user. Behind him was Jamie, triple amputee who couldn't sit on her decimated butt cheeks and who instead leaned against a portable pole magnetically fixed to either relative ceiling or relative floor, and lastly, Colo, demurely folded up in their chair, a non-Earth student taking Anthropology 425 as part of an Outward Bound degree course. Colo's green skin and six major appendages had long ceased to be remarkable to Daniel, who had grown up on Star Trek: The Next Generation reruns in his bio-family's holopod. Colo had been the one to call this meeting, as was their weekly duty.

Science fiction and disability

"Ham just fixed my stuck wheel, he's putting away his gear. Should be here soon."

Clara signalled her response, an appreciation for their mechanic, with swift fingers. Her tiny dark digits emerged from the pouch she used to keep her small body safe, since her thermal self-regulation was inadequate to the leaching cold right next to the vacuum.

Colo was dramatic, as ever, throwing back their long torso so the one remaining regulation chair around the table creaked and protested. At that point, Ham emerged. A smile creased his nut-brown skin upon seeing his comrades.

"All together! All together now!" Colo couldn't contain their excitement again. Daniel and Clara looked on indulgently, while Jaime threw a quick glance of fortification up toward the loose end of her pole.

"So what's the plan for the next docking?" She asked, accompanying her speech with a quick slide down Ham's living arm, to make sure he felt included in their discussion.

Daniel had their new itinerary ready on his tablet.

"Here's what we discussed last week. Entry on Centauri 7, Jamie in full limb drag establishes visitor credentials, talks about a child to give up, and visits with Un-Perfect Camp 37. Scope. Map. Then she comes back, and we prepare dark entry, once we figure out the guard holiday schedule for 37. Any comments, news, issues?"

They discussed the plan, one not dissimilar from many unsuccessful and a few successful raids. If the personnel of the holding camps were thin on the ground and inattentive, they had always been able to rescue some of the U-Ps. Some children, some grown, but kept like babies in beds, voiceless, agency-less, rarely able to see themselves as part of any group.

Colo took notes, acted as scribe. They got way too excited by planned future actions and needed something to focus on to be fully present in these meetings. Colo's people also had warehoused their cripples, but not for as long and never as systematically as Earth's people, and they were still unused to the normality with which Earthlings and their seeds discarded precious fellow humanoid life in holding tanks. The proposed liberation would be Colo's third raid, so they were still an activist greenhorn. Their limbs fluttered, and the others watched on and patiently waited till they scrolled and corrected the auto-transcription.

Clara had much to say about fine-tuning the selection process. She wanted more U-P6, the ones labelled 'useless lives,' a category that had remerged from Nazi Germany's catalogues around year 2035, shortly after the complete privatisation of old Earth.

"They are so hard to move, though, Clara. I want to rescue them, but we could get out 3 or 4 U-Ps for each U-P6 we liberate." Daniel wanted to be reasonable, but he couldn't figure out how to bring this argument home to Clara.

She signed back, "The other U-Ps usually have language, can sing to one another from one bed to the next. The 6s have nothing there, and so much to give us."

She was right, of course. Each category 6 had been able to modulate new speech and communication protocols, had been able to enrich the neuro-net of practices immensely, more than any U-Ps that had been able to adapt to their jailor's communication styles.

Ham pushed his good hand onto the table, fingers wide. They all watched the open palm and the waving digits. Each fingertip wove a song, a colour, a flower opening – one for Daniel, one for Clara, one for Jaime, one for Colo.

Late that night, Daniel dreamed of the rescue. He witnessed himself rolling past locked doors, dark and light eyes looking out at him, pleading arms, fingers, mouths open and stretched tongues, vibrating, reaching out into the unreachable corridor. Tears streamed down his face as he bypassed them, careful not to roll over outstretched hands reaching through bars. He remembered his own liberation, a regular U-P, hoisted aboard a tricked-out electric chair, the rescue he had so long heard about in myths and fables passed from cell to cell at night, as little boys, girls, and others tried to soothe themselves to sleep.

His re-education had begun in Ham's arms, in Clara's eyes, and culminated when they gifted him with his own specifically manufactured bay at the oval table.

He had been given a choice: rehome on one of the sanctuary planets. Or join the resistance, fight the normals, and liberate their people one by one. The choice had not been a hard one.

A tenday later, Daniel stood outside Camp 37, his graphite wheels whisper-quiet on the glass-like obsidian pavement, even in the near-Earth gravity of the small planet. Inside, Jaime had already disengaged a relatively weakly secured guard routine, had bypassed codes and electric locks with an hour's work, once the guards were either out for a night in the local bars or asleep, nodding over the latest telenovela beamed in from Earth's entertainment districts. Security was lax, as the objects of imprisonment were not valuable commodities – their lone value lay in insurance claims, not in any labour capacity.

A click. The lock in front of Daniel disengaged and swung inward.

Here ends this story fragment. To continue this narrative is to take sides, to engage, to identify, beyond the secure parameters of the potential suspense and narrative drive of a fully formed story. Interdependence is one core value of disability culture observations – and so this chapter uses user-focused, interactive, interdependent, and open forms as a way of marrying formal elements of storytelling to ways of knowing (or productive unknowing) disability. Tell your own story, maybe another fragment, maybe an ending, maybe a new beginning. Write with a partner, if that feels more supportive, tell the story orally if you prefer.

Go on your own story journey now. As you enter the inner worlds of Daniel, Jamie, Clara, Ham and Colo, see their emerging skin-shapes as invitations. Who would you like to be, or who would you like to meet? What are their thoughts, being part of this rescue mission, the break into the facility to 'free their people'? Why are they in the fight? What is their backstory, their motivation, and their breaking point?

'Free our People' is one of the rallying calls of grassroots disability rights movements, and organisations like the real ADAPT, a US-based group that uses actions like sit-ins in senate offices, etc., as tools to draw attention to the plights of warehoused disabled people. Here is their mission statement:

> ADAPT is a national grass-roots community that organizes disability rights activists to engage in nonviolent direct action, including civil disobedience, to assure the civil and human rights of people with disabilities to live in freedom.
>
> *(ADAPT website 2017)*

In this *ADAPT in Space* future story, who is behind bars, who awaits our team on the other side of the slowly swinging gate? Use your own imagination to flesh out the scene: will there be a love interest, and if so, of which gender/sexuality arrangement? Will there be racialised and class narratives of who is behind bars, who without, who cares for whom, who are the prison guards? What kind of U-P6 people will the team find in the camp? What are the differences between U-P6 and U-Ps, in your mind? What will their options be for liberating them, for establishing contact, for communication consent? What happens when they have

Science fiction and disability

to leave some U-Ps behind, appendages full of U-P6s? What will go on inside your chosen hero when one of the U-Ps shouts out a heart-wrenching plea for freedom – or, maybe, if they are to be left behind, for death? Would you assist them?

Many of the ethical and moral dilemmas and deep-seated ideas of 'lives not worth living' come to the fore in our communal and different narrations of disability. Issues that arise include

- complex issues of valuing people with communication differences and with cognitive differences
- pain and isolation
- mental distress associated with and not associated with mental health difference
- matters specific to acquired disability or veteran status
- effects of racialisation and colonialism on denigrated humanity
- effect of being undervalued on one's own sense of self, and much more.

As you are unspooling your own story, see where the understories are, the basements or hidden corridors that link parts of stories together. Transection and intersections, travels and encounters are the driving forces of much creative writing, so allow yourself moments of surprise in the telling of what is happening on the other side of the gate and in the retreat back to the starship.

Follow one character as they are trying to connect with the freshly freed prisoner. What concepts of freedom and responsibility make sense to someone who has been incarcerated all their lives? What survival strategies might they have honed, in a place with rationed food, set times of observations, little and highly codified markets of affection, warmth, and commodity? How can these strategies adapt to life in a free-er disability culture community, rattling about in space? Does hierarchy, traumatic stress, or fear affect newly freed people as they integrate with the shipmates? How do people find ways to be together, to survive and thrive? Are any of their tools and strategies particular to disability status, or do the team adapt tactics from other social justice movements? Think of something very practical like 'the human mic' as a way to amplify quiet voices between cells (an instrument much used in the Occupy movement of the early 2000s, where lack of electricity created a way of amplifying a speaker's voices through echo). Or think of the tactic of pill hording, preparing a (final) exit path for desperate folks in the folds of mattresses or under loose tiles, or maybe just as a way of reminding one's self of the possibility of (even complicated) ways of establishing and fantasising control.

Maybe you'll find yourself encountering aliens. Engage non-realist forms of embodiment and enmindment, i.e. ways of being that are not known in the world we live in, and touch them to the lives of people whose bodies and minds were or are denigrated, seen as tragic, or lost. How can you shape new worlds, with new openings for difference?

These are some questions to get going with, resources for engaging with important disability culture questions. You can spin on Jaime's or Daniel's story while taking a bath or having a meal, you could talk with someone about it, maybe even slip into their voices. Or you could analyse a TV show with disabled characters. Do you see Ham anywhere when you turn on the TV or read a book? Or Clara? Why would Jamie be a not unlikely figure in mainstream cinematic representation of 'positive images' of disabled people? How do the people here relate to highly visible disability representations in science fiction, such as actor Dominique Pinon as John Vriess, the motorised-wheelchair-using mechanic in *Alien: Resurrection*, or Professor Xavier in the *X-Men* franchise?

Think about the interiority of the people you are fantasising stories around. In the fragment here, Daniel is the emotional centre, and we get just a few glimpses into some of the other characters, based on Daniel's past interactions and observations. How would this story look like if Ham were the narrator? What sensations might be foregrounded, which might be less important? Or Colo? Or an as of yet unknown character, either a rescuer or an escapee, or both, like Daniel? In conclusion: this story has no conclusion. It is open; it points the way to new narratives; it offers incompletion as a linking strategy. Disability authors have begun to reclaim disability from the often stereotypical and one-dimensional uses in mainstream texts. Collections like *Accessing the Future: A Disability-Themed Anthology of Speculative Fiction* (Al-Ayad & Allan 2016) address these openings for thinking disability differently in genre literature.

At the same time, activists of all kinds are embracing again the value of storytelling as a way of generating and sharing knowledges, as a form of analysis in its own right. *Octavia's Brood: Science Fiction Stories from Social Justice Movements* (2015) is an example of this kind of inquiry. Evoking Octavia Butler, an African-American US science fiction writer and a form of fictional sociologist, the two editors, Walidah Imarisha and adrienne maree brown, worked with activists in multiple fields to explore the use of genre narrative as a way to communicate the need for and the opportunities of change.

ADAPT in Space sees itself in that heritage, embracing the capacities of all humans to tell stories, and to rehearse actions and reactions in them. Storytelling is an activist tool, a way of making change. Participatory artistic practices can allow us to feel things, to feel thing differently, and to invent new appreciations for the diversity of humanity and beyond. The storytelling round table is prepared; your adapted and comfortable seat is waiting. No open fire in the space station, but everything else goes.

References

ADAPT. 2017. *ADAPT website*. Accessed 1 May 2018. Available: http://adapt.org/.
Al-Ayad, Djibril, and Allan, Kathryn, ed. 2016. *Accessing the Future: A Disability-Themed Anthology of Speculative Fiction*. Accessed 1 May 2018. Available: Futurefire.net.
Imarisha, Walidah, and brown, adrienne maree, ed. 2015. *Octavia's Brood: Science Fiction Stories from Social Justice Movements*. Chico: AK Press.

23
Environments, ecologies, and climates of crises
Engaging disability arts and cultures as creative wilderness

Bronwyn Preece

Due to a mutation in one of my genes, I (self-) identify as a (dis)abled woman.

I am corollary thesaurus-ised as a FREAK of nature,[1] thus opening a critical lens through which I can examine notions of estrangement of both disability and environment.

This chapter is established on the premise that Western orientations towards our perceptions of the 'environment,' 'ecology,' 'nature,' and 'wilderness' are synonymous with many of our societal perceptions of disability. Estrangement, practices of othering, individualisation, and objectification permeate our relationships with(in) all of these categories of experience. This chapter will simultaneously and immediately plunge into the paradoxes which accompany identification/differentiation with disability and [the] ecological environment as they pertain to the context of the larger, interdependent global framework. The role/risk of anthropocentrism in the discussion will be addressed, tackling the question of whether the performance of ecological and disabled identities is dependent on the presence of the human. And, further, are we performing notions of 'ecological selves' (termed by philosopher Arne Naess), or are we as 'selves' being performed by ecology? Are – and/or how are – we performing and/or being performed by a self-disabling ecology? The lenses of the chapter will widen and narrow, moving from foci through focus: personalised through my own performance experience and approach.

I am an improviser. I am poet. I am eARThist. I work largely site-specifically, site-sensitively. I am an animist. I experience the world as alive. Exploring notions of place-based ethical encounters and reciprocity with the "more-than-human world" (Abram 1997), my work comes with an understanding that my engagement must negotiate as transparently as possible the human-centredness of my vantage point. Jane Bennett (2010) argues that this thus elicits a degree of healthy anthropomorphism necessary to address this understanding. I maintain, though I am able to resonate and communicate on a variety of levels with the other-than-human world, that I remain human in empathetic encounter with this dynamic animism. My felt and experiential perspectives, my engagement with the world, still might avail themselves to an uneven reciprocity (see Barbara Hillyer 1993; Wallace Heim 2012).

Following a particular improvisational performance, I had an insight which metaphorically problematised the boundaries of (my)self in concert with a wider frame. As I articulated it: *"If I truly believe that I am inextricably part of earth, then what is disability performing through my ecological body at this time; and what is an ecological self performing through disability?"*

My epiphanic moment was prompted as I reviewed video footage of a delineated 'solo' improvised show, entitled *one disclaimer....* During the performance, I could not make sense/could not place/could not contextualise my shaking hands and voice within it. Through disclamation, I was trying – both ironically and unsuccessfully – to deny their existence. I realised that the few moments of performance synthesis that occurred were when I simply genuinely let my body shake – to express itself 'naturally' – with me giving it/myself my full attention.

Through both a delineated performance space, and the "performance of everyday life" (Goffman 1959), *I had come to recognise my body is a vibrant metaphor for our diseased and disabled ecological condition.* I was a mover and a shaker, *shaking.* David Abram reminds us that "[h]owever determinate one's genetic inheritance, it must still, as it were, be woven into the present" (Abram 1997, 50). This necessarily prompts a receptivity to the textures and shapes of the given present which transforms into "a spontaneous creativity in adjusting oneself (and one's inheritance) to those contours. It is this open activity, ... by whichever animate organism necessarily orients itself to the world" (Abram 1997, 50).

As an animate organism, the potential for interrogating my perception from – and through – performance, offered the opportunity to transform my perspicacity into a new improvisatory relationship. *Performance eARTh.* "[T]o give permission to the artist within your disabled body is an outrageous act of defiance," claims Bonnie Klein, co-founder of Vancouver's Society for Disability Arts and Culture (cited Johnston 2012, 5). My improvisational defiance would, in turn, reveal both convivial and contradictory outcomes. As Brandon Larson (2013) remarks "[n]ot only is the choice of metaphor an ethical choice, it is also performative, which enlarges its significance even more" (Larson 2013, 141). He continues, suggesting "that the metaphors we choose are not merely cognitive: they lead to actions in the world that have consequences" (Larson 2013, 141) (Figure 23.1).

My moment of insightful arrest established a potentially inconsistent usage and/or double-edged metaphor: the valuing of disabled perspectives for what they might facilitate as means to engage practically with the climatic crisis, whilst equating the condition of crisis with disability. This critical juncture of these seemingly opposing vantage points/narratives in the paradox of ecological|disability provides the intersectional creative crux of my work, and the larger paradox of the global situation as a whole. My performance work *does* hold in its awareness the established problematics that have been cited about using metaphor vis-à-vis disability (see Sontag 1989; Sandahl 2001; Sandahl & Auslander 2005). Whilst valuing this argument, I engage in explorations which examine the potential benefits of employing disability metaphors as a tool for empowering and provoking change. Here, there is potency for understanding and communicating experiential feelings across bodies: trans-corporally.

Ecology is commonly understood as the study of the relationships between organisms to one another and to their environment or physical surroundings or "the science of the *living* environment" (Odum 1959, 4, emphasis added). Now, the term has been arguably appropriated to be synonymous with notions of interconnection: its basis still one which, again arguably, favours individuation. Often used interchangeably, ecology "has become vaguely synonymous with 'environmentalism,' even though for decades it was used exclusively to refer to a formal scientific pursuit" (Keller & Golley 2000, 3). Stemming from biology, the ecological lens – the science of studying living organisms – is engaged in examining systems

Environments, ecologies, and climates of crises

Figure 23.1 Bronwyn Preece, site-specific improvisation, Huddersfield, United Kingdom, 12 May 2015. Image by Franc Chamberlain

by way of studying the individual nature of living animals and plants in interaction. Ecology, so defined and understood, bifurcates and dichotomises. I am cautious around 'ecological' terminology, in that it is grounded in what Tim Ingold observes about the dominant narrative. He suggests:

> An understanding of the unity of life in terms of genealogical relatedness is bought at the cost of cutting out every single organism from the relational matrix in which it lives and grows. In this understanding, life presents itself to our awareness not as the interlaced meshwork ... but rather as an immense scheme of classification.
>
> *(Ingold 2011, 163)*

The more often destructive, rather than beneficial, ramifications of natural classification – shared with disability communities – is addressed in part by Eugene T. Gendlin, who asserts that "We need not think of nature as artificially constructed out of separate pieces, although it is useful (and dangerous) to construct and reconstruct them" (Gendlin 1998, 38). This paradox of the employment of ecology-as-lens is perhaps best captured by J. Baird Callicott's comment: "If it weren't for ecology we would not be aware that we have an 'ecologic crisis'" (Callicott 2005, 1169).

Though I can find rapport with many of the demands of the environmental movement which is trying to address what is commonly referred to as the ecological crisis, in addition to steering away from using ecology, I avoid, even more so, the words environment, wilderness, and/or nature. "In the wilderness myth, the body is pure, 'solo,' left to its own devices, and

283

Bronwyn Preece

unmediated by any kind of aid" (Ray 2009, 48). Though not the case with the now-common British and European usage of the term "rewilding" (Monbiot 2014) – a term that remains site specific, and arguably an attempt to 'un-Other' – these terms seem to emphasise an 'out there' or distanced orientation, steeped in a complicated legacy of privileged White-Western Romanticism, Enlightenment, and more recent conservation protection efforts (see Evernden 1992; Morton 2007; Finney 2014). Timothy Morton remarks that "putting something called Nature on a pedestal and admiring it from afar does for the environment what patriarchy does for the figure of Woman" (Morton 2007, 5). He calls this an act of paradoxical "sadistic admiration" (Morton 2007, 5). Lucy Lippard continues:

> In the last twenty years or so, the word "environment" has replaced and demythologized a great part of what was once considered Mother Nature, but it allows us to maintain the separation: humans are the center, *surrounded* by everything else, reflecting the way Western culture has been built in opposition to nature.
>
> *(Lippard 1997, 12, original emphasis)*

As a female improvising (with) disabilities, "there is another predator out there: exhilarating sensual identification with landforms and processes is countered by social fear and oppression" (Lippard 1997, 17). Sarah Jaquette Ray identifies a systemically embedded view she calls the "disability-equals-alienation-from-nature-trope" (Ray 2009, 61). As a woman, I *do* experience "sensual identification with landforms" (Lippard 1997, 17). And as I claim this, I am not suggesting that men cannot experience the same affinity – in fact, my inclusive argument does not posit a binary between male/female connectivity with/ as earth. Through my experience of reflections through these landforms, I am better able to relate to my 'own' body – through my dis*abling* distance/proximity. These reflections always have to contend with perspective and access, and within a disability frame are often constructed through a polarising discussion which focuses either on "ignoring the limitations of the body or triumphing over them" (Kafer 2013, 142; see also Akhila Vimal C. in Chapter 27 of this book on representations of disability that rely on overcoming disability). It is through discussions of access (not limited solely to the physical, gendered, or raced, but also financial and the 'sacred') that areas such as mountaintops, steep cliffs, and remote extremes associated with our constructions of a Western conquerable wilderness evoke the ability to understand our cultural concepts of nature as being largely built by and for the able-bodied. Thus, what is rendered is an assumed inaccessibility on the part of the non-normative body. Kafer (2013) asks, "[h]ow might we read disability into these formations?" (Kafer 2013, 130). Petra Kuppers deduces that disability "is one of the organising principles of what we think it means to be human, and how a society organizes itself" (Kuppers 2014, 9). And what it means to be human is contingent on being of this world, of these formations. Disability thereby becomes a shared ecology. Bruce Henderson and Noam Ostrander (2010) remark that

> it is not facile to assert that we are all involved in disability now, whether in our present state, in our relationship with the world around us, both personally and politically, or in our own futures.
>
> *(Henderson & Ostrander 2010, 2)*

Disability and the ecological register resonate without much effort, or as Morton puts it, "the ecological thought is also friendly to disability" (Morton 2010, 85).

Mutation – arguably, the genetic property of many disabilities – is a natural phenomenon. I do not consider all disability the 'product' of mutation; however, this is a term which relates to my personal relationship/entry point to exploring this arena of thought/practice/living. One of the processes of mutation, for example, is known as "genetic polymorphism" (Suzuki 1997, 132) and "is a fundamental characteristic of a vibrant, healthy species, a reflection of its successful evolutionary history and continued potential to adapt to unpredictable change" (Suzuki 1997, 133). Peggy Phelan (2005) similarly remarks, "it is necessary to think of disability as both a natural condition in all human life and as a social interpretation that informs and illuminates the phantasm of normative and 'proper' bodies" (Phelan 2005, 324).

My improvisatory process, by relating earth-as-bodied-Body, permits me a liminal leap into the site of the phantasmal. As I do, I engage with questions about what constitutes notions of the normative and proper. The social interpretation of disability (to which I am contributing and challenging) advocates through disability studies for an embracing of the disabled person into the social/built environment as a recognised necessary phenomenon on a continuum. By so doing, it dissolves to some extent the estranged and othering status so often attributed to disability. However, that being said, the social model of disability is premised on an uncomfortable and paradoxical perpetuation of viewing the social environment as the sole built environment. Much as with nature, disability exists as a social creation (see Kafer 2013). So, naturally, a world in balance holds disability as part of, not separate from, its activities. Tobin Siebers claims the "disabled body seems difficult for the theory of social construction to absorb: disability is at once its best example and a significant counterexample" (Siebers 2001, 57). Ato Quayson (2013) upholds this observation, remarking that disability simultaneously oscillates between "a pure process of abstraction" and "a set of material conditions" (Quayson 2013, 206). Bree Hadley further contends that "this paradoxical positioning of the disabled body is a personal, political and ethical issue not just for themselves, but for their spectators and for society at large" (Hadley 2014, 7).

I am, therefore, now able to address what might have been understood earlier as a potential contradiction within my epiphany, when I equated the current condition of crisis to disability, while simultaneously appreciating dis|abled perspectives for what they might facilitate as means to engage practically with the socially ecological climatic crisis (see Abbott & Porter 2013; Wolbring 2014). I posit that a disabled world is in fact one that has disrupted the (ecological) balance. By paradoxically trying to institutionalise norms, on a sweeping scale – ranging from monocultures, to economic structures, to international patenting laws, to sanctioning dominant narratives – a disabled world is one that seeks to horizontalise through homogenisation. In so doing, the qualities of variability inherently needed to ensure survival are revoked. Eli Clare accurately cautions, however, that it:

> would be all too convenient and neat to suggest that without disability, humans recreate ourselves as a monoculture—a cornfield, wheat field, tree farm—lacking some fundamental biodiversity. Environmentalists have named biodiversity a central motivation for ecosystem restoration and a foundation for continued life on the planet. But to declare the absence of disability as synonymous with a monoculture disregards the multiplicity of cultures among humans. It glosses over the ways in which culture and nature have been set against each other in the white Western world.
>
> *(Clare 2014, 214)*

Incorporating the above flag, Clare does declare, much as I do, that: "the bodies of both disabled/chronically ill people and restored [ecosystems] resist the impulse toward and the

Bronwyn Preece

reality of monocultures" (Clare 2014, 215). Euro-American attitudes about nature, explains Patricia Limerick, are expressed largely in a "historical 'model' that has 'all the flexibility and variation of a conveyor belt; it gives very little room to variations in groups and individuals or in places or times'" (Limerick 2000, 173). Abram addresses how this perpetuates a cycle of normalisation, which then feeds overconsumption as a means to compensate:

> the mass-produced artifacts of civilization, from milk cartons to washing machines to computers, draw our senses into a dance that endlessly reiterates itself *without variation*. To the sensing body these artifacts are, like all phenomena, animate and even alive, but their life is profoundly constrained by their specific "functions."
>
> *(Abram 1997, 64, original emphasis)*

The effect and affect are the production of populations drawn into a dynamic of dulling their senses. The search for variety leads to taking up the material project in its more physical and substantive form. The dulled norm is countered through the acquisition of more things, new products, more stuff. These objects massage our relationships to temporal frames of use, life, and decomposition. Phelan remarks that, "we are simultaneously alive to our death and deadened to aspects of our life" (Phelan 2005, 324). Her apt observation edgily applies here. So, too, does Stacy Alaimo's (2016) persistent reminder that: "It is how objects are entangled—economically, politically, and substantially across bodies, ecosystems, and built environments—that matters, not how each object exists in isolation" (Alaimo 2016, 187).

These accumulative acts could be termed as material dis-attachments, ecological dis-placements: actively displacing our relationships to what the term ecology is meant to convey. Through them, I am/become, *more than ever*, attached to that carton of milk and the dirty laundry of our washing machines. From within this frame, Kuppers' (2016) locates the current agency – and necessity – of disabled/disability activism:

> Living in precarious times, this is the core feature of our [disability culture] activism: getting together, as best as we can, and acknowledging relationality, to each other, to land, acknowledging joy and sadness, connecting ourselves to a world of cultural production that needs our presence.
>
> *(Kuppers 2016, n.p.)*

Though tension between current discourses of disability cultures and environmental restoration remains (Clare 2014), people with disabilities are actively positioned to advocate on behalf of variance, deviance, and mutability. They embody the double-edged metaphoric tools which may – with a linguistic nod to both Audre Lorde and the etymology of the term ecology from the Greek *oikos* 'house' + -logy (Oxford English Dictionary n.d., n.p.) – be described as simultaneously dismantling and rebuilding the house of the Master ecology. David Abbott and Sue Porter (2013) remark that the lived experience of interdependency "provides a neat bridge between the environmental and disability movements" (Abbott & Porter 2013, 851). However, with this understanding comes an uncomfortable bedfellow:

> Constant reference to environmental causes of disability renders those who are disabled passive recipients of harm and implies their inability to be full participants in environmental justice work. It removes agency from those identified as disabled, especially when those working for disability rights are not part of the environmental justice conversation.
>
> *(Johnson 2017, 83)*

And further, the 2016 World Social Forum framed this tension as such:

> One the one hand, there is a tendency for non-disabled environmental justice advocates to highlight the disabling impacts of resource extraction or contamination in ways that treat the tragedy of disabled bodies as self-evident. On the other, white, liberal disability rights frameworks oriented towards the celebration of the disabled body often prevent us from recognizing and organizing against disablement caused by environmentally unjust projects and models. How to move forward with these tensions in mind?
>
> *(World Social Forum 2016, n.p.)*

The moving forward necessitates an awareness of the interplay of the past as crucial in understanding our present-into-future. David Fancy demands that the performance community address how we may continue "to develop theories and practices of performance that are informed by an understanding of participation that does not situate agency or cause solely within human bodies?" (Fancy 2011, 62).

Advocating from and as a site of performance, through the tiered complexities of disability – both directly/indirectly – has engaged in me a subjective reciprocal relationalism. *My body is of earth. I perform and am performed by earth. I am simultaneously soil and soiled by and as earth*: I am *this* active and temporally extended (de)composition. In William Bryant Logan's *Dirt: The Ecstatic Skin of the Earth*, he remarks that soil chemists have been trying to pin down exactly what humus is (which I consider here, as our *grounded* animate interlocutor) for decades, without success:

> Radical disorder is the key to the functions of humus. At the molecular level, it may indeed be the most disordered material on earth. No two molecules of humus may be alike. Though no one has difficulty recognizing a humus molecule, it is quite likely unique, because it works upon fractal principles. Simple geometries define any given part of it, but the modes for the combining of these shapes produce a vast array of different manifestations at different scales. For humus, similarity is rampant, but identity nonexistent.
>
> *(Logan 1995, 16)*

Corroboratively digging this analogy into the ecology-disability frame, I am an animated, embodied intersection of this underpinning chemistry, wherein "intersectionality as a theory references the tendency of identities to construct one another reciprocally" (Collins 2003, 208). As Donna Haraway remarks, "...becoming human, becoming humus, becoming terran, has another shape – the side-winding, snaky shape of becoming-with" (Haraway 2016, 119). I am the metaphor of our soil: ecologically disabled in the adaptive agency found by trying to navigate its/our simultaneous life-giving potential and overly resourced, dirty extraction. I am, once again, met by Phelan's (2005) assertion that "we are simultaneously alive to our death and deadened to aspects of our life" (Phelan 2005, 324).

I have been forced to explore my wanting to dismiss an identification with the term ecology, while I simultaneously, purposefully, enact societal gestures/behaviours perceived (to a certain degree) as embodying an ecological ethic. Through improvisation, I am trying to straddle this very *performative* binary: a collision of worldviews and semiotics. Within this, I am enjoying the manoeuvrability of the term disability: wherein the remaking of dis*abilities* necessarily becomes multiple. Dis-ability, by proxy takes up the ecological (and feminist)

Bronwyn Preece

project of interconnection, leaving me with an understanding that none of the labels are strictly my own:

> disability citizenship and aesthetics can model a form of being in space and in relation that aligns with many ecological thoughts, but can foreground access and its diversity, questioning notions of the pristine and too-carefully-guarded boundaries (of all kinds), of virgin land and heroic forays.
>
> *(Kuppers 2007, 31)*

Deep Ecologist and Buddhist scholar Joanna Macy has extensively studied General Systems Theory as corroboratory with the Buddhist appreciation of a dependently co-arising world. She offers process descriptors which can be understood as the intra-permeability of disability-within-ecology:

> When perturbations in the environment persist and produce a continual mismatching between input and encoded norms, the system either becomes dysfunctional or hits on new behaviors which are adaptive to the new conditions. These are then stabilized at a new level of negative feedback. In the process the system has altered its norms and complexified its structure for greater adaptability. The novelty-producing feedback is called "deviation-amplifying"; the movement is toward differentiation and more improbable steady states.
>
> *(Macy 1991, 76)*

Clearly articulated, an ecosystem is based on continually adapting to change, to difference – the process of which is not assimilation or sublimation, but rather displacing the possibility of fixed 'norms.' Thus, deviance becomes the mechanism towards establishing improbable balance. In this case, I am equating deviance with the properties of the disabled body, to be interpreted as reason to value the insights emanating from such perspectives. I note that Macy does not directly reference disability. However, her remarks corroborate with the premise which supports the denial/suppression of the natural integration of disability is what ironically creates a 'disabled planet' (understood as being one that aims to achieve homogenisation, thus invoking the term's usage in more conventional sense). Dis-Ability is thus a complexifying and improvisatory agent:

> A wild population of any species consists always of individuals whose genetic constitution varies widely. In other words, potentiality and readiness for change is already built into the survival unit.
>
> *(Bateson 1972, 451)*

In this sense, through the provocatively adaptable improvisatory frame, Henderson and Ostrander (2010) argue that disability studies exist always as a form of performance studies (see also Sandahl & Auslander 2005; Hadley 2014; Kuppers 2014). Similarly, Baz Kershaw (2008) and Bonnie Marranca (1996) argue that so too is the study of ecology one of performance. Adele H. Bealer remarks that

> Identifying the performative consequences of a variety of discursive paradigms, eco-performance theory might also discover opportunities for transgressive intervention in the gaps and spaces that open between performance as doing and performativity as social construction.
>
> *(Bealer 2012, 5)*

Rooted in a reciprocal discursivity, I contend therefore that as I approach the discussion of the relationship(s) between performing disabled and ecological identities, necessarily any of my observations will remain human. *Will remain as those of a White woman*. It is with 'exceptional' privilege that I am able to explore my being-with-and-of-the-world, from this perspective.

My apprehension of my human perspective as a unique privilege does not automatically answer the questions: Is the performance of ecological and disabled identities dependent on the presence of the human? Are we performing notions of 'ecological selves,' or are we, as 'selves,' being performed by ecology? And, further, are we performing and/or being performed by a self-disabling ecology? A renewed look at 'performance' is thus essential, to address the question of whether I perceive the more-than-human world as performing performers.

The line is blurry.

I could signal the flamboyant courting rituals of birds or the waggle dance of bees, as examples which confound my human deciphering. With David Attenborough ringing in my head, these displays appear to be performances-out-of-the-ordinary realm of the everyday – as something more specialised – particularly characterised and amplified by each individual animal. Such a display appears through our human perceptions, to be an amplification of the everyday, and therefore arguably, a performance. However, I argue that the bird's, or the bee's, behaviour is necessarily improvisatory. The animal is responding and accommodating the present context of the moment. Their movements, as Chamberlain interprets, may "indicate an evolutionary continuity from insect behaviour to human dance – particularly in its non-literal aspect" (Chamberlain, Lavery & Yarrow 2012, 23). The non-literal, and interrelated, evolutionary animal-human connection finds Maxine Sheets-Johnstone asserting that "[d]ance is older than man, in his bones as it were, in the form of an evolving empowering morphology and qualitative kinetics" (2009, 324). In such cases, I would argue that the essence - if not the term - of performance is present within the actions of the bee and bird.

This same bird or bee, *in situ*, is perhaps negotiating the disabling/disability factors that may influence the performance equation: such as deforestation or air pollution. The effects of the climate crisis have quite possibly forced the need for an exaggerated form of performance – an acceleration of the improvisatory – unto the more-than-human world: inextricably a co-performative paradigm.

In "Interspecies Improvisation" (2016), sound improviser David Rothenberg makes mention of the noted and rapid changes that have been occurring within the "songs" of the South Pacific Humpback Whale population. He credits this occurrence to several whales which "got lost" (Rothenberg 2016, 519). He does not question what might have prompted such directional differences, but rather focuses with marvel on how quickly the whales significantly adapted their own songs and affected the songs of those whales amongst whom they now found themselves. Though his angle of enquiry holds much merit, I do find it shocking, if not sadly ironic, that a practitioner of sonics would not have perhaps questioned if (human-made) sound may have forced the whales off course. Could the magnitude of underwater sonar or the dense swirling plastic gyres not be contributing factors to the disturbance of the whales' echolocational abilities? I suggest – much as Cornell University marine bioacoustics expert Christopher Clark asserts in "How Ocean Noise Pollution Wreaks Havoc on Marine Life" (Schiffman 2016) – that such environmental factors well might have been.

Articles in *Current Biology* (Garland et al. 2011) and *Nature* (Noad et al. 2000) report a desire for novelty on the part of the whales, as the factor for their changing songs. "Cultural transmission" and "cultural revolution" feature, respectively, in their titles. As much as this may be true, neither article affords any ecological speculation about the cultural dimension. Though I acknowledge that this might have been beyond their purview, neither of these articles asks why the whales may have been off course, nor if/how we may have been implicated in rendering them so, a line of thinking I think should be considered. Their dis-(echo)-location was taken as a given, as if part of 'normal' anthropocentric parlance, with humans resuming their space, arguably, as distanced spectators. By highlighting this point, I admit, however, that I am tending towards two assumptions, the first being that I believe that 'environmental' factors influenced the whales' behaviour, and the second being my willingness to accept that, in fact, the whales were indeed off course. In conjunction with my first assumption, the latter may appear inadvertently to non-facetiously dismiss the possibility that the whales may have been travelling in different directions to meet representatives in order to consider different courses of action or they might have been meeting to check out whether sound and plastic pollution were common across the oceans. The potentiality for anthropocentric – if not anthropomorphic – interpretations must continuously come into check. However, the gauge, as a human respondent, is limited at best.

I cannot conceive of the performance of ecology and disability in the absence of the human because the human is inextricable from earth. Through this interconnection, our human performances of ecology and disability are continuously informing and being informed by/effected and affected by the other-than-human world, and so they cannot be conceived of apart. Paradoxically, my apprehension of ecology as a worldview, from which I cannot be made or am separate from, becomes objectified when I chose to name or discuss 'it.' And yet, here I transfer the same qualities of invoking an essence bequeathed upon the more-than-human, to best understand my performance as human. Similarly, performing an 'ecological self' is contingent on being performed by ecology. Though I, human, might not be present in a plastic gyre in the Pacific, a piece of plastic that I used very well might be. In turn, the plastic gets consumed by an albatross, or becomes the leaching home of hermit crab, which in turn, and thus, and then...:

> One bottle cap—such a negligible bit of stuff to humans—may persist in killing birds and fish for hundreds (thousands?) of years. There is something uncanny about ordinary human objects becoming the stuff of horror and destruction; these effects are magnified by the strange jumbling of scale in which a tiny bit of plastic can wreak havoc on the ecologies of the vast seas.
>
> *(Alaimo 2016, 130)*

Thus, we all are engaging in 'ecologically' performing the simultaneity of being performed by a self-disabling ecology. The human does not necessarily have to be physically present in one site to affect another. *On land. In sea.* Concurrently, the improvisations of the animate world, near and far, shape and in-form me:

> The potential for a revised responsiveness in one's connections with distant voices and lands is possible, brought about by the assemblage of conversations in a space imbued with the aesthetic, and in which an ethical response is not pre-figured, but improvised and formed through those exchanges.
>
> *(Heim 2006, 208)*

Environments, ecologies, and climates of crises

All at once we are embedded within a discussion of trans-corporeality. Intriguing dimension is found by specifically approaching the above considerations through globe-spanning aesthetic practices. Improvised exchanges are metered and mattered through this (oft malignant) web. Alaimo remarks that:

> Toxic bodies may provoke material, trans-corporeal ethics that turn from the disembodied values and ideals of bounded individuals toward an attention to situated, evolving practices that have far-reaching and often unforeseen consequences for multiple peoples, species, and ecologies.
>
> *(Alaimo 2010, 22)*

We have produced our own toxins. We are metabolising ourselves through our own productions and, according to Kershaw (2012), performance compulsions. We have created our own diseases: Multiple-Chemical Sensitivity, otherwise known as Environmental Illness, among others. As Morton remarks, industrial society has produced "asbestos, radioactivity, and dioxins, which have truly opened the body to its environment, albeit in the negative" (Morton 2007, 108). All this comes in tandem with the invention of the environment: "born at exactly the moment when it became a problem" (Morton 2007, 141). Gregory Bateson accurately observes that "Conscious man, as a changer of his environment, is now fully able to wreck himself and that environment—with the very best of conscious intentions" (Bateson 1972, 446).

Nancy Tuana (2008) provides the example of drinking a drink from an aluminium (derived of earth) can. The can is then incinerated. The sensing and permeable body, reciprocally animate, inhales the fumes:

> The parts of the plastic become as much a part of my flesh as parts of the coke that I drank. Once the molecular interaction occurs, there is no divide between nature/ culture, natural/artificial. These distinctions, while at times useful, are metaphysically problematic, for there are important migrations between and across these divides that can be occluded.
>
> *(Tuana 2008, 202)*

The lines of contingency and agency become marred, at times, through and by an overwhelming sense of imprisonment, of occlusion. The rhetoric/knowledges of intra-connection and interdependence all of a sudden don't exist as windows to freedom, but as the most oppressive of understandings. Through oppression, from oppression, the task of my improvisations, our performances, my and our disability is perhaps best articulated, with a nod to Stephen Bottoms and Matthew Goulish's *Small Acts of Repair* (2013), as means to hold and fold these feelings into 'small *acts* of (potential) repair.' And in so doing, I am reminded by Morton that we are "duty bound to hold the slimy in view" (Morton 2007, 159).

I do.

Acknowledgements

Please note that this chapter is compiled from, and directly cites, the author's PhD, entitled "Performing Embodiment: Improvisational Investigations into the Intersections of Ecology and Disability" (anticipated completion 2019).

Bronwyn Preece

Note

1 The thesaurus of the New Oxford American English Dictionary, clearly, and in uppercase, draws a connection between ecology and mutation when the thesaurus offers as synonym for mutant: FREAK (OF NATURE). The British version uses all lowercase, and drops the brackets.

References

Abbott, David, and Porter, Sue. 2013. "Environmental Hazard and Disabled People: From Vulnerable to Expert to Interconnected." *Disability & Society*. 28 (6): 839–852.

Abram, David. 1997. *The Spell of the Sensuous*. New York: Vintage.

Alaimo, Stacy. 2016. *Exposed*. Minneapolis: University of Minnesota Press.

Alaimo, Stacy. 2010. *Bodily Natures: Science, Environment and the Material Self*. Bloomington: Indiana University Press.Bateson, Gregory. 1972. *Steps to an Ecology of Mind*. Northvale: Jason Aronson Inc.

Bealer, Adele. 2012. "Reading Out Loud: Performing Ecocriticism as a Practice of the Wild." *Interdisciplinary Studies in Literature and Environment*. 19 (1): 5–23.

Bennett, Jane. 2010. *Vibrant Matter: A Political Ecology of Things*. Durham: Duke University Press.

Bottoms, Stephen, and Goulish, Matthew. 2013. *Small Acts of Repair: Performance, Ecology and Goat Island*. London: Routledge.

Callicott, J. Baird. 2005. "Natural Law and Natural Rights." In Bron R. Taylor ed. *Encyclopedia of Religion and Nature*, 1. New York: Continuum, 1168–1169.

Chamberlain, Franc, Lavery, Carl, and Yarrow, Ralph. 2012. "Steps towards an Ecology of Performance." *University of Bucharest Review, Literary and Cultural Studies Series*. 14: 6–38.

Clare, Eli. 2014. "Meditations on Natural Worlds, Disabled Bodies, and a Politics of Cure." In Serenella Iovino and Serpil Oppermann ed. *Material Ecocriticism*. Bloomington: Indiana University Press, 204–220.

Collins, Patricia Hill. 2003. "Some Group Matters: Intersectionality, Situated Standpoints, and Black Feminist Thought." In Tommy L. Lott and John P. Pittman ed. *A Companion to African-American Philosophy*. Malden: Blackwell, 205–229.

Evernden, Neil. 1992. *The Social Creation of Nature*. Baltimore: The John Hopkins University Press.

Fancy, David. 2011. "Geoperformativity: Immanence, Performance and the Earth." *Performance Research*. 16 (4): 62–72.

Finney, Caroline. 2014. *Black Faces, White Spaces: Reimagining the Relationships of African American to the Great Outdoors*. Chapel Hill: University of North Carolina Press.

Garland, Ellen C., Goldizien, Anne W., Rekdahl, Melinda L., Constantine, Rochelle, Garrigue, Claire, Hauser, Nan Daeschler, Poole, Michael, Robbins, Jooke, Noad, Michael J. 2011. "Dynamic Horizontal Cultural Transmission of Humpback Whale Song at the Ocean Basin Scale." *Current Biology*. 21: 687–691.

Gendlin, Eugene T. 1998. *The Process Manual*. Chicago: University of Chicago Press.

Hadley, Bree. 2014. *Disability, Public Space Performance and Spectatorship: Unconscious Performers*. Basingstoke: Palgrave Macmillan.

Goffman, Erving. 1959. *The Presentation of Self in Everyday Life*. Middlesex: Penguin Books.

Haraway, Donna. 2016. *Staying with the Trouble: Making Kin in the Chthulucene*. Durham: Duke University Press.

Heim, Wallace. 2012. "Can a Place Learn?" *Performance Research: A Journal of the Performing Arts*. 17 (4): 120–127.

Heim, Wallace. 2006. "Navigating Voices." In Gabriella Giannachi and Nigel Thrift ed. *Performing Nature: Explorations in Ecology and the Arts*. Bern: Peter Lang, 199–216.Henderson, Bruce, and Ostrander, Norm ed. 2010. *Understanding Disability Studies and Performance Studies*. London: Routledge.

Hillyer, Barbara. 1993. *Feminism and Disability*. Norman: University of Oklahoma Press.

Ingold, Tim. 2011. *Being Alive: Essays on Movement, Knowledge and Description*. New York: Routledge.

Johnson, Valerie Ann. 2017. "Bringing Together Feminist Disability Studies and Environmental Justice." In Sarah Jaquette Ray and Jay Sibara ed. *Disability Studies and Environmental Humanities*. Lincoln: University of Nebraska Press, 73–93.

Johnston, Kirsty. 2012. *Stage Turns: Canadian Disability Theatre*. Montréal: McGill-Queen's University Press.

Kafer, Alison. 2013. *Feminist, Queer, Crip*. Bloomington: Indiana University Press.

Keller, David R., and Golley, Frank B. 2000. *The Philosophy of Ecology: From Science to Synthesis*. Athens: University of Georgia Press.

Kershaw, Baz. 2012. "This Is The Way The World Ends, Not...?': On Performance Compulsion And Climate Change." *Performance Research: A Journal of the Performing Arts*. 17 (4): 5–17.

Kershaw, Baz ed. 2008. *Theatre Ecology*. Cambridge: Cambridge University Press.

Kuppers, Petra. 2016. "Different Rhythms: Land-Based Disability Performances in Precarious Times." MLA Conference paper, Austin, Texas, 7–10 January 2016. Accessed 7 June 2016. Available: www.academia.edu/20061601/Different_Rhythms_Land-Based_Disability_Performances_in_Precarious_Times_MLA_2016_talk.

Kuppers, Petra. 2014. *Studying Disability Arts and Culture: An Introduction*. Basingstoke: Palgrave Macmillan.Kuppers, Petra. 2007. "Outsides: Disability Culture Nature Poetry." *Journal of Literary Disability*. 1 (1): 22–33.

Larson, Brendon M.H. 2013. "The Metaphorical Links between Ecology, Ethics, and Society." In Ricardo Rozzi, Steward Pickett, Claire Palmer, Juan J. Armesto, and J. Baird Callicott ed. *Linking Ecology and Ethics for a Changing World: Values, Philosophy, and Action*. Ecology and Ethics 1, Dordrecht: Springer Science and Media, 137–145.

Limerick, Patricia. 2000. *Something in the Soil: Legacies and Reckonings in the New West*. New York: Norton.

Lippard, Lucy R. 1997. *The Lure of the Local: Senses of Place in a Multicentered World*. New York: The New Press.

Logan, William Bryant. 1995. *Dirt: The Ecstatic Skin of the Earth*. East Rutherford: Riverhead Books.

Lorde, Audre. 2007/1979. "The Master's Tools Will Never Dismantle the Master's House." In Audre Lorde *Sister Outsider*. Berkeley: Crossing Press, 110–113.

Macy, Joanna. 1991. *Mutual Causality in Buddhism and General Systems Theory: The Dharma of Natural Systems*. Albany: State University of New York Press.

Marranca, Bonnie. 1996. *Ecologies of Theater*. Baltimore: John Hopkins University Press/PAJ.

Monbiot, George. 2014. *Feral: Rewilding the Land, Sea and Human Life*. London: Penguin Books.

Morton, Timothy. 2010. *The Ecological Thought*. Cambridge: Harvard University Press.

Morton, Timothy. 2007. *Ecology without Nature: Rethinking Environmental Aesthetics* Cambridge: Harvard University Press.

Noad, Michael J., Cato, Douglas H., Bryden, M.M., Jenner, Micheline N., Jenner, K. Curt. 2000. "Cultural Revolution in Whale Songs." *Nature*. 408: 537. Accessed 22 October 2016. Available: www.nature.com/nature/journal/v408/n6812/full/408537a0.html.

Odum, Eugene P. 1959. *Fundamentals of Ecology*. 2nd ed. Philadelphia: W.B. Saunders Company.

Phelan, Peggy, 2005. "Reconsidering Identity Politics, Essentialism, & Dismodernism: An Afterword." In Carrie Sandahl and Philip Auslander ed. *Bodies in Commotion: Disability and Performance*. Ann Arbor: University of Michigan Press, 319–326.

Quayson, Ato. 2013. "Aesthetic Nervousness." In Lennard J. Davis ed. *The Disability Studies Reader*, 4th edn. London: Routledge, 202–213.

Ray, Sarah Jaquette. 2009. *The Ecological Other: Environmental Exclusion in American Culture*. Tucson: University of Arizona Press.

Rothenberg, David. 2016. "Interspecies Improvisation." In George E. Lewis and Benjamin Piekut ed. *The Oxford Handbook of Critical Improvisation Studies*, 1. New York: Oxford University Press, 500–522.

Sandahl, Carrie. 2001. "Performing Metaphors: AIDS, Disability, and Technology." *Contemporary Theatre Review*. 1 (1): 49–60.

Sandahl, Carrie, and Auslander, Philip ed. 2005. *Bodies in Commotion: Disability and Performance*. Ann Arbor: University of Michigan Press.

Schiffman, Richard. 2016. "How Ocean Noise Pollution Wreaks Havoc on Marine Life." *Yale Environment 360*, 31 March 2016. Accessed 7 December 2017. Available: http://e360.yale.edu/features/how_ocean_noise_pollution_wreaks_havoc_on_marine_life.

Sheets-Johnstone, Maxine. 2009. *The Corporeal Turn: An Interdisciplinary Reader*. Cambridge: Imprint Academic.

Siebers, Tobin. 2001. *Disability Theory*. Ann Arbor: University of Michigan Press.

Sontag, Susan. 1989. *Illness as Metaphor and AIDS and Its Metaphors*. New York: Picador.

Suzuki, David with McConnell, Amanda (1997) *The Sacred Balance: Rediscovering our Place in Nature* Vancouver, BC: Greystone Books.

Tuana, Nancy. 2008. "Viscous Porosity: Witnessing Katrina." In Stacy Alaimo and Susan Hekman ed. *Material Feminisms*. Bloomington: Indiana University Press, 188–213.

Wolbring, Groegor. 2014. "Ecohealth Through an Ability Studies and Disability Studies Lens." *Ecological Health: Society, Ecology and Health Advances in Medical Sociology*. 15: 91–107.

World Social Forum. 2016. "Working at the Intersection of Environmental Justice and Disability Justice." Discussion Workshop, August 12, 2016. Montréal, QC. Accessed 19 September 2016. Available: https://fsm2016.org/en/activites/working-at-the-intersection-of-environmental-justice-and-disability-justice/.

Part V
Activism, adaptation, and alternative futures

24

Changing representations of disability in children's toys as popular culture

Katie Ellis

Toys always mean something.

(Barthes 1993, 53, emphasis added)

In 1972, Roland Barthes wrote that these meanings are inherently tied to the "myths or the techniques of modern adult life" (Barthes 1972) In other words, toys are tied to society and culture. More recently, English journalist and television presenter James May described children toys as the "story of everything" and recommended future archaeologists look to the toy box for insights into previous generations in his 2009 documentary *James' May Toy Stories* (Bainbridge 2010, 829).

I began my 2015 book *Disability and Popular Culture* with an investigation of disability popular culture in the context of children's toys. I saw toys as important popular culture artefacts because "they embrace the past, present and future" (Ellis 2015a, 15). Toys hyperbolise taken-for-granted cultural constructions (Seiter 1995, 10) to reflect the zeitgeist, draw on nostalgia, and give an insight into what we think the future will be like.

This cultural function of toys notwithstanding, with a few exceptions (Garland-Thomson 2004; Ellis 2010; Ellis 2015a; Fitzgerald, Drury & Stride 2018), within critical disability studies, children's toys have gone significantly underexplored, despite their close link to social and cultural constructions. Yet within popular culture itself, the representation of disability in children's toys is an important topic of discussion, with several adult bloggers reflecting on the significance of the un/availability of disabled toys in their childhood (Disability Horizons 2013; Miller n.d.; Atkinson 2015a), and parents of disabled children calling on the toy industry to improve representations, to give their children a toy to identify with (Atkinson 2015b). Even children with disability have likewise taken to online platforms to encourage toy manufacturers to include disability diversity in their toy lines (Shang & Shang 2014). While calls for improved and increased representations of disability in children's toys have taken place for some time, significant momentum was achieved in 2015 when UK journalist and mother Rebecca Atkinson began the online community #toylikeme. Atkinson acknowledged that

Katie Ellis

disability inclusion has come a long way because of legislative and environmental changes, but that we still had further to go:

> Thanks to the Disability Discrimination Act, disabled children can no longer be refused entry to toy shops, schools or soft play centres on the grounds of their wheelchair being a fire hazard or bothersome to other children. In terms of ramps, lifts and buildings constructed with equality in mind, the country has never been more accessible. But what about the rights of disabled children to be positively represented in the cultural sphere? To see their lives and experiences reflected in the media they consume?
>
> *(Atkinson 2015c, n.p.)*

As Atkinson explains, the cultural sphere, and particularly media and popular culture, have just as significant an impact on whether people with disabilities feel included in public spaces.

Despite a history of problematic representations, people with disability integrate popular culture in creative ways in their everyday lives. There are four key stages in this process that can be applied to other forms of disability in popular culture. First, in the absence of disability-themed toys, people will make their own by altering mass-produced products or by attempting to mass produce and market these toys to a wider audience. (This process of adaptation is akin to the ways in which disabled people adapt other objects, cultural phenomenon, and places to their needs, for example, as in the adaptation of musical instruments discussed by Alex Lubet in Chapter 25.) While smaller companies have varying degrees of success, larger companies such as Mattel, Lego and Hasbro adopt different strategies. The second stage therefore occurs when these larger companies offer mass-produced disability toys; however, they often do so under a charity model of disability and donate funds to disability charities. Despite this, some people respond positively to the toys. However, others protest even using toys to further advance the social position of people with disability. Toy manufacturers leverage both positive and negative feedback as a form of "viral advertising" (Rogers 1999) to keep their product in the popular media and therefore increase sales. The final stage occurs when consumers turn these mass-produced products into popular culture by meaningfully integrating them into their everyday lives. Increasing these so-called "producerly" (Fiske 1989, Ellis 2015a) activities of consumers is taking the form of spreadable media, whereby audiences share media that means something to them online and, in the process, create new representations, meanings, and texts.

This chapter provides a brief overview of the significance of children's toys to disability and popular culture. This paper traces the social, cultural, and medical history of disability toys to explore what they communicate about society's view of disability, from ableist representations to social inclusion. The chapter therefore takes a Gramscian approach to popular culture to recognise and interrogate both the problematic and subversive aspects of disability and popular culture using children's toys as a case study. Throughout the chapter I draw on several cultural artefacts including online forums and blogs to illustrate the shifting nature of disability representation in children's toys.

Theories of popular culture

Antonio Gramsci's critique of popular culture and hegemony offers some useful tools in the study of popular culture and a way to reconcile the notions of subordination and resistance addressed throughout this chapter. Under this framework, popular culture is a site of struggle between subordinate groups and the ruling class. Cultural hegemony describes the way ruling classes manipulate subordinate groups into accepting the ideology of their own domination via cultural products. Gramsci, however, did not view hegemony as a given; rather, it is a process whereby concessions are made to oppositional ideas (Gramsci 1971). Gramsci described this struggle as a "compromise equilibrium" whereby the "leading group should make sacrifices of an economic-corporate kind" (Gramsci 1971, 161). This chapter argues that disability in children's toys as an example of disability popular culture is a site in which disability oppression can be debated, rather than simply reinforced.

Communications scholar John Fiske pointed out that not all mass culture becomes popular culture. Popular culture is the text that is meaningfully integrated into people's lives, while mass culture is the text that is mass-produced and distributed. Meaning making is central to whether a text, object, or artefact became popular culture (Fiske 1989). The compromises identified by Gramsci are described as a pluralisation, evasion, and resistance of dominant or preferred meanings by Fiske. Producerly popular culture refers to the ways mass culture is turned into popular culture and recognises both the problematic aspects of popular culture, as it reinforces the dominant ableist ideology, and the ways this ideology is vulnerable, and in some cases rejected, by users of popular culture (Fiske 1989).

Henry Jenkins extends Fiske's distinction between popular and mass culture to argue participatory online media has a prominent role in the study and creation of popular culture. He identifies a trend which he calls "spreadable media" (1999), whereby audiences share media that means something to them online to create new representations, meanings, and texts. He makes an overt connection between spreadable media and Fiske's producerly popular culture:

> Material that spreads is producerly, in that it leaves open space for audience participation, provides resources for shared expression, and motivates exchanges through surprising or intriguing content. People want to share media texts which become a meaningful resource in their ongoing conversations or which offer them some new source of pleasure and interest. They want to exchange and discuss media content when the material contains cultural activators, when it offers activities in which they can participate.
>
> *(Jenkins 2013, 227)*

Drawing on Fiske's concept of the producerly, throughout *Disability and Popular Culture* I called for a more in-depth examination of the producerly aspects of disability popular culture, particularly in light of the conversations taking place in online and spreadable media. In addition to the ways people create popular culture from mass-produced culture through a process of meaning making and integration into their everyday lives, it is important too to recognise that popular culture changes – it is not a constant representation. As Nachbar and Lause argue, popular culture comprises two distinct values – the transitory and concentre. Transitory values reflect the popular zeitgeist at moments in time, whereas concrete values persist across time (Nachbar & Lause 1992, 5).

Disability is popular (Manaseri & Raphael 2014), and it is represented often in media and culture; however, researchers within the domain of disability studies have struggled with the study of disability in popular culture. Critiques have tended to focus on negative representations and persisting stereotypes (Mallett 2009; Ellis 2015b) without looking to the ways people have meaningfully integrated popular culture into their everyday lives. The remainder of the chapter will consider children's toys as an important site of disability and popular culture, beginning with the polio epidemic and the ways mass-produced items were manipulated to reflect the realities of children experiencing polio.

Katie Ellis

History of disability toys

Facilitating children's identification with toys, and therefore society at large, is a key theme that runs throughout activism and calls for increasing and improving disability representation in children's toys. This motivation is also clear in the first half of the twentieth century, when toys began to be used in children's hospitals to explain medical procedures and offer reassurance to children during the polio epidemic, for example. A collection of early examples of disability toys originated at the Lord Mayor Treloar Hospital in Hampshire. The hospital opened in 1908 to treat children afflicted with tuberculosis and later treated and educated children during the polio epidemic in the West. This epidemic has been identified as a key moment in the formation of disability popular culture because of the influence it had on children of that era who would go on to became disability artists or activists (McKay 2013). While rooms of children in iron lungs dominate the cultural imagery from this era, several entries in the Science Museum's History of Medicine are of interest to the current discussion. The first image is labelled "ceramic teaching doll to show treatment for polio, England, 1930–1950" (Science Museum n.d., n.p.)

The entry explains toys and dolls were modified to explain and personalise polio treatments:

> Staff at the hospital used… everyday-looking toys to prepare and encourage children and their families. The dolls helped to personalise the process. They were dressed in hospital clothes, some accompanied by their teddy bears, and in beds made with hospital sheets and blankets. One was even cocooned in a tiny iron lung. These mini-patients were an attempt to create reassurance in the face of quite drastic and sometimes painful treatments.
> *(Science Museum n.d.)*

The same doll appears several times in the museum's digital archives, lying on a bed, sitting in a chair, and wearing an arm splint. A later entry is of a different doll wearing splints; this one was used with infants being treated for hip dysplasia at the same hospital between 1940 and 1960. These dolls are important early examples of an emerging cultural recognition that children respond to and are reassured by toys, particularly ones that reflect their reality.

An image search for 'polio doll' in the Science and Society Picture library yields five results. Each doll is described as a 'teaching doll.' While disability toys have moved on to become more commercial in nature, the use of dolls and teddy bears to explain medical procedures remains; for example, the Science Museum also includes entries for teddy bears with cochlear implants created during the 1990s, and the American Girl doll company offers a service within their doll hospital to attach hearing aids to existing American Girl dolls (American Girl 2017). Similarly, Rebecca Atkinson traces the real momentum behind the #toylikeme community as the moment she posted an image of a Tinker Bell toy with a home-made hearing aid attached (Atkinson, 2015e) (Figure 24.1).

In an attempt to discover whether disability toys were available commercially at the same time these polio dolls were being adapted from existing ceramic and fabric dolls, I conducted a content analysis of every Billy and Ruth toy catalogue produced between 1930 and 1963. With the exception of doctors' and nurses' kits popular during the 1940s, the first disability-themed toy to appear was a Three Blind Mice Talking Toy in 1955. Six years later, the Mr Magoo Toy Car first appeared (Mueller n.d.). This toy is catalogued as a significant cultural artefact on the website *Everybody: An Artifact History of America*. This site attempts to chronicle the presence of people with disability throughout America's history. The toy is noted as significant because it prompted one of the first disability rights protests.

300

Representations of disability in children's toys

Figure 24.1 © Rebecca Atkinson / #ToyLikeMe / Beth Moseley Photography

People with disability and blindness and vision impairment in particular protested the doll because it "ridiculed and satirized people who were blind or had low vision" (Everybody: An Artifact History of America n.d., n.p.). This transmedia character maintains its cultural significance for the disability community, who continue to protest Mr Magoo's various media incarnations (Copeland 1997). The Mr Magoo characterisation is now being protested as ridiculing ageing.

Moving into the 1970s, disability-themed toys began to be popular in the mainstream via the release of several action figures ascribing to an amputee and cyborg aesthetic. The toys – G.I. Joe's Mike Power, Atomic Man, the Jay J. Armes action figure, and the Six Million Dollar Man – reflected the cultural value on hyper-masculinity and resourcefulness evident during the time of the Vietnam War. Representations of cyborgs dominated popular culture during this time. To begin with Mike Power, Atomic Man, this toy was released during a time when the G.I. Joe franchise was losing popularity. The G.I. Joe franchise is illustrative of the ways toy manufacturing reflect both cultural values and economic imperatives. Released in the mid-1960s, G.I. Joe initially embraced a military aesthetic; however, as the military began to lose cultural currency amongst anti-Vietnam protests in the late 1960s, Joe was rebranded as a civilian (Walsh 2005). Then in the mid-1970s, as the cyborg gained popularity, the first G.I. Joe to be given a name, Mike Power, Atomic Man, was released. Described as part man, part

Katie Ellis

machine, Mike Power's back story referenced the bionic franchises, hyper-masculine resource-fulness, and the inspirational disability narrative:

Mike Power was born with disabled limbs. He refused to accept them and spent his life developing atomic parts for his body. His atomic leg allowed him to run 200 miles per hour, his atomic arm could lift 10,000 pounds and his atomic eye could see through six feet of solid steel. He decided to join the Adventure Team and demonstrated his abilities, convincing G.I. Joe he had what was needed.

(G.I. Joe wiki n.d.)

The Jay J. Armes action figure was similarly resourceful:

No matter what the situation or crisis required, a kid could modify his Jay J. Armes doll with: 2 suction cups for climbing walls; a wrist-locked magnet for hanging onto steel structures; an implanted machete to cut his way out of tough situations; a pair of false hands for undercover roles, so as to look undistinguished from the rest of the crowd; a prosthesis that converts to a pistol; and a pair of spring loaded hooks.

(Miller n.d., n.p.)

The bodies of these action figures, although 'disabled,' are the site of action. Accessories attach directly to their bodies as hyper-effective prosthetics. Leaving aside the problematic aspects of the superhuman characterisation of these cyborg, superhuman representations, people with disability report meaningfully integrating these action figures into their everyday lives as an important site of identification (Miller n.d.). However, by the end of the 1970s, they were no longer available.

During the 1980s, at the height of the popularity of Cabbage Patch dolls, Mattel released a series of disabled, Cabbage Patch-style Hal's Pals, described here:

In addition to Hal, who doesn't have a left leg and is the only doll who has been named, there is a ballerina wearing hearing aids, a boy in a gray warm-up suit in a wheelchair, and a girl with leg braces and canes. The fifth disabled Pal, a girl, is visually impaired and comes with a red-tipped cane and guide dog. The two other dolls, a preppy boy and a Madonna look-alike, do not appear disabled. However, they can be bought with the various accessories, such as the wheelchair.

(Inquirer Wire Services 1986, n.p.)

Named after Hal O'Leary, director and founder of the Winter Park Handicapped Sports and Recreation Program in west Denver, Colorado, the dolls were available via mail order and promoted to paediatricians and physical therapists. At the time of their release, Mattel insisted the dolls were ultimately intended for a mass audience, yet they were marketed specifically towards children with disabilities, and a portion of profits was donated to charity. However, these dolls were not well received in the mainstream market. Toy-industry analyst Paul Valentine predicted the dolls longevity would be short-lived because children did not like to feel different. He posited that children with disability would be made to feel even more different from the mainstream by these dolls and would not embrace speciality disability dolls that were not part of mass culture (Valentine cited Timberlake 1986). Down Syndrome Dolls, released during the early 2000s, were received in the same way. These dolls, released by Downii Creations and HEST, were designed to look like they had Down syndrome, with Downii Creations boasting

302

13 features and HEST 9 (Hareyan 2008). However, the dolls, while designed for children with Down syndrome, were not embraced by this group (Cafferty 2012) and were protested online (Faulkner 2008). Protests against disability entering the children's media domain are not unusual (Ellis 2016). While neither doll had any intrinsic or essential meaning, the negative public reactions reveal a lot about the social position of disability (Ellis 2012).

Only a few years earlier, Mattel's 1996 foray into disability dolls, with the colloquially termed 'wheelchair Barbie,' represents the most widely recognised disability representation in children's toys. The officially named 'Share a Smile Becky' sold out in under two weeks. Originally conceived as Barbie's friend the school photographer, there have been several incarnations of Becky – Becky the school photographer, Becky the camp counsellor, and Becky the Paralympic athlete. The doll was released amidst positive media coverage of children with disabilities playing with toys like them and with large donations to charities (Mattel 1997). Significantly, Mattel described the doll in the following way:

> Barbie® doll's hip and very cool disabled friend who is a photographer for her high school yearbook. She comes with a pretend camera so she can take "pictures" at all school events. Becky doll uses a red and silver realistically designed wheelchair and keeps in style wearing a trendy fashion ensemble accessorized with red stud earrings, red framed sunglasses, and a brown backpack that hangs on the back of her wheelchair.
>
> *(cited Ellis 2015a)*

Although likely an unintended and overlooked aspect of the doll's creation, Becky's wheelchair was so realistic of the disability experience that it was excluded from public space in the same way actual wheelchair users are. The chair was too large to fit into the elevator of the Barbie Dreamhouse, and Mattel would not retrofit the environment to be accessible. With the release coming only six years after the Americans with Disabilities Act, Mattel was heavily criticised for the accessibility faux pas (Gilje 1997). However, the mix of positive and negative press worked as a viral advertising strategy, keeping Becky in the news. Barbie historian Mary Rogers argues Becky is the most successful example of this strategy, as there was an extended period of positive and negative coverage of the doll (Rogers 1999).

This release can be tied to both the focus on cultural diversity within the Barbie franchise during the 1990s (see du Cille 1994 for a discussion of multicultural representations) and the introduction of disability legislation, such as the Americans with Disabilities Act, throughout the world during this decade. Share a Smile Becky is a key example of producerly popular culture. The doll was mass-produced and created with the intention of making money; however, little attention was paid to its specific access needs within the Barbie universe. Indeed, even negative publicity around this was considered free advertising for Mattel. However, this mass-produced doll was turned into popular culture by children and adults who meaningfully integrated it into their lives.

Increasingly, producerly popular culture spreads throughout online media in a phenomena Jenkins calls "spreadable media" (2013). The power of spreadable media has had significant implications for disability in children's toys, through both community platforms such as #toylikeme and equal parts consumer- and producer-based transmedia.

Transmedia: Ghoulia Yelps

Transmedia storytelling is the use of multiple media platforms to provide several points of entry to a single story world. Typically, transmedia narratives can each stand alone but when taken together offer multiple points of entry to provide a more comprehensive overview of the narrative. For example, Monster High is a fashion doll franchise created by Mattel in 2008 and released to the public in 2010. Equal parts science fiction and Barbie, the dolls are the offspring of canonical monsters such as Frankenstein and Dracula. In addition to the Monster High dolls, the franchise traverses a number of other mediums, including a web series, video games, and graphic novels. On top of this official representation, user-generated content adds significantly to the story world, with fan sites hosting discussions online.

Ghoulia Yelps is a Monster High student described as the daughter of zombies. Zombies are significant in the Monster High world because they are typically discriminated against. Ghoulia Yelps has been widely interpreted as exhibiting characteristics of autism. Yet Ghoulia Yelps, like Sheldon Cooper in *The Big Bang Theory*, is never officially described as having autism (see Walters 2013). Despite this, fans have identified key aspects of her character description as evidence. While she professes to be a fussy eater and her pet peeve is 'last minute schedule changes,' her 'Monster Quirk' encompasses several cultural stereotypes of autism:

> I cannot function without a proper schedule and I do not process last minute schedule changes very well. My Zombie nature also means that I walk rather slowly, have trouble making facial expressions and can only speak…. well…. Zombie.
>
> *(Monster High, n.d.)*

In an example of collective intelligence (see Lévy 1997), fans both identify with and criticise this description, offering insight to their own experiences with autism and inadequate cultural representations. Henry Jenkins describes "convergence culture" as a new media site where the "power of the media producer and the power of the media consumer interact in unpredictable ways" (Jenkins 2006, 2). Content flows across multiple platforms while consumers seek out new information from multiple sources in such a way that "every important story is told" (Jenkins 2006, 219).

Monster High Dolls is an online community of Monster High dolls fans. Within this community, a page is dedicated to debating whether Ghoulia Yelps has autism (marjol3in1977 2012). A fan identifying as having autism professed to identify with Ghoulia Yelps and posed the following idea:

> It seems to me that Ghoulia has a form of autism: she fits perfectly in the characteristics of Asperger syndrome.
>
> *(comment on marjol3in1977 2012)*

In response, people began identifying instances where they either identified with Ghoulia Yelps' feelings and behaviours or examples of autism-like behaviour, listing representations across the franchise related to the importance of routine and time management, difficulty dealing with sudden changes to plans, her so-called zombie language as a metaphor for difficulties communicating with others, her friends' willingness to learn her language and the discovery that she is intelligent, fussy eating practices, and finally, the overall ethos of Monster High being about accepting flaws and differences. The discussion offered multiple points of entry to the narrative to facilitate a new type of representation of autism.

The community also discusses the need for positive portrayals of autism, the diversity of symptoms amongst people who have autism, and whether or not toys have any impact. For example, when some members of the community questioned that Ghoulia could have autism because of her so-called 'normal' behaviours and close friendship with another Monster High character Cleo, the value in using a doll to discuss these issues was hotly debated.

#toylikeme

#toylikeme therefore emerged in the context of this history of disability representation. The group both targeted mainstream toy manufacturers like Mattel, Playmobil, and Lego and featured community members who created their own disability toys by altering mass-produced products in the same way people did during the polio epidemic. #toylikeme have made major inroads in highlighting the significance of this issue, with both Playmobil and Makies implementing disability-themed toy lines immediately in response to the popular campaign. Playmobil posted a Facebook message detailing their response to the campaign.

> You may have seen or heard about Toy Like Me in the news and on social media.... We always take on board a lot of feedback from children and fans across the world and design our toys to reflect this. The Toy Like Me campaign has been inspiring for us – we've listened to our audience and are delighted to offer our full support. We are in the planning stages to release a PLAYMOBIL set which will include characters with disabilities, with part of the profits to be donated to a charity hand-selected by Toy Like Me. And moving forward, we will be looking into including more characters with disabilities in our ranges. We receive a lot of positive comments from guardians of deaf and disabled children on how well our toys stimulate their learning and creativity, so we are thrilled to be able to champion their representation in the toy box.
>
> *(Playmobil UK 2015, n.p.)*

This release is remarkably similar to the strategy adopted by Mattel when Share a Smile Becky was released. However, where Mattel was criticised for attempting to market towards the disability community, Playmobil and #toylikeme have received what appears to be universally positive feedback.

Under Atkinson's leadership, #toylikeme targeted Lego as particularly significant because of its cultural sway as one of the largest toy manufactures in the world. Children all over the world play with Lego; it is a much-loved brand in the #toylikeme community, being featured often in the community photo album. A commitment to positive disability representation from Lego "could really have an amazing impact on the self-esteem of kids with disabilities to see they are valued by a super brand," Atkinson told me in an email. Lego is often complimented for being progressive and reflecting both racial and gender diversity (Bologna 2014, Shop n.d.; Brown 2010). Disability diversity has not always featured in this ethos. Indeed, discriminatory language was used to describe new character Turg as "Part frog, part chicken, part back-of-the-bus window-licker" in 2015 (Newsbeat 2015, n.p.). Window-licker, a derogatory term describing someone with a physical or mental disability, was voted the third most offensive disability-related word in a 2003 poll by British disability website Ouch! (Ouch Team 2003). Lego claimed no knowledge of this history, issued an apology, and altered TURG's description (NewsBeat 2015). However, their Duplo Community People Set released shortly after this gaffe was criticised for including an elderly wheelchair-using character. Promotional images which depict an elderly man being pushed in a grey wheelchair by a younger character reinforce medical images of disability. In a press release, Atkinson argues the figure "does little to celebrate or educate children about the realities of disability" (2015d, n.p.), describing the character as a disability-related blunder on par with the window-licker gaffe.

This negative disability publicity ultimately worked in the same way as Mattel's viral advertising strategy where negative publicity is leveraged to keep the brand in the popular media. After years of refusing to respond to the #toylikeme campaign, Lego quietly developed a wheelchair minifig for release at the 2016 Nuremberg toy fair (Beaumont-Thomas 2016). The quiet announcement was soon amplified by an interested and engaged online community. The story was spreadable, and the figure made popular before it was even released because it was meaningfully integrated into the lives of so many people. Amongst the celebrations of a disabled minifig, it was almost forgotten that Lego had actually released a number of what could be described as disabled Legos, often to capitalise on certain historical or media moments. There have been pirates, cyborgs, and even Darth Vader (Graham 2016) – a figure widely recognised within disability studies as problematic (Norden 1994). These characters have come to be recognised as archetypes perpetuating the notion that disabled people are evil or that they have become disabled as a result of their evil activities.

Conclusion

Throughout this chapter, I used disability representation in children's toys as an example of disability popular culture. While historically disability has been subject to negative representations in popular culture, people with disability remain enthusiastic consumers of popular culture. Therefore, representations of disability in popular culture are a key example of the ways popular culture is a site of both subordination and resistance. Within this tradition, several key tendencies emerge: first, the ways mainstream toys have been adapted into the so-called disability toys to offer children a point of identification and belonging; second, the ways toy manufactures have responded to calls to improve disability diversity by adopting both a charity model of disability and viral advertising strategies to leverage negative publicity; and finally, despite problematic aspects of children's toys as disability popular culture, the importance of disability representation in children's toys is widely recognised as an important site of mass-produced culture and communicated via spreadable media.

Extending the concept of incorporation and resistance, the chapter offered a history of disability in children's toys throughout the twentieth and twenty-first centuries. The popular culture of disability toys began as a history of medical culture, with the use of toys to explain medical procedures during the polio epidemic. As specific disability toys began emerging in mass culture throughout the twentieth century, some, such as Hal's Pals and Down Syndrome Dolls, were created specifically for children with disabilities, while others – notably the Jay J. Armes and Mike Power, Atomic Man action figures and Share a Smile Becky – were intended for the wider market. The production of each toy can be directly tied to a particular historical era. While some toys were protested for their problematic representation of disability, either by the disability community or the mainstream population, others were integrated into the toy market without much notice. Finally, some have achieved an almost icon-like status. In this context, #toylikeme is particularly interesting. Toys prompted by this community are not the first disability toys ever produced; however, the group is the first to gain such a momentum in positioning people with disability as a consumer group interested in seeing themselves represented in popular culture.

References

American Girl. 2017. *Doll Hospital.* Accessed 8 December 2017. Available: www.americangirl.com/shop/ag/doll-hospital.
Atkinson, Rebecca. 2015a. *Rebecca Atkinson: Children Should Be Able to Play with a Toy That Reflects Their Deafness or Disability.* The Limping Chicken. Accessed 15 November 2017. Available: http://

limpingchicken.com/2015/04/24/rebecca-atkinson-children-should-be-able-to-play-with-a-toy-that-reflects-their-deafness-or-disability/.

Atkinson, Rebecca. 2015b. *Why #toylikeme Think It's Time Lego Left Disability Stereotyping Abehind*. Rebecca Atkinson. Accessed 3 March 2016. Available: http://rebeccaatkinson.co.uk/why-toylikeme-think-its-time-lego-left-disability-stereotyping-behind/.

Atkinson, Rebecca. 2015c. "Why Do You Never See a Lego Mini-Figure with a Disability?" *The Guardian*. Accessed 3 March 2016. Available: www.theguardian.com/commentisfree/2015/dec/22/lego-mini-figure-disability-toy-disabled-children.

Atkinson, Rebecca. 2015d. *Lego Duplo Rile Parents, Children's Charities and #Toylikeme Campaigners with Release of Stereotype Wheelchair Figure* [Press Release].

Atkinson, Rebecca. 2015e. "Deaf News: Deaf Tinkerbelle Toy Goes Viral". *The Limping Chicken*. Accessed 12 June 2018. Available: http://limpingchicken.com/2015/05/13/deaf-news-deaf-tinkerbelle-toy-goes-viral/.Bainbridge, Jason. 2010. "Fully Articulated: The Rise of the Action Figure and the Changing Face of 'Children's' Entertainment." *Journal of Media & Cultural Studies*. 24: 829–842.

Barthes, Roland. 1993. *Mythologies/Roland Barthes; Selected and Translated from the French by Annette Lavers*. London: Vintage.

Beaumont-Thomas, Ben. 2016. "Lego Unveils First Ever Minifigure in Wheelchair." *The Guardian*. Accessed 30 December 2017. Available: www.theguardian.com/culture/2016/jan/27/lego-unveils-disabled-minifigure-promobricks-nuremberg-toy-fair.

Bologna, Caroline. 2014. "Letter From LEGO To Parents In The '70s Makes An Important Point About Gender." *Huffington Post*. Accessed 30 December 2017. Available: www.huffingtonpost.com.au/entry/lego-letter-from-the-70s_n_6212362.

Brown, Joe. 2010. "Hollywood's Racism Exposed... By Lego." *Gizmodo*. Accessed 30 December 2017. Available: www.gizmodo.com.au/2010/09/hollywoods-racism-exposed-by-lego/.

Cafferty, Diana De Rosa. 2012. *A Doll Like Me: Do Children with Down Syndrome Prefer to Play with Dolls That Have the Physical Features Associated with Down Syndrome*. Unpublished MS Thesis, University of California.

Copeland, Jeff. 1997. "Blind Protest Mr. Magoo Movie." *E!News*. Accessed 8 December 2017. Available: www.eonline.com/news/34792/blind-protest-mr-magoo-movie.

Disability Horizons. 2013. "Toys with Disabilities and Why They Matter." Disability Horizons: A 21st Century View of Disability. Accessed 9 February 2014. Available: http://disabilityhorizons.com/2013/05/toys-with-disabilities-and-why-they-matter/.

Du Cille, Ann. 1994. "Dyes and Dolls: Multicultural Barbie and the Merchandising of Difference." *Differences*. 6: 46–68.

Ellis, Katie. 2016. *Disability Media Work: Opportunities and Obstacles*. New York: Palgrave Macmillan.

Ellis, Katie. 2015a. *Disability and Popular Culture: Focusing Passion, Creating Community, Expressing Defiance*. Surrey: Ashgate.

Ellis, Katie. 2015b. "Disability in Television Crime drama: Transgression and Access." *The Journal of Popular Television*. 3: 243–259.

Ellis, Katie. 2012. "Complicating a Rudimentary List of Characteristics: Communicating Disability with Down Syndrome Dolls." *Media Culture Journal*. 15. Accessed 1 June 2018. Available: http://journal.media-culture.org.au/index.php/mcjournal/article/viewArticle/544.

Ellis, Katie. 2010. "Dolls with Disabilities: Playing with Diversity." In Nanette Norris ed. *Unionist Popular Culture and Rolls of Honour in the North of Ireland During the First World War and Other Diverse Essays*. New York: The Edwin Mellen Press.Everybody: An Artefact History of America. n.d. "Mr Magoo Toy Car, 1960s." *Everybody: An Artifact History of America*. Accessed 4 December 2013. Available: http://everybody.si.edu/media/749.

Faulkner, Lorraine. 2008. *Disability Dolls*. Accessed 13 December 2009. No longer available: http://whatsortsofpeople.wordpress.com/2008/06/26/disability-dolls/.

Fiske, John. 1989. *Understanding Popular Culture*. London & New York: Routledge.

Fitzgerald, Hayley, Drury, Scarlette, and Stride, Annette. 2018. Representations of the Sporting Female: Queering Paralympic Barbie. In Louise Mansfield, Jayne Caudwell, Belinda Wheaton, and Beccy Watson ed. *The Palgrave Handbook of Feminism and Sport, Leisure and Physical Education*. London: Palgrave Macmillan, 667–680.

Garland-Thomson, Rosemarie. 2004. Integrating Disability: Transforming Feminist Theory. In Bonnie Smith and Beth Hutchinson ed. *Gendering Disability*. New Brunswick: Rutgers University Press, 73–103.

G.I. Joe wiki. n.d. "GI Joe Meets The Amazing Atomic Man!" *G.I. Joe Wiki*. Accessed 7 February 2014. Available: http://gijoe.wikia.com/wiki/GI_Joe_meets_the_Amazing_Atomic_Man!.

Gilje, Shelby. 1997. "Barbie's Friend Finds Doors Closed." *Seattle Times*. Accessed 4 December 2013. Available: www.washington.edu/doit/Press/06.07.97.times.html.

Graham. 2016. "Disability and LEGO: Five Minifigures with Disabilities." *All About Bricks*. Accessed 15 March 2017. Available: http://allaboutbricks.blogspot.com.au/2016/01/disability-and-lego-five-minifigures.html.

Gramsci, Antonio. 1971. *Selections from The Prison Notebooks of Antonio Gramsci/Edited and Translated by Quintin Hoare and Geoffrey Nowell Smith*. New York: International Publishers.

Hareyan, Armen. 2008. *Using Dolls to Reduce the Stigma of Down Syndrome*. Accessed 12 June 2018. Available: www.emaxhealth.com/7/22865.html.

Inquirer Wire Services. 1986. "Dolls with Disabilities Introduced By Mattel." *Philly.com*. Accessed 8 December2013.Available:http://articles.philly.com/1986-06-04/entertainment/26043710_1_girl-with-leg-braces-hal-s-pals-disabled-children.

Jenkins, Henry. 2013. *Spreadable Media: Creating Value and Meaning in a Networked Culture*. New York: New York University Press.

Jenkins, Henry. 2006. *Convergence Culture: Where Old and New Media Collide*. New York: New York University Press.Lego Shop. n.d. "Explore the World and Beyond at The Research Institute!" *Lego Shop*. Accessed 30 December 2017. Available: https://shop.lego.com/en-US/Research-Institute-21110.

Lévy, Pierre. 1997. *Collective Intelligence: Mankind's Emerging World in Cyberspace*. New York & London: Plenum Press.

Mallett, Rebecca. 2009. "Choosing 'Stereotypes:' Debating The Efficacy of (British) Disability-Criticism." *Journal of Research in Special Educational Needs*. 9: 4–11.

Manaseri, Holly, and Raphael, Raphael. 2014. Popular Culture and Disability. *Review of Disability Studies: An International Journal*. 10: 6–7.

Marjol3in1977. 2012. "Ghoulia Yelps Autistic? What Do You Think?" *Monster High Dolls*. Accessed 14 April 2017. Available: www.monsterhighdolls.com/forum/topics/ghoulia-yelps-autistic-what-do-you-think.

Mattel. 1997. "Mattel Launches School Photographer Becky; Barbie Doll's Friend Who Uses A Wheelchair." *PR Newswire*. Accessed 4 December 2013. Available: www.prnewswire.com/news-releases/mattel-launches-school-photographer-becky-barbie-dolls-friend-who-uses-a-wheelchair-75963267.html.

McKay, George. 2013. *Shakin All Over: Popular Music and Disability*, Ann Arbor: University of Michigan Press.

Miller, Chuck. n.d. "J.J. Armes Action Figures – Turning Disability into True Ability." *The Journal of Antiques and Collectables*. Accessed 7 February 2014. Available: www.journalofantiques.com/April07/playing_around.html.

Monster High. n.d. "Ghoulia Yelps | Monster High." *Monster High: Everyone is Welcome*. Accessed 30 December 20107. Available: http://play.monsterhigh.com/en-au/bios/ghoulia.html.

Mueller, Richard. n.d. "Toy Catalogues." *Antique Toy Collections*. Accessed 6 February 2014. Available: http://antiquetoycollections.info/pages/catalogs.asp.

Nachbar, Jack, and Lause, Kevin. 1992. *Popular Culture: An Introductory Text*. Bowling Green: Bowling Green State University Popular Press.

Newsbeat. 2015. "Lego Apologises for 'Window Licker' Toy." *BBC*. Accessed 3 March 2016. Available: www.bbc.co.uk/newsbeat/article/33079474/lego-apologises-for-window-licker-toy.

Norden, Martin. 1994. *The Cinema of Isolation: A History of Physical Disability in the Movies*. New Brunswick: Rutgers University Press.

Ouch Team. 2003. "Worst Words Vote". *Ouch!* Accessed 3 March 2016. Available: www.bbc.co.uk/ouch/play/worst-words-vote.shtml.

Playmobil UK. 2015. "Facebook Status." *Facebook*. Accessed 30 December 2017. Available: www.facebook.com/PlaymobilUK/posts/780597118704513.

Rogers, Mary. F. 1999. *Barbie Culture*. London Thousand Oaks: SAGE Publications.

Science Museum. n.d. "Ceramic Teaching Doll to Show Treatment for Polio, England, 1930–1950". *Science Museum: Brought to Life Exploring the History of Medicine*. Accessed 2 February 2014. Available: www.sciencemuseum.org.uk/broughttolife/objects/display.aspx?id=5894.

Seiter, Ellen. 1995. *Sold Separately: Children and Parents in Consumer Culture*. New Brunswick: Rutgers University Press.

Shang, Melissa, and Shang, Yingying. 2014. "American Girl: Release an American Girl with a disability". *Change.org.* Accessed 26 January 2014. Available: www.change.org/petitions/american-girl-release-an-american-girl-with-a-disability.

Timberlake, Cotten. 1986. "Hal's Pals May Have Very Limited Appeal, Toy Analyst Says." *AP News Archive.* Accessed 8 December 2013. Available: www.apnewsarchive.com/1986/Hal-s-Pals-May-Have-Very-Limited-Appeal-Toy-Analyst-Says/id-adb38ba1986fd9e51ffc8241f4190aef.

Walsh, Tim. 2005. *Timeless Toys: Classic Toys and the Playmakers Who Created Them.* Kansas City: Andrews McMeel.

Walters, Shannon. 2013. "Cool Aspie Humor: Cognitive Difference and Kenneth Burke's Comic Corrective in The Big Bang Theory and Community." *Journal of Literary & Cultural Disability Studies.* 7: 271–288.

25

Economies of scales (and chords)

Disability studies and adaptive music

Alex Lubet

Introduction

This chapter contemplates adaptive music: that is, the means by which physically disabled people with hand/arm impairments modify conventional performance practice and conventional musical equipment in order to play musical instruments. The focus is upon differences between adaptations prescribed in medical settings, under the guidance of health professionals, and adaptations developed by disabled people themselves. Of particular interest are the contrasting economics and sociocultural/class implications of health professional-driven versus disabled people-driven adaptations. These are of more than purely musical interest and may offer lessons for the entire field of disability arts and, indeed, the entire field of disability studies.

The reader's patience is requested here, as background in disability studies in music and contrasting models of disability, along with examples of adaptive music, by necessity precede our key discussion. I have endeavoured to make this chapter accessible to non-musicians, a group that includes many disabled people wrongly deprived of the opportunity to make music. It is my hope that reader's patience will be amply rewarded.

A brief and highly personal history of disability studies in music

At the risk of hubris, it is acknowledged that I introduced the field of disability studies in music (Straus 2011, ix). While the article Straus cites as "pioneering work" (2011) appeared in 2014, my first disability studies publication, "Disability Studies and Performing Arts Medicine," dates from 2002. That the latter appeared in a medical journal, *Medical Problems of Performing Artists* – strange or even hostile territory for a field that largely defines itself in opposition to the "medical model of disability" (Shakespeare & Watson 2001, 17) – was indicative of my perspective in disability studies that, then as now, might be regarded as an outlier. The desire to engage health professionals has gained in prominence in recent years, as their counterpoints to the "strong social model of disability" have enriched the field. Occupational therapy appears to be particularly open to disability studies perspectives (Cuff et al. 2014). Interacting with health (and other) professionals unfamiliar with disability studies or disability rights is

Disability studies and adaptive music

a personal priority, which owes in no small part to my chosen, lifelong profession, music, in ways that shall be elaborated here. While I chose music, like many others in disability studies and the disability community, disability studies of music appears to have chosen me, a result of serious injuries, major surgeries, and years of litigation.

In light of my interest in engaging health professions, I have chosen not to publish in music journals and edited volumes on music. I concluded long ago that music as a research field was ableist in ways that rendered its publications inaccessible to many readers with disabilities, excluded from participation in educational and communal musical activities that foster the ability to read music notation and understand music terminology.

My principal research concern is music making (and music education) as a human need and human right (2011a), which people with disabilities are often denied, and thus who understandably do not read music journals. This by no means implies that other disciplines are free of ableist barriers to disabled readers (some considered by other authors earlier in this book). But, as a musician, I have chosen my battle, in the hopes of reaching readers on or beyond music's margins, who might contribute to making music praxis more accessible.

Since my first publications, a large body of scholarship in disability studies in music has emerged. Unlike – and sometimes in opposition to – my work, much has appeared in journals in the traditional disciplines of musicology, music theory, and ethnomusicology and presents little or no challenge to these fields' orthodoxies (Iverson 2012). There are also two large edited volumes devoted to disability studies in music Lerner and Straus' *Sounding off: Theorizing disability in music* (2006) and Howe, Jensen-Moulton, Lerner, and Straus' *The Oxford Handbook of Music and Disability Studies* (2016).

I am critical of the principle direction of disability studies in music, in the (mostly) humanistic disciplines of musicology, music theory, and ethnomusicology (2013). Much of disability studies in music is preoccupied with proclaiming works of music (Straus 2011, 45–102) and music theories (Straus 2011, 103–124) as disabled: portrayals of disabled characters in, for example, operas (Jensen-Moulton 2012), and highly successful 'supercrips' who are not representative of the lives, educations, and careers of most disabled people who participate or attempt to participate in music (as Misener, Quinn, and Bodin discuss in Chapter 6). The latter may be observed in the contrast between representing deafness in music through the example of percussionist Evelyn Glennie (Straus 2011, 145–149) – an extraordinary talent – versus the non-triumphal narratives of ordinary musicians contending with hearing loss (Miller 2011, 17–46). My focus has thus been on the actual lives of musicians, music students, and potential musicians, who, by virtue of their disabilities, have been partially or wholly excluded from participation in music, or "musicking" (Small 2011).

In a way, it is more accurate to characterise the disability studies I criticise, focused on aestheticised sound – compositions, performances, and theories – as the disability studies of music, with my work, emphasising living, musicking, humans, characterised as the disability studies of musicians. The latter has stronger affinities with the social sciences than with musicology – more recent and radical "new musicology" (Kramer 2003) notwithstanding – or music theory. Among established music disciplines, the disability studies in music I propose and practice intersects most strongly with ethnomusicology, whose parent disciplines include anthropology. The foremost ethnomusicologist of disability, Michael Bakan (Bakan et al. 2008, 168–69), acknowledges that autism is a category of difference that challenges the norms of his field, observing that "people on the autism spectrum destabilize the terrain upon which ethnomusicologists are accustomed to constructing and deconstructing difference and otherness, structure and agency." He does not, however, address or even name his discipline's legacy of ableism (Lubet 2011b, 8–9).

311

By contrast, the applied fields of music education (see, for example, Rathgeber 2017) and especially music therapy – the latter sometimes harshly critiqued from a disability studies perspective (Straus 2011, 157–159; Cameron 2014) – are among the music disciplines that take disability studies – and accept criticism – most seriously. For example, *Voices: A World Forum for Music Therapy* devoted a special issue to disability studies (Hadley 2014), including the aforementioned savaging article by Cameron. Among disability studies criticisms, especially of music therapy, is that these professions view disability from a medicalised – that is individualising, pathologising, and curative – rather than a sociocultural – that is, a minority rights – perspective.

Social and medical models of disability apropos musicians

Fundamental to disability studies are the binary perspectives termed the medical and social models of disability. They are, typically with little nuance (Cameron 2014), regarded as opposed, the medical model viewed negatively, the social model positively. Fields seen as medicalising disability – including non-medical but individualising practices such as special education and social work – are even deemed "not disability studies" in Simi Linton's canonical *Claiming Disability* (1998, 132–156). Nonetheless, fields including occupational and music therapy have been eager to incorporate disability studies perspectives.

While discussion of the social model has always dominated disability studies, it has long had its critics, both disability studies opponents (Harris 2001) and disability studies scholars, including Wendell (1996), Shakespeare and Watson (2001), and Siebers (2008). What critics of the strong social model of the British founders of disability studies have in common is a more nuanced and less dichotomous, though still sociocultural, perspective on relations between disability (social oppression) and impairment (embodied negative difference) (Shakespeare & Watson, 2001, 11–12). These critics hold that the disadvantages of disability reside not only in discrimination and denial of rights, but in negative personal experiences of pain and limits/loss of function (Shakespeare & Watson 2001, 12). Shakespeare and Watson in particular, at times, espouse the value of medical and other individualised interventions for enhancing the quality of life of disabled people (Shakespeare & Watson 2001, 16), an idea unremarkable in non-academic/non-activist discourse. They also provisionally endorse the limited efficacy of the medical model (Shakespeare & Watson 2001, 17). They report that medical treatment that enhances mobility has been opposed in strong social model scholarship (Shakespeare & Watson 2001, 15), a position that would doubtless mystify many, including disabled people, outside disability studies.

I have never claimed a disability identity. My history of major injuries, surgeries, and chronic illnesses is substantial, but my limited personal experience of social oppression, lost opportunities, and impaired function has not, in my opinion, measured up to minoritised disability status. My interest in disability studies began in 2000, resulting from 3.5 years of workers' compensation litigation (*Alex Lubet, Employee, v. University of Minn.* 2002), following spinal neurosurgery, which convinced me that my sociolegal difficulties were worse than the physical, although the latter were substantial, pre- and post-surgery.

Apropos this chapter's focus, I have long relied upon health professionals (including an even more serious spinal neurosurgery in 2013) to regain and maintain the functioning of my arms and hands and continue as a performing instrumentalist. Such bodily interventions are seemingly opposed at least in the fiercest iterations of the strong social model. Early in my engagement with disability studies, I naively posted on a listserv, praising the physical therapy that enabled me to play instruments again. I was rebuked by a noted disability studies scholar for

Disability studies and adaptive music

seeking rehabilitation rather than accommodation, although it is hard to imagine anything other than medical intervention that would have restored my ability to perform, or why anyone would eschew or decry such benign, beneficial treatment.

Adaptive music

For performing musicians, maximisation of mobility and sensory function is understandable, desirable, and necessary. But medical and therapeutic interventions to enhance bodily performance are not always possible, desirable, or worth the risk. Other means of enabling disability music performance other than body modification might be termed adaptive music.

The focus of this chapter henceforth is to investigate means of adaptation and their agents, both medical professionals and disabled people, sometimes in conjunction with engineers and designers. Of particular concern are the implications of agency, whether disabled musicians or others with different interests guide the process.

The impetus for this research was Woldendorp and van Gils' 2012 *Medical Problems of Performing Artists* article "One-Handed Musicians – More Than a Gimmick." The article is remarkable for two reasons. While it concerns hand and arm impairments only (as does this chapter), it is comprehensive as to the Western instruments for which adaptations are prescribed, and discussions of some instruments are speculative rather than precedented. Even more exceptional is that the article was written by physicians rather than occupational or music therapists.

These doctors work at the Centre for Rehabilitation and Music in the Netherlands, dedicated to adaptive performance for musicians with disabilities, both amateur and professional, as well as disabled aspirants to instrumental performance. The work of the Centre is affirmation of the value of medical praxis to disabled musicking as well as an admirably holistic view of medicine that values the arts as fundamental to quality of life.

The Centre is apparently unique in its specific mission as a health facility addressing musical adaptation. A programme at the University of Colorado Denver (Assistive Technology Partners n.d.) offers similar, more disability-diverse, services, but without a dedicated music facility. Elsewhere, there are programmes for rehabilitation of injured musicians, notably Minneapolis' Performing Arts Medicine Clinic (where I was a patient), principally those whose impairments do not meet the criteria of disability and are presumably temporary or manageable (Allina Health 2018). (While there are not – and may never be – universally accepted criteria for disability, I employ the Americans with Disabilities Act's definition; "a physical or mental impairment that substantially limits one or more major life activities." The impairment must be permanent, whether continuous or intermittent (ADA.gov, 2009).) The New Orleans Musicians' Clinic and Assistance Foundation (2018) addresses all medical needs – not necessarily performance-related – of that city's music community and is not limited to performers in economic distress.

There is little indication the Centre – henceforth our focus, owing to its mission – employs a broadly sociocultural orientation to disability. However, it incorporates two notable elements of disability health praxis that transcend medicine's central tenet of cure. The first is the recognition that music is an important aspect of quality of life, including, in some cases, livelihood, regardless of (dis)ability. Further, its goal is not the elimination/amelioration of impairment, but its musical accommodation.

Any medical unit dedicated to disability accommodation is extraordinary. However, it is impossible to address the needs of a person whose impairment and chosen musical instrument, both highly idiosyncratic, except in a manner that is individualised or – in, disability

313

studies terms – medical. While such individualised attention to impairment stands in contradistinction to the strong social model, the sheer number and variety of cases discussed in Woldendorp and van Gils (2012) demonstrate that the Centre provides services valued by many disabled people.

A comprehensive discussion of the nature of all the accommodations employed by the Centre is beyond the purview of this chapter. Suffice it to say that

1 They fall into two basic categories: (a) assistive apparatus that enable performance on unmodified instruments and (b) modified musical instruments
2 The Centre attempts to provide adaptations for all Western musical instruments, and
3 While the Centre employs occupational, physical, and speech therapists –and, as Woldendorp informed me via email, a music therapist –the authors make no reference to medication or surgery.

Typical apparatus prescribed by the Centre include stands and straps that support wind and brass instruments, when muscle weakness demands this (Woldendorp & van Gils 2012, 232), and prostheses that enable right-hand amputees to play bowed string instruments (235). They also prescribe one-handed woodwinds: recorder, flute, and saxophone (Woldendorp & van Gils 2012, 234). There may be other adaptive instruments in other families not mentioned, but, as a rule of thumb (pun neither intended nor avoided), some woodwinds may be adapted, while strings, brass, percussion, keyboards, and woodwinds that require only a special strap or stand are accommodated with supplemental equipment.

DIY (do it yourself) adaptive music

Were upper body mobility-impaired people dependent upon health practitioners for musical adaptations, there would be few, if any, such disabled musicians. There are, however, many such musicians and a long history of adaptive music. This owes to disabled people having taken responsibility for their own musical accommodations, both as individuals and groups.

Though much needed, there is no comprehensive database of DIY musical accommodations. The largest collection I know, some dating back to the nineteenth century, is from the unfortunately named "Deke's Wonderful World of Weirdness" (n.d.). I have also long collected examples, some included here. My emphasis here is professional musicians, some well-known.

The musical adaptations disabled people have developed themselves, some with designers but many not, fall into three categories: (1) modified instrumental technique, without special apparatus or instruments, (2) assistive apparatus that enables performance on unmodified instruments, and (3) modified musical instruments.

Disability adaptations of instrumental technique only, without special apparatus

Importantly, many adaptations require only alternative playing technique and no special equipment whatever, something not discussed in Woldendorp and van Gils (2012) and presumably not part of the Centre's practice. Examples are far too numerous to discuss here, but the level of impairment addressed ranges from a few immobilised fingers on one hand – a relatively minor disability for many people, but devastating to, for example, a professional guitarist – to congenital double arm amputation.

Among the most famous hand/arm disabled instrumentalists is jazz guitarist Django Reinhardt. Having lost the use of two left-hand fingers in a fire in his teens, Reinhardt adapted his technique and became "widely regarded as the first European to become a major influential jazz musician" (Givan 2014). Unable to play many simple chords, Reinhardt nonetheless adapted an idiosyncratic virtuoso technique (Lubet 2011b, 45–51; Reinhardt & Grappelli 2015).

Reinhardt's piano counterpart was American Horace Parlan. Right side hemiplegic due to childhood polio, Parlan used his immobile but well-positioned second and fifth fingers like vibraphone mallets, shifting much of the melodic responsibility to his left hand (Lubet 2011b, 51–56). Arguably most remarkable was not Parlan's work as a leader and soloist, but as sideman for greats including Charles Mingus and Archie Shepp (Shepp 1994), who might have chosen any number of accomplished two-fisted pianists, for whom fuller harmonic voicings were possible, but opted instead for Parlan's taste and creativity.

The most significant physical impairment for a string, keyboard, or percussion player would surely be double arm amputation or paralysis. Nonetheless, Nicaraguan-American guitarist/vocalist/composer Tony Melendez, born without arms as a result of his mother's thalidomide use during pregnancy, plays with his feet, tuning his instrument to accommodate chords he can play with the toes of his left foot, and holding a pick with the toes of his right. He may be best known for a performance he gave for Pope John Paul II in Los Angeles in 1987 (Melendez n.d.).

DIY disability instrumental performance apparatus

Like some Centre patients, some disabled instrumentalists require unconventional equipment to play. Unlike equipment prescribed at the Centre, either commercially manufactured or commercially customised, DIY equipment is typically either homemade or repurposed.

One-handed electric bassist Bill Clements uses both adapted technique – he taps the strings hard enough and turns up the volume sufficiently on his amplifier that he does not need to pluck – and a user of extremely simple technology. To mute the open strings – that is, those unfretted by the left hand – such that they do not ring when not played – typically, a right-hand assignment – Clements repurposed a sock, hair tie, or underwear, tying it around the first fret (at the top of the neck). More recently, Clements has begun using a 'fret wrap' (Gruv Gear 2018), an inexpensive commercial mute, mostly used by two-handed bassists. Clements, a virtuoso by any standards, can be seen playing using a hair tie (Clements 2007) or fret wrap (Clements 2012).

There are numerous one-handed guitarists, amateur and professional, many quite accomplished. They often use DIY prosthetics that either hold conventional picks or incorporate picks. Nashville-based Tony Memmel, a below-the-elbow congenital left-hand amputee, uses arguably the simplest and cheapest possible prosthetic, a strong, repurposed tape, to hold a conventional pick with his right arm. Perhaps the archetype of DIY disability musical accommodation, curiously, it is not without commercial implications, as the tape's manufacturer, Gorilla Glue Co., is one of the artist's sponsors. Memmel is seen performing and taping his pick on his website (Memmel n.d.).

Georgia-based guitarist Lefty Williams, a congenital below-the-elbow right hand amputee, employees a more intricate homemade prosthetic of his own design. On his band's website (Williams n.d.), he calls the entire prosthetic a 'pick,' though it comprises both a conventional guitar pick and an elaborate holder, made of common, inexpensive parts, mostly from hardware stores. He provides detailed instructions for "How I make a pick"

(William n.d.), which also include a list of tools and photos that demonstrate that Williams is both a skilled guitarist and 'handy' (again, pun neither intended nor avoided).

Both Memmel and Williams incorporate disability advocacy into their musical work. Memmel's work especially appears to be largely motivational/inspirational – with a preponderance of such engagements listed on his website calendar – in a manner that troubles disability studies scholars and disability activists concerned about "inspiration porn" (Gagliardi 2017). However, it can be argued that both artists render a service to the amputee community in sharing useful information about disability musicking. (I am undecided as to whether Memmel's videos are inspiration porn, document valuable services, or both. It is not always an easy call.)

Adaptive musical instruments in non-clinical settings

While disabled performers typically play conventional instruments, with modified technique and/or prosthetics, occasionally an artist will use a customised instrument, such as those offered at the Centre; this is done without medical consultation. Likely the most famous such performer is Rick Allen, drummer for the British band Def Leppard. Allen lost his right arm in an auto accident. He plays with a partially (originally entirely) electric drum kit (Def Leppard, 2015a), built to his specifications by the Simmons company (Amendola 2002). The outstanding feature of this kit is that drums typically played with the left hand are operated with foot pedals. There are videos that tour Allen's drum kit (Def Leppard 2012; 65 Drums 2017). Others show him soloing (Def Leppard 2015b) and discussing his work on behalf of wounded veterans (Public Domain TV 2014).

Professor David Nabb, of the University of Nebraska at Kearney, is the best-known one-handed saxophonist (University of Nebraska Kearney 2018a). Unable to play with his left hand due to a stroke, he performs on a toggle-key saxophone designed by Nabb and instrument builder Jeff Stelling. A much-honoured advocate for disabled musicians, Nabb founded the One-Handed Woodwinds Program (University of Nebraska Kearney 2018b), which makes instruments available to disabled musicians. Nabb performs and discusses his disability and his instrument in a TED talk (Nabb 2017) and at UN-K (University of Nebraska Kearney 2018c).

Throughout Nabb's appearances, he stresses the high cost and labour-intensiveness of building instruments like his, a characteristic it surely shares with Rick Allen's drum kit (Rose 2016). In a 2015 lecture to my Music, Disability, and Society class, I asked Nabb, whom I had only seen playing alto saxophone, if he owned instruments of other sizes. He replied that he did not, less because of the cost – $25,000 (far more than an excellent conventional saxophone) – than because of the year it takes Skelling to build one. Were he to commission a second instrument, Nabb said it would deprive another disabled player from having one.

Currently, one-handed woodwinds are limited to saxophones (in addition to the Nabb/Stelling instrument, there are two other systems), recorders, and flutes (Woldendorp & van Gils 2012, 233). All are extremely expensive (Nabb 2006, 160) and professionally designed and built, in contrast to DIY inventions for one-handed string playing.

Disability self-advocacy in music

In addition to medically based programmes like the Centre for Rehabilitation and Music and the Performing Arts Medicine Clinic are self-advocacy programmes led by disabled musicians. Canada's Vancouver Adapted Music Society (2018) offers people with significant physical disabilities opportunities to perform and record. Notably, the VAMS studio includes technologies enabling those without use of their hands, including "a range of innovative breath-operated musical equipment that allows people with high-level disabilities to sample the magic," enabling musicians to compose, an alternative to real-time performance (Disability Foundation 2009).

The Long Island-based Coalition for Disabled Musicians (Coalition for Disabled Musicians, Inc. 2018) offers support for physically disabled performers and sponsors three bands. An innovative feature of their work is "tag-team" performance, in which musicians with limited endurance share playing engagements.

Another Way to Play (Thomforde 2018), the website of disabled music educator Valerie Thomforde, offers links to information about adaptive musical instrument praxis, including modified playing technique, supplemental apparatus, and modified instruments, including a one-handed ocarina and a recorder that is adaptable to all manner of hand impairments (including Thomforde's). Particularly notable is the advocacy for 3-D printers as an affordable means of manufacturing adaptive equipment.

Discussion

The most immediately notable difference between medical and DIY disability musical accommodations is one of economics. Every accommodation used by the Centre as per Woldendorp and van Gils (2012) requires an equipment or instrument purchase. While many of these, such as a prosthetic bowing (of a string instrument) hand or an adapted saxophone, recorder, or flute (Nabb 2006), are certainly extremely costly, none come without a price. While some disabled musicians whose accommodations were designed outside health institutions utilise costly devices, such as Rick Allen's drums and David Nabb's saxophone, these are exceptions, used by accomplished professionals who acquired their disabilities after establishing careers. A simpler, less costly accommodation seems impossible and the investment surely worth the high cost. Unlike the DIYs by the disabled guitarists and bassist discussed earlier, chosen from a much larger cohort, Allen and Nabb constitute their entire cohort. Notably, Nabb's saxophone is mentioned in Woldendorp and van Gils (2012) as apt for prescription. It is reasonable to regard such high costs, who pays notwithstanding, as typical of medical services in modern, industrialised nations.

In contrast, most DIY accommodations cost little or nothing. Given especially that some of the aforementioned musicians are acknowledged virtuosi, such as Django Reinhardt and Horace Parlan (Lubet 2011a, 45–56), it appears that cheap or free accommodations are at least as effective as those medically prescribed. Even the commercially available fret wrap that bassist Bill Clements now prefers to his earlier DIY choices sells for $US11.99 on amazon. com (Gruv Gear 2018).

There are other subtle insinuations of class difference in the contrast between medical and DIY accommodations. One is the choice of instruments. While Woldendorp and van Gils (2012) address all of Western musical instrumentation, there is little mention of guitar, a vernacular music favourite. The apparent neutrality toward instrument choice - addressing all Western musical instruments but with a lack of focus on popular favourites like guitar - represents classical bias, since the overwhelming majority of Western instruments are associated with the symphony orchestra. (The same instrumental bias also marginalises non-classical music in nearly all Western music curricula in higher education. If every instrument of the symphony orchestra must be taught, along with classical piano, organ, and voice, the remaining resources available for teaching and equipping any other music will almost always be limited to inadequate. Poorly funded programs in, for example, jazz, can then be faulted for failing to flourish while being starved.)

By contrast, DIY accommodations are mostly for guitar, bass guitar, or steel/slide guitar, and occasionally keyboards or fiddle (folk violin). Medical music adaptations are thus more oriented toward classical music, DIY adaptations almost exclusively for vernacular idioms.

The genre implications of medical versus DIY musical adaptations are supported by additional evidence. The DIY examples I have compiled are almost exclusively artists working in vernacular idioms: jazz, folk, rock, country, and gospel. The sole exception is David Nabb, who mostly plays classical saxophone, but some jazz. While the Centre is unique in its mission, there is an entire specialty of performing arts medicine, whose principle emphasis is music. Its nuclei are the Performing Arts Medicine Association, whose annual meeting is in conjunction with the Aspen (classical) Music Festival, and the journal *Medical Problems of Performing Arts* (*MPPA*), where Woldendorp and van Gils' (2012) work appears. The overwhelming majority of the journal's articles concern classical musicians.

In "The Popular and 'Proper' Performing Arts," former *MPPA* editor Ralph Manchester writes,

> [W]e have devoted most (but not all) of our attention in the performing arts healthcare field to the classical forms of the performing arts. ... [T]here have been articles on various forms of popular music and dance in most years but not in all issues.
>
> [T]he relative number of articles on classical versus popular music and dance has been the inverse of their presence in modern culture as a whole. ... Performing artists in both the classical and popular genres can probably benefit from a ... broadening of our horizons.
>
> *(Manchester 2012, 180)*

Since the appearance of Manchester's editorial, 10 out of 183 articles in 16 issues of *MPPA* have concerned popular music. There are also articles on non-classical dance forms. The inverse presence Manchester references remains. Manchester's 2013 editorial was not the first to express concern over this imbalance. Two earlier editorials speculate as to the reasons for this classical music – and thus, I would argue, class – bias. Writing in 2006, Manchester observes that

> In large part, this focus probably owes to the fact that most of the larger and better established performing arts organizations are devoted to these better-established arts traditions. It is much less difficult to study a group of students in a music school or musicians in a professional orchestra than it is to track down a similar number of pop musicians and follow them over time. Several dozen to several hundred classical musicians show up at the same place for months to years at a time; non-classical musicians tend to gather in smaller groups and often move around more.
>
> *(Manchester 2006, n.p.)*

There is an unspoken class bias here. Symphony orchestra musicians, unlike nearly all their brethren working in vernacular idioms, often have salaries, benefits, and union contracts that guarantee regular employment. Acknowledging that there is a problem, Manchester further observes that

Disability studies and adaptive music

> [R]acial, ethnic, and socioeconomic diversity is typically more prevalent in the non-classical world, especially as it relates to historical, underrepresented minorities. It does not have to be that way, but in many communities that is what happens.
>
> *(Manchester 2006, 45)*

Class – and therefore racial – bias is even more obvious in "Medical Problems of Nonclassical Musicians" (Brandfonbrener 1995), a 1995 editorial by Manchester's predecessor and *MPPA* founding editor Alice Brandfonbrener. Brandfonbrener observed that since *MPPA*'s founding in 1986, there had been only 6 articles on non-classical music: 2 on rock, 1 on bagpipers, 2 on marching band, and an editorial (by Brandfonbrener) on jazz. (I would not count the marching band articles and did not in my earlier tally of more recent articles. Marching bands belong to the same classical music education system as concert bands and orchestras.) This paucity, which she bemoans, is, she claims, because

> This is the music that many physicians grew up with, continue to listen to, and occasionally perform. It is familiar and comfortable and it stimulates our emotions.
>
> *(Brandfonbrener 1995, 1)*

It requires little imagination to associate these physicians and the music they love with class privilege and European heritage, although Western classical music now also looms large in Asian/Asian-American cultures, groups Manchester appears not to regard as underrepresented. A connection between disability and poverty (Eide & Ingstad 2017) – and thus vernacular culture and cheap or free DIY musical accommodations – is equally obvious.

References to disability – as opposed to treatable injury and illness – are even rarer in *MPPA* than discussions of vernacular musics. A search for the title or abstract keyword disability in *MPPA* yielded only four title keywords (including an article by me and a review of my *Music, Disability, and Society* by David Nabb (2014)) and 16 abstract keywords.

Finally, with few exceptions, there is a contrast between composer-performer relationships in classical versus vernacular musics that makes the latter more open to disability accommodation. Contemporary classical music performance practice (regardless of the era in which the music was composed) is grounded in loyalty to the notated score in a manner that limits interpretive latitudes. Substantive changes to a composed work expressly for the purposes of disability accommodation are rare and limited to keyboard instruments (Brofeldt n.d.), where, unlike the playing of jazz pianist Horace Parlan, the impaired hand is never used, even if it has some function.

In contrast, wide latitudes of interpretation are virtually required in all the vernacular traditions referenced earlier and many others worldwide. Often, skilful employment of such freedoms, including improvisation, is a standard by which the quality of performance is judged. Interpretation exists in classical music as well, but choices are restricted by the canonised score. In vernacular musics, performers are expected not simply to interpret, but to make compositional choices, not merely how a work is played, but what is played (Lubet 2011a, 42–68). This applies to extant works, such as popular songs, open to substantive modification, or to the demands of/ for original compositions. The expectations of either modification or composition invite disabled performers to choose what they play, according to what their bodies encourage.

Conclusions

While performing arts medicine has paid little attention to disability musicking, the work of the Centre for Rehabilitation and Music provides a model that should be emulated, stressing

Alex Lubet

accommodation (and non-invasive therapies) over chemical and surgical procedures. The conventions of medical praxis, though, make the process of accommodation costly, regardless of who pays. Perhaps unintentionally, the work of the Centre is oriented toward classical music, with class/racial implications.

In contrast, disabled musicians have invented numerous DIY accommodations costing little or nothing, enabling artists, even noted virtuosi, to perform numerous idioms, across class/racial boundaries. Performing arts medicine has much to learn from these artist/inventors. One possible collaboration would blend DIY ingenuity, the work of institutions like the Centre, and the power of medical informatics to create a free and open, well-indexed database of adaptive musical resources.

One lesson of this chapter is that there are no fields, even medicine, that are "not disability studies," as per Linton (1998, 132). The work of the Centre reaffirms the potential of sociocultural perspectives in health fields, such as occupational and music therapy. Finally, although the reflections here upon class, race, wealth, poverty, disability accommodations, and performing arts medicine are not economics per se, they point to an as yet unfulfilled need for a disability studies of economics.

References

65 Drums. 2017. *How Rick Allen Uses Electronic Drums (Def Leppard), 2017.* Accessed 13 January 2018. Available: www.youtube.com/watch?v=ZWhnW84-voc.

ADA.gov. n.d. *Americans With Disabilities Act of 1990, As Amended.* Accessed 13 January 2018. Available: www.ada.gov/pubs/adastatute08.htm#12102.

Alex Lubet, Employee, v. University of Minn., Self-Insured/Sedgwick Claims Management Servs., Employer/Appellant, 2002, USA.

Allina Health. 2010. *Performing Arts Medicine Clinic.* Accessed 13 January 2018. Available: www.allinahealth.org/Courage-Kenny-Rehabilitation-Institute/Programs-and-services/Performing-Arts-Medicine-Clinic/.

Amendola, Billy. *Def Leppard's Rick Allen. Modern Drummer,* August 2002. Accessed 13 January 2018. Available: www.angelfire.com/band/rickallenthundergod/rickallen.html.

Assistive Technology Partners. n.d. *Adapting Musical Activities for Persons with Disabilities.* Accessed 13 January 2018. Available: www.ucdenver.edu/academics/colleges/medicalschool/programs/atp/Documents/AdaptingMusicalActivitiesforPersonswithDisabilities.pdf.

Bakan, Michael B., Koen, Benjamin, Kobylarz, Fred, Morgan, Lindee, Goff, Rachel, Kahn, Sally, and Bakan, Megan. 2008. "Following Frank: Response-Ability and the Co-Creation of Culture in a Medical Ethnomusicology Program for Children on the Autism Spectrum." *Ethnomusicology.* 52 (2): 163–202.

Brandfonbrener, Alice. 1995. "Medical Problems of Nonclassical Musicians." *Medical Problems of Performing Artists.* 10: 1–1.

Brofeldt, Hans. n.d. *Piano Music for the Left Hand Alone.* Accessed 13 January 2018. Available: www.left-hand-brofeldt.dk/.

Cameron, Colin. 2014. "Does Disability Studies have Anything to Say to Music Therapy? And Would Music Therapy Listen if it Did?" *Voices: A World Forum for Music Therapy.* 14 (3). n.p. doi:10.15845/voices.v14i3.794.

Clements, Bill. 2012. *Fret Wrap.* Accessed 13 January 2018. Available: www.youtube.com/watch?v=ulV-oFH4AQw.

Clements, Bill. 2007. *Bill Clements.* Accessed 13 January 2018. Available: www.youtube.com/watch?v=eskvyuzF1-Y.

Coalition for Disabled Musicians, Inc. 2018. *Coalition for Disabled Musicians, Inc.* Accessed 14 January 2018. Available: www.disabled-musicians.org/performance-schedule/.

Cuff, Sharon, McGoldrick, Kathleen, Patterson, Stephanie, and Peterson, Elizabeth. 2014. "The Intersection of Disability Studies and Health Science." *Transformations: The Journal of Inclusive Scholarship and Pedagogy.* 25 (2): 37–50.

Def Leppard. 2015a. *Rick Allen.* Accessed 13 January 2018. Available: www.defleppard.com/member/rick-allen/.

Disability studies and adaptive music

Def Leppard. 2015b. *Rick Allen Drum Solo - Live Nottingham Arena 13th December 2015.* Accessed 13 January 2018. Available: www.youtube.com/watch?v=Y8xsua4NZ88.

Def Leppard. 2012. *Tour of Rick Allen's Drum Kit.* Accessed 13 January 2018. Available: www.youtube.com/watch?v=YS53IJAqquw.

Dickerson, D. n.d. *Deke's Wonderful World of Weirdness.* Accessed 13 January 2018. Available: www.dekedickerson.com/weird-armless.php.

Disability Foundation. 2009. *Vancouver Adapted Music Society's CD-Quality Recording Studio.* Accessed 14 January 2018. Available: www.youtube.com/watch?v=AA7ZlDuQinA.

Eide, Arne, and Ingstad, Benedicte. 2017. *Disability and Poverty: A Global Challenge.* Bristol: Policy Press.

Gagliardi, Katy. 2017. "Facebook Captions: Kindness, or Inspiration Porn?" *M/C Journal.* 20 (3). Accessed 13 January 2018. Available: http://journal.media-culture.org.au/index.php/mcjournal/article/view/1258.

Givan, Benjamin. 2014. "'Django's Tiger:' From Jazz to Jazz Manouche." *Current Musicology.* 98. Accessed 13 January 2018. Available: https://currentmusicology.columbia.edu/article/djangos-tiger-from-jazz-to-jazz-manouche/.

Gruv Gear. 2018. *Gruv Gear FretWraps String Muter.* Accessed 13 January 2018. Available: www.amazon.com/s/ref=nb_sb_ss_i_1_4?url=search-alias%3Dmi&field-keywords=gruv+gear+fretwraps&sprefix=gruv%2Caps%2C148&crid=BP4JMU19LCJ7).

Hadley, Susan. ed. 2014. "Special Issue on Music Therapy and Disability Studies." *Voices: A World Forum for Music Therapy.* 14 (3). n.p. doi:10.15845/voices.v14i3.794.

Harris, John. 2001. "One Principle and Three Fallacies of Disability Studies." *Journal of Medical Ethics.* 27 (6): 383–387.

Howe, Blake, Jensen-Moulton, Stephanie, Lerner, Neil, and Straus, Joseph, ed. 2016. *The Oxford Handbook of Music and Disability Studies.* New York: Oxford Handbooks.

Iverson, Jennifer. 2012. "Review: *Extraordinary Measures: Disability in Music* by Joseph N. Straus; *Music, Disability and Society* by Alex Lubet." *Journal of the American Musicological Society.* 65 (2): 611–621.

Jensen-Moulton, Stephanie. 2012. "Intellectual Disability in Carlisle Floyd's of Mice and Men." *American Music.* 30 (2): 129–156.

Kramer, Lawrence. 2003. "Musicology and Meaning." *The Musical Times.* 144 (1883): 6–12.

Lerner, Neil, and Straus, Joseph, ed. 2006. *Sounding Off: Theorizing Disability in Music.* New York: Routledge.

Linton, Simi. 1998. *Claiming Disability: Knowledge and Identity.* New York: New York University Press.

Lubet, Alex. 2014. "Tunes of Impairment: An Ethnomusicology of Disability." *Review of Disability Studies: An International Journal.* 1 (1): 133–146.

Lubet, Alex, 2013. "Extraordinary Measures: Disability in Music. By Joseph Straus." *Music and Letters.* 93 (4): 635–639.

Lubet, Alex. 2011a. "Disability Rights, Music and the Case for Inclusive Education." *International Journal of Inclusive Education.* 15 (1): 57–70.

Lubet, Alex. 2011b. *Music, Disability, and Society.* Philadelphia: Temple University Press.

Lubet, Alex. 2002. "Disability Studies and Performing Arts Medicine." *Medical Problems of Performing Artists.* 17 (2): 59–62.

Manchester, Ralph. 2006. "Diversity in Performing Arts Medicine." *Medical Problems of Performing Artists.* 21 (2): 45–47.

Manchester, Ralph. 2013. "The Popular and the 'Proper' Performing Arts." *Medical Problems of Performing Artists.* 28 (4): 179.

Melendez, Tony. n.d. *Welcome!* Accessed 13 January 2018. Available: www.tonymelendez.com/English/Welcome.html.

Memmel, Tony. n.d. *Tony Memmel.* Accessed 13 January 2018. Available: http://tonymemmel.com/wp/.

Miller, Cherrise, ed. 2011. *Making Music with a Hearing Loss: Strategies and Stories.* Gaithersburg: AAMHL Pub.

Nabb, David. 2017. *The Case for Adapted Musical Instruments | David Nabb | TEDxLincoln.* Accessed 13 January 2018. Available: www.youtube.com/watch?v=j2v28JGfphQ.

Nabb, David. 2014. "Music, Disability, and Society, by Alex Lubet." *Medical Problems of Performing Artists.* 29 (2): 118.

Nabb, David. 2006. "Interview with Maarten Visser." *Medical Problems of Performing Artists.* 21 (4): 159.

New Orleans Musicians' Clinic & Assistance Foundation. 2018. *New Orleans Musicians' Clinic & Assistance Foundation.* Accessed 13 January 2018. Available from: https://neworleansmusiciansclinic.org/.

Public Domain TV. 2014. *Awesome Interview with Def Leppard Drummer Rick Allen.* Accessed 13 January 2018. Available: www.youtube.com/watch?v=xrgv21Y7r2M.

Alex Lubet

Rathgeber, Jesse. 2017. "A Place in the Band." In Zack Moir and Matt Brennan ed. *The Routledge Research Companion to Popular Music Education*. London & New York: Routledge, 369–381.

Reinhardt, Django, and Grappelli, Stephane. 2015. *Django Reinhardt & Stéphane Grappelli - Jattendrai Swing 1939 - LIVE!* 2015. Accessed 13 January 2018. Available from www.youtube.com/watch?v=ANArGmr74u4.

Rose, Beth. 2016. "The Importance of a One-Handed Saxophone." *BBC News*, 2 June 2016. Accessed 13 January 2018. Available: www.bbc.com/news/disability-36168077.

Shakespeare, Tom, and Watson, Nicholas. 2001. "The Social Model of Disability: An Outdated Ideology?" In Sharon N. Barnhart and Barbara M. Altman ed. *Exploring Theories and Expanding Methodologies: Where We Are and Where We Need to Go?* Bingley: Emerald Group Publishing Limited, 9–28.

Shepp, Archie. 2014. *Archie Shepp Quartet Featuring Horace Parlan* 1994. Accessed 13 January 2018. Available: www.youtube.com/watch?v=uK76sWSmwMY.

Siebers, Tobin. 2008. *Disability Theory*. Ann Arbor: University of Michigan Press.

Small, Christopher. 2011. *Musicking: The Meanings of Performing and Listening*. Hanover: Wesleyan University Press.

Straus, Joseph. 2011. *Extraordinary Measures: Disability in Music*. New York: Oxford University Press.

Thomforde, Valerie. 2018. *Another Way to Play*. Accessed 16 January 2018. Available: https://another waytoplay.org/.

University of Nebraska Kearney. 2018a. *Dr. David Nabb*. Accessed 13 January 2018. Available: www.unk.edu/academics/music/fs/david_nabb.php.

University of Nebraska Kearney. 2018b. *UNK One-Handed Woodwinds Program*. Accessed 13 January 2018. Available: www.unk.edu/academics/music/unk-one-handed-winds-program.php.

University of Nebraska Kearney. 2018c. *Faculty Impact - Dr. David Nabb*. Accessed 13 January 2018. Available: www.youtube.com/watch?v=TVL9ZtFv6oc.

Vancouver Adapted Music Society. 2018. Accessed 14 January 2018. Available: www.vams.org/.

Wendell, Susan.1996. *The Rejected Body: Feminist Philosophical Reflections on Disability*. New York: Routledge.

Williams, Lefty. n.d. *Lefty Williams Band*. Accessed 13 January 2018. Available: www.lefty-music.com/home.

Woldendorp, Kees, and van Gils, Willemijn. 2012. "One-Handed Musicians-More than a Gimmick." *Medical Problems of Performing Artists*. 27 (4): 231–237.

26

Accidental leaders

Inclusion, career pathways, and autonomy among dancers with disabilities

Sarah Whatley

Introduction

Dance is an art form where the body is always on show, always on display. Dancers with different physicalities are therefore always performing their disability (Garland-Thomson 2009). For dancers with other kinds of impairments, whether sensory, cognitive, or a condition that is apparently invisible – such as chronic illness – disability can be something that each dancer will relate to differently. For some, identifying as a dancer with a disability can be important, whilst for others they prefer to eschew a disability identity. For those with invisible disabilities, the artist can find herself in a paradox whereby she wants to transmit something of her condition as it can determine how the choreography takes shape (whether or not 'disability' is subject matter) whilst not wanting to be viewed as anything other than a professional artist on her own terms and in her own right.

The involvement of dancers with disabilities in dance is acknowledged as enriching the field in general. As Kuppers observes:

> Disabled performers have successfully and visibly taken up the medium of dance to expand the possibilities of images, spaces and positions for their bodies. In their work with bodies in public spheres, they attempt to break through stereotypes of passive disability.
>
> *(Kuppers 2008, 25)*

Several inclusive dance companies are now gaining recognition for producing high-quality and popular performances, even if there is still some way to go before inclusion is the norm, and differently abled dancers are able to find work in all and any dance companies alongside their non-disabled peers. However, for nearly all dance artists with disabilities, their journey towards a career in dance is often quite different from the non-disabled dancer. This journey reflects the current state of training for a career in dance, which, despite various initiatives over recent decades, remains inaccessible for many students with disabilities. The reasons vary but may be due to self-perception and self-doubt, as well as assumptions by teachers, parents, and those in training organisations who perceive that elite training is incompatible with inclusion (Aujla & Redding 2013). As Aujla and Redding point out (2013), the lack of technical training, the content of dance training sessions – in particular the movement material used – and teachers' lack of knowledge in how best to train young dancers with disabilities are further barriers for young dance students.

Whilst dance training programmes focus on developing dancers who are technically and creatively proficient, and increasingly include education about what it means to find work and sustain work within the creative sector, dancers with disabilities often develop their own resources that prepare them for careers in the dance profession. On one hand, the reliance on their own resources, which can be augmented by working collaboratively with other dancers in similar positions, enables many to be enterprising and attuned to the challenges of a career that is usually piecemeal and 'portfolio'-based. But the reality of having reduced access to training underscores the inequality that continues to persist in a cultural practice where narrow views of what a dancer should look like, and move like, continue. Austria-based performance artist Elisabeth Löffler recounts the story of her early experiences of thinking about her career choices:

> I remember very well how the career officer laughed at me, when I told him that I wanted to become a singer. Three years later the director from a private acting school suggested I make radio plays instead of starting an acting career, so nobody would have to look at me. ... Looking back, I'd say there was a lack of Role Models I could refer to, but by accident I started to dance, and in this one week in Cologne in 1996 I figured out that this was what I wanted to do with my life, and that it was worth putting all my energy into it. I was twenty-six, At the beginning of trying to join classes, most of the artists rejected me and wouldn't let me participate in their classes, and I'm still not always successful. But nowadays the teachers are slowly changing their minds.
>
> *(Löffler 2017, 12)*

Those dancers who do participate in and complete dance training programmes – whether at a conservatoire or as part of a degree course – tend to take on a large part of the responsibility themselves for their navigation through the course and supporting the (likely) non-disabled faculty make suitable adjustments. Consequently, they can – or perhaps should – have a profound impact on established methods and perceptions of what a dance training should be, promoting diversity and variation that extends into the professional dance context. As Ben Evans, head of Arts and Disability for the British Council, states:

> Think about it. Artists with unique experiences of and perspectives on the world make new and unique art. Artists who have not gone to the same dance & drama schools, conservatoires and arts colleges as everyone else (often because they can't), bring new aesthetic ideas. Explorations of difference or 'otherness' help us all understand the complex society in which we live.
>
> *(Evans 2017, 6)*

Nonetheless, those dancers with disabilities who do sustain careers are relatively few and through their resilience are often perceived as ambassadors or leaders, even if they see themselves as 'accidental leaders,' which places responsibilities on them that they may not have chosen for themselves.

In this chapter, I will draw on the work and experiences of a number of disabled dance artists, most of whom are either based or have worked for at least some of their professional career in the UK, to discuss how this community of dance artists have effectively taken ownership of their working practices and how their modes of making and performing demonstrate how dance is a powerful mode for their self-expression. I deliberately foreground the words from the dance artists themselves to acknowledge the importance of their own direct experience and as an often untapped source of valuable knowledge. I will base this in a brief discussion on the current position of routes into and out of dance training courses in the UK for dancers with disabilities and note how some dance companies are taking on the responsibility themselves for training disabled dancers. For example, Stopgap Dance Company provides a training programme specifically to address the way the dance training framework is designed for the non-disabled dancer. My aim is thus to show how dancers with disabilities find ways to navigate through what continues to be a largely exclusionary landscape, from which emerges a triad of conditions that variously impact on how dancers build a career in dance; training accessed 'piecemeal' or 'on the job,' peer support through the wider disabled dance 'community of practice' (Lave & Wenger 1991), and reliance on their own self-learning, as autodidacts. I will conclude with some thoughts about how dance training structures may evolve in the future to dismantle discriminatory practices that are rooted in a narrow dance aesthetic.

Towards equal participation

Dancers with disabilities may choose to study dance and pursue a career in dance for a variety of reasons. Indeed, as I will explore, some may have found themselves in the dance industry more by accident than by choice. But whilst their pathway into dance may have begun with an interest in (or recommendation to pursue) the therapeutic properties of dance, which are variously described but tend to focus on physical, cognitive, emotional, and/or social benefits as well as reducing stress and encouraging self-expression (as described by Justin Lee, Shawn Goh, Sarah Meisch Lionetto, Joanne Tay, and Alice Fox in Chapter 8, and Sue Cheesman in Chapter 9 of this book), their working life is as artist, thereby challenging any presumption that their practice is primarily 'therapeutic,' even if positive for their sense of identity, agency, self-esteem, and so on.

For many dancers with disabilities, their lives are often continually mediated by medical care. Dancers talk about their regular visits to hospital, to physiotherapists and the familiar experience of being "poked, prodded and corrected by doctors" (Malin 2017, 14). The additional physical demands placed upon dancers may lead medical professionals to advise against a dancing career, even if dancing may be recommended as a form of physical therapy. The expertise of medical professionals is of course vital for many with disabilities to be able to live well even if the biomedical model of disability, as examined by disabled artists/ theorists (Kuppers 2003; Shakespeare 2010), by those situated principally within disability studies (Davis 2002; Sandahl & Auslander 2005; Mitchell & Snyder 2006; Henderson & Ostrander 2010; Siebers 2010), and by those in the medico-legal profession (Abberley 1987; Reinders 2000; Sloan 2000; Hintermair & Albertini 2005; see Alex Lubet in Chapter 25) is challenged. The medical model of disability is based upon a normative idea of the human body, so treatment and care for bodies that diverge from the 'norm' tends towards reducing difference so that the individual can fit more easily into social structures. Conversations with dancers in the context of various research projects (including *Moving Matters*, 2008; *InVisible Difference; Dance, Disability and Law*, 2013–2016; *Resilience and Inclusion: Dancers as Agents of Change*, 2016–2017) revealed that the models of disability were problematic for dancers who find the 'modelling' of their experience of living in the world unhelpful, and as a model for viewing and analysing their dance work, constraining. In conversation, dance artist and wheelchair-user Caroline Bowditch asked to have simply a 'human model' (Bowditch 2013) to avoid feeling pressure to align with a single model of disability. Bowditch is a good example of a dance artist who has established a successful international career, and for many years in the UK, and is regarded as a leader and 'role model' (Aujla & Redding 2013, 83) even though she has described herself as an 'accidental leader' (Bowditch 2013), having negotiated the triad noted earlier and her commitment to advocacy for the disabled dance community through taking up leadership roles within national bodies that represent disabled dancers. As an autodidact, she had to find a way of choreographing and performing with her own unique body, leading her to work with Scottish Dance Theatre between 2008 and 2012 as Dance Agent for Change, providing her with 'on the job' training in a mainstream dance company, accompanied by support from her community of practice.

Access to training

One of the challenges for dancers with disabilities finding a route into a dance programme is that a dance training assumes a baseline from which all dancers develop, and that leads to a normalising experience, so dancers who do not easily fit into a normative model either adapt to conform or resist conformity; neither is particularly conducive to thriving. Indeed, as Stopgap Dance Company's executive producer Sho Shibata observes,

> Because the training framework used in the workforce pipeline is designed solely with non-disabled dancers in mind professional disabled dancers face a disadvantage and are in short supply. It used to be the case that the industry ignored this inequality and simply claimed that disabled people just didn't turn out to be great dancers.
>
> *(Shibata 2017, n.p.)*

Ironically, those dancers who have developed successful careers have built a practice out of their individual way of moving and making work, which questions what value a dance training might be for the dancer who is already the expert in her own body's capacity for movement. The dance sector is not yet able to offer an individualised, bespoke training opportunity.

In universities, undergraduate and postgraduate taught courses offer a diet of practical activity and academic study, sometimes with a relationship with a local or regional cultural centre or dance company. A conservatoire training, or training in one of the many tertiary vocational dance schools, focuses very much on the acquisition of technical skills and the ability to be versatile and adaptable to a number of different dance styles. These tend to be primarily Western theatre styles – classical ballet, contemporary dance – but have broadened in recent years to include street dance, urban dance, non-Western forms, and a wide range of somatic-informed practices that promote a focus on a more holistic approach to dance training. Many courses will include contact improvisation (CI) – a practice based on the premise of physical and aesthetic disorientation (Davies 2010, 45). By exploring fall and recovery, and multiple balance points, CI "constitutes disability praxis, and a disability aesthetic in dance actualism fosters new ways of looking at different bodies" (Davies 2010, 44). Whilst it is important that CI is a form in which many dancers with disabilities feel more included, it does little to disrupt the view that other dance practices are not available to them.

The majority of dance students enter training through audition, having gained experience of dancing at school, in youth dance groups, or through classes in the private school sector, and so are at least to some extent familiar with the physical, emotional and psychological demands that a dance training will place upon them. However, dance activities for children often

> encourage students to aspire toward a traditional concept of an "ideal shape" and assessments are designed to judge how close they can get to these set shapes. But this is particularly unattainable for disabled people who have physiques that are far from the average and many of them feel discouraged from progressing through training because of this.
>
> *(Shibata 2017, n.p.)*

The barrier this imposes for disabled dancers at the entry level is then reinforced at tertiary and industry levels, "because they tend to lean toward the traditional pedagogical stance" (Shibata 2017, n.p.).

Many courses are designed to maximise studio-based learning, and students are expected to take responsibility for being physically prepared and ready to move. Traditional technical development in dance is delivered through classes where a cohort of students follows the direction, demonstration, and/or instructions from a teacher who will address the whole class, observe and offer individual feedback from time to time, but feedback which is potentially relevant for many of the learners. This description does no more than sketch out what may be regarded as broadly a 'typical' experience for the pre-professional dance student. However, because there is an expectation of familiarity with the dance training system and an assumption that studio-based learning is mostly delivered in groups, the culture tends towards promoting (however accidentally) homogeneity rather than variation, to the extent that any student who 'stands out in a crowd' and does not easily conform to the established regime may feel out of place and less able to participate. Consequently, it is in this context, the dancer with a physical or cognitive disability, or with an invisible disability, may feel discriminated against, even if unintentionally, as their experience of 'difference' may leave them unable to easily merge into a group that may appear to privilege or prioritise sameness.

However much an inclusive philosophy may be emphasised, the student with a different physicality, sensory or cognitive impairment may thus be concerned that her difference (I adopt the feminine pronoun throughout simply for ease, not to imply any gender bias) is made hyper-visible, not least because the numbers of students with disabilities continue to be at best marginal. Consequently, a disabled student may be the only one in a class cohort, potentially identified by her difference, which may extend beyond her physical/sensory/cognitive difference to her prior dance experience, which is also likely to be outside of the conventional pathways into a training programme (if indeed there was any experience at all). Moreover, as dance students are often encouraged to work towards a 'neutral body,' regarded as the ideal place from which learning or relearning can begin, and which neutralises habits – often seen as negative – the dancer with a different body will discover, or be aware of, the impossibility of neutrality, reinforcing that the "dancing body is constructed, and even in supposed neutrality is embedded with values" (Roach 2015, 112). Once again, difference is emphasised, and a difference that is inscribed into the body and not a difference that the student will wish to, or be able to, dilute or erase.

Labels

Underpinning much of the discussion about difference and disability is the question of labels and how dance artists identify (or not) with the disability label, and labels may inadvertently deter dancers from pursuing a particular pathway. The terms 'inclusive' and 'integrated' tend to be used interchangeably in dance. For the dancer with a disability, the label may be an invitation and may set up expectations that are not always realised in how a course is organised, delivered, and assessed. A course would need to consider carefully its curriculum, in terms of content, organisation, timetabling, and pedagogy. It may also suggest to the non-disabled learner that the course is training for a specific practice ('inclusive/integrated dance') and not relevant for them. Labels can then work against the aim of promoting equality and the creation of a context where all learners can learn and benefit on an equal basis. Paradoxically, applying the term 'integrated' may prepare participants to expect a setting where those dancing are more different than would ordinarily be found within a 'non-integrated' setting. As noted earlier, normative categories can extend more into the dance environment than in other arts practices where the body is more 'on show' (hyper-visible) as the primary site of creative expression.

Inclusive dance tends to use the term 'inclusion' as a politically charged message, to argue that the dance does not discriminate on the grounds of disability (or on age, race, and so on). Looking beyond the training environment, dance companies are beginning to think more about the use of these terms. Some companies consciously resist such labels to make the point that the work 'stands in its own terms' without a pre-warning to an audience that it is different, which can impact on expectations about the work that will be seen (Whatley 2007). For instance, Candoco describes itself as "the contemporary dance company of disabled and non-disabled dancers" (Candoco: About Us n.d.). By removing the label, there is a move towards the work being seen and critiqued in its own terms, as art work and not work to be 'admired' for how it transcends or overcomes the body's limitations or judged within a paradigm of dance therapy. But judgement of dance as a performing art is always rooted in what is seen and perceived by others, so how the individual is 'read' by others is key to how we are perceived as a person in the world. As Garland-Thomson observes, the reading of our body by others informs assumptions around ability or lack of ability and status in the world (Garland-Thomson 2009, 49). She points to the way notions of value are attached to the body, and the non-impaired body holds a higher value than an impaired body in its ability to read in a framework of normative body communication (2009). The disabled body is thereby interpreted through an ableist framework of understanding rather than through a non-verbal vocabulary of its own devising. Thus, meaning transmitted through the non-verbal vocabulary of dance will always be overshadowed by this framework, and it is in this framework of meaning making that the disabled dance student enters the institution and finds herself with a responsibility to try and undo the dominant ableist dance milieu.

Independence versus autonomy

Undertaking a training in dance will often focus on developing the student's ability to work independently. Independence can simply describe a working pattern that is based on self-employment, and often part-time or project-based work that is unconnected with a single company or organisation. Or it can designate the individual's self-determinacy, whereby the dancer aligns herself with a particular artist 'movement' that is consciously distant from dominant and mainstream working practices and aesthetics. For dance students with disabilities and who require some kind of support for their learning, the pathway towards independence requires a balance between reinforcing what was likely to be a more familiar situation whereby the student was used to being dependent on others and encouraging autonomy to avoid compromising the individual agency of the student. For those students who require some assistance for their learning in the dance studio, there are practical aspects for them to manage, which again lead to an uneven experience – such as the time it takes to prepare for studio work and the time it takes to transition into other parts of their studies – so are required to develop strategies for working that place additional demands on their route towards independence. These needs, whilst sometimes resulting in the need for more resources, are a question of equal rights for those with disabilities to access training. As Löffler recounts, she has taken many years

> to convince the government that dance art and disability aren't a contradiction, and that disabled dancers are also worth supporting. …. I just want the same rights of education as non-disabled students, as well as accessibility to education, rehearsal space, wardrobes, and of course stages.
>
> *(Löffler 2017, 12)*

Löffler is not unusual in taking up an advocacy role to persuade those in positions of power and authority to recognise what is needed and make adjustments as necessary.

Each dancer has a very different experience of finding her way in to dance, so looking for themes or what might be common for all dancers is difficult – hence the question, what would, or should, a training programme provide, and what are we training dancers for? Will a training programme designed with the non-disabled, normative body ever serve the needs of the dancer with a different body? The experience of Tanja Erhart illustrates how it is not possible to treat the (dancing) body as uninfused with social, gendered, or any other identities, and thus why a training programme designed for the 'majority' will fall short for those with different bodies and limit their full participation. Erhart's insightful observations also unpeel the many layers that combine to shape her working life:

> Our bodies are fluid, we're not one body but many, and they are not defined by what they are, but by what they can do. Nothing is fixed, everything is in constant change. And this fluidity of the body is something I've realised through dancing, and the possibilities that come into a space when I bring my crutches and my wheelchair…. For me the process goes like this: I come in to the space with my movement equipment (crutches and wheelchair) ready if needed, then I listen to the task, ask questions if needed and make decisions on which tool to use to best fulfill the task. And as the class or creative process goes along, these tasks and exercises change, so I might need to change my movement equipment. And if that happens, the time issue becomes key, because I need to figure out where the equipment is and then go/hop/crawl/roll there and make myself ready with the new tool. And this all takes effort and energy, so sometimes I decide to stick with what I have and who I am right then, and stay focused on that. And I do this even though I might be really interested in changing. So skill-gaining in all my three different bodies, is key to them becoming my embodied differences. And it all takes time, curiosity, training and a huge desire to dance. I'm not one, but many, in a very obvious way; as an amputee with various equipment to help me move, but also to do with my invisible disabilities, like my tumours, diabetes, chronic infection and so forth, which shape what I do and what I can't do.
>
> *(Erhart 2017, 21)*

Erhart refers to her 'three different bodies,' reinforcing the fluidity of the body and how all bodies are in a process of continual change. Her expertise has been acquired through the triadic process of self-learning, peer support, and discovering how to work with her 'multiple bodies' and with her 'movement equipment' in the professional working environment. The knowledge she has gained about how to work as a dance artist has implications for how training programmes need to take account of the additional time and tools required, if a course is going to be viable and accessible for the dancer with a different body.

Crutch dancer and choreographer Claire Cunningham describes how she rethought her relationship with her body through dance. Her formative training was in music, and whilst she recalls how she did not consider herself as disabled, had no experience of working with other disabled people, and had no encounter with the disability arts community, she did want to do something to help disabled people think about the arts as a career choice. She formed a company that worked with disabled participants, to find ways to perform and to be more employable as a performer. She was able to access free aerial training, which led to her working with British integrated dance company Blue Eyed Soul and which brought her into contact with choreographer-director Jess Curtis, now a long-term collaborator. It was working with Curtis and her first encounter with contact improvisation that offered her a new way of thinking about her body, how she could use her crutches, and how to use her weight differently. Further training with fellow crutch performer Bill Shannon and more aerial training meant working out a training regime for herself for the first time, which also led her to developing her own 'crutch technique' using the crutches as pivot points, finding spirals and new connections in her body. She found breakthroughs in the physics of her body and new ways to develop muscle strength. Her increased technical ability prepared her for working as an independent artist, supported through 'unofficial' mentors and a wider community of disabled artists who fed into her awareness of what it meant to be disabled. Having previously wanting to disassociate with disability, she acknowledged that her impairment was her source material for her work, and her crutches allowed her to develop a virtuosic dance technique (Cunningham 2013).

Cunningham's experience is particular to her journey but not atypical in terms of the triad process and a series of unexpected connections, discoveries, and opportunities, which often characterises the pathway into professional work for many dancers with disabilities. Cunningham shifted from resisting an identity of disabled to recognising that her physical impairment was fundamental to her arts practice, enabling her to develop a successful career. What her experience also points to is that a more conventional, normative dance training would be inadequate and inappropriate for the dancer with a unique body, who, in Cunningham's case, uses crutches and thereby determines the unique nature of her training needs. However, whilst the individualised nature of each working dancer's experience points to a landscape whereby a training programme that is suitable for all disabled dancers is hard to imagine, I do not wish to imply that a single artist's experience can be generalised. Moreover, Cunningham demonstrates a determination and persistence that is arguably a requirement of all working dance artists, but the additional challenges presented to those with disabilities amplify these qualities, which may account for the relatively low numbers of working disabled dance artists. Conversely, some dancers with disabilities may elect to follow a more conventional pathway in dance. For example, Annie Hanauer and Kate Marsh both took degrees in dance, and as Hanauer asserts:

> I've always felt that first and foremost, I'm a dancer. I've been dancing since I was a child … and (surprising no one more so than myself) I've earned a living as a performer, and also as a teacher and choreographer, since I entered the professional world. When I work I emphasise the fact that I'm a dancer, because I know that usually someone else will emphasise the woman-with-one-arm part for me.
>
> *(Hanauer 2017, 10)*

Kate Marsh elected to study for a BA degree in Dance and Related Arts in the UK in the 1990s but had not anticipated a career as a performer, as she discusses in her doctoral thesis (Marsh 2016, 2). She describes how she was

> interrupted from a career trajectory that seemed to offer only dance administration or dance therapy, by a workshop with the relatively newly formed CandoCo Dance Company. I had never experienced or seen work including dancers with disabilities away from a therapeutic context and the ethos and practice of (the subsequently rebranded) Candoco resonated strongly with my lifelong experience of impairment.
>
> *(Marsh 2016, 2)*

She recalls a strong sense of being one of a small minority of disabled dance graduates before embarking on working with Candoco. She notes how she became aware of some key shifts in the way dance including disabled people was performed and perceived, with the emergence of several inclusive dance companies – for example, Stopgap Dance Company (UK, 1997-), Axis (USA, 1987-), Touch Compass (NZ, 1997-), Restless Dance (AUS, 1991-) – and initiatives concerned with access and participation in dance. "I developed a sense of belonging in the dance sector and a feeling that my impairment should be no obstacle to progressing in dance" (Marsh 2016, 2) she says.

Marsh collaborates in much of her practice with dancer Welly O'Brien, who also works extensively with Candoco. O'Brien became an amputee after losing a leg in an accident in her late teens. She took part in a workshop with Candoco three months later when she was learning to walk again. She remembers; "It was the first time that I had taken my [false] leg off for a few minutes in front of a group of people and not felt funny about it. It changed my attitude to myself" (cited Stanford 1999, n.p.). She had not considered a dance career before that time, so her entry into dance came after her disability and through the encouragement of Adam Benjamin and Celeste Dandeker, the co-founders of Candoco. Her experience led her to recognise the value of dance to provide rehabilitation after an injury, saying "it helps people adapt to their new body make up or shape" (cited Smith 2015, n.p.). Her dance training was therefore 'on the job', whilst working with Candoco and her subsequent portfolio career mirrors that of many other independent dancers, working freelance with other inclusive companies. She acknowledges the 'trial and error' of finding the right training opportunity but believes that there is always a way in, whatever one's physicality (cited Smith 2015, n.p.).

Underpinning a lot of O'Brien's experience is the question of 'control' because of her relationship with her prosthetic leg, both in everyday life and in the context of her dancing career. She chooses to perform without her prosthetic, explaining,

> Maybe I don't wear it because I still think of it as a functional thing rather than a part of me. I feel much more 'me' and free without it. My body is more relaxed so therefore feel it's easier for me to move in a more natural way.
>
> *(O'Brien 2016)*

O'Brien's dancing career has always been as an amputee, but she recently reflected on her career, saying,

> What worried me was that I've spent 20 years thinking I was an ok performer and doing alright in my practice, but I started to wonder has it only been about my disability? Am I still valid if I am not making my disability explicit? How am I perceived then?
>
> *(O'Brien 2017, 20)*

Sarah Whatley

O'Brien seems to be reflecting a self-doubt that may arise from questioning whether she really 'belongs' in the predominantly non-disabled professional dance sector.

Given that there are relatively few working dance artists with disabilities in the UK and few dance companies that include dancers with disabilities, the community is small, and those with established careers have often worked together. Each of those discussed thus far has worked with Candoco, as has David Toole, who joined the company in the early days and has since worked in a variety of contexts including taking a leading role in the London Paralympic Games Opening Ceremony in 2012. His journey also reveals an experience that draws on the triad described earlier. Toole talks about how he was born with a condition, sacral agenesis, which led to him having his legs amputated when he was 18 months old. His early schooling gave him a taste of performing, but his first job was with the post office, where he worked for nine years. It was by chance that he was given a leaflet for a workshop at Yorkshire Dance, and through persuasion, went along and found himself dancing with other disabled and non-disabled dancers. He recalls, "The first couple of hours I was there I thought, 'What am I doing? But I found a way into it'" (cited Snow 2017, n.p.). The workshop was led by those who were setting up Candoco, and Toole notes that he eventually spent a week with the company making a piece and realised it was what he wanted to do. He was asked to join the company. He left his job as a postman – temporarily, although he never went back – enrolled on a dance course at the then Laban Centre in London, and his performance career began (Ahad 2013, n.p.).

In common with other dancers with disabilities, Tool found strategies to help him develop his career that were particular to his own body, developing a unique movement vocabulary. He recalls:

> I would use some of the "tricks" I used around the house to achieve things. Standing on one hand to reach a light switch for example looked impressive when moved away from the wall and incorporated into the choreography. I wouldn't think twice about leaping off my wheelchair, landing on my hands and 'running' across the stage.
>
> *(Toole 2017, n.p.)*

His learning has been primarily 'on the job' acknowledging that physically he now needs to change the way he works (Toole 2017, n.p.), aware that his individual dance practice places particular pressures on his body and needs adjusting accordingly.

The artists mentioned here, along with many others, demonstrate the possibility of moving towards an autonomous practice, one that is carving out a career route that is not dependent on traditional training and education routes into the dance workforce. More by need than by design, many combine learning through experience, accepting opportunities when they arise and developing new pathways into work. Whilst autonomy provides tools and strategies to help disabled dance artists develop and sustain their careers, their experiences are yet to inform and fundamentally change training practices and choreographic methods. But this needs the custodians of established pathways including the trainers, educators, and institutional directors to take note and be prepared to make changes for sound educational and ethical reasons. In an environment where non-disabled gatekeepers are making decisions about how dance is accessed, taught, and promoted, the dancer with a disability is marginalised, awaiting access to be 'given.' Consequently, the same 'voices' or gatekeepers are positioned to distribute the development opportunities for dancers with disabilities, forcing the individual to rely on her own resources, networks, and support structures.

Conclusion

Because the dancer's body is the medium in which the dancer works, and the movement of the dancer's body, however mobile/immobile, is what shapes the dance, dancers with disabilities are acutely aware of their body's capacity for movement. Their individual body and how it moves becomes source material, creating unique movement material. What may be perceived by others as a limitation is often experienced by the expert dancer as potential gain or advantage, revising the assumption that disability is a lack or deficit. However, whilst dancers with disabilities may resist the weight of the traditional aesthetic in dance that favours a body that conforms to the idealised and unnatural view of the slim, white, flexible dancer and discriminates against any body that is perceived as different or deviant, training for a career in dance remains out of reach for many. As Hanauer points out,

> We need institutions who accept disabled dancers to study, because there are people waiting to teach them and an industry that values their skills. And we need an industry that really does value their skills … The epitome of success for a disabled dancer is not to blend in. And I've trained to be a dancer and I've worked professionally for a while now, so it shouldn't really be surprising that I might appear skillful in some way.
>
> *(Hanauer 2017, 10)*

The lack of training impacts on the number of disabled dancers in the professional field. As Shibata states: "The problem of under representation in any field is often a result of systemic disadvantage, and it's no different in the dance industry" (Shibata 2017, n.p.).

Disabled dance artists have taken control of their working practices by engaging with the triad of self-learning, learning on the job and peer support, enabling them to develop successful careers, but this should not let dance training programmes 'off the hook.' Dance institutions should ensure that inclusivity is at the core of all provision, reconsidering and revising course design and curriculum content and underpinning values accordingly. Training structures need to look beyond traditional methods that have done little to challenge an aesthetic that promotes the 'flawless' dancing body and an ethos that may inadvertently discriminate against difference. Could the introduction of 'translation techniques' or 'crutch dance techniques' make way for a radical shift in pedagogy without undermining the individual artist developing an autonomous signature practice? Such changes would show how dance is a site for equal rights for disabled people, removing social inequalities, ensuring a future wherein/whereby disability is no barrier to access dance training whilst promoting a vibrant and diverse dance ecology.

References

Abberley, Paul. 1987. "The Concept of Oppression and the Development of a Social Theory of Disability." *Disability, Handicap & Society*. 2 (1): 5–19.

Ahad, Nick. 2013. "The Big Interview: David Toole." *Yorkshire Post*, 22 April 2013. Accessed 30 April 2018. Available: www.yorkshirepost.co.uk/news/the-big-interview-david-tool-1-5596967.

Aujla, Imogen, and Redding, Emma. 2013. "Barriers to Dance Training for Young People with Disabilities." *British Journal of Special Education*. 40 (2): 80–85.

Bowditch, Caroline. 2013. Conversation on 26/11/2013.

Candoco. 2018. *Candoco Dance Company*. About Us. Accessed 23 May 2018. Available: www.candoco.co.uk/.

Cunningham, Claire. 2013. Interview taken on 18/7/2013.

Davies, Telroy. 2010. "Mobility: AXIS Dancers Push the Boundaries of Access." In Bruce Henderson and Noam Ostrander ed. *Understanding Disability Studies and Performance Studies*. Abingdon: Routledge, 43–63.

Davis, Lennard. 2002. *Bending Over Backwards: Essays on Disability and the Body.* New York: New York University Press.

Erhart, Tanja. 2017. "…I See Myself as a Dancer of Three Different Bodies: Tanja with Crutches, Tanja with the Wheelchair, Tanja without Crutches or Wheelchair." In Kate Marsh and Jonathan Burrows ed. *Fresh Perspectives 7: Permission to Stare, Arts and Disability.* IETM; International Network for Contemporary Performing Arts in partnership with the British Council, 20–22.

Evans, Ben. 2017. "Forward by the British Council." In Kate Marsh and Jonathan Burrows ed. *Fresh Perspectives 7: Permission to Stare, Arts and Disability.* IETM; International Network for Contemporary Performing Arts in partnership with the British Council, 6.

Garland-Thomson, Rosemarie. 2009. *Staring: How We Look.* Oxford: Oxford University Press.

Hanauer, Annie. 2017. "…There Are More of Us Than You Think, and We're Out Here Dancing." In Kate Marsh and Jonathan Burrows ed. *Fresh Perspectives 7: Permission to Stare, Arts and Disability.* IETM; International Network for Contemporary Performing Arts in partnership with the British Council, 10–11.

Henderson, Bruce, and Ostrander, Noam, ed. 2010. *Understanding Disability Studies and Performance Studies.* New York: Routledge.

Hintermair, Manfred, and Albertini, John A. 2005. "Ethics, Deafness, and New Medical Technologies." *Journal of Deaf Studies and Deaf Education.* 10 (2): 184–192.

InVisible Difference: Dance, Disability and Law. Accessed 23 May 2018. Available: www.invisible difference.org.uk/.

Kuppers, Petra. 2008. "Deconstructing Images: Performing Disability." *Contemporary Theatre Review.* 11 (3–4): 25–40.

Kuppers, Petra. 2003. *Disability and Contemporary Performance – Bodies on Edge.* London: Routledge.

Lave, Jean, and Wenger, Etienne. 1991. *Situated Learning: Legitimate Peripheral Participation.* Cambridge: Cambridge University Press.

Löffler, Elisabeth. 2017. "…Moaning Never Helps When You Want to Change the World." In Kate Marsh and Jonathan Burrows ed. *Fresh Perspectives 7: Permission to Stare, Arts and Disability.* IETM; International Network for Contemporary Performing Arts in partnership with the British Council, 12–13.

Malin, Vicky. 2017. "…Everything is Wiggling." In Kate Marsh and Jonathan Burrows ed. *Fresh Perspectives 7: Permission to Stare, Arts and Disability.* IETM; International Network for Contemporary Performing Arts in Partnership with the British Council, 13–14.

Marsh, Kate. 2016. *Taking Charge – Dance, Disability and Leadership: Exploring the Shifting Role of the Disabled Dance Artist.* Unpublished PhD Thesis, Coventry University.

Mitchell, David T., and Snyder, Sharon L. 2006. *Cultural Locations of Disability.* Chicago: University of Chicago Press.

O'Brien, W. 2017 "…It Dawned on Me That Some of the Audience Hadn't Realized I Was Disabled." In Kate Marsh and Jonathan Burrows ed. *Fresh Perspectives 7: Permission to Stare, Arts and Disability.* IETM; International Network for Contemporary Performing Arts in partnership with the British Council, 20.

O'Brien, Welly. 2016. Conversation on 16/10/2016.

Reinders, Hans. 2000. *The Future of the Disabled in Liberal Society: An Ethical Analysis.* Notre Dame: University of Notre Dame Press.

Resilience and Inclusion: Dancers as Agents of Change. Accessed 23 May 2018. Available: https:// invisibledifferenceorguk.wordpress.com/blog/.

Roach, Jennifer. 2015. *Multiplicity, Embodiment and the Contemporary Dancer: Moving Identities.* Basingstoke: Palgrave Macmillan.

Sandahl, Carrie, and Auslander, Philip, ed. 2005. *Bodies in Commotion: Disability and Performance.* Ann Arbor: University of Michigan Press.

Shakespeare, Tom. 2010. "The Social Model of Disability." In Lennard Davis ed. *The Disability Studies Reader.* New York: Routledge, 266–273.

Shibata, Sho. 2017. *Why Can't Disabled People Dance?* New Internationalist: The World Unspun. Accessed 30 April 2018. Available: https://newint.org/blog/2017/02/27/why-cant-disabled-people-dance/.

Siebers, Tobin. 2010. *Disability Aesthetics.* Ann Arbor: University of Michigan Press.

Sloan, Phillip. ed. 2000. *Controlling Our Destinies: Historical, Philosophical, Ethical, and Theological Perspectives on the Human Genome Project.* Notre Dame: Notre Dame University Press.

Smith, Carmel. 2015. "Interview: Welly O'Brien – a Year of Frida." *London Dance*. Accessed 30 April 2018. Available: http://londondance.com/articles/interviews/welly-obrien/.

Snow, Georgia. 2017. "Interview: David Toole: 'It's Still Difficult to Get Serious Training for Disabled Arts." *The Stage*. Accessed 30 April 2018. Available: www.thestage.co.uk/features/interviews/2017/david-toole-its-still-difficult-to-get-serious-training-for-disabled-arts/.

Stanford, Peter. 1999. "Can Wheelchair Users Dance?" *The Independent*, 10 September 1999. Accessed 30 April 2018. Available: www.independent.co.uk/life-style/the-arts-all-the-right-moves-1117837.html.

Toole, David. 2017. "David Toole: I Incorporated Tricks I Used Around the House into My Dance." *WhatsOnStage*. Accessed 30 April 2018. Available: www.whatsonstage.com/london-theatre/news/david-toole-enormous-room-dancer-disabled_42966.html.

Whatley, Sarah. 2007. "Dance and Disability; the Dancer, the Viewer and the Presumption of Difference." *Research in Dance Education*. 8 (1): 5–25.

27

Performing disability

Representation and power in 'Classical' Indian dance

Akhila Vimal C.

This chapter considers disability and performance in India. It focuses on classical dance forms, the canonical texts that describe them, and their relationship with disability. In particular, it considers contemporary practices whose creators claim to capture dimensions beyond the subjectivity of the 'normal' body and map out the marginalised/excluded 'Other' bodies in an Indian context, and some of the challenges, paradoxes, and concerns these extensions of classical dance forms raise.

In India, 'classical dance forms' is an umbrella term that has been used since the early twentieth century to refer to a number of performances that claim to be codified according to the rules of the *Nāṭyaśāstra*. Attributed to a sage named Bharata Muni and dated between the second century BCE and the second century CE,[1] the *Nāṭyaśāstra* is the earliest available Sanskrit treatise on *Nāṭya* - theatre - and allied subjects like music, dance, and instruments. It is often regarded as a theoretical text, a prescriptive manual as well as descriptive text. Forms that are qualified as 'classical' draw from the *Nāṭyaśāstra* and other manual texts that emerged from it to construct the idealised dancer's body as part of the inherent power play that exists in many aspects of Indian culture. These texts have a complex relationship to disability. Through their codified structure of what constitutes the 'normative' body, they have defined disabled bodies by what they are not. People with disabilities, these scriptures argue, cannot perform aesthetically. According to *Nāṭyaśāstra,* dance has come to the world to create beauty, "*śobhāṃ prajanayediti nṛttaṃ pravartitam*" (Bharata Muni n.d., 4.261). This can be accomplished only through a fully formed 'beautiful' body. This means classical performance in India is integrally connected to a visual culture in which the able body and its perfectness have always mattered – precisely because of the hegemony of concepts based on 'beauty' as normality. The visibility of excluded/marginalised bodies has been mediated in order to establish a normal and dominant standard of the body.

This construction of normative bodies in the *Nāṭyaśāstra* and the dance informed by it is directly linked to Hindu Sanskrit tradition that designates disability as the repercussion of sinful acts in the previous birth. The fundamental notion of Indian philosophy is relayed on the notions of karma and the effect of that in one's life. Karma means action work or deed, which decides your future life and rebirths. Indian philosophy largely discusses disability as the consequence of misconducts of previous births. The *Mahabharata*, the popular Hindu epic, describes disability and illness as the result of wrong doings in the past and current lives. In it, Krishna says that Dritarashtra, the blind king of Hastinapuri, is blind because of the sins he committed in previous life. Similarly, Chandeswara's thirteenth-century law text *Smritiratnakara* argues that the sins of previous life are a cause of illness and disability. The *Garuda Purana*, one of the major Puranas, centres on karma and rebirth, details that the nature of disability that one will accrue in his rebirth corresponds to his sinful actions. Persons with disabilities are considered to be bad omens due to these sinful acts and their consequences. These texts carry references prohibiting the presence of disabled persons from auspicious and religious events and in any professions that engage with the public. Texts also refer to excluding them from all domains of life, especially professions like medicine (*Charakasamhita*), law (*Manusmriti*), politics (*Arthashastra*), astrology, dance, performing arts, and priesthood.

Responding to this tradition, contemporary classical performance in India has attempted to break the stigma of disability, propagated by the manuals and interpretations of *Nāṭyaśāstra*. A nominal degree of inclusivity and sensitivity to 'Other' bodies has now entered the imaginary of classical performance. Indeed, the canon appears to have become capacious enough to even bring disabled bodies within performance contexts and the stage. There are now a number of disability performance groups and disabled performers who engage on different terms with the disability culture such as Ability Unlimited from Delhi, Blind Opera from Kolkata, the dance group of Shree Ramana Maharishi Academy for the Blind from Bengaluru, and individual performers like Sudha Chandran.

In this chapter, I limit my enquiry to two practitioners who work within the medium of Bharatanatyam, one of several Indian 'classical' dance forms.

The first case study focuses on eminent Bharatanatyam performer and actress, Sudha Chandran. Chandran had been training as a Bharatanatyam dancer when she lost her legs in a car accident in 1981. She decided to use prosthetic limbs that had been recently introduced in India, to continue performing as a Bharatanatyam dancer. In addition to the circuits of professional/trained performance, Chandran captured the wider public attention in India not only due to her grit and determination but also due to her decision of using the prosthetic limb for dancing. Chandran's career trajectory is crucial since she foregrounded the idea of disabled performers in India and instead moulded the discourse and popular perception around disability performances in the country. Chandran's performance raises the questions around her continuing relationship to her disabled status and her desire to transcend it. At the time when Chandran re-entered the circuits of professional classical dance, as today, the pressure of appearing as an 'able' body was high. Dance became the tool to prove her virtuosity as a dancer. In the process, it overrules the recognition of the agency and identity of the disabled body. Chandran's trajectory and subjectivity raise the question: can all performances featuring a disabled body/bodies be termed as disability performance? Can we identify Chandran's performance as disability performance?

As the second case study, I will analyse the performances of the group Ability Unlimited Foundation, Delhi, and their engagement with the repertoires of disability performance. Syed Sallauddin Pasha, the non-disabled choreographer of Ability Unlimited, and the sole spokesperson of the group, has actively courted the media positioning of the group's repertoire as 'Bharatanatyam on Wheels' and as a 'New Nāṭyaśāstra.' Pasha's group includes young dancers with varying levels and forms of disability, especially deaf female dancers and wheelchair-bound male dancers. Pasha self-consciously positions his troupe as the 'first of its kind in the world.' In analysing the group's performance, I explore the seeming contradiction of claiming the authority from the text and labelling one's performance after a text that denies the entry of disabled body on stage. Can the 'New Nāṭyaśāstra' accommodate the possibility

Akhila Vimal C.

and problems of performing disability? I investigate whether Ability Unlimited is actually reinterpreting the form, or if it is, in fact, reclaiming the notion of the perfect body classical dance by performing it 'better than' an able-bodied dancer.

Transcending disability: Sudha Chandran

In 1981, at the age of 16, Sudha Chandran, an actress and dancer trained in Bharatanatyam, met with an accident, resulting in the amputation of her foot. She started performing with her prosthetic leg. Chandran had trained under Ramaswami Bhagavatar, a renowned Bharatanatyam teacher from Mumbai, India, since the age of three. Even after her accident and the fitting of the prosthetic leg, Chandran continued the training under him for the next 35 years. That she trained under a teacher who only taught able-bodied performers is a fact that Chandran cites as a measure of her ability to perform as an able-bodied performer. She went on to become one of the first disability performers in Indian context. The discourse on disability performance aesthetics in India thus needs to take account of Chandran's journey, especially the stigma of being one of the first classical dancers who insisted on continuing with performances, albeit now, as a disabled person/performer. Chandran's re-entry into the arena of professional classical performance was also marked by her insistence on 'transcending' her disability – by performing like an able-bodied dancer – and her self-image as a disabled person/performer, an approach different from that favoured by other disabled performers in other cultural contexts (Garland-Thomson 2000). This raises the question of the terms on which a disabled performer is accepted in the classical spectrum of dance: is this possible only once she has transcended her disability and performs as an able body? How does the disabled person/performer negotiate this new form of identity? In the case of Chandran, her identity as an upper-caste woman helped in bringing an 'authenticity' to perform Bharatanatyam even though she is disabled. Indian classical dance forms are focused on upper-caste, beautiful-bodied performers. Thus, Chandran's challenge was mitigated to an extent due to her 'appropriate' credentials within traditional social and caste hierarchies. Her endeavour was therefore to create an ideal, beautiful, non-disabled body through her performance. Regarding how this new identity as a disabled person defines the self-image of the performer, Chandran says, "I try to dance as perfect as possible like any other able-bodied dancers and I don't want to and like to carry the identity of disabled dancer" (Chandran, 2018). Her statement gestures towards at least two discourses that seem to be working dialectically: her new identity as a disabled person and her training in classical dance. It is crucial to remember that her career as a dancer had started much before she lost her leg and returning to the arena of performance after the accident was undoubtedly a decision requiring a lot of courage on her part. However, given her training in classical dance, Chandran chose to build upon this training, instead of 'unlearning' what she had been taught as a dancer, to suit her new condition. On her return, as a young dancer, she was determined to reclaim her space as a classical dancer. Chandran's insistence on the return to an aesthetic and performance on par with her pre-disability period underscores her refusal to challenge the fundamentals of Indian 'classical' performance described in *Nāṭyaśāstra* through her new identity as a disabled person/performer.

Chandran made her cinematic debut with the film *Mayuri* (Peacock) in the south-Indian language Telugu. The film draws heavily from her life; its plot is driven by her attempts to transcend her disability and dance once again, as gracefully, and one might add, as naturally as a peacock. Reiterating this 'victory' over her disability, Chandran states that,

338

I am someone who breaks the stigma always, and I am proud that I could set a role model for many like me who had to stop dancing or doing something because they have a disability. A girl from West Bengal, who had gone through an amputation, later started dancing and she is often called Mayuri of West Bengal. I don't know what in fact people achieve by identifying as a disabled. I don't think about it unless someone brings it up. I consider my life as an achievement that I could do it because I surpass my disability.

(Chandran 2018)

A sequence from a *Padam*, an *abhinaya* - that is, an expressive piece in the genre of Bharatanatyam, as distinct from expertise demonstration pieces also familiar to the form, in this case, focused on the Hindu god, Shiva – by Chandran and her troupe demonstrates how Chandran, as the sole disabled dancer in the troupe, surpasses her disability in her working methodology and performance.

In the beginning, two performers are standing in the centre stage, Chandran and a male performer positioned in the standing posture. When the music starts, they walk towards the back and turn and sit on *Aramandi* (a basic pose within Bharatanatyam wherein the dancer bends at the knees, forming a 60-degree angle between the knee and the thigh), positioning their hand on the thighs. Then both the performers move to the centre, and three female performers join the couple and the group begins the piece. Chandran and the male performer who occupies centre stage stand at the back; with one hand on the chest and the other above their heads, these central figures turn frontward holding the *mudra* (hand gestures) of God Shiva's *damru* (a small percussion drum held in the hand). Meanwhile, the background dancers perform moves demanding greater legwork – stretching one leg into the front and sitting on the other and pirouetting while their hands echo the same *mudra* as Chandran and her partner. Next, all the performers on stage together do the same *adavu* (the basic unit of movement) of Bharatanatyam, the right hand above the head while the left hand moves front and backwards in accordance with rapid leg movement.

In the next stanza of the music, the performers emote and express the lyrics that narrate the qualities of Lord Siva with *mudras* and fast *adavus* and facial expressions. Then, Chandran and her partner execute the *Tatti Metti Adavu* of Bharatanatyam, a set of foot movements executed on a beat. They repeat the *mudras*– the hand gestures of Shiva's *damru* (drum) accompanied by appropriate facial expressions. At this point, the accompanying performers hold a pose facing the audience. At the end of Chandran's sequence, these dancers pirouette once again, with their arms akimbo and end the motion by the holding the pose in *Aramandi*. Next, all the performers, including Chandran, assume the pose of the Nataraja – the dancing form of Shiva – one leg raised at the waist level and bent at the knee, with the foot inclined towards the other knee and attendant hand gestures. The performance ends with a pose where Sudha Chandran stands bending one leg and holding the meditation mudra of Shiva while other performers stand behind her in a line moving their hands, depicting the aura of Shiva.

This description of a vignette of Sudha Chandran's performance demonstrates the range of movements she undertakes as well as the ways in which the troupe presents a piece. Though Chandran dances with her prosthetic leg, her movements 'invisibilise' her disability. The costume used in Bharatanatyam – a wide, pleated skirt extending all the way to the ankles – also helps her propagate the aesthetic of able-bodied in her performance by covering her prosthetic leg. For instance, the *Tatti Metti Adavu* in Bharatanatyam requires immense foot movement– 'tatti' means to tap with a flat foot, and 'metti' means a striking movement with the toe and the heel. For *metti*, one must first be on the toes – either a jump on the toes or just striking a toe – and then flatten the feet while the toes are already firm on the ground. Chandran uses the foot movement like the *tatti metti* frequently in her performance. Moreover, while doing poses, she holds the live leg up in support of her prosthetic leg and vice versa. Though Chandran uses foot movements and other dance techniques, she does not project her prosthetic leg during her performance. She also extensively and intensively uses the facial expression in her performance while supporting performers focus on body movements. Facial expressions are one of the major elements of Bharatanatyam. In Chandran's performance, one could see the balance of both body movements and facial expressions following the style of Bharatanatyam.

Masking disability through the virtuous performance of a disabled body is Chandran's way of addressing disability. However, her identity as a disabled person has bestowed her with the status of a 'unique' performer. Disability, here, is important as a threshold that needs to be crossed. In a social media interview, she stated that accident was almost fatal, but it transformed into "a blessing in [her] life" (Team Social, 2016). In Chandran's aesthetics, disability helps her to be uniquely identified as a performer because of her insistence on and demonstration of transcending it. Through her mastery and demonstrable expertise, Chandran seems to insist on respecting and stabilising the normative structure of the classical dancerly body (Kuppers 2010). Disability is something that marks her as a performer, but masking it makes her a classical dancer.

For Chandran, the relationship between classical dance, the dancerly body, and canonical texts derives its intensity not so much from a textual source but as much as the dance pedagogical model centred on the *guru-shishya* system, in which the guru is the revered teacher of the dance form. Thus, in response to questions about the text of the *Nāṭyaśāstra* denying the entry of disabled body on stage, Chandran is unequivocal about the sources of authority that ground her practice and claims ignorance about what *Nāṭyaśāstra* proscribes. She clarifies that not being a 'theory person,' she merely follows "what my teacher taught me to do" (Chandran 2018). This unquestioning obedience to the teachings of the guru is something that is widely echoed by practitioners of Indian classical dance.

In the case of Chandran, while she denies understanding of theoretical manuals, like the *Nāṭyaśāstra,* she follows the very idea of classical that is proposed by the interpretation of the text. While this raises the question of the power of texts, it also draws our attention to the modes by which the canon of Indian classical dance is propagated, with regard to *guru-shishya* model. The transmission of knowledge through a guru and being submissive to the lineage of the guru is something that all the areas of knowledge in India have blindly followed. When Chandran says that she does not follow the text, she is instead following the traditional lineage of the guru she learnt the dance from. The aesthetic of an able-bodied performance is thus replicated and its structures preserved. Therefore, instead of centring her identity, the disabled body of Chandran centres the classical aesthetic of Bharatanatyam.

To transcend disability and deny disabled identity works for Chandran in a context where disability as an identity is not a well-accepted subjectivity, and one continues to compare her ability with able-bodied performers even today. Chandran's practice and her performative persona make it clear that it is by transcending her disability that she aims to recoup her status as a performer. Her negotiation of disability paints it as an obstacle to be overcome, an approach that those who identify as disabled consider problematic (Garland-Thomson 2000). In the context of India, and as early as 1984, however, Chandran's career opened up the space of classical performance for others who want to dance with disability setting a framework on which anyone can build new structures. Chandran occupied a significant space within popular imaginary of India as a classical dancer. Her position as a classical dancer with a prosthetic leg was something that was accepted positively instead of the negative stigma that disability generates in Indian society. Her positive attitude towards dance encouraged other disabled persons to approach the stage fearlessly and cite her as a model.

Foregrounding disability: Ability Unlimited

Ability Unlimited is a Delhi-based dance group established by Syed Sallauddin Pasha, a trained Bharatanatyam dancer, who is not disabled, who has claimed to be working with disabled performers for more than three decades. Among other things, Pasha also claims a number of world records. Pasha, through working with disabled performers, created world records, and he is a Limca Book of Records holder for creating 100 dance theatre productions and directing 10,000 dance performances with persons with different abilities. His student Gulshan Kumar entered the Guinness Book of World Records for spinning his wheelchair 63 times in one minute in 2011. The website of Ability Unlimited claims that the troupe is the "world's first professional dance company to innovate classical dances on wheelchairs for differently abled" (Ability Unlimited, 2007). Ability Unlimited's performance of disability in the contemporary Indian context also raises challenges to the normative formation of the 'classical' dances of India. Pasha's dance productions include vignettes from India's leading Hindu epics as well as pieces that he choreographs to showcase a particular form or impressionistically present India's living heritage, such as yoga, for example. The repertoire thus includes 'Bharatanatyam on wheelchairs,' 'Sufi dance on wheelchairs,' 'Yoga on wheelchairs,' 'Bhagawad Gita on Wheelchairs,' 'Ramayana On Wheels,' and 'Chariots of the Gods.' Due to this neat packaging of the officially authorised forms of Indian 'culture,' Pasha's group enjoys international recognition and takes part in international cultural exchange tours organised by the Indian Council for Cultural Relations.

Analysing the performance of Ability Unlimited draws attention to the issue of classical dance and the question of the disabled body in it, and how the disabled body is restructured – in the extreme, in some cases – to fit in the structure of the classical performance. It also draws attention to the issue of the identity and agency of the disabled performer in the group, given that Pasha is the non-disabled founder, choreographer, and the spokesperson of the group, speaking for disabled performers.

In one performance, Ability Unlimited present a sequence from *Tillana*, the last item of *Bharatanatya Kacheri*, a kind of concert where the performers follow a sequence of eight to twelve performances starting with a piece performed to seek blessings from the gods. *Tillana* is a rhythmic piece that typically concludes these concerts, mainly focused on rigorous *adavus* and body movements. In this work, the male performers are wheelchair dancers, and the female performers are deaf. The stage lights up; in the centre of the stage there are two female performers sitting, positioning their hands above the head and looking to the corner, and three other deaf performers stand behind them with the same hand pose while bending their body to the side. Meanwhile, two wheelchair performers are positioned beside them on both sides. When the music starts, performers standing on the centre stage jig to both sides, stretching hands to the same side while holding the *mudras*. While the wheelchair dancers spin their wheelchairs and get to the back of the stage, a fifth wheelchair dancer moves forward from the back to join them, moving his wheelchair up and down as the female performers circle around him. Then he puts his head on the wheelchair and stays upside down for around thirty seconds. The female dancers continue moving in a circle, doing one of the steps from the second sets of *adavu* called *Nattadavu*, wherein the heels are used as a pivot for stretching and hitting of the legs around him, and other wheelchair dancers perform on the side. Then, the female performers hold their hands and move sideways, stretching their body and legs in the same direction, creating a circle. All five wheelchairs go to the back of the stage, and female performers come forward in a parallel line with the male dancers and stand facing them, moving synchronously. The female dancers perform the leg movement, stretching one leg to the front and sitting on the other, while their hands echo the same *mudra* as the wheelchair dancers. Next, the female dancers move to the back, while the wheelchair dancers roll their chairs in the forward direction, and both groups create parallel horizontal lines, after which wheelchair dancers in the front and deaf dancers in the back together move to form parallel vertical lines facing each other. Then they perform the *Teermanam adavu* of Bharatanatyam which concludes in the sequence steps called *jati* – a step repeated thrice in a fast pace. In the *Teermanam adavu,* the upper body, including hands, neck, and eyes, has to follow while legs take the turn. While ending the *Teermanam adavu,* all the performers keep up the fast pace, and the wheelchair dancers move their torso while forcefully moving their wheelchair up and down and making circles according to the rhythm. Towards the end of the performance, the female dancers move to the back and sit there while the male dancers take 30-second spins with their wheelchairs. They move fast, following steps, and rapidly form a dancing cluster and create collective postures. Subsequently, the cluster disperses and yet again initiates the *Teermanam adavu* to conclude the dance and thereafter create a combined image of a chariot.

In *Bodies in Commotion: Disability and Performance*, Carrie Sandahl and Philip Auslander ask: "How does the work of disabled performing artists transform the artistic genres in which they work? What new genres are they creating?" (Auslander & Sandahl 2005, 1). The performance of Ability Unlimited demonstrates the rigorous process that the performers have to go through to fit into the mould of Bharatanatyam dancers. Performances of Ability Unlimited set the able body as a reference point, and performing 'better than' an able body has been set as the standard. "When we say/see that a disabled body can do all the movements just like an able body, the latter becomes the yardstick against which the value of the former is measured" (Vimal 2017, 327). Instead of destabilising the normative body, the disabled bodies are used to elevate normative expectations. Lalitha Venkat (2012), an eminent dance critic, wrote a review describing Pasha's 'Bharatanatyam On Wheels' as follows:

> Even able-bodied people cannot do half these movements… Poses were apt, turnings were precise and synchronisation good. In the highly innovative choreography, wheels became the extension of the limbs and the audience did not miss the legs in any way… Pasha's challenge was to replace the legs with the wheel and yet make it move with life and his amazing group of young dancers brought life to that vision.

In terms of what the audience can expect from a disabled dancer who performs classical dance, Pasha's aim seems to be the same as Sudha Chandran. He wants the audience to forget that they are disabled while watching his show. The art critics and audience follow the cues he offers them to make meaning of the performance. The identity of a disabled dancer is questioned and compared with every movement because the choreographer and audience still want them to follow the 'standard.'

Unlike Chandran, Pasha, the non-disabled choreographer of the group, knows the 'importance' of claiming the authority of the text in the cultural context of India. Drawing on this source of 'ancient' authority and high culture, Pasha positions 'Bharatanatyam on Wheels' as the 'New Nāṭyaśāstra.' Pasha in an interview stated that when he decided to work with disabled bodies, he created his own theories from available methodologies and proposed a different *Nāṭyaśāstra* for disabled performance. Pasha states,

My training in Bharatanatyam was for more than two decades and I am familiar with the nuances of Bharatanatyam, so I didn't change anything that *Nāṭyaśāstra* said and I stick to what [it] said while training them and I followed the basic rules and framework of dance that is mentioned in *Nāṭyaśāstra*. What you need for dancing Bharatanatyam is two legs which are not there in my artists, so I have to do some alternation in order to make the fit in the repertoire. I wanted it to be Bharatanatyam if I do more alteration then it won't be the same form anymore and I believe that my show is a complete Bharatanatyam on Wheelchair. I believe that through the training that I provide, the differently abled performer can master in the art of Bharatanatyam.

(Pasha 2017)

Given the way the *Nāṭyaśāstra* deals with the disabled body, one could ask what could be the role of 'new' but also still '*Nāṭyaśāstra*' in disability performance of Ability Unlimited? By mentioning the *Nāṭyaśāstra* in his performance, Pasha is not just referring to a text or manual. Rather, he refers to the method he used in creating 'Bharatanatyam on Wheels' and sometimes the specific performances that present it as a new driving text framing the dance.

In *Nāṭyaśāstra* there are references to what kind of body and mental fitness one needs for getting into classical dance and become a complete dancer or even a dancer. And when it comes to my group, my artists are not complete and they have a physical disability and I took that as a challenge and let Bharata Muni writes his own *Nāṭyaśāstra* and let me write mine.

(Pasha 2017)

For Pasha, the hegemony of the text is something that makes a performance authentic and thus the 'Bharatanatyam on Wheels' is a text itself in a revised way. The revision is not in the structure and technique that imposes beauty and ability into the performance; it is in putting or 'allowing' the disabled body to be present in a space where their ability and identity will be compared against that of the able-bodied performer. Therefore, 'Bharatanatyam on Wheels' as a framing text provides information on how disabled performers have to reconfigure their bodies to the extent that audience and critics forget their disabled identity to succeed in classical Indian dance.

Dance pedagogy, Ability Unlimited, and agency

In Indian classical dances, as in other traditional forms of learning, knowledge transmission takes place through paradigms of *guru* (revered teacher) and *shishya* (acolyte/initiate). These traditional forms of knowledge transmission were predicated on the idea of the learned teacher and a worthy student submitting to this human repository of knowledge. While devotion to the *guru* continues to mark the learning of classical dance in India, in the case of Ability Unlimited, the imbalances of power and position are amplified.

Pasha freely refers to the group's performance as "my show" (Pasha 2017). It suggests ownership of the dancers' bodies, a freedom that is then used to tweak, twist, and, reportedly, also abuse these bodies to create a performance – a fact that deeply undermines disability culture, agency, and subjectivity. According to newspaper reports, Pasha's students have spoken out, publicly accusing him of sexually, physically, and financially exploiting them. Ten dancers, including Gulshan Kumar, the world record-holder, have filed a complaint to this effect. Another female student also filed a case against him for sexual abuse

(Menon 2017). However, commentators on the performance or the group, such as Venkat (2012), and thus the audience following their interpretations, do not seem to note this power imbalance. This imbalance is amplified because, in addition to the sovereignty of the teacher typical in an Indian context, Pasha also holds the power of an able-bodied dancer who created a space where disabled performers can access Indian classical dance. The situation becomes even more complex when taking into account that the choreographer also fits into the non-performable body as a result of other aspects of his own identity. As Lalitha Venkat (2012) recounts in a review of Ability Unlimited's performance, Pasha, recalling his experience from 30 years previously, has said that his teacher refused to teach him Bharatanatyam because of his religious identity as a Muslim. This motivated him to do his own research and work with disabled performers as a choreographer.

Pasha's is the only voice that comes out of Ability Unlimited, as the performers are not available to speak for themselves. He is the sole point of contact with regard to information about the group. Indeed, Pasha makes sure that the group's identity and Pasha's identity are conflated – the group effectively does not exist beyond Pasha's identity. Attempts to interview the performers result in scripted answers under the tight supervision of Pasha. The absence of the performer within the discursive or self-referential mode of performance testifies to Pasha's control over their subjectivity while speaking for them and reinterpreting classical dance for them. It raises questions as to whose aesthetic and identity the troupe is performing – Pasha's image of a disabled body, the imagery of an able-bodied dancer, or an alternative aesthetic?

The website of Ability Unlimited suggests that Pasha "uses therapeutic theatre to cross physical and mental barriers," and that "Dr. Syed S Pasha [is] revered as 'Father of Indian Therapeutic Theatre' for persons with disabilities" (Ability Unlimited 2007). Analysing the performance, the demands of Pasha's choreography and teaching sit awkwardly with the idea that this type of dance is 'therapeutic' work, to treat the deficits for disabled persons, rather than virtuous. The gruelling training of even able-bodied Bharatanatyam dancers is well-known:

> Training in Bharatanatyam usually follows an abnormally rigorous method of body-rendering as it focuses on a highly stylised 'body'. It is not clear how the training and stylisation of Bharatanatyam empower the disabled performers...The extreme codifications of Bharatanatyam stand against the idea of the disabled body.
>
> *(Vimal 2017, 327)*

Watching Pasha's students perform with 'high' standards, 'better than' able-bodied dancers, is something that challenges his claim of a therapeutic method.

Pasha's use of the disabled body in Bharatanatyam, on the grounds of bringing bodies that were hitherto prohibited into the performance, does not challenge the ideal body. It compares disabled body's performance with a non-disabled body performing Bharatanatyam. By citing his earlier exclusion from mentorship due to his religious identity, Pasha stages a return by creating more nuanced disqualifications on stage. Accompanied by these disabled bodies that he strictly controls, he enters spaces that were earlier supposedly barred to him. The spectrum of Indian classical dance disallows any non-dancerly body, whether it is because of caste, religion, or physical disability on stage. Pasha breaks the structure in as 'ideal' a way as possible, enabling his inclusion within certain spaces while perpetuating an aesthetics that refuses the disabled body its full agency. As a result, as I have argued elsewhere, "it is not clear how the training and stylisation of Bharatanatyam empower the disabled performers"

(Vimal 2017, 327). Pasha's choreography and methods are thus profoundly problematic in the context of disability performance. His continuing success with state patronage thus gestures to two ideas: firstly, his product-oriented 'therapeutic' training method, which channels disabled bodies into highly demanding performances, and secondly, his tapping into state definitions of Indian 'culture' and disability.

Conclusion

Is all performance by a disabled body disability performance? As Rosemarie Garland-Thomson has noted,

> Disability performance art is a genre of self-representation, a form of autobiography, which merges the visual with the narrative. As a fusion of both seeing and telling disability performance art foregrounds the body as an object both to be viewed and to be explained. The disabled body is not only the medium but the content of performance.
> *(Garland-Thomson 2000, 334)*

When we look at the performances of Chandran, can we read them as reflective of her identity? Does her dance contribute anything to disability culture? While transcending her disability to make a career in dance and the entertainment industry, her trajectory lends itself to the scripts of the inspirational overcomer, the extraordinary individual who excels despite her impairments. When we come to Pasha and his group, his marketing strategy is more nuanced than Chandran's strategy, as Ability Unlimited feeds into the state definition of disability through claiming classical and textual authority. The performance of Ability Unlimited projects a grand spectacle using epic narratives like the *Ramayana* and *Mahabharata*, which accomplish the need of the nation's 'devotional aesthetics' surpassing the needs of disability culture.

The definition of disability In India, through the performance of Ability Unlimited or Chandran, flows into the state discourses of how the nation wants to define and patronise disabled bodies. Launching the Accessible India Campaign, in December 2015, Indian Prime Minister Narendra Modi attempted to push forward the usage of the term *'Divyang,'* where he claimed that persons with disabilities are imbued with certain extra power, *divyatha* (divinity), which is why as a mark of respect for them, we should use the word *divyang* (divine bodied) instead of *viklang*, the commonly used Hindi word for persons with disabilities. He suggested that such persons be called as qualifiers of divinity, instead of disease (Salelkar, 2016). Thereafter, government departments were instructed, from 2016 June onwards, to use the word *divyanga* as a substitute to *viklang* in all their communications (Sharma 2016). This extremely condescending and patronising usage disenfranchises the identity of disabled through divinity.

Over the course of this chapter, I have traced the Indian Sanskritic imagination of the disabled body through the text of *Nāṭyaśāstra* and how it is still transmitted into the contemporary classical dance practices of India. When I began this research, my objective was to look beyond the classical norms that I carry from my learning process. Indian classical dance is all about developing a grammar and transmitting it to students. In the case of disabled performers, however, dance is a winding tool, rather than a freeing practice, which never allows them to experience their own body or establish an expanded aesthetics but instead forces them to tweak and restructure their ability to follow a grammar. The performances and texts that I discussed here follow this trajectory of Indian classical dance and thus continue to veil the performer's bodily agency as disabled. As a performer who identifies as disabled, I envision a pedagogy and practice that anticipates a disabled performer's expression – what she/he/ze wants from a dance rather what others want to see from her/him/zir. This is highly critical in India, where claiming the identity and space as a disabled is considered as a privilege to which most disabled people in the country do not have access. A space where I can decide what my dance should be, and where disabled performers can create their own dance, is indeed a long and tortuous path that is still to be trodden in an Indian context.

Note

1 There are many discussions and controversies regarding the time and authorship of the *Nāṭyaśāstra*. Scholars like Paul Njero mentioned the time of the text as the first century BCE. Manmohan Ghosh, on the other hand, pointed out the time as the fifth century CE. The authenticity of Bharata Muni as the sole author of the text is also questioned. Scholars point out that it could have been a genealogical group of people who took up the work of composing the treatise, generation after generation.

References

Ability Unlimited. 2007. *Ability Unlimited.* Accessed 22 May 2018. Available: http://abilityunlimited.com/.

Chandran, Sudha. 2018. Personal Interview. 09 January. Delhi.

Garland-Thomson, Rosemarie. 2000. "Staring Back: Self-Representations of Disabled Performance Artists." *American Quarterly.* 52 (2):334–338.

Kuppers, Petra. 2010. "Accessible Education: Aesthetics, Bodies and Disability." *Research in Dance Education.* 1 (2): 119–131.

Menon, Vinod Kumar. 2017. "Differently-abled dancers accuse dance guru of sexual abuse." *Mid-Day.* Accessed 22 May 2018. Available: www.mid-day.com/articles/disabled-young-dancers-allegations-sexual-abuse-financial-misappropriation-syed-pasha-dance-guru/17949189.

Muni, Bharata. n.d. *Nāṭyaśāstra.*

Pasha, Syed Sallauddin. 2017. Personal Interview by Phone. 24 December.

Salelkar, Amba. 2016. "Divyang vs viklang: Disabled, disenfranchised but divine." *Indian Express.* Accessed 22 May 2018. Available: http://indianexpress.com/article/blogs/divyang-vs-viklang-disabled-disenfranchised-but-divine/.

Sandahl, Carrie, and Auslander, Philip, ed. 2005. *Bodies in Commotion: Disability and Performance.* Ann Arbor: University of Michigan Press.

Salelkar, A. 2016. *Divyang vs Viklang: Disabled, Disenfranchised But Divine.* New Delhi: The Indian Express.

Sharma, Aman. 2016. "Department of Empowerment of Disability Affairs to Incorporate the Word 'Divyang' in Hindi and English names." *The Economic Times.* Accessed 22 May 2018. Available: https://economictimes.indiatimes.com/news/politics-and-nation/department-of-empowerment-of-disability-affairs-to-incorporate-the-word-divyang-in-hindi-and-english-names/articleshow/52408370.cms.

Team Social. 2016. "Sudha Chandran's Story about Her Accident Will Leave You Inspired." *The Times of India Blog.* Accessed 22 May 2018. Available: https://blogs.timesofindia.indiatimes.com/everything-social/sudha-chandrans-story-about-her-accident-will-leave-you-inspired/.

Venkat, Lalitha. 2012. "Dancers with Unlimited Abilities." *Narthaki: Your Gateway to the World of Indian Dance.* Accessed 10 June 2018. Available: www.narthaki.com/info/rev12/rev1173.html.

Vimal C., Akhila. 2017. "Prosthetic Rasa: Dance on Wheels and Challenged Kinesthetics." *Research in Drama Education: The Journal of Applied Theatre and Performance.* 22 (3): 325–331.

28
Disability arts in an age of austerity

Bree Hadley

Is the current "age of austerity" (Summers 2009) impacting on art, culture, and media practices by and about people with disabilities, and, in particular, on art-based protest practices by people with disabilities? In recent years, much has been written about austerity as neo-liberal economic, political, social, and ideological agenda (Harvey 2005; Barnett 2010; Seymour 2014). Much has been written about the way groups effected by local and global governmental shifts towards austerity are protesting, presenting themselves, and being represented by others (Fritsch 2013; Goodley, Lawthom, & Runswick-Cole 2014; Runswick-Cole & Goodley 2015; della Porta 2015; Kokoli & Winter 2015; Beresford 2016; Dodd 2016; Giugni & Grasso 2016; Berry 2017). The question of whether disabled artists are adapting their practices to address these changing cultural circumstances has received less attention (Hadley 2017) and is thus the topic I focus on in this chapter.

Disability in an age of austerity

Austerity has become a central component of economic policy in the US, UK, Europe, and elsewhere in the last decade. In the literature, the emergence of this policy is tied to the global economic crisis caused by the collapse of the US banking and mortgage markets in 2008, which precipitated similar crises in European banking systems and led governments around the world to institute policies to reduce government debt and deficit (Berry 2017, 1). The initial tenants of industrial capitalism in the nineteenth century had given way to a more entrepreneurial form of capitalism characterised by emphasis on individuals and corporations working the market to drive consumption in the late twentieth century. In many countries, governments partnered with corporates to grow capacity. In the early twenty-first century, however, governmental capacity to regulate markets, and bail out collapsed companies, institutions, and systems to keep markets running, reached its limit. "[T]he reckless nature of capitalism had," as Goodley, Lawthom, and Runswick-Cole put it, "led to economic meltdown" (Goodley, Lawthom, & Runswick-Cole 2014, 980). In many countries, governments responded by implementing cuts to welfare, benefits, health, and housing subsides as part of a neo-liberalist political philosophy that stresses individual responsibility, activity, and rights within a market-driven system, in which the state's primary role is to provide institutional frameworks to support and sustain the market (Harvey 2005, 2). In principle, this meant praising the neo-liberal individual who "ensures their own self-care through market relations" (Fritsch 2013, 146). In practice, as Kokoli and Winter argue, "it meant the reduction of the welfare state" (Kokoli & Winter 2015, 158). The discourses around these cuts separated citizens into what politicians in the UK characterise as 'strivers' and 'scroungers' (Kokoli & Winter 2015, 158), or what politicians in my own context in Australia call 'lifters' and 'leaners' (Lynch 2016).

For critics, the problem with neo-liberalist austerity policy is that it impacts the poor, unemployed, and disabled members of society instead of the privileged members of society who precipitated the crisis in the banking and market systems (Harvey 2010; Goodley, Lawthom, & Runswick Cole 2014; Dodd 2016; Berry 2017). "Acceptance of such policies rests," Kokoli and Winter note, "on the public's willingness to assume responsibility for the economic crisis and mounting national debt, rather than blaming the free-market economics, hedge funds, mortgage schemes, and privatization, which actually precipitated the crisis" (Kokoli & Winder 2015, 159). An acceptance that positions the poor, unemployed, and disabled as responsible for their own misfortune perpetuates the growing wealth gap and amplifies stigma. In this sense, though austerity is framed in the public sphere as a matter of economics, it is intimately connected to social policy, social practice, and the ideologies that underpin them (Kokoli & Winter 2015, 158; Berry 2017, 9). For disabled people, accepting austerity policy means accepting negative representations of themselves in the press and in public debate as the people most likely to be 'leaners,' 'malingerers,' or 'scroungers' responsible for government debt. This, in turn, creates pressure to become what Goodley, Lawthom, and Runswick-Cole (2014, 981–982) following David Mitchell (2014) describe as the "able-disabled" person able to overcome their impairments to become as productive and useful a citizen as possible. Though governmental discourses position austerity as "smart, simple, intuitive, a virtue" (Dolmage 2017, 112), and necessary for the "common good" (Berry 2017, 10), for disabled people and their advocates it is a flawed approach that addresses a crisis by fixing the individuals impacted by it – forcing them to become more productive and useful to fix their own problems – rather than fixing the issues in the system itself. Paradoxically, this approach asks disabled people to become more productive whilst cutting the support they might have used to enter the workforce and become a more productive taxpaying citizen. The cultural stigma and the economic stigma enter what Dodd (2016, 154) characterises as a mutually reinforcing downward cycle.

The literature out of the UK in particular in the last five years provides examples of the adverse impact that austerity policies are having on disabled people, from reduced access to basic necessities like food, housing, and healthcare (Brawn et al. 2013; Dodd 2016), to increased stigma, hate crime, sickness, and instances of suicide (Walker 2012; Beresford 2016). Briant et al. (2013), for instance, found a content analysis of press coverage showed a shift in representations of disability between 2004/05 and 2010/11, not just a 43 per cent increase in coverage, but "increased discussion of disability as a benefit problem, and of disabled people as a burden on the state" (Brian et al. 2013, 878).

Though austerity is a worldwide phenomenon, there are, of course, differences in how the policy plays out in different countries. In Australia, for instance, Miller and Hayward (2017) have noted the "strange case" of the new National Disability Insurance Scheme, designed to offer disabled people agency in determining their care arrangements – albeit by marketising service provision – introduced at the same moment that public discourse stresses the need for Australians to be 'lifters' not 'leaners' to limit government spending (Lynch 2016). Globally, though, the fear of cuts to service provision is felt amongst all disabled communities, and

348

news outlets like *The Guardian* regularly feature stories about the loss of citizenship disabled people are feeling as a result of austerity agenda driving current policy changes (Ryan & Domokos 2017). For Briant et al. (2013), Kokoli and Winter (2015), Runswick-Cole and Goodley (2015), Beresford (2016) and others, this increased stigmatisation of disabled people in the current age of austerity constitutes what Dodd (2016) calls a "disablist austerity" (Dodd 2016, p153). State and media surveillance pressures disabled people to strive to be inspirational overcomers who take as much responsibility for their self-care as they possibly can, as an act of good faith to the taxpayers who support them, or risk stigmatisation and other consequences (Kokoli & Winter 2015, 160).

Disability arts in an age of austerity

As artist Aiden Moesby has argued, "[a]s Disabled Artists we are doubly damned in the current economic climate" (Moesby 2016a). Those who work in the arts have always had precarious employment, and this is only increasing in the current climate (Federici 2008; Kokoli & Winter 2015, 164). The press regularly reports on funding cuts for arts organisations, and, as a result, employment cuts for arts workers. The damnation is doubled for disabled artists facing not just these sector-wide cuts, but simultaneous cuts to the financial and disability supports that facilitate their engagement in the workforce. Mager (2014) highlights the case of Jenny Sealey, the internationally renowned artistic director of Graeae Theatre Company and co-director of the opening ceremony of the 2012 London Paralympic Games (for further discussion of representations of disability in Paralympic games, see Misener, Bodin, and Quinn in Chapter 6 of this book). Sealey has been impacted by cuts to the 20-year-old Access to Work Scheme, which supports disabled people to join the workforce in the UK, including cuts to packages used to access services such as sign language interpreters for events, meetings, and day-to-day engagement in the office environment. Sealey had her allowance for this critical support cut by more than half, adversely impacting her national and international arts projects and her company's bottom line, as they had to pay for interpreters, particularly for the overseas training, production, and performance for which she now receives no support.

In this context, it is not surprising that disabled artists have been using their expertise in arts-, culture-, and media-based protest practices to speak back to authorities, and to the general public, the authorities call on to accept and advocate for their austerity agenda.

A part of this has been calls to reconsider cuts to disability arts funding. For instance, when Creative Scotland recently announced they would no longer provide regular funding to companies specialising in theatre for, with, and by people with disabilities – including recognised companies such as Lung Ha and Birds of Paradise – arts workers and arts-based activists started a petition calling on them to reconsider (BBC Scotland 2018).

Another part of this has been disabled artists calls to consider what artists can do to contribute to the protest against cuts in the current austerity climate. Dave Lupton – who writes and draws cartoons under the name Crippen – has represented disabled artists' reaction to cuts to disability funding, and disability arts funding, in the work he creates for his blog on Disability Arts Online. In one cartoon, for instance, he presents a politician saying, "Let's see them try to survive outside residential care homes," alongside a disabled person with arms and legs with tags like "Independent Living Fund" and "Local Authority Assistance" being literally cut off (Lupton 2012a). In other cartoons, he highlights the impact for disabled artists, as those doubly damned by the cuts. In one, a pair of policemen outside the Prime Minister's residence at 10 Downing Street are confronted by a man in a wheelchair dragging a guillotine to protest cuts to another disability arts company's funding, with police enquiring "And may I tell Mr Cameron what you want to see him about ?!" (Lupton 2012b). Crippen is particularly scathing on the question of if arts funding agencies are directing support towards the 'able-disabled' privileged in an austerity climate. In one cartoon he draws a professional looking wheelchair user in a suit telling a more disheveled looking wheelchair user "Sorry, son. I'm afraid that you're not exactly what the public want to see!" outside an Arts Council funded Disability Arts Resource Centre, as a worker puts up a sign saying, "User Group Criteria – Must be: white, middle-class, educated, articulate, photogenic" (Lupton 2008). Crippen also calls on the disability arts community to generate ideas for protests that could attract both disaffected members of the disabled community and the public to the cause. He suggests that the disability arts community could be uniquely positioned to "protest without switching people off and being associated with violent confrontation, whilst at the same time getting in people's faces and making an impact" (Lupton 2010b). In one blog, Crippen calls on fellow artists to conceptualise a symbol, based on the black triangle – representing disabled people murdered during the Holocaust – being carried by participants in a recent protest organised by John McArdle of the Black Triangle Anti-Defamation Campaign in Defence of Disabled Claimants. "Envisage an MP opening an envelope in the future and a Black Triangle falls out" (Lupton 2010a) he suggests. Respondents to Crippen's posts note both positive and problematic connotations of the symbol, including co-option of symbols used by other groups. They propose addition of colours or slogans like "Never again" to try to amplify the message and debate the relative merits of turning the symbol up to emphasise the positive, if pointed, message versus turning the symbol down to show the message is negative and/or the desire to turn current attitudes upside down (Lupton 2010a). Though respondents to Crippen's blog posts note challenges and opportunities for disabled people when protesting – the challenge of developing symbols and symbolic actions that represent everyone, the challenge of getting out on mass to do actions, the opportunity social media presents to protest from home – the consensus and the volume of contributions to the conversation highlight the topic's importance for disabled artists (Lupton 2010b).

Changing forms of protest

Blogs like Crippen's show that disabled artists are committed to protesting the double impact of austerity cuts on them. To date, however, there has been no attempt in the scholarly literature to ascertain if the current 'age of austerity' is changing protest aesthetics in disability arts, or, more broadly, if the changing stages of capitalism can be aligned with stages in the development of arts-based protest designed to draw attention to the inaccessibility of social systems and institutions for disabled people. In the design field, Jay Dolmage (2017) has attempted this, looking at how the stages of capitalism align with the stages of development of disability accessible building and urban design. This suggests that tracing the relationships between capitalism and disability arts, culture, and media practice – particularly at potentially pivotal moments, such as in the wake of the global economic 'crisis' – could be a useful exercise.

According to Dolmage, industrial capitalism's relationship to disability culture is characterised by the image of the "steep steps" (Dolmage 2017, 111) as a metaphor for the exclusion of disabled people from "government buildings, art galleries, monuments, and other cultural and public spaces" (Dolmage 2017, 109) under this form of capitalism. This exclusion has been tackled in various types of protest performance actions – Alison Lapper crawling through a mall demonstrating the plight of the disabled individual (Siebers 2010), Aaron Williamson laying out an obstacle course of construction tape and cones in *Barrierman* to complicate movement through space for able-bodied people (Williamson 2009), or Jeff Preston's practice of 'stairbombing' where disabled people tape off stairs in a public building to give a sense of what inaccessibility feels like (Preston 2011; Hadley 2015). These interventions all offer a visceral example or experience of what it means to be excluded for the passer-by who sees the work or finds themselves excluded by the barriers in the work.

For Dolmage, twentieth-century capitalism's relationship to disability is represented through the logic of the "retrofit" (Dolmage 2017, 111). The retrofit is about making spaces work for people in ad hoc ways, as in the case of lifts retrofitted over stairs in theatres and cultural institutions (Hadley 2015). The inadequacy of ad hoc approaches is protested by artists like Jess Thom, who performs as Touretteshero, whose landmark *Backstage in Biscuit Land* dealt directly with "being refused entrance to theatres because of impairment issues" (Hambrook 2015; Lobel & Thom Chapter 19). The logic of the retrofit is also evident in efforts to retrofit or reconceptualise plays to change their representation of characters with disabilities, or include characters with disabilities, in part to protest historical stereotyping and exclusion (Hadley 2014). The retrofit highlights late capitalism's inability to deal with its own flaws, problems, and crises (Dolmage 2017, 108). It fixes the individual instance of the problem, instead of fixing the systemic problem, in the same way austerity policy is seen to do by its critics. The retrofit is often seen as enough, and as a fair, defensible, charitable approach to dealing with a problem, without actually dealing with the ideologies behind the problem (Dolmage 2017, 109). The logic of the retrofit is the logic of disabled people being forced to adapt as best as they can, often with limited resources and large amounts of creativity (as described in Lubet in Chapter 25 of this book). "Unfortunately," Dolmage notes, "this 'fixing' provides little opportunity for continued refitting, for a developmental and progressive process" (Dolmage 2017, 109). It is this more progressive approach that artists like Thom call for in their theatricalised critique of the logic of ad hoc accommodation as the main approach to access to the theatre for disabled people (Lobel & Thom Chapter 19).

The concept of Universal Design – as design that includes access to urban spaces and places as part of its core construction and aesthetic – is, for Dolmage, the mode of the hoped-for future in which all bodies will be able to survive, thrive, and become (Dolmage 2017, 109). In advocating this approach, late neo-liberal capitalism appears to advance in its relation to disability culture. In disability arts, the logic of Universal Design is represented in the construction of new platforms for disseminating art in public spaces and places, such as the portable Nebula platform that Access Arts Victoria has constructed in Australia to enable disabled artists and audiences to access work at a location that suits them (Access Arts Victoria, n.d.). Dolmage, however, highlights that even a Universal Design approach is not without its challenges when it comes to the hoped-for future of disability culture. The approach, which emphasises the best accessibility at the best cost, can itself get caught in the austerity agenda, hide continuing challenges, and create new ones. In particular, Dolmage (2017) notes, if Universal Design – or even retrofit – is seen to solve a problem, such as the problem of access to a building such as a library, it can be used to justify cuts to services, such as the library assistants who once collected and delivered books to disabled people unable to access the library. In this way, Dolmage says, Universal Design can "camouflage other forms of administrative discrimination" (Dolmage 2017, 109). It can cause an unwitting return to what Runswick-Cole and Goodley (2015, 163) following Lauren Berlant (Berlant & Seitz 2013) call a "cruel optimism." For Berlant, "cruel optimism is a double-bind in which your attachment to an object sustains you in life at the same time as that object is actually a threat to your flourishing" (Berlant & Seitz 2013). This is the phenomenon Dolmage points to when he warns that Universal Design may be desirable, but, paradoxically, may also be a

Bree Hadley

threat to the flourishing of disabled people if it hides cuts to other supports justified on the basis that Universal Design has diminished the need for them.

Following this logic, the double damnation that disabled artists feel in an age of austerity is akin to the disappointment of cruel optimism. In the past two decades, advances in disability arts seemed to offer pathways forward, beyond protest and lament at the prejudice disabled people suffer in the public sphere, towards innovative new aesthetics (Hambrook 2015). The current precarity, however, threatens continued access to funding and other forms of support required to capitalise on the work of the last two decades and move further towards true inclusivity (as noted by Austin, Duncan, Goggin, MacDowall, Pardo, and Paterson in Chapter 20 of this book). For some, the profundity of feeling this disappointment creates becomes a catalyst for new forms of art-based protest about the austerity agenda and the backwards step in disability inclusivity it is believed to bring.

Representation, self-representation, and protest in an 'age of austerity'

Though it is too early to construct a staged, schematic analysis of the way twenty-first-century neo-liberal capitalism is impacting on disability art, culture, and media practice, some trends are emerging (Hadley 2017).

The first trend is an increased desire amongst disabled artists and their allies to take issue with mainstream television and theatre representations of disability. Many artists, scholars, and activists have taken issue with the recent proliferation of 'pity porn' television programmes that focus on the flaws of the individual rather than the flaws of the system, or suggest that disabled people need to be 'supercrips' to help themselves within the system (Runswick-Cole & Goodley 2015, 166, see also Misener, Bodin and Quinn's discussion of the 'supercrip' in Chapter 6) – programmes like *Benefits Street* in the UK or *Struggle Street* in Australia. Theatre productions have drawn similar criticisms. For instance, Colin Hambrook singles out *Kill Me Now* by Brad Fraser, about a father sacrificing his career for a son secretly planning to commit suicide, riddled with stereotypes, and subject to complaint when presented at the Park Theatre, as "the kind of theatre that should be shot down as soon as it rears its vituperative head" (Hambrook 2015). Like current press reports, these programmes and performances present what Beresford calls "misery accounts" (Beresford 2016, 423) of austerity. They depict disability as a result of individual medical misfortune, something disabled artists have tried to avoid in recent decades, favouring instead work that sheds light on the social, institutional, and ideological construction of disability (Hadley 2014). These works may acknowledge the impact of cuts, show sympathy, and claim to offer a glimpse into the reality of the individual's experience, but unlike the Black Triangle protests mentioned earlier, for example, they focus more on one person's plight than on comprehensive analysis of failures in social, political, and economic systems (Beresford 2016, 424).

The second trend is a desire amongst allies to present alternative representations in response to the 'pity porn' narratives proliferating in theatre, television, and the popular press. The work of these allies is typically presented in realistic and/or traditionally theatrical stories designed to engage the spectator's empathy – again, a mode that disabled artists themselves can tend to eschew because it emphasises individual plight rather than politics (Hadley 2014). The ally's aim is often to create a counterpoint to the 'pity porn' representational practices they know disabled people contest. In *Jamie's Lighthouse*, for example, playwright Elinor Rowlands "tells the story of a young man with Asperger's Syndrome and ADHD who is forced to live with his mother due to governmental cuts and decides that 'he wants to live underwater because the noise is different there'" (Lovell 2016). The familiar reality

352

of the 'pity porn' narrative is extended via a hope of a future escape to a different reality, in a theatrical manoeuvre designed to convey the feeling of being stuck in an uncertain, discomforting, and difficult circumstance, and confront spectators with the impact the austerity cuts are having on disabled people, in a way that at least metaphorically suggests other realities may be possible. In a play called *Occupation* for the ARC Stockton Arts Centre, Pauline Heath goes further in trying to push the spectator to see the immediate reality and also see beyond the individual reality represented in the 'pity porn' narrative. Heath directly addresses "the impact of austerity on disabled people's lives" (ARC 2015) in a work based on anecdotes, workshops, and research with disabled people. Set at a protest rally, *Occupation* presents the "poignant and outrageously shocking personal experiences of disabled people and their families" (ARC 2015) – a young person, a parent, a professional, and a returned soldier – with "a powerful mix of statistics and reflections from Miss Maple, a democracy super sleuth based on 'the joker from the Theatre of the Oppressed'" (ARC 2015). The inclusion of multiple disabled characters, together with theatricalised accounts of larger-scale statistics, is a strategy to show that this is a shared problem not a single individual's plight. The showing at the ARC Stockton Arts Centre also included video stories from multiple individuals, and moments of audience interactivity, such as a game show (ARC 2015). In this respect, though created by an ally, *Occupation* incorporates the multiplicity of styles, the direct intervention and interaction with spectators, and the emphasis on the social construction of disability that many disabled people preferred in their self-representations in recent years (Hadley 2014). In both these cases, the avowed desire of the allied playwright is to prompt spectators to recognise that "we all have a role to play in analysing the messages we are fed" (ARC 2015) and reflect on the attitudes towards disabled people that popular press and 'pity porn' programmes tend to reinforce in the public sphere.

Though produced by allies, rather than disabled artists themselves, these works attempt to break through the mainstream media categorisation of disabled people as superhuman inspirations or scroungers. By presenting characters in multiple worlds, or multiple characters, and making things more "mucky around the edges" (Partridge 2016), as Partridge puts it, these works emphasise the importance of presenting more than singular, stereotypical representations of disabled people.

The third trend in arts-based activism worth recognising is the even more pronounced emphasis on symbolism, collective action, and connection with spectators seen in protests and protest performances by disabled people themselves. These protests frequently use the symbolism, stylised action, and public space intervention strategies that disabled artists have often favoured, not just because traditional narrative so easily re-enacts stereotypes, but because they are more accessible to the artists and the audiences they want to reach (Hadley 2014). The main difference to the anti-austerity plays produced by mainstream artists and allies is that these protest performances do even more to move beyond individual actions and stories – a solidarity approach to activism, in which one individual with whom we can identify stands for the larger whole – and towards collaborative or collectivist approaches – a provocation approach to activism, which aims not or not just to prompt identification but to push its spectators and participants to act in service of a cause (Giugni & Grasso 2016, 6).

In protests to cuts, disabled people have frequently sought to find provocative collective actions they can perform together to alert the public to their cause. Protestors have used a range of more or less confronting symbols and symbolic actions to engage the public in the streets, and in imagery shared online via social media platforms. In Bolivia, disabled protestors crawled through the streets wearing nappies, laid on their backs on crosses/crucifixes, and suspended themselves in chairs from bridges to highlight the precarity of their situation

(Viney 2016). In Greece, D/deaf protestors wore white gloves, and wheelchair-using protestors carried black balloons, the symbolism combined with chants and slogans highlighting their concerns (Gatopoulos & Becatoros 2016). Though varying in the provocativeness of the chosen symbolic action, these examples all show a clear desire towards collective action, rather than a singular exemplar story, to prompt the public to reflect on the reality the cuts are creating for a range of different disabled people.

In disabled artists' protest performances, symbolic actions and the sense of the collective have also been critically important. In *Figures*, for instance, filmmaker, installation artist, and activist Liz Crow sculpted hundreds of small human figures out of river mud, placing them along streets and foreshore. "Figures sets out to make visible the stark human cost of austerity," Crow says, "and to urge action against it" (Crow cited Crayshaw 2015). There were 650 figures, representing the 650 electoral districts, and thus 650 members of parliament, whose decision to accept austerity policy impacts on the lives of disabled people. "Though made in the same form," Crayshaw explains, "each figure differs in its detail, representing both common humanity and the individual" (Crayshaw 2015). After touring the work from London to Bristol over the course of a number of days, Crow allowed a bonfire to burn the figures, and while the fire burnt the figures to ashes to be scattered into the sea, a series of 650 stories of disabled people's experiences of austerity drawn from campaigns, parliamentary records, and other research were read aloud. The symbolism of the work, showing both the individual and collective impact of austerity policies, was designed to give spectators a visceral sense of "the firing and crushing of human aspiration" (Crayshaw 2015).

Around the same period, activist artist Vince Laws made poems out of a series of a hundred stories of disabled people who had died as a result of cuts to disability support collected by the Black Triangle Campaign (Laws 2015). Created for Dandifest! in Norwich, the poems included accounts of starvation, suicide, heart attacks, and other deaths attributed to the impact of austerity policy, often after a person had been assessed as fit to work. Though less symbolic than Crow's intervention, Laws' work again highlights both the individual and cumulative collective impact of austerity policies, and their impact on human lives.

A year later, as Disability Associate at the Salisbury International Arts Festival in 2016, Aiden Moesby demonstrated the stigmatisation to which disabled people are subject in a climate of austerity by means of "interventions which highlight issues around disability in a playful and gently provocative manner" (Moesby 2016b). Moesby took on the role of a representative of *The Bureau of Audience Discrimination*, creating comic encounters with spectators, to convey a sense of the "everyday experience of those with disabilities encountering seemingly random and contextless barriers and discrimination" (Moesby 2017). Wearing a lab coat and carrying a clipboard, Moesby would, for example, single out people wearing sunglasses and ask them to move to stand in a specific space, to call attention to the way disabled people are often singled out of the crowd in theatres, transport hubs, and other spaces and places. In tandem with this intervention, Moesby presented sandwich boards with headlines from a fictitious *The Daily Compulsion* newspaper to further highlight the attitudes to disability that audiences continue to display in festivals as in daily life (Moesby, n.d.a; Moesby n.d.b.; Moesby 2016b). Headlines like "it's people like you," "you look normal to me," and "pull yourself together" typified the attitudes that lead the public to question disabled people's right to support. Headlines like "please mind the barriers" flipped the perspective to give non-disabled people a sense of the barriers disabled people need to mind and move around in daily life. Another headline, "every time I'm in a queue I always imagine what I'm going to say about a hundred times" put spectators in mind of the way disabled people feel ahead of appointments in which they need to perform disability in particular ways to access benefits.

The headline "Gas is off, Taps are off, Plugs are off, Lights are off, Kettle's off, Cooker's off, Heaters are off, Right, we're off" highlighted basic human rights being lost. With this addition to his intervention, Moesby drew attention to words spoken so regularly in the press and in the public sphere that they roll through the mind and off the tongue without even really being registered by audiences whose "eyes glaze over" (Moesby 2017), but still cause pain for the many disabled people subject to such discourses from all sides.

In a piece called *Take Care* for the No Limits Festival in Berlin, Jeremy Wade also took an interventionalist approach to push participants to consider their words, actions, and attitudes. Dressed as a battlefield nurse, Wade hosted a three-day symposium and invited artists, activists, support workers, and academics to join him in performances, conversations, and lectures advocating for the establishment of The Future Center for Critical Care. Wade described the work – which took a 1988 quote from Audre Lorde, "self-care is a form of political warfare," as its starting point (Lorde cited Wade 2017) – as "a hybrid of art, activism, and social work" (Wade cited Hansom 2017). In the current political climate, Wade claims, "[c]are has been sold down the river like everything else – the neo-liberalist agenda wants us to take matters of support and health into our own hands. Systems are crumbling. Governments are telling us we must fend for ourselves" (Wade cited Hansom 2017). In this work, Wade wanted his battlefield nurse's lectures, conversations, interventions, and calls for collaboration in the future centre to show care "not just as a medical issue but also as a political issue" (Wade cited Hansom 2017; Wade 2017). Whilst acknowledging that care "can be part of the neoliberal agenda of self-improvement," Wade wanted to allow participants to reflect on an alternative paradigm, in which care "...can be embodied as a consensual and attentive communication in the pursuit of interdependence" (Wade cited Hansom 2017). As with the other artists' interventions analysed here, Wade's activism was designed not to prompt identification with a particular individual's plight, but to prompt collective action "to disrupt the isolation and competition that capitalism perpetuates" (Wade 2017).

Other artists have invited participants to join real grassroots protest movements to combat the problems the current economic and political climate is creating for disabled people. In Graeae Theatre Company's musical *Reasons to be Cheerful*, directed by Jenny Sealey, long-time activist, songwriter, and singer John Kelly and his band The Blockheads perform the songs of Ian Dury as protest music, in a performance set against signs and placards reading "stop the cuts," "fuck the system," and other anti-austerity slogans. The musical's signature song, "If It Can't Be Right Then It Must Be Wrong," sought to rally audiences against cuts to support for D/deaf and disabled people (Woodward 2017). Kelly has a history as an activist – and also an adaptor, having launched technology to allow people with disabilities to play guitar and other instruments of the sort Alex Lubet describes (in Chapter 25 of this book). As part of the project, he released protest singles, taught younger artists to write protest music, and invited the public to contribute their own protest music, played to audiences before and after the performances of *Reasons to be Cheerful*. In adopting this co-creative approach, and in inviting a broader community to contribute music to a protest movement, Kelly was acknowledging the changed climate of activism, in which "[w]e have Twitter and Facebook so people don't think they have to go out on the street to protest" (Kelly cited Scarlet 2017). For Kelly, petitions, street protests, social media protests, performances of protest music and theatre, and joining boards and groups advocating for change "all plays a part" (Kelly cited Scarlet 2017). As Christopher Balme argues in *The Theatrical Public Sphere* (2014), traditional theatres can too easily be relegated to private spaces with minimal impact beyond their own subscriber audiences; adopting and adapting the techniques of co-creative citizen protest movements seen on social media platforms as much as on the streets is necessary to ensure impact in the public sphere.

Kelly, like other disabled artists (Hadley 2017), heeds this advice. By using the musical and its signature protest song as a platform to launch a "grassroots protest movement seeking to produce 100 such songs with Graeae's community" (Woodward 2017), Kelly, Sealey, and the company sought to activate public interest in political activism. The more people involved, the more likely the work would attract both members of the disabled community and the public at large to the cause in the way commentators like Crippen advocate.

Impairment narratives?

Though the first three trends evident in anti-austerity protest performances are perhaps not surprising, the fourth, a return to characterising disability in terms of pain, impairment, and crisis, may be. As I have noted elsewhere (Hadley 2017; Hadley 2014), analysis of disability stereotypes in screen, stage, and social performance, literature, and the visual arts has revealed how such tropes – whether played as tragedy or as inspiration – tend to reinforce a medical rather than a social model of disability. In response, disabled artists have often deployed stylised aesthetics, physical action, live art, performance art, comedy, and direct connection with spectators in their efforts to subvert the stereotypes that conventional narratives create and draw attention to the social construction of disabled identities (Hadley 2014). Interestingly, however, recent practice protesting the austerity agenda has returned to issues of pain, impairment, and concrete physical problems (Hadley 2017).

The earliest to note this trend was Disability Arts Online editor and commentator Colin Hambrook. According to Hambrook (2015), in the early 2000s, there was a shift away from an anti-discrimination emphasis in disability arts towards a new set of work, created with more funding, and accessible to a wider range of audiences, which introduced aesthetically innovative forms and formats "to challenge perceptions and prejudices" (Hambrook 2015). The work was often "designed to emphasis the positivity of disabled people's lives" (Hadley 2017). In his summary of trends in 2015, however, Hambrook noted a change. Festivals such as the SICK! Festival in UK – "branded as a festival that confronts the physical, mental and social challenges of life and death" (Hambrook 2015) – together with work by artists like Jess Thom in *Backstage in Biscuit Land* (as described by Brian Lobel and Jess Thom in Chapter 19) – had returned to a focus on pain and impairment. For Hambrook (2015), this trend was apparent not just in the artwork, but in the commentary of bloggers on the Disability Arts Online website, such as Sophie Partridge. According to Partridge, the current climate of government cuts "has taken its toll on the health of many of us" (Partridge 2016). Reflecting on her own work, Partridge notes that, "[t]t is perhaps ironic that having to an extent 'denied' my impairment in any obvious way in my creative work, recently it has re-asserted itself big time in my life" (Partridge 2016). For Partridge, the fact that impairment issues reasserting themselves in life would lead to impairment issues reasserting themselves in her art is logical. "[A]rt by its very nature, IS political," Partridge argues, and is reflected in "what we include in our picture / poem / prose and / or performance and what we chose to leave out" (Partridge 2016). This includes the choice to more or less explicitly show ticks, tremors, idiosyncrasies, and other signs of pain and impairment in more or less positive accounts of disability experience.

In the works discussed in this chapter, produced primarily in Hambrook and Partridge's UK context, this renewed emphasis on impairment is clear. Though Crow's *Figures* is symbolic and collective, it does feature real narratives recounting real pain. In his poems, Laws literally quotes accounts of pain, suffering, and death. Though Moesby and Wade provide less direct accounts of suffering, their works still engage with pain and impairment, stressing the loss of basics like food, housing, employment, and care, and the pain it brings, whilst calling others

Disability arts in an age of austerity

not to simply acknowledge the problem but to join a collective community committed to fighting the problem. In protest works in my own context in Australia, I have observed a similar emphasis on pain, impairment, and problems. The Bolshy Divas, for example, explicitly focus on these issues when they create memes to circulate via social media platforms to "mimic and undermine public policy, reports, and advertising" (cf. Soldatic & Love 2015; Hadley 2017). This includes, for example, parodic job advertisements for the 'able-disabled' citizens the current policy climate prefers in a newspaper named *The Daily Token* and mocked-up open protest leaders to the minister with headers that feature a hand clawing at a shower curtain next to the phrase "Funding that allows you to shower only once a week? That's enough to drive anyone psycho" (Bolshy Divas 2014), amongst other parodies. Each of these protests to current service cuts calls attention to the negative, sometimes at the level of the single disabled individual, always at the level of disabled people as a stigmatised social group, and calls on those who encounter the work to join the fight to change the situation.

For Hambrook, this shift "is something that needs further and deeper discussion" (Hambrook 2015). The increase in work that highlights impairments, combined with the concurrent increase in work that calls spectators to collective action in place of and/or in addition to creating identification with specific situations and incidents, highlights the difficulties artists with disabilities see with current austerity policy. The logic and efficacy of this response to the current age of austerity notwithstanding, there is still risk inherent in the practice – not least, as Hambrook says, the risk of "a careering back to medical model language" (Hambrook 2015). The emphasis on pain, impairment, problems, and the volume of disabled people experiencing problems risks protest work being read in terms of individual problems rather than in terms of ideological, social, and political problems. Perhaps more critically, it risks protest work being read as the work of leaners, scroungers, or malingerers unable to live up to the ideals of the 'able-disabled' person who plays their part in the austerity agenda, in line with the attitudes that programmes like *Benefits Street* and *Struggle Street* inculcate in their audiences. This, in turn, risks turning audiences off in the way Crippen (2010b) warns, seeing performances go unattended, public space actions go unseen, and social media posts go unread by a public schooled to believe people should bear the primary responsibility for their own self-improvement as part of their role as a productive citizen.

Though Hambrook (2015) is correct to point to the risk here, the factor that offsets the risk in the work analysed here is the way this shift to focus on impairment has been accompanied by a concurrent shift from individual identification-based activist techniques to collective call-to-action-based activist techniques. This concurrent shift works against audience tendencies to read accounts of pain and impairment as an individual misery stories, unfortunate, especially if they are not easily and cost-effectively overcome by medical treatment, but unrelated to or unlikely to be resolved by change in the current social and political system. Whilst individual stories are sometimes featured in disabled artists' anti-austerity protest performances, they are counterposed with symbolic, interactive, and co-creative calls for spectators to see the bigger social and political picture behind the individual stories and become an ally to the cause, rather than simply register the realities of singular sad experiences with regret, sympathy, and frustration that is soon forgotten or folded into the broader narratives circulating within the current climate of austerity.

Conclusion

In this chapter, I have sought to identify and understand trends in the way disabled artists are using their art, culture, and media practices to protest the impact the current age of austerity is having on disabled people and call on the public to join them in fighting for this cause. The most interesting changes to practice emerging as part of disabled artists efforts to speak back to austerity policy include a shift in content – in particular, an increased amount of content on pain, impairment, and problems – and a shift in style – in particular, an increased interest in approaches that call on spectators to act as part of a collective struggle, instead of simply acknowledging concern for a certain individual's struggle. In hybrid art, activism, and social intervention works, artists like Liz Crow, Aiden Moesby, and Jeremy Wade in particular have engaged with individual stories but engaged these stories in combination with other symbolic and social interventions that call on spectators to join a collective conversation about human rights, care, and the shape of the communities of the future. In doing so, their protest performances push spectators to reflect on large-scale social issues, ideologies, and power relationships, as well as small-scale personal experiences, in tandem.

In the disability studies literature, recent commentary has questioned the way scholarship, theorisation, advocacy, and activism over the three decades have moved away from large-scale accounts of social experiences to more sophisticated accounts of specific examples of such experience (Runswick-Cole & Goodley 2011; Shildrick 2012; Goodley 2013; Dodd 2016). "Analysis of austerity by writers from critical disability studies has produced cultural insights but is almost exclusively limited to the rhetorical or discursive aspects of the problem" (Dodd 2016: 158), as Dodd puts it. The risk here is that analysis of specific examples of exclusion experienced by individuals can prompt acknowledgement of that person's struggle, but, without broader social context, can fail to call for action to address an issue that is impacting more people in more ways than the public might suspect. Clearly, the situation for disability art, culture, and media studies is slightly different. These practices, and the scholarship of these practices, cannot offer large-scale statistical analyses of the impact of government policy on disabled people. These practices can, however, offer new and more nuanced approaches to protesting the issues, including approaches that – whilst they do return to focus on pain, impairment, and problems – push spectators to go beyond the identification with individual stories that characterised solidarity-based activist movements and towards the calls to collaborative action that characterises collectivity-based activist movements. In this way, they can make their own contribution to maintaining focus both on large-scale social, political, and economic issues and on specific examples of these issues in activism moving forward. Though enacted in different ways by different artists, the strategies seen in current art-based protests against the global austerity agenda use actions in public spaces, including online spaces, to try to engage both disabled and non-disabled spectators in the anti-austerity movement. Though it is too early to tell if, and if so, how, these adaptations to practice will continue to evolve to try to speak back to an economic, political, and social reality that is also currently evolving, they do provide examples of the ways in which disabled artists adapt and change their practices in the hopes of having greater impact on their current audiences in their current cultural climate.

References

Access Arts Victoria. n.d. Nebula, Access Arts Victoria. Available: www.artsaccess.com.au/nebula/.
ARC Stockton Arts Centre. 2015. Occupation. ARC Stockton Arts Centre, September 2015. Accessed 1 February 2018. Accessed 30 January 2018. Available: http://arconline.co.uk/occupation-0.
Balme, Christopher. 2014. *The Theatrical Public Sphere*. Cambridge: Cambridge University Press.
Barnett, Clive. 2010. "Publics and Markets: What's Wrong with Neoliberalism." In Susan Smith, Rachel Pain, Sallie A. Marston, and John Paul Jones III ed. *The Sage Handbook of Social Geographies*. London: Sage, 269–296.

BBC Scotland. 2018. "Rethink Urged Over Cuts to Disabled Theatre Funding." *BBC Scotland*, 29 January 2018. Accessed 3 February 2018. Available: www.bbc.com/news/uk-scotland-42857886.

Beresford, Peter. 2016. "Presenting Welfare Reform: Poverty Porn, Telling Sad Stories or Achieving Change?" *Disability & Society*. 31(3): 421–425.

Berlant, Lauren, and Seitz, David. 2013. "Interview with Lauren Berlant." *Society and Space: Blog*. 9 April 2015. Accessed 3 February 2018. Available: http://societyandspace.com/2013/03/22/interview-with-lauren-berlant/.

Berry, David ed. 2017. "Cultural Politics, Austerity and Responses. In Berry, David ed. *Cultural Politics in the Age of Austerity*. London & New York, Routledge, 1–22.

Bolshy Divas. 2014. *Bolshy Divas* Website. Accessed 1 December 2015. Available: http://bolshydivas.weebly.com.

Brawn, Ellie, Bush, Marc, Hawkings, Caroline, and Trotter, Robert. 2013. *The Other Care Crisis: Making Social Care Funding Work for Disabled Adults in England*. Report by Scope, Mencap, National Autistic Society, Sense, and Leonard Cheshire Disability. Accessed 1 February 2018. Available: www.scope.org.uk/Scope/media/Documents/Publication%20Directory/The-other-care-crisis-1.pdf?ext=.pdf.

Briant, Emma, Watson, Nick, and Philo, Gregory. 2013. "Reporting Disability in the Age of Austerity: The Changing Face of Media Representation of Disability and Disabled People in the United Kingdom and the Creation of New 'Folk Devils'." *Disability & Society*. 28 (6): 874–889.

Crayshaw, Gill. 2015. "Figures: A Mass-Sculptural Performance to Make Visible the Human Cost of Austerity." *Shoddy Exhibition: Disability Art Project: Textiles, Recycling, Heritage, Now*, 26 November 2015. Accessed 2 February 2018. Available: https://shoddyexhibition.wordpress.com/2015/11/26/figures-a-mass-sculptural-performance-to-make-visible-the-human-cost-of-austerity/.

della Porta, Donatella. 2015. *Social Movements in Times of Austerity: Bringing Capitalism Back Into Protest Analysis*. Cambridge, Polity Press.

Dodd, Steven. 2016. "Orientating Disability Studies to Disablist Austerity: Applying Fraser's Insights." *Disability & Society*. 31 (2): 149–165.

Dolmage, Jay. 2017. "From Steep Steps to Retrofit to Universal Design, from Collapse to Austerity: Neo-Liberal Spaces of Disability." In Jos Boys ed., *Disability, Space, Architecture: A Reader*, London and New York: Routledge, 102–114.

Federici, Silvia. 2008. "Precarious Labor: A Feminist Viewpoint." *In the Middle of a Whirlwind*. Accessed 30 May 2014. Available: http://inthemiddleofthewhirlwind.wordpress.com/precarious-labor-a-feminist-viewpoint/.

Fritsch, Kelly. 2013. "The Neoliberal Circulation of Affects: Happiness, Accessibility and the Capacitation of Disability as Wheelchair." *Culture & Society*. 5 (1). Available: doi:10.5195/hcs.2013.136.

Gatopoulous, Derek, and Becatoros, Elena. 2016. "Disabled Greeks Protest as More Austerity Looms." *Ekathimerini*, 2 December 2016. Accessed 29 January 2018. Available: www.ekathimerini.com/214257/article/ekathimerini/news/disabled-greeks-protest-as-more-austerity-looms.

Marco, and Grasso, Maria T. 2016. "Introduction- Austerity and Protest: Debates and Challenges." In Maria T. Grasso and Marco Giugni ed., *Austerity and protest: Popular contention in times of economic crisis*. London: Routledge, 1–16.

Goodley, Dan, Lawthom, Rebecca, and Runswick-Cole, Katherine. 2014. "Dis/ability and Austerity: Beyond Work and Slow Death." *Disability & Society*. 29 (6): 980–984.

Hadley, Bree. 2017. "Disability, Sustainability, Austerity: The Bolshy Divas Art-Based Protests Against Policy Paradoxes." *CSPA Quarterly*. 18: 34–37.

Hadley, Bree. 2015. "Participation, Politics and Provocations: People with Disabilities as Non-Conciliatory Audiences." *Participations: Journal of Audience and Reception Studies*. 12 (1): Available: www.participations.org/Volume%2012/Issue%201/11.pdf.

Hadley, Bree. 2014. *Disability, Public Space Performance, and Spectatorship: Unconscious Performers*. London: Palgrave Macmillan.

Hansom, Joey. 2017. "Who Cares? Jeremy Wade Examines What We Can Learn from Disability Culture." *Siegessaeule*, Art & Politics, 9 November 2017. Accessed 5 February 2018. Available: www.siegessaeule.de/no_cache/newscomments/article/3623-who-cares-jeremy-wade-examines-what-we-can-learn-from-disability-culture.html.

Hambrook, Colin. 2015. "2015: The Year Impairment Issues Returned to the Fore." Blog-Colin Hambrook. *Disability Arts Online*, 17 December 2015. Accessed 6 February 2018. Available: www.disabilityartsonline.org.uk/editorial-blog?item=2659.

Bree Hadley

Harvey, David. 2010. *Social Justice and the City*. Atlanta: University of Georgia Press.

Harvey, David. 2005. *A Brief History of Neoliberalism*. Oxford: Oxford University Press.

Kokoli, Alexandra M., and Winter, Aaron. 2015. "What A Girl's Gotta Do: The Labor of the Biopolitical Celebrity in Austerity Britain." *Women & Performance: A Journal of Feminist Theory*. 25 (2): 157–174.

Laws, Vince. 2015. "UK Welfare-Related Deaths: The Black Triangle List." Blog- Vince Laws. *Disability Arts Online*, 30 April 2015. Accessed 6 February 2018. Available: www.disabilityartsonline. org.uk/vince-laws-blog?item=2517.

Lovell, Kate. 2016. "A Clear Sense of Direction – Elinor Rowlands." *Disability Arts Online*, 5 February 2016. Accessed 6 February 2018. Available: www.disabilityartsonline.org.uk/ Elinor-Rowlans-a-clear-sense-of-direction.

Lupton, Dave. 2012a. "A happy New Year from Cameron and His Cronies!" Blog- Crippen. *Disability Arts Online*, 17 December 2012. Accessed 6 February 2018. Available: www.disabilityartsonline. org.uk/?location_id=6&item=1655.

Lupton, Dave. 2012b. "A Cut Too Far." Blog-Crippen. *Disability Arts Online*, 8 October 2012 Accessed 6 February 2018. Available: www.disabilityartsonline.org.uk/crippen-cartoon-blog?item=1550.

Lupton, Dave. 2010a. "Crippen Looks At the Possible New Symbol for the Disabled People's Movement!" Blog- Crippen. *Disability Arts Online*, 4 October 2010. Accessed 6 February 2018. Available: www.disabilityartsonline.org.uk/crippen-cartoon-blog?item=760.

Lupton, Dave. 2010b. "Crippen Looks to the Arts for a Different Way to Protest." Blogs-Crippen. *Disability Arts Online*, 14 December 2010. Accessed 6 February 2018. Available: www.disability artsonline.org.uk/crippen-cartoon-blog?item=822.

Lupton, Dave. 2008. "Criteria." Blog – Crippen. *Disability Arts Online*, 11 March 2008, Accessed 6 February 2018. Available: www.disabilityartsonline.org/crippen-cartoon-blog?item=134.

Lynch, Anthony. 2016. "Now is the Turn of the Right: 'Ditch the Base'." *Social Alternatives*. 35 (2): 56–61.

Mager, William. 2014. Will Changes to Disability Work Grants Affect Deaf People the Most?" *BBC Ouch Blog*. Accessed 6 February 2018. Available: www.bbc.com/news/blogs-ouch-29800825.

Miller, Pavla, and Hayward, David. 2017. "Social Policy 'Generosity' at a Time of Fiscal Austerity: The Strange Case of Australia's National Disability Insurance Scheme." *Critical Social Policy*. 37 (1): 128–147.

Mitchell, D. 2014. "Gay Pasts and Disability Future(s) Tense. Heteronormative Trauma and Parasitism in Midnight Cowboy." *Journal of Literary & Cultural Disability Studies*. 8 (1): 1–16.

Moesby, Aidan. n.d.a. "Salisbury International Arts Festival – Disability Associate." *Aiden Moesby* Website, 23 March 2017. Accessed 6 February 2018. Available: www.aidanmoesby.co.uk/portfolio/ salisbury-international-arts-festival-disability-associate/.

Moesby, Aidan. n.d.b. "Aiden Moesby." *Disability Arts International* website. Accessed 6 February 2018. Available: www.disabilityartsinternational.org/artists/profiles/aidan-moesby/.

Moesby, Aidan. 2016a. "Stronger Together." Blog – Aiden Moesby. *Disability Arts Online*, 6 June 2016. Accessed 6 February 2018. Available: http://disabilityarts.online/artists-union-england/.

Moesby, Aiden. 2016b. "Disability Associate at Salisbury International Arts Festival." Blog-Aiden Moesby. *Disability Arts Online*, 5 June 2016. Accessed 6 February 2018. Available: www.disability artsonline.org.uk/?location_id=1233&item=2748.

Partridge, Sophie. 2016. "Blending the Personal and the Political." Blog- Sophie Partridge. *Disability Arts Online*, 8 March 2016. Accessed 6 February 2018. Available: www.disabilityartsonline.org.uk/ sophie-partridge?item=2705.

Preston, Jeffrey. 2011. "Operation: Stairbomb London." *Jeffrey Preston* Website. Accessed 6 February 2018. Available: www.jeffpreston.ca/2011/04/18/operation-stairbomb-london/.

Seymour, Richard. 2014. *Against Austerity: How We Can Fix the Crisis They Made*. London: Pluto Press.

Siebers, Tobin. 2010. *Disability Aesthetics*. Ann Arbor: University of Michigan Press.

Soldatic, Karen, and Love, Terence. 2015. "New Forms of Disability Activism: Who On Earth Are the Bolshy Divas?" *ABC Ramp Up*, 11 July 2012. Accessed 5 December 2015. Available: www.abc. net.au/rampup/articles/2012/07/11/3543571.htm.

Ryan, Frances, and Domokos, John. 2017. "'I Was A Citizen, Now I'm Nothing': Disabled Readers on Life Under Austerity." *The Guardian*, Benefits, 30 May 2017. Accessed 6 February 2018. Available:www.theguardian.com/society/benefits/2017/may/30/all.

Runswick-Cole, Katherine, and Goodley, Dan. 2015. "Disability, Austerity and Cruel Optimism." *CJDS*. 4 (2). Available: doi:dx.doi.org/10.15353/cjds.v4i2.213.

Scarlet, Mik. 2017. "John Kelly: So Many Reasons To Be Cheerful." *Disability Arts Online*, 29 August 2017. Accessed 6 February 2018. Available: http://disabilityarts.online/magazine/opinion/john-kelly-many-reasons-cheerful/.

Summers, Deborah. 2009. "David Cameron Warns of 'New Age of Austerity'." *The Guardian*, 27 April 2009. Accessed 6 February 2018. Available: www.theguardian.com/politics/2009/apr/26/david-cameron-conservative-economic-policy1.

Wade, Jeremy. 2017. *Take Care*, No Limits Festival. Accessed 6 February 2018. Available: http://take care.no-limits-festival.de/en/.

Walker, Peter. 2012. "Benefit Cuts Are Fuelling Abuse of Disabled People, Say Charities." *The Guardian*, 5 February 2012. Accessed 6 February 2018. Available: www.theguardian.com/society/2012/feb/05/benefit-cuts-fuelling-abuse-disabled-people.

Williamson, Aaron. 2009. *Barrierman*, Aaron Williamson Website. Accessed 6 February 2018. Available: http://aaronwilliamson.org/portfolio/barrierman/.

Woodward, Carl. 2017. "Jeremy Corbyn Backs New Anti-Austerity Song By Members from Ian Dury's Band The Blockheads and Graeae Theatre Company." MrCarlWoodward.com. Accessed 6 February 2018. Available: www.mrcarlwoodward.com/news/jeremy-corbyn-backs-new-anti-austerity-song-members-ian-durys-band-blockheads-graeae-theatre-company/.

Viney, Steven. 2016. "Bolivia Disability Protests: Demonstrators Hold Sit-ins, Clash with Security Forces Amid Demands for Benefits." *ABC News*, 12 June 2016. Accessed 6 February 2018. Available: www.abc.net.au/news/2016-06-12/bolivia-disability-protests-met-with-violence-amid-demands/7501914.

29

Conclusion

Practicing interdependency, sharing vulnerability, celebrating complexity – the future of disability arts, culture, and media research

Bree Hadley, Donna McDonald, Sarah Austin, Kath Duncan, Gerard Goggin, Lachlan MacDowall, Veronica Pardo, Eddie Paterson, with collaborators Dave Calvert, Jori De Coster, Shawn Goh, Alice Fox, Ann M. Fox, Andy Kempe, Petra Kuppers, Justin Lee, Alex Lubet, Sarah Meisch Lionetto, Ann Millett-Gallant, Tony McCaffrey, Laura Misener, Bronwyn Preece, Megan Strickfaden, Joanne Tay, Matthew Reason, Nancy Quinn, and Sarah Whatley

If there is an element that unites the diverse examinations of disability arts, culture, and media that come together in this collection, it is engagement with the way disability experience is enacted, re-enacted, and re-envisaged in art and media practices. In Part I, Kirsty Johnston, Donna McDonald, Janice Rieger, Megan Strickfaden, Sarah Kanake, Laura Misener, Kerri Bodin, and Nancy Quinn investigate problems with the way disability has been represented in the performing arts, the visual arts, and popular media. In Part II, Andy Kempe, Justin Lee, Shawn Goh, Sarah Meisch Lionetto, Joanne Tay, Alice Fox, Simon Hayhoe, Sue Cheesman, Susan Hogan, and Morgan Batch consider engagement with disability in arts outreach and therapy contexts. In Part III, Matthew Reason, Dave Calvert, Tony McCaffrey, Amanda Cachia, Ann Millett-Gallant, and Ann M. Fox analyse contemporary disability arts practices, their aesthetics, and the way audiences read and respond to these practices. In Part IV, Brian Lobel, Jess Thom, Eddie Paterson, Kath Duncan, Sarah Austin, Gerard Goggin, Lachlan MacDowall, Veronica Pardo, Jori De Coster, Petra Kuppers, and Bronwyn Preece present creative, multivocal, multi-perspectival, and at times pointed reflections on working in disability arts, culture, and media practice and working to open up new ideas about the future through disability arts, culture, and media practice. In Part V, Katie Ellis, Alex Lubet, Sarah Whatley, Akhila Vimal C., and Bree Hadley offer accounts of change, adaptation, and the way disabled people take leadership in responding to the trends, technologies, and cultural phenomena around them. The voices and perspectives are

362

The future of disability arts, culture, and media research

diverse, the research methods used to develop accounts of disability experience are diverse, and the resultant reflections are diverse. What all the contributors ultimately share, however, is a desire to offer insight into disabled experience and the way disability art practice and scholarship attempts to challenge, change, or recreate expectations about disabled experience across a range of countries, artforms, and contexts.

Researching disability as day-to-day lived experience

The challenges involved in researching disabled experience have been well documented in the past three decades (Oliver 1992; Barnes 1996; Stone & Priestley 1996). In a disability arts, culture, and media research context, constructing accounts of disabled experience requires reflection not just on the scenarios, interactions, and attitudes seen in the work, or in the production of the work, but on the deeper ideologies about disability these practices reveal. Responding to mainstream representational tendencies that often depict disability in terms of trauma, tragedy, special insight, inspiration, and overcoming, the authors contributing to this collection are suspicious of anything that casts these dominant accounts of disability experience as self-evident without delving into, discussing, and disrupting the ideological status quo.

> Third person narratives regarding disability are constructed around themes of powerlessness, and inspiration. These stereotypes are not only inaccurate but potentially dangerous. By telling 'ourselves sideways, crooked and "crip"' (St. Pierre & Peers 2016), opportunity is created to disrupt ableist notions and construct authentic understandings of lives informed by disability.
>
> *(Nancy Quinn)*

> Disability arts/culture/media research should grapple with the words, images, and dramaturgies of interaction that define disabled bodies – the problematic ones, the potentially transformative ones, and the ones that have the potential to go either way depending on how the spectator perceives and interprets them – to make a difference in the way disabled people are positioned in the public sphere. In doing so, it should also make a difference in the practice and politics of representation more broadly.
>
> *(Bree Hadley)*

> Disability arts/culture/media research should disturb canonical thought about representation. It should be contextual, understanding that representation and culture can be changeable and situational. It should be capacious, open to that which might not initially seem connected to disability. Finally, it should emphasise disability as a creative force, as a catalyst to be appreciated.
>
> *(Ann M. Fox)*

Trying to discuss, question, and disrupt the status quo remains a challenging task. As Jori De Coster's account of one disabled woman's attempts to perform her disabled identity in Chapter 21 demonstrates, disability experience is a complicated and at times contradictory experience of power, disempowerment, and negotiation with people, systems, and institutions to try to obtain power or overcome disempowerment. These negotiations are not a one-time process, but an ongoing series of self-performances, pushing for more inclusive practice in daily life, in the art, culture, or media industries, or in art, culture, and media representational practices. These negotiations can result in educational moments, in which disabled people explain why they need a service, adjustment, or accommodation, or why they are worried about a certain representation of, or response to, disability experience. These negotiations can result in empowering moments, in which disabled people feel understood. Equally, though, these negotiations can result in angry or traumatic moments as disabled people rile as barriers, injustices, and the larger experience of discrimination, marginalisation, and exclusion they create. Navigating these daily negotiations with an inaccessible world, disabled people make decisions based on needs, interests, and desires – the need to maintain the relationships one depends on for survival, the interest in expanding these relationships, and the desire to reframe these relationships. Disabled artists, disabled researchers, and their allies respond to this challenge, with what can sometimes seem like overwhelming emotion, at least from the point of view of non-disabled fellow artists and researchers unfamiliar with the energy it takes to navigate these seemingly small, individual, one-off but in fact all too regular barriers on a daily basis. It is the process of negotiating this daily experience of disability that informs and becomes a generative force in contemporary art, culture, and media production practices by disabled people, a critical step in their efforts to reshape attitudes to disability. It is the process of negotiating this daily experience that disability arts and media research – no matter the artform, topic, or context it takes as the specific subject of consideration – needs to understand, unpack, and make apparent.

> As an Indian artist, I realise that identifying as a disabled is a challenge that each one of us is passing through every day. As a performer, who identifies as disabled, due to a sporadically weakened vision, I envision a pedagogy and practice that anticipates a disabled performer's expression-what she/ze/he wants from a dance rather what others want to see from her/zir/him.
>
> *(Akhila Vimal C.)*

> Disability arts/culture/media research should be constructed with and through the lens and voices of the lived-experience. Disability sport offers the opportunity to express the embodied experience of disability and research that constructs narratives of the experiences of sport to offer the space to 'crip' sport as has been done in arts communities.
>
> *(Laura Misener)*

> Disability arts/culture/media research should produce, critique and, disseminate narratives about and representations of disabled and d/Deaf people, in their own words and images. Such media should also perform on global stages.
>
> *(Ann Millett-Gallant)*

Vulnerability, complexity, and uncertainty

Though arts and media practices provide a useful platform to explore this daily process of negotiating power, disempowerment, and position in an ablest world, researching these practices can still be a challenge for both disabled and non-disabled scholars. Disability arts research often requires researchers, their collaborators, and their subjects – artists, media makers, and everyday people – to break through the intense pressure to be seen as "able-disabled" (Mitchell 2014). It requires researchers and their participants to break through the pressure to show capacity to cope with and overcome barriers, to be accepted in a society that values productivity. It requires revelation of difficulties, anger, and exhaustion, as well as revelation of power, pleasure, and joy, whilst attempting to avoid reversion to or conversion of results into a medical model discourse that casts difficulties as tragic, traumatic, individual realities with little relation to broader social realities. This remains difficult and risky to do – for disabled researchers, disabled research participants, and the allies, advocates, and activists whose identity, action, and attitudes are also often on display when they engage in this form of research.

As Donna McDonald notes, reflecting on her own research, and her own attempts to provide new narratives that challenge dominant accounts of d/Deafness via analysis of d/Deaf characters in novels, memoirs, and other creative modes, negotiating these issues in arts and academic work often leaves researchers faced with the daunting prospect of breeching their own privacy.

> This was a troubling hurdle as I did not want my memoir to be an exercise in disability tourism for the curious but merely idle reader. I was mindful, too, of the 'Catch-22' involved in writing my memoir. My parents' benchmark for my 'success' as a deaf woman was the degree to which I blended in with, and integrated into, the hearing world and yet, to answer the questions of others about my deafness, I was required to elevate myself above the tidewater of anonymous integration. Given that personal privacy was being sacrificed, I wanted my memoir to matter, to grab the reader's attention and give them pause to reflect, to wonder, and perhaps even to provoke them into asking more questions that might bring about an improved understanding of the lives (and needs) of deaf people.
>
> *(McDonald 2014a, n.p., cf. McDonald 2014b)*

Part of the challenge here remains the challenge of collecting, narrating, and critiquing disability experience via traditional research methods. As Lennard Davis reminds us,

> When it comes to disability, "normal" people are quite willing to volunteer solutions, present anecdotes, recall from a vast array of film instances they take for fact. No one would dare to make such a leap into Heidiggerian philosophy for example or the art of the Renaissance. But disability seems so obvious – a missing limb, blindness, deafness. What could be simpler to understand? One simply has to imagine the loss of the limb, the absent sense, and one is half-way there.
>
> *(Davis 1997, 2)*

Prevailing paradigms of research have not always paid attention to the ways in which researchers and their research methods – which struggle to capture the difficult-to-convey nuances of disability experience that non-disabled people who are not part of disability culture may not be aware of, and to do this without reverting to problematic language – disenfranchise disabled people. Interviews, focus groups, surveys, and commentary about artwork are all readily reduced to dominant themes, with anecdotes that serve as exemplars, at the expense of nuance, contradiction, and paradox in accounts of disability as both a potentially traumatic and a powerful feature of one's identity, as something one both wishes to disclose about and has difficulty disclosing about. Traditional research methods are often inaccessible, anxiety-inducing, or at the least unable to capture accounts of experience in a wide range of signs, symbols, languages, and translations, from a wide range of voices, presenting accounts that are conflicted in themselves or in relation to each other. Finally, as the debate about disability research methods more generally in the early 1990s demonstrated, many disabled people find traditional research methods exploitative, and would like to see the development of more emancipatory research method that offer them more agency in research aims, methods, and outcomes (Oliver 1992; Barnes 1996; Stone & Priestley 1996).

Disability arts/culture/media research should aim – like all research – to be excellent, rigorous and challenging. It should also be humble; recognising how historically the academy has been implicated in suppressing the voices, rights and lived experiences of people with disabilities. It should avoid the 'god trick' and acknowledge its own situated and partial perspective.

(Matthew Reason)

Disability arts/culture/media research should be open and responsive, recognising that disabled artists engaged in cultural negotiations produce fresh insights into disability, culture, and society. To draw out these insights, it must resist the temptation to apply ill-fitting research paradigms, proceeding instead from the principle that the terms on which the work should be explored, examined and valued are intrinsic to the work it-self, and cannot be imposed without detriment.

(Dave Calvert)

One cannot remain unmoved by the beauty of disability arts or the conviction of its message. Researchers may describe disability culture using clinical language in an attempt to convey academic neutrality; but there is a greater responsibility to speak plainly so that more can understand its value and worth.

(Justin Lee)

Disability arts have immense aesthetic, expressive, and emancipatory value that is often hard to capture because of its intangible nature. Disability arts research thus plays a critical role in legitimising the worth of disability arts and advocating for more emphasis to be given to it in future.

(Shawn Goh)

The challenge of inclusive research methods – methods that acknowledge perspectivality, allow polyvocity, use plain language and/or creative methods to convey nuances of experiences that elude conventional methods, while maintaining rigour – is the real challenge of disability arts, culture, and media research. Many still feel their ability to make, research, and publish research is restricted by a system in which – despite increased interest in disability in the arts and in academia in the last three decades – funding and publication opportunities are still gatekept by authorities with limited lived experience of disability, and still assessed against conventional criteria. Such opportunities are thus often still designed to serve non-disabled authors' efforts to become leaders in the field via conventional research more than disabled authors efforts to become leaders in the field via creative new modes of research. Nearly 30 years after the debate about emancipatory disability research, a surprisingly large amount of disability research is still led by non-disabled people, with little day-to-day experience of disability culture, beyond their direct research engagement with participants they perceive as subjects rather than equals. Disabled people are secondary researchers, paid research assistants, consultants, or participants not leaders. This is particularly prevalent in some of the health, social services, and community services sectors' research that artist researchers encounter in surveying the field. The need to ensure this situation changes – in the academy, as much as in the arts and media industries – remains a pressing priority for many in the field.

All disability research must have a liberatory pragmatic connection, if not an explicit component. Arts and media are basic human rights. Disability research should advance the cause of participatory access for all.

(Alex Lubet)

Disability arts/culture/media research should challenge established orthodoxies and provide space for the voices and experiences of those with disabilities to be present, heard, and valued. Research should be respected for its work on examining where social oppression continues, and for arguing for disabled and d/Deaf people having equal rights to independent living and inclusion in their communities.

(Sarah Whatley)

Disability arts/culture/media research should provoke acts of reckoning, protest and change. It should be valued alongside other research as a significant contributor to understanding and responding to the global-wide struggle by generations of disabled and d/Deaf people to gain a good education, a secure job, and the affection, respect and love of friends, colleagues and family without having to perform staggering, contortionist-like feats of 'normalcy.'

(Donna McDonald)

In disability arts and media research, scholars are typically highly cognisant of these issues. They are committed to avoiding exploitation, misinterpretation, and misrepresentation and are interested in the creative new research models established researchers in the field like Petra Kuppers (2011) have used to open up the possibilities for new research methods in the field.

As yet, though, scholars in disability art and media studies field have not had their own in-depth debate about what emancipatory research methods in our own field does, could or should look like, or about accepted approaches, methods, and mechanisms to ensure disabled people have agency in disability arts and media research. Though discussed and debated around programs at conferences, the literature in the field has yet to have debate on this issue at scale. This means many d/Deaf, disabled, and divergent-identified artists and academics still feel excluded from criteria used to determine merit, integrity, and quality, deployed in academia, as well as in dominant arts practices, and arts training, institutional, and funding frameworks. This also means many non-disabled artists and academics – those who are cognisant of the issues, ready to contribute to the development of methods that allow field to become more inclusive, and guard against the traps of past practice and research that tended to reduce disabled experience and relegate disabled people to the status of research subject rather than research leader – still feel anxious and uncertain about their mode and ethics of their engagements (Leighton 2009). Whilst this shared vulnerability, complexity, and uncertainty can be uncomfortable, many disability arts and media researchers are also now starting to recognise its potential as a productive component of research conversations moving forward.

Interdependent, shared, situated research practices

This collection offers insight into the diversity of approaches, methods, and mechanisms used to research disability arts and media practices today. Some contributors adapt conventional approaches to research to their needs, using them to articulate issues in a way they hope will be meaningful to readers. Others "disrupt traditional research power hierarchies and facilitate multisensory modes of research dialogue" (Macpherson & Fox 2016, 373). They work together to try to advance the field to be inclusive of a wider new range of research approaches, methods, and reporting mechanisms. They demonstrate the potential of research models that allow different stakeholders to engage in a continuing reflective conversation in which artists and researchers with disability and artists and researchers without disability alike are invited to reflect upon their own views on aesthetics, representation, reception, and the arts and media industries in terms of their relationship to disability issues. Research models that allow those working in this field to be alive to moments of engagement between artists and scholars – and spectators, advocates, and allies – and that have the potential to animate what Bree Hadley calls a "dialogics of difference," characterised by "productive, unpredictable, improvisatory encounters" (Hadley 2014, 186) with the potential to alter the public sphere. Research models that allow conventional scholarship but at the same time allow movement into moments of co-authoring, collaborative authoring, collage authoring, and comingling of art with research, when and as necessary to build on perspectives emerging from the encounter between different stakeholders and their different perspectives and contributions. Research models that include consideration of how we might best collaborate with disabled artists, and disabled people, using our own arsenal of arts-based methods, to make and shape our research while being both reflexive and critical. Models that acknowledge our identifications, with disability/non-disability, or as researchers, performers, and audience members. Models that implicate us all in self-reflection on practices – from the ways in which we hold meetings and events, to our practices of consent and collaboration, to how we view and 'read' performance, to how we send an email, or how we undertake a polyvocal writing process, and so on. Models that share the burden of self-disclosure, amongst disabled and non-disabled stakeholders in the research. Models that recognise that collectively researching a personal and public and sensitive and ego-baring and vulnerability-making topic like disability in arts, culture, and media practice in contemporary society is a challenge, that there will be dissensus and conflict as much as consensus. Research models that recognise that this may need to come out in alternative, multivocal, and multimedia modes of expression – like those explored in Part IV of this collection in particular – to capture the nuance, contradiction, and paradox in accounts of disability as both a traumatic and a powerful feature of one's identity.

> Inclusive arts research provides creative opportunities between artists with learning disabilities and their non-disabled collaborators. It can make understanding and multiple meanings through collaborative, artistic forms of inquiry. It advocates and actively values the immersed, situated, subjective nature of the researcher and the research process.
>
> *(Alice Fox)*

> Disability arts/culture/media research should engage, stretch, cartwheel, immerse, reverse/forward…and question, and question, and question disciplinary divides… Creative terrains should foster inclusive exploration with fresh vigour and inspiration. Embodying and celebrating themes of intersectionality and interdependency, the impact of such work should remain prescient, applicable, accountable, and accessible.
>
> *(Bronwyn Preece)*

> Disability arts/culture/media research should take place in the streets, in rehearsal rooms, theatres, studios, workplaces, schools, universities, beyond the built environment, and in the minds/bodies of people with disabilities in mutual, interdependent relationships with others. It should open up spaces of queer/crip futurity, explore the potential of the impotential, and contribute to new ecologies of the posthuman.
>
> *(Tony McCaffrey)*

> Disability arts/culture/media research should acknowledge the increasing value of creative scholarly outputs as dynamic forces that shift society towards change. Seemingly small outputs in the form of, for example, short films, music, exhibition and dance performed within the public realm provoke reflection, promote meaning, and lessen ableist attitudes.
>
> *(Megan Strickfaden)*

The value of interdependent, shared, situated, collaborative, and creative research practice is something the contributors in Part IV of this collection in particular pursue. It is something Lobel, Thom, and de Coster attempt with their dialogic approach, something Austin, Duncan, Goggin, Pardo, Paterson, and MacDowall attempt with their collaboratively authored approach based on workshops and ongoing correspondence, and something Kuppers and Preece attempt with their creative approaches. They adapt academic practice in the name of inclusion, in the same way the musicians, dancers, performers, and media activists that Ellis, Lubet, Whatley, Vimal, and Hadley discuss in Part V attempt to do in arts and media practice. In each case, a diversity of disability experience, as well as disabled and non-disabled voices in dialogue about issues, problems, and pathways forward, provide insight into the way disabled people negotiate to make themselves heard, while at the same time acknowledging that it is almost impossible to do justice to the range of lived experience within our communities from any one single perspective. The most creative contributions embody some of the 'crip aesthetics' Reason, Calvert, McCaffrey, Cachia, Millett-Gallant, and Fox consider in Part III, in practice that can be provocative and disruptive of the representational canons Johnston, McDonald, Rieger, Strickfaden, Misener, Quinn, and Bodin critique in Part I, and inclusive in the way Kempe, Lee, Goh, Meisch Lionetto, Tay, Fox, Hayhoe, Cheesman, Hogan, and Batch advocate in Part II.

What these contributions start to point to are new modes of artmaking, knowledge-making, research, and engagement – often based on collaboration – that are open to consensus, dissensus, debate, contradiction, alteration, adaptation, and celebration, and that do not all need to align into a singular account to have an impact. These contributions point to the possibility of new models of disability arts and media research, based on needs, interests, dialogues, and debates, in which multiple voices and demands become interdependent and perform their interdependency. In doing so, these contributions offer interesting glimpses of potential futures and potential future research models for a maturing field. These models open pathways to a potential future of polemical, confrontational, crip activist research of the sort Phil Smith describes:

> It will be a virulent research.
> It will be a pissed off research…
> And it will all be done – these researches, these languages, these ideologies – by those whose voices and signs and silences and lives have not been heard or seen or attended to by the normative educational institutions in our culture – institutions that destroy not just the lives of people with disabilities, but the lives of all of us.
>
> *(Phil Smith 2006, 58)*

Equally, these models open pathways to a potential future in which polemical research can exist in productive dialogue with more conventionally educational, empowering, and emancipatory research of the sort Michael Oliver, Colin Barnes, and others have been calling for since the 1990s (Oliver 1992; Barnes 1996; Stone & Priestley 1996). These models point to potential futures in which research led by disabled people can exist in productive dialogue with research that acknowledges that no one disabled person can recognise, reflect on, and speak to the whole, diverse, intersectional, interdependent reality of disability experience. Futures in which research by disabled people can exist in productive dialogue with research by non-disabled allies, advocates, and supporters who work with disabled people day-to-day, encounter the barriers day-to-day, and thus experience a sense of commonality with those for whom they do this work. Futures in which research by a range of allies, from true social

Bree Hadley et al.

justice allies, to advocates motivated by altruism, and even those motivated by desire for self-advancement in an increasingly popular form of research, exists in productive dialogue, enabling readers to reflect, critique, and draw their own conclusions on a range of different accounts of disability experience. Futures in which the fact that fellow contributors may query approaches, aims, or outcomes is accepted, and even celebrated, as a result of a common recognition that negotiation, heat, conflict, and compromise will be amongst the most productive and impactful elements of the research.

> Disability arts/culture/media research honors a full range of emotional facets of living, including joyful and affirming perspectives, giving contrast to the dour approaches to disability that dominate the mainstream, and the long histories of disability oppression. It benefits from including arts-based and trickster methods as ways of knowing and discovering ways of being alive.
>
> *(Petra Kuppers)*

> Disability arts practice demands that we resist any comfort zone of polite exchange in order to grapple with the complexities of the social contract between disabled and non-disabled identities. Disability arts promises to wreak havoc, to disrupt and be loud and unruly. In doing so, it resists dominant narratives around disabled identities and disability research should underpin this artistic and creative agenda.
>
> *(Sarah Austin)*

> Disability arts/culture/media research should offer the possibility to break open conventional (normalised) ways of seeing and understanding and create awareness about the continuous emergence of life and being, its frictions, and its entanglements with power relations. It should make visible these frictions, and the cracks of everyday (dis/abled) life, and offer the possibility to (self) reflect, learn and activate for change.
>
> *(Jori De Coster)*

> Disability arts/culture/media research should be accessible and revolutionary. We are demanding equality, space for diverse voices, and professional careers for Australia's most exciting performers, writers and media makers. Join the uprising or get out of our way.
>
> *(Kath Duncan)*

What the diversity of different approaches that come together in this collection alert us to, above all, is the fact that the research modes of the future need to remain open to radical thinking. Research modes of the future need to keep tearing things up, or moving forward in different ways, accepting that failed approaches as much as successful approaches have a part to play. Disability arts, culture, and media research is not simply about themes, politics, or ideologies present in the work but about revealing the ways in which the work attempts to think about alternative futures. Moving forward, then, disabled and non-disabled researchers need to acknowledge the power of working together to bring disabled and non-disabled scholars, activists, artists, and audiences challenged by contradiction, conflict, and uncertainty into a space where they can feel comfortable to share the burden of being vulnerable together, in order to open up what may at first be fragile paths towards uncertain potential futures. Interdependency, and active commitment to performing interdependency in our artistic and research relationships, is a necessity in setting the stage for this challenging but vital work.

This collection flags the possibilities of potential future modes of disability arts, culture, and media research. It invites readers to join this community of scholars, activists, artists, and audiences in the rigorous, disciplined, collaborative, creative, and destructive work the field demands. These possibilities are reflected in many of the chapters that have come together here – in contributions that explore different modes of research production, in contributions that place voices and views in dialogue, and in editorial decisions that avoid collapsing or cohering very different contributing voices into a completely homogenous collection. The work the authors share here demonstrates how these research modes can contribute, not just to disability arts, culture, and media practice, but to cultural practice more generally – both creative cultures in drama, dance, music, film, television, visual arts, and the media, and everyday cultures in a range of educational and social institutions.

> Research into disability and the arts shows that mainstream education and theatre can benefit from the insights gained when the experiences of families living with the everyday challenges of disability are considered. Action taken to enrich their cultural lives can inform and enrich society as a whole and in doing so moves society towards becoming more just.
>
> *(Andy Kempe)*

> Disability arts research brings a variety of perspectives to disability policies and practice, and enhances the development of practical applications that will help build a strong and inclusive cultural sector. It examines and challenges social, political, and aesthetic discourses, leading to transformative change within the multi-dimensional field of arts and disability.
>
> *(Joanne Tay)*

> Disability arts research can play a vital role in contributing to the development of an inclusive cultural scene and to fostering awareness of transformational models such as the social model of disability and the creative case for disability.
>
> *(Sarah Meisch Lionetto)*

The invitation, to the reader, is to consider how they could insert their voice into the conversations started here. How they could become part of a community of researchers – artists, scholars, audiences, policymakers, able, disabled, intersectional, and interdependent on each other in a range of creative, collaborative, and sometimes contested or contradictory ways – that can come together to provide more nuanced accounts of what disability experience means to the many people whose lives are in some way marked by it.

References

Barnes, Colin. 1996. "Disability and the Myth of the Independent Researcher." *Disability & Society.* 11 (1): 107–112.

Davis, Lennard J. ed. 1997. *The Disability Studies Reader.* London & New York: Routledge.

Hadley, Bree. 2014. *Disability, Public Space Performance and Spectatorship: Unconscious Performers.* London & New York: Palgrave MacMillan.

Kuppers, Petra. 2011. *Disability Culture and Community Performance: Find a Strange and Twisted Shape.* London: Palgrave MacMillan.

Leighton, Fran. 2009. "Accountability: The Ethics of Devising a Practice-As-Research Performance with Learning-Disabled Practitioners." *Research in Drama Education: The Journal of Applied Theatre and Performance.* 14 (1): 97–113.

Macpherson, Hannah, and Fox, Alice. 2016. "Listening Space: Lessons from Artists with and without Learning Disabilities." *Environment and Planning: Society and Space.* 34 (2): 371–389.

McDonald, Donna. 2014a. "The Reluctant Memoirist. Griffith Review. 33." Accessed 29 June 2018. Available: https://griffithreview.com/articles/the-reluctant-memoirist/.

McDonald, Donna. 2014b. *The Art of Being Deaf: A Memoir.* Washington, DC: Gallaudet University Press.

Mitchell, David T. 2014. "Gay Pasts and Disability Future(s) Tense. Heteronormative Trauma and Parasitism in Midnight Cowboy." *Journal of Literary & Cultural Disability Studies*. 8 (1): 1–16.

Oliver, Michael. 1992. "Changing the Social Relations of Research Production?" *Disability, Handicap & Society*. 7 (2): 101–114.

Smith, Phil. 2006. "Split-----ting the ROCK of {speci[ES]al} e.ducat.ion: FLOWers of lang[ue]age." in >DIS<ability studies." In Scot Danforth and Susan L. Gabel New York eds. *Vital Questions Facing Disability Studies in Education: Disability Studies in Education Vol 2*. New York: Peter Lang Publishing, 33–61.

Stone, Emma, and Priestley, Mark. 1996. "Parasites, Pawns and Partners: Disability Research and the Role of Non-Disabled Researchers." *The British Journal of Sociology*. 47 (4): 699–716.

St. Pierre, Joshua, and Peers, Danielle. 2016. "Telling Ourselves Sideways, Crooked and Crip: An Introduction." *Canadian Journal of Disability Studies*. 5 (3). Accessed 29 June 2018. Available: cjds.uwaterloo.ca/index.php/cjds/article/viewFile/293/509.

30
Plain language summary

Bree Hadley and Donna McDonald

In this book Bree Hadley and Donna McDonald have asked artists and researchers from around the world to talk about the arts and media practices of disabled and d/Deaf people.

Bree is a researcher from Australia. Bree is mainly interested in the performing arts and the media arts – theatre, dance, music, television, film, and the Internet.

Donna is also a researcher from Australia. Donna is mainly interested in the visual arts – painting, photography, and exhibitions at galleries and museums.

Bree, Donna, and the friends they have asked to write parts of this book are all interested in the stories about disabled people we see in theatres, cinemas, museums, or the media.

They think it is important to study these stories. This is because these stories teach the audience who see the stories how they should think about, talk about, and treat the disabled people they meet in their daily lives.

Some of the writers in this book talk about their ideas in complicated words that can be difficult for people who are not university researchers to understand. Some of writers in this book talk about their ideas in words that are easier to understand – for example, they share a record of a conversation about these ideas, or they share a short story that they think would help the audience to think about disabled people more positively.

In this chapter, Bree and Donna have summarised the ideas the writers share in the book.

They hope this will make the ideas easier to understand for D/deaf and disabled people who are not university researchers, including people with learning and intellectual disabilities.

This is something that other researchers have tried to do in the past.

In his book *Theatres of Learning Disability: The Good, The Bad, The Ugly*, published in 2015, researcher Matt Hargrave asked his friend Ruth Townsley to write an easy-read summary of the ideas in his book. Matt knew this summary would not be right for everyone who wanted to understand the ideas in the book. But Matt thought it was important to try to include a summary that could help some of the performers with learning disabilities he wrote about in his book understand the ideas in his book.

Bree and Donna thought it would be a good idea to try to do this for their book too.

Introduction

In the **Introduction**, Bree and Donna talk about why they asked 40 artists, activists, and university researchers from around the world to talk about disability arts and media practices in their book.

Bree and Donna explain that researchers have been studying the stories about disabled people we see in theatres, cinemas, museums, or the media for more than 30 years.

Some writers have talked about the upsetting stories about disabled people they have seen in their day-to-day lives. Other writers have talked about how disabled people have started to make their own plays, performances, pictures, films, and stories to show the barriers that make it difficult for disabled people to feel like they are fully included in society. Other writers have talked about positive stories disabled people present through their art.

Some writers talk mainly about projects where disabled people produce these performances, paintings, exhibitions, films, or digital stories as a professional job. Other writers talk mainly about projects where disabled people participate in the arts for fun or to help them feel better.

In the Introduction, Bree and Donna introduce the reader to these writers and their ideas.

A lot of the writers talk about the same things. Most believe that disabled people do not need to be fixed by a doctor to lead happy lives; they just need society to do a better job of including disabled people. Most believe that artwork can help disabled people fight for this goal.

A few of the writers fight about the best words to use to describe artwork by disabled people. A few of the writers also fight about if it is better to talk mostly about disabled people who do arts as a professional job or better to talk mostly about disabled people who do arts to feel better.

Bree and Donna thought it would be good to have a book with a lot of different writers talking about their different ideas. This would help readers who have not thought about artwork by disabled people before to understand these ideas without having to read hundreds of books.

Part I: Disability, identity, and representation

In the first part of the book, Bree and Donna ask writers to talk about the stories about disabled people presented in theatre, museums, books, and the media in the past.

Kirsty Johnston is a researcher from Canada. Kirsty has written a lot about disabled characters in plays presented in the theatre, including in her own book, called *Recasting Modernism: Disability Theatre and Modern Drama*, published in 2016.

When people ask about her research, Kirsty says that even when she goes to see a play with disabled characters in it, she does not see any disabled people on the stage playing the characters, and she does not see any disabled people in the audience watching the play.

Kirsty says this is a problem. A lot of plays include disabled characters. Sometimes these characters are presented as the crazy, crippled, or the bad guys in the story. Sometimes these characters are presented as the victims of a tragedy in the story. This makes the audience think this is what it is really like to be a disabled person in real life.

This is very difficult to change, Kirsty says. Many theatre makers do not think disabled people can be good actors. When they need somebody to play a disabled character, they ask a non-disabled actor to play the disabled character. Many theatre teachers do not let disabled people into their classes to learn to be good actors.

Plain language summary

There are now some theatre companies that have been set up to allow disabled people to present their own plays, with positive stories about disabled people, and with support for disabled people to come and be part of the audience.

Kirsty is happy that theatre makers and researchers are starting to pay more attention to the companies that are doing this. For Kirsty, this is very important, to make sure that the theatre industry gets better at including disabled people in the future.

Donna McDonald is a painter and a researcher from Australia.

Donna thinks pictures of disabled people in paintings tell a story about what it is like to be a disabled person. These pictures often tell a stereotyped story about what it is like to disabled person. The pictures make the viewer look at disabled people with pity. They make the viewer scared of disabled people or scared of becoming a disabled person.

Donna talks about examples of paintings that presented disability this way in the past. Donna talks about her feelings when she looks at these paintings.

Donna then talks about her feelings when she looks at more recent paintings which tell different stories about what it is like to be a disabled person.

By talking about the way viewers have looked at different paintings, in different museums and galleries, at different points in time, Donna hopes that we can all learn to think a bit more about how we feel when we look at pictures of disabled people in paintings in the future.

Janice Rieger and Megan Strickfaden think old photographs, objects, and documents presented in museum exhibitions are important because they tell us what people thought about past events at the time and what people think when they remember past events now.

They compare the National Gallery of Australia, where Janice lives in Australia, and the Canadian War Museum, where Megan lives in Canada.

At the Canadian War Museum, Janice and Megan saw a lot of pictures and stories about soldiers who had been injured in wars. The word disability was not used in describing the soldiers. Instead, words like 'wound' and 'rehabilitation' were used. The museum told a medical story about disabled people being fixed by doctors.

At the National Gallery of Australia, Janice and Megan did not see as many pictures or stories about disabled people. The museum staff were able to tell Janice and Megan which painters had a mental health problem. The museum staff also sometimes used old-fashioned and upsetting words to describe paintings that showed pictures of disabled people.

Janice and Megan think it is important that museum exhibitions tell more stories about what it is like to live as a disabled person in society and teach their staff to talk positively about pictures and stories of disabled people, to show they care for disabled people in society.

Sarah Kanake writes about books that tell a story about Down syndrome.

A lot of books about Down syndrome talk about the relationship between a mother and a child with Down syndrome. They talk about how the mother feels when she is told her child has Down syndrome. They do not talk about how the child with Down syndrome feels.

Sarah tried to tell a different story about what it is like to have Down syndrome, in her own book, *Sing Fox To Me*, published in Australia, where Sarah lives, in 2016.

Some readers liked Sarah's story. Some readers did not like Sarah's story. They said the main character in Sarah's story, Samson, was too aware of his own feelings for someone who had been born with Down syndrome.

Sarah says the readers who did not like her book have very low expectations about what people with Down syndrome are able to do in their lives.

Laura Misener, Kerri Bodin, and Nancy Quinn write about the Paralympic Games and the stories the media likes to tell about disabled people who participate in the Paralympic Games.

Laura, Kerri, and Nancy are researchers from Canada who have seen and read a lot of stories about the Paralympic Games in the media, in Canada, and around the world.

These stories talk about how upsetting it is to have a disability. They talk about how good it is to see disabled people doing really well in the Paralympic Games in spite of their disability. They talk about these disabled people as 'heroes' who inspire non-disabled people to do really well in their lives too.

These stories say the best disabled people are the 'heroic' disabled people who do not let their disability stop them doing well at sports.

Laura, Kerri, and Nancy do not think these stories help disabled people in their day-to-day lives.

Part II: Inclusion, well-being, and whole-of-life experience

In the second part of the book, Bree and Donna ask writers to talk about programmes that allow disabled people to participate in arts and cultural activities for fun or to feel better.

Andy Kempe, a researcher from England, talks about 'relaxed' performances.

In a 'relaxed' performance, a theatre company 'relaxes' the rules about how people should behave in the theatre. The audience gets more information about what will happen in the play before they come to the theatre. There is no pressure to sit still, be quiet, or stay for the whole play. This can be good for disabled people and their friends and families who want to come to see a play without worrying about fitting in and following the rules.

Andy writes about a 'relaxed' performance of *Beauty and the Beast* at the Corn Exchange Newbury in England in 2017 for children with autism and their families.

Andy says that theatre companies need to think about all the details of the performance very carefully when they are creating a 'relaxed' performance. This is important to make sure the children, the parents, and the other people attending the performance all have a good time.

Justin Lee, Shawn Goh, Sarah Meisch Lionetto, Joanne Tay, and Alice Fox write about arts programmes for disabled people run by arts companies, councils, charities, and health services.

Justin, Shawn, Sarah, and Joanne are researchers and artists from Singapore.

This means they write mainly about arts programmes for disabled people they see in Singapore.

Justin, Shawn, Sarah, Joanne, and Alice say that arts programmes that help disabled people have fun, feel better, or feel part of the community offer a good service for disabled people.

In Singapore, though, these art programmes sometimes spend too much time thinking about how to provide a good service for disabled people and not enough time thinking about how to make interesting art that asks the audience to think about disability in different ways.

Sue Cheesman is a dance teacher and researcher from New Zealand.

Sue writes about her work with a community dance programme called Encompass, run by Touch Compass Dance Company in New Zealand, over the last 15 years.

Sue says community dance should not focus on dance as a treatment or therapy for disabled people. It should focus on creating interesting new types of dances and on developing the skills to create interesting new types of dances, to allow everyone to achieve their creative potential.

Sue writes about how she has worked with the Encompass ensemble to do this.

Sue says working in partnership with the disabled people participating in the Encompass ensemble is important to ensure everyone can express themselves through dance.

Plain language summary

Simon Hayhoe writes about the process the Deaf Service at Yosemite National Park in the US used to add new features and services to make sure d/Deaf people could enjoy the park.

Simon writes about a five-step process which starts with changing the way we value d/Deaf and disabled people in our society.

The first step is connecting with d/Deaf and disabled people as friends, classmates, or workmates. The second step is learning more about how d/Deaf and disabled people think, speak, and behave. The third step is using this information to come up with new features and services that could make a visit to a cultural site more enjoyable for d/Deaf and disabled people. The forth step is adding the new features and services. The fifth step is assisting d/Deaf and disabled people to move through the cultural site with the help of the new features and services.

Simon says this process worked well to make it easier for d/Deaf people to visit Yosemite National Park in the US.

Simon thinks other parks, museums, and historical buildings could use this same process to make sure that d/Deaf and disabled people can enjoy their visit in the future.

Susan Hogan is an arts therapist from England.

Susan writes about her work in art therapy, and her research into art therapy, over the past 20 years.

Susan explains that art therapy is based on psychological principles, which the art therapist uses to help a person with a mental health problem deal with the difficulties they have in their life.

Susan noticed very early in her art therapy career that these psychological principles are often based on men's way of seeing their lives rather than on women's ways of seeing their lives. For example, if society says being a wife and mother should be most important to a woman, then psychological principles and treatments will start with the idea that a woman's difficulties in her life might be to do with her desire to be a wife or mother. Psychological principles and treatments will interpret the symbols and stories in the woman's art in terms of that desire.

Susan says art therapy techniques should be adapted to make sure they are not based on these types of assumptions about what men and women might want in their lives.

Susan thinks everyone is different, and if arts therapy celebrates this difference, it will be able to do more to help people.

Morgan Batch is a researcher in Australia.

Morgan is interested in stories about people with dementia presented in plays and performances in the theatre. Dementia is a medical condition where a person, often an older person, has difficulty remembering the things that have happened in their life.

Morgan says most studies about performance and dementia talk about how taking part in a performance project can help people with dementia with their memory problems.

Morgan looks at a much bigger group of plays and performances about people with dementia.

Morgan finds that stories about people with dementia almost always say that these people are very different to normal people, that they have become like young children again, and that this means the medical condition of dementia is a very scary medical condition.

Morgan says this is a problem, because it 'dehumanises' people with dementia, making it seem like these people are not proper human beings anymore.

Part III: Access, artistry, and audiences

In the third part of the book, Bree and Donna ask writers to talk about the way audiences respond to artwork by disabled people.

Matthew Reason is a researcher from England.

Matthew writes about five different ways spectators watch performances by people with learning disabilities (as they are called where Matthew lives in England) or intellectual disabilities (as they are called in other countries).

These five ways of watching include looking at disabled people as 'no different' to other people; looking at disabled people as more interesting because they are 'different' to other people; looking at disabled people to see the similarities between disabled and non-disabled people; looking at disabled people because they are more real and authentic than non-disabled performers pretending to be somebody else in a play; and looking at disabled people because they are doing interesting new styles of performance that all theatre makers might be interested in using in the future.

Matthew thinks understanding the way people watch performances by people with learning or intellectual disabilities is important. It helps spectators go beyond watching people with learning or intellectual disabilities simply because they look different. It helps people see similarities, differences, and interesting new styles of performance in the work.

Dave Calvert is also a researcher from England, and Dave also writes about the way spectators watch performances by people with learning or intellectual disabilities.

Dave explains that society has often seen learning disabled people as 'fools' or 'idiots.'

Dave says this has made it difficult for spectators to know how to react to performances by learning disabled people. This is because spectators are not certain if the learning disabled performers are just performing their own personalities, or if the learning disabled performers are pretending in the way other actors do when they perform certain personalities on the stage.

Dave talks about performances that play with this uncertainty, make spectators think about this uncertainty, and think about the way they see learning disabled people both in performances and in day-to-day life.

Dave thinks this is a good thing if it can make spectators think about the stereotypes that society has about learning disabled people and the abilities of learning disabled people.

Tony McCaffrey is a theatre maker and researcher from New Zealand.

Like Matthew and Dave, Tony also writes about significant performances by people with intellectual disabilities over the last 50 years.

Tony talks about how stories about intellectually disabled people presented on stage and on screen have changed over time and how this has helped change attitudes towards intellectually disabled people.

Tony says that current work by intellectually disabled performers is very important.

Current work by intellectually disabled performers is allowing intellectually disabled people themselves to play an important role in how they are seen in society, as well as showing interesting new styles of performance.

Amanda Cachia is a curator and researcher who lives in the US.

Amanda writes about her group exhibition, *Sweet Gongs Vibrating*, at the San Diego Art Institute in the US in 2016.

In the exhibition, Amanda wanted viewers to experience the artworks through touch, and through hearing, not just through their eyes, the way they normally would in a gallery.

Amanda thought this was important to allow a more diverse group of people to enjoy visiting an exhibition in an art gallery, including blind people.

The difficulty was that the art gallery was worried that people touching the art, and even swinging on some of the art, would break the art.

The gallery put up signs asking that people not touch the art.

Plain language summary

This experience allowed Amanda to think about some rules and principles she could use in future exhibitions to balance the needs of those viewers wanting to touch the artwork and the needs of artists and art galleries worried about viewers wanting to touch the artwork.

Ann Millett-Gallant is an artist and researcher from the USA.

Ann writes about the work of a disabled, feminist artist Persimmon Blackbridge.

Ann says Persimmon's art shows a 'crip aesthetics.'

A 'crip aesthetics' is a specific style that can be seen in some artwork.

It is a style that asks the viewer to think about the meaning of the artwork and think about the meaning of images of pain, impairment, disability, and pride in being a disabled person within a community of disabled people they see in the work.

The sculptures, photographs, and other artworks that Persimmon has created use a 'crip aesthetic' to ask the viewer to think about what it is like to be a disabled person in a society that does not include disabled people, people with mental health problems, and other minorities.

Ann M. Fox is also a researcher from the US.

Ann writes about portrait artist Riva Lehrer's paintings of Lennard Davis, a disability researcher from the US, and Carrie Sandahl, a theatre researcher, teacher, and artist from the US.

Ann says Riva's paintings are interesting, because her pictures include symbols that ask the viewer to think about Lennard and Carrie's expertise in their jobs, as well as symbols that ask the viewer to think about Lennard and Carrie's relationship to disability.

Though it was a risk for Lennard and Carrie to let Riva paint them, Ann thinks the paintings provide a very good picture of what it is like to be a person with a disability.

The paintings make it clear that we can present disabled people in a positive way, showing that the person has done many important and memorable things in their life and that the person can be remembered both for their disability and for their broader life.

Part IV: Practices, politics, and the public sphere

In the fourth part of the book, Bree and Donna ask writers to talk about their own arts practices. Most of the writers choose to do this in a conversational, collaborative, or creative way.

Brian Lobel is an artist and researcher living in England. **Jess Thom** is an artist living in England.

Brian and Jess share a record of a conversation they had about Jess's experience of taking her show *Backstage in Biscuit Land* to the Edinburgh Fringe Festival in 2014.

Jess is a person with Tourette syndrome. People with Tourette syndrome make noises, gestures, and movements – including sometimes rude noises – without wanting to do this. These are called 'tics,' and they are not something the person has a choice about doing or not doing.

In the past, Jess has been told she cannot come to the theatre or that she cannot sit with the main audience to watch a performance in the theatre, because her 'tics' could be annoying to other members of the audiences.

In the *Backstage in Biscuit Land* show, Jess talked about these experiences of being excluded.

Though it was difficult for Jess to take her show to The Edinburgh Fringe Festival, it taught everyone a lot about how disabled people could be better included in the festival in the future.

Sarah Austin, Kath Duncan, Gerard Goggin, Lachlan MacDowall, Veronica Pardo, and Eddie Paterson are artists and researchers from Australia.

Sarah, Kath, Gerard, Lachlan, Veronica, and Eddie have read an article which says that disability theatre is a 'last avant garde.' This article says disabled theatre makers are the last group of people producing experimental new styles of theatre performance that we still know very little about, because we now know quite a lot about how women, queer people, people of colour, and other groups make experimental theatre performances about their own lived experiences.

They are working on a research project which asks disabled theatre makers in Australia to share some of their experiments in producing interesting new styles of performances.

They write about some recent shows by the Quippings performance troupe and the Rawcus theatre company in Australia.

They explain how the disabled theatre makers producing these shows have experimented with new styles to present a more positive story of what it is like to be a disabled person.

Sarah, Kath, Gerard, Lachlan, Veronica, and Eddie find that these theatre makers are doing excellent experimental shows, but that their ability to continue making excellent experimental shows is increased when they have better funding to help make the shows.

Jori de Coster is an anthropologist from Belgium. This means Jori studies the way people live their lives.

In this book, Jori writes about Danielle, a Belgian Congolese woman who has low vision.

Jori met Danielle during her research into how disabled people perform their own identity in spaces, places, and cities that are not inclusive of disabled people.

Jori uses a lot of Danielle's words to describe the struggles Danielle feels in trying to fit in and find a place for herself in Belgian society. This includes struggles with her husband, children, and family relationships, struggles with disability service providers to get the support she needs to live her life, and struggles with spaces and places not set up for people with low vision.

Having spent a lot of time with Danielle over the past few years, Jori has learnt a lot about Danielle's struggles to feel like she fits in in society.

Jori thinks sharing Danielle's lived experience can help us all better understand the way people like Danielle work to make a place for themselves in society.

Petra Kuppers is an artist and researcher who lives in the US.

For Petra, storytelling is a tool that artists, activists, and disabled people in the community can use to help readers understand their experience living in a society that excludes them and the things that could be done to create a different and more inclusive society.

Petra shares the first part of a science fiction story. In the story she imagines a different society, where disabled people have different struggles, sources of support, and relationships. The story is set in a future where new technology – like spaceships and space travel – is part of the characters' world.

Petra shares only the first part of the story.

This is because Petra wants the reader to think about where the story could go next and about what a society that is more inclusive of disabled people could look like.

Bronwyn Preece is a performance maker and researcher from Canada.

Bronwyn is interested in the environmental movement, which encourages people to think about their relationship to the natural world and their relationship to each other in the natural world.

Bronwyn writes about how her environmental ideas connect with her identity as a disabled person, a performance maker, and an environmental activist.

Bronwyn's writing blends philosophical language and performance language.

This helps the reader learn about some of Bronwyn's ideas, how Bronwyn talks about these ideas, and how Bronwyn creates new relationships between herself, her body, and the environment around her in her performances.

Plain language summary

Part V: Activism, adaptation, and alternative futures

In the fifth part of the book, Bree and Donna ask writers to talk about the way disabled people adapt arts practices and argue for their inclusion in arts practices, to try to make sure that more disabled people can participate in the arts in the future.

Katie Ellis is a researcher from Australia.

Katie writes about the history of toys. Katie says toys – and in particular, dolls – have been popular for more than a century. Until recently, though, the toys that companies manufacture for children have not usually included dolls with disabilities.

Katie talks about how disability activists have called for companies to create a #toylikeme for disabled children.

Katie talks about parents who have adapted toys and dolls so that their own children with disabilities, and other children with disabilities, can have a toy like themselves to play with.

Katie also talks about companies who have produced toys and dolls with disabilities.

Katie says the companies sometimes get it wrong, creating toys with disabilities, or descriptions of toys with disabilities, that people find offensive.

Alex Lubet is a researcher from the US.

Alex was one of the first people to write about disability, music, and musicians.

Alex writes about how musical instruments can be adapted so that people with disabilities can play them.

Alex says there are two ways to adapt musical instruments for people with disabilities. The first way is changing the technique used to play the instrument, or creating tools that can be used to play the instrument, so it is possible for people with, for example, only one hand to play. The second is to change the instrument itself.

Alex says that when medical professionals change the instrument, or the way we play the instrument, the solutions they come up with can often be so expensive that disabled people cannot afford them.

Alex then talks about some examples of disabled musicians who changed their instrument or the way they play their instrument on their own, at much less cost.

Alex thinks it is important to consider things like cost when we talk about changing musical instruments to make it possible for disabled people to play them. If we do not think about the cost, we will end up with instruments that very few disabled people can afford, so this will not really help more disabled people play musical instruments.

Sarah Whatley is a researcher from England.

Sarah writes about dance training for people with disabilities.

Sarah says that there have been some projects in schools and in the dance industry to try to make dance training more inclusive of people with disabilities.

While this is good, Sarah does not think this has really changed things. People with disabilities still find it difficult to become dancers through traditional dance training programmes.

Sarah shares the thoughts of some professional disabled dancers in England. Sarah finds that these dancers have had to come up with their own approaches to training and developing a career in dance in order to succeed. These dancers have become accidental leaders in the dance field. They did not start thinking they would be a leader, inventing a new way to train and work in dance, but they had to do this to succeed in their career.

Sarah thinks this is both good and bad. This is good, because these dancers have led the way, and showed the industry that disabled people can have careers in dance. But this is also bad, because it takes a lot of time, and energy, and effort to create a career in dance without the support of dance schools, dance companies, and a dance industry ready to accept a disabled dancer.

Akhila Vimal C. is a dancer and researcher from India.

Akhila says classical dance in India is based on rules set out in a book called the *Nāṭyaśāstra*.

These rules are all about how to present a beautiful body, doing beautiful movements, which the audience will enjoy. These rules do not allow for the possibility of disabled dancers.

Akhila talks about dancer Sudha Chandran and choreographer Syed Sallauddin Pasha and his company Ability Unlimited and their attempts to show that disabled people can do classical Indian dance.

Akhila says the work of these dancers is celebrated in India.

For Akhila, though, the work of these dancers always seems to be about how disabled people can overcome their disability, and do classical dance movements just as well as non-disabled dancers. This is disappointing for Akhila. Akhila thinks it would be better if disabled people were allowed to develop their own new styles of dancing, and be celebrated for those new styles of dancing.

Bree Hadley is a researcher from Australia.

Bree writes about the way disabled artists are reacting to cuts in the amount of money available for disability support services in a lot of countries around the world.

Bree says disabled people have started to use their arts practices to help them draw attention to their protests against the government funding cuts.

Bree says disabled people have also started to create performances to draw the audience's attention to the way the government funding cuts are hurting them in their day-to-day lives.

Bree thinks it is interesting that these performances concentrate on how difficult it is to be a disabled person. In the last 20 years, disabled performance makers have concentrated on the positive parts of being a disabled person, and the positive part disabled people can play in creating new styles of performance. They have concentrated on ability, not on disability.

Bree is not sure how spectators and society at large will respond to this return to negative stories about what it is like to be a disabled person.

Conclusion

In the **Conclusion**, Bree Hadley, Donna McDonald, and some of the other writers who have shared their ideas in this book talk about their study of disability arts, culture, and media practices.

The writers say that studying disability arts, culture, and media practice is difficult.

In the past, books about disability were mainly written by people who did not have lived experience of disability, in words that were difficult for a lot of disabled people to understand.

In the present, this is changing. But writing a book about disability arts, culture, and media practice still means asking disabled artists to share a lot of information about what it is like to be disabled. This can be difficult. Even with interpreters, captioners, audio description, and other communication supports, it can be hard for disabled artists to explain their work, and explain why they do their work, in words that non-disabled readers will understand. This can also be upsetting. Even if the researcher and the reader are sympathetic, it can be hard for disabled artists to talk about the difficult, challenging, and frustrating parts of being a disabled artist.

Plain language summary

In the Conclusion to this book, the writers suggest that artists and researchers, disabled people and non-disabled people, need to find new ways to work together to study disability arts, culture, and media practice and support each other in dealing with these difficulties.

Each of the writers shares their own ideas about what research into disability arts, culture, and media practice should look like, what it should achieve, and how it can help make sure disabled people are fully included in society in the future.

Index

3D printing 209

Abbott, David 286
Ability Unlimited 15, 341–3; and dance pedagogy 343–5
'able-disabled' people 348, 350, 357, 364
ableism: and dance 120, 328; and ethnomusicology 311; and everyday life 76, 116, 298–9, 363, 368; internalised 255, 257; and psychiatry 222; and the arts 232, 235–6; and theatre 21, 29; and sport 74, 80; and war exhibition 56–58
able-bodied people: and dance 116, 120, 338–40, 342–4; and everyday life 76, 219, 284; and sport 9, 75, 77, 80–83; and the arts 110; and war exhibition 56–57
"ablenationalism" 194
Abnormally Funny People 243
abuse: of disabled people 16, 170, 221, 343; of the self 221; against women 141
accessibility: and cultural spaces 54, 102–3, 129, 227; and dance 118, 329; and everyday life 81, 284; and the Fringe Festival 243–6; and sport 74, 82; of the theatre 22–3, 29–31; and toy design 303; and Yosemite National Park 130–4
access aesthetics 22, 31–2
Accessibility for Ontarians with a Disability Act 82
Accessing the Future: A Disability-Themed Anthology of Speculative Fiction (Al-Ayad and Allan) 280
activism: dementia-related 149; in disability arts 123, 227, 263, 286, 353–6, 358; in theatre 191; and intellectual disabilities 194; and exhibition 203–4, 209; and children's toys 300
actors with intellectual disabilities: and Back to Back Theatre 190; and contemporary theatre 189–90; and Mind the Gap Theatre 190; support for 193; and Theater HORA 190
Adams, Rachel 2
ADAPT 278
ADAPT in Space 278–80

adaptation: of children's toys 298, 300, 306; of cultural institutions 127, 351; of dance 118, 326, 331; of disability arts 109, 347, 351, 358, 362, 369; of musical instruments 310–320, 355; of musical performance techniques 314–320; of technology 270
adaptive music: described 313–4; disability studies and 310–20; DIY (do it yourself) 314; instruments in non-clinical settings 316; introduction 310; *see also* music
Adorno, Theodor 177, 179
advertising: of arts events 243, 248; of art therapy 107; of children's toys 298, 303, 305–6; of disabled artists 243, 248, 345; mimicry of 357; of Paralympic Games 74, 79–80; of theatre 23, 28, 156, 158, 257
advocacy: of disability arts 108, 111, 244, 316–7, 326, 329; in disability studies 1; for people with dementia 152; tools of 255
aesthetic distance 180, 290
aesthetics: access 22, 31–2; of authenticity and presence 170–2; of blindess 44; crip 218–226, 369, 379; dance 120; "disability aesthetics" 40, 42, 110, 251–2, 259, 260–1, 288; *Disability Aesthetics* 37, 40, 218, 220; haptic 216; of identification 169–70; models 253–4; of no difference 164–6; performance 198, 338; political 260; post-dramatic 173–4; postmodern 11; protest 350; of resistance 260; of radical difference 167–9; traditional 109; of universal humanity 164–6; of watching learning disabled theatre 164; of visual arts 36
affect: in theatre performance 166, 171–2, 191, 197, 199; in exhibition 203; and reading narrative 36, 70
"Age is Just a Number, Init? Interrogating Perceptions of Age and Women within Social Gerontology" (Hogan) 144
ageing 301, 144, 148–51
age of austerity: and changing forms of protest 350–2; and disability 347–9; and disability arts 349–50; protest in 352–6; representation in 352–6; self-representation in 352–6

385

Index

agency, for disabled people: in dance 123, 325, 328, 337, 341, 343–4, 346; in determining care arrangements 348; in disability research 365, 367; in museums 49, 213; in narrative characters 62, 122; and the body 141, 287, 291; in theatre 156, 168–9, 171–2, 190, 193, 195–6, 199, 239; in visual art 232, 237; in activism 286; and adaptive music 313

Aladdin 94–7

Alaimo, Stacy 286

Al-Ayad, Djibril 280

Albert, Lyle Victor 26

Alice in Wonderland 40, 93, 98

Alien: Resurrection 279

Allan, Kathryn 280

Allen, Rick 316–7

Alliance for Inclusion in the Arts in the U.S. 23

allies of disabled people: 9, 17, 219, 252, 256, 352–3, 364–5, 369–70

All Our Kin (Stack) 267

"All you have to do is call and I'll be there" (Taylor) 232

Althusser, Louis 137–8

Alzheimer's Disease 149–51

Alzheimer's Disease: Coping with a Living Death (Woods) 151

Americans with Disabilities Act (ADA) 130–1, 303

American Theatre 25

Amici Dance Theatre 115

amputee(s): and children's toys 276, 301, 314–6, 329, 331; in theatre 166; and veterans 55

Angels in America (Kushner) 239

Another Way to Play 317

anthropocentrism: and the environment 281, 290; and puppetry 157

Anzaldua, Gloria 219

Aramandi 338

architecture, accessible: of cultural heritage sites 125, 130, 133–4; of museums 50–6, 58; of public buildings 350–1, 377; of theatre venues 21–2, 31–2; and Universal Design 102–3, 132, 351–2

Architectural Barriers Act 130

Aristotle 192

Armstrong, John 36

art(s): community *see* community arts; digital 8; disability-informed standards of 110; for diversion, recreation or product sales 107; education 40; funding 104; and health 10, 36–7; inclusive 6; live 152, 154–7, 199, 204, 248, 255–6, 259, 356; media 9, 121–2, 152, 158, 169, 173, 203, 218, 224–5; participatory 102, 144, 280; overcoming personal challenges in 107; painting(s) 37–46, 51, 53, 56, 100, 108, 110, 223–4, 227–8, 233, 235–6, 238–9; performance 8, 14, 26–7, 37, 218, 227, 324, 345, 356, 100, 107–8, 113,

257, 262, 271–2, 293; puppetry 153, 155–8; in Singapore 100–11; suitable for broader political and social goals 110–1; subversive 8; as 'therapy in a different form' 107

artefact(s) 48–55, 58–9, 234, 237, 297–8

art history 36–40, 43, 45, 67, 167, 216, 228, 251

Art, Museums, and Touch (Candlin) 214

Art and Dementia programme 54

'art as a service': 9–10; consequences of 107; paradigm 100–11

artists: biography of 39–40; non-disabled 108; work of 39–40

The Art of Being Deaf 36

Arts Access Aotearoa, New Zealand 115

The Arts and Disabilities: A Creative Response to Social Handicap (Lord) 102

arts and disability 6, 9, 254, 371; in Singapore 100–11; accessible infrastructure 102–3; art as 'therapy in a different form' 107; arts funding policy 104–5; central planning and voluntary sector implementation 105–6; consequences of 'art as a service' 107; creation of disability identity and culture and 109; crystallisation of an 'arts and disability' field 104; disability agenda by non-disabled artists 108; disability-informed standards of beauty and art 110; for diversion, recreation or product sales 107; downplaying disability as irrelevant and de-politicised 108–9; emergence of 102–9; expressive, aesthetic, and emancipatory potential of 109–11; inclusive programming 103; normalising disabled artists 108–9; structural reasons for the instrumentalisation of 104; suitable for broader political and social goals 110–11; VWOs and 106–7

arts funding policy 104–5

Art Therapists' Association of Singapore (ATAS) 106–7

art therapy: 4, 10, 100–2, 107; gender representation in 137–45; identity in 137–45; power in 137–45

Art Therapy: An Introduction (Rubin) 4

artworks: across history 40–5; time and place and 40–5

ASD 89, 91–3, 96–8

Asperger syndrome 89, 96–9, 304

asylum: for people with intellectual disabilities 192; theater within 192

athlete(s)

Atkinson, Rebecca 297–8, 300

Atomic Man 301, 306

Attenborough, David 289

audience, inclusive 92–3

audio description 32–33, 227, 382

Auslander, Philip 3, 22, 341

austerity: and disability 347–9; and disability arts 349–50

Austin, J.L. 200
Austin, Sarah 379–80
author(s) 36, 62–3, 71, 183, 220–2, 230, 252, 263, 272, 280, 311, 358, 368–370
Authoring Autism (Yergeau) 194
authorised touch 212–3
autistic spectrum disorders (ASD) 33, 58, 89, 91–3, 96–8, 104, 194–5, 197–8, 272, 304, 311, 376
autonomy *see* independence
avant garde *see Disability and the Performing Arts in Australia: Beyond the Social Model*
The A Word 183
Axis 115, 331

Baade, Clement 257
Backstage in Biscuit Land 244
Back to Back Theatre 163–4, 168–9, 171, 189–90, 199
Baggs, Amanda 220
Bakan, Michael 311
Baker, Cooper 204, 207
Baldwin, Neil 183
Barbie: "Liminal Barbie" 224–5; and Monster High dolls 304; and 'Share a Smile Becky' 303, 305–6; 'wheelchair Barbie' 303
Barnaby Rudge (Dickens) 63
Barrier Man (Williamson) 350
barriers: in the theatre 22, 30–2, 53, 344, 351, 364; in society 82, 91, 107, 109, 114–6, 259–61, 311, 354, 369, 374; to capital 127, 254; natural barriers 130; and the Architectural Barriers Act 130; to arts and education 254; for dancers 324, *see also* discrimination
Barthes, Roland 297
Batch, Morgan 377
Bateson, Gregory 291
Bealer, Adele H. 288
beauty: and aesthetics 220; and crips 255; and dance 336, 343; and disability 40, 42; and disability arts 366; disability-informed standards of 110; and fragmentation 236
Beauty and the Beast 89–99; autism as a case in point 91–2; devil in the detail 97–8; emergence of RPs 89–91; impact of RPs 95–7; towards an inclusive audience 92–3; vital preparations 93–5
Beckett, Samuel 244
The Beestings: Rethinking Breast-Feeding Practices, Maternity Rituals, and Maternal Attachment in Britain and Ireland (Hogan) 143
The Beggars 40
Bel, Jérôme 189, 195–6, 198
Belluso, John 25
Benefits Street 352
Benjamin, Adam 117
Bennett, Jane 281

Bennett, Lucy 120
Berlant, Lauren 351
Beyond Victims and Villains: Contemporary Plays by Disabled Playwrights (Lewis) 24–5
'*Bhagawad Gita* on Wheelchairs' 341
Bharatanatya Kacheri 341
Bharatanatyam 337–41
bias: ableist 29, 78, 165, 194, 204, 237, 284; class 318–9, 215, 237; classical music 317–8; epistemological 193; gender 32, 75, 78, 80, 144, 194, 237, 257, 284, 327; racial 165, 194, 319, 284, 328
The Big Bang Theory 304
binary: and dementia 10; capacity/incapacity 193; in dance 116–7; in theatre 193; ability/disability 194; disabled/non-disabled 218; and gender 257, 284; performative 287; medical and social models of disability 312
biography: autobiography 26, 183, 232, 345; of an artist 39, 101; of Mat Fraser 28
biosocial model, of sport and disability 77–8
Birds of Paradise 349
The Birth of Venus 224
Blackbridge, Persimmon: background 218; "Queering the Crip or Cripping the Queer?: Intersections of Queer and Crip Identities in Solo Autobiographical Performances" 218–20; work of 220–5
Blackman, Barbara 45
Blackman, Charles 43–5
Black Triangle Anti-Defamation Campaign in Defence of Disabled Claimants 350
blindness: and visually impaired people 13, 23, 32, 44, 54, 58, 165, 203–4, 215, 267–8, 270–1, 301, 364–5; later in life 127; and *The Parable of the Blind Leading the Blind* 40–1; and Barbara Patterson 43–4; and Barbara Blackman 45; from war 53; and Canadian National Institute for the Blind 56; and *Marking Blind* 207; and Three Blind Mice Talking Toy 300; and Dritarashtra 337; and museum design 56, *see also* Braille
The Blockheads 355
Blue Eyed Soul 330
Bodies in Commotion: Disability and Performance (Sandahl and Auslander) 3, 22, 341
bodily narratives of sporting impairment 78–82
body: ageing 149; of children's toys 302; corporeal 22, 75, 218, 225; and crip aesthetics 225, 369; and dance 115–8, 259, 323, 326–33, 336–8, 340–45; disabled 65, 76–8, 82, 102, 229, 235–6, 248, 256, 265, 282–8, 291, 314; and exhibition 203–5; embodiment 82, 116–7, 121–2, 190, 227–31, 233–9, 279; and the environment 228; female 141, 256; Gothic 71; homosexual 219; maternal 143; medical 325; modification 313; and performance

387

Index

152–3, 156, 198, 258; and spirituality 273–4; sporting 75–7, 80–81; and theatre 172; in visual art 220–28
Bodin, Kerri 375–6
Bogdan, Robert 2
bonding 105, 111, 128, 133
Boss of the Pool (Klein) 69
Botticelli, Sandro 224
Bottoms, Stephen 291
Bourdieu, Pierre 126, 128
Bowditch, Caroline 326
Bowering, Jeff 151
Bowker, Peter 178
Bradsworth, Hannah 257
Braille 54, 102, 127, 211, 265–6, 270–71
Brantley, Ben 28
Breast Cancer Radiation Mask (McPeake) 206
Brecht, Berthold 24
Brecht, Stefan 197
Brew, Marc 119
British Council (BC) 104
Broke Her 78 Records (McPeake) 206
Brother Rick Curry 25
brown, adrienne maree 280
Brown, Jax Jacki 251
Brücker, Mathias 196
Büchner, Georg 24
Building and Construction Authority (BCA), Singapore 102–3
Bulmer, Alex 30–1
Bunton, Chris 253
Buried Child (Shepard) 24
Butler, Judith 219
Butler, Octavia 280
Buxton, Michael 257

cabaret 252, 255, 257
Cachia, Amanda 378–9
Callicott, J. Baird 283
Calvert, Dave 163, 198, 378
Cameron, David 350
Camic, Paul 4
Campbell, Lucy 165–6
Canada's Vancouver Adapted Music Society 317
Canadian Broadcasting Company (CBC) 81
Canadian National Institute for the Blind (CNIB) 56
Canadian Theatre Review 26
Canadian War Museum (CWM) 52–3; forgetting at the 54–5; silencing at the 55–6
cancer 247
Candlin, Fiona 212–5
Candoco 115, 331
canon: disability studies 312; dramatic 25, 239; of Indian classical dance 336–7, 340; monsters of the 304; musical score 319; painting 224; portraiture 228; representational 363, 369

capacity: for coherent speech 150; of disabled people 79, 117, 123, 144, 184, 197, 246; mental incapacity 180–2, 192–3, 197; for movement 116, 326, 333; of people with autism 90
capital: cultural 126, 128, 257; human 126–8; inclusive 10, 125–9, 133, 135; non-economic 126, 134; technical 126
capitalism 347, 350–2, 355
care: act and acting of 199–200; conclusion in a novel 71; giving 237; givers 33, 69, 91, 94, 103, 139, 142, 151–8; by mothers 68; and museums 48, 50, 55–9; of self 348–9, 355; settings 65, 67, 91, 102, 151–8, 170, 186–9, 191–3, 349
Careers: in dance 323–6, 330–33, 337–8, 340, 345, 381; in music 311, 317; in performance 246–7, 331, 370, *see also* employment
Carlson, Licia 167, 176–7
Carr, Liz 244
Carroll, Jerome 174
casting, and disability theatre 27–9
Cattanach, Ann 4
Cavendish, Dominic 27–8
Center for Digital Storytelling (CDS) 122
Centre for Rehabilitation and Music 313, 316, 319
Chandran, Sudha 15, 337–41
Chappell, Catherine 117–18, 121
character(s): arc 192, 279–80; with autism 171, 183, 304; in dance 122, 157; deaf 365; with dementia 150–58; with Down Syndrome 62–72; in dramatic literature 239; with epilepsy 21; evil 306; in opera 311; in theatre 93–6, 171–4, 181–5, 254, 305, 351–3, 22–5, 28–30; in television 27, 98; transmedia 301
charity: cases 5, 8, 39; groups 9; model of theatre 189; model of disability 192, 298, 306; profits donated to 302, 305
Cheesman, Sue 376
Chemers, Michael 2
childbirth 143–4, 154
childhood: 138, 139, 220, 229
children: who are actors 171; art classes for 233; with autism 89–99, 104; and dance 327, 330; of Deaf adults 230, 321, 232; with Down Syndrome 62–72; and parent relationships 6, 62–72, 153–4, 157, 268; of people with dementia 154, 158; and poverty 264, 270, 271; raising 265–77; with special needs 103, 106; separated from their mothers 139; therapy for 140, 142; toys for 297–305; young 102–3, 210
children's toys: changing representations of disability in 297–306; cultural function of 297
children with autism, access to the theatre for 89–99
choreography, *see* dance
Christina's World (Wyeth) 40, 41–3

chronic: deterioration 149; illness 219, 285, 312, 323; infection 329; pain 249
Chute, Hillary 230
Circle Stories (Lehrer) 227–9
citizenship: "absent citizen" 49; disability 58, 228, 288, 349, 357; full 76; good 192; protest movement 355; useful 348, 357
Claiming Disability (Linton) 312
Clare, Eli 227, 285
Clark, Christopher 289
classical music *see* music
'Classical' Indian dance: Chandran, Sudha 337–41; overview 336–8
Clements, Bill 315, 317
Clift, Stephen 4
climate: of activism 355; austerity 349–50, 354, 356–7; of crisis 281, 289; economic 349; industry 13, 261; political 82, 355; production 5
Close, Chuck 39
Cloudstreet (Winton) 68–9
cognitive: decline 10, 150, 153; dissonance 169; impairment 24, 103, 168, 180, 183, 186, 190, 195–7, 279, 323, 327; justice 137; power 150; skills 107
Colborne, Jez 11, 166, 178
Coleridge, Samuel Taylor 232
Collette, Morwenna 251
comedy 26–7, 169, 243, 249, 255–7, 356
Coming Down the Mountain (Haddon) 69
"coming out" 108, 219, 221–3, 368
"Coming Out Crazy" (Blackbridge and Gilhooly) 221–2
Common Ground Stopgap 115
communication: through art 110; and ASL 135; and autistic spectrum disorders 91–2; and dance 115, 118, 345; difficulties and impairments 223, 279, 150; through technology 134–5, 269, 382; scholarship 299; skills 101, 107; spaces 192, 198, 268
community arts: and 'art-as-service' paradigm 100–7, 111; dance programmes 114–23; performance artist 37; theatre 26, 163, 190, 196
Compagnie de l'Oiseau Mouche 189
complexity, and disability arts research 364–7
concentre values 299
Concerto for the Left Hand: Disability and the Defamiliar Body (Davidson) 3
consent 130, 152, 238, 278, 368
contact improvisation (CI) 326
Contained 173
contemporary theatre: and actors with intellectual disabilities 189–90; for people with intellectual disabilities 192
"convergence culture" 304
Cook, Fiona 251
co-option 5, 6, 350
Corn Exchange Newbury (CEN) 89

corporeal, *see* body
coup de théâtre 200
Courier 132
Cowie, Elizabeth 137
crafts: for diversion 107; for recreation or product sales 107
Craven, Sir Philip 80
creative: adaptions of music artists 250; autonomy 195, 203; collaboration 259, 355, 357; leaders 253; methods and processes 14, 17, 32–3, 100, 103, 114, 117, 122, 176, 195, 365–6; research 17, 367–9; self-determination 254; solutions 135, 250; thinking 7, 10–13, 82, 104, 115, 172, 252, 282, 305, 315, 328–9, 351, 356, 362–3, 370–71; wilderness 281; writing 8, 279
Creatrix Tiara 255–6
crip: activist 369; community 238; described 218; drag 5; and everyday life 363; Kafer on 219; McRuer on 219; time 196; feminist 219; futurity 228; relationships 239; performance space 225; queer 194, 218–9, 368; Sandahl on 219; sport 364; 'supercrips' 74, 79, 82, 311, 352
'Crip Aesthetics' 12, 218–26, 369
"cripistemologies" 190–91
Crippen 349–50, 356–7
crippled/s 24, 38, 41, 218, 229, 238, 277, 374
"crippled metaphors" 25
Cripple of Inishmaan (McDonagh) 24
The Cripples 40
"cripping up" 28, 29
Crip Theory: Cultural Signs of Queerness and Disability (McRuer) 219
crisis: economic 219, 347–8; ecological 282–3, 285, 289; equating with disability 282, 356, *see also* climate
criticism: arts 40, 102, 342; dance 342–3; theatre 28, 32–3, 154
critical spectatorship 178–80
Crossing Boundaries (Gibbs) 211
"Crossing the Line" 189
Crow, Liz 354
"cruel optimism" 351–2
Crutchfield, Susan 3
cultural capital 126–7
cultural hegemony 298–9
culture 1–7, 263
culture: ableist 76; Aboriginal 50; arts 101–5, 249, 347, 349–50, 352, 357, 362–3; "convergence culture" 304; Deaf 109; disability 23, 26, 37, 109, 116–7, 123, 164, 228, 257, 278–9, 282, 286, 337, 343, 345, 350–51, 358, 362–3; high 342; of inclusion 57; Indian 336, 341, 345; mass and popular 82, 109, 141, 219, 233, 250, 260, 263, 284, 297–8, 299–306; material 48, 50–52, 59, 272; medical 306; mono 285, 286; sport 77;

389

Index

theatre 90; visual 204, 218, 220, 225, 336; and
    women 141; *see also* accessibility *and* access
    aesthetics
Cunningham, Claire 330
curation 12, 39, 42, 44, 48, 50, 59, 102–3, 204,
    207, 211, 214–7, 220, 312; *see also* exhibition
curative violence 192
The Curious Incident of the Dog in the Night-Time
    (Haddon) 22, 27
Current Biology 289
Curtis, Jess 330
cyborg(s) 301, 302, 306, 219

D/deaf artists 30–2, 110, 215, 254–5, 261, 337,
    341–2
D/deaf arts 253
D/deafness 23, 32, 36, 75, 100, 101, 103, 108,
    127, 132–5, 204–5, 230, 232, 252, 259,
    305, 311, 354–5, 364–7 *see also* Yosemite
    National Park
Dacre, Kathy 30
The Daily Compulsion 354
Daily Telegraph 27
The Daily Token 357
DanceAbility International 115
dance: activist movement 118; ballet 115, 326;
    Bharatanatyam: 15, 337–44; burlesque 255–6;
    choreography 121, 323, 332, 342, 344–5;
    classical Indian 336–46; community 118–20;
    contemporary 115, 326, 328; creative cultures
    in 371; education 104, 117–8; integrated/
    inclusive 114–23, 176, 197; mainstream 117;
    popular music and 318; and storytelling 257,
    259; theatre 155; therapy 101
dance pedagogy, and Ability Unlimited 343–5
dancers with disabilities: access to training
    326–7; choosing dance as career 325–6;
    independence *vs.* autonomy 328–32; labels
    327–8; overview 323–5
Dancing Colours 121
Dancing Wheels 115
Dandeker, Celeste 331
Darcy's Utopia (Weldon) 66
Dark Horse 173
Darth Vader 306
Darwin, Charles 143
Davidson, Michael 3
Davies, Telory 197
Davis, Lennard 230–2, 365
Deaf West Theatre 32
Dear Evan Hansen (Pasek, Paul and Levenson) 24
death 67–71, 149–51, 156, 286–7, 353, 356–7
death ending in the Down Syndrome novel
    67–71
Death of a Salesman (Loman) 153
Death with Dignity Movement 150
debility 194

de Botton, Alain 36
December 12th (Sexton) 64
de Coster, Jori 363, 380
Dee dee NiHera 222
DeFelice, Robert 218
Def Leppard 316
de Groot, Raphaëlle 207–9
dehumanisation 149, 157–8
Deleuze, Gilles 48, 176–7, 274
dementia: challenge of reframing 158;
    dimensions of 148–50; as drama 152–8;
    narrativised as metaphor, stereotype, and
    'other' 150–2
Derbyshire, Jan 26
design, accessible, *see* architecture
d'Evie, Fayen 203
Devlin, Harriet 257
D-Generation: An Exaltation of Larks 155–8
diagnosis: general 181, 239; of Down Syndrome
    62–7, 70–71; of dementia 149, 153; of
    intellectual disabilities 198
*Diagnostic and Statistical Manual of Mental
    Disorders* 91
dialectic of vulnerability 185–6
dialectics and learning disability 180–3
"dialogics of difference" 368
dialogue: 12–14, 57, 108, 123, 140, 191, 216,
    252, 274, 367–71
Dickens, Charles 63
difference: aesthetics of no 164–6; bodily 6, 10,
    30, 76, 109, 225–6, 235, 251, 256, 329; class
    214; cognitive 91, 219, 327; in dance 114–5,
    117, 120, 122; dialogics of 368; linguistic 109;
    and otherness 324–5, 327, 333; radical 167–9;
    stigmatising 44
*Digital Disability: The Social Construction of
    Disability In New Media* (Goggin and Newell) 3
digital storytelling 121–4
dignity 39, 106, 111, 150, 229, 245
directors 23, 27, 31–3, 93, 117, 120–21, 131–2,
    134, 164–8, 172–3, 190–2, 195–9, 202, 244,
    252–8, 302, 324, 330, 349
Dirt: The Ecstatic Skin of the Earth (Logan) 287
disabilities: intellectual 23, 62–4, 70–71, 100,
    107, 176–7, 181–3, 187–200, 323, 327;
    learning 90, 116, 163–174, 176–84, 185–7,
    193–4, 196–8, 222–5, 248, 257, 368; physical
    58, 127, 194, 317, 323, 327, 343–4; sensory
    103, 134, 219, 323, 327
disability: adaptations of instrumental technique
    314–5; in an age of austerity 347–9; athletes
    with a 74–83; community 76–83, 100,
    108–9, 114, 237, 301–6, 311; culture 109, 116,
    123, 257, 278–9, 286, 337, 343–5, 350–1,
    365–6; as day-to-day lived experience 363–4;
    deepening understanding of disability images
    over time 43–5; downplaying as irrelevant

and de-politicised 108–9; and ecology 284; hagiography 227; in popular culture 299; medical model of 75–6; as a metaphor for spiritual concerns 40–1; and museums 50–1; representations, in children's toys 297–306; and science fiction 276–80; sentiment *versus* historical reality 41–3; in Singapore 100–11; social interpretation of 285; social model of 76–7; studies 285–8, 297, 299, 306, 310–2, 316, 320, 325, 358; and adaptive music 310–20; studies as performance studies 288

disability art(s): activism 224, 227; in an age of austerity 347–358; and 'art-as-service' paradigm 100–2; in Australia 13; and the avant garde 251–262; community 330; contexts 258–61; and dance 117, 119, 120; and emancipation 109–11; and environment 281–2; and festivals 247, 250; in Singapore 108–9; study of 1–9, 12, 15–17; and theatre 23, 26, 28–29, 31, 164–5, 166

"Disability, Care and Debility: Radically Reframing the Collaboration between Non-Disabled and Learning Disabled Theatre Makers" 198

Disability, Culture, and Identity (Riddell and Watson) 3

Disability, Public Space Performance and Spectatorship: Unconscious Performers (Hadley) 3, 22

Disability Aesthetics (Siebers) 3, 37, 40, 167, 218, 220

disability agenda, and non-disabled artists 108

Disability and Contemporary Performance: Bodies on Edge (Kuppers) 3

disability law 1, 9, 130–32, 134, 138, 150, 180–82, 246, 249, 250, 312, 325

disability-led practice 6, 123

Disability and New Media (Ellis and Kent) 3

Disability and Popular Culture (Ellis) 297

Disability and the Performing Arts in Australia: Beyond the Social Model 251–61; aesthetics models 253–4; disability innovations 253–4; funding 259–60; infrastructure 259–60; practice 259–60; process 259–60; Quippings 252, 254–5; Rawcus 252, 257–8; *Risky Business* 252, 255–7; *Song for a Weary Throat* (Rawcus) 252, 258–9

disability apropos musicians: medical models of 312–13; social models of 312–13

disability art 1–7; and austerity 349–50; expressive, aesthetic, and emancipatory potential of 109–11; supporting creation of disability identity and culture 109; *see also* art(s)

disability arts research: challenge of inclusive 366; and complexity 364–7; interdependent 367–71; shared 367–71; situated 367–71; and uncertainty 364–7; and vulnerability 364–7

Disability Culture and Community Performance: Find a Strange and Twisted Shape (Kuppers) 3

Disability in Art History 37

disability-informed standards of beauty and art 110

disability in museums: dis/ordered assemblages of 48–59; embodied and material case study research 51–2; forgetting at the CWM 54–5; forgetting at the NGA 55; National Gallery of Australia (NGA) 53–4; overview 48–50; power and care in museums 57–9; remembering, forgetting, and silencing in museums 52–3; remembering at CWM 53; silencing at the CWM 55–6; silencing at the NGA 57

disability innovations 253–4

disability sector: central planning and 105–6; voluntary sector implementation and 105–6

disability studies *see* disability

"Disability Studies and Performing Arts Medicine" 310

disability theatre: access aesthetics 31–2; casting 27–9; disability theatre reception 32–4; dramaturgy 24–7; five aesthetics of learning 163–74; overview 21–3; and production 23; reception 32–4; training 29–31

Disability Theatre and Modern Drama: Recasting Modernism 3

disability-themed toys 298; history of 300–3

disabled artists 108–9

The Disabled Body in Contemporary Art (Millett-Gallant) 3, 40

disabled performers 21–9, 100, 121, 163–6, 170–72, 177, 187, 243, 254, 260, 316–7, 319, 323, 337–8, 341–6

Disabled Theater 189, 195–6, 198–9

Disabled Theater (Umathum and Wihstutz) 3

"disablist austerity" 349

discourse: ableist 56–58; against discourse 273; alternative 118; biosocial 78; care 155; on childbirth and motherhood 144, 154; critical discourse analysis 81; on dementia 148–9, 152–3; on disability 116, 170, 191, 195, 286, 312, 345; on disability arts 337–8, 371; dominant public 32, 80, 107, 116, 163, 144, 348; Foucault on 138; generational 153–4, 157–8; government 348; scientific 195, 364

discrimination against disabled people: and the Disability Discrimination Act 58, 298; in everyday life 77, 109–10, 131, 312, 364; medical 144; and design 351; and *The Bureau of Audience Discrimination* 354; and disability arts 356

disease 149, 154, 282, 291, 345

dis-ease 141, 220

divergent: artists and academics 367; neurodivergent 167, 194, 256–7, 259; performers 252, 254–5, 261

391

Index

diverse: audiences 203, 211, 217, 254–5; bodies and performance 116–23, 228, 258, 333; disability experience 363, 369–70; identity 219, 257; services 313

DIY (do it yourself): adaptive music 314; disability instrumental performance apparatus 315–6

Dodd, Jocelyn 3

Dokter, Ditty 4

Dolmage, Jay 350–1

Dostoevsky, Fyodor 21, 23

Down, John Haydon Langdon 191–2

Downii Creations 302

Down Syndrome (DS): arts practitioners with 197, 259; diagnosis 62–7, 70–71; dolls 302–3, 306; novel 62–73

Down Syndrome (DS) novel: conclusion 67–70; diagnosis 64–7; mother trauma narrative 70–2; no story without a syndrome 63; overview 62

drama, dementia as 152–8

dramaturgy 24–7

Dreamcatcher (King) 63, 68

Duncan, Alex 121

Duncan, Kath 255, 260, 379–80

Earlswood Asylum 193

earth 228, 268, 274, 277–8, 282, 284–5, 287, 290–91

eARThist 281

Eckersall, Peter 3

ecology: definition of 282; and disability 284; and environmentalism 282–3

economic: access and inclusion 14, 76, 92, 255, 257; crisis 219, 347–50; development 104–5; stress 313; structures 106, 126, 134, 183, 192–3, 211, 216, 243, 260, 285–6, 299, 301, 311, 317–9, 347, 352, 358–9

Edinburgh Fringe 243–4

education: dance 114–124, 104, 332–3, 324–33, 337–8, 343–5, 349, 367; of deaf people 205, 367, 369; of disabled people 30, 40, 82, 91–98, 102–8, 111, 118–9, 126, 129–30, 135, 182, 193, 195–8, 252–4, 260, 274, 324, 329, 367; drama 22–3, 29–33; institutions 369, 371; museum 51; music 311–2, 317, 319; and self-learning 325–6, 329, 333; in theatre 33; of tactile engagement 216; and teaching 15, 36–7, 40, 45, 69, 95–7, 104, 107, 115–20, 123, 127, 192, 205, 229, 249, 271–2, 274, 318, 323–4, 300, 327–8, 340, 343–4; unlearning 338

Edwards, Kim 62, 63

Edwards, Rachel 257

Eileen's Palette (McPeake) 206

Einstein on the Beach (Wilson) 197

Ellis, Katie 3, 297, 381

emancipation, and people with intellectual disabilities 189, 191, 193–4, 200

embodiment, *see* body

empathy 36, 39, 127, 140, 142, 167, 191, 228, 352

employment 82, 104, 106, 117, 183–4, 223–4, 254, 260, 264–6, 271, 318–9, 325–6, 331–3, 349, 356–7 *see also* career

empowerment 7, 8, 52, 63, 77, 102, 104, 143, 194, 363–4

Encompass education and outreach programme 117–19, 119–20; performance opportunities within 120–2

enfant sauvage 197–8, *see also* autistic spectrum disorders

Enforcing Normalcy (Davis) 230

Enke, A. Finn 230

enmindment 190, 279

Environmental Illness 291

environmentalism, and ecology 282–3

epilepsy 21–4

Epstein, Marcy 3

The Equalities Act 82

equity 9, 74, 83, 194

Erhart, Tanja 329

Ervin, Mike 25, 227

An Essay Concerning Human Understanding (Locke) 182

essentialism: biological 77, 80; reductive 144

ethics: of care 57–8; in film 183; in research 367; and sport 78; in therapy 140; trans-corporeal 291

ethnicity 77, 126, 129, 130

ethnomusicology 311, 320–1

Evans, Ben 324

Evans, Kathy 71

Everybody: An Artifact History of America 300

exhibition 12, 44, 48, 50, 52–4, 57, 111, 127, 203–4, 207–8, 209–17, 222–3

experience: bodily 77–80; lived 6, 15, 36, 62, 65, 77–9, 83, 118, 149, 195, 234, 252, 258–9, 260, 286, 363–4, 366, 369; social 75, 92, 96–8, 218, 358

experimentation 13, 110, 197, 215, 257

exploitation 23, 28, 34, 183–4, 186, 367

Extraordinary Bodies: Figuring Physical Disability in American Culture and Literature 3

The Extras 27

family relationships: 28, 33, 45, 65–7, 69–71, 89–90, 94, 97, 126–8, 151–8, 163–4, 183, 225, 232, 239, 264–8, 271–3, 367

Family Photograph (McPeake) 206–7

The Father 154

Faulkner, William 63–4

feminism: and approaches to art therapy 140–42; critiques 10, 137, 139, 237; movement 219, 220–22, 253; theory 40, 77, 118, 219, 287

Feminist Queer Crip (Kafer) 219
Fences (Wilson) 24
Ferris, Madison 28
festivals 33, 101, 103, 119–21, 156, 189, 243–4, 249–50, 318, 354–6
Figures 354
film 145, 152, 160, 279, 338
Fiske, John 299
Fitzgerald, Maureen 132
"Five Diagnoses" 225
Flanagan, Bob 219
Flesh and Blood 183
Florence, Janice 119
Foal's Bread (Mears) 63
Fornes, Maria Irene 24
Foucault, Michel 137–8
4:48 Psychosis (Kane) 24
Fox, Alice 252, 376
Fox, Ann M. 379
Frankenstein (Shelley) 232
Fraser, Brad 352
Fraser, Mat 26, 244
freakshows 37, 200
Freakery: Cultural Spectacles of the Extraordinary Body 2
Freak Show 2
Freeman, David 26
Freie Republik HORA 195–6
"From the Inside Out" 223
FTH:K 32

Gallant, Ann Millett 3
galleries 8, 12, 37, 44, 51–9, 101, 103, 203–17, 220, 222, 225–7, 229, 233, 350
Galloway, Terry 218
Gardner, Lyn 33
Garland-Thomson, Rosemarie 2–3, 164, 180, 227–8
Garuda Purana 337
gaze, the 38–9, 43, 141, 163, 166, 169, 173, 231, 233, 238, 268, *see also* staring
gender representation, in art therapy 137–45
General Systems Theory 288
genetic polymorphism 285; *see also* mutation
Genova, Lisa 152
Genzlinger, Neil 28
Gervais, Ricky 27
Ghoulia Yelps 303–4
Giant Spectrum (Baker) 204, 207
Gibbs, Anne 211
Gilhooly, Sheila 220–2
The Glass Menagerie 28
Glennie, Evelyn 311
Goffman, Erving 189
Goggin, Gerard 3, 379–80
Goh, Lily 110
Goh, Shawn 376

Goodey, C.F. 181
Gorilla Glue Co. 315
Goulish, Matthew 291
government: agencies 78, 111, 131, 180, 350; funding 106, 255, 257, 356; policy 55, 58, 104–5, 115, 130, 329, 345, 347–8, 352, 355, 358
Graeae Theatre Company 31, 245, 349, 355
Gramsci, Antonio 298–9
Grant, M. Shane 25
Great Hall of the Metropolitan Museum, New York 51
Gregson, Sarah 90
Grehan, Helena 3, 168
Guatarri, Félix 176–7, 179
Gunter, Ben 25
Gutenberg printing press 38
Guttman, Ludwig 75
Guven, Nilgun 257

Ha, Lung 165, 349
Haddon, Mark 69
Hadley, Bree 3, 22, 251–2, 312, 368, 373–4, 382
Halifax Explosion of 1917 55–6
Hal's Pals 302, 306
Hambrook, Colin 352, 356–7
Hanauer, Annie 330
Handbook of Art Therapy (Malchiodi) 4
Handbook of Inquiry in the Arts Therapies (Payne) 4
haptics 209; *see also* touch
haptic activism 203–4
Haraway, Donna 287
Hargrave, Matt 3, 32, 178, 193, 373
Hasbro 298
Hauser, Arnold 39
Häusermann, Julia 189
Have You Been Watching (Dark Horse) 173
Hayhoe, Simon 377
Hayhow, Richard 172, 198
health: diagnosis 181, 224, 265; discipline 40, 45, 149, 239, 366; maintenance 78; memoir 64; mental 137–145, 221–2, 226, 243, 247–9; professionals 155, 310–14; services 102, 104, 106–7, 221–2, 226, 269, 271, 313, 317–8, 320, 347–8; and well-being 101, 126, 138, 178, 243, 355–6; World Health Organisation 82
Hearing Difference: The Third Ear in Experimental, Deaf, and Multicultural Theater (Kochhar-Lindgren) 3
Heavy Load 178–9
Hegel, Georg Friedrich 179
Hellman, Lillian 239
Henderson, Bruce 3, 284
heritage 25, 55, 103, 125–6, 129, 130–31, 135, 232, 272, 280, 319, 341, 359

Index

hero(es), disabled people represented as 49–50, 52, 56, 67–8, 70, 74–5, 78–9, 103, 106, 244, 288
Hickey-Moody, Anna 3, 197
High, Rachel 255, 256
Hijinx Theatre 163, 171
history: art 36–40, 43, 45, 67, 167, 216, 228, 251; cultural 139, 228; of disability 22, 82, 163, 170, 176–7, 180–7, 232, 257, 239, 298, 305; of disability-themed toys 300–3; escaping from 176–8; family 267, 272; of human capital 126–8; local 265; in museums 48, 50–58, 213; national 267; natural 132; personal 68, 232, 312; psychiatric 194; theatre 23–7, 189, 194, 197
Hogan, Susan 4, 377
Holman, Winnie 24
Holocaust 27
Hood, Kate 251, 260
Hoptman, Laura 42
hospital 41, 64, 75, 107, 138, 143–5, 191, 201, 300, 325
housing 104, 134, 227, 243, 250, 264–5, 276, 313–20, 347–8, 351, 356, 364
Houston, Andrew 26
Howe, Blake 311
Howlround 33
"How Ocean Noise Pollution Wreaks Havoc on Marine Life" (Schiffman) 289
How To Do Things With Words 200
Hughes, Nym 222
humanity 41, 158, 164, 166, 228, 232, 268–9, 279–80, 354
Hunter, Kelly 93
Hyper Real exhibition 57

ideology: ableist 299; biosocial 78; cultural 298; medical 76; political 165
identity, in art therapy 137–45
"idiocy": sedimented history of 180–3
The Idiot (Dostoevsky) 21–2, 23
"If It Can't Be Right Then It Must Be Wrong" 355
imagination 45, 93, 96, 115, 152, 224, 258, 272, 278, 319, 345
impairment, *see* disability
impairment narratives 356–8
improvisation 117–21, 197–8, 258, 282, 287, 290–91, 319, 326, 330
inclusion: in the arts 190, 195, 204, 227, 230, 233, 239, 248–9, 259–60, 284, 298, 363, 371; in the arts in Singapore 101–4, 110–11; dance 114–123, 323–333, 337, 344, 352–3; in the Down Syndrome novel 62–72; inclusive capital 126–134; of learning disabled musicians 179; in the museum 51–2, 57–9; in sport 74–83; theatre 21– 3, 29–33; theatre for children with autism 89–99; research methods 366–9
inclusive audience 92–3

inclusive capital 126–7; developing through the Deaf Service at Yosemite 133–4; five stages of developing 127–9
inclusive programming 103
independence: and agency 123, 199; and living 367; and personhood 195, 237; versus autonomy 328; and self-determination 254, 261
Independent Living Fund 349
independent artists 330–1
industry: arts 260–61; dance 325–7, 333; entertainment 345; theatre 31, 89, 246
Ingold, Tim 283
innovation 5, 8, 31, 195, 252, 260
In One Skin (Olsson) 63
"inspiration porn" 316
installation 203, 211, 227, 229, 232, 235, 237–9, 354
institution: barriers 30; educational 369; insitutional care 64–69, 75, 139, 153, 155–6, 189, 190–200, 313, 315, 317, 320, 350; medical 22, 50; psychiatric 220–24; residential 105, 151; social 22, 145, 371
"institutional theatricals" 189
instruments, musical, *see* adaptive musical instruments
instrumentalist, musical 105, 315
instrumentalisation as an arts and culture policy 10, 104, 107
integrated/inclusive dance 114–17
intellectual/learning disabled artist 32, 163–174, 176–187, 193, 198, 257
intellectual/learning disability theatre 163–174, 198–9
InterACT Disability Arts Festival, Auckland 120–1
interdependence 227, 239, 263, 276, 278, 291, 355
interdependent disability arts research 367–71
International Day of Persons With Disability 252
International Olympic Committee's (IOC) *Handbook of Sports Medicine* 76
International Paralympic Committee (IPC) 74
intersectionality 10, 13, 16, 149, 194, 217, 228, 251, 282, 292, 368–9, 371
internships 260, 274
The Iron Lady 152

Jack and the Beanstalk 94
Jackson, Shannon 23, 193
Jacob, Jennifer 132
Jacob, Wendy 205
James' May Toy Stories 297
Jamie's Lighthouse (Rowlands) 352
Japanese Noh *monogurui* plays 24
Jay J. Armes action figure 301–2, 306
Jenkins, Henry 304
Jensen-Moulton, Stephanie 311
Jewel (Lott) 62–3, 64, 69, 70
Johnston, Kirsty 1, 3, 374–5

394

Jones, Lizard 222
Jones, Phil 4
Journal of Child Psychotherapy 142
Joynt, Chase 230
judgement 33, 41, 91, 116, 120, 128, 192, 238
Julian, Anthony 255
Juro, Kara 24
justice: social 111, 122, 135, 166, 244, 279, 370; sense of 128; injustice 135, 166, 184, 364

Kafer, Alison 218, 219
Kahlo, Frida 39
Kanake, Sarah 375
Kane, Sarah 24
Kapuscinski-Evans, Jess 251, 255
Kelly, John 355
Kempe, Andy 376
Kent, Mike 3
Kershaw, Baz 288
Kill Me Now (Fraser) 352
Kim, Eunjung 192
King, Stephen 63, 68
King Lear (Shakespeare) 25, 153
Kirby, Michael 171
Kirkpatrick, Diane 39
"Kiss and Tell" 222
Kitt, Tom 24
Kleege, Georgina 227
Klein, Bonnie Sherr 224, 282
Klein, Robin 69
knowledge 36–40, 42, 44, 49–51, 55, 58–9, 65, 118, 125–8, 137, 145, 179, 181–2, 187, 190–91, 196, 204, 214, 235, 239, 251, 263, 271, 280, 291, 324–5, 330
Knowles, Christopher 197
Kochhar-Lindgren, Kanta 3
Kruger, Barbara 141
Kumar, Gulshan 341
Kunst-und Wunderkammer (Cabinet of Wonders) 38
Kuppers, Petra 3, 4, 22, 25, 115–16, 176, 195, 254, 284, 367, 380
Kushner, Tony 239
Kwok, Joon-Yee 252

Laban Centre 332
labelling of disabled people 58, 108, 156, 172, 225, 288, 327–8
Labine, Greg 26
Lady Aoi (Yukio) 24
Lady Eats Apple 189, 199–200
Lambert, Joe 122
Lapper, Alison 350
Larson, Brandon 282
Larson, Jonathan 24
'the last avant garde', *see Disability and the Performing Arts in Australia: Beyond the Social Model*

leadership 29, 31, 123, 196–7, 253, 305, 323–33, 357, 362, 366–7
'leaners' 348
learning disability, *see* disability
Learning Disability and Contemporary Theatre: Devised Theatre, Physical Theatre, Radical Theatre (Palmer and Hayhow) 198
Lee, Harper 63
Lee, Justin 376
Lego 298, 305
Lehrer, Riva 220; background 227–8; *Circle Stories* 227–8
Le Père (Zeller) 154
Lerner, Neil 311
Levenson, Stephen 24
Lewis, Victoria Ann 24, 25, 30
LGBTQI, *see* queer
life, quality of 153, 312–3; everyday 45, 79, 167, 260, 264, 266–7, 271–2, 282, 331
'lifters' 348
Lilit, Kochava 255, 256
Limerick, Patricia 286
"Liminal Barbie" 224–5
Lincoln, Abraham 131
Linton, Simi 312
Lionetto, Sarah Meisch 376
Lion in the Streets (Thompson) 24
The Lion's Face 155
The Lion King 90
Lipkin, Joan 25
Lippard, Lucy 284
The Little Foxes (Hellman) 239
Living in the Labyrinth: A Personal Journey Through the Maze of Alzheimer's (McGowin) 151
Lobel, Brian 379
"Local Authority Assistance" 349
Locke, John 182
Löffler, Elisabeth 324
Logan, William Bryant 287
Lomnicki, Tekki 227
Long Day's Journey into Night (O'Neill) 239
Long Island-based Coalition for Disabled Musicians 317
Lord, Geoffrey 102
Lorde, Audre 286
The Loss of Self (Cohen & Eisdorfer) 151
Lott, Brett 62–3, 64, 69
Love Poems 64
Lubet, Alex 381
Lupton, Dave 349–50
Lynzaat, Joshua 257

McArdle, John 350
McArthur, Park 227
McCaffrey, Tony 378
McCarthy, Siobhan 26
McDonagh, Martin 24

Index

McDonagh, Patrick 180
McDonald, Donna 251, 365, 373–5
McDowall, Lachlan 379–80
McEvoy, Mike 258
McNamara, Julie 251–2, 255–6
McPeake, Aaron 206–7
McRuer, Robert 218–9
Macpherson, Hannah 252
Macy, Joanna 288
Mahabharata 336–7
Mahadeo, Gem 255
Mainwaring, Sarah 193
Mairs, Nancy 219
Makeham, Paul 252
Makies 305
Making An Entrance: Theory and Practice for Disabled and Non-Disabled Dancers (Benjamin) 117
Malchiodi, Cathy 4
Manchester, Ralph 318
Mann, Jon 36–7, 40–1
Manning, Lynn 25, 26
Marcon, Sonia 255
marginalisation: of disability arts 243, 317; of disabled artists 243, 247, 332, 336; of disabled people 32, 43, 45, 76, 101, 120, 169, 247, 261, 263, 345, 364–5
marketing, *see* advertising
Marranca, Bonnie 288
Marsh, Kate 330–1
Martin, Darrin 209
Marvellous 178, 183; and the dialectic of vulnerability 185–6; and performativity 183–5
Marx, Karl 126, 128
mass culture, *vs.* popular culture 299
Materials and Media in Art Therapy (Moon) 4
Matley, Paul 257
Mattel 298, 303–5
Maxwell, Victoria 26
May, James 297
Mayuri 338
meaning making 18, 48, 299, 328
Mears, Gillian 63
Media: mixed 224–5, 231; multi 169, 203, 218, 368; new 121–2, 227, 304; social 33, 121, 128, 134, 243, 305, 308, 321, 340, 350, 353, 355, 357
Mee Jr. Charles 26
medical: conditions 41, 43; discipline 45, 337; gaze 163; institutions 22, 50, 233, 310; interventions 219; model of disability 44, 53–6, 75–6, 81–2, 102, 107, 116, 126, 298, 305, 312–4 325, 356–7,364; narrative of dementia 148–50, 153, 155; services 133, 316–8, 320; technology 66; understanding of autistic spectrum disorders 91, 195
medicine: sports 76–9; history of 300; performing arts 110, 313, 316, 318–20;

knowledge of 65; practice of 139, 144, 239, 265, 270, 300, 306, 325, 355
media: future of para-sport and 82–3; narratives of sporting impairment 78–82; studies 1–7
"Medical Problems of Nonclassical Musicians" 319
Medical Problems of Performing Artists 310, 313
Medical Problems of Performing Arts (MPPA) 318
Meditation Gong–After Derrick (McPeake) 207
Meet Fred 173
Melendez, Tony 315
Mellis, Gaelle 251
melodrama 24–5, 67
Memmel, Tony 315–16
memoir 36, 39, 64, 151, 224, 365
memory: 23, 45, 49, 51–3, 57–8, 72, 98, 125–6, 148, 153–5, 221, 264, 267, 271, 377
The Memory Keeper's Daughter (Edwards) 62–3, 64–5, 69, 70
mental health: gender representation in 137–45; identity and 137–45; puerperal insanity 143; power and 137–45
mentoring 30, 119
methodology 7, 78, 106, 113, 147, 197–8, 219, 251, 264, 339
Meyyappan, Ramesh 108
Mia 169, 172–3
A Midsummer Night's Dream 93
migration 272, 291
Mike Power 301, 302, 306
Miller, Arthur 153
Millett-Gallant, Ann 379
Mind the Gap Theatre 163, 168–71, 189–90, 199
Mingus, Charles 315
minority group 2, 109, 170, 215, 221, 312, 331
Misener, Laura 375–6
"Mistaken Identity" 225
Mitchell, David 3, 36, 96, 230
mobility: impaired 23, 32, 53–55, 153, 276, 314; physical 50, 128–9, 143, 312–3; virtual 128
Moesby, Aiden 349, 354
Monster High 304
Moomsteatern from Malmö 189
Moon, Catherine Hyland 4
moral: agenda 101; conclusion 68; dilemmas 279; identity 150; knowledge 125, 127–8; values 41, 63, 126, 138, 164, 191–3, 269
Morton, Timothy 284
Mother Courage (Brecht) 24
motherhood 141–5
Mothers Make Contemporary Art (Hogan) 145
mother trauma narrative 70–2
movement: artistic 103, 118, 253, 328; in artwork 204–7; of the body 263, 333, 339–42, 326 351; in dance 116, 119–22, 324; disability rights 76, 114–5, 117, 222, 254, 278, 286; environmental 283; euthanasia 150; in health treatment equipment 329, 102; as integrated

396

knowledge 263; Paralympic 74; punk 179; as signatures of autistic spectrum behavior 197; social justice 122, 194, 219, 279–80, 355–6, 358; vocabulary 332
Mud (Fornes) 24
Multiple-Chemical Sensitivity 291
multisensorial: access 12; art 56, 203, 207, 217; engagement 204, 210, 216
multimedia 12, 169, 203, 218, 368
multiplicity 236, 285, 334, 353
multivocal 362, 368
Muni, Bharata 343, 346
Muscular Dystrophy Association of Singapore (MDAS) 107
Museum of Contemporary Art San Diego 205
Museum of disABILITY History, Buffalo, NY 50
museums: disability and 50–1; forgetting in 52–3; history of touch in 213–14; power and care in 57–9; remembering 52–3; sensory transition 214; silencing in 52–3; and unauthorised touching 215
music: classical 317–20; disability 313–9; education 100, 102, 271, 311–2, 319; protest 355; self-advocacy in 316–7; therapy 312, 320
musical instruments, *see* adaptive musical instruments
"musicking" 311, 313, 316, 319
musicology, *see also* ethnomusicology
Music, Disability, and Society (Nabb) 319
mutation 285 *see also* disability
My Teddy Brownie (McPeake) 207

Nabb, David 316–9
Naess, Arne 281
Nagel, Erica 33
narrative: dominant 79, 257; dementia 148–50, 153, 155; digital 121–4; impairment 356–8; mother trauma 70–2; pity porn 353; plot 63–70, 90, 153–4, 192, 338; sporting impairment 78–82; study of 36–8; visual 36–47; tragedy 75, 80–83, 151, 228, 287, 363
"narrative prosthesis" 3
National Accessibility Branch (NAB) 131
National Arts Council (NAC), Singapore 104
National Autistic Society 91, 94
National Disability Insurance Scheme 348
National Gallery of Australia (NGA) 52–4; forgetting at 55; silencing at 57
National Theatre for the Deaf 32
Nattadavu 341
Nature 289
nature *see* environmentalism
Nāṭyaśāstra 336–8, 340, 342–6
negotiation: among performers 12, 259; between performer and spectator 180; of disability 340, 363–4, 366; of support 193; with ticket-sellers 22; and transport 121

Neo, Alecia 103
neurodivergent 194, 256, *see also* autistic spectrum disorders
New, Ryan 258
Newell, Christopher 3
Newhouse, Imogen 255
New York Times 28
Next to Normal (Kitt and Yorkey) 24
Nickel Arts Museum 50
Nielson, John Shaw 44
Nixon, Nicholas 151
non-disabled artists 108
normalcy 57, 101, 108, 110, 198, 227, 230, 256, 326, 367
The Notebook (Sparks) 152
"Nothing about us without us" 23
Not I (Beckett) 244, 249
novels 21, 62–72, 96, 151–2, 220, 223–4, 227, 230, 278, 304, 365
Nussbaum, Susan 25, 29, 227

Objects Unknown: Sounds Familiar (Martin) 209
O'Brien, Welly 331
"Observations on an Ethnic Classification of Idiots" 191
The Observer 28
Occupation 353
Octavia's Brood: Science Fiction Stories from Social Justice Movements 280
Oddlands 189
Oedipus Rex (Sophocles) 24, 27
O'Leary, Hal 302
Oller, Maria 165
Olsson, Kristina 63
Once I Saw It All (McPeake) 206
"One-Handed Musicians–More Than a Gimmick" 313
O'Neill, Eugene 239
On the Verge 178
open access 227, 243–4, *see also* access aesthetics
oppression of disabled people 167, 177, 194, 284, 291, 299, 312, 367, 370
orchestra 317–9
O'Reilly, Kaite 28
Ostrander, Noam 3, 284
'Otherness' 49, 63, 82, 116, 150, 167–9, 243, 256, 263, 273, 311, 324, 336–7
Ott, Katherine 234–5
Ouch! website 305
outreach, *see* community arts
Outsider Art 167
The Oxford Handbook of Music and Disability Studies (Howe, Jensen-Moulton, Lerner and Straus) 311
Oxford Textbook of Creative Arts, Health, and Wellbeing: International Perspectives on Practice, Policy, and Research (Clift and Camic) 4

Index

Padam 338
pain 222, 229, 235–8, 249, 269, 279, 300, 312, 355–8
painting(s) 37–46, 51, 53, 56, 100, 108–10, 223–4, 227–8, 233–6, 238–9
The Painting of a Disabled Man—Study on the Representation of Disability and its Relevance to the Present (Schönwiese & Flieger) 38
Palmer, Jon 172, 198
Pangdemonium Theatre Company 108
Panofsky, Erwin 37–8, 40, 43–4
Papalia, Carmen 227
The Parable of the Blind Leading the Blind 40–1
The Paralympic paradox 80
parallax gap 178
paralympics 74–83
para-sport: bodies, and legacies of media representation 74–83; media and future of 82–3
Pardo, Veronica 379–80
parenthood 33, 62–72, 90, 94–8, 120, 138, 142, 153–4, 157, 169–70, 297, 353
Parlan, Horace 315, 317
participatory arts, *see* arts
Pasek, Benj 24
Pasha, Syed Sallauddin 15, 341, 343–5
Paterson, Eddie 379–80
Patterson, Barbara 43
Paul, Justin 24
Payne, Helen 4
people with disability: case of Danielle 263–74; described 263; and self-discovery 266–8; and sense of belonging 268–71; *see also* disability
people with intellectual disabilities: asylum for 192; contemporary theatre for 192; and emancipation 194
perception *see* judgement
performativity: learning disability and 180–3; *Marvellous* and 183–5
performers with a disability, *see* disabled performers
Performing Arts Medicine Clinic 313
Perring, Giles 171
personhood 195, 237
Phantom of the Opera (Webber) 24
Phelan, Peggy 285
Philoctetes (Sophocles) 24
P.H.*reaks: the Hidden History of People with Disabilities (Lewis) 26
Pieter Bruegel the Elder 40
pity porn narrative 353
Playmobil 305
Playwrighting 23–6, 28–30, 100, 182, 227, 352–3
Points of Contact: Disability, Art, and Culture (Crutchfield and Epstein) 3

poetic(s): narratives 9; searching for the 172; metaphor 259
poetry, *see* arts
Poke, Kerryn 258
policy, *see* government
politics: 38, 101, 167, 170, 190, 194, 203–4, 216–7, 228, 251, 253, 256, 260–1, 352, 363, 370
pollution: 289–90
popular culture: Antonio Gramsci's critique of 298–9; disability in 299; *vs.* mass culture 299; theories of 298–9
Porter, Sue 286
The Portrait of a Disabled Man from the 16th Century 38
Portrait of Carrie Sandahl: A Project in Four Parts (Lehrer) 229, 232–9
post-dramatic aesthetics 173–4
Post-modernist but not Post-feminist! A Feminist Post-modernist Approach to Working with New Mothers 142
poverty 16, 41, 81, 104, 254, 260, 264, 267–71, 319–21, 348, 359
power, in art therapy 137–45; *see also* empowerment
Preece, Bronwyn 380
pregnancy 141–5
Preissing, Christophe 235
prejudice, *see* discrimination
Prerogitiva Regis 180
Preston, Jeff 351
pride 10, 101, 109, 194–5, 218–9, 226, 237, 255, 379
privacy 365
Problems of Identity: Deconstructing Gender Issues in Art Therapy (Hogan) 4, 137–42
problem solving 117, 119, 260, 274
Process in the Arts Therapies (Cattanach) 4
producerly popular culture 298–9, 303
production, and disability theatre 23
prosthetics: cane 224, 266, 268, 271, 302; crutches 27–8, 41, 193, 229, 237, 329–30, 333; DIY 315; exhibition 215–6; eye patches 25; hooks 25; peg legs 25; wheelchair 28, 32–3, 42, 50–8, 79–81, 227, 230, 246–8, 276, 279, 298, 302–6, 326, 329, 332, 337, 341–2, 349–50
protests 39, 219, 277, 298, 300–3, 347–58, 367; *see also* movement
Prowd, Leisa 258
Prozac Highway (Blackbridge) 220
psychology 24, 101, 107, 116, 137–42, 153, 176, 256, 264, 326
psychiatry 222
Puar, Jasbir 194
public sphere 22, 26, 70, 163, 244, 252, 261, 323, 348, 352–3, 355, 363, 368
publicity, *see* advertising
puppetry, *see* arts

quality of life, *see* life
Quayson, Ato 285
queer: queer: appropriation of 194; artists 32; cabaret 252; crip 219, 256, 368; friendly 255; gender 32–3, 75, 77, 227, 230, 254, 256–7, 305; homosexual 219–22; in relation to autism 195; lesbian 219–26; LGBTQ 219, 222, 237; men 254; theory 40, 218–9
"Queering the Crip or Cripping the Queer?: Intersections of Queer and Crip Identities in Solo Autobiographical Performances" (Blackbridge) 218–20
Quinn, Nancy 375–6
Quippings 252, 254–5

Radio 69, 272, 324
Ramayana 341, 345
Ramps (McArthur) 227
Randall, Nora D. 222
Rawcus Theatre Company 252, 257–8
Ray, Sarah Jaquette 284
realism: 25, 69, 82, 183, 224, 279, 352
Reason, Matthew 378
Reasons to be Cheerful 355
Reasons to be Graeae: A Work in Progress (Sealey) 31
Recasting Modernism: Disability Theatre and Modern Drama (Johnston) 374
reciprocity 23, 118, 269, 281
recreation 76, 107, 111, 133, 302, *see also* sport
Redmayne, Eddie 27
reflection 31, 45, 95, 97, 144, 168, 178, 187, 264, 271, 362–3, 368
reform 46, 253, 255, 359
rehabilitation 53, 56, 75, 77–8, 104, 116, 131, 134, 224, 313, 316, 319, 331
"Rehabilitating unauthorised touch, *or* why museum visitors touch the exhibits" 212
Reinhardt, Django 315, 317
'relaxed performance' (RP): emergence of 89–91; impact of 95–7
religion 126, 130, 172, 266, 270, 272–3, 292, 344
Renaissance
Rent (Larson) 24
representation: in age of austerity 352–6; in children's toys 297–306; of gender in art therapy 137–45; of para-sport bodies in the media 74–83; self-representation 352–6
Re-Presenting Disability: Activism and Agency in the Museum (Sandell, Dodd and Garland-Thomson) 3, 37
respect 23, 39, 44, 117, 123, 163, 171, 345, 367
Restless Dance Theatre 115, 331
reverse integration 197
re-wilding 284
rhetorical listening 194–5
Riddell, Sheila 3
Rieger, Janice 375

rights: civil 76, 114, 194; disability 76, 114–5, 117, 222, 254, 278, 286; gay 194; human 37, 48, 50, 81, 139, 222, 278, 355, 358, 366; women's 194
"right to maim" 194
Riisik, Louise 258
The Rime of the Ancient Mariner (Coleridge 232)
risk: and portraiture 227–40, 247; taking 121–2, 144, 247, 257, 357; and vulnerability 126, 151, 185–6, 370
Risking Happiness 155, 157–8
The Risk Pictures (Lehrer) 229, 230–2
Risky Business (Quippings) 252, 255–7
Rix, Peter 63
The Road (Soyinka) 24
Roche, David 26
Romanticism 284
Rothenberg, David 289
Rowbotham, Rupert 90
Rowlands, Elinor 352
"The Royal Hospital: Unladylike Behaviour" 221
Royal Shakespeare Company 27
Rubin, Judith 4
Runswick-Cole, Katherine 347–9, 351–2, 358–9

saints 41; *see also* hero(es)
salaries, *see* employment
Sandahl, Carrie 3, 22, 25, 218–19, 341
Sandell, Richard 3
scars 221, 234
Schmidt, Yvonne 193, 195–6
Schoolgirls and Angels 40
Schwartz, Stephen 24
Schweizer Grand Prix/Hans-Reinhart-Ring 189
science fiction, and disability 276–80
Scraping the Surface 26
'scroungers' 348
Sealey, Jenny 31–2, 245, 355
'seductive fiction' 140
self, performance of 264
self-reliance, *see* independence
sense of belonging, and people with a disability 268–71
sense of inclusion 125–9
sensory disabilities *see* disabilities
Sex Pistols 179, 187
Sexton, Anne 64
Shaban, Nabil 31
Shakespeare, William 24, 27, 93, 153, 181, 232
Shameless: The Art of Disability 224
'Share a Smile Becky' *see* Barbie
shared disability arts research 367–71
Shattering the Glass Menagerie (Sandahl) 25
Shea, Theresa 63, 66
Shelley, Mary 232
Shepard, Sam 24
Shepp, Archie 315

Index

Sheppard, Alice 230
Sher, Antony 27
Shibata, Sho 326
Shonibare, Yinka 253–4
Shoot! (Manning) 25
Shyamalan, M. Night 152
sickness 223–4, 243, 348, *see also* pain
Sideshow USA 2
Siebers, Tobin 3, 40, 218, 220, 251, 285
Sifis, Eva 251
sign language 32–3, 103, 108, 110, 121, 127, 132–3, 255, 349, *see also* D/deafness
silence 50, 52, 55–8, 195, 232, 263
Silvers, Anita 167
Singapore: arts and disability in 100–11; structural reasons for instrumentalisation of art in 104
Singapore International Foundation (SIF) 104
Sing Fox to Me 63, 71–2
Sins Invalid 32
situated disability arts research 367–71
Small Acts of Repair (Bottoms and Goulish) 291
Smith, Adam 126
Smith, Phil 369
Smritiratnakara 337
Snyder, Sharon 3, 36
Social Communication Emotional Regulation Transactional Support Model (SCERTS) 92
The Social History of Art (Hauser) 39
social model of disability 76–7
social services *see* health
soldiers 43, 53–8, 316
song 110, 153, 173, 231, 254–60, 289, 319, 355–6
Song for a Weary Throat (Rawcus) 252, 258–9
soundscape 52, 103, 239
The Sound and the Fury (Faulkner) 63–4
Sounding off: Theorizing Disability in Music (Lerner and Straus) 311
Soyinka, Wole 24
Sparks, Nicholas 152
special needs 100, 103–5
speculative fiction 280
spectators: diverse audiences 203, 211, 217, 254–5; and spectatorship 22–3, 71, 157, 163–87, 192, 196, 233–5, 240, 252, 259, 268, 285, 290, 352–8
"speech act" 200
spirituality *see* religion
sport 50, 74–83, 302, 364; *see also* recreation
sporting impairment: bodily narratives of 78–82; media narratives of 78–82
"spreadable media" 299, 303
Stack, Carol 267
Stage Left Theatre 32
Stage Turns: Canadian Disability Theater (Johnston) 3, 29

Staging Stigma: A Critical Examination of the American Freak Show 2
'stairbombing' 351
stand-up/sit-down comedy 26
staring 22, 42–3, 46, 65, 166, 168–9, 180–81, 223, 228–9, 272, 334
Staring: How We Look (Garland-Thomson) 3, 37, 40
State of Grace 155
Stelling, Jeff 316
stereotypes 30, 36, 44, 50, 57, 59, 68, 75, 79–80, 150–51, 158, 172, 179, 195, 197, 247, 257, 280, 299, 304, 323, 351–3, 356, 363
Stevenson, Prue 258
Stewart, Susan 222
stigma, *see* discrimination
stigmata 64, 65, 71
Still Alice (Genova) 152
Still Sane (Blackbridge and Gilhooly) 220–2
Stoke Mandeville Games 75–6
Stonum, Anna 227
Stopgap Dance Company 120, 325–6, 331
storytelling, *see* narrative
Straus, Joseph 311
Strickfaden, Megan 375
'strivers' 348
stroke 149, 224, 316
Struggle Street 352
Study 5, A New Place 207
Studying Disability Arts and Culture: An Introduction (Kuppers) 4, 37, 117
suffering, *see* pain
suicide 150, 159, 186, 221, 273, 348, 352, 354
Sulan, Kate 251, 258
A Summer Evening in Des Moines (Mee Jnr.) 26
Sunnybrook: A True Story with Lies (Blackbridge) 220, 223–4
Super Discount 193
Supervision of Dramatherapy (Jones and Dokter) 4
surgery 312, 314, *see also* medical
survival 279, 285, 288, 364
sustainability of the arts 16, 117, 257, 261
Swaffer, Kate 151
Sweet Gongs Vibrating: artwork examples at 204–10; authorised touch at 210–16; overview 203–4
symbolism 138, 353–4
symptoms 65, 140, 152, 153, 304, *see also* medical

tabula rasa, see autistic spectrum disorders
Tainted Wedding Ring (McPeake) 206
Take Care 355
Tatti Metti Adavu 338
Tay, Joanne 376
Taylor, James 232
tax-payers 348–9
teaching 15, 36–7, 40, 45, 69, 95–7, 104, 107, 115–20, 123, 127, 192, 205, 229, 249, 271–2,

400

274, 318, 323–4, 300, 327–8, 340, 343–4; *see also* education

technology: adaptive 270–71; assistive 313; captioners 31–3, 94, 134–5, 257; information 135; listening devices 33, 133; medical 66; and translators 198

television 22–3, 27, 79, 98, 183, 219, 272–3, 297, 352, 371

The Tempest 93

Thatcher, Margaret 152

Theater HORA 189, 190, 195, 198

theatre: accessibility 22–3, 29–31; actors with intellectual disabilities in 190–3; advertising 23, 28, 156, 158, 257; affect in 166, 171–2, 191, 197, 199; agency in 156, 168–9, 171–2, 190, 193, 195–6, 199, 239; artistic management 23; barriers in 22, 30–2, 53, 344, 351, 364; casting and disability 27–9; characters in 93–6, 171–4, 181–5, 254, 305, 351–3, 22–5, 28–30; charity model of 189; for children with autism 89–99; community arts 26, 163, 190, 196; criticism 28, 32–3, 154; dance 326, 336; history 23, 24, 27, 189, 194, 197; inclusion 21– 3, 29–33; relaxed 33, 89–91, 94–5, 97, 244–5; venue architecture 21–22, 31, 32

Theatre and Disability (Kuppers) 4, 22, 195

Theatre Access NYC 33

Theatre Breaking Through Barriers 32

The Theatre of Visions: Robert Wilson (Brecht) 197

Theatres of Learning Disabilities (Hargrave) 193

Theatres of Learning Disability: Good, Bad, or Plain Ugly? (Hargrave) 3, 32

Theatres of Learning Disability: The Good, The Bad, The Ugly (Hargrave) 373

therapy: art 101–2, 107, 111, 137–145; dance 120, 328, 331; drama 152; music 312; psychotherapy 36–7, 45; occupational 310; physical 325; remedial 40; theatre 189

The Theatre Times 154

The Theatrical Public Sphere 355

The Theory of Everything 27

"The Popular and 'Proper' Performing Arts" 318

Thom, Jess 26, 244–50, 351, 379

Thompson, Judith 24

Three threads an a thrum (for D.B.) 205

tickets 93, 107, 108

Tillana 341

TimeSlips method 156

To Kill a Mockingbird (Lee) 63

Tolan, Kathleen A. 25, 29

Tomlinson, Richard 31

Tonso, John 258

Toole, David 332

Totems and Familiars 229

touch: tours 32–3, 51, 54, 204; and tactile engagement 203, 208–217 *see also* haptic

Touch Compass Dance Company 331; and Encompass education and outreach programme 117–19; Encompass programme 119–20; integrated dance 114–17; performance opportunities within Encompass programme 120–2

touring 189, 190, 249, 354

Tourettes Syndrome 12, 244, 351

Townsley, Ruth 373

toys, *see* children's toys

#toylikeme 305–6

tragedy narrative 75, 80–81, 151, 228, 287, 363

Trahan, Julia 218

training, and disability theatre 29–31

trans-corporeal 291

transgender 230

transgression 75, 288

transmedia storytelling 303–4

trauma 75, 80, 228, 287, 363, 279, 363–5, 368

Trauma Narratives and Herstory (Andermahr and Pellicer-Ortin) 70

Tribes 108

trickster methods 370

Tuana, Nancy 291

Tuesday's Child (Evans) 71

Turnbull, Joe 29

The Tyranny of Expectations of Post-Natal Delight: Gendering Happiness (Hogan) 143

The Tyranny of the Maternal Body: Maternity and Madness (Hogan) 143

Two Women (Juro) 24

Umathum, Sandra 3

uncertainty: and disability arts research 364–7

Understanding Disability Studies and Performance Studies (Henderson and Ostrander) 3

The Unfinished Child (Shea) 63, 66

Unimaginable Bodies: Intellectual Disability, Performance and Becomings (Hickey-Moody) 3, 197

Union 121

Universal Design, *see* architecture

Unlimited Festival 243

Unseen: Constellations 103

Valentine, Paul 302

The Value of Art Therapy in Antenatal and Postnatal Care: A Brief Literature Review (Hogan, Sheffield, & Woodward) 142

Vancouver Adapted Music Society 317

Vancouver's Society for Disability Arts and Culture 282

Venkat, Lalitha 341

venues 89, 93, 102, 163, 243, 246, 254–5

verbal: abuse 170; non-verbal 64, 328; responses 92; speech impairment 64, 150, 232, 150; speech therapist 314

Index

Verrent, Jo 33
veterans, *see* soldiers
Vimal, Akhila C. 382
"viral advertising" 298
virtuosity 74, 122, 337
visible: disabled people 45, 67, 177, 232, 244,
   247–8, 261, 279, 328; impairments 22, 24, 80,
   225, 229, 259; invisible disabilities 21, 74, 80,
   116, 222, 229, 243, 256, 259, 323, 327, 329
vision centric 203
vision-impaired, *see* blindness
visual arts *see* arts
The Visit (Shyamalan) 152
visual narratives: artworks across history, time,
   and place 40–5; history 38–9; separating
   the artist's work from the artist's biography
   39–40; visual narratology 36–8
visual narratology 36–8
Vital Xposure 252
voice: disabled people's 33, 264, 344, 366–7,
   369–71; giving dementia a 152, 155–8;
   marginalized 51, 120, 122–3, 163, 166, 168,
   222, 236, 244, 277, 279; multivocal 118, 362,
   368; polyvocal 368
Voices: A World Forum for Music Therapy
   (Hadley) 312
Voluntary Welfare Organisations (VWOs)
   104–7, 111
volunteers 33, 90, 94, 95, 107, 119, 215, 365; *see
   also* internships
von der Borch, Danielle 258
voyeurism 163
vulnerability, and disability arts research 364–7
VWOs pursue therapeutic outcomes 106–7

W!LD RICE 103
Wade, Cheryl Marie 25–6, 29, 219
Wade, Jeremy 355
Wallin, Scott 169
Walloch, Greg 218
Water Under Water (Rix) 63, 68
Watson, Keri 36–7, 40–1
Watson, Nick 3
ways of watching: aesthetics of authenticity and
   presence 170–2; aesthetics of identification
   169–70; aesthetics of no difference (or
   aesthetics of universal humanity) 164–6;
   aesthetics of radical difference 167–9;
   aesthetics of watching learning disabled
   theatre 164; post-dramatic aesthetics 173–4
Webber, Andrew Lloyd 24
*Welcome to My World: A Concert by People with
   Disabilities* 104
Weldon, Fay 66
'*We're People Who Do Shows': Back to Back
   Theatre – Performance Politics Visibility* (Grehan
   and Eckersall) 3

Whatley, Sarah 381
*What the Hell Happened to My Brain? Living
   Beyond Dementia* (Swaffer) 151
wheelchairs 329, 28, 32–3, 42, 50–8, 79–81, 227,
   230, 246–8, 276, 279, 298, 302–6, 326, 329,
   332, 337, 341–2, 349–50, 354
Wheeler, Tim 168
"Where All Bodies Are Exquisite" (Lehrer) 228
whole-of-life experience, *see* life
Wicked (Schwartz and Holman) 24
Wihstutz, Benjamin 3
Wildsmith, Heather 90
Williams, Lefty 315–6
Williams, Raymond 164
Williams, Tennessee 25
Williamson, Aaron 350–1
Wilson, August 24
Wilson, Robert 197
Winslet, Kate 27–8
Winton, Tim 68
Wooden Spatula (McPeake) 207
work, *see* employment
World Health Organisation 82
World War II 75
Woyzek (Büchner) 24
writers, *see* author(s)
Wyeth, Andrew 40

X-Men 279

Yardi, Sarita 126, 128
Year of the King: An Actor's Diary and Sketchbook
   (Sher) 27
Yellow Ribbon Project 106
Yergeau, Melanie 194–5
yoga on wheelchairs 341
Yorkey, Brian 24
Yosemite National Park: access and inclusion
   at 130–3; access at 130–3; bonding 133;
   case study 129–30; developing inclusive
   capital through the Deaf Service at 133–4;
   disability access at 125–35; five stages
   of developing inclusive capital 127–9;
   inclusion at 130–3; inclusive capital 126–7;
   information 134; learning 133; space and
   place 134
You Have Been Watching 173
You Spin Me Round 256
youth 10, 29, 100, 103, 115, 119, 122, 153,
   229, 326
YouTube 38, 121
Yukio, Mishima 24

Zeller, Florian 154
Zeilig, Hannah 148–51, 160
Žižek, Slavoj 172
zombie(s) 149–51, 156, 159, 304

402

Milton Keynes UK
Ingram Content Group UK Ltd.
UKHW031955060324
438929UK00018B/662